Exchange and Production:

Competition, Coordination, and Control

Second Edition

Exchange and Production:

Competition, Coordination, and Control

Second Edition

Armen Alchian
and
William R. Allen
*University
of California,
Los Angeles*

Wadsworth
Publishing Company,
Inc.
*Belmont,
California*

Economics Editor: John Mahaney
Production Editor: Larry Olsen
Designer: Dare Porter
Technical Illustrator: John Foster

Printed in the United States of America
1 2 3 4 5 6 7 8 9 10—81 80 79 78 77

ISBN-0-534-00493-8

L. C. Cat. Card No. 76-54602

Preface

The test of any science is its ability to explain the events of the real world in a coherent, consistent fashion. Economics passes that test. This book presents, at the introductory level, an exposition of economic analysis with persistent emphasis on its empirical meaningfulness and validity.

Economics is relevant to the everyday activities and situations of our personal lives. We find, from some thirty years of experience in teaching, that students show keen interest and even excitement in discovery of economic theory—mainly because, we believe, the theory is made pertinent and convincing by repeated, realistic applications within their own range of experiences. At the same time, major questions of national policy are considered again and again without a loss of continuity of interest.

Of course, in any such book much must be left out; to cover everything is to learn little about anything. But the fundamental principles and theorems of analysis are included and stressed and repeatedly applied. The propriety in stressing the few fundamentals is, we think, illustrated by the statement of an economist, Alain A. Enthoven, who has worked very successfully at the highest levels of national policy in the Department of Defense:

. . . the tools of analysis that we [in Defense] use are the simplest, most fundamental concepts of economic theory, combined with the simplest quantitative methods. The requirements for success in this line of work are a thorough understanding of and, if you like, belief in the relevance of such concepts as marginal products and marginal costs, and an ability to discover the marginal products and costs in complex situations, combined with a good quantitative sense. The economic theory we are using is the theory most of us learned as sophomores. The reason Ph.D's are required is that many economists do not believe what they have learned until they have gone through graduate school and acquired a vested interest in marginal analysis. ("Economic Analysis in the Department of Defense," *American Economic Review,* 53 [May 1963], p. 422).

The instructor will find that the scope of the theory covering choice, demand, exchange, and supply has been extended to behavior beyond the old, narrow, wealth-maximizing behavior in simple private-property markets. The scope of costs, and their relation to various dimensions of outputs, includes modern industrial techniques of mass-production economies. Furthermore, recognition of the role of information and the costs of acquiring it and the costs of transactions and agency relationships have enabled economists to discern a unified theory of economics valid for both individual behavior and for fluctuations in national aggregates of employment and income.

But the test of a text is the text itself—not promises and self-advertising in the preface. So we add only that questions appear at the end of each chapter, and answers to most questions are at the end of the book. Question numbers in boldface type in the margin at the end of major sections throughout the chapters indicate the best places to study the answer.

We must record appreciation to an unnamed host of economists, mostly of the past two centuries, who developed the analysis presented here. The temptation for living economists to think all modern analysis was discovered by them is something that gets easier to resist as one gets older. To all, living or dead, we express our admiration and appreciation for being able to put their ideas in this text and for having benefitted from them. We also wish to thank Robert Mc-Closkey (University of Chicago), Tim Ozenne (University of Washington), and David Gay (University of Arkansas, Fayetteville), who read the manuscript for the publisher and provided many helpful comments.

Armen Alchian
William R. Allen

Contents

0

How Much Mathematics and Graphs?

"How much mathematics must I know to understand economics?" Only arithmetic, but one must also be able to read charts and graphs. Arithmetic or graph reading are less a cause of confusion than is *interpretation* of quantitative relationships between economic magnitudes. Therefore, this Note presents interpretations along with the arithmetic and chart reading. If you can follow it, you are adequately prepared. The arithmetic, chart reading, and interpretation are presented by simple examples in imaginary economic contexts. Numbers are chosen primarily to make computations and relationships easy to see, rather than to reflect reality.

Imagine we are producing "tees" for golf balls—little wooden devices on which the ball is placed prior to striking it 250 yards down the middle of the fairway. To make one tee costs, we assume, $1.00, counting all material, labor, etc. Costs of producing two, three, four, etc., tees per day are in Table 0–1. The more tees produced in a day, the greater the total cost of that day's output. Two tees cost $1.90, and three cost $2.70. "Total costs" and "tees produced" both change in the same direction. The change of two magnitudes in the same direction is called a *positive* relationship. Another example would be daily caloric intake and one's weight—usually assumed to be positive, for more of one means more of the other. (Nothing is assumed about *causal* connection in saying a relationship exists. Whether or not any causality runs either way from one magnitude to the other is not our concern here.)

An example of a *negative* relationship is age and strength for people over about 30 years: As age increases, strength decreases. For younger people, the relationship is positive: A youth gets

Table 0–1. Output of Tees and Costs

Tees Produced Daily	Total Costs
10	$1.00
1	1.90
2	2.70
3	3.40
4	4.00
5	4.70
6	5.50
7	6.40
8	7.40
9	8.60

stronger as he grows. But after some age, strength ceases to grow and then decreases with age. Thus over the *entire* range of age, the relationship with strength is at first positive, then possibly zero (indicating no change in strength as age increases), and then negative.

We can picture relationships with graphs. Figure 0–1 portrays the relationship that is assumed between costs and number of tees. The height of each bar indicates *total costs* of the number of tees to which it corresponds. Each bar has an upper shaded section showing how much higher it is than the neighboring bar of one less unit of output. The shaded part of the bar portrays the *increment* to total costs consequent to producing one more. We could draw a smooth line along the tops of the bars to indicate total costs without showing a lot of bars; this is done in Figure 0–2 to make a cleaner looking chart. You will see that the line passes through several dots. You may interpret the *line* between the dots as guiding the eye from point to point, or the line

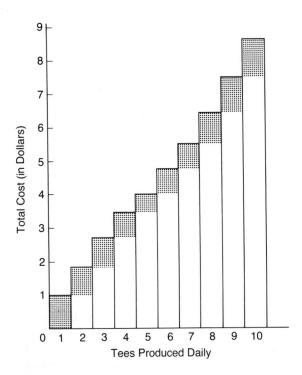

Figure 0–1. Bar Chart of Total–Cost–Output-of-Tees Relationship

Shaded sections denote how much cost increases with each unit increase in daily output. Relationship between total cost and tees produced is positive, *for both increase (or decrease) together.*

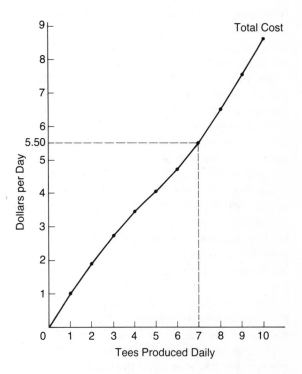

Figure 0–2. Line Chart of Total-Cost–Output Relationship

Line chart shows more clearly how total cost varies with daily output of tees. Height of line at each output measures daily total cost. Upward slope, called positive slope, indicates positive relationship.

may represent the costs of producing fractional amounts. For example, if three tees are produced in two days, this is 1.5 tees per day. So fractional amounts of even nondivisible things do make sense, if interpreted as a *rate* of production per day. Even though only discrete or "integral" amounts of some good can be produced, we can still speak of fractional amounts per some unit of time.

So far in interpreting a chart, we have taken a point on the horizontal axis and then read up to the line to find the value of the corresponding variable in which we were interested. We first found five units of tees on the horizontal axis, and then by reading up directly above that point we saw the cost was $4. Usually the graph can also be read the other way. Suppose you were told that $4 could be spent on producing tees.

How many could be produced? To answer, find $4 on the vertical scale, then go horizontally across the chart to the curve and drop straight down to the horizontal axis to an output of five tees.

We now direct attention to three different aspects of costs as different outputs of tees are considered. Three different, important concepts, *total, average,* and *marginal,* must be understood. The *total* costs of Table 0–1 are again shown in Table 0–2, along with *average cost* per tee and *marginal cost* of tees. The *average* cost is the total cost per day divided by the number of tees per day. For two tees, the total cost per day, $1.90, divided by 2, is 95 cents per tee. And for five tees the average cost is 80 cents. Compute the average cost of five and of six tees. If you agree with the numbers shown, proceed; if not, give up.

The continuing scholars should next look at the *marginal* costs column of Table 0–2. These are the *differences* in the *total* costs of producing two different quantities of tees—differing by one tee. For five tees a day the total cost is $4.00, and for six tees is $4.70; the difference, called the *marginal cost,* is 70 cents. This is shown in Figure 0–1 as the shaded section of the bar for six units.

This simple concept of change, difference, or increment in cost associated with *one* unit larger output is *"marginal* cost." It is the *change* in one variable (here, total cost) associated with a *one* unit change in the other (in this case, output of tees). This could have been called the "incremental cost when six are produced rather than five," or the "marginal cost of producing six rather than five," but it is in fact called the *"marginal* cost at, or of, six." Note carefully that it is not the total cost of producing six, for that is $4.70, and it is not the average cost of producing six,

Tees Produced Daily	Costs		
	Total	Average	Marginal
1	$1.00	$1.000	$1.00
2	1.90	.950	.90
3	2.70	.900	.80
4	3.40	.850	.70
5	4.00	.800	.60
6	4.70	.783	.70
7	5.50	.785	.80
8	6.40	.800	.90
9	7.40	.825	1.00
10	8.60	.860	1.20

Table 0–2. Costs and Output of Tees

Total costs increase with number of tees produced daily. Average costs are total costs divided by number of tees produced daily. Marginal cost is increase in total costs for *one* unit increased output.

for that is 78 cents per unit. It is the *increase* in total cost of six over the cost of five.

We shall use these concepts extensively. Unless you *always* keep these three *concepts*—(1) total, (2) average, and (3) marginal—clearly separated, you will almost certainly not acquire a good grasp of economic principles. Hint: Never use the term "cost" by itself; always identify it with "total," "average," or "marginal," so that you won't confuse one with the others. Let's test your ability to *interpret* and apply these concepts. Someone asks the question, "What is the cost of six tees?" If you try to answer that question as it stands, you have just missed the point. What cost? Total, average, or marginal? Each is different. But there lurks still another potential ambiguity. What is meant by the "marginal cost of six tees?" It means, as we have said, how much more total costs are than if only five are to be produced. In the present example that seems clear enough. But to see how things can get muddied up in other contexts, we give you the following example.

Imagine a retail store with four clerks. Total sales are $2000 per day for the total of all four clerks—with some selling more than the $500 average and some less. Add a fifth clerk to the sales force, and sales increase by $200 to $2200. Now it is *erroneous,* but tempting, to infer that the new person is not as productive as the first four. If you were to look at the details you would discover that he had $800 of sales, which is more than for any other clerk. His presence enabled the store to sell $200 more by getting customers who otherwise would have decided not to buy, but he also managed to attract customers away from the other clerks, because of his superior looks and personality. *His* sales were $800, but that is not called his marginal sales or the marginal sales of the fifth person. The marginal sales with a fifth person were $200. Average sales were $440 with five people ($2200/5). And what about his $800? Is that *necessarily* comprised of $600 of sales taken from other clerks plus $200 of new customers? Not necessarily. All of the $800 may have been from old customers attracted from other clerks, while the other clerks scrounged around to get the extra $200 in sales. As we use the term, "marginal sales with a fifth person" is *not* to be interpreted as what *a* particular person or any other one did, but only as the *change* in the *total* results of having a *team* of five clerks rather than a team of four. "Marginal sales" or "marginal costs" or "marginal whatever" will always be interpreted that way—as the *change in total* of one variable consequent to having *one* more of the other variable.

We do not give any name to the $800 of sales of the fifth person. In fact, often it cannot even be detected or conceived. For example, you have a team of four men rowing a boat with a trailing net to catch fish. You add a fifth man to row or help tend the net. How can you make any meaning of what the fifth man himself caught? You can't. The only possibility is the meaning we have given—the change in the *total* consequent to having five rather than four.

Turn your attention to the possible quantitative *behavior* of these magnitudes. Looking in Table 0–2 at larger outputs of tees, you will notice marginal costs *increase* after their earlier initial decreases at small outputs of tees. Taking the total costs as correct data, check the average cost and marginal costs calculations.

To exercise your arithmetic talents a bit more, consider how "averages" *must* behave relative to "marginals." Suppose that as you increase output by one unit, from eight to nine, the total cost *increase* (the marginal cost) is greater than the average cost at eight. What will be the average cost of nine? To see what is meant by the question, look at the output of eight tees. For that output, average cost is 80 cents. Now the question is, "What will happen to the average cost of output, if you know that when you expand output from eight to nine, the *increase* in total cost, 90 cents (i.e., the *marginal* cost), is greater than the average cost (80 cents) at eight?" Isn't this exactly like asking what will happen to your average test score if the points earned on your next test are higher than your present average? Won't it raise your average? And if one more test adds *fewer* points than your existing average, the average will be pulled down. We repeat, if the marginal exceeds the average, the average will rise; and if it is less than the current average, the average will go down. Hence the answer to the question is, "The average will be rising if the marginal is greater than the average." To verify this, look at the marginal costs for tees ranging from 7 to 10. For all those, the marginal cost is greater than the average, and the average cost rises in that output range.

If you examine all the marginal costs for tees 0 through 6 you will see that the marginal cost is less than the average, so the average falls with increases in outputs. Where the marginal value exceeds the average value, the average must always increase. And if the marginal value of the variable is less than its average, the average must decrease. Only if the marginal value equals the average will the average remain unchanged.

To familiarize yourself with graphic presentation and analysis, examine Figure 0–3, which shows bars for total costs; superimposed are the marginal costs, this time at the bottom of each bar. The marginal cost bars are exactly the same as the shaded sections at the top of the total cost bars in Figure 0–2. We quickly see that the marginal costs at first decrease and then increase. Note also that the *sum* of all the marginal costs up through seven tees is the total cost of seven units. This equality between the sum of marginal costs and the total cost is true for every output, by definition. Also shown are average costs per unit of each output, as dots connected by a line. You can see that average costs decrease so long as marginal costs are less than average costs, and that average costs rise when marginal costs have risen above average cost.

The same figure is repeated as Figure 0–4 but with lines rather than bars. The total cost of seven units of output is shown in three ways: (1)

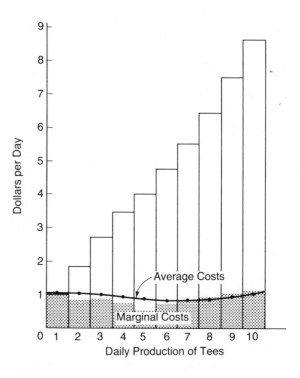

Figure 0–3. Bar Chart of Total and Marginal Cost–Output Relationship

Shaded sections show marginal costs. Average costs are shown by line through dots, to avoid cluttering graph. Average costs fall when marginal costs are less than average cost; and rise when marginal cost exceeds average cost.

by the *height* of the total cost line at 7; (2) by the *area* under the marginal cost line from the first through the seventh—the sum of the marginal costs; and (3) by the shaded area of a rectangle whose base is the horizontal axis from 0 through 7 and whose height is the average cost of seven. The average cost of seven ($.785), shown by the height at 7, multiplied by 7 will be the total cost ($5.50, rounded to 3 figures). If you

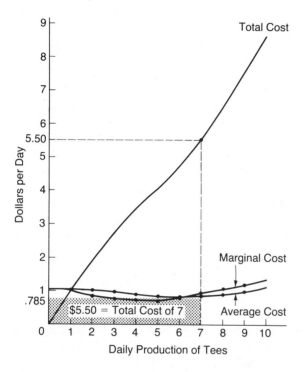

Figure 0–4. Line Chart of Total, Average, and Marginal Cost Relationship with Output Rate

Rectangular area with height at average cost and base at output rate is measure of total cost. Area under marginal cost curve is also measure of total cost.

see that both the area *under the marginal cost curve* and the *rectangular area* formed by the average cost curve height at 7 units represent the total cost, then you have passed the hardest arithmetic and graphic interpretation test.

As evidence of your talents, examine the new data in Table 0–3. The first two columns show prices and the number of tees that can be sold. The lower the price, the more that can be sold at any price. Complete the empty spaces in

Table 0–3. Sales Price and Number of Tees Sold Daily

Tees Sold	Price of Tee	Sales Receipts or Revenue (Dollars)		
		Total	Marginal	Average
1	$10	$10	—	10
2	9	18	+8	9
3	8	24	+6	—
4	7	28	—	—
5	6	30	—	—
6	5	30	—	—
7	4	28	−2	—
8	3	24	—	—
9	2	18	—	—
10	1	10	—	—

Complete the table and plot the results in Figure 0–5. Negative marginal sales receipts indicate that total sales proceeds diminish at lower price despite increased number sold. Sales proceeds are typically called "revenue."

the columns labeled "marginal receipts" and "average receipts"—which you will see is the same as price, because each unit is sold at the same price. Do not be surprised to get some *negative* marginal receipts. And in any event do the arithmetic without worrying much about why the relationship is shown as it is.

On the partially completed graph in Figure 0–5, some of the points have already been placed. Put in the rest of the dots for the average receipts and for the marginal receipts and connect the points in each set with a smooth line. Then draw in the *two* alternative areas representing total receipts for four tees at a price of $7. Do the same for eight tees at a price of $3. Which has the larger area?

Finally, some algebra. If you put $100 in a bank that pays interest at the rate of 5 percent per year, at the end of one year you will have $105.

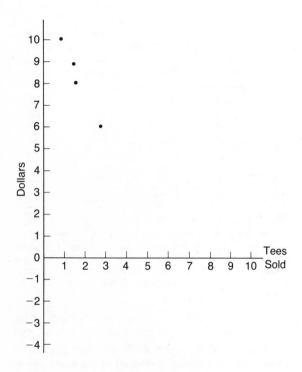

Figure 0–5. Exercise Graph for Receipts–Units-Sold Relationship

You are to complete set of dots and draw lines of average costs and marginal costs. Relationship of price and units sold is negative. Is relationship between total sales receipts positive, negative, or both?

At the end of two years you will have earned another 5 percent of the $105 with which you ended the first year, so you will have 5 percent of $105 added to the $105, a total of $110.25. How can this be written in algebraic form? At the end of the first year you will have $100 + ($100 × .05) = $105 which can be written as $100(1.05) = $105. At the end of the second year, the amount is multiplied again by 1.05. Therefore the initial

amount of $100 will in two years be $100(1.05)(1.05) = $110.25 which can be written as $100 $(1.05)^2$. This is what is meant by compounded interest, compounded once a year for two years. The initial investment is increased by 5 percent by the end of the first year and then that entire amount (initial principal plus accumulated interest) earns interest the next year and grows by another 5 percent, or by the multiple 1.05. Succinctly, it grows to 100(1.05)^2$ = $110.25. In three years it will grow to $100(1.05)(1.05)(1.05) or $100 $(1.05)^3$ which is $115.76. In ten years it will be 100(1.05)^{10}$ which is $162.89. If you understand this, with only some minor hesitancy, by writing it down and checking it, all will be well. For the concluding twist, suppose you want to have $150 in six years at 5 percent interest compounded annually. How much must you invest *now* so that the value will grow to $150 in six years? The answer is obtained by noting that a present amount, P, will grow in six years at 5 percent interest compounded annually to $P(1.05)^6 = F$, where F denotes some future amount. In the example we have $P(1.05)^6 = \$150$. So dividing through by $(1.05)^6$ we have $P = \$150/(1.05)^6 = \$150/1.34 = \$111.93$. Of course, computing the value of $(1.05)^6$ is tedious, but don't worry. You won't have to, because we have tables in which to look up the answer.

You have now demonstrated adequate knowledge of arithmetic graphics and algebra. If some of the concepts are a little unfamiliar, don't worry. So long as you understand them, later exercises will make them familiar and easy. It really is easy—or will be. Your instructor will probably help make it easy and will cleverly take you on to more mathematics with no trouble at all.

1

Scarcity, Competition, and Social Control

Societies have prospered despite almost universal ignorance of economic analysis. So why trouble yourself with formal analysis of what has been going on more or less successfully for thousands of years? Although economic analysis alone will not resolve the economic problems of the world, it *can* reduce the probability of your clumsily making your life worse. And you will be less susceptible to confusion from common incorrect claims and half truths.

Examples of these are numerous. Among them are: Minimum wage laws help the unskilled and minorities (p. 406); automation reduces available jobs (p. 394); unions protect employees from employers (p. 396); producers profit by making goods with short use-lives (p. 155); "equal pay for equal work" aids women, minorities, and the young (p. 408); used-book markets reduce the royalties of authors (p. 156); "free" medical care increases aid to the poor (p. 118); government regulatory agencies protect the consumer (p. 327); strict liability on producers for defective products protects the consumer (p. 329); the environment should not be harmed (p. 427); employers' contributions to social security are borne by employers rather than employees (p. 393); price controls reduce consumers' costs (p. 91); American agriculture produces a surplus of wheat because it is so productive (p. 332); reducing unemployment requires creating more jobs (p. 384); free-tuition education costs students less than high-tuition education (p. 118); the draft is cheaper than a paid-volunteer military (p. 412); the superstars among professional athletes are overpaid (p. 412). The list could go on.

In addition, as a broader generalization, many people see a world of economic confusion unless some central government planning agency collects and digests a wide variety of information, and then issues directives and coordinates policy. However, the collecting of diverse information into one central agency does not mean that it will be better understood or better used, or that activities will be better coordinated. On the contrary, even if bits and pieces of information remain dispersed among individual holders, efficient coordination and organization of economic activity is achieved. Indeed, among the achievements of economics has been:

1. Discovery and analysis of the different ways in which our individual goals and activities can be consistently coordinated without central planning; and
2. Understanding of the method that characterizes the system under which we live, a system without a central collector of information and issuer of directives, a system that despite—or possibly because of—that absence operates with remarkable efficacy.

And do not suppose that economics applies only to grubby questions of "business" and "finance." We are, in fact, studying fundamental issues of the organization and functioning of a society rather than merely a productive activity.

Finally, although economics is not best approached as a how-to-do-it study of financial tricks, it can nevertheless help you to invest your wealth better—and you will have much to invest.

Give economics a try. It may well prove worthwhile and even entertaining. Economics is better than pot at dispelling (and sometimes generating) anxieties—and it's legal. Like pushers, we intend to make it habit-forming.

Magnitudes of
Our Problem of
Economic Control

The size and complexity of the American economy is awesome: 215 million people, in 70 million households, with a labor force of over 90 million (one-third women) and 13 million business units (including 10 million single proprietorships, 1 million partnerships, and 2 million corporations). Collectively they produce and market an uncounted diversity of goods and services worth $1.4 trillion annually (an average of $6500 per person)—over 25 percent of the world's total. If staggering to the imagination, is it beyond coordination? To be sure, for personal matters, individual, independent decision-making may be tolerable. But to coordinate the economic activities of millions of individuals in an intricately interdependent society, must not a planning agency be in charge?

In actuality, the economic activity of American society generally has *not* been centrally planned or directed by any economic czar, government or private. No one poses detailed questions or provides answers on an economy-wide basis to organize the use of resources; no one designates how much of each good and service should be produced and who shall obtain how much of what. No agency ensures that food reaches every city—yet, people eat. No "Big Brother" directs essential economic functions—yet, things get done. (Paradoxically, when some economic czar is given governmental power to control some good, such as oil, results can border on chaos.)

If you conclude that governments are a common source of disruption, you are not wrong. But you would be wrong if you thought that all or most government activity is disruptive while all private activity is efficient. Neither is true. The truth is that a decentralized economic system based on private wealth-seeking does, to an astonishing extent, coordinate production and consumer demands among millions of independent people.

The Scarcity Constraint

Since the fiasco in the Garden of Eden, most of what we get is by sweat, strain, and anxiety. We want more than we have any realistic prospect of obtaining. Even the wealthiest societies are in a state of *scarcity,* and doubtless will remain so—but not because they produce the "wrong things" or do not fully use their productive potential. Despite religious and philosophical exhortations to abandon materialistic desires for more, our wants and goals remain incompletely fulfilled. The idea that any society is becoming saturated with goods and services is fantasy (one that was popular in the 1960s). And the opposite view (popular in the 1970s) that we are again becoming a world of scarcity is equally distorted—because ours has been a world of scarcity ever since Eden.

The limitations on production possibilities are portrayed by the guns-and-butter example in Figure 1–1. In 1977, society could produce a maximum of OG_{77} guns, if no resources were devoted to butter; alternatively, if all resources were used for butter, OB_{77} units could be produced, with no guns. *All* feasible output combinations of guns and butter are bounded by the curve between G_{77} and B_{77}, the production-possibility boundary. That boundary describes the known limits of the

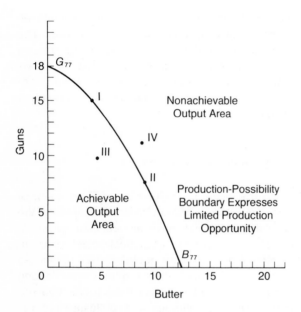

Figure 1–1. Scarcity, Efficiency, and Choice Illustrated by Production-Possibility Boundary

The curved line portrays limits on amounts of guns and butter producible in the economy. Any point on the line (for example, I or II) can be produced. No combination of guns and butter outside the curved line (say, point IV) can be achieved by the economy given its productive powers and preference for leisure. Less would be produced if the productive resources were unemployed or used inefficiently—as, for example, at point III. In some manner society selects a point on the boundary or inside it. Productive efficiency means that the economy is on the production boundary. We shall be studying the means for determining what pushes the economy to that line and to what point on that line. Why the curve has the shape shown here will be discussed later. If you are interested in the environment, you can replace "butter" by "clean air" and see that there is a tradeoff between steel for guns and cleaner air. The same kind of limitation and tradeoffs are applicable.

society's productive powers, given tastes for leisure and work, organizational methods, property rights, knowledge, and productive resources. By definition, an economy has organized its resources with *productive (technological) efficiency* (that is, without waste) if it is some place *on* the production boundary, but it is inefficient (wasteful) if *inside* the boundary. If it is inside, falling short of its production possibilities, it is badly coordinated.

The diagram also illustrates *substitutability* in production. Starting inefficiently someplace inside the boundary, the community *could* produce more of *both* goods; but starting efficiently on the boundary and moving to another point on the boundary necessitates producing more of one good only at the "cost" of *reducing* output of the other.

But at which point on the boundary "should" the economy be? If it is at a "best" combination of guns and butter, it is *economically efficient*. If the community is at some "wrong" point *on* the line, it is economically inefficient, although productively efficient. Economic efficiency, then, is more difficult to achieve than productive efficiency. The notion of economic efficiency rests on a normative criterion of "best" or "goodness." (Normative criteria are "oughts"—what people *ought* to do, how they *ought* to behave, what they *ought* to want.) Thus, productive efficiency, which pertains to the alternatives we *can* produce, is shown by any position on the boundary line, whereas economic efficiency pertains to the particular *preferred* alternative on that line.

Growth is represented by an outward shift of the achievable boundary, for example, to the 1987 boundary shown in Figure 1–2. Growth means

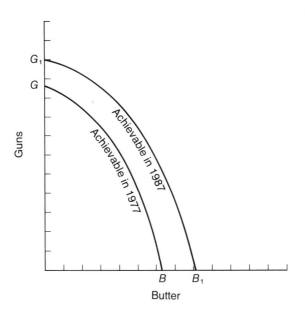

Figure 1–2. Growth of Economic Productive Powers of the Economy

A richer, more productive economy is represented by a production-possibility boundary that is higher and more to the right, as for 1987 compared to 1977. Growth can occur in several ways. A great production-possibility boundary is usually induced by a larger labor force. (But does the output per person increase? That cannot be indicated by this diagram, which gives only the social totals.) Moving the frontier outward involves restricting current consumption by saving either to create more productive goods or to invest in knowledge and inventions. (Problem: Suppose the two boundaries intersected. Which would represent greater productive power?)

that society can produce more. But does the society become "better"? That depends on what it does with its greater productive power. Not all people agree on what is "better" or "best." People compete for the political power to impose their conception of what is "best."

Costs Are Forsaken Alternatives

Our capabilities are limited. We cannot have all of everything we want. As individuals and as a coordinated group, we must select some combination of feasible outputs, because to choose more of one thing means to have less of another. We thus define *cost: the cost of any act is the most valuable alternative thereby forsaken.* So *choice* and *cost* are different facets of the same thing—scarcity. Throughout all economic analysis, by the *cost* of any act is meant the highest valued of the alternative options necessarily forsaken.

To emphasize this, in economics costs are often called *opportunity costs.* A purchaser of a hot dog forsakes claims to other goods worth the equivalent of the price of the hot dog, say 75 cents. But the money price is usually only part of the costs. The purchaser may have spent five minutes waiting in line, and that time could have been used for something else. No extra money expenditure was involved, yet an opportunity to use that time in some other way was forsaken. If alternative use of the time was worth the equivalent of what could be bought for 15 cents, the cost of getting and consuming the hot dog is at least 90 cents (75 cents + 15 cents).

To extend the scope, suppose while buying the hot dog I tarried and joked with the vendor for another minute and kept three other people from being served so quickly. They lost the value of what they could have done with that minute of time. If that were worth 2 cents to each of three people in line, the cost of my hot dog is 6 cents more, or 96 cents, of which I bore only 90 cents while externally imposing 6 cents worth of costs on other people.

Cost then is not necessarily measured only by what is paid in money. It is *all* the forsaken options a person incurs and those he forces others to incur. If I put a lot of onions on my hot dog and foul up the atmosphere in a close conversation with my friend with a loss of purer air of a value to him of 3 cents, the costs of my purchase and consumption of the hot dog mounts to 99 cents, of which I bear 75 cents through sacrifice of market purchasable options and 15 cents of use of my time spent in line, with 9 cents worth of costs imposed on other people and my friend.

Obviously, costs are not always measured by an expenditure of claims on marketable resources by paying money. Nor are they always borne by the particular person responsible for the act.

What do we conclude from all this?

1. The cost of an act is the value of the best alternative opportunity thereby forsaken.
2. Some costs do not involve money expenditures.
3. Some costs may be borne by other people, and in that event are called *externalities*.
4. Many social philosophers think that a person performing some act should be cognizant of all the costs, and some philosophers also argue the actor should bear those costs in order to restrain actions that are not worth the costs (other opportunities forsaken) they involve. Under what conditions those costs are recognized, borne, and affect behavior will be discussed extensively in the remainder of this book.

5. Costs are derived from personal value of possible opportunities; they do not determine those values. Thus, prices and values of goods are the source of costs. As we shall see, market prices are determined by use values rather than by costs.

Actions, production, and consumption are expanded up to the point at which their costs rise to the value of the action. Because these actions or output are expanded up to the point their costs (forsaken use values) equal the perceived or anticipated selling value of the service, many people have been led to think costs determine prices. In fact, output and costs are incurred up to the value of the output or action. If this is not clear now, it will become clear later and will then be a test of how well you have grasped—or this book has taught—economic principles.

The Problem of Production

To think that the problem is to choose desired combinations on our production boundary in the light of values and costs is to overlook the task of even reaching that boundary. The idea of simply choosing some output from our productive capability is romantic. Who can make butter, let alone a gun? One person may know how to breed, feed, and milk cows. Does he also know

1, 2
3, 4
5, 6 *

---

* These numbers direct you to the questions at the end of the chapter. You should refer to these questions—and to the selected answers at the end of the book—when their numbers appear in the margin of the text. Asterisked questions at the end of chapters are not answered at the end of the book.

how to make a modern milk processing plant? To make the stainless steel, the engines, and gases in the refrigerating equipment, the thermometer, trucks to carry milk, and on and on? Indeed, is there any final consumer good that *one* person can or knows how to produce? It boggles the mind to think of the number of people, the incredible variety of specialized bits of knowledge, and the technical skills necessary to provide butter for the market. How is the incomprehensible mass of detailed, separately held knowledge, ability, and work harnessed and coordinated to yield the vast output of consumer goods? Hardly anyone knows who the final recipient will be—or even what final goods our particularized bits of knowledge and services will help produce. We may work with benevolence for a small circle of friends, but our work cannot be relied on to induce all the specialized productive activities that are beneficial to the masses whom we do not know and in ways we cannot forecast. It is an amazing achievement of the capitalistic market-exchange system that it harnesses the powerful motive of self-interest in such peaceful particularized, productive activities that so enormously benefit mankind at large rather than permitting self-interest to lead to junglelike, parasitic, destructive behavior. Without that peaceful control and coordination of self-interest for productive gains, a few of us would be living in the poverty-stricken, painful, brutish, short-lived, ignorant Stone Ages, while most of us would never have experienced life at all.

Competition, Coordination, and Control

With scarcity and unlimited wants, competition among people—and therefore interference with other people—is inescapable. A world of scarcity is a world of competition, and conflicts among competing people must be resolved. One means of resolving such conflicts has always been violence, although the state has usually claimed violence for itself alone, with a view to compelling its citizens to use nonviolent modes of competition. Whether violent or nonviolent modes prevail, the question remains: What mode of competition among greedy people is best?

Note that the question is not how to eliminate competition, for as Arnold Palmer said, "If you aren't competing, you're dead." The scientific questions are, "What are the different kinds of competition, how do they operate, and what are their effects?" The (unsolved) ethical question is, "What is a 'good' society?" Economics can help answer the scientific question, but it cannot decide what is the "good" society.

Violence as a Form of Competition

Before condemning violence (physical force) as a means of social control, note that its threatened or actual use is widely practiced and respected —at least, when applied successfully on a national scale. Julius Caesar conquered Gaul and was honored by the Romans; had he simply roughed up the local residents, he would have been damned as a gangster. Alexander the Great, who conquered the Near East, was not regarded by the Greeks as a ruffian, nor was Charlemagne after he conquered Europe. Europeans acquired and divided—and redivided—America by force. Lenin is not regarded in Russia as a subversive. Nor is Spain's Franco, Cuba's Castro, Nigeria's Gowon, Uganda's Amin, China's Mao, our George Washington.

Within a nation, successful application of violence is a jealously guarded monopoly of the government—indeed, a monopoly necessary for its continued existence. The question of concern to us is, "For the defense of what *other* forms of competitive behavior should the government's violence be threatened or used?"

None of what has been said is in defense of every past or present government nor in praise of physical force. It is simply a nonromantic recognition of its crucial role.

**Control by Religion,
Law, and Ostracism**

Although formal law and state police power are most conspicuous, they are not always the most pervasive or most effective form of social control. Religious doctrines usually promise punishment or rewards in a next life, a prospect that throughout history has been an extremely powerful influence on behavior. Social ostracism for violations of customs and rules of conduct is also a powerful control, as we learn when we are snubbed or left isolated on occasions of our "uncivilized" behavior. No matter how much they differ from society to society or from period to period, standards of morality and propriety seem essential to the continuance of human society.

Techniques of social control differ in effectiveness. Some can be escaped by migration to a new society. Society's intolerance of any behavior can the more readily be ignored the less it is associated with government power, that is, physical force. When the state and the church operated together, each had greater power than when they operate separately. A government's power is less pervasive in a so-called free-enterprise, private-property system than in a socialist system. This fact does not make free enterprise the better system, for you may believe that greater political control over people is desirable in order to restrain their "bad" behavior. Societies in which political authorities control most resources, production, and distribution are called *socialist* or *command* societies, as distinct from *private-enterprise* or *free-market* economies, in which individual contracts play a decisive role.

**Control by Competition in Exchange
and Production of Private
Property**

People are quite predictable in their response to opportunities of gain. Thus, although few have thought of it in this way, an offer of exchange is a powerful competitive social control. If the bulk of property rights are privately owned and can be traded with few constraints, the coordination of competitive behavior is strongly encouraged. Let Adam Smith, the great eighteenth-century Scottish economist, comment:

Man has almost constant occasion for the help of his brethren, and it is in vain for him to expect it from their benevolence only. He will be more likely to prevail if he can interest their self-love in his favor, and show them that it is for their own advantage to do for him what he requires of them. Whoever offers to another a bargain of any kind, proposes to do this: Give me that which I want, and you shall have this which you want, is the meaning of every such offer; and it is in this manner that we obtain from one another the far greater part of those good offices which we stand in need of. It is not from the benevolence of the butcher, the brewer, or the baker, that we expect our dinner, but from their regard to their own interest. We address ourselves not to their humanity but to their self-love.

We shall investigate this and some other kinds of competition in detail, with possibly surprising implications.

Controls, Competitive Criteria, and Survival Traits

Suppose you had to distribute 200 Rose Bowl game tickets (or admissions to your college) without selling them. What form of competition would you use? The authors, red-blooded male chauvinists, would award tickets to the 200 most beautiful women they found. (Why are admissions at your college not allocated that way—or perhaps to some extent they are?) Certainly, a system using beauty is discriminatory. But *all* competition—like all choice—is discriminatory by intention.

If you think beauty is a frivolous criterion, consider an alternative rationing device: first come, first served. All applicants could run a race, with tickets going to the first 200 at the finish line. Silly? Replace "finish line" with "box office at the Rose Bowl" or "registration desks" for popular college classes or "gasoline stations" during so-called oil shortages, and then ask if it is silly. The only difference is that, in these other instances, there is no single starting time, so some people start earlier and wait at the finish line—in rain, cold, and darkness.

Economics does not say what competition is silly, fair, or best. If "fair" competition meant an equal random chance (which it need not), then names could be drawn from a bowl (including names of those who did not trouble to apply). Would you want everyone to have that kind of "equal chance" to be your surgeon, mate, juror, waiter, parents, employer, or movie performer? But we have selected men for the armed forces that way. To further complicate an already complex problem, what is to stop the selected recipients of our Rose Bowl tickets from passing the tickets on to others, according to their own criteria? Or selling them? It is extremely difficult to ensure that one's criteria, selected so reasonably and with the purest of hearts, will be effective all the way through the allocative procedure.

If "first come, first served" were used for allocating such things as food, the people best able to withstand the rigors of standing in line or whose time was less valuable would have better prospects. They would stand in line up to the point where the marginal cost of so doing equals the value of what is obtained. (Remember the meaning of costs.) If food, wealth, or social popularity were awarded more to relatively tall people, height would increase over time. And if beauty were the selected criterion, beauty would tend to increase. Or if personality and rhetorical ability were important as rationing criteria, as they are in politics, society would tend to be distinguished for its personable, articulate people. If productivity were an important allocative criterion, as it is, more resources would be offered to the most productive people; the society would be richer, as would the more productive individuals.

In the gamut of economic problems of *every* society, there is always scarcity, competition, and discrimination; that is, there is social control. This is the fundamental axiom of our analysis, and the behavior stemming from it is our subject matter.

Names color our view of the thing named. *Capitalism, free enterprise,* and *private-property market system* are synonyms, but with different connotations: different mental associations and attitudes. They all refer to a system in which people have private-property rights to production and consumption goods. But the term *capitalism* (first used by Karl Marx) is the standard term used by economists. Why? (1) Because to economists it reminds them that present prices of goods reflect the anticipated values of the future as well as the present services obtainable from existing goods. Just as the price of an automobile reflects the anticipated future services from the car, so prices of all goods reflect the anticipated values of future services. This process of pricing assets in the market to reflect future anticipated values of income streams or consumption services is called *capitalizing,* and we shall explain the process in considerable detail later, in Chapter 7. (2) It also suggests that the price is revealed and obtained in a market where one can sell private property. The availability of a market; the right to exclusive use of authority to decide uses; to buy and sell these entitlements in exchange for others; and the capitalization of values of future services into the present market price of private property goods in open competition with others are all connotations of the term *capitalism.*

Socialism will denote a system in which income-producing goods (machines, land, buildings) and durable consumer goods (houses) are the property of the government and are not salable in the market at market prices.

Between capitalism and socialism there is an intermediate situation in which private property exists for most resources but the state exercises extensive control over what can be done; it prohibits some people from selling certain goods in the market in competition against those who are politically protected and have favored access to the market. This kind of state reservation or monopolization by a politically favored group is often called a *mercantilist system.* As we shall see, it, too, comprises a significant portion of the American economy.

No system is exclusively capitalist, mercantilist, or socialist. Every known society is a mix, with the mixture differing among countries. In the United States, the roads, post office, schools, and police are heavily—though not exclusively—socialistic (not exclusively because we have private schools, private delivery systems, private roads, and private security guards). In predominantly socialist economies, some goods are privately owned, like furniture, clothes, cars, but not all sources of income-producing goods are.

We will not use the terms *free enterprise, free markets,* or *free society* because they suggest "free" has some clear meaning that everyone

7, 8
9, 10
11, 12
13, 14
15

agrees to—when in fact it does not. We avoid comparing "freer" or "less-free" societies and instead investigate differences in cultural attributes, personal behavior, ability, and costs of individual life styles.

Attributes of Economic Analysis

Before going further let's note two attributes of economic analysis that have been implicit in what has so far been said:

(1) Economic analysis is scientific, not normative. It helps to explain what conditions will lead to what consequences: "If A, then B." It does not forecast that A will occur. *If* demand for cars falls, *then* price will fall. But if condition A is met and consequence B follows, the economist is not ordained to pass final judgment on the desirability of B: This is a normative issue. Economics gives no ultimate criteria for determining whether consequences are good or bad, just as chemistry has none for determining whether more rapid oxidation under heat is good or bad. Although many scientists (including economists) will offer all sorts of ethical assessments, what economic *theory* says must be distinguished from what an individual economist may prefer. The former is what counts, not the latter.

(2) To be valid, economic theory must identify and be built on something common to all people and societies. What is common amid all the diversity? Human nature! All people are assumed to have some identifiable similarities of preferences. It is not contended that economic theory has identified (or needs to identify) all the traits that comprise human nature. And it is certainly not assumed that all people are alike in every respect. It is assumed, indeed, that they have different productive capabilities and different tastes. Yet, some virtually universal regularities and general human preferences have been sufficiently demonstrated to yield a theory which is powerful in explaining social phenomena throughout the world. In the next chapter are described those regularities of human nature on which economic theory rests.

16, 17
18, 19
20

What you are to learn is economic *theory* and how to *use* it. You will pick up some facts and further information to provide a context for its application. But do not confuse theory, which is an essential part of any science, with the institutional and empirical data to which the theory is applied. Applications of theory require efforts to learn that theory. Vacuous chatter—appropriate perhaps for cocktail parties and TV talk shows— is neither our goal nor our method.

Summary

1. Production of goods and services is always less than the total amount of goods and services desired. Scarcity is the situation in which the quantity of available goods and services does not match people's desires.
2. The limited production capability can be expressed by a production-possibility boundary, which indicates the maximum amount of a good that can be produced relative to specified amounts of all other goods.

3. Choice, the availability of alternative situations, creates the concept of costs: The cost of any act is the most preferred (highest valued) alternative opportunity thereby forsaken. In a world of scarcity, every chosen act has a cost: the highest valued alternative opportunity thereby forsaken.

4. Some part of the costs of an act by a person may not be identified with a current expenditure of money, and some costs may be borne by other people.

5. People's desires for more goods and services lead to interpersonal conflicts of interest. The process of resolving that conflict is called competition. It often takes the form of striving to offer people opportunities that they will prefer over those offered by other people. All forms of striving to enhance one's situation are competition.

6. Scarcity and competition are inseparable.

7. Instead of futilely complaining about the existence of competition, seek to understand the different forms of competition and differences among their consequences, and what forms of competition are more feasible with given institutional means of controlling societies.

8. *Capitalism* is the name for a society in which the dominant rights and entitlements to use or alter goods and services are exchangeable private property entitlements.

9. *Socialism* denotes institutions in which the productive resources are owned and controlled by the government.

10. *Mercantilism* is a system in which government regulates the use or possible sale of goods and services that are nevertheless held under private property entitlements.

11. Economic analysis and theory are strictly descriptive and analytic, not prescriptive or moralizing.

Questions

1. "If people were reasonable, strikes and wars would not occur." Do you agree? If so, why? If not, why not?

2. a. If there is more than one opportunity to be forsaken, which forsaken opportunity is the cost?

   b. How are opportunities made comparable so that one can determine which one is the cost?

   c. Can there be production without costs?

*3. What is the cost of your college education?

4. "The time involved in purchasing something cannot be considered part of the cost since the time would have passed anyway. Hence to count the value of time as part of the cost of any action is fallacious." Evaluate: What is meant by the value (or cost) of time?

5. Are costs the same thing as the undesirable consequences of some action? Explain why not.

6. What is meant by an equality between private and social costs?

7. Name three honored statesmen who obtained their status by successfully competing in the ability to use violence and who, had they failed, would have been punished for treason or crimes against mankind.

8. a. What kind of competition is permissible in seeking political office but is not permissible in private business?

   b. What kinds of competition are permissible

in seeking admission to college but not permissible for grades in this course?

c. What kinds of competition are approved for business but not for admission to fraternities?

9. "Government dominates in coercive violence." "Government is a social agency for resolving interpersonal conflict."

a. Are those two propositions correct and compatible statements of fact?

b. What evidence can you cite for your answer?

10. a. If you had the power to decide, what forms of competition would you declare illegal?

b. What forms of competition are made illegal by laws establishing price ceilings, minimum wages, fair-employment practices, pure food and drug standards, private-property rights, and by socialism?

11. Competition for admission to colleges uses mental ability, athletic ability, good looks, residence, willingness to pay, alumni status of parents, color, sex, religious belief. Why?

*12. On the average, who do you think are most honest—politicians, businessmen, or teachers? Why? What is your evidence? Can you think of any reasons why dishonesty would be more surely detected and punished in one of these professions? If successful, would dishonesty be more rewarding in one rather than the others?

13. "A more equal distribution of wealth is socially preferred to a less equal distribution."

a. Explain why you agree or disagree.

b. What is meant by "socially" preferred as contrasted to "individually" preferred?

*14. a. What does "equality of opportunity" mean?

b. How could you determine whether it exists?

c. Is there equality of opportunity to get an "A" in this course?

d. How would you make it equal, if it is not?

e. What is the difference between increasing opportunity and equalizing it?

15. "Under socialism, cooperation will replace competition."

a. Is the quoted proposition correct?

b. What evidence can you cite to support your answer?

c. What is the difference between cooperation and competition?

16. "Food is grown, harvested, sorted, processed, packed, transported, assembled in appropriately small bundles, and offered to consumers every day by individuals pursuing personal interests. No authority is responsible for seeing that these functions are performed and that the right amount of food is produced. Yet food is available every day. On the other hand, especially appointed authorities are responsible for seeing that such things as water, education, and electricity are made available. Is it not paradoxical that in the very areas where we consciously plan and control social output, we often find shortages and failure of service? References to classroom and water shortages are rife; but who has heard of a shortage of restaurants, churches, furniture, beer, shoes, or paper? Even further, is it not surprising that privately owned businesses, operating for the private gain of the owners, provide as good, if not better, service to

patrons and customers as do the post office, schools, and other publicly owned enterprises? Furthermore, wouldn't you expect public agencies to be less discriminating according to race and creed than privately owned business? Yet the fact is that they are not." How do you explain these paradoxes?

17. The economic system is alleged to have an effect on the fundamental social and cultural characteristics in a society. Among these are patterns of speech, expression, religion, travel, marriage, divorce, inheritance, education, legal trials, art, literature, and music.
    a. Do you believe these characteristics are in any way different under capitalism than under socialism? Why?
    b. Can you cite evidence for your answer?

*18. Economic ideals of the Middle Ages were influenced by Christianity and by Aristotle's doctrines. Among those ideals were:

"(1) The purpose of economic activity is to provide goods and services for the community and to enable each member of society to live in security and freedom from want. Its purpose is not to furnish opportunity for the few to get rich at the expense of the many. Men who engage in business with the object of making as much money as possible are no better than pirates or robbers.

"(2) Every commodity has its 'just price,' which is equal to its cost of production. No merchant has a right to sell any article for more than this price plus a small charge for the service he renders in making goods available to the community. To take advantage of scarcity to boost the price or to charge all that the traffic will bear is to commit a mortal sin.

"(3) No man is entitled to any larger share of this world's goods than is necessary for his reasonable needs. Any surplus that may come into his possession is not rightfully his but belongs to Society. St. Thomas Aquinas, the greatest of all medieval philosophers, taught that if a rich man refuses to share his wealth with the poor, it is entirely justifiable that his surplus should be taken from him.

"(4) No man has a right to financial reward unless he engages in useful labor or incurs some actual risk in an economic venture. The taking of interest on loans where no genuine risk is involved constitutes the sin of usury.

"It would be foolish, of course, to suppose that these lofty ideals of an economic system largely devoid of the profit motive were ever carried out to perfection." (E. M. Burns, *Western Civilizations, Their History and Culture,* 5th ed. New York: W. W. Norton, 1958.) What do you think of these ideals? If you disagree with any, how would you express your ideal? After completing this course, answer these questions again.

19. What is meant by
    a. The logical validity of a theory?
    b. The empirical validity?
    c. Does either imply the other?

20. "The free-enterprise, capitalist system is free in that it involves no imposition of force or compulsion." Do you agree? Explain your answer.

2

Choice and Exchange

**The Unit of
Analysis Is the
Individual**

Groups, organizations, communities, nations, and societies are best understood by focusing on the incentives and actions of their members. A business, union, or family may be formed to further some common interest of its members, but group actions are still the results of decisions of individuals. Therefore, do not ask, "Why does the U.S. government, or General Motors, or some union, behave as it does?" Ask instead, "Why does the decision-maker decide as he does?" Economics analyzes behavior by assuming a person adapts to environmental changes so as to more fully satisfy his preferences or goals. Economics studies also how he changes the environment. Although people differ in significant and sometimes intriguing ways, all of us share much in our aspirations and expectations; in how we view options and weigh alternatives; in how we respond to circumstances and incentives. Fundamental regularities in behavior can be largely summarized with a few central *behavioral postulates.* To characterize "human nature" so starkly may at first seem oversimple, but it yields an impressive payoff.

   Throughout this book, our analysis is based on several postulates about regularities in human behavior. Some are introduced here—evaluative and choice characteristics. Later, in Chapter 8, their resourcefulness, or productive characteristics, will be indicated.

**Postulate 1.
For each person, some
goods are scarce.**

A *good* is anything that anyone wants. Anything is a good if at least one person wants it. There are two classes of goods: (1) *free* goods and (2) *economic,* or *scarce,* goods. A free good is not scarce, that is, no one would give up any amount of anything to have more of it. The classic example of a free good, for most of us, most of the time, is air: no one has to forego an alternative to inhale. You can have all the air you want even at a zero price; it is costless. However, air is not a free good to astronauts, deep sea divers, and city residents on smoggy days. In such cases, someone does have to give up something if additional air or better air—or *any* air—is to be had. Economic goods are those of which people want more than is available. People will pay something to get more of an economic good. Thus, even as wealthy as it is, America is a society of scarcity.

   Beware of confused usages of *free.* It does not mean an economic good distributed to some people at a zero money price; on the contrary, such economic goods are scarce and thus costly, for example, "free" education, "free" public libraries, "free" campsites, "freeways," and "free" beaches are not free goods. More of anything to one person means less of that thing to other persons, or less of other goods to that person. Charging a zero money price does not magically make a good plentiful to satiation. Indeed, paradoxically, a zero money price on an economic good, as we shall see, makes it even "scarcer."

Hereafter, when we speak of a *good,* we shall mean scarce (economic) goods, that is, goods of which people want more than they have and thus for which they are willing to give up something. By this definition, *goods* include more than just those things that can be conveniently bought in a market. A good is anything, including an objective or goal, of which a greater amount or degree of attainment is desired: love, friendship, esteem, virtue, athletic skill, beauty, speedy trials, and freedom of speech are as much goods as are milk, nylon, music, and gasoline.

Postulate 2.
Each person desires many
goods and goals.

No one wants only one good. We want more of this and also more of that. But to have more of this and more of that, we must forsake some amounts of other goods. Nature is niggardly; we are not provided all we want of every good we want. Therefore, selective, discriminatory *choices* among opportunities are required.

Postulate 3.
Each person is willing to forsake
some of an economic good to
get more of other economic goods.

A person is willing to forsake *some* of any good if a sufficiently large increase in some other goods can be obtained. No one steadfastly refuses to give up even the tiniest portion of some good despite what he could get in return. A sufficiently large reward of some other goods would induce a person to part with *some* (not necessarily all) of any given good.

The smallest amount of some good—for example, wine—that a person would insist on receiving in order to give up, say, one egg is called one's *marginal personal use value* of an egg: It is the amount of wine he regards as just substitutable (that is, equivalent) to that egg. Turned around, it is also the *largest* amount of wine the other person would be willing to *give up* to get that one more egg. "Marginal" refers to *one more* unit—a marginal egg.

It may be surprising that the personal use value of one good is measured, or expressed, as units of some other good. But no good has an intrinsic, or built-in, "absolute" value. In economics, *value* is always defined, measured, and expressed in terms of amounts of some other good. For example, we measured the value of eggs in terms of wine and vice versa; that is, we dealt with the *relative* values of eggs and wine. (Again, in economics there is no other kind of value.) And because the value of a good is defined and measured solely in terms of what we are willing to pay for it, it follows that the value is not necessarily equal to the cost of producing the good—although we shall discover circumstances in which the cost and the value tend to be brought to equality.

Although generally our economic analysis will be of trade-offs among ordinary marketable goods and services, it applies as well, as we said, to trade-offs involving *all* goals, objectives, ideals, and principles. Each of us on occasion sacrifices *some* degree of integrity for some (sufficient) increase in income or safety or popularity or power.

All desired things—standards of morality as well as trinkets in the marketplace—are marginally substitutable for each other. This is a fact of human behavior, which here we neither praise nor condemn.

We again remind you that goods include all desired entities, conditions, and traits: truth, virtue, health, beauty, safety, responsibility, politeness, decency, self-respect, or whatever goals, ideals, and principles you may have. Everyone is prepared to, and does, sacrifice *some* amount (not necessarily all) of honesty or truthfulness for *more* safety, pleasantness, or beauty. People forsake *some* of one ideal for some *more* of another. Each of us is *less* faithful to an ideal or principle if we can get *more* income, a *safer* or a *more* pleasant life, or a *greater* attainment of other esteemed goals. Like it or not, so-called inviolable or moral ideals are violated or compromised by each of us. Imagine a world where no one ever told the slightest lie, or hid the slightest truth, no matter what the resultant gain in security or social pleasantness (or grades?). All goals and ideals are competitive and substitutable in *degrees* of achievement or fulfillment. This is a fact of human behavior that we simply recognize without praising or condemning it. Though in our subsequent analysis, usually we shall deal with trade-offs among amounts of ordinary marketable goods with only occasional reference to trade-offs among degrees of achieving goals or ideals, economics is narrowly materialistic in neither its underlying conceptions nor its real-world application. Notice carefully the emphasis on *more* versus *less;* it is *not* a question of *all* or *nothing* of a good.

Postulate 4.
The more one has of any good, the lower its personal marginal valuation.

The personal value placed on a good is not random, totally unpredictable, or constant. Experience, education, and psychological traits affect the valuation. It also depends on the amount of the good a person already has: *the more of a good one has, the less of other goods one is willing to pay to get an additional unit*—that is, the less is his *marginal* personal value for that good. As we have more of any good, the extra units are put to the less valuable uses.

Postulate 5.
Not all people have identical tastes and preferences.

Even people who have identical amounts of the same goods are not likely to place the same personal marginal values on them. Nor can we say that with equal amounts they are equally well off. One person's gloried asceticism is another's stultifying poverty.

Postulate 6.
People are innovative and rational.

People will try new things in hopes of improving their situation, and among their perceived opportunities they will choose consistently in the sense that if situation A is preferred to B and B is preferred to C, they will, when presented with a choice between A and C, choose A. That innovative yet consistent behavior when selecting from among perceived options is what we mean by saying people are resourceful and rational. (In more rigorous terminology of logic, the term *transitive* refers to consistent choice of A, as in the above example. Nevertheless the term "rational" to describe that transitive consistency has become common in economics.)

These six easy postulates are the features of human behavior on which we shall rely initially. They can be shown in graphic form as *personal marginal use-value* curves. In Figure 2–1, the height of one such curve, *VV,* shown by thin vertical strips, expresses our imaginary person's marginal valuations of successive units of *X*, or, say, eggs. For example, a twentieth egg (if he already has 19) is as valuable to him as having 9 more *Y*, or, say, glasses of wine; and the marginal value of a thirtieth egg is 5 more units of wine per month. We here speak of the value or worth of an egg in units of wine rather than in dollars to again emphasize that value is not merely a monetary phenomenon.

Postulates 2 and 3 (desire for more than one good, and substitutability among goods, respec-

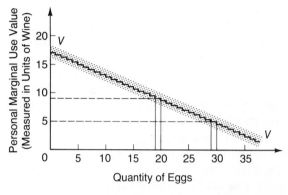

Figure 2–1. Diminishing Marginal Personal Value Schedule
As more of any good, say eggs, is had, the marginal value decreases. The straight line is used as a simple special example for numerical and graphic simplicity. The value is defined and measured in terms of some other goods, here units of wine.

tively) say that a gain or loss of eggs can be offset by a loss or gain of wine or other goods. The downward slope of the valuation curve portrays postulate 4 (marginal personal value of a good falls as its amount increases). Postulates 2 and 3 say that there *is* a curve expressing a person's value (in units of wine) of marginal amounts of eggs, while postulate 4 says the curve has a *negative* slope; that is, height decreases with more eggs.

Although we do not know the particular numerical measures for any person's valuation curve, such a curve nevertheless summarizes much. First, the curve *slopes downward:* the marginal personal value of *X* decreases as *X* increases. That is, as his holdings of *X* get larger, the payment he is willing to make for an additional one is smaller.

Second, the *position,* or height, of the whole curve depends in part on how wealthy a person is, how much he has of other goods. The wealthier the person, the more likely is the curve to be higher. The wealthier one is, the more of other goods he will give to get a unit more of a given good. In sum, what a person is willing to pay (his personal value) for a unit more of X depends on (1) the number of eggs he possesses and (2) his total wealth of all goods. The former affects his *position* along the valuation curve, while the latter affects the *height* of the whole curve itself. In the case of a so-called "superior" good, the whole marginal value curve shifts upward with greater wealth or income; with a so-called inferior good, the curve shifts downward with larger wealth or income. Examples of superior goods are presumed to be diamonds, fine wine or imported beer, clothes, food, automotive elegance, and face-lifts; examples of inferior goods may be cheap brands of beer or cosmetics, as individual wealth or income increases, its possessor puts a smaller valuation on marginal units of such items.

Third, personal value curves are *not identical* for everyone, even for people of the same wealth. Tastes or preference patterns differ. But they all are characterized by *diminishing* (downward sloping) marginal value curves.

To this set of formal postulates about behavior, it is useful to add one observation about our behavior. None of us can perfectly foresee the future or the full consequences of our present actions. We act with uncertainty about outcomes. We state this obvious fact in order to avoid the impression that economic analysis assumes people act with perfectly complete information without ever making errors or allowing for that possibility. Indeed we devote a substantial amount of effort and time to getting better information and

1, 2
3, 4
5, 6
7, 8
9

we do so in a very wide variety of ways, many of which we will examine later in the course of study.

Let us begin to use our postulates.

Trade without "Surplus" Goods

It is commonly believed that people trade because they have a *surplus* of some goods. But trade is induced without surpluses. (Indeed, what *is* a "surplus"?) In fact, people sell goods that are still useful to them—yet, they deem themselves better off by trading. Mutually beneficial trade can occur when people put different marginal valuations on any good. If I am willing to pay more (up to my personal value) to get a book from you than you are willing to accept for it (your personal value), a sale of the book to me at some price below my personal value and above yours would make us each better off. This is the reason for exchange.

Figure 2–2 illustrates the analysis with personal value graphs for Ms. A and Mr. B. Initially, each has 20 eggs per month. The valuation curves differ: With their present numbers of eggs, Ms. A puts a *higher* value on a marginal egg than does Mr. B (a value of 12 units of wine compared to 6 wine). Our first major principle is that *mutually* advantageous trade opportunities exist when the respective personal *valuations differ* at the initial amounts of eggs. Some eggs are sold to the person with the higher marginal personal value of eggs (Ms. A), until she gets a quantity of eggs at which her personal valuation decreases to equal that of the increasing value of eggs to the seller (Mr. B).

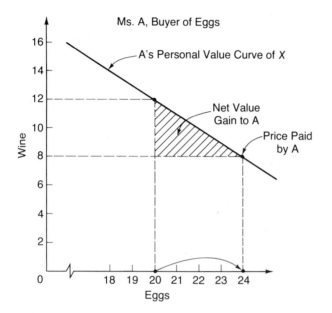

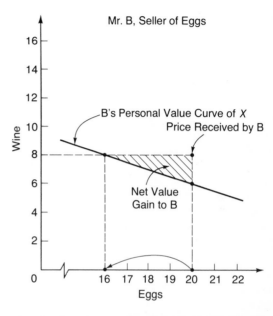

Figure 2–2. Gains from Exchange

Ms. A is happy to buy some additional eggs at a price below 12 wine, and Mr. B gains if he can sell eggs at a price above 6 wine. Ms. A gains by obtaining an egg (to 21 per month) for a price of 10 wine, which she values at 11 wine. Her gain is indicated graphically by the lined area under her marginal value line. When she has bought two to have 22 eggs, her valuation of another egg (the twenty-third) is

reduced to less than 10 wine. At a price of 10 wine, Ms. A will not choose to buy more than 2 eggs, bringing her total amount to 22. The gain to Mr. B is shown by the cross-hatched area above his curve between 20 and 18 eggs. That gain is the amount of wine he is paid in excess of the amount of wine that the egg he sold is worth to him (20 wine—13 wine).

In our illustration, Ms. A is happy to buy some additional eggs at a price *below 12* wine, and Mr. B gains if he can sell some eggs at a price *above 6* wine per egg. By their own personal valuations, both traders are better off at a trading price of, say, 8 wine per egg. Ms. A gains by obtaining her twenty-first egg, which she values at 11 wine, for a price of 8 wine, and she gets a gain on the twenty-second and twenty-third egg, which she values more than 8 wine. Her total gain is indicated graphically by the lined area un-

der her marginal value line. But if she has 24 eggs per month, her marginal valuation of another egg is equal to 8 wine. At a price of 8 wine per egg, Ms. A will buy up to 4 eggs to have 24 eggs per month. Mr. B is willing to sell 4 to Ms. A at a price of 8 wine each, since he values his twentieth, nineteenth, and eighteenth egg at less than 8 wine. His gain from the sale of eggs is represented by the hatched area above his curve. Exchange continues until the marginal personal values of eggs to both parties are equalized, so

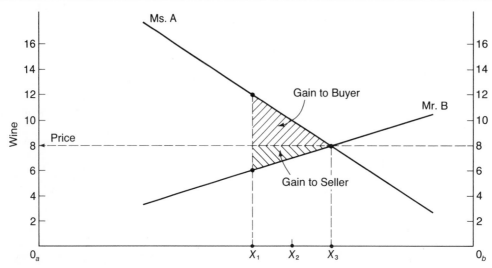

Figure 2–3. Gains from Exchange: Superimposed Marginal Value Lines

Reversing and then superimposing the graphs of Figure 2–1 shows the gains from trade more clearly and portrays exchange in terms of a demander and a supplier, with the person with the lower value on eggs being the seller to the demander—the person with the higher value for more eggs. This diagram shows that the supply of eggs to Ms. A is simply to be interpreted as the demand for that good by other people—here Mr. B.

that no further gains from exchange are feasible. At that price the number of eggs the buyer wants to buy equals the number the seller is willing to sell.

The size of the gains from trade can be analyzed more fully by superimposing the two personal valuation graphs of Figure 2–2. This we do in Figure 2–3. Simply flip the graph for Mr. B around to read from *right to left* and place it so that the *total* number of eggs available for both persons (40 units) is given by the entire length of the base of the diagram, 0_a to 0_b. The number initially possessed by Ms. A (20 units) is indicated by the distance from the left side, 0_aX_1, while that possessed by Mr. B (also 20 units) is measured by the remainder of the base (from the right origin, 0_b, leftward to point X_1).

It is easy to see that the marginal personal value placed on a marginal egg at point X_1 (where each party has 20 eggs) is greater for Ms. A than for Mr. B. That difference reveals that both parties would gain by trade in which Ms. A bought some eggs from Mr. B, moving to position X_2. The gain to Ms. A is in her lined area and the gain to Mr. B is his area. Ms. A's area is below her valuation curve of eggs and above the line indicating the price she pays for the eggs. The gains from trade are measured in units of the good wine, paid as the price, and the areas indicate how the total gains are divided.

These gains from exchange are equal to an amount of Y represented by the lined areas. The "mere" exchange of some eggs for some wine benefits the two parties just as if there had been a magical, costless increase of wine (distributed in accord with the sizes of the lined areas). Trade is as productive as the creation of more physical goods.

We cannot generally predict the actual exchange rate, or negotiated wine price of eggs, but there are limits to what that price can be. It must be between the respective initial marginal valuations of the traders. Any intermediate ratio would induce some trade. And the traders will have an incentive to continue exchange until they reach the distribution point X, at which their valuation lines intersect. A price that would move them to that point is indicated by the intersection height of the two valuation curves: in our illustration, 8 wine = 1 egg.

From all this we deduce a necessary condition for the gains from exchange: *Marginal valuations* placed on the same good differ among people. A sale of some eggs from the person who values them less to the person who values them more is mutually advantageous. The trade brings the marginal valuations of all parties toward equality, with the buyer moving down his valuation curve and the seller moving up his curve to a common level of valuation and price. *Both* traders gain in this process of redistributing goods between themselves, for each trader puts a higher value on what he obtains (buys, imports) than on what he gives up (sells, exports).

When the process of exchange has eliminated any difference in personal valuations—Ms. A and Mr. B each believe at point X_3 in Figure 2–3 that, at the margin, 8 wine is worth exactly 1 more egg—there is no longer a basis for further *mutually* beneficial trade. Further exchange could, indeed, make one person better off, but the other would be made worse off, by selling something he valued more highly than what he bought. Starting at point X_1, this would involve "overshooting" the equilibrium point, moving to the right of X_3. Moving from some distribution point like X_1 to X_3 is often called an *efficient* reallocation of goods; moving beyond X_2 is called *inefficient*.

Propriety of Trade

Should we permit and applaud such conduct? How could one object to Ms. A and Mr. B engaging in uncoerced exchange that makes each person better off? Many in fact believe that individuals should not have this option of exchange to reach positions that are deemed not "really" desirable but are chosen through ignorance or improper standards of conduct. It might be argued that if Ms. A and Mr. B were the only people in the community and each of them considers the redistribution of eggs and wine to be desirable, then "social welfare" has been increased by the exchange. But third parties often deem many exchanges undesirable. Restrictions on gambling or the sale of pornographic literature, or the licensing of occupations all prevent some pairs of individuals from entering into what they would consider to be mutually advantageous exchanges. Perhaps you think it silly (or worse) to prohibit or restrict gambling, pornography, and such—but how about restricting university research contracts with the Department of Defense (for research in biological warfare and thermonuclear weapons and all that), and how about restricting my activities as a part-time doctor equipped only with a course in first aid? Economics explains exchange, but it does not prove that a given exchange should be permitted.

10, 11
12

Money, Markets, and Middlemen

Few persons buy or sell a good for anything except money. A baker does not normally sell bread for meat or flour or vegetables. He sells for something that everyone can actually recognize, store, and transfer at the lowest costs of recognition, storage, and transfer: money. The more transferable, divisible, and easily recognizable a good is, the lower the costs of exchanges are. A good that minimizes those costs can serve both as (1) a common means of payment and (2) a common measuring unit of personal values and prices. A good with those properties would become money. Money enhances our productive power by making exchange cheaper. Anything that enhances our productive power is itself a productive resource. Obvious as that might seem, it was not apparent to the Greek philosopher Aristotle and the many since who, like him, believed that money is sterile and nonproductive.

When deciding what to buy and from whom, you would not sample goods and the prospective services of people at random times and places. You can more cheaply compare personal valuations and negotiate sales in a market at a specialist's store.

Cheap, swift means of communication and cheap, secure transportation have made markets more effective. Sellers advertise their wares and location and terms of exchange. Whatever is said

in criticism of advertising, its major role is to reduce the overall costs of searching for *information* about goods and for completing exchanges. In our example with Ms. A and Mr. B, we tacitly assumed that A and B knew each other, could readily communicate, recognize the qualities of preferred goods, transport the goods, and write contracts of sale covering foreseeable performance contingencies—all at *no cost.*

Figure 2–3 portrayed that ideal case of costless discovery and completion of exchange opportunities. But in the real world we must recognize the costs of finding trade possibilities, of assessing the true characteristics or quality of goods, and of negotiating exchanges. In addition to the explicit price Ms. A pays for X, she also incurs the personal costs of discovering, arranging, and completing exchanges. The actual gross cost to her is higher than the price by the costs of the related shopping activity. Similarly, if the seller performs some of those shopping activities for Ms. A, his actual net revenue will be the cash price proceeds *minus* his personal marketing costs. The effect of these *transaction-arranging costs* is to reduce the extent and the gains of trade. In Figure 2–4(a) all of the cash price—let it be \$8 instead of wine—paid by Ms. A is received by Mr. B. But suppose the self-provided shopping costs are \$1 per unit for Mrs. A and 50 cents per unit for Mr. B, a total of \$1.50 per unit. The net gain from trade now is shown by the (reduced) lined area for Ms. A, between her valuation line and her total costs (price plus personal shopping activity costs). For Mr. B, the gain is the (reduced) lined area between his personal valuation line and his net proceeds line. Exchange goes from X_1 only to X_3, rather than to X_2, where the valuation lines intersect—because

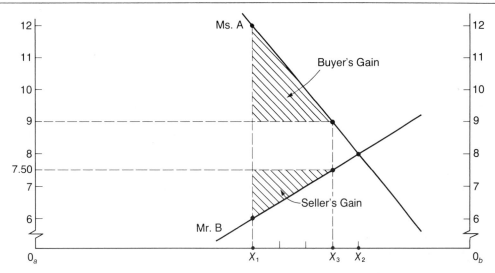

Figure 2–4(a). Exchange with Positive Transactions Costs but No Middlemen

If each unit of X involved a transaction cost (in addition to its price) of $1.50, the lined areas show the gains from the restricted feasible trade.

the costs of trade are no longer zero. These costs reduce the extent and the gains of exchange compared to what they would have been in an unreal world of costless trade information and activity. But the use of money reduces those transactions costs.

Are there other devices than money that reduce marketing costs? The costs of marketing—$1.50 for each unit sold when Ms. A and Mr. B perform their own exchange services—can be reduced to a lower total, say, 75 cents, when done by middlemen, who are *market and commodity specialists.* If Ms. A and Mr. B try to make the sales themselves, without resort to the specialized knowledge of market intermediaries, their total costs will usually be higher. A middleman who can reduce the shopping information

and transactions costs below $1.50 will permit greater gains to both Ms. A and Mr. B with greater exchange, as shown in Figure 2–4(b).

To be sure, the price paid by Ms. A will be higher—say, $8.50 (instead of $8.00, as in the ideal, costless case)—and the price received by Mr. B will be $7.75 (instead of $8.00). But the true cost (including all the transaction costs incurred by Ms. A) is lower because of the middleman: $8.50 instead of $9.00 (i.e., $8.00 + $1.00 equivalent of self-service costs). And the net received by Mr. B is higher: $7.75 rather than $7.50 (i.e., $8.00 − 50 cents equivalent of self-service costs). The people who ignore the value of the middleman's exchange-facilitating services believe that the difference between the price paid by the consumer and the price received by the producer is

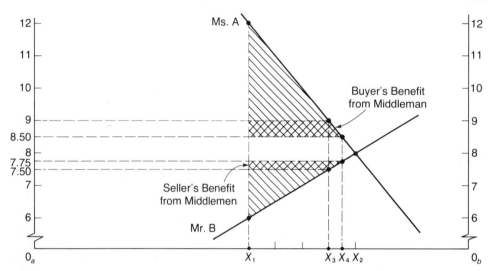

Figure 2–4(b). Greater Gains from Exchange with Positive Transactions Costs and Middlemen

By lowering transactions costs, the middleman allows the trader's gains to be greater than if there were no middleman.

The increase in trader's gains is indicated by the double hatched areas for each trader. More trading will take place with middlemen. Instead of trading from X_1 to X_3 as in Figure 2–4(a), trade will increase to X_4.

a rip-off of the two parties, an exploitative wedge that raises costs to the buyer and lowers proceeds to the seller. In fact, middlemen do the opposite. They reduce gross costs to consumers and increase net proceeds to producers, by performing marketing functions at lower costs. Each trading partner benefits; the middleman covers his costs of marketing by the difference ("markup") between the buyer's retail price and the seller's wholesale price.

This payment for cost-reducing, exchange-facilitating intermediary services accounts for the mark-up difference between retail and wholesale prices (and between "bid" and "ask" quotes in stock markets). Services whose costs are covered in those "spreads" include building space where

transactions can occur, inventories for prepurchase inspection and demonstration of goods the middlemen predict consumers will want, quick delivery, record keeping, advertising, light and heat, insurance, assurances of quality, return privileges, and postpurchase maintenance services. By contrast, discount houses permit (or require) consumers to perform more of these activities of exchange—collecting information from other sources about the quality of goods, self-delivery, obtaining credit, and self-insurance for performance and servicing.

In reducing costs of exchange and providing better service, middlemen—retailers, warehousers, salesmen, brokers, advertisers, and a host of other marketing and financing specialists—are as productive as the actual initial producers of "real" goods. They are not parasites and cost-increasers.

The useful scope of middlemen's services depends on the costs of services that customers are willing to perform themselves and the risks they are willing to bear, the length of the work week, and other factors that we explore later. It also depends on restraints on competition.

13, 14
15

Restraints on Open-Market Competition

In our example, the middleman got 75 cents for each unit sold—the markup between his retail and wholesale prices, $8.50 and $7.75. Assume this was a very profitable spread for him, with the costs of all his activities associated with serving the market, including normal competitive wages for himself, coming to only 30 cents a unit with a profit of 45 cents a unit. Some others, seeing his performance and rewards, might venture into the same business. Their entry would be sustained only if they could sell at lower retail prices and pay higher wholesale prices than the first middleman, or could offer better services to customers. Any of this competition would reduce the profits of that first middleman, who would object to "unnecessary, inexperienced, low-cost, cut-throat, excessive" competitors. The possibility of still other new entrants into the middleman's market would eliminate profits, leaving only normal competitive wages to the first middleman—a less pleasant prospect for him.

That is how open-market competition works. But open markets are not a universal condition. Our initial middleman need not acquiesce to that competition passively. He has several optional tactics in trying to restrict entry—some crude and some sophisticated, but each at one time or another used successfully.

Threats of Violence and Force

To be realistic, we may as well start with what is sometimes a most effective procedure. A threat to damage the new entrant's person or property unless he quits is not genteel. But there are threats against anyone who crosses a picket line in seeking work, or who provides medical, dental, legal, airline, or public utility services for pay without a license. On a picket line, the threat of violence is privately administered; in the other cases, the threat is from government agents—courts and police, who are "legitimate" specialists in applying force. Violence and force are widely applied—sometimes with the help of the state or with acquiescence of the state. (Read that again. Note that we did not suggest what is right or wrong morally. Economics has no basis for decreeing that force or coercion is proper in, say, the medical case and improper in the labor picket case.)

Compulsory Licensing and Self-Regulation

Entry restraints on new, lower-cost or higher-quality competition enables the incumbent group to maintain its income above competitive levels. Under the guise or intent (it doesn't make much difference) of protecting consumers from shoddy products or unscrupulous, corner-cutting, quack sellers of goods or services, a protective law permits only "approved" (duly licensed, properly trained, reliable, ethical) traders. The law usually is administered by a state board staffed by experts, who—naturally—are selected from those already in the business and who automatically get licenses under a "grandfather clause" exempting everyone already in the business. This board determines when "public necessity and convenience" warrants more sellers. Predictably, the number of new licenses is small, for standards of "consumer protection" must be kept "high." Prices are thereby maintained at a level sufficient for the few, more "respectable" practitioners to enjoy a standard of living they deserve. A (very) few examples are provided by liquor stores, pharmacies, lawyers, doctors, banks, barbers, airlines, taxis, accredited schools, and morticians. And some consumers do benefit, especially relatively wealthy people who normally buy from well-established, more expensive firms, while poorer people are protected from lower-priced sellers.

Cartel–Monopoly

An industry with the means—often legal—to control the offering of services of existing members or to restrain the entry of new competitors is a *cartel*. To be effective, violators or nonmembers must be detected and punished, sometimes by invalidating licenses or franchises. But enforcement is not easy. Agents and spies (called *commissioners*) are hired to detect illegal acts like price cutting, favors, and special services. Some of our most respected industries qualify: among them airlines, railroads, radio and TV stations, medicine, law, producers of tobacco, wheat, cotton, corn, milk, and peanuts, and colleges in athletic competition.

Cartel members must pay the political powers for that legal protection—payments in the form of fees for franchises, licenses or special taxes, purchases of $100 dinners honoring politicians, charitable contributions to approved public causes, or free services to special groups. (Consult your local politician, state board member, or member of a regulated industry to learn of additional devices.) These payments will just about exhaust the excess of the future anticipated earnings over what could have been earned in an open market—not forgetting the costs of legal services in obtaining the protective legislation. If state-protected cartels can have earnings in excess of competitive returns, is it surprising that most cartels must contribute to political parties? It is not always clear whether an industry's political power is a prior fact in establishing such legislation, or is a result of the ability to pay for the legislation out of protected cartel income. We conjecture that the larger the number of firms in the business, the more likely is the former case.

Still, no one escapes competition. Even in the striving to form a cartel there is competition among potential members over the conditions. Sometimes consumers who will be harmed are able to exert political power to persuade politicians not to grant legal restrictions that would create a cartel. And even if a cartel is formed, the members will have incentive to cheat in terms of quality, secret rebates, and in ways we shall explore later.

Who Regulates the Regulators—In Whose Interest?

A particularly vivid and quite typical example of the effects of cartel regulation is the Interstate Commerce Commission (ICC). Prior to about 1880, open entry into railroading resulted in the overbuilding of lines, because investors had been too optimistic about the demand for rail services.

Investors suffered losses; as prices were cut below the costs of long-run maintenance, rails and equipment were slowly used up and not replaced. Railroaders persuaded Congress in 1887 to pass the Interstate Commerce Act, so that the government could prohibit price cutting below "just and reasonable" minimum rates, to be publicly posted to prevent secret price cuts. The ICC became the first agency to maintain a price-fixing cartel. But it did not control entry into the transportation business. Other forms of transportation, like barges and trucks, took away some rail customers—more rapidly than would have been possible had the railroads not prohibited themselves from pricing competitively. Because the railroad interests insisted that these new competitors, too, be regulated, the ICC is now authorized to approve rates and market entry by interstate "public-hire" truckers. Public-service surface transportation (rails, trucks, barges) is a restricted industry in which competitors could not lower prices or raise quality of services to what they would be on an open market. Thus, many firms do their own private trucking, because it is not controlled by the ICC and hence is less costly. Competition is indeed pervasive.

Nevertheless, closed markets and price fixing are asserted—and widely believed—to be in the public interest. Are you better off because every moving company is forced to charge the same noncompetitive rate? Are shippers (and consumers) of large bulk products better off when the rails are prohibited from lowering their normal high rates to provide lower-cost bulk service than do barges or trucks—a restriction now imposed on the rails by the truckers and barge owners? Do not confuse the costs of administering controls with the resulting losses imposed on society. Although the expense of administering the ICC is less than $100 million, the cost to society of this inefficient use of transport has been estimated to exceed $5 billion annually. And the ICC is not unique; the Federal Power Commission and the Federal Communication Commission, to name only two, also are similar.

Lest you think ill of government and political restrictions, consider an example generally deemed desirable: restrictions on pollution of rivers and the atmosphere. The pollution problem arises from the absence of clearly defined, easily transferable *property rights* in water or air. Did such rights exist, they would restrain people from abusing resources, i.e., using them in other than their most valuable ways. But in the absence of such rights, government intervention can act as a substitute for them to prohibit lower valued uses of those resources (pollution) and require compensation for any use. In this context government can help clarify property rights to permit better control of such goods through market prices and exchange, or it may instead politically direct how goods shall be used. We shall later be able to analyze effects of each type.

16, 17
18

Ethics of Free Markets

As we noted earlier, economics does not demonstrate that open market competitive exchange makes people better off in a moral or "absolute," "objective" sense. Economics explains how exchange makes transactors better off *in their own estimation*. If a transaction is entered into on the basis of inaccurate and inadequate information, then the contention that a buyer preferred to get what he actually got is open to doubt. Possibly the disappointment prevents the same mistake in the future. As an alternative preventive, could someone else make a better choice for the individual? Others may know more about technical consequences, but they may know little about— or disagree with—the individual's preferences.

Often it is argued that young people ("minors") sometimes do not make sufficiently informed decisions and therefore should be controlled "for their own good." Medical care, food, drugs, and education are areas in which minors—and sometimes adults—are prohibited from entering into mutually agreeable exchanges of goods and services with whomever they please.

Various critics and would-be restrainers of open-market trade attach more weight to regrettable consequences for those who would make unfortunate choices (unfortunate at least in the eyes of the critics and restrainers) than to the forsaken gains for those who would make happy choices, if permitted to choose. Others who make the opposite evaluation favor a larger range of individual responsibility as desirable in itself. Which, if either group, is necessarily more humane, is beyond the scope of economics to say.

Some opponents of open-market trade, further, contend that even with correct information many consumer choices are simply improper. People "ought" to prefer classical to modern music, opera and theatre to TV and movies, sensible housing to flashy cars. "We" who advocate a tax-supported national theater are saying in effect that taxpayers do not spend their money appropriately; but critics allege that "we" are seeking to force others to pay for a theater so that "we" may indulge our tastes at their expense. (Would the issue be changed if "we" were "college teachers" and "tax-supported theater" were "tax-supported college"?)

Freedom: As You Like It

This evaluation of the right to voluntary exchange of goods in the open market is part of the clash between the capitalist and socialist cultures. We have been careful not to express the matter as "free versus unfree" or "democratic versus undemocratic." The socialist could say that people are freer in Russia, because they are free from the task or risk of making uninformed choices. They are freed from the danger of making certain kinds of later-regretted choices, just as you and I are "freed" (prevented) from the risk of hiring a quack to perform an operation or advise us about our illnesses, or from the possibility of buying whole milk with too low a cream content, or from all sorts of possibilities of acquiring inferior things—substandard food, substandard airplane flights, substandard houses. We are supposedly protected from our own folly; we are "freed" from doing or acquiring things that someone thinks we *really* do not want. This may seem an unusual meaning of "free," but it is a widely accepted meaning in Russian *and* American life. It is easy to allege that one's proposed restrictions on other people are those that really give them "more freedom," promote "good" and prevent "bad" consequences. Restraint from doing what is "bad" is, some of us think, no restraint on "true" freedom. But different individuals have different notions of what is good and what is bad. Thus, to use the term "freedom" is to beg questions.

Nor do we speak of democratic versus undemocratic economic rights. Democracy is a way of allocating political power, not a criterion of what is done with it. A dictatorship that is undemocratic could enforce economic and legal rules that are conducive to what some might call a desirable society. A democracy can, by majority revision of various economic and legal rules, produce an "undesirable" society. It is *not* perfectly self-evident to all that democracy as such is more conducive than *any* other system to the emergence or continuance of a society that many would call "free," "open," or "desirable."

Criticisms of Methodology

It is sometimes erroneously charged that economic analysis assumes an unwarranted degree of rational calculation in human economic behavior. It does not. Economics does not explain how people *think;* it identifies predictable, observable patterns of *behavior.* People need not be aware of the principles of economics when they engage in exchange. Sticks and stones, birds and bees obey the law of gravity even though they do not know what it is; humans obey this same law before they have learned about it. Nothing in economic theory rests on any premise that people are logically consistent in their *thought processes.* Instead, it is the theory and analysis of economic behavior that is logical. And that analysis will be empirically valid if the behavior it implies is observed.

Self-Interest and Greed

Where in the preceding postulates can you find the assumption that humans are interested *only* in their own individual wealth or welfare? The assumption isn't there, and properly so. We did assume that humans are greedy—meaning that each wants *command over* the decision about uses of more goods rather than of less. But a person may want control over more goods in order charitably to help others. It is not assumed that he is oblivious to other people or unconcerned about their welfare or not benevolent. If these assumptions had been made, the resultant theory would be immediately falsified by the fact that people do engage in charity, are solicitous of other people, do consider the effects of their behavior on other people, and do sacrifice marketable wealth for leisure, knowledge, and contemplation.

What *is* meant by "selfish" man is that one of the "economic goods" he seeks is the right to choose among options that will affect ensuing affairs. In short, the *right to make choices* about the future is a desired thing, an "economic good." However, as with all other goods, as the cost of that right is raised, the less of that choice will be retained. The lower is the cost, the more will be retained. Raise my salary enough, and I'll let you determine what kind of clothes I wear to work, or where I work, or how my retirement fund is invested.

Utility-Maximizing Behavior

The preceding set of postulates is often misleadingly called the "utility-maximizing" theory of human nature. The term suggests there is something called *utility*—like mass, height, wealth, or happiness—that people maximize. And indeed during the early history of economic analysis, it was assumed that goods provided utility or usefulness in some measurable, psychological sense. Although that misleading psychological conception has been abandoned, the name "utility" has stuck. So it is now simply a name for the ranking of options in accord with any individual's preferences.

Once *utility* no longer is thought to have an objective, measurable meaning, saying that a person "maximizes" utility may seem an elaborate camouflage of our ignorance of why people behave as they do; for whatever a person does, could he not be said to be "maximizing his utility"? Yes, but only if we were unable to specify what entities are goods and goals and if we could not classify situations according to higher or lower costs of acquiring goods. In fact, we *can* make specifications of goods and relative costs and therefore *can* provide meaningful, refutable theorems. And we shall give many in this book. For the moment, consider an example. Saving

19, 20
21, 22
23

lives may be a good. But consider two different situations. In one, you can save a life by jumping into a pond and pulling out a child; in the other, you must jump into a raging torrent with 99 percent probability of drowning yourself. Now, what does our theory tell us? The probability that a given number of people will jump into ponds to save lives is higher than that they will jump into torrents.

Finally, economics is "value free" in that it is scientific and analytical in explaining what happens; it makes no judgments as to what is desirable for people—or what should be. Nevertheless, economists as individuals are not value free. Like everyone else, they have preferences and prejudices about what ought or ought not to be, and those opinions are as fallible and personal as the judgments of those who know nothing about economics. Though the economist may be better able to discern the consequences of some proposed act, he is not superior in evaluating the propriety of that consequence. Often, what passes for analysis is merely a personal view. Distinction among facts, analysis, and value judgments are important in all of one's experiences. The authors have their conscious and unconscious personal views about what ought, or ought not, to be. But we have made great efforts to make them detectable as personal views, rather than to pass them off as conclusions of scientific economic analysis (although we have perhaps done so with less than total success).

Summary

1. The unit of economic analysis is the individual who acts within the economy, not the institution within which he acts.
2. *Postulates of Behavior:*
   (1) For each person, some goods are scarce.
   (2) Each person desires many goods and goals.
   (3) Each person is willing to forsake *some* of an economic good to get *more* of other economic goods.
   (4) The more one has of any good, the lower its personal marginal valuation.
   (5) Not all people have identical tastes and preferences.
   (6) People are innovative and rational.
3. The future is not perfectly foreseeable.
4. To say a person places a value on a good means he is willing to sacrifice some of some other goods to get more of that good.
5. Self-interest means a person values the power of choice over options that will affect his situation.
6. Differences in the personal valuation of goods for any two persons means that reallocating portions of these goods by trade can move each person to a preferred situation, provided the costs of discovering these people, of negotiating the exchange contracts, and of transporting the good do not exceed the difference in personal values.
7. Goods will be traded from the lower valuing person to the higher valuing person.
8. Each person will increase (or reduce) his amount of any good relative to other goods until his personal marginal value for increments of the good are reduced (or increased) to equality with the market price.
9. At equilibrium each person has the same marginal personal valuation of a good as every other person—a value that is also equal to the market exchange price.
10. Each seller (or buyer) has an incentive to restrict other sellers (or buyers). In the absence of arbitrary obstacles or legal restrictions, the prospect of profits will entice new sellers into the market. Existing sellers (or buyers) have incentives to reach agreements to avoid cutting (or raising) price. The government will be appealed to as a means of keeping out new competitors—under the guise of protecting consumers. The gains from being a legally protected cartel will, in part at least, be taken by government officials or be absorbed in the costs of getting political protection.
11. Market prices do not measure the value of the total amount of a good; they measure only the marginal value—the increased value from an additional unit (an increment) of the good.
12. For trade to occur it is not necessary that one party have a surplus of some good while another has an insufficiency.
13. Exchange of two goods between two parties occurs because each party has a different marginal value on each good. The higher marginal valuing party gets more of the good that he values more highly, and the other party receives the other good that he values more highly.
14. Economic analysis does not prove that trade is a good thing. It only shows the conditions that lead people, if given the opportunity, to engage in exchange.

Appendix: Preference
Maps and Utility Lines

The postulates characterizing the economically relevant attributes of human behavior can be described by preference maps.

In Figure 2–5, point A denotes a combination of two goods, X and Y. The amount of X is measured by the horizontal distance to the right from the vertical axis, and the amount of Y by the vertical distance upward from the horizontal axis. Point B denotes a different combination of goods X and Y. It contains more X but no more Y than does combination A: It lies directly to the right of point A. On the other hand, combination C contains more Y than point A, but no more X.

According to our postulates, the combination denoted by point B is preferred to that of point A; also, point C is preferred to point A. We mean that, if offered a choice between options A and B, our person would choose B, since it has more X and no less Y. The preference of B over A means that X is an economic good. Similarly we assert he would choose C over A, which means that Y is an economic good.

To indicate his preference pattern or ordering, we could arbitrarily assign some number to point B, say 76, and assign a smaller number to point A, say 49. A point assigned a higher number is preferred to a point assigned a lower number. We shall *arbitrarily* attach the term *utility* to that preference indicator. Perhaps the term *preference* or *choice index* would be better, but the convention of economics dictates *utility*.

Now consider Figure 2–6. A curved line labeled U_1U_1 runs through point B. At point B is a little "triangle," the length of whose vertical side measures the decrement of Y, $\triangle Y$, that would be the

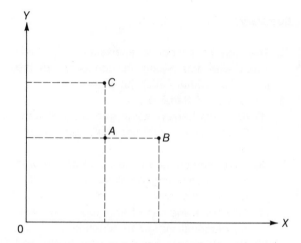

Figure 2–5. Combination of Goods X and Y

Points A, B, C denote different combinations of X and Y. The combination denoted by B has more X and the same amount of Y as the combination at A. C has more of Y. If point B is preferred to A, X is an economic good. Similarly, if point C is preferred to A, Y is an economic good. (Why?) If B is not preferred to A, X is either a free good or a "bad" (rather than a "good"). But we have defined X and Y to be goods and, in particular, economic goods. How could you portray diagrammatically the personal value of a unit of X at point A? Would it be greater or less than at B? At C? (See Figure 2–6 for the answers.)

most our person would be willing to sacrifice to get the small increment (horizontal side) of X, $\triangle X$, with the person initially at combination B. The ratio of $\triangle Y$ to $\triangle X$, $\triangle Y/\triangle X$, is indicated by the *slope* of the hypotenuse of that triangle, which is the slope of the curved line U_1U_1 at B. The flatter that slope, the less is the decrement, $\triangle Y$, that our person is willing to sacrifice for the increment $\triangle X$ of X. The less is $\triangle Y/\triangle X$, the less is the substitution value of an X (in terms of Y) and the greater is the substitution value of a Y (in terms of X). Remember that the personal sub-

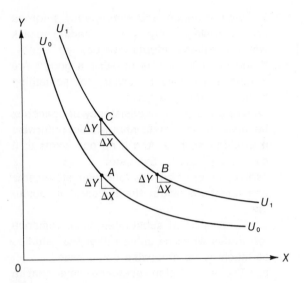

Figure 2–6. Convex Constant-Utility Curves for Some Person

Any point on U_1U_1 is preferred to any point on U_0U_0. At each point, the slope of the curve measures, by ΔY, this person's valuation of ΔX, a uniform increment of X. Slope at B is less than at A; and at A is less than at C. Also, the slope of a curve diminishes along the curve as one moves from upper left to lower right. That is, personal substitution valuation of X decreases as one moves from much Y and little X to less Y and more X.

stitution value of a unit of any good *is* the amount of his "equally preferred" change of some other good. The slope at point *A* is steeper than at *B* (with reference to the *X* axis). This means the value of an *X* at combination *A* is greater than the value of an *X* at *B*.

The slope of the line through point *C* is steeper than at *A*. The value of a unit of *X* is greater (in terms of *Y*) at *C* than at *A*. Our person has more *Y*, and the more he has of a good (the amounts of other goods being unchanged), the less is its personal value. That steeper slope indicates a reduced personal substitution value of a unit of *Y*

relative to *X*: It takes more of an increment in *Y* to offset the unit change in *X*. Remember that the larger $\triangle Y$ is for a unit change in *X*, the *lower* is the personal substitution value of *Y* (and the greater the personal substitution value of *X*).

Line U_1U_1 marks combinations of *X* and *Y*, all of which are equally preferred (that is, equally desired, have the same utility) with point *C* or *B*. All combinations of *X* and *Y* through which U_1U_1 goes are equally desirable. In terms of our preference indicator, utility, all points on U_1U_1 have the same utility index.

Every point above and to the right of line U_1U_1 is preferred to any point on that line, since every point above it represents a bigger combination than any point directly below or to the left of it. Every point below the line is less preferred than any point on the line. A curve, U_0U_0, drawn through *A*, shows all combinations indifferent to *A*. And every point on U_0U_0 is less preferred than any point on the line U_1U_1. (Be sure you see why!)

How does a convex sloped constant-utility line describe the postulates? First, it has two dimensions—two goods—not just one, which reflects postulate number 1. Second, any basket with a larger amount of either good (lying to the right or above) will be on a constant-utility curve with a greater index of utility—which means that more of *X* (or of *Y*) is preferred. This is postulate number 2. Some goods (here, *X* and *Y*) are scarce. Third, the U_1U_1 lines (constant-utility, or indifference, curves) have *negative slopes*—which means that some increment of *X* will make up for some loss of *Y*, and vice versa. That negative slope expresses our third substitutability postulate. Fourth, the slopes of the successive indifference curves that one crosses, from left to right, get flatter. At each point the *slope,* which is the personal substitution valuation of *X,* decreases the more of *X* one has. This is postulate number 4. Also, as one moves up vertically—indicating more *Y* for a *fixed* amount of *X*—slopes of successive indifference curves get steeper, which means his personal substitution value of *X* increases as *Y* is increased. But this is the same thing as saying that his personal substitution value of *Y* decreases as *Y* is increased.

The personal substitution value of good *X* is measured by the slope of the indifference curve at any point. It is *not* measured by how much the utility of the person increases as he gets one more unit of the good *X.* Why not? Because we define the personal substitution value to be that slope. And, anyway, no one has yet discovered a generally acceptable, objective method of measuring increases in utility so as to make them comparable among different people. Lacking any such interpersonal comparability of a measure of utility, we must not pretend one exists—unless we want to get into all sorts of errors in comparing measures that simply cannot be compared.

24, 25
26, 27
28

Questions

1. "The college football team has a goal."
   a. Is it the social goal of the "team," or is it the common individual goal of each member of the team?
   b. Are you sure that each member has only that goal and not also one of playing more of the game himself?
   c. Is it helpful to talk of one goal being preferred over another?

2. In trying to understand some policy enforced at your college, why is it misleading to ask why the college adopts that policy?

3. If you don't smoke, is tobacco a good? Are purchase and sale necessary for something to be considered a good?

4. "A free good is an inconsistency of concepts, because no one wants what is free; otherwise it wouldn't be free. And if no one wants it, it can't be a "good." Evaluate.

*5. Explain or criticize the following statements and questions about the substitution postulate:
   a. "Every student substitutes some romance for grades when he dates rather than studies as much as he otherwise could have."
   b. "The substitution postulate says that a student does not seek the highest possible grades."
   c. Does the substitution postulate deny that water, food, and clothing are more basic or more needed than music, art, and travel?
   d. "There is no hierarchy of wants." What does that mean? Can you disprove it?
   e. Is travel in Europe a substitute for formal academic education? for some food? for a bigger house or new clothes or medical care? For what would it not be a substitute?
   f. "I'd like to play poker with you again tomorrow night, but I don't think my wife would like it." Is this consistent with the substitution postulate? Is the wife's utility being compared with the husband's? Explain.

6. Explain the difference between the statements, "People act in accord with certain fundamental propositions" and "People consult or refer to such propositions for guid-

ance in choosing their behavior." Does either interpretation assume "free will" or independence from other people's behavior or tastes?

7. In testing a person's preference between two known options, it has been suggested that if a person agrees to let some unknown party choose for him, then he is indifferent between the two options. Do you think that is consistent with the postulates listed in the text?

8. Suppose that I am indifferent if given a choice among the following three combinations of steaks and artichokes:

	Steaks		Artichokes
	(pounds per year)		
Options A:	100	and	30
B:	105	and	29
C:	111	and	28

a. What is my marginal personal value of steak (between options A and B)?

b. What is my marginal personal value of artichokes (between B and C)?

c. If the amount of meat in A were doubled to 200, what can be deduced about the amount of meat required in B to make its personal value equal to A?

*d. Using your answer to (c), compute my personal marginal valuations between the new A and the new B. Is that consistent with the fourth postulate?

9. Postulates were used to characterize some aspects of human nature and behavior.

a. Do you think any of them are also applicable to nonhuman animal life? For example, which of the postulates would validly apply to the behavior of monkeys, ants, bees, tigers, and birds?

b. Which postulates, if any, do you think serve to distinguish human from nonhuman behavior?

c. What evidence can you cite to support your answers?

d. Do you think the human race would survive if it lost the attribute described by postulate 3 while some animals retained it?

10. "Economic analysis shows that to permit trade is better than to prohibit trade." Does it?

11. A parent gives each of his two children some milk and meat. The two children then exchange with each other, one drinking most of the milk and the other eating most of the meat. If the parent does not permit them to make that exchange, which of the postulates (if any) is he denying? Or does the explanation rest on some new postulate not made explicit in the text?

12. "Trade between the Mediterranean and the Baltic developed when each area produced a surplus of some good."

a. What do you think this quotation, from a widely used history text, means?

b. Can you propose an alternative explanation of that trade?

13. Some discount stores advertise that they can sell for less because they buy directly from the manufacturer and sell to the consumer, thus eliminating many middlemen. What is the flaw in this reasoning?

14. "Middlemen and the do-it-yourself principle are incompatible." Explain.

15. It is estimated that 25 percent of the price a housewife pays for a head of lettuce goes to the farmer, while the remaining portion is for middlemen and distribution costs.

    a. Would you, as a farmer, necessarily prefer to have your percentage raised? Explain your answer.

    b. Would you, as a consumer, prefer to see his percentage raised? Explain.

16. Which of the following are compatible with open (or free) markets:

    a. A lawyer must get permission of present lawyers before he can engage in that trade.

    b. Medical doctors must pass a state examination before being allowed to sell medical services.

    c. Selling is prohibited on Sunday.

    d. Pure food and drug laws restrict the sale of "impure" foods and drugs.

    e. Consumption, manufacture, or sale of alcoholic beverages is prohibited.

    f. Dealers and agents must be certified by the U.S. Securities and Exchange Commission before they can act as middlemen in buying and selling stocks and bonds—that is, before they can be security dealers.

17. Suppose you succeed in leading an army of "liberation." Upon taking office as dictator, you abolish all existing monopoly rights.

    a. Would you then grant new monopoly rights?

    b. If you did, how would that benefit the government (you)?

    c. If you didn't think of doing that, who would suggest it to you?

18. You are campaigning for mayor or councilman in your home town, in which the taxi service (or, for that matter, garbage service, milk delivery, electric power, water, gas, etc.) is provided by anyone who wants to operate a taxi business or drive his own cab. In other words, the taxi service is provided by an open market. You campaign for more government control of taxi drivers in order to ensure better quality of service.

    a. If elected, would you initiate a system of giving just one company the right to perform the service? Why?

    b. If so, how would you decide which company?

    c. Would that company be one of your campaign financiers?

    d. In California the right to sell liquor is restricted by the state government to far fewer stores than would prevail otherwise. Would you be surprised to learn that the liquor dealers are a political "lobby" and source of "power" in state politics? Why?

    e. What generalization does this suggest about a source of political power?

19. "All goods or goals are incompatible. And at the same time they are compatible." Can you make sense of that?

20. "It is well to remind ourselves from time to time of the benefits we derive from a free-market system. The system rests on freedom of consumer choice, the profit motive, and vigorous competition for the buyer's dollar. By relying on these spontaneous economic forces, we secure these benefits: (a) Our system tends automatically to produce the kinds of goods that consumers want in the relative

quantities in which people want them. (b) The system tends automatically to minimize waste. If one producer is making a product inefficiently, another will see an opportunity for profit by making the product at a lower cost. (c) The system encourages innovation and technological change. . . . I regard the preservation and strengthening of the free market as a cardinal objective of this or any Administration's policies." (President J. F. Kennedy, September 1962, speaking to business magazine and newspaper publishers.) Is it surprising and confusing that while extolling the virtues of an open, competitive economic system, businessmen and politicians restrict markets—for example, by controlling allowable imports of sugar so as to maintain sugar prices in the United States above the open-market level—in order to maintain larger wealth for incumbent businessmen and their employees? A confusion between freedom of competition and freedom from competition is suggested. What explains this praise of the virtues of a system of private property and open markets with simultaneous attempts to suppress it?

21. Your college allots some parking space for your car while a friend is allotted a desk in the library stacks. Suppose that you and he would each be better off if you were to trade your parking space for his desk space.

*a. This kind of trading is almost invariably prohibited by the college authorities. Why?

*b. If you were the college president, why would you prohibit it?

*c. Would you consider solving the whole problem by simply selling parking space to one and all at the market-clearing price, like a downtown parking garage? Why?

22. "Economic theory is built on an idealization of man: that he has tremendous computational power, a detailed knowledge of his desires and needs, a thorough understanding of his environment and its causal relationships, a resistance to acting on impulse or by habit." Explain why this statement incorrectly characterizes economic theory.

23. Suppose it were claimed that a denial of college facilities to some speaker is a denial of the right of free speech. Show how that argument confuses free resources with free speech.

24. The following combinations of X and Y are all equally valued by Mr. A, i.e., he is indifferent among them.

Equal-Value Combinations	X	Goods	Y
A	9	and	50
B	10	and	40
C	11	and	34
D	12	and	30
E	14	and	26
F	17	and	21
G	21	and	17
H	26	and	13
I	33	and	10
J	40	and	9
K	47	and	8
L	57	and	7

a. What postulate is expressed by the fact that there is more than one combination of the same utility to Mr. A?

b. Do these combinations conform to the postulates?

c. What postulate is expressed by the negative slope of the line connecting these combinations (the *iso-utility line*—sometimes called an indifference curve, to connote that the person is indifferent among the combinations on this line)?

d. What postulate is reflected in the curvature (not the slope) of the iso-utility line?

25. How could you show graphically, on the diagram you drew for question 24, the meaning of postulate 2?

26. If I regard each of the following combinations as equally preferable, which postulate is denied?

		Goods		
		X		Y
Options	A	100	and	70
	B	105	and	69
	C	110	and	68
	D	115	and	67

27. Suppose that Mr. A is indifferent between A and C of the following three options.

		X		Y
Options	A	100	and	200
	B	110	and	180
	C	120	and	160

If he is given a choice among the three options, prove that, according to the postulates, he will choose option B over either A or C. (The proof is easy—but it is not easy to discover that proof.)

28. What refutable proposition is suggested by the statement, "A has more utility than B"?

3

Demand:
The Relation of
Price to Amount
Demanded

If there is no national authority to compute per-capita shares of available food, gasoline, shoes, tires, or pencils and ration them accordingly, what makes the total private consumption decisions match available social totals? Apparently something does. And why does it sometimes fail? To answer that and many other queries we use an analytical device that, for many purposes, adequately incorporates all the fundamental behavior postulates from Chapter 2. This device, *demand,* is a *relationship* between the amount of a good demanded and its market price.

Of course, the amount of a good we want depends on a lot of other things, too. For example, a person's demand for automobiles will depend on his wealth, his current income, his age, his health, the price of gasoline, the costs of garage space, where he lives, the prices of public transport service, to name just a few. In addition to all those, one thing that surely affects how many automobiles he wants to have is the price of automobiles themselves. The price of something itself is a major, though not the sole, determinant of the amount of that good demanded. Even if that price doesn't vary much, whatever the price is affects the amount demanded. The principal factors we shall investigate are the price of the good itself, the income or wealth of the person, and prices of some close substitutes and of jointly used complementary goods.

Demand versus Amount Demanded: The First Law of Demand

Table 3–1 illustrates the *demand relationship.* It lists a schedule of possible prices with the

Table 3–1. Demand Schedule

Price	Quantity of Eggs
$1.00	1
.90	2
.80	3
.70	4
.60	5
.50	6
.40	7
.30	8
.20	9
.10	10

amounts demanded at each price. At lower prices, amounts demanded are larger; at higher prices, amounts demanded are smaller. The two statements are converse expressions of the *first law of demand.* This whole list of prices *and* associated amounts demanded is called the *demand schedule*—or *demand* for short. The particular amount at any one price is called the *amount demanded*—*not* demand, because the latter term refers to the whole *schedule of amounts and prices.* (Observe this distinction if you want to avoid a lot of misleading terminology and erroneous analysis.) At a price of $1, the amount demanded (*not* the demand) is one egg weekly. At a price of 90 cents the amount demanded is two eggs weekly. And if the price were 80 cents, the amount demanded would be three eggs a week.

According to the table the lower the price, the larger is the amount demanded. This is the first law of demand. It can be expressed in various ways, some more elegant and general and less open to misinterpretation. For example, some people correctly counter that sometimes when

Table 3–2. Demand and Personal Use Values

Price	Quantity	Total Personal Use Value	Marginal Personal Use Value
$1.00	1	$1.00	$1.00
.90	2	1.90	.90
.80	3	2.70	.80
.70	4	3.40	.70
.60	5	4.00	.60
.50	6	4.50	.50
.40	7	4.90	.40
.30	8	5.20	.30
.20	9	5.40	.20
.10	10	5.50	.10

Table 3–3. Personal Values Demand, and Market Revenues

1	2	3	4	5
Price (p)	Quantity (Q)	Total Personal Use Value	Marginal Personal Use Value	Total Market Value or Revenue (TR)
$1.00	1	$1.00	$1.00	$1.00
.90	2	1.90	.90	1.80
.80	3	2.70	.80	2.40
.70	4	3.40	.70	2.80
.60	5	4.00	.60	3.00
.50	6	4.50	.50	3.00
.40	7	4.90	.40	2.80
.30	8	5.20	.30	2.40
.20	9	5.40	.20	1.80
.10	10	5.50	.10	1.00

the price of a good rises they continue to consume as much as ever. But, of course, if the price were *much* higher, they would cut down on their consumption. The law of demand does not state that every person will reduce his consumption with every rise in its price. It is only to show the basic principles in operation that we use a numerical example with a different amount demanded at every price. All that the law of demand says is that at some higher price, possibly much higher, he would consume less. The law does not predict a continuous response in amount demanded for any price rise, no matter how small. All that is assumed is the proposition just stated: For any amount of consumption at a given price, *some* higher price would make the person reduce his consumption of that good. This permits some intervening range of price over which that person does not change his amount demanded. But certainly there is an upper limit to that range of nonresponse, above which he will reduce his consumption of the good.

Personal Use Valuations (Total and Marginal) and Market Expenditures

Because it gives alternative prices and the quantities demanded at each price, the demand schedule permits us to compute total, average, and marginal values in personal use of a good to the demander, as in Table 3–2. Since the person demands one egg a week when the price is $1, we infer that the use value of that egg equals at least the value of $1 of other things that could have been bought with that dollar. If the price were 90 cents per egg, the person would choose to buy two eggs per week. Since he could have chosen to demand only one egg, but demanded two eggs, that second (that is, marginal) egg must be worth at least 90 cents of *alternative* possible purchases. The $1 use value of the first egg plus the 90 cents value of the marginal egg gives a total use value of at least $1.90. But while the use value of the two eggs to this individual approximates $1.90 ($1 + 90 cents), the market expenditure required to buy the eggs is $1.80 (90 cents × 2) (column 5 of Table 3–3).

At a price of 80 cents each, three eggs are demanded. Since that third egg is demanded, it must have a value equal at least to the price of 80 cents. So the *total* use value of the three eggs is $1 + 90 cents + 80 cents = $2.70; the additional use value from obtaining an extra (marginal) egg—that is, the *marginal* use value of eggs when three are demanded—is 80 cents. This is the difference in the total use values of two eggs and of three eggs. The *expenditure* on the three eggs is 80 cents × 3 = $2.40.

Use value is given in terms of money only for simplicity; use value is actually interpreted in terms of the quantity of other goods that the person regards as no more than equally desirable. That is, we say that the marginal use value of eggs is 80 cents when we demand three eggs. Why 80 cents? Because by spending 80 cents on that marginal egg (which physically is no different from any of the other eggs), the person thereby forgoes buying other things obtainable with the 80 cents. And by choosing that third egg the person indicates that those other things are not of greater value to him than the marginal egg. But note that the marginal use value of eggs is not constant—it decreases as the number of eggs gets larger. Value, then, is not an "absolute"— it is not an intrinsic, constant, built-in attribute of either the good or of the inputs that produced it.

Remember, personal use value is to be interpreted and measured in terms of the quantity of other goods that a person regards as equally desirable. Remember also that economic goods include *all* things that we would like to have— friends, cleanliness, health, honesty, social amenities, beauty of person and environment—and not merely marketable things like milk, shoes, cars, etc. In economics, the measure of value is all-inclusive, even though it is often expressed in terms of just one of the goods: dollars. Finally, remember also that value is not some "mystical," inherent attribute of a good. To repeat, the value to any person of one more unit of a good is simply the amount of other goals, goods, or desirable things that are equally desirable.

We can now explain the connection between use value and demand. If the price per egg is 80 cents, three eggs are demanded each week, according to that unchanged demand (the schedule, remember, not the amount demanded). We have seen that to this person one egg has a marginal use value of $1. For that one egg, the consumer obtains a "surplus" of 20 cents, that is, a surplus of personal use valuation ($1) over the market price (80 cents). Similarly, a second egg could be bought for that price of 80 cents, although it has a personal use value of 90 cents— thus, a "consumer's (buyer's) surplus" of 10 cents. There is no surplus from the third egg: personal valuation equals price. And if the price were lowered to 70 cents, consumer's surplus would increase: 30 cents on a first egg, 20 cents on a second, and 10 cents on a third, with zero surplus now on a fourth. Thus, the person extends his amount demanded to that at which the surplus on the marginal unit is zero; that is, an amount is bought at which marginal use value is reduced to market price. And at that desired quantity at a given price, the *total personal use value* (column 3 of Table 3–4) will exceed the total revenue, or expenditure (column 5). This

Table 3–4. Demand, Personal Values, Market Revenue, and Consumer Surplus

1	2	3	4	5	6
		Total Personal Use Value	Marginal Personal Use Value	Total Market Value or Revenue	Consumer Surplus
Price	Quantity				
$1.00	1	$1.00	$1.00	$1.00	$ .00
.90	2	1.90	.90	1.80	.10
.80	3	2.70	.80	2.40	.30
.70	4	3.40	.70	2.80	.60
.60	5	4.00	.60	3.00	1.00
.50	6	4.50	.50	3.00	1.50
.40	7	4.90	.40	2.80	2.10
.30	8	5.20	.30	2.40	2.80
.20	9	5.40	.20	1.80	3.60
.10	10	5.50	.10	1.00	4.50

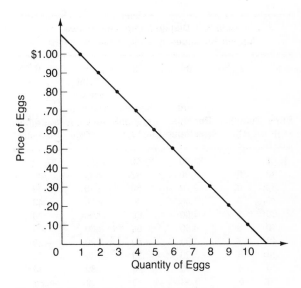

Figure 3–1. Ms. A's Weekly Demand for Eggs

The dots chart a demand relationship between the price of eggs and the quantity of eggs demanded at each price (see Table 3–1). (We connect all of these points on the demand schedule to get a continuous demand curve, as shown by the black line drawn through the dots).

difference between value and expenditure is the consumer's surplus (column 6).

We only pretend to know the exact personal marginal use value schedule for any person. But we do know one crucial characteristic of that schedule: Marginal use value diminishes as quantity of the good increases. And this suggests that the lower the price, the more will be demanded. This is our first, fundamental law of demand—probably the most useful proposition in all of economics: "The higher the price, the smaller the amount demanded in the market," or, "Whatever the quantity of any good demanded at any particular price, a sufficiently higher price will decrease the amount demanded." More generally, "The community's consumption of any good will be decreased (or increased) if its unit price is raised (or lowered) sufficiently."

Figure 3–1 is a diagram of the demand sched-

ule in Table 3–1. Price is measured on the vertical axis and quantity of eggs demanded on the horizontal. At each price, the amount demanded is that which equates the buyer's marginal use value to the price. But do not confuse the buyer's *total use* value (column 3 of Table 3–4) with *total market* value (column 5). Contrast the numbers in those two columns of Table 3–4. Total use value is expressible as the sum of successive marginal use values along the buyer's demand schedule (for example, at a quantity of 5, total use value of $4.00 equals marginal use values of $1 + 90 cents + 80 cents + 70 cents + 60 cents). But the total market value of each quantity is the product of that quantity times the unit price at which that

54

Table 3–5. Demand, Personal Values, Market Revenues, and Marginal Revenues

1	2	3	4	5	6
Price (p)	Quantity (Q)	Total Personal Use Value	Marginal Personal Use Value	Total Market Value or Revenue (TR)	Marginal Revenue
$1.00	1	$1.00	$1.00	$1.00	$1.00
.90	2	1.90	.90	1.80	.80
.80	3	2.70	.80	2.40	.60
.70	4	3.40	.70	2.80	.40
.60	5	4.00	.60	3.00	.20
.50	6	4.50	.50	3.00	.00
.40	7	4.90	.40	2.80	—.20
.30	8	5.20	.30	2.40	—.40
.20	9	5.40	.20	1.80	—.60
.10	10	5.50	.10	1.00	—.80

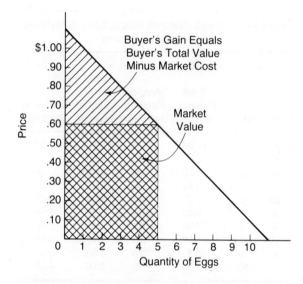

Figure 3–2. Total Market Value and Total Personal Value in Ms. A's Weekly Demand for Eggs

This figure shows the same demand curve as in Figure 3–1. If the price of eggs is 60 cents, our consumer would buy five eggs per week. The entire shaded area represents her total use value of those five eggs. The crosshatched area represents the total market value of those same five eggs, while the upper triangular lined portion is consumer's surplus.

quantity would be bought. The buyer's marginal use value is brought down to equality with price by buying an amount at which marginal use value equals (or just barely exceeds) the market price of a unit.

To picture all this, look at Figure 3–2, which is an elaboration of Figure 3–1. We again draw the down-sloping demand curve, and we add a horizontal price line. Let the price be 60 cents, so the quantity demanded is then three. *Total market value* is price × quantity (60 cents × 5 = $3.00) which, geometrically, is *height (P) × base (Q)*, or the crosshatched rectangular area. *Total use value* is the total area under the demand curve to the quantity of three—the area indicated by the vertical shading lines. In the figure, the total use value area thus includes the rectangular total market value area and also the triangular area lying below the demand curve and above the price line, marked by positively sloping lines. That excess of use value over market value is *consumer surplus*.

Needs versus Amount Demanded

Needs claimed to be "vital" or "urgent" or "crying" or "minimal" or "critical" are nonsense. Indeed even the term "needs" is misleading. The amount of anything we demand depends on its price. The higher the price of any good, the less of it I will demand—the less will be my needs, if you wish. There is no particular amount of a good that I must have. Always, we will choose less if the price (value of forsaken alternative) is large enough. Even the conception of some minimum necessary amount of food for sustaining life is not useful. What quality of life? How long a life? How probable a continuation of life?

Imagine a poverty-stricken person. He says he has the bare necessary amounts of goods. Yet if he were offered more food for a sacrifice of some of his clothes, would he refuse on the grounds that no amount of more food would make less clothing tolerable? Or turning it around, would he be unwilling to part with any small part of his remaining food for a lot more clothing or other comforting goods? Indeed, *everyone,* no matter how poor, will be willing to give up some more of one good if offered enough more of some other goods. There is no minimum amount of any good such that a person could not tolerate any *less*—not even a part of one's life. (If life seems inviolate, how many of you risk life by traveling at high speeds or in airplanes, or by smoking or doing other things that have a probability of shortening your life?)

The amount of any good we choose to have (whether or not you call it "need") depends on what you can get if you forsake more or less of

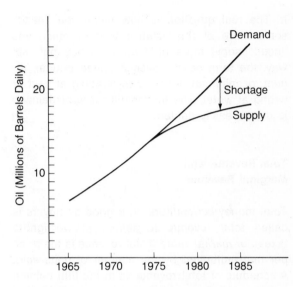

Figure 3–3. Fallacious Interpretation of Demand

This figure is a sample of a common but incorrect method of portraying demand and supply conditions. The graph shows "demand" exceeding "supply" after 1975 as if some deficit or shortage will occur. The fundamental error in this portrayal is that the amount of oil that will be demanded in the future will depend on the price. The price will affect the amount demanded in each year and will affect the line of historical amounts actually demanded in each year. A higher price will lower that line, which is misleadingly labeled demand. It should be labeled amounts demanded in future years. That line is not fixed. It will be higher or lower depending on the prices that prevail in the future. And so will the amounts supplied. Indeed, the open-market price will adjust so that the two lines depicting the amounts demanded and the amounts supplied will in fact coincide—as they did in the past solely because the price adjusted so as to equate the amounts demanded and consumed with the amounts supplied. Never use the above kind of diagram to portray demand and supply or to suggest that the future portends some shortage or deficit. Such a disparity would reveal only that the market price is going to be prevented from clearing the market (as we shall demonstrate later).

it. The real question is how much you "need" some more of this relative to how much you "need" some more of that. And once put that way, the term *needs* (even if called critical, urgent, or minimal) becomes misleading at best or wrong at worst. The fundamental law of demand is not so easily denied.

11, 12
13, 14

Total Revenue and Marginal Revenue

Total money expenditure on a good by buyers is called *total revenue to sellers* (if we ignore taxes), or *market value.* Total revenue is the price per unit multiplied by the number of units sold. A schedule of total revenue is in the fifth column in Table 3–5. This table is the same as Table 3–3 with a sixth column added.

If one egg is sold at $1, total revenue is $1. If the price were 90 cents, two eggs would be sold with a market value, or total revenue, of $1.80. The *increase* in total revenue of 80 cents (= $1.80 − $1) is *marginal revenue* (MR) (column 6). *Each* egg is purchased at 90 cents: The buyer pays 90 cents for the second, but also only 90 cents (that is, 10 cents less than before) for the first. The seller receives 10 cents less on the first unit, which reduces the 90 cents receipt on the second to a net revenue increase of 80 cents.

The cut in price that permits selling one more unit is a price cut on *every* unit. So, although the quantity of the good demanded is larger at the lowered price, total proceeds do not increase by the amount of the market value of the extra unit sold. Indeed, at a price of 50 cents, the total market expenditure ($3) is no larger than at a

price of 60 cents. At still lower prices, the total market revenue actually would decrease. In that range of prices, a cut in price reduces the price on so large a number of units that the cut on those units more than offsets the price for the extra unit sold.

The Marginal Revenue column (6), then, lists the *changes* in total revenue or total expenditure between prices that are just sufficiently different to induce exactly a *one unit* change in the amount demanded. (The listed prices in the table change the amounts demanded by *one* unit.)

Of the six columns in Table 3–4, the first and second together form the demand schedule. From them we can compute all the others. And we shall use all these columns to explain widely used pricing and sales tactics. In your mind, keep the personal use values of columns 3 and 4 distinct from the market values of columns 5 and 6.

Quantity Purchased Equates Marginal Use Value to Price, Not to Marginal Revenue

We have seen that a consumer, if he can buy any demanded quantity at the same price per unit, will purchase that amount of which his marginal use value is equated with the market price. If the price is 80 cents, Table 3–4 indicates that the quantity demanded is three. If the selling price were 70 cents, the amount bought would be increased to four, with marginal use thereby reduced to 70 cents. But what of marginal revenue? Total revenue is now $2.80 (= 4 units at 70 cents each) compared to $2.40 (= 3 × 80 cents); so marginal revenue, when four units instead of three are bought, is $2.80 − 2.40 = 40 cents. The price of the fourth unit (and of each of the other three) is 70 cents, while the marginal revenue (the difference in revenue in exchanging four units instead of three) is only 40 cents. The value of the fourth unit to the buyer is the 70 cent price, not the 40 cent increase in expenditure. No one forced the consumer to buy the fourth unit—he could have bought only three units (or any other amount) at 70 cents each. He would not have paid 70 cents for that fourth unit if he himself valued it at less than 70 cents. And he would value a fifth unit at less than 70 cents.

While the buyer extends his quantity demanded at a given price to the point where his marginal valuation equals the price, the seller, who quotes the market price, is sensitive to marginal revenue. For in order to induce the buyer to purchase four units instead of three, the seller must reduce the price from 80 cents to 70 cents on all units. Total receipts are then $2.80 instead of $2.40, a net increase (marginal revenue) of only 40 cents.

15, 16

Changes in Amount Demanded When Price Changes Are Not Changes in Demand

Demand, let it never be forgotten, is the *entire schedule*—or geometrically, the *entire curve*—of potential unit prices and the amounts demanded at each unit price. Suppose that a demand is unchanged over time; that is, the demand curve does not move. Now, let the price of the good change. Because the price changed, the amount demanded changes. If the demand schedule remains unchanged but the price increases, the demander moves up the unchanged schedule, so the *amount* he demands diminishes; as price falls, he slides down the constant curve. But the demand (schedule) has not changed.

Of course, the demand (schedule) can shift over time. For example, it may increase; that is, the whole curve may move upward and to the right so that, at any given price, more would be demanded than before—perhaps because the demander's income has increased. Thus, in Figure 3–4a, we start with price OP_1, demand D_1, and amount demanded OQ_1. Now, if demand increases, with the schedule shifting to D_2, the demander is willing to buy a *larger amount* (OQ_2) at the *original price* (OP_1)—or he is willing to pay a *higher price* (OP_2) for the *original amount* (OQ_1).

To be sure of the very important distinction between changes in demand (schedule) and changes in amount demanded, meditate on Figure 3–4b. As before, we start with demand D_1, price OP_1, and quantity OQ_1. If price is reduced to OP_3 while demand (schedule) is unchanged, we slide down D_1 and increase quantity demanded to OQ_2. Alternatively, suppose price is unchanged while the demand (schedule) is increased to D_2. Again, quantity demanded increases to OQ_2. In both cases, we have an increase in quantity demanded. In the first instance, quantity demanded increased because price decreased and we moved down the unchanged demand (schedule); but in the second illustration, amount demanded increased even at an unchanged price, because the demand (schedule) increased.

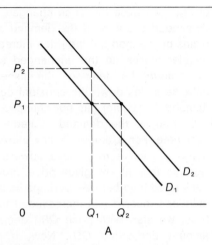

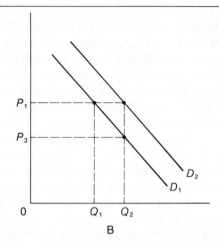

Figure 3–4. Increased Demand

Increased demand means a shift to the right (or upward) of a whole demand curve. It does not mean a movement down along an unchanged demand curve when price falls (as along curve D_1 in B, from Q_1 to Q_2 when price falls from P_1 to P_3).

Demand increase means more is demanded than before at any given price, or a higher price is obtainable for any given amount being sold, as when Q_2 increases instead of Q_1 at P_1, or as P_2 is feasible rather than P_1 at Q_1 in panel ˙.

Meaning of Change in Price and Change in Quantity

Let us now look at what happens when the demand schedule remains unchanged but price changes cause changes in the amount demanded. We shall see that the nature and measurement of changes in price and quantity is a little trickier than we have thus far admitted.

Say the price of eggs rises from 50 cents per dozen to 60 cents. This is an increase in the money price of eggs. But suppose that the money price of widgets rises at the same time by the same proportion, from, say, $2 to $2.40. Then, if eggs are paid for with widgets, the price of eggs has in fact remained constant. Before the price

increased, four dozen eggs sold for as much money as did one widget; after the price increased, the "terms of trade" of eggs for widgets is still 4 to 1: The market price of eggs had not changed relative to the market price of widgets. Moreover, if the money price of widgets had increased to more than $2.40, then, although the money price of eggs had gone from 50 cents to 60 cents, their relative price would have *fallen*. (It is often alleged that prices are "sticky on the downside"—they go up more readily than they go down. However true this may be of *money* prices, it cannot be true of *relative* prices. If the price of widgets rises relative to the price of eggs, it follows that the price of eggs falls relative to the price of widgets.)

Hereafter, we shall assume that money prices

Table 3–5. Demand Schedule, Total Market Value, and Elasticity

Price	Amount Demanded	Total Revenue	Marginal Revenue	
$1.00	1	$1.00	+$1.00	Total Sales Value Moves
.90	2	1.80	+ .80	Opposite to Price Change:
.80	3	2.40	+ .60	Elastic Demand in This Range
.70	4	2.80	+ .40	of price
.60	5	3.00	+ .20	Unchanged Total Proceeds:
.50	6	3.00	0	
.40	7	2.80	− .20	Unit Elasticity between Prices
.30	8	2.40	− .40	of 60 Cents and 50 Cents.
.20	9	1.80	− .60	Total Sales Value Changes in
.10	10	1.00	− .80	Same Direction as Price Change: Inelastic Demand in This Range of Price.

of all other goods remain constant except the price of the good under discussion. Thus, if the money price of eggs alone changes, then the price of eggs relative to the prices of other goods has changed correspondingly.

Amount demanded, too, is subject to more than one interpretation. In Table 3–4, the amount demanded at a price of 90 cents is two per week—which is a rate of 104 per year or about nine per month. All express the same rate. And we could say the same for more expensive and more durable goods. How can one consume more than one car? Replace it more frequently or use it more intensively or buy a more expensive, impressive model—or simply own two of them. The principles of demand hold whether *amount* refers to amount owned, rate of consumption, rate of purchase, or frequency of replacement.

17, 18

Elasticity of Demand

It is widely recognized and sometimes lamented (by sellers) that an increase in the supply of a good drives down its price along the demand schedule so that total sales revenues (price times quantity sold) may be reduced. This appears to be true, for example, for some food products, alcoholic beverages, and tobacco. How responsive quantity demanded is to a change in price is summarized by the concept of *elasticity*.

Elasticity of demand at some specified price is the ratio of (1) the percentage change in quantity purchased as a result of (2) a small percentage change in the price. In Table 3–5, for example, if the price is reduced from $1.00 to 90 cents, a 10 percent reduction, the quantity demanded is increased from one to two, an increase of 100 percent. Putting +100 percent over −10 percent gives a ratio of −10. Because the quantity change is in the opposite direction from the price

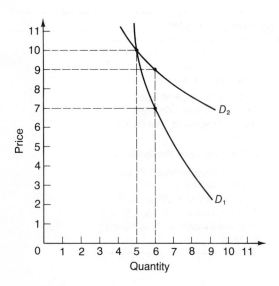

Figure 3–5. Differing Elasticities of Demand

D₂ requires a price cut of only $1 to sell one more unit, while D₁ requires a cut of $3. D₂ is more responsive to price. Its elasticity at that price range is about 2 (a 10 percent cut in price gives a 20 percent change in amount demanded). But D₁ requires a 30 percent cut in price to give a 20 percent increase in amount demanded. Its elasticity is measured at about 20/30 = .66, less than for D₂. The marginal income at the sixth unit is +$4 (=$54 − $50) for D₂ and is −$8 (=$42 − $50) for D₁.

change, the ratio is negative. However, hereafter we will simply ignore the minus sign and refer to the absolute value of the ratio. So the elasticity at that part of the demand schedule is 10.

At a price change from 70 cents to 60 cents, a reduction of 14 percent, the quantity demanded increases from four to five, an increase of 25 percent. The ratio of the percentage change in quantity to the percentage change of price is 25/14 or about 1.8 (and the marginal revenue is positive, 20 cents, but much less than the 60 cents price).

Next, estimate the elasticity in the 60 cents to 50 cents price interval, for another unit increase in the quantity, from five to six. The ratio of the percentage change in quantity to the percentage change in price is .166 to −.166, which gives an elasticity of 1. Note that the marginal revenue is zero; total receipts are unchanged at 30 cents. Finally, a 33 percent price reduction from 30 cents to 20 cents induces a 12.5 percent increase in quantity sold, from 8 to 9 units. The elasticity is 12.5/33 = .38.[1] The marginal revenue is negative: −60 cents.

The elasticity of demand at some particular price interval depends on both the slope, or steepness, of the curve and the actual amount being demanded at that price. Two diagrams will help to show how these two factors affect the elasticity (and the marginal revenue from a price change): Figure 3–5 shows the effect of the differences in the slope of the demand curve, while Figure 3–6 shows the effect of the actual initial amounts demanded.

Three features of elasticity should be noted:

(1) Elasticities are not the same throughout the demand schedule.[2]

---

[1] Because we have used rather large percentage changes between prices in this example, the arithmetic measures of elasticity will differ slightly, depending on the size of the price change. These differences disappear for small-percentage changes in price and quantity. The concept of elasticity is usually referred to in two alternative forms: a point and an arc elasticity. These will be understandable only to those familiar with calculus. Point elasticity is based on continuity of demand and defined as $dx/x \div dp/p$ of the function, while arc elasticity is $\Delta x/x \div \Delta p/p$. Point elasticity is the limiting value of arc elasticity.

[2] As an aside and to avoid misunderstanding, we note that the elasticity measure changes along the demand schedule despite the fact that the slope of the demand schedule is constant. All along the demand schedule a 10 cent change

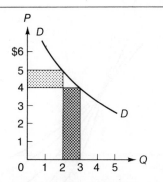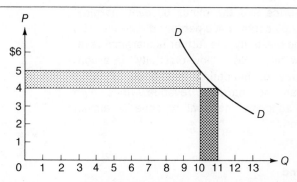

Figure 3–6. Demand Elasticities and Sales Revenue

The left curve is more elastic, even though in both curves a price drop of $1 induces a one-unit increase of amount demanded. On the left curve it changes total sales value from $10 to $12, an increase of $2. Marginal revenue is $2. The $4 price receipt of the third unit is offset by the $1 price cut on each of the two units already being sold. The percentage increase in quantity was 50 percent, while the price decrease was only 20 percent. But with the curve in the

right-hand diagram the situation is different. The same 20 percent decrease in price with one unit increase in quantity gives only a 10 percent increase in quantity. Total sales value changes from $50 to $44, a decrease of $6. The $4 price receipt on the eleventh unit is offset by the $1 price reduction on each of the 10 units already being sold. In each case the value of the extra units sold is weighed against the reduction in value of the initial quantity, and the reduction is larger the larger the number already being sold.

(2) The elasticity is greater than 1 whenever a price cut increases total receipts; that is, whenever marginal revenue is positive. The elasticity is less than 1 whenever the total proceeds are

in price gives a one unit change in amount demanded. The ratio of the *absolute* change in Q to the *absolute* change in P is constant. This is *not* the ratio of the *percentage* changes in P and Q. At small quantities and high prices, a one unit change in amount is a larger percentage of quantity than at the larger base amounts. For example, at two units, the one unit increase to three units is a 50 percent increase in amount demanded. But at nine units, the increase of one unit in response to a price cut of 10 cents is now only about 11 percent in amount demanded. Similarly, the change in price is small or large in relation to the initial price from which the change is considered. What is important is the *percentage* change in amount and the associated *percentage* change in price.

In mathematical terms, point elasticity for continuous functions is defined as $dx/x \div dp/p$ of the demand function $x = f(p)$, while $\Delta x/x \div \Delta p/p$ is called arc elasticity. Point elasticity is the limit of arc elasticity as $\Delta p \to 0$.

reduced (that is, the marginal revenue is negative) by a price reduction along the demand schedule. Only where the elasticity is −1 does the total revenue not change as one more is sold.

(3) The larger the elasticity, the closer is the marginal revenue to price. For example, at the $1.00 to 90 cent price segment, the elasticity is 10, and the marginal revenue is 80 cents, or only about 10 cents below the new price—an 11 percent difference. At from 70 cents to 60 cents the elasticity is only 1.8 and the marginal revenue is 20 cents, about 40 cents less than the new price —about a 66 percent difference. And where the elasticity is 1, the marginal revenue is zero—at the price of 50 cents, a spread of 100 percent below the new price. Even worse, at prices around 30 cents to 20 cents, the elasticity is .38 (less than 1) and the marginal revenue is negative: minus 60 cents. The difference between the

20 cents price and the minus 60 cent marginal revenue is 80 cents, a 400 percent difference. The smaller the elasticity, the further is marginal revenue below price. So a "low elasticity" is a convenient way of indicating that price is much larger than the marginal revenue, while high elasticity suggests marginal revenue is almost equal to price.[3]

The Second Law of Demand

The second law of demand is that the longer the time for adjusting to a price change, the greater will be the responsiveness of amount demanded. The adjustment by demanders will be greater after a week and still greater after a month, until eventually full adjustment is achieved. Why? In time, more people learn about the price change. Also, the slower the rate at which consumption is revised, the lower are the adjustment costs. For example, if the price of water were doubled, consumption would immediately decrease some— but would decrease by a great deal more within a few months, after people had made adjustments in associated activity and in water-using equipment, as we shall elaborate on later.

This principle is shown by the set of intersecting demands in Figure 3–7. The successive de-

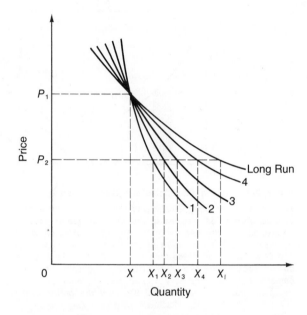

Figure 3–7. Effect of Time on Price-Elasticity of Demand
The longer the time after a price change, the greater the effect of that price change on the amount consumed—shown by the flatter curves for more elapsed time after a price change.

mand curves (1, 2, 3, etc.) show the responses after price falls from p_1 to p_2; in one "day" the rate is up to X_1, after two days it is X_2, etc., until it ultimately reaches the long run adjustment, X_l.

It is not necessary to know the exact quantities and elasticities in all these demand relationships. To draw some important explanations or implications about how our economy operates, we need only know the *direction* of effects. Direction is indicated when we know that demand curves are (1) negatively sloped with respect to price, and (2) more responsive to more prolonged price changes.

[3] In our numerical example, the elasticity was lower as we moved down the demand schedule to lower prices. That need not be true. The demand could be such that at lower prices elasticity is greater. For those familiar with algebra, the exact relationship is: elasticity = $P/(P - MR)$. This relationship is approximated rather than exactly satisfied by our examples because we have used unit differences in quantity to compute the elasticity and marginal revenues. For the exact relationship, calculus is necessary.

Elasticities of demand with respect to prices are extremely difficult to estimate. A price will change in response to a demand curve shift—indeed possibly because the demand curve has shifted. The resulting change in the price will change the amount demanded because of a slide along the new demand curve; in addition, the quantity will have changed because of a change in the position of the demand curve. The total change in amount bought will not be the result only of a change in price along a fixed demand, as is necessary to measure elasticity of demand. The change in amount demanded is the result of two changes: change in price and in whatever changed the position of the demand curve. Separating these two effects in the change in quantity is usually not possible.

22, 23

Economists and statisticians have nevertheless devised some ways to attempt to adjust for this fundamental ambiguity and have estimated elasticities of demand for various goods. The elasticity of demand for gasoline was recently estimated to be between about −.5 and −.8, meaning that a one percent rise in price would decrease the amount demanded by between .5 and .8 percent. Experience during the recent fuel shortage during the 1973–1974 oil embargo indicates that was not a bad estimate. (Question: If you were the sole seller of gasoline in some country and knew the elasticity of demand for gasoline at present prices were between .5 and .8, would you contemplate raising the price by reducing the amount supplied? Can you see that it would increase the total receipts?) Demands for tobacco, alcoholic beverages, and electricity have been estimated to have elasticities of less than one near the current prices—at least for periods of time ranging up to a year. After a longer inter-

Table 3–6. Some Estimated Price Elasticities of Demand

Foreign travel by U.S. residents	4.1
Medical care insurance, long run	3.6
Intercity rail, long run	2.7
Airline travel	2.4
Lamb meat	1.8–2.0
Auto insurance	1.6
Automobiles	.8–1.5
Shoe repairs	1.5
Peaches	1.5
Apples	1.3
Radios and TV, long run	1.3
Butter	1.3
Chicken	1.2
Radios and television	1.2
China, glassware, utensils	1.2
Beef	.8–1.1
Shoe repairs, short run	1.1
Local bus and transit	1.0
Pork	.7–1.0

Residential electric power, cotton, corn, citrus fruit, potatoes, eggs, milk, margarine, shows, steel, physicians, legal services, funeral services, new cars, and gasoline, both long run and short run (.5 to .8) } less than one

Data drawn from H.S. Houthakker and L.D. Taylor, *Consumer Demand in the United States: 1929–1970,* Cambridge, Mass.: Harvard University Press, 1966; and L.W. Weiss, *Case Studies in American Industry,* New York: John Wiley, 1967. Also reported in D.A. Worcester, Jr., "On Monopoly Welfare Losses: Comment," *American Economic Review,* Vol. LXV, No. 4 (December 1975), p. 1016.

val greater adjustments can be made so that the elasticity may be substantially greater for the longer period.

Table 3–6 shows several estimated elasticities. These are elasticities in the interval of prices existing at the time the studies were made. From these estimates it cannot be deduced how different the elasticities would have been at prices far different from the actual prices at the time. These elasticities are for each type of good, not for particular brands. (If elasticities were estimated for goods by particular brands, would they be higher or lower?)

Elasticity of demand can also be defined with respect to income, that is, the ratio of the percentage change in amount demanded in response to a small percentage change in income. These elasticities are usually positive, unlike the negative price elasticity of demand. Statistical studies indicate that income elasticities of demand for food and drink and rent of housing space and clothing are less than one, but greater than one for durable goods and travel abroad. These studies also suggest a positive correlation between price and income elasticities: that is, high price elasticities and high income elasticities seem to be more commonly associated than not. But if this is true, it has not yet become a well-established generalization.

Some Illustrations of the Laws of Demand: Response to Price Change with an Unchanged Demand Schedule

Demand for Food

Higher beef prices will induce people to economize on it, buying less beef and more of other things. Other sources of protein—eggs, poultry, fish, cheese, milk—are obvious. Less obvious is the fact that we can substitute some more vacation for less food enjoyment, since we enjoy both food and travel.

However, we really should not speak of demand for "food," since no one buys "food" as such. We buy particular commodities. For each of these, purchases are affected by price. But even if we do talk conveniently of the "demand for food," the law of demand asserts that, with an unchanged demand (schedule), the amount of food consumed is reduced at a higher price.

Demand for Wood

If wood prices rise, we substitute plaster, plastics, steel, aluminum, copper, glass, paper, coal, oil, and electricity; less wood will be demanded at the higher price. You and I may not consciously respond very much, if at all, to a 10 percent rise in the price of wood. But industrial product designers will shift in varying degrees to substitutes. The things we buy will be made with less wood and more of other material. Nor must every person revise his purchase rate with every little change. Some people are on the margin of choice between one good and another; and, as prices change, some people shift their choices, even with an unchanged demand (schedule).

Demand for Water

Water is an especially powerful example. Although people cannot live without it, they will *reduce* (not eliminate) their use of water at a higher price. We all could use more water, and we all could get by with less. People in arid regions use less water, but not because they couldn't use more; rather, they don't want more at its high price. They *choose* to consume less water and to use the money not spent on more water for other, more desired purposes.

In the United States the average per capita daily purchase of water varies from 230 gallons in Chicago to 150 in New York and Los Angeles, down to 120 in San Diego and 110 in Boston. Among the reasons for these differences are differences in industrial uses. Chicago has steel and oil-refining industries, which use a great deal of water; New York City businesses—finance, retail, apparel—are light water users. And the cost of water had something to do in determining the locations of those industries.

By the law of demand, one way to get reduced consumption is to let price rise. If water prices are higher, water will be more worth saving. In New York City, 10 percent of the total water consumption is estimated to be from leakages in street mains. At higher prices for water, it will pay to reduce that loss. Also, water meters, which make people pay according to use, are not yet universally used. If they were, people would have stronger incentives to conserve water (by repair and modification of faucets and water-using equipment).

At higher water prices, residences will have smaller gardens and lawns. More sprinklers will be used because they use less water. Gardeners will sweep, rather than wash lawns and sidewalks. Rock gardens, paved and brick patios will become more common. Automobiles will be washed less often. Water will be softened, because soft water washes as well with less water. None of these changes would reflect a change in tastes, but only the fact that the price of water is higher. It has been estimated that a doubling of water prices would reduce total domestic water consumption by 30 to 50 percent within a year. (Translate that into elasticity terms.)

Still more ways of conserving water exist. In many cities, industrial users take about half the

Table 3–7. Variations among Firms and Products in Industrial Consumption of Water, per Unit of Output

Product or User and Unit	Draft (in gallons)		
	Maxi-mum	Typical	Mini-mum
Steam-electric power (kw-h)	170	80	1.3
Petroleum refining (gallon of crude oil)	44	18	1.7
Steel (finished ton)	65,000	40,000	1400
Soaps, edible oils (pound)	7	. . .	1.5
Carbon black (pound)	14	4	0.25
Natural rubber (pound)	6	. . .	2.5
Butadiene (pound)	305	160	13
Glass containers (ton)	670	. . .	120
Automobiles (per car)	16,000	. . .	12,000
Trucks, buses (per unit)	20,000	. . .	15,000

Source: H.E. Hudson and Janet Abu-Lughod, "Water Requirements," in Jack B. Graham and Meredith F. Burrill (eds.), *Water for Industry* (Washington, D.C.: American Association for the Advancement of Science, 1956), Publication No. 45, pp. 19–21.

water. Their demand for water is probably more responsive to price than is that of domestic users. Table 3–7 shows great differences in water use even within the same industry. The *maximum* column presents amounts used in the most profligate plants, while the *minimum* column shows the least amount used per unit of output produced. Note the tremendous range in the first three industries, which happen also to be the heaviest industrial water users. Many industrial firms use water for cooling purposes on a once-through basis without recirculation in cooling units. Some steel mills use 65,000 gallons of water per ton produced, but the Kaiser steel mill (in the Los Angeles area) uses only 1600 gallons. One soap plant in the same area has recirculatory cooling towers to reduce water consumption from about six million to less than half a million gallons per day. At higher water prices, the greater savings on reduced use of water would make recycling worthwhile. Clearly, even the amount of water "needed" varies with price!

There are still more ways to adjust water usage to price. The largest user of water in Southern California is agriculture, which uses approximately 80 percent of the water—at prices lower than urban dwellers pay, even after the costs of distribution and purification. What would farmers do if the price of water were to reflect its higher value in city uses? Some would go out of business—which is to say that some of the water used by farmers is worth more elsewhere. Higher water prices indicate some water now used to grow watermelons, lettuce, and celery, for example, would be more useful elsewhere. Less would be grown in Southern California and more in areas where agriculture is cheaper, and shipped to Southern California, because shipping produce would be cheaper than shipping in the water. Some areas would decline as people found it preferable to move to places where water is cheaper or took up tasks that use less water. (That is, after all, the reason that the Western deserts are sparsely populated.)

When the price rises, will you discover how to use less? Some people make a living by giving that information: commercial salesmen of water-recycling equipment, water softeners, automatic faucets, fertilizers, irrigation and sprinkling equipment, air-conditioning machinery, hardtop patios, chemicals that reduce evaporation, washing machines that use less water, etc. Every rise in water prices enhances their business prospects. Salesmen make it their business to detect ways in which their equipment is more economical. Teachers may believe that most worthwhile knowledge comes from schools and books, but an incredible amount of information about practical matters is provided by salesmen—because it is to their personal interest to inform potential customers. Though users may not presently know how to alter their use of water, rubber, energy, sugar, steel, or gasoline in response to a price change, were the price to change they would be swamped with information by salesmen about new uses or substitutes. But as long as we think only of using more or using less in the same old customary ways, we will underrate price effects on amount demanded.

Demand for Gasoline or Energy (or Anything!)

The gasoline supply to the United States and the world was reduced in 1974 by 10 percent below its normal past growth rate. No one (well, hardly anyone) believed the resultant higher price would sufficiently restrict consumption. As prices of gasoline increased people decided which were the less valuable uses to be forsaken. But politicians and many business people did not believe that higher gasoline prices would be effective in telling us what uses to restrict. For example, they proposed to prohibit high school students from "wasteful" driving to school.

Once prices are allowed to rise to their market-clearing level, they reflect the most valuable marginal uses. Is it desirable to compel people to restrict consumption in still other ways? The current market price of the amount actually available is already restricting use to the available amount. Asking people to restrict consumption more than they are induced to do by a free-market price that reflects demand and supply is to ask them to reduce their gasoline use so that it can be used elsewhere in *less* valuable ways. Such *required* "conservation" (which compels diversion of goods to less-valuable uses) gives some politicians more power over economic resources. We emphasize this because market prices are a means of control and coordination of people in competition for scarce resources—and so is political power. Market prices and political power are competing systems for control.

A price rise of about 50 percent was sufficient to restrict the amount demanded to available supplies in the same way as for water, food, wood, or pencils. As the costs (price) of using gasoline rose, we stopped the extra driving which was worth less than its costs. We reduced speed (and the *reduced* speed limit to 55 m.p.h. is not necessary to reduce speed more than is worthwhile); we combined more of our shopping in one trip; we turned off the engine more often rather than let it idle; we flew between cities and rented cars; we drove in our smaller second car; we accelerated less rapidly; we took fewer and shorter joy rides; we tuned our engines better. All that many of us did immediately. And most purchases were of smaller new cars. The same measures were taken with higher prices for heating oil. At higher costs we wear more clothing, have better insulated houses, accept lower indoor temperatures, and warm fewer rooms. Although the responses to a higher price are varied and numerous, we were moving up the demand schedule as prices rose. All the reductions in the amount of gasoline used and those adjustments described above are the results of a higher price. They are not the results of a reduced demand schedule.

Alleged Exceptions to the Laws of Demand

Some people talk of counterexamples to the laws of demand. They point out that people could conceivably be insensitive to price or that they could buy more of some things even when the price rises. Indeed, they conceivably could; almost anything is conceivable. But the law of demand says that actually they do not.

An exception to the law of demand is alleged to occur when the price of, say, wheat falls and buyers think, "It will fall further. If I wait longer I can buy cheaper." By this reasoning, a lower price has presumably resulted in *fewer* purchases—an apparent contradiction of the law of demand. But has the price fallen relative to other relevant prices? On page 581 we discussed relative price behavior with respect to eggs and widgets. But prices need not be relative only to other *goods;* they can be relative to other *times,* as well. Future prices of the wheat are expected to be even lower. Therefore, relative to *expected future* prices, the present price has *increased.* People who have the alternatives of buying now or buying later transfer their purchases from relatively high-price times to relatively low-price times—exactly as implied by the law of demand. Remember, it is *relative* prices that count.

Another alleged exception is a prestige or "conspicuous consumption" good—like Mumms champagne, Balmain clothes, Rolls Royce cars, Orrefors crystal, or whatever the "elite" display. Presumably, possession of such goods sheds prestige on the user. Desire for such prestige could increase the demand schedule but it could not produce a demand schedule that is *positively sloped.* Let the price of the prestige good be higher, and less of it will be bought. Otherwise, what would prevent the price from rising without limit? The prestige value of a good simply *shifts* its demand schedule *upward.* But the new, higher demand curve still has a negative slope. The pursuit of prestige is consistent with the laws of demand.

Also cited as contradictions of the law of demand are occasions when a higher price is asked to make the buyer believe the item is better. Similarly, anyone who proposes to sell something far below its current market price will have more problems making a sale than a seller asking the market price, for the low price immediately stirs up doubts about the genuineness or quality of the item. These are sensible doubts, given the fact that price usually reflects quality. If I offer to sell my nearly new Plymouth for $2000, a potential buyer will hesitate, suspecting the quality of the car or my ownership. If he can satisfy himself that the lower price is not the result of lower quality, he will buy the car more readily than if I asked $4000. An inferior quality good is sold at a lower price because only then will anyone buy it; at the same prices, everyone would prefer the better item. The public's association of higher price with quality is a consequence, not a refutation, of the law of demand.

**Income Effects
on Demand**

Factors other than price affect the amount demanded, and these should not be neglected. Changes in income or wealth will change (shift) the demand function. A larger income will induce more consumption of most goods: for example,

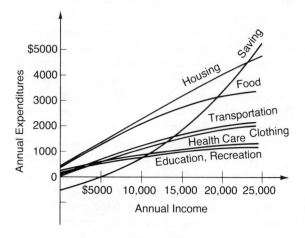

Figure 3–8. Income Effect on Demand for Services

The lines show that expenditure rates on general classes of goods and services are related to income—increasing with income but at a lower proportionate rate. Amounts demanded are clearly related to income and therefore not only to price. Of course, a combination of a price change and income change can affect the amount demanded, possibly in opposite directions if the lower price is for some good that is a significant part of the goods a person produces and sells in getting his income.

The variation of saving, from negative rates at low incomes to highest rates at high incomes, is deceptive if you think it shows that people whose annual incomes over the years average about $5000 or less do not save. Because incomes fluctuate not unexpectedly over the years and because a person tends to consume according to his longer-run income average, savings will show large residual fluctuations as income fluctuates transiently from year to year.

transportation, food, housing, medical care, education, travel, champagne, and prestige goods. Figure 3–8 shows how consumption of some services increases at higher incomes. On the other hand, as income or wealth increases, one's demand for some goods decreases: Candidates might be rump roasts, "soul" food, hamburger, or low-grade gasoline. Goods for which demand is greater at higher incomes are called *superior* goods; goods for which demand decreases with increases in income are called *inferior*. Sometimes a *price* change also causes a substantial change in a person's income, such as for a good that is a substantial part of a person's endowment (property) or source of income. If an owner of a natural-gas well experiences a big rise in the selling price of his gas, his higher income will get him a larger house which uses more gas for air conditioning. Because he sells the gas at a higher price, his income increases enough to shift his demand schedule upward. This shift more than offsets the higher price he must now pay as a gas consumer himself, and thus, on the new, higher demand schedule his amount demanded increases from what it was on the old schedule at the old lower price. The increased price of a good that is both a source of a person's income and a good he consumes has two effects —an *endowment effect* (increasing his wealth and hence his demand for gasoline) and a *substitution effect* (sliding up the demand curve). In our example, not enough of a substitution effect occurs away from gas in response to the higher price to completely offset the greater endowment effect. So, at a higher price he consumes more gas because of the large natural gas endowment income dominance. Unless we separate these two effects of a price rise, we may erroneously suppose a demand function to be unchanged when in fact it has shifted because of the price-change's effects on a person's wealth.

Another kind of income effect also occurs. Even if a good is not a person's source of income, a price fall in that good is accompanied

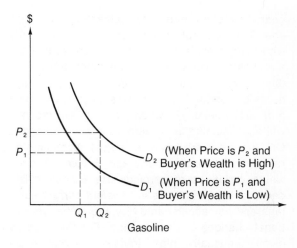

Figure 3–9. Price Effects on Wealth Can Shift Demand Curve Enough to Offset Price Effects on Amount Demanded

by an *expenditure-releasing effect.* The lower price of a good being purchased gives "savings" on the former rate of purchase. But since this released purchasing power is usually small, and of course is distributed over the total purchases of all other goods, its effect on the demand schedule for the lower-price good itself is usually negligible.

Income Changes: Transient or Permanent?

Just as the effect of a price change on consumption varies in magnitude according to the duration of the new price, so does the effect of a change in earnings: the longer the duration, the greater the effect. Many people know their earnings will vary from week to week and even year to year, probably around some average, so they gear their consumption to that anticipated average. They do not revise consumption instantly with every transient variation in income. Is there a real estate salesman who consumes only on the days he sells a house, consuming nothing on days he sells nothing? Do business people consume only on weekdays, when earning an income, while consuming at a zero rate on weekends? On the contrary, people adjust consumption rates to a long-run average income around which variations of earnings are expected. Because of this, variations in *transient current* earnings are not accompanied by the same proportional changes in consumption. For the reasons given, unusually high transient earnings go mostly into accumulation of cash or bonds or repayments of past debts, for example. As a result, at transiently high incomes, consumption does not increase in proportion to the temporarily higher income. People save more to smooth over later expected low incomes. During transiently low earnings they dip into accumulated reserves or use up inventories.

If you look again at Figure 3–8, you will see that consumption of some things increases less than proportionally with income, while saving increases more than proportionally. Such relationships are deceptive if expenditures are charted against a particular annual income that has transitory extreme high or low earnings: Current consumption is relatively insensitive to current transitory income, while the residual of the current temporary increase—savings—is sensitive. But when lasting changes in average income occur, people adjust their consumption more fully. Although some goods—like travel, education, medical care—appear to be insensitive to transient

changes in income, they also appear to increase more than in proportion to *permanent* or longer-run anticipated average income. In sum, when studying the effect of income, one must be very careful to identify whether the recorded income level is transient or long-lasting.

Direct Evidence of Validity of Laws of Demand

Have you noticed that prices of fruits and vegetables are lower when the crop is in season and the supply is large? The greater amount can be sold only at a lower price. If prices of perishable crops did not fall at the peak of the harvest season, the first law of demand would not be true. Likewise, if poorer-quality goods sold for the same price as better-quality goods (assuming everyone agrees on standards of quality), the first law of demand would not be true. Merchants have clearance sales at lower prices; to induce you to buy, someone who seeks your business will lower the price—not raise it. Indeed, in response to several polls and questionnaires, most people said they would not reduce the amount of gasoline they used just because price went up. They said they had to have transportation. (How much? At what cost?) In fact their statements indicated a low level of economic sophistication. Their actual social response—as the data showed—was to reduce the amount of gasoline demanded at a higher price, as predicted by the first law of demand. The amount of reduction has been even greater in the long run, as predicted by the second law of demand.

Indirect Evidence
of Validity

Usually the power of a law is corroborated by indirect, unexpected implications rather than by direct evidence. Why is a larger proportion of good-quality California oranges and grapes shipped for sale in New York while a larger proportion of the poorer-quality remains in California? Are New Yorkers richer or more discriminating? Possibly—but then why is the quality *ratio* higher even in the poor districts of New York than in California? The question can be posed for other goods: Why do Asians import disproportionately more expensive American cars rather than cheaper models? Why are "luxuries" disproportionately represented in international trade? Why do young parents go to expensive plays rather than movies more often than do young couples without children? Why are "seconds" (slightly defective products) more heavily consumed near the place of manufacture than farther away? Why must a tourist be more careful buying leather goods in Italy than Italian leather goods in the United States? Why is most meat shipped to Alaska "deboned"? The answers are implications of the law of demand. Let us see why.

Suppose that: California grapes cost 5 cents a pound to ship to New York, regardless of quality; that production of grapes is 50 percent "choice" and 50 percent "standard"; and that in California the choice grapes sell for 10 cents a pound and the standard for 5 cents a pound. The cost of shipping grapes to New York raises the New York buyer's cost to 15 cents for choice grapes and to 10 cents for standard grapes. One pound

of choice grapes in New York costs the same as 1.5 pounds of standard, whereas in California it costs the same as 2 pounds of standard. New Yorkers pay a lower price for choice relative to standard, and therefore, in accordance with the first law of demand, consume relatively more choice grapes than do Californians. In California, where standard grapes are cheaper relative to choice grapes, a larger fraction of standard grapes should be consumed. And it is so.

Total Use Value,
Consumer Surplus, and
Total Market Value

In Figure 3–2, total use of value of a given amount of a good was represented by the entire area under the demand curve out to that quantity. And the total use value consists of the two components: consumer surplus and total market value. If we were to hold the demand curve constant and slide down it by lowering the price, what would happen to those three measures?

If we compare Figures 3–10a and 3–10b, it is clear that, in moving down the unchanged demand curve, the total use value must increase, as will consumer surplus. It is not as obvious that total market value may increase, remain constant, or decrease. But that is what the numbers of column 5 in Table 3–4 tell us. And that helps us to resolve a "paradox of value" that long troubled some people. How could a commodity like diamonds be so much less useful than a commodity like water and still be so much more expensive?

Suppose that the commodity in Figure 3–10a is

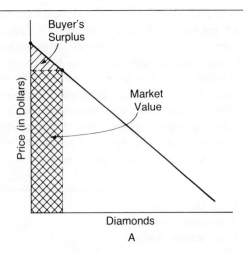

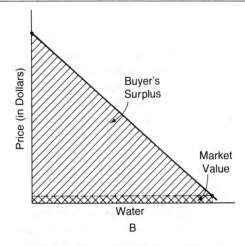

Figure 3–10. Total Personal Value, and Total Market Value

The total personal value of diamonds is small relative to that of water. The total market value of water can be less than that of diamonds as illustrated in the above figures. The greater the amount of any good, the greater its total personal value, but the total market value may decrease if the demand is inelastic.

diamonds and that the commodity in Figure 3–10b is water. For present purposes, it is not necessary (although it is convenient) for the two demand curves to be identical. But let the amount of diamonds be sufficiently small that the price (and the marginal use value) is "high"—the amount demanded is near the vertical axis—and suppose that the amount of water is so large that the demander is far out along his demand curve. Then the total use value of water (the lined area under the demand curve) can be larger than the total use value of diamonds, despite a very low price of water and a very high price of diamonds—and despite a total market value of water that is not only small but may be decreasing as the amount of water available increases.

Pricing Tactics: A Preview

To further demonstrate the power of a demand schedule to summarize basic consumer behavior, one more aspect of behavior hidden in that demand schedule should be exposed to permit later explanation of some pricing tactics. Suppose a seller were faced with our demand schedule of Table 3–1. He sets a price of 50 cents. His costs of supplying eggs are 25 cents each. He receives $3.00 with a cost of $1.50 for six eggs, a profit of $1.50. Next, suppose the seller offers two more eggs at 30 cents each, on condition that the first six are bought at 50 cents each. If the seller could use such a pricing tactic, he would get 30 cents on each of the extra two units, without a price cut on the six units already salable at 50

32

cents. His marginal revenue (total revenue *increase*) would now be 30 cents on the seventh egg and 30 cents on the eighth. He has no off-setting price cut on the first six units. On each of those last two units, he obtains a net gain of 10 cents that he could not have obtained had he also cut the price on the first six units.

In our example the seller could do still better, with a multipart schedule of prices: He tells the buyer, "You may buy one egg at 99 cents. You may then buy a second egg at a price of 89 cents for the second egg, after you have agreed to buy the first one for 99 cents. A third egg may then be purchased for 79 cents; a fourth for 69 cents; a fifth for 59 cents; a sixth for 49 cents; a seventh for 39 cents; an eighth, or as many thereafter as you wish, at 29 cents each." How many will the buyer buy? The correct answer may be surprising.

This customer will buy a first egg, since to her one unit is worth at least $1.00, and she can buy it for only 99 cents, with a one-cent gain of useful value as compared to not buying it (although her gain is not as great as it would be were she able to buy each for 29 cents). A second egg has a marginal use value, to her, of 90 cents, but will cost only 89 cents, giving another one-cent gain of value in use. Similarly, each successive additional unit purchased adds one cent of use value over the costs, until she has purchased eight units. A ninth would have a marginal use value of only 20 cents, but would cost 29 cents. Her total consumer surplus would be 8 cents, one cent on each of the eight eggs.

If the price had been a simple 30 cents per egg regardless of quantity purchased, she would still have bought only eight eggs and her gain (consumer surplus) from this single price would have

been equivalent to $2.80: the sum of the 70-cent value gain on the first unit (worth $1.00 but purchased for only 30 cents), and the 60-cent gain on the second unit (worth 90 cents but costing only 30 cents), and so on with successive gains of 50 cents, 40 cents, 30 cents, 20 cents, 10 cents, 00 cents on the eight eggs). But under multipart pricing, the seller gets more of the gains from market trade. Who *should* get more is unanswerable.

It might at first be surprising that with multipart pricing the buyer still buys up to the eight units she would have bought at the single price. Be careful not to think that the buyer will purchase fewer eggs simply because a multipart price schedule costs her a lot more money than does the single 30-cent price: $5.12 for eight eggs weekly with a multipart price schedule ($5.12 = 99 cents + 89 cents + ... + 29 cents), compared to only $2.40 at a 30-cent single price. Why indeed does she buy the same number of eggs in each case? Because that additional $3.72 ($5.12 − $2.40) is a reduction in her consumable income that she would have spent on everything else she buys. The sliding-scale price system simply makes her $3.72 poorer for those other purchases. If she spends about $200 a week on all her consumption, that $3.72 is about a 2 percent reduction in her consumable income power. Thus she would cut back roughly 2 percent on all of her purchases—including eggs. (Although she really would buy fewer eggs, because her demand schedule for eggs would have shifted back a little bit, nevertheless, for all practical purposes, this 2 percent income effect on her demand for eggs is too small for us to notice in her buying behavior.)

Thus, whether price is a constant, single per-unit-price or a sliding, multipart-scale, we once again see that the consumer buys amounts that equate her marginal personal value to price. That is, she buys the amount that brings her marginal personal value down to equality with price of the last unit. Nevertheless, a buyer certainly prefers a uniform *low* price to a multipart scale of prices, whereas a seller would certainly use the multipart price schedule, if possible, rather than the single price system. Later we shall investigate circumstances under which multipart pricing can be employed successfully.

33

Summary

1. Demand is the whole schedule of alternative possible prices and amounts demanded at each price. The term demand refers not to any one of those amounts at a given price, but rather to the whole schedule.
2. Marginal personal value of a good is the change in total personal value from a unit change in the amount of that good.
3. Personal value is always measured as an amount of some other goods that are equally desired to the amount of the initial good being valued.
4. As larger amounts of the good are held, marginal personal value diminishes.
5. The amount demanded at any price is the amount at which the marginal personal value is brought to equality with the price.
6. The first fundamental law of demand states: "The demand for any good is a negative relationship between price and the amount demanded," or, "Whatever the quantity demanded at a given price, there is a higher price that will induce a reduction in the amount demanded."
7. The elasticity of demand with repect to price is a measure of the responsiveness of amount demanded to changes in price. In general, the ratio of the relative (percentage) response in amount demanded to the relative (small percentage) change in price is the measure of elasticity near that price. An elasticity greater than "one" implies that a reduction in price increases the total receipts, in the neighborhood of that price.
8. The greater the elasticity, the closer is marginal revenue to price.
9. The second fundamental law of demand asserts the elasticity of demand is greater in the longer run than in the shorter run.
10. At a lower price more of the item will be put to current uses, new uses will be discovered, and more people will use the good.
11. "Need" is a word often used to suggest absolute minimum requirements, when in fact the amount "needed" depends on the cost of having more.
12. Incomes affect the amount demanded at any price. Hence incomes affect the demand schedule.
13. Price changes have a substitution and an income effect on the amount demanded.
14. Alleged exceptions to the laws of demand usually result from changes in amounts demanded because of a price change being confused with a change in the demand schedule because of nonprice factors.
15. Effects of price or income changes depend on how long the price or income stays at the new amount.

16. Consumer or buyer gain from trade (called consumer surplus) is the difference between total personal value of the amount bought and its market cost. Do not confuse the total market cost with the total personal use value.

17. Not all market prices permit one to buy whatever amount he demands at that price. Sometimes (under situations to be explored later) a sliding schedule of prices forces a buyer to pay a per-unit price that depends on how much he buys, usually to permit the seller to get a larger share of the gains from trade.

Questions

1. The following is characteristic of Mr. A's market demand for pencils. Each price is associated with the number of pencils he would buy each year.

Price	Quantity	Total Revenue
$1.00	1	$1.00
.90	2	1.80
.80	3	2.40
.70	4	——
.60	5	——
.50	6	——
.40	7	——
.30	8	——
.20	9	——
.10	10	——

   *a. Complete the total revenue.
   b. At a price of 60 cents Mr. A would own five.

At a price of 50 cents he would own six. At each of these two prices, he would have a total of $3.00 in pencils. Does this mean that he attaches no value to a sixth? What value does he attach to a sixth?

2. The demand schedule of the preceding question shows that at a price of $1, the annual consumption is 1 unit. At a price of 90 cents, the annual consumption is 2 units.
   a. Can it be said that this person wants *each* one of those 2 units more than he wants 90 cents' worth of annual expenditures on any other goods?
   b. Note that at the price of $1, he spent annually $1.00 on this good; whereas at a price of 90 cents he spent $1.80 or 80 cents more than previously. Do you still say he values the extra unit at approximately 90 cents, even though he spends only 80 cents more?
   c. Explain why. In doing so, explain what is meant by "value."

3. Can Table 3–1 be read as follows: "A person sees a price of $1, and he therefore buys one egg. The next hour he sees the price has fallen to 80 cents; so he dashes out and buys three. A couple of hours later, the price rises to 90 cents; so he buys two." If it can't be interpreted that way—and it can't—how is it to be interpreted?

4. For goods like shoes, a rise in price will reduce the number of pairs of shoes a person will want. Since the price at which he can sell used shoes is low relative to the new-shoe price, he will not sell some shoes in order to reduce his stock of shoes. How does he adjust his stock of shoes to the

new, lasting, higher cost of shoes? (Hint: How does a person adjust his stock of clothes to his new demand after experiencing a reduction in demand consequent to a reduction of his income?)

5. Consumption is a rate concept, even though the good being consumed may be held as a stock or finite amount of goods. True or false?

6. To say that a person purchases and consumes water at a *rate* of 50 gallons per day, or 350 per week, is to say the same thing in two ways. What is the equivalent statement in terms of rate per year?

7. Mr. A currently uses water at a rate of 3650 gallons per year at the present price. Suppose that his demand doubles, so that his rate increases to 7300 gallons per year. How many more *gallons* of water will he consume during the first week of higher demand?

8. "According to the law of demand, the lower the price of vacations, the more vacations I should take. Yet I take only one per year. Obviously the law of demand must be wrong." Is it?

9. There are *three* conceptions of the amount demanded: (1) The rate of *consumption;* (2) the quantity a person wants to *buy* in order to increase his current stock; (3) the quantity a person wants to *own*. As an example of each: (1) a person may consume eggs at the rate of 6/7 per day (which does not necessarily mean he buys and eats a fraction of an egg each day); (2) on Saturday he buys a half-dozen eggs; (3) he may own an average of three eggs in his refrigerator. Normally, explicit distinctions between rates of purchase and consumption are not necessary since they are closely related. Which of these three measures is a rate of activity and which is a "stock"?

10. Using the demand-schedule data in problem 1, suppose that these refer to number of diamond rings he would want to own at each price. He now owns four rings.
a. How many more would he *buy* or *sell* at each possible price?
b. If the equilibrium price in the market turned out to be 30 cents, how many would he want to buy or sell and how many would he then own—assuming he has four initially?

11. Explain how each of these is a denial of the law of demand and the basic postulates of economics:
a. "The budget of the Department of Defense covers only our basic needs and nothing more."
b. "Our children need better schools."
c. "Nothing is too good when it comes to education."
d. "America needs more energy."

12. Why is it nonsense to talk about urgent, critical, crying, vital, basic, minimum, social, or private needs?

*13. A book was entitled *Social Needs and Private Wants*. Would the title have suggested something different if it had been *Social Wants and Private Needs?*

14. Diagnose and evaluate the following news report: "Our city needs more golf courses, according to a report submitted to the City Recreation and Park Department by the National Golf Foundation. The survey discovered that many people do not play as often

as they would like because of the lack of courses." Does this differ from the situation of filet mignon steaks, champagne, and autos?

15. a. For the demand schedule in Problem 1, compute the marginal revenues.

b. Compute also the marginal personal use values at each quantity.

c. To which of the preceding concepts, marginal revenue or marginal personal use value, does a buyer equate the price by his choice of how many to consume?

16. Why is the marginal revenue always less than price (except at first unit)?

17. An increase in *demand* (the demand *schedule*) is shown graphically by a demand curve (to the right of) (above) (below) (to the left of) the old demand curve. Select correct options.

18. Which of the following would increase the demand for wigs?

a. A raise in one's salary.

b. Higher price of hats.

c. Having a swimming pool.

d. Rise in cost of hair care.

e. Getting divorced.

f. Number of other people who wear wigs.

g. Lower price of wigs.

19. Are the following statements correct or incorrect? Explain your answers.

a. "A 1 percent rise in price that induces a 3 percent decrease in amount taken indicates elasticity greater than one."

b. "A 1 percent fall in price that induces a 3 percent increase in amount purchased indicates an elasticity of greater than one."

c. What is wrong with asking whether a 1 percent rise in price induces a 3 percent decrease in demand?

20. "Elasticity is a measure of the percentage increase in demand for a one-cent change in price." There are two errors in that statement. What are they?

21. In the graph below, which of the three demand curves has the greatest elasticity at price p_1? At price p_2? Does the elasticity change as the price changes along each curve?

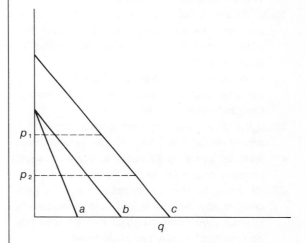

22. a. If the price of gasoline rose 100 percent, automobile manufacturers would make changes in the designs or operating characteristics of automobiles. True or false?

b. What effect would that price rise have on gasoline consumption?

c. Would the effect be more extensive at the end of one year or at the end of three years?

23. Explain how what is often called "impulse" buying is consistent with the laws of demand. Explain why habitual buying is also consistent. Suggest some behavior that would not be consistent.

24. Does the demand for children obey the fundamental theorem of demand? The demand by immigrants for entry to the United States? The demand for divorces? The demand for pianos? The demand for beautiful women? The demand for a winning college football team? The demand for "A's" in this course? The demand for appendectomies?

25. a. Because we represent a demand curve with precise numbers, does that mean that people have these numerical schedules in their minds?
b. What essential property illustrated by the demand-schedule data does characterize their behavior?

26. If the price of candy rises from $1 to $1.25 a pound while the price of ice cream rises from 50 cents to 75 cents a quart, in what sense is that a *fall* in the price of candy?

27. "If the price of gasoline rose by only 10 percent, many people would not immediately change their consumption." Explain why this does not refute the law of demand.

28. Economics asserts that people prefer more to less. Yet there are waiting lists of people seeking small apartments in slum areas while bigger, better apartments do not have a list of applicants. How can people want smaller, less luxurious apartments rather than bigger apartments without violating our postulates about people's preferring more economic goods?

29. a. As your wealth or income increases, what happens to your demand (schedule) for gasoline?
b. If you own a dairy farm and the price of milk went up, would you consume more or less milk?

30. Why is it that when a couple goes out, the probability is greater that they will attend an expensive theater if they have infants for whom a baby sitter is necessary than if they are childless.

31. Let p_1 be the price of a higher-quality version of a good, and p_2 be the price of a lower-quality version. Both prices are the prices in the United States. Let T_1 and T_2 be the transport costs of these goods to a "foreign" market. Show that if $T_1/T_2 < p_1/p_2$, then *relatively* more of good "1" will be shipped; if the inequality is reversed, relatively more of good "2" will be shipped. "Relative" to what? In your answer, what do you assume about demand conditions in domestic and in "foreign" markets?

32. A Governor of California once asserted that the reduction of Mexican labor in California did no harm, because the total value of the crop harvested was larger than before. Evaluate the relevance of that criterion. (The same was true when the Arabs reduced the amount of oil sold in 1973.)

33. A competitor of the authors of this text claims his text is "invaluable." Does that sound consistent with economic analysis?

4

Market Prices as Social Coordinators

In this and the next four chapters let us conveniently assume that there is a fixed amount of consumption goods. (Later we will investigate their production.) How are they distributed among members of the community? One method is a supposedly all-knowing, or sufficiently powerful, central rationing agent that decrees the allocations. But without such an agent, the responses of individuals to the market prices of respective goods can bring the amounts demanded into equality with the amounts available.

If the total amount demanded is greater than the amount available, there is a so-called shortage: The amount available falls short of what people wish to buy at the selling price; or, put the other way around, the quantity demanded is excessive—*at the going price*. The price is too low to equate quantity demanded to quantity available. But a sufficiently higher price will restrain quantity demanded to match the available supply, thereby eliminating the shortage (but, of course, not eliminating "scarcity"). And if the price is too high, the amount available exceeds the quantity demanded—producing a "surplus."

A sufficiently higher price will eliminate a shortage; a sufficiently lower price will correct a surplus. Such equilibrating prices occur through the normal market activity of individuals who are free to buy and sell in quantities and on terms to which any two people agree. To understand how market-determined prices match demands with supplies without central authority, and to understand the effects of the matching process and its influence on production, we first use a "toy" problem, or what scientists call a *model.*

Why use a model or a "toy" problem? We can answer best by an analogy: Someone studying automotive mechanics must first master the basic principles of the internal combustion engine, described in terms of pistons moving in cylinders, compressing gas, which, once ignited, expands and moves the pistons, thus providing power to turn wheels. Only when those principles are understood can one understand a real engine with all its other essentials—a cooling and lubrication system, carburetor, ignition and distributor, exhaust muffler, and all the rest that make that system work. The operation of the market exchange process, too, is supported by a mass of essentials and accessories—middlemen, inventories, advertising, business firms, government regulations, etc. So first we outline the basic exchange principles. Then we shall examine how the accessories affect the working of that exchange system. Do not treat abstract, "toy" examples as simplistic and irrelevant to the real world. Properly used, they systematically introduce us to the complex and confusing real world.

Market Demand

Start with a society of four people, A, B, C, and D. Their demands for automobiles are in Table 4–1. (All the automobiles are alike.) The total community or market demand expresses our first theorem of demand: Greater amounts are demanded (needed?) at lower prices. The market amount demanded is the sum of the individual amounts demanded at a common price.

Suppose seven cars exist, all initially owned by A. The following is one of many possible scenarios of exchange sequences. (Suppose, for simplicity, that no person's wealth, and hence his

Table 4–1. Car Ownership Demands of A, B, C, and D

| Price | Quantity of Automobiles | | | | |
	A	B	C	D	Total Market
$1000	2	0	1	1	4
900	2	0	1	1	4
800	2	0	1	2	5
700	2	0	1	2	5
600	3	0	1	2	6
500	3	1	1	2	7
400	3	1	2	2	8
300	3	1	2	3	9
200	3	1	2	4	10
100	4	2	2	4	12

demand schedule, is changed significantly by the succeeding sequence of trades.)[1] A would sell some cars even if he could get only $100 per car. How many? Three if C and D each extravagantly offer $900 a car, A will delightedly sell one to each. Then B more shrewdly offers only $400 for a car; again, A sells. This leaves A four cars, and B, C, and D have one car each. C then buys another car from A at, say, $300—a price as high as $400 is acceptable to C, and A sells because he would rather have any amount over $100 than a

fourth car. Finally, though D would have paid as much as $800 to get a second car, he initially offers A only $300 for a second car; but A has no cars to "spare" unless he can get $700. B, however, if alerted to this negotiation, would offer his car to D for $600, even though he just bought it. And C, who values his second car at only $400, would undercut B's price by asking for only $500. Neither A nor B would cut their prices that far. So C would sell to D for $500.

In the final market-clearing equilibrium A ends up with three cars, B with one, C with one, and D with two. Everyone is content with his pattern of goods, given his preferences and wealth: There are no further mutually acceptable revisions. And, at every step in the sequence, both the buyer and seller moved to preferred higher personally valued situations. Though many other starting allocations and sequences of trade could be imagined, all will yield to the same final distribution and to the same equilibrium-maintaining price, $500. There is always some price that makes the sum of the individual amounts demanded equal to the total available.

Market Supply and Demand: Graphic Interpretation

Analysis of pricing and exchange is aided with demand and supply diagrams. In Figure 4–1, individual demand curves, *AA, BB, DD,* for persons A, B, C, D, are added horizontally to get the total community demand, *TT.* The community supply of seven cars is shown by a vertical line, *SS.* The vertical supply line means that, regardless of

[1] Throughout this chapter we will operate under one very important assumption: No person ever acts as though he could affect the market price by himself holding off the market any units he owns. Whatever the number of the good a seller owns, he has, or believes he has, too few to significantly affect the potential selling price by refusing to sell some units. Later we shall modify that assumption. For the present we make it because it is often realistic and because it permits us to concentrate on the demand side of the exchange, and the way in which price (however determined) controls the allocation of the amount made available.

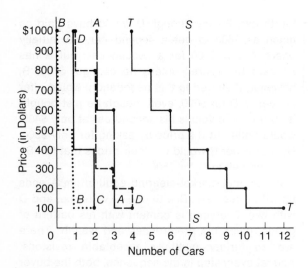

Figure 4–1. Individual and Total Community Demand

Individual and total community demand curves with existing stock of automobiles as the supply. The total demand curve, TT, is the sum of the horizontal distances of each of the individual demand curves at each price, the points of total quantity being connected by straight line segments. With a fixed number of cars available regardless of price, the supply curve, SS, is a vertical line.

price, the available amount is seven. The community demand intersects the supply at a price at which the number of cars demanded by A, B, C, and D is three, one, one, and two, respectively, for a total of seven. This diagram easily indicates there is a price that matches amounts demanded with amount supplied.

Figure 4–1 shows that at any price above the equilibrium price, $500, the community amount demanded would be less than the number available. If a law were to stipulate that cars could be purchased only for a price *above* $500, there would be a *surplus* of cars, with one or more cars

being offered for sale but no more being demanded. The allocative control provided by prices would be broken.

But the surplus would instantly become a shortage if the permissible price were somehow confined *below* the equilibrium price. Consumers would say their "needs" (at that low price) were not satisfied. Of course, if the price were higher, that "need" would be less urgent than the "need" for other things that could be obtained instead with that greater amount of money. The market equilibrium price will eliminate any "surplus" or "shortages." At that price, the amount individuals want (or say they "need") matches the total available: The market is "cleared." Shortages and surpluses occur if somehow prices are prevented from changing enough to equate the amounts demanded to the amounts available.

Adjustments to Changes in Supply

If total supply were reduced, a rise in price would reduce the amounts demanded to match the smaller supply. For example, suppose one of A's cars is destroyed by fire. The community supply is decreased to six, represented by shifting the supply line leftward to six on the quantity scale in Figure 4–2. The intersection of demand with the smaller supply now requires a higher equilibrating price, $600. How is the higher price brought about? If A's loss of the car does not reduce his wealth significantly (as we assume in this example), he will seek a replacement. Since no one is willing to sell a car at the price of $500, there would be a "shortage" (of supply) or, to put it in different words, an "excessive amount demanded" at that $500 price: Seven are demanded;

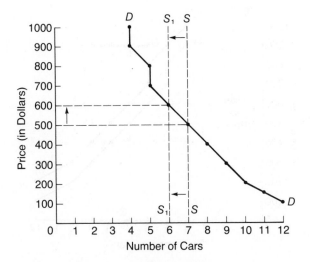

Figure 4–2. Reduced Supply Raises Price

Reduction in supply is shown by a shift of the supply curve to the left. The total market demand line is now labeled DD. The rise from $500 to $600 facilitates a redistribution of cars from those who value a car less than $600 to those who value a car at least at $600. Without the option of bidding higher prices in response to a reduction in supply, cars would not be reallocated according to relative personal valuations.

six exist. But A has only two cars; he still values a third car at $600. That is, he prefers a third car more than any other things he could get with $600. By offering $600 for purchase of a car, A could buy a car from B who prefers $600 to his second car. A could thus move to what is now a preferred position, although not what he preferred before the fire.

The fire and subsequent exchange has benefited B. It may seem unfair that others gain from A's loss. But to refuse a gain to B through trade is to condemn A to the worsened postfire situation, unless you condemn someone else to bear

the loss—and *someone has* to bear it.[2] By offering to buy a car from B for $600 and thereby improving B's situation, A was also able to improve his own.

If a price ceiling of $500 is imposed, B is prevented from "gouging" A, or, as it is sometimes said, "profiteering from A's misfortune." We might think we were doing A a favor by preventing him from paying more than $500. But he cannot get a desired third car at that price. A shortage would be created—by the prohibition of higher prices, not by the burning of a car, which reduced the supply.

Adjustments to Changes in Demand

Suppose again that there are seven cars, and that a newcomer, E, joins the community. His added demand increases the community market demand (shifts the demand curve to the right) and requires a higher equilibrating price (See Table 4–2 and Figure 4–3.) E is willing to pay as much as $900 for a car. How much *must* he pay? No one is willing to sell at the old equilibrium price of $500, but B will sell at $600—he prefers $600 to the car.

Don't be deceived by the numerical details. The specific numbers serve only to illustrate the *relationships* among prices, amounts demanded, and personal values. Two things are crucial for understanding how price in a market-exchange economy controls the amounts demanded and facilitates redistribution of goods: the *direction* in which price affects amounts demanded; and

[2] Voluntary insurance is a method for distributing the loss over all coinsurers, rather than concentrating it on one person.

Table 4–2. Car-Ownership Demand Schedules
of A, B, C, D, and E

	Quantity Demanded		
Price	A,B,C,D	E	Total
$1000	4	0	4
900	4	1	5
800	5	1	6
700	5	1	6
600	6	1	7
500	7	1	8
400	8	1	9
300	9	2	11
200	10	2	12
100	12	3	15

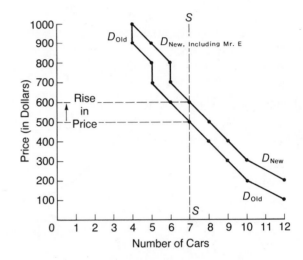

Figure 4–3. Higher-Price Effect of Increased Demand

The important conclusion is not merely that price is increased, but that the higher price permits a reallocation of an automobile to E, the higher-valuing person, from B, who prefers $600 to an automobile.

the *direction* in which the amount of a good in a person's possession affects his marginal personal values.

[1, 2 3, 4 5, 6 7]

Knowing the laws of market demand and exchange, we can now interpret some real situations as examples of how the system works.

Pareto-Efficient Allocations

If any achievable redistribution of goods would make someone better off without hurting anyone else, surely we would say, "Move to the new allocation." Any distribution, a change in which would *have* to hurt someone, is called a "Pareto-efficient" distribution, after Vilfredo Pareto, the nineteenth-century Italian sociologist who first emphasized it in his studies. If a situation could be changed so that some would benefit without hurting others (say by more than compensating them for any initial undesirable effects) the initial situa-

tion would not have been a Pareto optimal one. Though the Pareto-efficient distribution would seem to be a reasonable, widely acceptable normative, ethical standard, it is neither widely accepted nor regarded as reasonable. Nevertheless, for the moment we will contemplate it.

Given the demands of persons A, B, C, and D in our example earlier, the resulting distribution of three, one, one, and two cars respectively to each of them is a Pareto-efficient distribution. You could not devise any subsequent sale of a car that could benefit each of any two parties, or anyone else, as each judges the result. (Try it; it's impossible. We safely offer $1000 to anyone who can.)

But from any other allocation you could find exchanges with a resultant "gain from trade" split between the buyer and seller. We have not assumed or shown that there should be more (or less) equality in the initial or final results. (And we have not shown—nor can it be shown—that all real market situations lead to "Pareto-efficient" results.)

The Pervasive Illusion That Cost Determines Price

Many prices misleadingly appear to be set by costs of production instead of competition among demanders. This very widespread illusion can be illustrated with an increased demand for meat.

For some reason, people's desire for meat increases. Housewives reveal that increased demand by buying more than formerly. As sales increase, butchers' inventories are depleted more rapidly than expected. Normally a butcher, like any retailer, carries an inventory large enough to take care of *more* than the average of daily sales in order to accommodate transient increases in sales without running out of stock or having to raise prices late on those days when his inventory approaches depletion. Stable, predictable prices are convenient to housewives when they plan what to buy and where to buy it; such prices spare them the extra costs of shopping around and making last-minute revisions in their plans in response to unexpectedly and temporarily high or low prices. Hence inventories help increase the efficiency of the market system by assuring immediate supply at more predictable prices. (Highly predictable prices can be assured by legally controlling them, but that reduces the market's effectiveness in assuring immediate supply.)

Furthermore, in reality most customers come to sellers at a rate varying randomly around some constant *average*. Not only do buyers come at random intervals but the amounts purchased by each customer vary at random around his own, possibly constant, average. Thus while the basic consumption demand has not necessarily changed, the timing and amounts purchased do vary, so actual sales in any one day will vary at random around some stable mean. Sellers know this and do not treat every change in sales volume as a change in underlying consumption demand. As a result, when the underlying consumption demand really has shifted, sellers will not be able to detect it immediately. Any true shift in consumption demand will be masked by the daily transient purchase fluctuations. (We are ignoring the detailed marketing problems this causes, because we are interested in understanding how prices control consumption and allocation. The details of the *process* whereby demand changes are detected and price is changed do not fundamentally alter that allocative function of prices, as we shall now illustrate.)[3]

For the present it is sufficient to be aware that: (1) retailers maintain inventories, at least as buffers, to permit availability at relatively predictable prices despite transiently shifting purchase rates; and (2) they cannot immediately distinguish underlying shifts in aggregate consumption demand from daily, transient, reversible purchase variations.

---

[3] But demand changes do cause serious difficulties in the *production* processes, especially those in which services cannot readily be stored in a buffer inventory to smooth out the transient variations in amounts demanded, as we shall see later.

No butcher knows instantly that the consumption demand has risen for the community as a whole. All he knows is that *he* has temporarily experienced more meat sales at the existing price. He will buy more meat than usual the next day in order to restore his abnormally low inventory; and he will buy even more if he believes the increased sales will continue. If the aggregate demand for meat did increase, so that one butcher's increased sales was not transient or some other butcher's loss, then purchases by the aggregate of butchers from the packers (meat suppliers) will increase, and the increase will persist.

Packers also rely on inventories as a buffer to sales fluctuations. Packers restore inventories by instructing their cattle buyers (who travel among cattle raisers, fatteners, and stockyards) to buy more than usual. But with all the packers restoring their inventories, the cattle available is inadequate to meet the increased amount demanded *at the old price.* Either some buyers cannot get the amount requested, or they must boost their offer prices to persuade cattlemen to sell steers to them instead of to other packers.

This rise in offer prices may occur nearly simultaneously among the buyers, as if there were collusion among the cattlemen or buyers. The cattlemen let the buyers bid against each other until the price rises to a point where the packers will not want to buy more meat than is available.

In terms of our demand-and-supply apparatus, the *currently* available market supply curve of cattle is vertical (that is, it is not influenced by current price), as in our automobile example. An increased demand by packers for cattle (a demand that simply reflects the ultimate consumer demand for meat) implies a higher price but at the same quantity. Each packer is forced back up along his increased demand curve to that higher price, at which he buys less than he had planned at the old price. The total amount demanded is then no greater than before. Each packer must pay a higher price for cattle to avoid getting less than before. Competition among the packers has raised the price during the immediate period when cattle production could not be increased. Subsequently cattlemen will increase production of cattle up to that amount at which their costs rise to match the price they expect to get for the cattle. In this way prices, which depend on demand and supply, also set the limit to how much costs can be incurred.

Cattle raisers bask in the wealth of higher selling prices. But to packers this is a rise in *costs.* Why did their costs rise? The cost of existing cattle did not increase; nor the costs of getting cattle to market, of slaughtering, or of distributing meat. The higher price paid by wholesaler-slaughterers to cattlemen is essentially a result of the increased demand by consumers being expressed all the way through to producers, where it becomes evident as higher prices for cattle.

As the price of cattle has been bid up (higher *costs* to the packers), so packers must charge a higher price in order to allocate meat among competing retail butchers. Retail butchers, in turn, post higher prices to housewives. When housewives complain about the higher price, the butcher in honesty says that it isn't his fault. The price he pays to get meat has gone up. The butcher can say, "I never raise prices until my costs go up." And the packers can honestly say the same thing.

If housewives want to know who is to blame for the higher prices of meat, they can look in the mirror behind the butcher's counter. They might then say to each other, "If you didn't want more meat, I could have more." But that tactless observation is neither useful nor fitting in the competitive exchange system. The exchange system glosses over this facet of competition and makes it appear as if the higher price of meat were caused by the greed of butchers, packers, and farmers—not that of consumers. For example, in a period of inflation consumer prices appear to rise because all *costs* are rising, but fundamentally what has happened is that a large increase in the money stock has increased *demand,* and the larger demand has run up against limited stocks of productive resources—a topic we shall explore later.

Rental and Allocation

A clearer perception of the hidden conflict among competing demanders is obtained by explicitly distinguishing people whose demands have increased from those whose demands have not. A person who rents a house will feel the effect of increased demand by other people when his rent rises. A higher rent will reduce the amount or quality of housing he demands, which means he is induced to release some housing to those whose demands have increased. Since the renter does not own the house, he will not capture any of the higher market value of the house—or lose its value if the demand had instead fallen.

This can be analyzed graphically. In Figure 4–4, curve $D_a + D_b$ represents the community's demand for housing space *before* an increase. D_a is a demand that remains unchanged, and D_b is the initial demand by those whose demand will

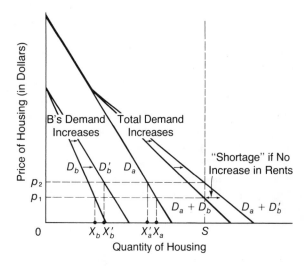

Figure 4–4. Change in Price of Housing Enables Reallocation of Housing Space among Competing Demanders, from A to B

When demand by group B increases while that of group A does not, the increased total market demand raises prices with less housing then being demanded by members of group A. Housing space equivalent to distance X_b–X_b' is transferred to group B from group A. That housing space is valued more highly by group B than by group A.

If rentals were held down by law at the old rental, a "shortage" of housing would appear as more housing than is available is demanded at that old rental. Allowing price to rise would eliminate the excessive amount demanded, which is the "shortage." Miami Beach recently imposed rent controls when demand for housing increased and rents started to rise. Immediately a shortage appeared. It is proposed that the rent controls be retained until the shortage disappears. Will it?

later increase to D_b'. Initially, the rental price is p_1, with X_a space rented by group A and X_b by group B. Now, let group B's demand increase to the curve D_b'. The new total demand, $D_a + D_b'$, intersects the existing housing supply at price p_2, greater than p_1.

If rents were held below p_2, a shortage would occur—the excess of the housing space demanded over the amount available, shown by the distance between the supply line and new demand curve at prices less than p_2. At *any* price below p_2 there simply is not enough to satisfy the amounts of housing demanded. If the rent is not suppressed, rental prices will be bid up to p_2, as frustrated demanders offer or tolerate higher rents to get demanded housing. While rents were rising, the housing market would be called "tight" or "strong" or a "seller's" market, and vacancy rates that normally exist to facilitate the normal flow of movers (like the inventories that stores maintain) would diminish.

When rents rise from p_1 to p_2, group B obtains a larger amount, OX'_b, instead of only OX_b. Members of group A end up with only OX'_a. Space goes from those whose demand did not increase to those whose demand increased. (We are leaving the effect on production or supply for later; however, any increase in housing production as a result of a price increase would lower the ultimate equilibrium price.)

As the price rises in response to the increased demand (represented by the shift to the right of the market-demand curve), all claimants for the more highly demanded housing will reduce their *amounts* demanded. That is, the higher price moves each of them to reduced amounts back up along their demand schedules, D_a and D_b. House *owners* receive more rent; their houses are worth more. Members of group A, whose demand did not increase, pay higher rents and use less housing space. Members of group B present a more complex result. Those whose demands increased most get more space than they were getting at the lower price; those whose demands have in-

creased only a little may end up paying higher rents and getting somewhat less space than originally.

Everyone will blame the owners for raising rents. But what enabled the owners to get higher prices? The *increased demand* by tenants in group B. The owners, in effect, tell the A people to meet the competition of the B's. The B's and A's may be friends and neighbors who complain to each other about the higher, "exorbitant" rents— never thinking to blame the competition among themselves for the higher price.

Objections to the higher prices are objections to the higher valuation of these goods by some other people. The *terms* of trade and the realizable *gains* from trade will vary from day to day. Trade enables each party to move to a situation preferred to *no* trade at all; but the gains from today's available trade, under new conditions of demand by other people, may be larger or smaller than yesterday's gains.

Tax on Fixed Supply

One of the important implications of demand and supply analysis is that no matter what may happen, if the demand and the supply schedule are unchanged, the price is unchanged. Returning to our automobile example, suppose the state legislature imposes a $200 tax on the sale of a car. What would that do to the price of cars? To answer that we must first discover what would happen to the demand and supply schedules. The supply was fixed at seven cars, and in no way depended on or could be affected by the price at which the cars could be sold. The supply line, or supply schedule, which here is a vertical line at seven cars, does not shift as a result of the tax. Nor does any consumer's demand to own cars. To each consumer the use value of cars is still the same. Thus the consumer demand curve and the supply curve have not shifted in response to that tax. Hence the sales price to a buyer will still be $500. What does happen is that each seller gets to keep only $300 of that price, with the remaining $200 going to the state. (Assume each buyer of a car does not expect to ever sell the car again; assuming otherwise would add complications that can be discussed only much later.)

If this scenario seems odd or incorrect, let us distinguish between two related demand schedules: one is the consumer's and the other is that part of the consumer's demand that will impinge on the seller's own wealth. Figure 4–5 shows a (net of tax) demand curve for cars that is exactly $200 lower than the consumer's demand at every quantity of cars. The upper demand curve is a smoothed version of the demand by consumers and the lower demand curve, exactly $200 lower, is the net of tax demand that sellers retain after the government tax. These two demands give different prices—one, the consumer's price, is *paid* by the buyer and the other, the seller's price, is *received and kept* by the seller, net of taxes. These two demand curves were formerly one and the same—with everything paid by the buyer going to the seller. Now a difference has been created. Though the tax does not change the total price paid by buyers, it reduces the seller's portion by $200. The market price paid by the consumer is unchanged, but the price received by the seller falls by exactly $200—because the supply schedule is a vertical line.

The seller cannot avoid that $200 fall in his

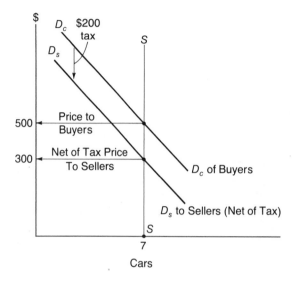

Figure 4–5. Effect of Tax on Demands and on Price with Fixed, Invariant Amount Supplied

Consumers' demand, reflecting use value of cars to consumers, stays unchanged with a tax. Demand impinging on sellers falls by the $200 tax. Consumers' price stays at $500 but price received by sellers falls to $300 because the vertical supply line represents fixed amount available despite price. If tax is to be paid to government by consumers, consumers' demand for cars is the same as if tax is to be paid to government by sellers. In the former case, buyers pay $300 to car sellers and $200 to government for a total price of $500, as before tax, and in the latter case, sellers pay $200 to government to retain $300 of price of $500, as before tax. With vertical supply (that is, total amount available does not vary with price) total price (tax plus proceeds to car seller) does not change. What changes is the portion of that $500 value that is distributed to the government from the wealth of the car owners at the time the tax is announced.

received price—or unchanged price to the buyer —because the supply of cars is fixed regardless of their price.

On whom the tax is levied makes no difference. Say the tax had been levied against the buyer rather than the seller: A demander is now required to pay $200 to the government when he buys a car, so he offers $200 less to the car seller. Since this will be true for every possible car buyer, the sellers cannot avoid a lower price. To refuse would mean no sale. Because the demand to have cars is unchanged, the total price buyers are willing to offer sellers (*and the government*) is still $500 for the *existing* seven cars. If the government extracts $200, only the remainder will be available to sellers. Again we have two related demand schedules, the consumer demand schedule and the *lower* partial demand to the seller after the buyer pays $200 to the government. The total purchase cost to the buyer is still $500, $200 to the government and the remainder, $300, to the seller. The gross purchase price is unchanged. The seller cannot get a higher net price. The query "Who pays the tax?" tends to confuse two separate things: the person who hands the money to the government should not be confused with the person who bears the corresponding reduction in wealth, in this case the car owners at the time the tax is announced.

To illustrate further, suppose a country has many landowners all with uniform areas of land renting for $100 per acre a month. The government levies a tax of $40 a month on the land. What happens to the rental value of land? Nothing happens to the amount paid by renters. No more land can be produced and none will disappear no matter what the rental income. Again, the supply schedule of land is a vertical line at the existing stock of land. It does not shift or change when the tax is levied. Nor does the demand for land by renters because the land use is still worth to renters as much as before. The equilibrium price paid by renters cannot change. However, the portion of the consumers' or rent-

ers' demand for land that accrues to the private landowners is now $40 lower per acre per month. A new demand schedule seen by landowners is $40 below the consumers' demand schedule at each amount of land, while the government takes the difference. The rental stays at $100, but only $60 is left for the private landowner while $40 is taken by the government, which has essentially declared itself a 40 percent owner of the value of the land. The landowners cannot increase rents. The rental values to renters are still the same as ever; the only difference is that $40 of that opportunity has been taken away from the owners. The best they can do is still $100, with a net of $60. If any landowners think they can raise the rent to renters, now that part of the rent goes to the state, they will find their opportunities no different from before. A higher rent will result in less land being rented and the unrented land will then be bid down in price back to the old $100 rental rate to renters.

To accurately perceive what is happening, treat the demand facing sellers as their *opportunity set.* That has not changed. However hard they may try to raise prices to renters they will find that the market-clearing gross rental is still $100 per month (with only $60 being retained by them). With unchanged demand conditions, and with the unchanged vertical supply of land, any attempt to increase rents will result only in some temporarily unrented land and a return to the old equilibrium price as the best of the available opportunities. Economic analysis does not say that *initially* people won't respond in various ways to some stimulus, but it does say the stimulus will shake up things only a while without changing the rental that can be sustained—unless demand or supply conditions change. This is not a complete analysis of the effects of land taxes. For example, we have not inquired as to the use of the tax proceeds. If used to improve the roads, schools, or environment near the land and thereby improve its usefulness, the consumer's demand for the land would shift upwards. In fact, if the value of those improvements equaled the tax cost, the renters' demand for that land would increase and the rent would go up by the amount of the tax. The landowners would net the same wealth as before because of that higher demand for their land.

The 1975 National Energy Act: Bad Economics and Good Politics

An especially timely example of erroneous economic analysis is provided by the National Energy Act of 1975. Congress mandated a rollback and continuing control of domestic crude oil prices below market-clearing levels on the mistaken presumption that prices would be kept down on gasoline, fuel oil, and other refined products obtained from crude oil. However, keeping the price of domestic crude oil low does not in fact keep down the price of the products refined from crude oil. The President, the Congress, Congressional staff advisors, the National Energy Board (but not the Council of Economic Advisors) erroneously thought that it would.

To illustrate the error with a specific example, suppose the products derived from a barrel of crude oil (for example, gasoline, kerosene, fuel oil, asphalt, plastics, chemicals, drugs, rubber, etc.) are worth $100 at their final market prices to consumers. Those final product prices are not controlled by law; they are market-clearing prices. Suppose also that all the costs of refining,

transporting, and distributing these final products amounts to $86, giving an excess of $14. (Those costs do not include that of obtaining crude oil.) Any processor who could convert a barrel of oil into products worth $100 at a cost of $86 would make a profit if he could purchase a barrel of crude oil at less than $14. Competition among refiners would bid the price of crude oil up to $14 as they competed for the available crude oil. The fundamental point is now clear: The price of a productive input is *bid up* to the value of what it provides consumers; in this way its value to consumers determines its price. In the present example, the $14-a-barrel value (and market price) comes from the $100 value of the refined products to consumers (minus the $86 of other costs of processing and distributing). Thus, by implication, if the price of the crude oil were kept down to $1 a barrel, any processor who got that oil for $1 would make a profit of $13, because the refined products would still sell for $100. The $100 value of the refined products depends only on the demand for them and their supply. *The supply of refined products is not changed whether the producer's (seller's) price of crude oil is kept down to $1 by law or bid up to its $14 value.* All that is affected is who gets that $14 value.

We have assumed that the crude oil will be taken from the ground regardless of the price obtained by the well owner; he will continue to sell the same amount whether he gets $1 or $14. Although this assumption is not entirely correct, we will hold it for the moment to simplify the analysis. We shall correct it shortly.

Since the supply of domestic crude oil, and hence the supply of its refined products, is not affected by the price received by the crude producer, the final product prices will be unaffected by what is paid for the crude oil. The price of refined products could not be increased, for to do so would mean that some amount would not be sold. That is why putting a legal price control on crude oil (or on any input) will not—and did not—keep down the price of the derived final products—gasoline, chemicals, plastics, and drugs obtained from crude oil.

When the 1975 National Energy Act was passed, members of Congress and of the Administration claimed that if the price to American producers of crude oil had been allowed to rise from the legally restricted price of $7 a barrel to the free-market value of $14 a barrel, the price of gasoline refined from that oil would rise about 17 cents a gallon.[4] (Since about 42 gallons of gasoline can be refined from a barrel of oil, a price rise of $7 a barrel divided by 42 gallons of gasoline comes to about 17 cents a gallon.) The error is, of course, in assuming that the cost of making something is the source of its value.

To see that costs do not determine value, reconsider the earlier automobile example. If it had cost $100,000 to make those cars—and only 7 were available—the price would be unaffected. (If you're still not not convinced, consider what determines the value of a Picasso painting.) The explanation is that only insofar as costs determine the *supply* available do costs (*indirectly*) affect price.

The demand for any good along with the supply available determines the price, its market value. If more of the good can be produced, people will incur costs to produce more until the

costs rise to the product's value. The production costs that it pays to incur are determined by the value of the good—not the other way around. The value to the consumer is not increased simply because one pays more to produce a good. If you never, never fall into that trap you will be a rare, but economically sophisticated, person. Under the National Energy Act crude-oil price controls, the refiners who are fortunate enough (or politically well enough placed) to command crude oil from a well owner for only $7 are getting oil worth $14 a barrel in refined form (net of $86 of other costs), netting a gain of $7 a barrel. And since the supply of crude oil, and hence of refined products, is unaffected, as we assume here, the market price of the refined goods is not affected. To repeat, if the refiner had to pay $14 per barrel for the crude he would be making $7 less profit—now going to the crude oil producer —while the price of refined products is unchanged. Yet because people persistently think that costs of production determine the sale price —ignoring the fact that it is supply that interacts to set price—they believe the National Energy Act keeps down the price of gasoline by limiting the price of crude to refiners. It does nothing of the kind; an only effect was to withhold from the crude producers part of that $14 value per barrel and let it remain with the refiners. Such a simple wealth transfer from one party to another has no effect on the supply, and hence the price of gasoline or any other refined product is unchanged. Economic analysis doesn't enable us to explain why the public and so many politicians are trapped by that line of fallacious reasoning.

To correct our artificial assumption that the supply of crude oil was constant, we need only recognize that in fact crude producers would

---

[4] *The Wall St. Journal,* however, repeatedly pointed out the error—to little public effect.

produce more crude if they received a higher price. That increase in the supply of crude would increase the production of refined products, the prices of which would then be reduced. Far from keeping down the price of refined products, price controls on crude oil actually tend to raise them. But not very much, since they already reflect *world* supply and demand. We import crude oil at the world price of $14 a barrel because that is its value in terms of its refined products at free-market prices after allowing for refining and distribution costs. We also import refined products from foreign crude. For all these reasons it is apparent that the *supply* of oil and refined products to the U.S. market is essentially unaffected by price controls on domestic crude oil.

If you are mystified as to why price controls are imposed on crude oil producers, perhaps your local political scientist can help you. We can't. Let us add another mystery. The National Energy Act also authorizes political authorities to control the proportions of fuel oil, gasoline, and other products that are refined from crude oil. It is a technological fact that refiners can vary the ratio of gasoline, fuel oil, chemicals, and plastics derived from a gallon of crude by adjusting the refining process. By taking control over what is refined with the available crude, the political authorities can determine the supply of each type of refined product and hence their market prices and values. It is reported by the Act's advocates that this will enable us to make sure that not "too much" gasoline is produced at the expense of not having "enough" fuel oil. According to the Act's proponents it is highly probable that the authorization to reduce gasoline output in favor of more fuel oil for heating will be exercised. As Ralph Nader, a supporter of controls, said, "I

don't have an automobile." And he lives in a city in a part of the United States that has cold winters. Is the National Energy Act a means of transferring economic resources to the benefit of areas of the country like the East, which are colder, urban, and use the automobile less, at the expense of the warmer areas that use the automobile more, as in the West? Again, ask your local political scientist, not your economist.

Price Controls, Competition, and Discrimination

We can better understand how a free-market pricing system allocates goods if we try to get along without it for a while. Our analysis of the market pricing system suggests that everyone can buy all he chooses of any good, given his wealth, and can sell all he chooses at the going market price. According to our preceding analysis, there should not be waiting lines or shortages. But at the going, current market prices, you may find there *is* a long waiting list for some goods. In other situations, sellers find that at the market price there are *no* buyers. What has gone wrong with our analysis? (Do not ask, "What has gone wrong with the world?") One answer is that we failed to recognize legal or customary restrictions on permissible market prices. We assumed, not entirely correctly, that potential buyers and sellers could negotiate exchanges with each other at whatever prices they chose. If, as is sometimes the case, prices are restricted or controlled, we must modify our analysis. However, our laws of demand are not changed. We must not use them solely for open markets, which are markets in which everyone is allowed to buy and sell whatever they wish at mutually agreeable prices. In many parts of the world, and for many goods, the negotiable terms of trade are restricted by law or social controls. In New York City, the rents you can pay for old apartments are limited by law; in most cities, taxi rates are set by law, and taxis cannot legally collect higher fares during rain or snow or rush hours. All these cases are characterized by "shortages," waiting lines, or waiting lists.

To analyze what happens when price controls are effective, suppose that demand for, say, housing space increases and that rents or house prices were not allowed to rise.[5] The total amount demanded exceeds the available supply at the old, legal-limit price. A shortage, or, what is the same thing, an "excessive demand" develops.[6]

This situation can be analyzed with the demand and supply graphs of Figure 4–6, a diagram basically the same as Figure 4–4. The demand lines for A and B are shown as they were before a demand increase by B and also as they are after his increase in demand. At the old price, p_1, the total amount demanded exceeds the amount supplied, S. As long as the price is restricted to p_1, B will want more housing space; he complains of a shortage since he can't get as much space as he "demands" (or, as he is likely to say, "needs"). Two other effects will also occur: a wealth transfer and an increase in nonprice competitive discrimination.

[5] In a later chapter, we shall investigate the effects of legally imposed *minimum* prices.

[6] Although the legal maximum price of housing is deemed "fair," some demands are not met at that price. Any person caught in that situation could ask, "What is the meaning of a price at which I *can't* buy?"

Figure 4–6. Effect of Rent Control

Shortages are created by rent controls, resulting in transferral of wealth.

Wealth Transfer

The potential wealth transfer (increased market value of housing) is easy to discern. Suppose a tenant were allowed to sublease to others at uncontrolled prices, while the rent paid to the landlord is restricted to p_1. It would pay him to rent more space from A ($X_a - X'_a$) and pay a price of p_2 per unit of space, all of which space will go to B, as $X'_b - X_b$. A prefers this because he would rather have the extra money income than the space, and B prefers the extra space to the money. The greater market value of housing services would be captured by the old tenants. The part of the increased value kept by B would be ($p_2 - p_1$) X_b, and the part to A would be ($p_2 - p_1$) X_a.

This market-value increment occurs whether or not subleasing side-deals are legally permitted. If permitted, they enable a reallocation of housing space to help both B and A reach mutually preferred positions, but with no transfer of the increased market value of housing to the housing owner. If not permitted, the housing space is not reallocated so effectively, but the higher value is still retained by the tenants. Under rent controls, with or without uncontrolled subleasing, the increased income that would belong to the owners is "taken" from the owners by the legal rent limit, and the original tenants get that wealth from the owners. Hardly anyone has proposed that under rent controls tenants really be allowed to sublease at market-clearing prices —despite the gains that would accrue to tenants. Is it because this would make the whole element of wealth redistribution too transparent to be acceptable politically?

The preceding analysis is correct as far as it goes, but there is more. Any excess of the open market value over the controlled price of that housing space (or whatever the price controlled good may be) is something for which the suppliers and demanders will compete. As a result, efforts to get that value will induce extra costs that just match the marginal gain. The effect is simply to waste other resources (as we illustrated in the case of lawyers and other expediters acting as intermediaries to get enhanced prospects of being able to actually buy at the lower controlled price). And even more, producers will let the quality of the price controlled good deteriorate, rather than incur costs of maintaining its quality. In the long run, that excess of open market value over the controlled price will be dissipated by extra costs incurred by the buyers or by reduced product quality until its open market value is reduced to the controlled price.

In a price-controlled market, competing demanders resort to still other nonprice inducements to suppliers to get desired amounts. Those inducements, procedures, or forms of competition are not costless. Waiting in line, for example, is costly. One will wait until the personal cost of waiting plus the (controlled) money price is equated to the personal marginal use value of the amount of the good he can thereby get. A buyer of a good under a nonprice rationing system will incur a cost that in one form or another equals the marginal value of the amount of the good he gets.

But that cost to him does not take the form of a *transfer of goods from him to the seller.* By standing in line or doing whatever else enables him to get some of the good, he is not producing more valuable goods with which to pay the seller. Nonprice activities incurred by competing demanders do not contribute as much to the seller or to society as the output that would otherwise be produced and transferred to sellers by money prices. That is why the seller supplies poorer service along with the price-controlled goods. Demanders seek such goods up to the point at which the value of the goods they manage to get equals the sum of the controlled price plus the other costs they must incur. Demanders whose time is more valuable (that is, whose forsaken alternative output is more valuable) have *higher* costs for getting the price-controlled good than do other people whose time is less valuable (whose forsaken output is lower). People whose time is *less* valuable will stand in line longer and get *more* than those whose time is valuable. But everyone will be forsaking some production of goods by standing in line or doing whatever (non-productive) activities will get one higher on the rationing rating scale. That social waste is caused by the illegality of trade at mutually acceptable open-market prices.

We conclude that even under price controls, the demanders in fact incur a cost equal to the marginal value of what they get, a cost consisting of the payment to the seller plus the costs of other activities to get higher on the rationing scale. Those other activities are a social waste to the extent that they are less valuable to the sellers than the open-market price they could otherwise have paid to sellers without price controls.

Allowing prices to clear the markets yields more to the rich in marketable wealth than to the poor. But that is what is meant by being richer —having more marketable, exchangeable wealth. But whether rich or poor, buyers of any good pay for that use. They forsake claims to other goods they could have consumed, and those forsaken goods are worth more to the rest of society than the goods the rest of society gave up.

At controlled low prices purchasers get goods worth less to them than the marketable goods that would have been released by other buyers at higher, free-market prices. For example, because natural gas prices are controlled, those who live farther away from natural gas sources are not allowed to bid enough to get more gas for their more highly valued uses. Thus the East Coast gets less gas and must use higher-cost fuel oil, while, to those near the source, that gas has less use value than to Easterners. Why, then, do any consumers want price controls? For several reasons:

1. Some consumers believe—correctly—that, if the price were allowed to clear the market, their costs would increase. The sellers would gain that greater value. So present consumers prefer to take their chances in competing for the price-controlled goods in ways in which they may believe they have a relative advantage or are richer (being more willing or able to wait in line; knowing the right people; being of a favored ethnic type; having political power, etc.). Some people (chiefly the politically strong) find that price controls further enhance their power, particularly when, by weakening the effectiveness of market-exchange offers, controls allow these people to decide who gets what goods.

2. Some people are unaware of the above considerations and do not understand what prices do in directing exchange and consumption.

3. Some people do not understand the price-control effects on production and on the quality and quantity of products—a topic we will take up in later chapters.

4. Many people incorrectly believe that price controls can prevent inflation and protect the purchasing power of money. (They cannot, as we shall explain much later, in Chapter 19.)

Discrimination

As we know, suppression of open-market exchange pricing implies: (1) that the amount demanded will exceed what is available at any imposed price that is below the open-market price; and (2) exchange of goods from lower- to higher-valuing users is restrained, so total satisfaction is reduced. And we can now add: (3) nonmonetary and nonmarket criteria or payments or forms of competitive behavior will be more used for discriminating among competing claimants to the available goods, and may dissipate the higher value over the controlled price. As the authors discovered during the period when meat prices were restricted below market-clearing prices, their wives' beauty suddenly began to count more heavily in the butcher's eyes when he decided which customers could buy the available meat. Similarly, with controlled housing rentals, our wives were the ones sent to apply for an apartment that was to be vacated. As long as the landlord couldn't get a higher money price from less desirable people, why should he ignore the virtues of delightful tenants? When rentals and meat prices had been *un*controlled, the money offers from the "less desirable" types made it more costly for the butchers and landlords to exercise their preferences for loyal customers of long standing, or people who are nice, charming, or witty—or who are white, not foreign, etc. When not allowed to offer higher money prices, people, whether rich or poor, must resort to nonmonetary compensation to induce others to tolerate their "undesirable" features. But it is those nonmonetary features in which they are most deficient!

These facts should be kept in mind by "unpopular" people who believe that price controls will help them in nonmonetary, nonprice competition with people who are also richer in money. The disadvantageous personal characteristics, which they could counterbalance with offers of higher money prices, are no longer so effectively overcome under price controls.

That price controls lead to greater discrimination by personal characteristics can be seen in the increases in racial, religious, and personal discrimination, in personal favors, and in poor maintenance that occur in rent-controlled and publicly subsidized housing—all involving rentals at less than market-clearing prices.

If you want to give more importance in the distribution of goods to race, religion, and personal characteristics and to legalistic tactics, you should reduce the effectiveness of the money offer, as price controls do. People will then try to buy or acquire those more competitively powerful traits and techniques—at least some of what would have been paid as higher prices for the desired goods will now be spent in alternative strategies. In fact, even more may be spent (wasted?) on those alternative competitive techniques than would have been spent as direct payment for the goods under uncontrolled prices. For example, lawyers or "expediters" become important in getting political aid when prices are controlled and other criteria are used by the government for allocating goods—as in the allocation of radio and TV station licenses, airline routes, liquor licenses, national park campsites, taxi licenses, parking spaces on campus, library stack permits, admission to law or medical schools, faculty employment.

Every allocative system is discriminatory. In a capitalist, free-market system the discrimination is based heavily, sometimes solely, on the amount of money (other goods) offered as exchange. Thus the crucial question about prices is not whether particular prices are high or low, but how they permit market exchange to influence who gets and who produces what. The private-property system puts *more* goods where there are *more* dollar offers. Everyone can get some, up to the quantity that the person decides is worth the price he pays for that last unit.

Rich people can feed their dogs while poor children have little milk because the system permits people individually to decide what to do with their income and wealth. You may wish some people were not so wealthy or had different tastes in utilizing wealth. But do not expect to find a feasible system or mechanism that will promote the distribution of wealth holdings that conforms to your ideas of a better world. For the present, we take wealths as given—but we do not assume they are ordained as "naturally proper." In later chapters, we will see low income and wealth depend heavily on one's productivity.

Pro-Rata Rationing

Under price controls, the wastes from other kinds of nonproductive competition can be avoided by *rationing:* assigning specified portions of the available stock—to everyone. But each recipient would then be thwarted in seeking a more preferred *recombination* of goods by further exchange with other people, as in our automobile example. Rationing *with* price controls restricts exchange and hence the realization of these more preferred *combinations:* take your allotted share and no swapping.

If holders of ration coupons are allowed to sell them, then rationing changes the distribution of effective wealth among people (which is one reason it is sometimes advocated), for everyone is initially allotted an equal number of coupons. But it doesn't keep down the price paid by consumers! It doesn't because the transferable ration coupon becomes valuable by an amount

11, 12
13, 14
15, 16
17, 18
19, 20
21, 22
23, 24

equal to the difference between the "official" price and what the free-market price would be. That difference is the exact amount that would be offered for a coupon—or forsaken by using the coupon rather than selling it. Therefore, the total price for every consumer (money price plus coupon value) is just what the free-market price would be—except that there are additional transactions costs associated with dealings in the coupons. Also, there has been some shift in wealth among consumers according to the initial disbursement of the (valuable) coupon. Finally, the price-control also transfers some wealth (value of the price-controlled good) from sellers toward consumers.

Economic Rent

In this chapter our analysis of the operation of demand has been based on the assumption that the supply of goods is given. We were thus better able to understand the fundamental law of demand without getting into complications about production. To explain the concept of economic rent, we now make an even stronger restriction: We assume a good for which the supply is fixed and indestructible. No matter what happens to its price the *amount* of the good does not change—at least for the period under study. The classic example is often land. There it is and there it stays, no matter what rent may be paid for it or what price may be offered.

A misconception often arises when the supply of a durable good is *not* affected by its price. A higher price is said to lead only to unjustly enriching the owners; higher prices should be prevented, for they serve no function. Ignoring the question of "unjust" enrichment, we can say that the higher price, like it or not, does assign the existing goods to the highest-valuing users. If the price were not allowed to rise, other rationing techniques would be necessary, with different results.

There are two functions of market pricing: first, allocating existing goods; and, second, coordinating new *production* to demand. The concept *economic rent* is used to avoid confusion between these two functions. Although "rent" connotes a payment for housing space, *economic* rent is the name given to market receipts that affect neither the present nor the future amount of that good. In our earlier automobile example, in which the number of cars was fixed regardless of price, the entire price of a car was an economic rent. It is not called a "surplus"—that is, useless—because it serves the purpose of rationing the good to the highest-valued competing use. Any lower market price for that good would not accomplish that allocation. Although a price may not affect the amount of a good in existence, it does affect assignment to *particular uses*. The price is unnecessary (surplus) to keep the good in existence, but it is necessary for achieving allocation to highest-valuing users. Hence it is called economic rent: *economic* to emphasize that it serves an economic (scarcity-related) function, and *rent* because it does not affect the supply.

The price paid by a demander to get a resource away from some other user is a cost. Willingness to pay is a competitive way of revealing the use value of the good to the demander. If it has greater value with him than elsewhere, he will get the good. The entire price or rent of the land is in excess of the zero amount necessary to keep that land in *existence*. Yet to decide the *use* of that land the market rent is crucial and is a cost to the particular user.

But is land rent a true economic rent? Some goods thought to be indestructible really are not. Land is surprisingly perishable. Its valuable features include levelness, fertility, and absence of rocks, weeds, and bushes. Any farmer or ecologist knows how fast land can erode or become overgrown with weeds. Goods that have literally *no* preservation or maintenance costs are rare—indeed, nonexistent: We can think of no examples.

Quasi-Rents

Related to economic rent is *quasi-rent*: Any payment that does not affect the amount *currently* available but will affect the *future* amount is called a *quasi-rent*. Payments for many goods are quasi-rents. Even though the good is already in existence, future production depends on present prices, which help predict future prices for future supplies.

Land Rent—A Taxable Surplus?

In the belief that payments for some goods are unnecessary to create either the existing or the future supply, some people conclude that the market value of such a good is a surplus the holders of which should be taxed. Prominent are the "single-taxers"—followers of Henry George, a nineteenth century novelist and reformer, who believed that land rent is an economic rent and should be taxed away. (Somehow he overlooked

equally "pure" economic rents on other resources—for example, beauty and talent.)

Other doctrinaire advocates of taxing, or na-
tionalizing, land rents are the socialists. The
theorists of the leftwing of the British Labour
Party argue that landsite values reflect the actions of society as a whole and not the owners
of a particular parcel of land. Therefore, the site
rent should belong to all the people. But that is
true of *every* good, and this argument fails to explain why every person in the society should bear
the consequences of changes in value of every
parcel of land—even those he will never see or
perceptibly affect. Some people do not want to
carry the risks of gains or losses from all land
and instead prefer to hold titles to other goods.
Just as people with private-property rights differ
in consumption patterns, so people specialize in
the goods they prefer to own and on which to
bear the risks of changes in their value. But socialist doctrine does not permit private-property
rights in productive resources. Socialists say that
the people should have *non*transferable shares
in the value of certain goods—hence those goods
are *socialized,* that is, their full value is taxed and
used by government.

It has been argued that even if land rights
were socialized so that the land rent value went
to the government, the *use* of the land would be
unaffected, since the government could rent to
the highest-bidding user. But the reward for a
private owner to incur the costs, risks, and trouble
of discovering and actually putting the land into
the highest-valued uses is greater than for a salaried government employee in charge of the socialized land. Thus the government employee is
less likely to find or heed highest market-valued
uses. Whether this be good or bad depends in
part (and only in part) on whether you think the
highest market-valued use as judged by individuals competing in the market is a good or bad
criterion. It is not for economists to hazard judgments about that.

Smog Removal and Land Value

We earlier illustrated the use of demand analysis
by showing (1) how the rent of land is not affected by a tax if the consumers' valuation of
land use is not affected by the tax, and (2) how
the consumers' valuation of the land can be increased by the use of tax proceeds. Let us try
another, surprising example. If the smog were
magically removed, forever, at no cost, from the
center of a major industrial city, what would happen to the value of that land? Would it rise because of the increased value of that cleaner air to
tenants and users? If the value rose, would the
landowners capture some benefits of the cleaner
air? If the landowners did, would the tenants be
paying a higher rent for cleaner air by consuming
less of other goods because their rent was
higher? Might the renters be no better off than
before, enjoying cleaner air but having less of
other goods? The answer is essentially "Yes" to
all those queries. Let's inquire further. Would land
values fall in the nearby suburbs because people no longer have to travel so far for better
air? Again, Yes. If instead of being magically
costless, smog removal were very costly because
of expensive pollution control devices, should the
landowners bear the costs of cleaning the air?
Should they bear the costs of preventing further
deterioration? These last two queries are about
who *should* do something, so we leave the answers to you.

Maximum Value Allocation

Exchange is motivated by differing personal valuations and is based on material gain. Each of the traders considers himself to be benefited: Each puts a higher value on the things he obtains than on the things he pays (sells). A person who places a lower use value on a good than is placed on it by some other user will sell it and receive in exchange other goods worth more to him than the good he sold. If I sell you some *X*, then by your use value standards the *X* you get is more valuable to you than the *Y* you paid. And by my use value standards the *Y* I got has a higher use value than the *X* I paid. In *my* personal valuation, *I* got more than I gave up; and in *your* personal valuation, *you* got more than you gave up. This is often summarized by saying voluntary exchange puts goods to their highest personal use values. The total of use values is maximized. These possible exchanges are fully achieved in equilibrium.

This notion of *equilibrium* does not imply that there is some super person who knows it would be better if I had one more *X* than if you had one more *X* so that some total social valuation would be higher. That kind of social value judgment is not available from anything in economics or from any other source. Every one of us may be willing to declare what he thinks would be the best state of the world and distribution of goods. But not everyone else would agree; therefore, there is no socially accepted super value criterion, and economics does not—because it cannot—say that any kind of exchange is really better on the basis of some super ethical judgment. What economics can say is that with voluntary exchange each person moves to some combination of goods that each values more highly—until a redistribution of available goods is achieved which fully exploits the potential mutual gain of additional trade.

25, 26 27

Summary

1. The amount of any good demanded by each person in the community is equated to the amount available by the free-market price— one reached by open-market offers and bids among competing buyers and sellers—called an equilbrium price.
2. Shortages and surpluses are pricing phenomena in that the price is forcibly kept too low (shortage) or kept too high (surplus). Shortages or surpluses would be eliminated almost instantly by free-market prices.
3. Any allocation of goods among people such that it would be impossible to further redistribute the various goods to benefit any person without having to hurt some other person is called a Pareto-efficient allocation. Market exchange at free prices tends towards Pareto-efficient allocations.
4. When demand for a good increases, competition among buyers raises its price. If there are middlemen or agents, who transmit the demands to potential sellers or suppliers of the good, the higher price that must be paid for the existing amount by those middlemen will appear as higher costs to them of providing goods to their buyers. Hence the increased demand by the public for a good will usually first appear to the suppliers as a rise in their costs. The public will tend erroneously to interpret the price rise as caused

by a rise in costs, rather than the higher costs being caused by, and reflecting, the higher value placed on the goods by the increased public demand.

5. Any payment or marketable value of a good in excess of that required to continue the existence of the good is an economic rent.

6. A quasi-rent is a payment or market value that does not affect the amount of the good now in existence, but does affect the current or future rate of production and hence the future available amount.

7. With shortages resulting from price controls, nonmarketable forms of wealth or characteristics acquire a relatively greater role in determining the distribution of goods. If market prices are restricted, race, creed, age, sex, and personal characteristics are less capable of being offset by productivity for market trade.

8. Though existing market prices may have no effect on the amount currently available of some good, the price does affect the distribution of the good. A free-market price will move the goods to their highest-valued users so that everyone who sells some of a good will reach a preferred position.

9. If some goods are rented rather than bought outright, the goods will move to their highest-valued users, and the higher value of the goods will be captured by the owners rather than the former renters, who release some of the goods to the new higher-valuing users.

10. Under price controls, bidders and demanders for the good will pay the money price plus additional costs of other activities enabling them to get more goods until the money price plus those additional costs equal the marginal personal valuation of the goods acquired. This is wasteful because the value to the seller of the additional activities to enhance one's claims to the seller's goods does not equal his value of a direct money receipt.

Appendix: The Edgeworth Exchange Box

The Edgeworth Exchange Box, a powerful method for explaining the principles of trade, is named for Francis Ysidro Edgeworth, who first suggested it in his *Mathematical Physics* (1881). The box consists of a combination of two utility or preference maps (explained in the Appendix to Chapter 2) for two people, here called a Cuban and Hungarian, between whom there will be trade (without a middleman).

To construct an Edgeworth Box, the utility or preference maps of the Cuban and the Hungarian are superimposed as in Figure 4–7, *after* rotating one of them 180 degrees so that it appears upside down, with the conventional left-hand scale on the right side running from *top* to bottom. Here the Hungarian's map has been rotated so that *his* zero point, O_h, is in the *upper-right* corner. The length of each side of the box represents the *total* amount of X and Y available to these two people. The total amount of X is measured on the horizontal axis. O_cX_c represents the initial amount of X allocated to the Cuban as his initial amount of X; the remainder, O_hX_h (shown at the top of the box), is the amount of X initially held by the Hungarian. Note that the distance O_cX_c plus the distance O_hX_h exactly equals the width of the box, denoting the entire existing amount of X.

Similarly the initial division of Y between the

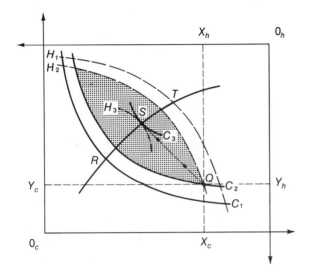

Figure 4–7. Edgeworth Exchange Box

two people shows that the Cuban has the amount O_cY_c, measured vertically up from the lower-left origin, O_c, for the Cuban; and the Hungarian has O_hY_h of Y, measured down from the upper-right origin, O_h, for the Hungarian. The distance O_cY_c plus O_hY_h equals the vertical height of the box, and denotes the total amount of Y.

Point Q in the box denotes the *initial* allocations of X and Y to the Cuban and Hungarian, with the horizontal distance of the point measuring the amounts of X available to the Cuban (on the left) and to the Hungarian (measured from the right). The vertical height to the point Q indicates the amount initially available to the Cuban, and the vertical distance down from the top side indicates the amount of Y initially available to the Hungarian.

The curved solid lines are utility isoquants, or indifference curves, for the Cuban. The dashed

curved lines are utility isoquants for the Hungarian; these may at first sight appear to be curved in the wrong direction, but remember that his map is turned upside down so that its origin is in the upper right, at O_h.

Point Q is on the utility isoquant, C_2, for the Cuban. Line C_1 is another of his indifference curves, but with lower utility, while C_3 is a higher indifference curve. Similarly point Q, measured with reference to the origin, O_h, is on an indifference curve, H_2, for the Hungarian. Turning the book upside down, you will see that the curves H_1 and H_2 are lower and higher indifference curves, respectively.

The *slope* of the indifference curve, C_2, as explained in the Appendix to Chapter 2, shows the Cuban's personal values of the commodities, or marginal rate of substitution between X and Y in consumption at point Q. If he could trade *some* X for *some* Y, at a rate of exchange indicated by the slope of the dashed, arrowed "trading" line emanating from point Q, he could move to higher utility on C_3, at point S. If the Hungarian were to get what the Cuban gave up—that is, if the Hungarian and the Cuban were to trade with each other—then the Hungarian would also be revising his combination of goods from Q along the dashed line to S. He, too, would be moved to *higher* utility, H_3. As long as they trade with each other along some dashed line that moves each to higher indifference curves, trade can be mutually agreeable. *And any dashed trading line that starts from a point like Q and runs inward into a football-shaped shaded area, bounded by the two indifference curves through point Q, will move both the Cuban's and the Hungarian's resultant mixture of goods to preferred combinations, that is, to higher utility lines for each person.*

In general, as long as the dashed straight trading line (the *slope of which measures the price for X, and Y,* at which the Cuban and Hungarian might trade) *cuts* the utility curves of both the Cuban and the Hungarian at point Q, it will pay each to move on that trading line in the direction that moves both to higher utility curves. The dashed trade line at point Q has a slope *between* that of (1) the Cuban's indifference curve slope through point Q and (2) the Hungarian's indifference curve through the point Q; this means that the proposed buying (and selling) prices of X (in terms of Y units) differ from the personal values placed on X relative to Y. Such a trading price will enable both parties to reach combinations with higher utilities.

Basis of Exchange

Through every point on the diagram there is an indifference curve for C, and there is also one for H. Wherever a curve of one man cuts a curve of the other man, some trade would improve each person's utility. Only for a special series of points do the utility curves of one person not *intersect* those of the other person. Instead, the curves are *tangent.* These special points form the *contract curve,* indicated by the thick line labeled RST. This contract curve line indicates *all* the combinations of goods X and Y for each person at which the indifference curve for the Cuban for that combination is *tangent* to the indifference curve for the Hungarian. At that point of tangency the curves have the same slope. Any initial allocation of X and Y between the Cuban and Hungarian (except those on the line RST) can be improved by trade along a trading line toward RST. In our diagrammed example, the straight trading

line from Q to S extends into the football-shaped enclosure bounded by two indifference curves of the initial situation. This is a line along which they could move by trading with each other, until they came to point S. If they moved along their trading line past S, they would each be moving to lower indifference curves (that is, to less-preferred positions). Once they have reached the RST line, they have exhausted the possibilities of *mutual* gain from trade with each other, no matter where they started from. The line RST is called the contract curve because it is to some point on this curve that their contracts for trade will take them. This tangency of the two indifference curves and the trading price line means that the price between X and Y equals the personal values placed on X relative to Y by both of the trading parties.

Once they have *reached* the contract curve, no further *mutually* acceptable revision of consumption patterns is possible. Moving *along* the contract curve means that one party gives up some of *both* goods to the other. That would be a transfer of wealth from one party to the other, not an exchange.

If we accept the premise that each party should be the judge of his own interests, then any distribution of goods between the two parties represented by a point *off* the contract curve is *economically inefficient:* things could be improved for everyone by trading and moving to a point *on* the contract curve at which no *jointly* beneficial *revision* is feasible. Hence any point on the contract curve is *economically efficient* in the sense that it is impossible to make a change that would improve the position of *both* parties. Economically efficient allocations of goods are those from which there is no possibility of improving the situation of someone without reducing the utility of someone else: That is, there is no waste. (We say *economic* efficiency, because later we shall identify a more restricted concept: *technical* efficiency.)

Questions

1. The demands to own by A and by B for good *X* are:

Price	A's Demand	B's Demand	Market Demand
$10	0	0	——
9	1	0	——
8	2	0	——
7	3	1	——
6	4	2	——
5	5	3	——
4	6	3	——
3	7	4	——
2	8	5	——
1	9	6	——

a. What is the market demand by A and B?
b. If six units of *X* are available, what will be the resulting allocation between A and B if open-market exchange is used?
c. With six units available, if price were legally imposed at $4, would there be a shortage, a surplus, or an exchange equilibrium?
d. If the price were legally imposed at $9, would there be a shortage, a surplus, or exchange equilibrium?
e. How can there be a change from a shortage to a surplus without any change in supply or demand?

2. In question 1 above, increase the amounts demanded by B uniformly by two more units at each price.
a. What will be the new open-market price?
b. What will be the allocation between A and B?
c. If the price is held at the old level by law, will there be a surplus or a shortage?
d. How can that surplus or shortage be eliminated?

3. "Demand and supply is a classification that is applicable to more than private-property market exchange. Demand and supply is applicable to every problem of allocating scarce resources among competing uses. In any given possible use, the usefulness of the resource in that use is what is meant by its demand, while its usefulness in all alternative uses (against which this particular use must compete) is the supply." Do you agree?

4. "Competition is never 'buyer against seller' but always seller against other sellers and buyers against other buyers."
a. Is this true for you when you buy food? Automobiles? Shoes? Sell your labor?
b. Can you cite a case in which it is not true?

5. Distinguish between the law of demand and the law of market price, which says price equates the amount supplied to the amount demanded. Which holds more generally?

6. A distinguished professor of law wrote: "Some people believe that every resource which is scarce should be controlled by the market. And since, in their view, all resources except free goods are scarce, all resources—even rights to radiate radio sig-

nals—should be so controlled. But surely some resources are 'scarcer' than others, and thereby possibly merit different treatment. It doesn't advance the argument very much to place a label of 'scarcity' on everything." Do you think economics should be studied by professors of law? Why?

7.

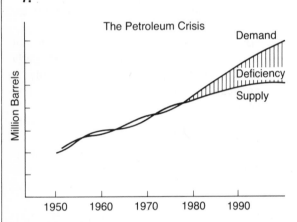

This chart is typical of scores that have appeared recently in the news media. It purports to predict that supply will fall short of future requirements and demand. A similar diagram was published in the 1950s by the U.S. Department of Labor purporting to predict a future excess supply of engineers above demand. Why, in fact, are such diagrams fallacious and just plain wrong? The answer is very simple and based on the principles given in this chapter.

8. When prices on the stock market fall, the financial pages report heavy selling; yet every share sold is bought by someone. Why don't they refer to heavy buying?

9. Which tactic would be more likely to get you a lower price on a new car: going to just one dealer and acting like a tough and aggressive bargainer; or going to several dealers and mildly asking for their selling price while letting it be known that you really intend to buy a car and are shopping around? Explain why. Can you cite any evidence?

10. The Council of Economic Advisers (to the President of the United States) once argued that keeping down the price of cattle could keep down the price of meat to the consumer. The Federal Energy Agency asserts that holding down crude oil prices reduces the price of gasoline (made from crude oil). Explain why economic analysis rejects these contentions.

11. "With open-market pricing, housing units are scarce or expensive, whereas with rent control the housing market is characterized by shortages." Explain.

12. Are the words "scarcity," "reduced supply," and "shortage" synonyms? If not, what is the difference?

*13. Do you think rent controls would be good or bad for each of the following: (a) Middle-aged couple who do not contemplate moving, (b) young married couple with two children moving to a new town, (c) black moving to a new town, (d) young person receiving a raise in salary, (e) old person in retirement, (f) person who likes to drink and smoke, (g) beautiful young woman, (h) homely immigrant, (i) Mormon in a Jewish community, (j) Jew in a Mormon community, (k) excellent handyman who likes to work around the house and care for gardens, (l) old couple who have saved wealth and invested in an apartment house.

*14. "Price controls give adequate housing to those in the lower-income levels who would otherwise not be able to afford it." Subject this proposition to economic analysis.

15. "In the capitalistic system, only money or market values count in allocating productive resources." Evaluate.

16. "In capitalism, commercialism dominates and suppresses social, artistic, and cultural values." Evaluate.

17. "Under open-market, private-property pricing, a person is allowed to make any kind of appeal to a seller to get some of the good— even offering money. Under price controls, the buyer is told that there is one appeal he cannot use—i.e., offer of a larger amount of other goods." True or false?

18. At the same price for each, you choose a color television set over a black-and-white set; but when a black-and-white set costs a third as much as a color set, you choose the black and white. In which case are you "discriminating"?

19. Which of the following choices involve discrimination? (a) Cadillac versus Chrysler, (b) Van Gogh versus Gauguin, (c) blondes versus brunettes, (d) beautiful versus homely people, (e) blacks versus whites, (f) Japanese versus Koreans, (g) filet mignon versus hamburger, (h) *all* choices.

20. You are collecting data for a cost-of-living survey. For each of the cases below, which "price" would you report as *the* price? Why?
   a. "List price, $125. Special discount to $90!"

b. "35¢ box of Kleenex for 29¢."
   c. "One cent sale. First for $1. Second for 1¢."

21. It has been argued that politicians tend to gain from price controls and hence they advocate them. What line of reasoning would support that argument?

*22. The military draft of the U.S. government involved price control—in which the maximum price that can be paid by the military services is set by law. As a result, the number of personnel demanded exceeds the supply *at that price;* but the buyers, instead of accepting the amount sellers are willing to provide at that proffered price, resort to a compulsory draft to satisfy their "excess" of demand. Graphically, in Figure 4-4 (p. 87), the price, military wages, is limited to p_1, at which the excess demand is satisfied by the draft. Who gains what by this system of price controls? (Before presuming that military personnel could not be obtained by a wage system, note that the permanent military officers, the leaders, are obtained by a voluntary open-market wage system. So are policemen and firemen.)

*23. Prices (tuition fee) for colleges are below the market clearing price in many colleges. Without inquiring why, explain how we know the price is that low. Applying the principles of competition when prices are kept below market clearing levels, indicate the kinds of non-price competitive payments or behavior (of competing student applicants) that acquire added influence. To whom are these other enhanced forms of competition for admission advantageous? Indicate (or conjecture) who captures the value of the excess of the market clearing price over the controlled price of the services of the colleges.

*24. News item: "Seoul, Korea (AP). The city government ordered the capital's 1500 restaurants not to sell any meal containing rice during lunch hours. The measure is designed to encourage the customers to take other food. South Korea is experiencing a serious food shortage because of a poor rice crop." Would open-market prices achieve the same result? How effective will this measure be?

25. "Allowing the prices of goods to rise when more of the good cannot be produced is immoral, because the higher prices do not induce a larger output. They merely give unwarranted profits to those who are lucky enough to own the goods. Either prices should be prevented from rising, or the government should take over ownership in order to prevent unjust enrichment." Do you agree with this analysis? If so, why? If not, why not?

26. Which of the following do you think contain some economic rent? Insofar as any of them contains rent, for what is that rent unnecessary? For what is it necessary?

a. The wealth of those who owned land in Palm Springs, California, from 1940 through 1975, when land values boomed.

b. Elizabeth Taylor's income.

c. The income of a genius.

d. The income of smart students.

e. The salary of the President of the United States.

27. "The rent for land in New York City is not a payment necessary to produce that land. It is a necessary payment to obtain use of the land. From the first point of view, it is an economic rent; from the latter point of view, it is a cost." Do you agree? If so, why? If not, why not?

5

Information Costs, Property Rights, Public Goods, and Philanthropy

So far we have assumed that it is costless (1) to obtain information about potential bids to buy and offers to sell, (2) to agree on contracts, and (3) to enforce contracts and property rights. We assumed also (4) private-property rights in all goods, (5) no acts of charity, and (6) no public goods (the consumption of which by some does not diminish the supply for others). And we assumed that (7) no seller was sufficiently large to significantly affect the price at which he could buy or sell, and (8) full information about the performance of goods and services was costless to obtain prior to purchase.

These assumptions were made in part to permit clearer demonstration of the gains from exchange, the basic principles of demand, and the role of price. But to comprehend many other features of our economic system, particularly its misunderstood marketing institutions, we must relax the assumptions and recognize more realistic features. Doing so, however, does not upset any prior conclusions. We now abandon these assumptions, one by one.

Costs of Collecting Information about Market-Clearing Prices, Goods, and Exchange Opportunities

Had the sale of cars in our example in the previous chapter involved used-car dealers instead of just the private parties, the sequence of prices in the exchange process would have been less erratic and nearer an equilibrating price. Cars could also have been more cheaply and quickly inspected. And when price increased, buyers would probably have complained that used-car dealers had unscrupulously raised prices. Used-car dealers do raise prices—but scrupulously, after demand increases. They must then offer higher wholesale purchasing prices to replenish their inventories. When demand changes, dealers must move *both* their selling and buying prices; otherwise, used-car lots would either overflow or empty. Used-car dealers can buy, sell, and survive in business only at *offer* and *asking* prices (called respectively *wholesale* and *retail* prices) that reflect the public's demand for cars. The spread between the offer and asking prices must cover their service costs if they are to continue making used-car transactions.

The existence of used-car dealers makes price fluctuations less erratic, thus reducing the extent that buyers and sellers would be misled about the value of the cars they want to buy or sell. Potential sellers of cars and potential buyers do not all come to the market in a nice, paired stream. Intervals between bids to buy and offers to sell vary irregularly. More thorough knowledge of the possible bid and offer prices will enable buyers and sellers to exchange at prices more accurately reflecting the equilibrating price. Dealers provide that service by purchasing inventories on a speculative basis, generally paying more than a private seller could get without costly search for a buyer, and selling for less than the total cost (price plus search cost) would be to buyers who did their own searching. Competition among used-car dealers reduces the retail-wholesale spread to the cost of their services.

Some observers of the economic scene, forgetting that information about potential bids and offers and the features and quality of various goods is not *instantly* available at *zero* cost, say markets are "imperfect." But information—like steel and wheat—is costly to produce and distribute. If markets in the real world operate in ways not accounted for by a theory that assumes costless information, then the theory itself is imperfect. If such valuable information is costly, we would expect substantial resources or institutions to be devoted to collecting and selling information about exchange possibilities. And they are: Used-car dealers, real-estate agents, employment agencies, retailers, salesmen, brokers, and wholesalers act not only as sellers of goods but also as efficient collectors and sources of information about goods, services, and potential buyers and sellers—as should be painfully obvious to those who try to bypass middlemen.

In summary, with respect to the costs of collecting information, note four central facts:

1. *Information about goods and potential buyers or sellers is not free.*
2. *The more completely and rapidly it is obtained, the greater its costs.* The less rapid a search is, the less costly is each unit of new information obtained. More rapid acquisition may or may not be worth the extra cost.
3. *Adjusting resources to new uses or customers is costly; and the more rapid the adjustments, the more costly.* For example, moving from one place to another or from one job to another uses up productive effort and resources.
4. *Information about attributes of goods and best available buying and selling prices is sometimes made less costly by inventories held by middlemen retailers.* Inspection of goods is easier and less costly if inventories are on display and if retailers competitively set what they believe are the equilibrium prices.

Recognizing these means of reducing costs of information about traders and goods enables us to see better how, and why, people adjust to persistently changing market demands and supplies.

Buffer Stocks:
Inventories and Price Predictability

Random, transient fluctuations in purchases by customers around some average occur from day to day. To buffer, or accommodate, those fluctuations, middlemen hold inventories. Though they appear to be "idle" or "unemployed" as inventories, they are economical information-providing or information-substituting uses of resources. Consider the problem facing a newsboy who expects to sell at a stated price a daily average of one hundred copies of a local paper—but not exactly one hundred each day. He has several options: (1) Spend money to predict who is going to buy copies each day; (2) stock fewer than one hundred and rarely have any unsold copies; (3) stock more and have copies left over; (4) stock one copy, and each time one is sold order another, getting special-delivery service. Customers prefer him to stock a quantity greater than the average sales, providing instant availability from inventories, despite a slightly higher cost of the newspaper (implied by each seller's ending up with extra copies). The higher cost to customers need not appear as a higher money price. It may appear as a smaller newspaper or as fewer retailers. But this will be less costly than if the sellers attempted to obtain *complete* information or make *instantaneous* adjustments in the number of papers with a stable price.

An apartment owner builds more apartments than he expects on the average will be occupied.

It pays to build more apartments to satisfy unpredictable demands rather than relying on instant fluctuations in rents to clear the market. In providing vacancies, he is catering to the desires of renters to move when they want rather than making plans and reservations far in advance. The situation is exactly analogous to a person's building a home with a large enough dining room to seat more visitors than he will ordinarily have. To say he has "surplus," "idle," or "unemployed" dining-room capacity is to consider only the cost of the extra capacity, overlooking its value and the higher costs of alternative ways of obtaining the same convenience or utility.

An inventory of empty apartments *per se* is not waste. It economizes on the high costs of *immediately* producing whatever a person wants. By producing in advance at a less rapid, more economical rate and holding resources available for contingent demands, we economize in having housing services at a cost that is worth incurring, taking into account the value of being able to move without planning long in advance and with lower search costs. We could reduce housing costs by building fewer apartments if we required more advance planning of people's activities and refused to allow them to adapt quickly to new situations, but this would reduce convenience and raise planning costs. For the same reasons, we see "excessive supply" of service stations, barber shops, dress shops, real-estate agencies, insurance salesmen, and car dealers. The "excessive" supply is an inspection, or convenience, supply. Imagine what it would be like to try to move in a community that had just as many apartments as families and every apartment was therefore now rented. "Costs" would be imposed on tenants who wanted to move. Vacant apartments are "waste" only in an imaginary world of perfect predictability of everyone's entire future at zero cost, or in a world where instant production to meet every momentary change in demand is no more costly than advance preparation.

Fire escapes, fire hydrants, first-aid kits, and fire extinguishers would be wasteful only if information about the future were free and available in advance. If instant production or adjustment or information were no more costly than slower production, adjustment, or gathering of information, there would be no "idle," "excess," "unemployed" resources. But instant adjustments *do* cost more. We therefore observe what might ignorantly be called "idle" resources.

It is commonly thought that an industry is "sick" because it has excess capacity which is almost never fully utilized (for example, barber shops and service stations). But it is naive to believe the full capacity should be constantly utilized. Some barber shops have chairs or barbers that are not utilized most of the time; but when demand peaks, they are utilized, and it is precisely the peak demand that is served by this apparent overcapacity. How would you like to live in a community in which there were just enough barbers to cut everyone's hair if the barbers were always "fully" employed? Would you like to have to plan your purchases of goods on some schedule that allowed you no opportunity to adjust to unexpected events? Would anyone argue that Palm Beach has too many hotel rooms because most of them are empty during the summer, or that there are too many ski resorts because they are idle most of the time, or that there are too many churches because all of them are empty almost all the time? If you think there are too many service stations, would you like the one that you buy from to be one of those that are abolished? Does Sak's Fifth Avenue have too many salesgirls because many or most of them are "idle" most of the time? Would you say two-bathroom houses are uneconomic because neither bathroom is fully utilized at all times? To ask any of these questions is to answer them all.

Not all forms of unemployment, or apparently idle resources, are explainable only as means of reducing the costs of adjustment, or of acquiring information more rapidly, or of predicting future contingencies. But we will see that many forms of apparently idle resources do in fact serve those useful functions.

Money, Price, and Time Costs

A seller could instantly and temporarily raise or lower the price as sales and inventories fell or rose so as always to clear the market to customers without their waiting in line. But imagine a restaurant in which the price of food to newcomers varied instantly to avoid their waiting in line. The more unpredictable prices were, the more resources people would devote ahead of time to looking for sellers with lower prices—but the more unreliable, and hence less useful, advance plans would be. Looking for places with lower prices is costly, and the higher the costs of search, the more people will prefer to stand in line a bit if that permits a more predictable price. Sellers will hold inventories as buffers to shorten waiting lines, to permit more predictable prices and better plans, and to reduce customers' search costs, especially where search or planning costs are high and inventory costs relatively low.

Waiting in line is not the only way that time enters the rationing process. Some goods require more time in the act of purchase or consumption than do others. Getting a haircut may cost $3, but it also takes about half an hour, whereas one can buy $3 worth of gasoline in about three minutes. The *total* cost of a haircut is greater than that of an equivalent *money*-valued purchase of gasoline. A round of golf may cost $10 and four hours, while $10 of nightclub entertainment takes only one hour. The money cost of a trip to Europe by air may exceed the boat price, yet the total cost may be less by air because of the smaller costs (in terms of loss of opportunities for other activities) by not being confined to a boat for five days.

Goods and services are rationed among competing claimants partly by the money price and partly by the time involved in its acquisition and uses. If the money price is lower, the waiting line will be longer until its time costs plus the money price clear the market. Some restaurants or stores give quicker service at a higher price, with a lower *total* price to buyers who value time more highly. People with high hourly wage earnings demand quicker service than those of equal income derived from, say, stocks and bonds, or those who have low hourly earnings.

[1, 2, 3]

Costs of Exchanging Property Rights

Market prices can guide the allocation of goods only if there are incentives to express and to respond to offers. If each person speaks a different language, or if thievery is rampant, or if contracts are likely to be dishonored, then negotiation and policing costs will deter market exchanges. If property rights in goods are weak, or ill-defined, their reallocation is less likely to respond to highest-valued uses. Who would offer as much for a coat if its ownership is unknown or it is likely to be stolen in the future? The higher market value for goods with strong ownership rights spurs individuals to seek laws that would strengthen their rights to goods they are able to control. However, not all jurists, politicians, or people in general have viewed with uniform sympathy the tendency to secure private-property rights. The greater private-property rights are, the more limited is the power of political forces over resource-use. History is a long story of fluctuations and variations in this development. At times private-property rights have dominated; at others, they have been weakened or replaced by socialism, government ownership, or communal or tribal ownership.

Property Rights

A person's property rights include his expectations that his decision about the uses of certain resources will be effective. The greater the probability those expectations will be upheld in one way or another (custom, social ostracism, or government punishment of violators), the stronger are his property rights. If, in using my goods, I deny your authority over your goods, I violate your rights to your goods. I can legally throw a rock through your window or tear down your house and dump garbage on it if, and only if, I obtain the rights from you. Private-property rights contain, in addition, the right to transfer or trade

rights with other people. In sum, two elements of private property are the rights to make decisions as to use and transferability of rights.

It is a mistake to try to contrast human rights and property rights. Property rights *are* human rights to the use of economic goods. To see a conflict between human rights to use property and civil rights is equally misguided. Civil rights do not conflict with human rights to use goods. A *genuine* difficulty arises from the differences afforded people in the protection of their rights. Protection of some people's rights more than other people's is a source of much discontent and open conflict. But this conflict is not one of property versus human or civil rights—it poses an interpersonal conflict about whose, if anyone's, rights are to be more thoroughly respected and enforced.

Rights to control goods are not always clearly assigned to particular people. If I burn refuse or operate a factory that emits smoke, foul smells, and airborne acids over your land, I am using my goods in ways that use your goods without your permission. When a neighbor walks his dog for its nightly relief, my property is damaged. When I drive my scooter with a blaring exhaust that sends sound vibrations across his property, I momentarily detract from its physical features. These actions use and change the characteristics of the goods other people are understood to own. This is often called excessive pollution, "nuisance," "invasion of privacy," a "tort," or "theft," or an "externality." They all are the same.

Thousands of years ago, man learned geometry and trigonometry and how to demarcate specific plots of land. Once it became possible to identify parcels of land, control and sale of land became possible. Today we are slowly learning how to monitor and police and exchange rights over radio waves just as we do land rights. Airlines keep track of planes with sufficient accuracy to measure, police, and exchange rights to moving cocoons of airspace. Water is still a relatively expensive item to control in its natural state, though not after it has been captured in reservoirs, canals, or pipes.

Undoubtedly, the future will bring new, economical metering, policing, or contracting devices for the control of air, water, streets, airspace, radio and TV frequencies, and that great treasure bed, the ocean floor. As the effective range of radar increases and boats become faster and use longer-range guns, greater distances from the shore can be policed and are being claimed by the nearest country—as has already been done for oil rights hundreds of miles into the North Sea and Caribbean. Peru is claiming and pricing rights to fish "its" ocean as far as 200 miles from its shore. This gives Peru an incentive to conserve ocean resources rather than permit overfishing, just as such rights now do for land use.

Another example of the 200-mile limit is the Iceland-Britain "cod war." British trawlers are fishing outside the 12-mile limit determined by the International Court at the Hague, a limit the Icelandic government does not accept. Britain would be willing to accept Iceland's 200-mile limit if the Icelandic government would permit British trawlers to collect up to a specified maximum tonnage of fish, but the Icelandic government wants a lower limit. (Do you wonder how much the Icelandic government might be paid to persuade them to permit the larger catch?)

Limitations of Market Prices

High costs of negotiating exchanges of property rights and of property-enforcement increase the prevalence of waiting lines, waiting lists, and other nonprice means of allocating goods. If collecting payments and policing the transactions for parking spaces costs more than the value of the parking spaces, the landowner has no incentive to rent space for parking. Either he gives away parking rights or lets no one park, depending upon the side effects. Pricing will occur only if devices are available (for example, parking meters with police enforcement) to lower the costs of collection and policing—or if the demand rises sufficiently to raise the parking value above those costs. Where labor is cheaper *relative* to land, such as in Europe as compared to the United States, or in U.S. cities as compared to suburbs, parking attendants to collect fees and police the space cost less relative to the value of the space. Therefore, parking-lot attendants are more common in Europe than in the United States, and in cities than in suburbs.

The *variety* of theater-seat prices is affected by the cost of ushers to enforce multiple-sectioned seating. If ushers' wages are high relative to admission values, fewer ushers will be used; this will make it more difficult to ensure that those who pay premium prices are the only ones in the premium seats. In Europe, or in "live" theaters, because wages are lower relative to theater-seat values, there will be a greater variety of price classes. Different seats within the theater will be priced more closely to the price that equilibrates demand with supply.

Parking meters permit cheaper metering of street parking. As yet, no one has devised an economical way for drivers who want to use the parking lane for a traveling lane to bid away that space from those who want to park, and so such transactions do not take place. However, society is not helpless, and as the excess of value for driving over parking becomes larger, laws are passed prohibiting parking in curb lanes during "rush" hours.

In the past, it was too costly to provide an electronic device whereby a receiver could pick up radio and TV programs limited to paying subscribers. Economical cables to permit pricing have now been developed, but the U.S. government still restricts their use. Nevertheless, pay-TV appears on the verge of enormous expansion.

Another example of economical mechanical market-exchange operations is the coin-operated vending machine. Some airport waiting rooms have coin-operated television sets; coin-operated devices control access to dormitory rooms and restrooms for travelers between flights. We have coin-operated rental typewriters at libraries, and pay telephones everywhere. (Why not "pay" drinking water fountains? But why pay for Cokes?)

When cheap transferability and well-identified rights do not prevail, the market-exchange system is weakened. Other forms of competition for controlling goods are then enhanced. Several examples come readily to mind. (1) The western states fight in the courts over use of water from various watersheds, but they don't fight about the use of forest timber, oil, iron ore, coal, or other "natural" resources—because rights to oil, lumber, and coal are privately transferable. Government agencies allocate water, but no agencies are required for wood or oil. (2) Street congestion

4, 5
6, 7
8, 9
10, 11
12

and behavior on public beaches are examples of behavior with "fleeting, undefined, nonexchangeable" right to space. Excessive pollution arises because expensive, ill-defined, or ill-enforced property rights to the resource being polluted prevent resource-use pricing. So other control methods must be devised—some good, some bad, some indifferent. (3) Cities upstream dump sewage, and cities downstream bear the consequences; so each city is tempted to build a pipeline farther upstream nearer the source to catch purer water.[1]

Allocation under Rights Other Than "Private Property": Nonprofit Institutions

Even in the United States (the epitome of the free-market system), not all market arrangements are based on private-property rights: consider nonprofit institutions. A *nonprofit* corporation has no "owners" who can decide to distribute gains to themselves as their own wealth, as they can in a for-profit proprietary corporation. Any profits must be spent in the enterprise to further its specified purposes. Most private colleges are nonprofit institutions, and resources are to be devoted solely to the aims of education. Many hospitals are nonprofit organizations; all their income is supposed to be used, not for the trustees, but for the stated aims of the foundation.

---

[1] The basic identity of congestion, pollution, and conservation and also their dependence on low transaction costs of transferable, well-defined property rights in the market will be explained and illustrated in later chapters.

Almost all religious and fraternal organizations and unions are nonprofit organizations.

Rose Festival Association

For each New Year's Day Rose Bowl football game in Pasadena, California, more tickets are wanted than are available at the price set by the sponsoring association. Some people offer higher prices to get seats, and yet the Rose Festival Association and the associated college authorities refuse those offers and persist in selling at a lower price to students, alumni, and Rose Festival Association affiliates (and to 2000 winners of a race to get to the Rose Bowl box office for a special "public" sale). Furthermore, the Association and the universities declare it illegal for anyone to resell his ticket at a price higher than he originally paid for it. (The authors know that many tickets *are* resold at $50 markups.)

Why does the Rose Festival Association refuse higher offers from eager bidders? Why does it reject greater wealth? One-third of the gate receipts are used to finance the association's activities, such as providing the game, the Rose Parade, and other civic affairs. The remaining two-thirds of the receipts are divided between the two participating universities and their athletic conferences. But no person can claim any *pro rata* part of the proceeds as being "his"; no one can spend the net proceeds in the way he could spend his privately owned wealth. In these circumstances, the operator-members of this association—those who set its policies and determine the specific activities—have less incentive to behave as if they were owners or were responsible to owners.

But someone has to set the ticket price. The person in charge could set a low price, so that more seats are demanded than are available. He might then, by virtue of his position, secure tickets and resell some at higher market-clearing prices, thereby unethically diverting wealth to himself. Being moral, he certainly eschews *this* line of "gain"—and uses another. By underpricing the tickets, he gets some for himself more cheaply, releasing a bit of his own wealth for other uses. Also, an excess demand for tickets permits him to favor some applicants. The "right" people get tickets at a price less than they *and others* are willing to pay. In return, he is invited to the best places and clubs; and when he buys a car or furniture, past favors are fondly and effectively recalled. A high enough price might leave empty seats—which would look bad even if it increased receipts to the Association. But in a privately owned corporation with private-property rights residing in stockholders, the *owners* (stockholders) will have a stronger incentive to reduce the discrepancy between realizable and realized income.

If there are several kinds of seats, which seats will be most underpriced? Primarily the kind that the manager and the association members would want—the best seats. You might think then that market-clearing prices would more likely be charged for inferior seats that go to people who are neither students nor alumni. And the facts agree.

One might suppose that the universities surely should want maximum receipts and therefore should oppose the underpricing of tickets. But the universities also are nonprofit, nonprivate-property institutions, and so the *individuals* who make the decisions act in the absence of private-property rights and their accompanying incentives. The university administration of athletic affairs is like the Rose Bowl administration. These same principles apply also to government agencies.

Other Nonprofit Associations

Nonprofit corporations—for example, RAND Corporation, Brookings Institute, Harvard University, and nonproprietary hospitals—have incentives to provide services in a more expensive, manager-beneficial manner. Costs are higher, because no one can claim the sacrificed potential savings in the way that owners of a private, for-profit organization can. Forgone personal wealth to the managers because of exercise of their own tastes is smaller. Managers have prettier secretaries, even at higher wages than required for less-attractive secretaries. If the managers prefer whites to equally productive but lower-priced reds, yellows, browns, or blacks, the managers can hire fewer of them and more whites. Performance standards for employees, and for their dismissal, are less severe. Furniture and equipment will be more luxurious than for employees doing the same quality of work in private, for-profit businesses. Such are the implications of economic analysis. And data being collected are slowly providing corroboration.

Only with respect to private property will market prices behave strictly as explained in earlier chapters. With nonprofit or government agencies, market-clearing prices are less likely; shortages or surpluses are therefore more likely. So is discrimination on nonprice criteria.[2]

[a] Chapter 9 explores production problems under alternative property rights.

Philanthropy

Philanthropy, or charity, totals billions of dollars in expenditures annually. Charitable foundations and colleges are prime examples of givers of wealth, as are religious groups and individuals. Musical concerts, museums, and libraries are deliberately available at below market-clearing prices because the donor wants to be charitable and to induce that particular kind of cultural activity. Almost every college provides services at less than cost, because they are supported by people who want to give education to (smart) young people. Because the price is low or zero, applicants must compete on some nonprice discriminatory bases. Do the results differ from market-price competition?

The *economics* of charity or gifts may seem contradictory. How can people give gifts if they are assumed to be selfish? Selfishness, however, was not assumed: The postulates of economic theory do *not* say that man is concerned only about himself. Each of us can be, and is, concerned about other people's situations. After disasters, many who were unaffected give to those who were harmed. I would prefer other people to be richer than poorer, even if it cost me something. I would give them a dollar if my personal use of it meant less to me than would its increase of their wealth—in *my* assessment of a most-preferred situation. The larger my wealth relative to the poor, the greater my willingness to contribute to the poor, just as a larger amount of candy increases my willingness to give up candy for Cokes. This implies the richer contribute more to the poor; and they do. Furthermore, "matching grants" would induce me to give still more, because each dollar I give up gets more than a

13, 14 15, 16 17, 18 19, 20

dollar to the poor. This implies that matching grants should be commonly observed in charity; and they are.[3]

Who Gains What from a Gift

A gift is equivalent to a sale at a price lower than the market-clearing price. The effects of such a subsidy are complex but can be seen if we apply our demand theory and personal-value concepts.

Suppose you were admitted to a college that charged a tuition below what it cost the college to provide your education. To analyze the effects on you, use the following five concepts, and associated values (the values given are assumed for illustration only):

A. The cost to the college of the education = $1000

B. The tuition charged = $700

C. How much you would have spent for tuition (possibly at another college) if tuition here were on a full-cost basis = $800

D. The full personal value you attach to the education here at the below-cost tuition college = $1450

E. The personal value you attach to the education you would have obtained if the low-cost tuition were not available = $1300

[3] Income-tax deductions for gifts are another way to reduce the donor's costs of giving money to other people—by making other taxpayers pay more to offset my reduced tax payments.

Taking these figures, we compute:

1. The cost of the subsidy borne by the subsidizer: A − B = $1000 − $700 = $300

2. The cash release of spending power to the recipient: C − B = $800 − $700 = $100

3. The gain in personal value of education to the student: D − E = $1450 − $1300 = $150

The total value of the gains to the student in cash and increased education is $250 (items 2 and 3: C − B and D − E), but this is $50 less than the net cost, $300 (item 1: A − B), to the college. From the student's point of view, the subsidizer wasted $50 because the student would rather have a $300 gift in cash to spend as he saw fit, rather than get $100 in cash plus $150 in the form of better education. The subsidizer may be fully aware of the student's preference, but he thinks the value of the increased education to the recipient is greater than the student does. By that subsidy the donor has induced the student to act in a way the donor prefers. But the student would be made just as well off, *in his own way of judging,* if he had received only a $250 gift in cash. From the recipient's point of view every gift in kind will involve some waste—if the recipient is induced to make changes in his way of life, changes he would not have made had he been paid strictly in cash.

Compare these results with those of another student with the following preferences. The second student is assumed to value this low-cost education at $1075 and would have spent $1100 on education if the alternative were full-cost tuition, which he values at $1200. Given these data, we can compute that he gets a $400 cash release (C − B = $1100 − $700) but a reduction in value of education attained of −$125 (D − E = $1075 − $1200). So he ends up with less education but more money for other things, a total gain as he values it of $400 − $125 = $275, which cost the college tuition subsidizer $300, a $25 waste from this student's point of view, though not necessarily in the subsidizer's scheme of things.

Foreign Aid

Every year the U.S. government grants aid (gifts) to some foreign governments, ostensibly for specific purposes. If the U.S. government gives $10 million to the Egyptian government to build a dam, what has Egypt gained? What would the Egyptians have done without the gift of aid? Suppose they had intended to build the dam anyway, financing it by domestic saving. Then the gift for the dam releases the wealth of the Egyptian government for other things. The gift purportedly "for a dam" is actually for general purposes—the Egyptian government now simply has $10 million more than it would otherwise have. Conceivably the government could lower taxes—thus giving the Egyptians that much more income for general consumption. Or the government itself could spend the extra funds.

Why, then, do we give the money "for a dam"? One possible answer is that otherwise they would not have built the dam, so that the gift does provide one more dam. A simple gift of $10 million with no strings on its use would have enabled the Egyptians themselves to decide what were the most valuable uses of that extra wealth. Of course, officials of both the U.S. and Egyptian governments understand all this, and the conditional form of the grant is employed primarily to try to induce the Egyptian government to behave more in accord with the judgment of the U.S. government.

To apply this analysis of gifts as inducements to behave as specified, look at your campus: Do the faculty have special parking rights not granted students? If so, deduce what gains the faculty get, with and without rights to sell their parking rights to students. Apply it also to student admission procedures.

Unintentional Charity

Intentional and unintentional gifts cannot always be distinguished from one another. Nor, as we shall see, does every allocation of resources made at less than a market-clearing price (even at a price as low as zero) yield a gain to the recipient. (Fortunately, intent is not necessary to the definition of what happens.)

For example, to operate a new television station you must obtain a license from the Federal Communications Commission (FCC). The explicit government price for a license is far, far less than its value—often millions of dollars less. Many applicants appeal to the FCC for a license.[4] How? In sales or leases of government-owned forests and oil lands, the "right" person is the highest bidder, with the proceeds going to the govern-

[4] The number of channels that can be used at one time is not a technologically fixed constant. It depends upon the kind of receiving and transmitting equipment. With more expensive and sensitive receivers and transmitters, the number of available channels could be greatly increased. And the possibilities with transmission by cable are enormous.

ment. But the law creating the FCC forbids allocating channels on that basis. Nor is "first come, first served" the rule (although it was for radio in the early 1920s). Instead, the commission chooses among applicants.

The applicant must show his community "needs" another station—over protestations of the owners of existing stations, the value of which would fall. Money that would have been paid to the government under price competition for that license is instead devoted, at least in part, to competition for the commission's favor. Since something worth millions is at stake, millions are spent in seeking the license.

What criteria do commissioners use for selecting licenses? "Respectability," "moral" reputation, post and future promises, dedication to "public service," and education. A newspaper publisher is attractive, for he is experienced in news collecting and dissemination. If he doesn't promise religious programs, if he plays mainly jazz and Western shows, with few if any "cultural," political, or news programs, or public "information," he might as well give up. His "antenna" must detect the preferences and tastes of the commissioners, and thus the kinds of programs he should offer. He must not offer explicit, detectable bribes to the commissioners or their staff. Of course, if in the past he hired some of the FCC technical staff to operate his other radio or television stations, if he is a former Congressman or employs one as legal counsel to advocate his case to the FCC, he shows that he recognizes able people and could therefore successfully operate a television station. The total value of the broadcast license accrues neither to the federal taxpayer nor to the winning applicant; instead, part is diverted to legal fees, publicity

costs, production of the kinds of programs the FCC prefers, and other expenses to win the license. Thus, even though the nominal price of the license is zero, the costs of getting it are substantial—not to mention the costs of the losing applicants.

The gift-value of the license can be measured by the jump in the stock prices of a company receiving a license. Fortunately for station owners, this wealth gain *is* transferable; they can sell that station and license to other people. (It's inadvisable to be so crude as to sell the "nude" license, without broadcasting equipment.) The presumed *motivation* of this rationing procedure is to "safeguard" the public and to provide to the public what is "good." Our discussion does not mean that the FCC commissioners act irresponsibly. They act as anyone else would who was constrained by the law to allocate a good by other means than price.

More examples are available. Competitive prices are not used initially to allocate licenses to operate (a) scheduled passenger airlines; (b) liquor stores in many states; (c) taxis in most cities; (d) banks in most states; and (e) sugar-beet, cotton, and tobacco farms in the United States. But these rights are salable once they have been awarded. For example, the "shield," the right to operate one taxi in New York City, sells for about $25,000.

Gifts of Nontransferable Property Rights

Some unintended gifts *cannot* be reallocated or resold: for example, the right to enroll in college or medical school; to enter the United States; to join some unions; to adopt a child; to play golf on a publicly owned golf course, to camp in a national park. These rights are allocated at zero or below market-clearing prices and are not transferable. (Consequently, there are "short-ages," and allocation is by methods discussed in earlier examples.) Whether or not the allocated item is subsequently resalable affects the extent to which the gift can be realized as an increase in the recipient's *general* wealth, instead of only as a gain in a *particular* kind of good. For exam-ple, when a municipally owned golf course un-derprices its services and has a waiting list, which is a "shortage" of playing space, those "lucky" enough to get access receive a particu-larized gain—if they haven't had to pay other costs to get on the reservation list. Or when chil-dren in some public-school districts are given free bus rides to school, who gains what? The parents of the children should be classed ac-cording to whether lacking free busing they would have provided transportation for their chil-dren or made them walk. The first group, now relieved of buying transportation, receives all the subsidy as a general wealth increase. The other parents get no gain in *general* wealth, only in the *particular* form of better transportation for their children.

These gifts might as well be resalable, or given as money by the donors, to the extent that the recipients already purchase the services given to them. If I am given a case of Coca-Cola each month by some kind-hearted person who thinks he is inducing me to drink more Cokes, he should note that since I already consume a case a month, I will reduce my buying of Cokes and use the released wealth for other purposes.

Public Goods

The hot dog I eat is one no one else will enjoy. The more I have of that good, the less, by neces-sity, someone else *can* have. Only my utility—no one else's—is affected by the amount of hot dogs *I* get. But, for some goods, the amount available to me does not reduce the amount for you. I can view a television program *and* you can, too (*once the program is broadcast*). The same holds for some parts of national defense: more for me is also more for you, unless it is a kind of local anti-missile defense for your town only. *Public,* or *col-lective, goods* are those for which consumption by one person in a given group of people does not diminish the amount of that good available for any other person in that group (once the goods are produced). For "private" goods, on the other hand, more for one person leaves less for someone else. Some goods have mixtures of pri-vate-good and public-good attributes: For exam-ple, a band concert; the space around the band-stand is limited, and a better space for some of us means a poorer space for others.

Examples of goods having almost exclusively public-goods attributes are mathematical theo-rems, TV and radio programs, songs, poems, technological ideas, and knowledge. One per-son's use of an idea does not leave less of it for anyone else.[5] For pure public goods, no one need give up some other goods in exchange, since

[5] However, *teaching* it to one person does not automatically teach it to everyone else. So knowledge is not a pure public good, because teaching it to me could mean not teaching it to you.

(once the pure public good is created) any person can have as much of the available amount as he chooses without anyone else having less. *There is no rationing problem—and thus no required rationing price—for the existing amount of the pure public good.* There is no reason to reserve the existing public-good service only to users with the higher personal valuations of the good—as must be done for hot dogs in a private-goods system—because everyone can simultaneously use all that exists.

Be careful not to jump to unwarranted conclusions, however. Some people think, for example, that pay-television is wrong, because the price charged for viewing a program would wastefully dissuade some potential viewers without making more available to others. This is correct as far as it goes, but it ignores some inescapable issues. Utilization of the service *once it is created* is only part of the problem. Another, prior problem is to decide how much and what kind of public goods to produce. *Production of public goods is not "free."* Advocates of pay-TV seek to make the viewers *directly* influential as to what and how much shall be *produced* and who should bear the costs. So even though existing public goods pose no *rationing* problem, there is the problem of determining how much and which public goods to produce and at whose cost. If no price is charged for a good, how is its value to society to be determined relative to other goods? By advertisers? Politicians? Voters? Potential users of public goods are tempted to conceal their valuations so someone else can be maneuvered into paying production costs; then, *once the good is produced,* those who do not pay

could use all that is available without having borne its production costs. But that tactic could be prevented *if the provider of the public good could exclude* any user that did not pay for use of the public good.

This problem of excluding nonpayers pertains to *all* goods, private as well as those having the technological characteristic of public goods. (And do not be misled by the terms, *private* and *public* goods. They are based on technological characteristics, not on the ownership structure or the costs of excluding nonpayers.) For example, private goods such as water, streets, use of radio frequencies, airspace for aircraft, pollution-free air are kinds of private goods for which exclusion of nonpaying users is extremely, sometimes impossibly, expensive.

The *only* unique consequence of a public good is the absence of a rationing problem for the *existing* supply of the public good. For purposes of getting production, the usual method, for all types of goods, is to exclude nonrevealers (nonpayers). The feasibility of using market prices as indicators of value of different amounts to be produced—which requires ability to exclude nonpayers—is not inherent in a distinction between public and private goods. For that purpose the distinction is not crucial. The ability to exclude is crucial, whether the good is a public or private good.

So far in this book we have considered only the rationing problem of goods. But it is useful to indicate briefly some of the considerations involved in production. If one unit of a public good is valued by two potential users at $10 and $20 respectively, and *both* can enjoy its services, that unit of service is worth $30, not merely the $20 of the single highest valuing user. The value of a unit of public services is the *sum* ($30) of *both* people's individual values. Another unit of the public good would be produced if it cost less than $30, but if that *sum* of the users' values cannot be brought to bear, too little would be produced.

Some goods with public-goods attributes are produced outside the normal market-exchange, private-property system by government and financed by taxes or by fees to users, as in England where radio and some television are provided by the government and financed by a tax on every receiver. In the United States, national defense is provided by government and financed by taxes. In cities and towns, police protection is financed by taxes, although in some cities private police forces are bought by those desiring more protection.

It is not demonstrable whether the solution to the problem of determining how much of which public goods to produce can best be solved by private or government methods. Each involves "undesirable features." To analyze this further, we must await the principles of production and its control.

31
33
35
37
39

Summary

1. Accurate information about buyers' and sellers' offers is not free. Nor is the creation and operation of a market costless. The more rapidly such information is collected, the more expensive it is. The more rapidly people adjust to new developments, the more expensive the adjustment. Information about buyers' and sellers' offers and the availability of goods is cheapened by middlemen and their inventories.

2. Buffer inventories reduce the costs of adjustments and information collecting. Buffer inventories are not idle, unemployed, or wasteful.

3. Shifts in demand may be transient or permanent. Transient shifts are more economically met by inventories and stable, predictable prices, while permanent shifts will call for price changes. Therefore, shifts in demand will first become evident through changed inventories and output, with price changes following the discovery that the shift is permanent.

4. Marketing and exchange costs are reduced lower, the more specific, secure, and transferable private-property rights are.

5. Under nonprivate-property rights less of the marketable value of a good accrues to the controller, so market values are given less heed in determining production, exchange, and allocation. The existence of philanthropy and charity is consistent with the economic laws of demand and supply. Charity involves some combination of (a) gifts in kind, (b) gifts of general purchasing power, and (c) waste from the recipient's point of view, though not necessarily from the donor's point of view. The recipient does not necessarily get a net gain since he may pay in equally costly activity to obtain priority of the nonmarket-allocated goods.

6. Public goods are those for which one person may have as much as is available without affecting the same amount available to other people. Prices could be charged for public goods as long as the price did not reduce the amount any one person would demand below the

amount available. Any price in excess of that would restrict consumption unnecessarily. A price, while not necessary for the rationing task (since there is no rationing problem) would serve as a guide to production of more or less of the public good. The price relevant for this valuation is the sum of the individual prices charged various users.

Questions

*1. It has been estimated that carrying a spare tire on automobiles costs the public about $150,000,000 or about $5 per car. Is this a wasted idle resource? What do you think it would cost if that figure were cut to zero by not carrying any spare tires at all? Do you think it would be cheaper to make tires more durable and to devote more resources to handling emergency "flats"?

2. You are planning to build an apartment with eight units. You are told you can add a ninth unit for an extra cost of $10,000; and, if the extra unit is occupied all the time, it will be worth $15,000. If occupied three-fourths of the time, it will be a break-even proposition.
   a. Would you then consider building more apartments than you could expect to keep always rented?
   b. Would you consider that apartment to be unemployed when not occupied?
   *c. Would you consider every unemployed person as a "waste"?
   *d. Why?
   *e. Is there any distinction between unfortunate and wasteful?

*3. a. Estimate the fraction of your wealth tied up in resources designed to ease your own unforeseeable changing demands or circumstances.
   b. How about the amount of money you hold; items in the medicine cabinet; food kept at home in the refrigerator, freezer, and in canned goods; general education? Are these idle, unemployed resources?

4. If a cheap enough method could be invented for metering the extent to which each motorist uses a street, would use of streets be rationed more with a price system? Do you know of any such cases now in use? Name two.

5. Shopping centers often provide free parking spaces. In effect, the shopping-center merchants provide free parking for some non-shoppers so that their customers will find adequate space. Some allege that the number of parking spaces is excessive (that is, more resources go into the provision of parking space than should) where the space that "should" be available is the amount that would clear the market when a charge is levied to cover the construction and maintenance cost of the parking space. However, policing "pay" parking space involves a cost of estimating charges, collecting fees, and prosecuting violators. Does the fact of that cost mean that it might be "better" to provide "too much" parking space than to provide the "right" amount with a price rationing system? Explain.

6. A owns and lives in a home near an area in which it is announced a series of 20-story apartments will be built. This will have only trivial effect on a view, since the land is all flat. A sues to prevent the construction on the contention that it will create extra traffic hazards and congestion. In court, A proves to the judge's satisfaction that his allegation is correct. As the judge, how would you rule? Why?

*7. A owns a hillside lot with a beautiful view. B, owner of the lot just below, plants trees that grow up to 50 feet in height and block A's view. A asks him to trim the tops. B refuses. A offers to pay for the trimming. B refuses. A offers $300 in addition. B refuses; B asks for $2,000. A sues for $5,000 damages to the marketable value of his property.

a. As the judge, how would you rule?

b. If, earlier, A had sued to force the person to trim the trees, how would you have ruled?

c. What will our courts really decide today in such suits?

8. The City of Palm Springs prohibits construction of any building whose shadow will fall on some other person's land between 9 A.M. and 3 P.M. Is that a restriction of private property or a strengthening of it? Explain.

9. A restaurant opens near an apartment. The cooking smells annoy the apartment tenants. The apartment owner sues for invasion of property rights.

a. You are on the jury. Would you find in favor of the restaurant or the apartment owner?

b. Would your decision depend upon whether or not the apartment owner lived in the affected apartments?

c. Do you know what decisions have actually been rendered in similar cases?

10. "The fact that some airplanes collide is evidence that there is too little air traffic con-

trol." Evaluate. (Hint: What would it cost to avoid all risk of air collision?)

11. A city passed a zoning ordinance prohibiting the owner of a large parcel of land from constructing homes on it because of a fear that the noise of a nearby airport owned by the city would be so disturbing to the new tenants that airport operations would have to be curtailed.

a. Whose rights were being curtailed by the zoning ordinance?

b. Under the definition of private-property rights, were the landowner's rights being taken from him?

*c. Can you suggest some other solution to the problem?

*d. If you were a taxpayer in that town and did not live near the airport, what solution would you have voted for?

*e. If you owned vacant land near the airport, what solution would you advocate? If your vote is different in each case, do you think you are denying the morality of decisions by voting? Why?

12. Ralph Nader, currently a popular exposer of defects, complains that a person who relieves himself in the Detroit River is fined, but industries that pollute the same river are not. He says also that muggers are punished but smoggers are not. These he cites as illustrating the inequities and irrationalities of our society and economy in its attitude toward big corporations. What has Nader overlooked in his condemnation?

13. Camping fees in almost all state and national parks are so low that people want more space than is available.

a. Why is the market price not at a market-clearing level?

b. How much space would people want at a market-clearing price?

14. In Los Angeles two closely situated golf courses, one privately owned and one publicly owned, are both open to the public.

a. Which do you think charges the higher price, and which do you think requires less or no advance reservation? Give your reasons.

*b. Who is benefited in what respects by each course's policy?

c. As land values rise around the course, which one do you think will be converted to housing or business first? Why?

15. "Californians are crazy. Near a beautiful California beach, there is a luxurious motel and a state-owned camping area. Despite the greater luxury of the motel facilities, scores of cars are lined up for hours each morning seeking camping sites, whereas at the motel there is hardly a day the rooms are all taken. This shows that Californians prefer outdoor, dusty camps to the luxuries of a motel with pool, TV, room service, and private bath." Do you agree? Explain.

16. Churches are typically nonprofit institutions. Can you think of a problem in allocation of church facilities that is solved without use of the price system?

*17. The college you now attend is almost certainly a not-for-profit institution. Are any of its resources allocated at less than market-clearing prices? (Hint: Library facilities? Athletic facilities? Counseling? Course admission? Campus space?) Who gains by the power to select admissible students?

*18. a. Why do college athletic conferences chronically have an enormously larger number of people wanting tickets than are available for the playoffs and important games?

b. Why are admission tickets for the Masters Golf Tournament (a most prestigious golf tournament) fewer than the number demanded by the public?

19. "When property rights interfere with human rights, property rights have to give in." This statement is reported to have been made by a lieutenant governor of California. What do you think it means?

20. "The imbalance between governmentally and privately provided services is evidenced by the fact that the family that vacations in its air-conditioned, power-braked, power-steered car passes through cities over dirty, badly paved, congested streets, not to mention the billboards obstructing the beauties of the countryside. When the family picnics with excellent food provided by private business, they must sit by a polluted stream and then spend the night in a public park that is a menace to health and morals and littered with decaying refuse. Private abundance and public poverty are facts that assail every observant person. A plentiful supply of privately produced goods and a shortage of publicly provided services is inescapable testimony to the lack of a social balance between private and governmentally provided services."

Without trying to prove that there ought to be less or ought to be more governmentally provided services, tell why the arguments, taken from a popular book advocating more governmentally provided services, are faulty and do not indicate anything at all about whether there is too little of governmentally provided services. (Hint: Note the use of the term "shortage"; what does it suggest? How are governmentally provided services rationed?)

21. The *New York Times* sponsors a charity appeal each Christmas and gives cash to selected poor families. The *Los Angeles Times* sponsors a charity appeal each summer to send children of poor families to summer camp. Given your choice, to which of these forms of charity would you contribute more? Why? Do you think people who choose the other way are mistaken?

*22 In 1950 many public-welfare and charitable aid organizations refused to help families that owned a television set—no matter how poor the family might be. The welfare workers claimed they were not supposed to finance luxury. What would have been your policy if you were dispensing the aid?

23. Suppose you are running a university and the faculty is asking for higher salaries, some of which you will have to grant at the sacrifice of buildings and activities. Now, the Ford Foundation gives you $1 million, the income of which is to be allocated exclusively to faculty salaries. Who gains what?

*24. The faculty of many colleges are given free parking space even in areas where parking space is not a "free good."
a. Who gains what?
b. What would be the effect if the faculty could sell their space to students?

*25. Immigration-quota rights to the United States are priced at "zero" instead of being sold at a market-clearing price to "acceptable" types of people. Who gains what? Why are these rights not sold at the highest price to acceptable people?

26. In 1963 the right of Northeast Airlines to offer commercial air service between New York City and Miami was rescinded by decision of the Civil Aeronautics Board, the U.S. government agency that allocates such rights.
a. What do you think happened to the value of the stock of Northeast Airlines upon news of that decision?
*b. At the same time, the price of the common stock of two other airlines remaining in service on that route, Eastern and National Airlines, jumped about 25 percent. Why was Northeast Airlines not allowed to sell its right to that route to National and to Eastern instead of having the right taken away from it?
c. Who gained what by the decision to take that right away from Northeast Airlines and let National and Eastern remain as the two carriers?
*d. As a final twist, after losing that right, Northeast Airlines reverted to the status of a "local-regional" airline, serving only the New England area. As such, it is entitled to federal subsidies. Who lost what by the transfer of flight rights by authority rather than by sale to other airlines?

*27. Some state governments, when disposing of property, sell at auction to the highest bidder. The right to form and operate a bank, a liquor store, a race track, or a savings and loan bank is not sold at auction to the highest bidder among a set of "acceptable" businessmen. Instead, the "winner" is selected by a board, much as judges choose the winner in a beauty contest.

a. What is your explanation for not letting the highest bidder win?

b. Who gains what?

c. Which system do you think increases the wealth of lawyers? Of politicians?

d. Explain why a system of controlled entry is conducive to strong political lobbying groups.

*28. The U.S. Congress has agreed with governments of foreign countries producing coffee to prohibit the import into the United States of more than a specified amount of coffee, thereby raising the price in the United States and increasing the total proceeds to foreign countries. (What is the elasticity of demand for coffee in the United States assumed to be?) Why would Congress agree to a law that raised costs of coffee to American consumers? Explain how this could be considered a form of foregin aid that does not appear in the federal government's budget record of taxes and expenditures.

29. There are reputed to be over 100,000 voluntary health and welfare organizations soliciting contributions from the general public, in addition to hundreds of individual hospital-support groups, as well as about 100,000 fraternal, civic, and veteran's organizations and some 300,000 churches which sponsor a variety of charitable activities, not to mention individual charities or gifts. A professor of public-health administration says, "It should not take over 100,000 voluntary agencies to provide private health and welfare services in the U.S." How many do you think it should take? Why?

30. "More of a public good can be produced without the production of other goods being curtailed." Evaluate.

31. Public goods are those for which (choose the correct statement): (a) several people can simultaneously enjoy the good; (b) it is impossible to exclude some consumers; (c) no consumer reduces the amount of the good available to others by his act of consuming the good; (d) prices should not be charged; (e) the government should provide the goods.

32. A theater performance with several simultaneous viewers is not a public good. Why?

*33. A melody is a public good. What is the best way to induce people to produce melodies?

34. "National defense is shared by everyone. More of it for one person does not mean less for someone else. Therefore, it is a public good and should be provided via government taxes and operation."

a. Does greater anti-missile defense for New York City mean greater defense for Houston, Texas?

b. Do more public concerts on the west side of town mean more on the east side?

c. Does it follow that public goods—those that give benefits to several people without less to anyone else—really do not exist?

d. Do external benefits mean that (i) more than one person benefits, or that (ii) a nonpayer benefits, or that (iii) those who benefit do so without any less of the service to someone else?

35. "Even if it were costless to exclude nonpayers from enjoying a public good, it does

not follow that nonpayers should be excluded." Explain why.

36. "Financing public goods by taxes is a means of excluding nonpayers, for nontaxpayers will be put in jail." True or false?

*37. "When a pretty girl wears beautiful clothes, the people who see her get a public good—for which they do not pay. Therefore the standards of dress for pretty girls should be regulated by law in order to induce sufficient amounts of well-dressed girls." Evaluate.

*38. The following is orthodox Chinese Communist (Marxist) economic doctrine: "The goal of socialist production is not profit but the satisfaction of social needs. Goods must be produced as long as they are needed by society, even if a loss is incurred. Not profits, but the calculation of assigned target goals and their fulfillment is the most important consideration. This follows from the Marxist-Leninist tenet that, contrary to capitalism which seeks maximum profits, the objective of socialism is the maximum satisfaction of the material and cultural requirements of society. This fact gives the Communist Party, as representative of society, the right to determine society's requirements and what the economy should produce."

However, in 1962 the Chinese Communists permitted some Chinese economists to publish the following ideas: "Profits should not be set against the goal satisfying social needs. The profit level is the best measure of the effectiveness of management. This would mean that no enterprise would operate at a loss because the output would be curtailed unless the state valued its product sufficiently to raise its prices, and no enter-

prise would try to exceed the output plan at the expense of profits. There would be less need for political participation in enterprise management decisions, if prices were more realistic, in reflecting either market values or costs. The capitalist evil connotations of profits are not present in socialism, because under socialism profit takes on an entirely different character, where it is a good thing."

But still later in 1962, the Communist Party authorities reaffirmed their initial orthodox doctrine and did so both directly and by indirection with an attack on "revisionist" ideas as exemplified by Yugoslavia, which engaged in what the Chinese Communists regard as backsliding policies—like adopting market pricing (permitting more prices to be set in the open market, decentralizing state enterprises and permitting more private property in farming and handicraft activities). In reaffirming their orthodox Marxist tenets, the Chinese Communists directed factory managers to adopt political and economic means to raise labor productivity and to overfulfill specified targets of gross value of outputs whenever possible.

In order to understand why the issues of "proper" pricing, the use of the market, and kinds of incentives are so crucial to the Communists, it is pertinent to understand the effects on the power position of the Communist Party politicians if the economists' 1962 proposal were adopted. What would those effects be? Explain why.

39. "Economic theory is applicable only to a capitalistic society." Evaluate.

6

Allocation of Consumable Goods over Time: Futures Markets

What we eat today we cannot eat tomorrow. After the summer's harvest of wheat, what is the most we should eat in the fall, winter, and next spring? No central planning agency sets maximum consumption limits for each month until the next harvest. How do we avoid famine before the next crop? Some people, who have neither delegated responsibility nor authority, devote their major activity to this task. In a private-property, free-enterprise system these people are acting for their own wealth; yet, in some mysterious way, their decisions influence our consumption over the year. In this chapter we shall see how. The example of wheat will bring out the essential details. Although we discuss only wheat, the principles apply to *all* goods, whether agricultural or manufactured.

The Forecaster in Commodity Markets

The wheat crop (assuming only one type of wheat) has been harvested. Must the farmers store it, gradually selling a bit each month until the next harvest? Not wanting to risk so much of their wealth in the form of harvested wheat, farmers prefer to sell it, letting someone else bear the risks of forecasting the future value of the wheat stock. Who buys the harvested wheat? The millers, who grind grain into flour, don't want to store a year's supply of wheat in advance. Even the housewives refuse to take on this duty, because they do not want to make commitments so far ahead. But there is a very simple inducement to someone to store wheat: If people refuse to store the harvested wheat, the price of wheat falls. This offers an increased prospect of profit

in buying wheat at the lower price, storing it, and selling it later at an anticipated higher price after some of the wheat is consumed. In a private-property, open-market system anyone may buy wheat at harvest time in a self-serving endeavor to profit by selling it *later at a higher price*. This buying for later resale is known as speculation.

Differences among people in the willingness to bear risk, in their talents and facilities for storing wheat, and in their estimates of future prices and of costs of storing wheat—all determine what the price of wheat will be after the harvest. Permitting any or all persons to buy stocks of wheat for speculative purposes keeps the price from falling further, thereby giving farmers a higher price than if some of these more optimistic buyers were not allowed to buy for speculation. And speculators' realized profits, if any, will be smaller. In the United States, anyone can buy and store wheat by telephoning a commodity-market broker who will arrange to have wheat purchased, stored in rented facilities, and insured against theft and spoilage.

Control of the Rate of Consumption out of Stocks

What determines the *rate* at which the stock of harvested wheat is consumed? Who tells speculators how much wheat to sell each month for consumption? No one. But *something* does: the present price of wheat relative to its expected future price.

Past experience, that prime source of knowledge, provides the basis for expectations of what the price of wheat will do between harvests. And the further the present price is from future expected prices the more will speculators want to hold currently, because profit prospects are increased.

The present (*spot*) price of wheat is also determined by the current consumption demand (schedule) and the supply of wheat. If current consumption demand should increase, the present (spot) price of wheat will rise and reduce prospects of profits from storing wheat, thus inducing storers of wheat to sell more wheat to current consumption channels. *The relationship between the present, spot, price for wheat and the expected future price affects the rate at which wheat will be released from storage into consumption.* There is a price in a market that closely approximates the expected future price. That is the price of a "futures" contract in the "futures" markets.

A commodity "futures" contract is a contract to deliver, say, wheat at some specified future time at a price *now* agreed upon but to be paid in the *future* at time of delivery. That currently agreed-to price is essentially a prediction of what the price of wheat will be at that future time. No one would make a "futures" contract now to receive future delivery if the price now agreed to were greater than he thought it would be in the future. Nor would anyone sell such a promise to deliver wheat at a price agreed upon now and to be paid later, if the agreed upon price were less than he thought it would be in the future. (In fact, hardly ever is the wheat actually delivered at that specified future date. Instead, as that time approaches, the two parties simply settle by a payment reflecting the extent to which the price of such contracts was an erroneous forecast of the price in the future.)

Futures Prices and Spot Prices

Suppose it is now September, and you can buy wheat (in 5000-bushel lots) for $4 a bushel for immediate delivery—on the "spot." Today's *spot* price of current wheat is $4. Today you can also make a *futures* contract for delivery of wheat to you upon payment of $4.50 per bushel, where both payment and delivery are to occur *next May*. That price, $4.50, agreed to now in September of this year but to be paid in May of next year, is called the September price of a *May futures*. The difference between the two prices (spot and futures), 50 cents, will, on the average, just cover storage, insurance, and interest costs of investment in holding wheat over the interval between September and May.

Future Expected Prices and Futures Markets

Prices in futures contracts on the commodity futures markets are reported in the financial sections of major newspapers. You may find, in September, something like the following for the wheat futures market (which is in Chicago).

Futures Contract Prices of Wheat in September 1976	
September 1976 (harvest)	$4.00
December 1976	4.15
March 1977	4.30
May 1977	4.50
September 1977 (harvest)	4.00
December 1977	4.15

These futures prices are predictions of the future spot prices. May is the last month before a new harvest. The summer harvest cannot be used in the *preceding* May to increase the amount available for consumption; if it could, the May price would be pushed down and the September price raised.[1]

Anyone who can make a better prediction of actual spot prices of wheat in the future can quickly reap a fortune. For example, suppose in September 1976 the *futures contract* price for a May 1977 delivery contract is $4.50. If you believe the price for wheat will go higher than $4.50 before May of 1977, you could buy now a *May 1977 futures contract,* for, say, 5000 bushels of May 1977 wheat at $4.50 a bushel—the wheat to be delivered to you and paid for next May. You agree to this contract now in September at the presently quoted *May futures price* of $4.50 per bushel. Then you nervously wait; *if* the spot price next May is higher than $4.50 you can insist on delivery of the wheat which you can sell at the higher price, reaping the difference as a profit. (If the price were lower, you would suffer a loss.)

Of course, for every buyer of a contract for future wheat, there is a seller who promises to deliver the wheat in the future. That seller may believe the price in the future will be lower than the current futures price (the market's present prediction of the price in May), and if *he* is correct *later* he can buy wheat at that lower spot price and deliver it to the buyer for the currently agreed-to higher price. (Actually, neither party will insist on delivery in this futures contract. In-

stead they will settle up with the loser, the poorer forecaster, paying the winner an amount equivalent to what the winner would have obtained had the delivery been carried out.) An important consequence of this speculative activity is that an increased demand for wheat to be delivered in the future pushes up the current futures price of a May contract from $4.50 toward that new predicted May price. It also raises the current spot price. How? A higher price for a May futures contract raises the profitability of storing more of the existing wheat for that future time. There is an immediate increase in demand to acquire wheat now to store until next May, driving up the *current* price of wheat. The higher current price of wheat reduces current consumption and more is retained for next May.

Suppose a different initiating cause of increase in the current price. Suppose, instead, that the demand for current consumption increases. The present price of wheat rises. Continued storage will be less profitable unless it is also expected that the price in the future will increase still further. A faster rate of consumption will leave smaller stocks and higher prices in the future. Currently, therefore, *futures* prices in the futures markets will be bid up.

Who are the main parties to futures contracts? Millers, who grind wheat into flour, must have sufficient wheat on hand to insure a smooth flow into milling operations. They also want an inventory of flour on hand to facilitate convenient delivery to flour buyers. But having wheat on hand exposes the millers to risks having to do with the market value of the stored wheat—changes that can offset profits from efficient milling and other services. How can they protect their income from the risks of big drops in the price of stored

[1] There is some downward pressure on May prices, for consumers will reduce current consumption in the expectation of buying and consuming more wheat at a lower price after the new crop is harvested.

wheat? There are at least three ways to do so, only the third of which is usually inexpensive enough:

1. Don't buy wheat in advance of your milling operations. But this will not permit efficient flow of production, and you won't survive in the milling business this way.
2. Find someone else to buy the wheat and store it in your place of business while you buy it from him as you use it. Any fluctuations in the value of the stock of wheat will be his risk. Unfortunately, this is too inconvenient and expensive, as you would discover if you tried it.
3. Hedge in futures markets. At the time you buy wheat (for later milling) *sell* a futures contract for the same amount of wheat. If the price of your wheat should fall in the future, you would lose money on that wheat. But because you sold future wheat via a futures contract at a higher price than the price now is, you will make a gain on the futures contract that exactly offsets the loss in the value of the wheat that you bought for storage for your milling operations. On the other hand, if the price of wheat should have risen in the future, you will then have to deliver at higher cost to you than you receive for the contract—giving you a loss on the futures contract exactly offsetting the gain on the value of the wheat you own in storage for milling operations. Remember, if you sell a futures contract and the futures market price goes up, you lose, but you gain from the higher value of the stored wheat you own. And when the futures contract price falls, you gain, and this offsets the loss that is due to the lower value of the wheat you are holding in storage. The gain (or loss) on the

futures contract offsets the loss (or gain) on the wheat you are holding, thus insuring you against any loss (or gain) consequent to shifting values of the wheat you hold in inventory.

In fact, unless there are such processors of storable raw materials, it is unlikely there would be enough people seeking to sell future contracts to maintain a market in futures contracts. Futures contracts would not survive if they were only devices for gambling. More desirable means of gambling are provided by horse races, roulette, craps, athletic events, lotteries, and cards!

**Illustrative Application:
Coffee Futures Markets**

To see the social consequences of futures markets, we can apply the above analysis to price movements from coffee futures. The scenario is only partly imaginary, being based on recent actual events.[2] The rumor spreads that the next coffee crop, now blossoming in Brazil, has been nipped by unseasonably cold weather. No one really knows how much the buds are affected, but there is an increased probability that next year's yield will be reduced. This implies greater (or surer prospects of) profits for those who own existing coffee today and who store it for next

[2] In addition to the coffee market, today there are organized open futures markets for at least the following goods: wheat, soybeans, oats, corn, cotton, barley, sorghum, sugar, cottonseed oil, soybean oil, hides, lard, eggs (frozen, powdered, and shell), potatoes, frozen chickens and turkeys, silver, tin, rubber, cocoa, platinum, pepper, flaxseed, copper, lead, zinc, wool, pork bellies, orange juice, and foreign monies. One for onions was outlawed! Instead of coffee, you could think of any of these goods.

year's prospective higher prices. Therefore, the present price of coffee to present consumers will rise as more of the presently existing coffee is withheld for future consumption to help offset the otherwise smaller future supply. Immediately, the consumption of coffee out of current stocks is reduced.

There is, of course, just as much coffee as there was before the news about a potential smaller crop. And yet the present price has risen. Congressmen, responding to housewives' protests, begin to demand public investigations. Sure enough, there is just as much coffee in existence *now* as before the rise, and greedy speculators have driven up the price.

If you were a speculator—and they're people of all types: dentists, carpenters, students, salesmen—what would you tell complaining Congressmen? What, according to economic analysis, were the sources and effects of the current price rise? Could you defend yourself and claim you deserve not censure but a medal for having benefited all mankind; or were you working against the interest of other people? Your defense might run something like this: "True, news of the cold weather suggested higher prices *next* year. I believed that if I bought some of this year's currently stored crop at present spot prices, I could later sell it at higher prices at a tidy profit. I believed the crop damage was severe and was able to buy claims to coffee from people who did not believe the future supply looked so bleak. I was not alone; many competed for current stocks of coffee. No one would sell existing stocks at a price less than he could get by holding until next year (allowing for the costs of storage, insurance, and interest). No coffee

would have been released from stocks for current consumption at the old price. So, immediately, the current price rose to attract some coffee out of storage and also to induce consumers to decrease consumption to match the smaller flow of coffee out of storage. All this is summarized in the first fundamental law of demand: Less will be consumed as price increases. However, quite incidentally and unintentionally, my action—like those of the many other similarly motivated, foresighted, more informed persons—augmented the supply of coffee for next year, by adding part of this year's stored stocks to next year's reduced harvest. The consumer next year will have more coffee to consume and at prices lower than if we speculators had not carried more coffee from this year over to next year. For that, the consumers should thank us—not condemn us!

"We speculators did not cause the reduced supply of coffee next year. Nature did that. There simply *is* going to be *less* coffee next year. The choice facing people therefore is: 'Shall we continue to consume coffee today *as if* there were not going to be less next year, and then reduce consumption next year by the full reduction in the harvest? Or, shall we reduce consumption this year in order not to have to reduce it so much next year?' The choice is *not* more coffee rather than less, nor is it lower prices rather than higher prices. It is 'when shall the available coffee be consumed?'

"If I must *defend* my actions rather than merely *explain* them, we speculators enabled people to be better off than otherwise, despite their protestations about the currently higher price of coffee. From the fact that next year's prices are predicted to be higher than this year's, I know that people *prefer* to give up a pound now in order to have one more next year. This is precisely what the higher futures price for next year's coffee means, relative to the present price this year. And if we are right in that forecast, we will make a profit; if wrong, a loss. The profitability of our activity is an acid test that people did want some coffee shifted to the future.

"As speculators, we have immediately relayed to people our prediction of less coffee relative to other goods next year. We are not responsible for that bad *event,* but we are responsible for anticipating the effects of impending unfavorable events so that people can more cheaply adjust to them—so they will be better off than if news of the coming crop failure were hidden until even more of the current crop was eaten up. We speculators are blamed for bad events because people confuse *news* of the event with the *event,* or because they sometimes think that news of bad future events is worse than not knowing about it.

"You say, But what if your predictions were wrong? Suppose only a few buds on each tree were damaged, while the hardier undamaged buds produced even bigger coffee beans—more than enough to compensate for the reduced number, so that the crop next year will in fact be even larger! Or suppose the cold snap did no damage at all. Or maybe the news about cold weather was simply false. After all, some South American governments have been known to issue false bad news about an impending coffee crop precisely to drive up the price of coffee now, so that they could sell some of their existing stock at higher prices. What then?'

"The answer is simple. If speculators or people who store coffee make mistakes in foresight, they will lose wealth, which, in part, pays the rest of the community for the error. Speculators will have paid more for the coffee than they will get when they sell it.

"I will not go so far as to say that any damage done to other people by our erroneous forecasts is made up to them by our losses—a transfer of some of our wealth to the rest of society. In part this is correct, but still perverse forecasts do more damage than our loss of wealth to the rest of society can offset. They do damage in the sense that if our forecasts had been more correct, everyone could have achieved a more desirable adjustment in his consumption patterns over time than he did in fact achieve. Obviously, the more accurate our forecasts, the better for us and for everyone else. The less accurate they are, the worse for us, and the less helpful to others. However—and this is crucially important—the results are not as bad for everyone else as they would be if everyone had to do his own forecasting and storing of stocks for his own consumption, thereby bearing the full consequences of his own forecasts—right or wrong.

"Clearly, then, the issue is not whether the forecasts of speculators are correct or incorrect in every instance. The issues are instead: (a) What systems exist for making and acting on better forecasts? (b) What systems exist for allocating coffee among people over time *and* for allocating the risks and consequences of the erroneous forecasts? Any system will have erroneous forecasts, but which one will have fewer of them? And who will bear the major burden of their consequences?"

And so by answering one question our scenario posed new ones, to which we turn.

Price-Forecasting Errors and Risks in Futures Markets

Do speculative markets, to which everyone has access, predict future prices more accurately than some other possible scheme? To find an answer, let us look at onions. The organized futures market in onions was abolished by federal law in 1959. Among those who wanted the markets closed were firms that specialize in collecting, storing, sorting, and distributing onions to retailers. Without an open futures market, information about onion conditions is less widely dispersed. Insiders, such as these processors, can benefit by their more exclusive access to information and opportunity to buy and sell onions. How they managed to induce enough congressmen to vote for that legislation is a question for your professor of political science. However, as it happens, this prohibition provided a fine opportunity to compare the behavior of prices with and without futures markets. The record is clear: With the organized futures markets for onions, the forecasts were more accurate than when they were closed. In particular, with open speculative markets, prices varied less between crops than without them. In other words, the forecasts of future prices—the futures prices—influenced spot prices more accurately toward what was going to happen, avoiding the large fluctuations that occur when spot prices respond to unforeseen events.

How should the consequences of forecasting errors be borne? It has been contended that only experts should be allowed to make speculative decisions; this would avoid the errors made by less-informed people. To this there are several considerations. First, if experts are now better-informed than the consensus of the markets, they could easily get wealthy very rapidly by speculating. The experts' superior information would help move the present spot and futures prices in the "correct" directions. Second, there is the problem of finding experts. When the government employs a group of specialists in this matter, the specialists are not automatically superior forecasters. The predictions of "experts" differ. If, despite these inherent difficulties, a group of experts were responsible for making forecasts and controlling the storage rates, who bears the losses when the forecasts are erroneous? Shall we require that each and every person, whether he wants to or not, shall bear, in proportion to his taxes, the changing wealth values of the stocks of stored commodities? If the speculative activity were a voluntary arrangement with open futures markets, those who want to bear more of the risk can hold more of their wealth in the form of stored goods, and those who want to be relieved of those risks can own other forms of wealth. This points up one fundamental feature of a capitalistic system: Individuals can adjust their patterns of risk-bearing, as well as their pattern of consuming goods. If you wish to avoid the wealth changes of certain goods, you can own other goods. Although it is impossible to completely avoid risks, choosing among types of risks is possible with open markets and private-property rights. But whether that is desirable, economics cannot say.

Having chosen not to bear the risk of wealth changes in a certain good, a person should not complain if its price later rises. His complaints would amount to the assertion that "hindsight is wonderful" and that insurance is wasted if the disaster that was insured against doesn't happen! (In this case, by not holding goods in advance of use, he has insured against decreases in their value.)

Some people mistakenly believe that speculation can be avoided by legally imposing fixed prices on commodities. This is identical to painting the thermometer to avoid a fever. Price controls do not prevent shifts in demand or supply. They reduce the opportunity of people to use exchange to adjust their differences in personal values among goods as well as among risks.

8, 9
10, 11
12, 13
14, 15

Speculative Markets under Different Economic Systems

Who will bear the profits and losses is an issue in all societies, and it cannot be evaded by abandoning a capitalist system. Only the method of allocation varies from system to system. In a capitalist system, individuals can negotiate among themselves, offering to exchange "this" risk of loss or gain for "that" risk. Just as people negotiate for the particular pattern of consumption goods they shall have, so they can negotiate about the pattern of risks they shall bear. Although the option of bearing no risk at all is open to *no* man, in a capitalist society risks may be exchanged for risks on other kinds of wealth. In a socialist system, the risks of value changes, for state-owned goods—or those owned by the people as a whole—are borne by everyone in accord with tax liabilities and access to state services. The risk patterns are not individually negotiable with other people.

If you believe a person should have less choice in his risk patterns, and if you think risks should be separated from the people who control the use of goods, you will prefer to reduce the scope of private property. But if you prefer a wider choice of risk patterns and a closer correlation between risk-bearing and control of use, you will prefer a greater range of private property. Risk and insurance are examined further in Chapter 9.

Summary

1. Allocation of goods between harvests is affected by present prices relative to prices expected to prevail in the future. A drop of spot prices immediately upon harvest induces some people to buy the crop and hold some of it in the expectation of a profit.
2. Futures markets are markets in which contracts are made in terms of future prices. Current *futures* prices negotiated in a futures contract—which is essentially a contractual agreement to compensate or be compensated for a price change—are predictions of what the future price of the good will be.
3. Not everyone has to carry his own consumption supply through the period between harvests. People who bear the risks of fluctuations in the market value of a good are called *speculators*. People who use large stocks of the good in their business can shift the major portion of risks of price changes to speculators by futures contracts. Without hedgers seeking to have speculators bear the risks of price changes, the futures markets would not survive.

4. Concurrent increases in the futures prices and in the present (spot) price of a good may reflect, not a smaller current stock on hand, but an anticipated smaller future stock or larger future demand. More of the current stock will be carried over to the future, by releasing less for current consumption, which raises current prices.

5. Higher predicted (futures prices) values for the future will attract goods from the present (by reducing present consumption), whereas lower expected future values will increase present rates of consumption of existing stocks, leaving less for the future. (Future goods cannot shift to the present; instead, less of presently available goods are shifted to the future.)

6. Economic systems differ in the determination of who will bear which risks of the changing values of existing goods. In capitalism, they are individually negotiable or voluntarily pooled. In socialism, they are pooled and borne by people more in accord with their tax liabilities and their access to state services.

Questions

1. What is the difference between a "futures" price and a futures spot price?

2. Which good will have a greater fall in its price as the crop is more fully harvested: one that will store readily or one that is more perishable? Why?

3. Today you can buy 100 bushels of wheat to be delivered today and paid for today. Does this involve a futures price?

4. A soybean processor buys in March 50,000 pounds of soybeans at $2.35 per 100 pounds. He expects to crush the beans into oil and "meal," and sell the soybean oil and meal in about two months. He sells "futures" in soybeans at the same time he buys soybeans, hoping to obtain some protection from wealth changes resulting from changes in the price of soybeans and soybean oil and meal. He sells futures in soybeans—say, May futures—to the extent of 50,000 pounds. Suppose the price of soybeans falls to $2 per 100 pounds in the interim, and therefore the price of soybean oil and meal also falls. Compute how this enables the processor partially to avoid wealth changes caused by fluctuations in soybean prices.

5. The following was reported in *The Wall Street Journal* in September 1976.

Prices of Maine Potato Futures (Chicago)	
November 1976	$4.70
March 1977	5.50
May 1977	7.50
November 1977	5.00

a. In what months does it appear that the new crop is harvested?

b. Explain the basis of your answer.

c. Approximately how much does it cost to store a bushel of potatoes for one month?

6. The Los Angeles Dodgers and New York Mets are in the playoff series for the National League baseball title. The winning team will then be host for the World Series, with consequent receipts to the owners of neighboring parking lots. I own a parking lot

near the Dodgers' stadium, and you own one near the Mets' stadium. If the Mets win the play-off, you gain; if the Dodgers win, I gain.

a. Into what kind of contract can we enter to reduce the risk each of us bears?

b. Have we exchanged or reduced risk? Can you construct a kind of "futures contract" that would accomplish the same effect?

7. "Short selling" consists of selling promises to deliver at a specified date in the future some goods that the seller does not now own. Newspapers sell short when they take subscriptions with advance payment. A house buyer sells short when he borrows money, for he is promising to pay money in the future—money that he does not now have. A college that charges tuition and room and board in advance is engaged in short selling; it sells something it has yet to produce. I sell short if I sell a promise to deliver 1000 bushels of wheat to you next year for a price currently agreed upon and in receipt for payment now from you. Why is short selling often regarded as immoral, improper, or bad?

8. There are no organized exchanges or futures markets for wine, raisins, dried peaches, coal, oil, gasoline, whiskey, or olive oil.

a. Does that mean there is no speculating in these commodities?

b. Who does the speculating?

c. Why aren't there futures markets for these goods?

9. "If the commodity 'futures' markets were closed, there would be less speculation and smaller fluctuations in the prices of goods.

Farmers could more reliably know what their crop would be worth, and consumers would be spared the price swings that are initiated in the speculative futures markets." Do you agree? If so, why? If not, why not? Can you cite any evidence?

10. A U.S. Senate Agriculture Committee recommended the prohibition of futures trading in potatoes in formal speculative markets.

a. Would such a prohibition stop speculation in potatoes?

b. What would be its effect?

c. Why, do you think congressmen were induced to advocate the prohibition of futures markets in potatoes?

11. The Chairman of the U.S. Securities and Exchange Commission proposed to prohibit or restrict short selling at times when the market prices are under "temporary pressure or distress." The presumption is that short selling destabilizes the market and induces larger downward swings than are justifiable in times of temporary distress. Suppose you were appointed by the President to decide when to restrict short selling in order to prevent it from pushing prices down lower.

a. How would you decide when a drop in prices was temporary and unjustified?

*b. Who would decide when a drop in prices was "justified"?

*12. Things similar to, but not identical to, futures contracts exist for stocks and bonds. These are known as *options.* An option is a right to purchase a stock before specified future time at the *current* price of the stock, regardless of how high the price of that stock may rise in the interim, before the option expires. An option is sold by a party who, in effect, is betting that the stock price will fall in the interim. If it does, he will not have to fulfill his promise to sell at the higher specified price, since the buyer of the option could buy more cheaply on the market. If the stock rises, the seller of the option will have to buy the stock on the market at the higher price and deliver it to the holder of the option for the lower contract price.

On August 1, 1976, you could have purchased an option on Uniroyal stock—giving you a right to buy that stock at a price of $8 per share any time during the following 10 months. That option (the right) would have cost you $21.

a. To what price would Uniroyal stock have to rise for you to have made money?

b. If the price rose to $10 in one month, would you have exercised your option?

c. Or if the price fell $1?

*13. "Futures markets are defended on the premise that it is better to be aware of impending events than to be unaware of them. But for events like impending crop disasters, earlier news merely shifts forward the effects and thereby spreads them over a longer interval, to no one's benefit. People might prefer to experience a short, intense period of less coffee in the future rather than have an earlier, longer-lasting though less intense reduction in consumption." What does economic theory say about this?

*14. "That speculators push up the price of a good is evidenced by the fact that the price often rises before there is any change either in the rate of consumption or the existing supply." Do you agree? If so, why? If not, why not?

*15. News item dated August 5, 1963: "The New York Sugar Exchange, where sugar futures prices soared and then dived in May 1963, will have to be placed under government supervision according to Rep. Leonor K. Sullivan (Democrat, Missouri), Chairman of the Consumer Affairs Subcommittee of the House of Representatives. Her report said in part, 'It was excessive speculation in futures, rather than manipulation, that stimulated the price advance and the subsequent price break. The investigation did not show indications of price manipulation on the part of any individual or groups of traders.' Mrs. Sullivan said the interest of consumers—'who are still paying higher prices for sugar and products containing sugar because of the market behavior'—requires some measures to dampen speculation." What do you think of Representative Sullivan's economic analysis? Explain. Similar proposals are made almost every year by some congressmen.

7

Capital Value, Interest Rates, and Wealth

**Present Value, Future
Value, the Rate
of Interest**

Many goods are durable: They yield services now and in the future. The present price of an automobile, refrigerator, house, shovel, reusable textbook, acre of land, or pair of stockings reflects the value of the anticipated, future services.

The current price, or *present value,* of any of these goods is *less* than the sum of the future values of the future services. For example, if an automobile will yield a service *this* year worth $100 now and a service *next* year worth $100 at that time, the value, or price, *now* of the automobile (the source of that series of services) is less than $200. Why less? One reason is that 100 units of a present good can be converted into more than 100 units of that kind of good later. For example, from 100 bushels of present wheat more wheat can be grown next year. After allowing for all the jointly used productive inputs, you will still have more than 100 bushels of wheat left over—say 105, a net gain of 5. Or a tree with 100 cubic feet of lumber will grow in one year to, say, 105 cubic feet. The remarkable ability to use resources today to get more value in the future is called the net productivity of investing. (None of this is in any way dependent on inflation. It occurs without inflation.)

To illustrate further, if you had 200 bushels of wheat now, you could (a) consume all 200 now, or (b) you could consume 100 now and *more* than 100—say 105—next year. The 200 now can be converted into consumption of 100 now and 105 a year from now. Thus, a present quantity of 200 is "equivalent" to (that is, exchangeable for) 100

now and 105 a year from now. The equivalent of 100 units this year and 105 a year hence is 200 *now,* the *present value.* We can put the same idea conversely: To consume 100 now and 105 next year does not require 205 now. With a net growth rate, of 5 percent, if you had 205 now you could consume 105 now, and the remaining 100 would increase to 105 in a year.

Put this in dollar prices: If each of the present 200 bushels of wheat is now priced at $1, you could consume $100 of wheat (100 bushels) now, and you could consume next year $105 worth of wheat (105 bushels of wheat, each worth at that future time, the same price, $1). That combination of the current $100 of consumption *and* next year's $105 of consumption, at an unchanged unit price of $1 a bushel, is valued today at less than $205.

We summarize: The present price, paid *now,* for a good to be delivered *later* is called the present value or present price of a *future* good. It is the price paid now for a good to be delivered, say, a year from now. The *present* price of a future good will be less than its *future* price or value at that time.

In considering the "premium" of the present price for a *currently* available good over the present price for the same kind of *future* good, we have emphasized the net productivity or growth from investing. There are additional reasons for the premium. A good-in-hand can be used in the event of unforeseen emergencies in the interim whereas a future good cannot. Thus a future good will sell for less now. Also, people may simply prefer to consume now rather than later.

The general fact that the present price of a future good is less than the present price of a present good and is also less than the expected future price of that good can be summarized in terms of a *positive rate of interest.* Usually we think of the interest rate as the rate at which an investment will grow over time. A dollar invested in a bank savings account may earn a 5 percent rate of interest per year—$1.00 will grow in one year to $1.05. You can think of the investment of $1.00 as a purchase of a claim to $1.05 to be available a year later. Viewed a bit differently, we invest a dollar and earn 5 percent per year on it, and when that accumulated interest is added to the initial investment, we have $1.05 in one year. Or, interpreted from the banker's point of view, if a depositor wanted $1.05 at the end of the year and the bank paid 5 percent interest per year, the depositor must initially invest $1 in the account.

Interest, present prices, and future prices of future goods are applicable to goods as well as to money. For example, if the price of a gallon of gasoline *available today* is 50 cents, and if you could make an agreement to pay 45 cents today to get a gallon *one year later* (presumably then selling at that future time for 50 cents), the implied annual rate of interest is

(50 cents − 45 cents)/45 cents = 11%.

The rate of interest can be interpreted—in fact, defined—as (a) the *premium* of the present price of current goods over the present price of the same goods *deferred* a year relative to (b) the present price of present goods. Few of us ever have occasion to make this kind of purchase, because we find it cheaper and more convenient to make commitments for future money rather than for specific goods. So we shall persistently use rates of interest on money.

Methods of Expressing or Measuring Rate of Interest

1. If you can lend me 90 cents and get $1 a year later, the rate of interest is 11 percent, because 90 cents today would return a payment of 11 percent more than was lent. You pay (lend) the 90 cents for my promissory note of $1 to be paid a year hence. The promissory note may say that I will pay you 90 cents plus 11 percent interest per year, or may simply say that I will pay you $1 in a year (with no explicit interest). No matter how written, the total future receipt is composed of repayment of the amount loaned (the principal) plus interest.

This fundamental way of interpreting the rate of interest is

$$P\,(1+r) = A,$$

which is to say that the present payment, P, will grow in one year at the annual rate of interest, r, to A, the future amount. In the example, 90 cents (P) will grow at 11.1 percent per year (r) to $1.00 ($A$).

$.90\,(1+.111) = \$.90 + \$.09999 = \$.999$ (or $1).

Rearranging the former equation, we get

$$(A - P)/P = r.$$

So, if A represents $1.00 to be obtained in one year and P, the *present price* of that future dollar, is 90 cents, the rate of interest works out to

($1 − $0.90)/$0.90 = 0.111 = 11.1% per year.

Consider a real illustration. Almost every week the U.S. government seeks to borrow money for short periods—say, one year. It does so by auctioning to bankers its promissory notes (called "Treasury certificates"), promising to pay $1000 in one year without any explicit interest. Suppose a successful bidder gets one for $900. What is the *implicit* rate of interest? By what percent of $900 will the $1000 repayment exceed the $900 loaned? The $100 excess of repayment is 11.1 percent of $900. Therefore, the annual interest rate is 11.1 percent. (The price for the last several years for such notes has varied from $900 to $970, implying interest rates between 11 and 33 percent.) Even though interest is not explicitly stated in these loan contracts, there is actually a positive rate, because the present price is less than the promised future repayment. The higher the present price paid, the lower the implicit interest rate.

2. The present price, *P*, of something deferred a year is often called its *discounted* value. The present price of a future amount is the "discounted" value, because it is less than the future amount due. This way of looking at the problem means merely that we solve the first basic equation for *P*, in which case we get

$$P = \frac{A}{(1 + r)}.$$

If *A*, the future value or amount due in one year, is $1 and the annual rate of interest, *r*, is known to be 11 percent, then *P*, the present price, must be $.901:

$$\$.901 = \frac{\$1.00}{(1 + .11)}.$$

So the amount, $1.00, deferred one year is now worth $.901 at 11 percent interest. Or, 90.1 cents at the annual rate of interest of 11 percent will grow to $1.00 in one year. Or, if $1.00 deferred one year has a price now of 90 cents, the implied annual rate of interest is 11 percent. These are all different ways of saying the same thing; they correspond to alternative expressions of the same equation.

Interest—The Price of Money?

The interest rate is often called the price of money. This nickname is misleading, for the price of $1.00 right now is, of course, $1.00. More accurately, interest is the price of, or payment for, *earlier availability*—sometimes also carelessly referred to as the price of time. The term *price of money* has become popular because people usually do borrow money with which to buy goods to have them now, rather than borrowing the goods themselves in exchange for more future money. They get less now than the future amount to be returned. That larger *future* amount (which includes interest) is paid for having the money earlier rather than later.

People lend more money if they can get a higher rate of interest. But almost everywhere and always, there are laws against "usury"—another word for interest. Christian dogma long considered interest as improper, unjust, and unsanctioned. Communist doctrine asserts interest is exploitation. When William the Conqueror ruled England, interest was illegal—except if collected by Jews, a convenience to William, who allowed Jews into England so others (especially William and his nobles) could borrow from them. Every society has "interest." It is impossible to find a satisfactory economic reason for the Christian and Communist doctrinal opposition to interest—when one understands that interest is a manifestation of preferences for earlier rather than later availability and of net productivity of investment. The Soviet Communists seem to have shed some Marxian confusions about economic fundamentals. Now they recognize interest, if you judge by their actions rather than their words. The Soviet government borrows money and pays a premium, and its investment policy recognizes the advantage of early over later availability. Instead of the term *interest rate,* Russia uses *efficiency index*—a rather clever term.

The Farther in the Future, the Lower the Present Value

The *more distant* the deferred receipt (or income or goods), the *lower* its present price, with a given rate of interest. At an interest rate of 6 percent the current price of $1 deferred a year is 94 cents—the amount that will grow at 6 percent in one year to $1. This is given by the formula

$$P = \frac{A}{(1 + r)} = \frac{\$1.00}{(1 + .06)} = \$.943.$$

To get the present price for $1 deferred *two* years, simply repeat the operation. If $1 deferred one year is now worth 94 cents, then deferring the dollar one additional year again reduces its present value by the same proportion. For two years, this is .943 × .943 = .889. A dollar due in two years would be worth 89 cents now. At 6 percent per year 89 cents will grow in one year to 94 cents, and then in the second year the 94 cents will grow to exactly $1. This can be written,

$$P(1 + r)\,(1 + r) = A,$$

where P represents the price now that will grow in two years, at the 6 percent annual interest rate, to the amount A.

Solving for P, we get

$$P = \frac{A}{(1 + r)\,(1 + r)} = \frac{A}{(1 + r)^2} = \frac{\$1.00}{(1.06)^2} = \$.89$$

Two years' discount is measured by the factor $1/(1.06)^2 = .89$; three years of discounting is obtained by multiplying the future amount due in three years by $1/(1.06)^3 = .84$. The present value of $1 deferred t years from today is obtained by use of the *present-value* factor, $1/(1.06)^t$. Multiplying an amount due at the end of t years by the t year present-value factor gives the present value (or present price, or discounted value) of the deferred amount, A, due in t years. These present-value factors are given in Table 7–1 for various rates of interest and years of deferment. The present-value factor *decreases* as t is *larger;* the *farther* into the future an amount is deferred, the *lower* is its *present* value. For example, the present value of $1 due in nine years, when the interest rate is 8 percent per year, is 50 cents. A dollar deferred nine years is worth 50 cents now—if the rate of interest is 8 percent. But it is worth less than 50 cents if it is deferred longer—or if the interest rate is greater.

Future Amount Corresponding to Given Present Value

Instead of working from future amounts to present values, we can reverse our perspective and derive (for any rate of interest) the future amount that will be purchasable for a dollar now. At 15 percent per year, $1 will get you $1.15 in *one* year; and in a second year, that $1.15 will grow to $1.32. Hence, $1 today is the present price or

Table 7–1. Present Value of a Future $1: What a Dollar at End of Specified Future Year Is Worth Today at Alternative Interest Rates

Year	3%	4%	5%	6%	7%	8%	10%	12%	15%	20%	Year
1	.971	.962	.952	.943	.935	.926	.909	.893	.870	.833	1
2	.943	.925	.907	.890	.873	.857	.826	.797	.756	.694	2
3	.915	.889	.864	.840	.816	.794	.751	.711	.658	.578	3
4	.888	.855	.823	.792	.763	.735	.683	.636	.572	.482	4
5	.863	.822	.784	.747	.713	.681	.620	.567	.497	.402	5
6	.837	.790	.746	.705	.666	.630	.564	.507	.432	.335	6
7	.813	.760	.711	.665	.623	.583	.513	.452	.376	.279	7
8	.789	.731	.677	.627	.582	.540	.466	.404	.326	.233	8
9	.766	.703	.645	.592	.544	.500	.424	.360	.284	.194	9
10	.744	.676	.614	.558	.508	.463	.385	.322	.247	.162	10
11	.722	.650	.585	.527	.475	.429	.350	.287	.215	.134	11
12	.701	.625	.557	.497	.444	.397	.318	.257	.187	.112	12
13	.681	.601	.530	.469	.415	.368	.289	.229	.162	.0935	13
14	.661	.577	.505	.442	.388	.340	.263	.204	.141	.0779	14
15	.642	.555	.481	.417	.362	.315	.239	.183	.122	.0649	15
16	.623	.534	.458	.394	.339	.292	.217	.163	.107	.0541	16
17	.605	.513	.436	.371	.317	.270	.197	.146	.093	.0451	17
18	.587	.494	.416	.350	.296	.250	.179	.130	.0808	.0376	18
19	.570	.475	.396	.331	.277	.232	.163	.116	.0703	.0313	19
20	.554	.456	.377	.312	.258	.215	.148	.104	.0611	.0261	20
25	.478	.375	.295	.233	.184	.146	.0923	.0588	.0304	.0105	25
30	.412	.308	.231	.174	.131	.0994	.0573	.0334	.0151	.00421	30
40	.307	.208	.142	.0972	.067	.0460	.0221	.0107	.00373	.000680	40
50	.228	.141	.087	.0543	.034	.0213	.00852	.00346	.000922	.000109	50

Each column lists how much a dollar received at the end of various years in the future is worth today. For example, at 6 percent per year a dollar to be received ten years hence is equivalent in value to $.558 now. In other words, $.558 invested now at 6 percent, with interest compounded annually, would grow to $1.00 in ten years. Note that $1.00 to be received at the end of fifty years is, at 6 percent, worth today just about a nickel. And at 10 percent it is worth only about .8 of one cent, which is to say that 8 mills (.8 of a cent) invested now would grow, at 10 percent interest compounded annually, to $1.00 in fifty years. Similarly $1000 in fifty years is worth today $8.52, and $10,000 is worth today $85—all at 10 percent rate of interest. *Forty* years from now (when you are about 60) $10,000 would cost you now, at 10 percent rate of growth per year, about $221. (See the entry in the column headed 10 percent and in the row for forty years.) Formula for entry in table is $1/(1 + r)^t$. (No inflation is involved in this table.)

value of $1.32 in two years. In terms of our formula, this can be expressed

$$P (1 + r) (1 + r) = A,$$
$$\$1 (1.15) (1.15) = \$1 (1.32) = \$1.32.$$

For three years, the term (1.15) enters three times, denoted $(1.15)^3$, and equals 1.52. Therefore, in three years $1 will grow to $1.52. In general, the formula is

$$P (1 + r)^t = A,$$

for any present payment, P, paid for an amount A available t years later. The multiplicative factor $(1 + r)^t$ is called the *future-value compounding factor*. Values of this future-value factor for different combinations of t and r are given in Table 7–2. For example, the future amount to which $1 now will grow—or be equivalently valued—in nine years at 8 percent rate of interest annually is $2.00, found in the 8 percent column at the row for nine years. Or, as another example, at 6 percent for five years, the compounded future amount is $1.34 at the end of five years. Notice that the entries in Table 7–2 are simply reciprocals of those in Table 7–1.[1]

1, 2
3, 4
5, 6

[1] The "rule of 72" is an ancient, quite accurate, and convenient financial rule: The number 72 divided by the annual rate of interest yields the number of years required for a present sum of money to *double* at compounded interest. For instance, an investment that increases at 8 percent a year will double every nine years—because 72 divided by 8 equals 9; or if it doubles in nine years, the interest rate must be 8 percent. (Test the rule in Table 7–2.)

Present Capital Value for Series of Future Amounts: Annuities

We can find the present value of a *sequence* of future amounts (or values of services) due at successive future times. Just as we add up the costs of individual items in a market basket of groceries, we add the *present values* of each of the future amounts. (We do *not* add up the future amounts themselves—we add their present values.) That sum is the present value of the whole series of amounts due at various future dates. Such a series might be likened to an oil well that each year on December 31 spurts out one gallon of oil that sells for $1.

To simplify the problem, first suppose that the series of dollars (spurts of oil) continues for only two years. If the interest rate is 6 percent, the present value of $1 deferred one year hence is 94 cents (see Table 7–1, column of 6 percent rate of interest for one year); and the present value of the $1 of oil due in two years is 89.0 cents (see the same table, same column, but now read the entry for year 2). The sum of the *present* capital values of the future amounts due is 94.3 cents + 89.0 cents = $1.83. To say that the rate of interest is 6 percent per year is another way of saying that $1.83 today is the value of the right to receive $1 in one year *and* another dollar at the end of the second year.

If the sequence of $1 receipts is to last three years, the *aggregate* present value is augmented by the present value of the dollar due in the third year. At a 6 percent rate of interest, the third dollar has a present value of 84.0 cents (see Table 7–1, column for 6 percent and row for year 3).

Table 7–2. Compound Amount of $1: Amount to Which $1 Now Will Grow
by End of Specified Year at Alternative Rates of Compounded Interest

Year	3%	4%	5%	6%	7%	8%	10%	12%	15%	20%	Year
1	1.03	1.04	1.05	1.06	1.07	1.08	1.10	1.12	1.15	1.20	1
2	1.06	1.08	1.10	1.12	1.14	1.17	1.21	1.25	1.32	1.44	2
3	1.09	1.12	1.16	1.19	1.23	1.26	1.33	1.40	1.52	1.73	3
4	1.13	1.17	1.22	1.26	1.31	1.36	1.46	1.57	1.74	2.07	4
5	1.16	1.22	1.28	1.34	1.40	1.47	1.61	1.76	2.01	2.49	5
6	1.19	1.27	1.34	1.42	1.50	1.59	1.77	1.97	2.31	2.99	6
7	1.23	1.32	1.41	1.50	1.61	1.71	1.94	2.21	2.66	3.58	7
8	1.27	1.37	1.48	1.59	1.72	1.85	2.14	2.48	3.05	4.30	8
9	1.30	1.42	1.55	1.69	1.84	2.00	2.35	2.77	3.52	5.16	9
10	1.34	1.48	1.63	1.79	1.97	2.16	2.59	3.11	4.05	6.19	10
11	1.38	1.54	1.71	1.90	2.10	2.33	2.85	3.48	4.66	7.43	11
12	1.43	1.60	1.80	2.01	2.25	2.52	3.13	3.90	5.30	8.92	12
13	1.47	1.67	1.89	2.13	2.41	2.72	3.45	4.36	6.10	10.7	13
14	1.51	1.73	1.98	2.26	2.58	2.94	3.79	4.89	7.00	12.8	14
15	1.56	1.80	2.08	2.40	2.76	3.17	4.17	5.47	8.13	15.4	15
16	1.60	1.87	2.18	2.54	2.95	3.43	4.59	6.13	9.40	18.5	16
17	1.65	1.95	2.29	2.69	3.16	3.70	5.05	6.87	10.6	22.2	17
18	1.70	2.03	2.41	2.85	3.38	4.00	5.55	7.70	12.5	26.6	18
19	1.75	2.11	2.53	3.03	3.62	4.32	6.11	8.61	14.0	31.9	19
20	1.81	2.19	2.65	3.21	3.87	4.66	6.73	9.65	16.1	38.3	20
25	2.09	2.67	3.39	4.29	5.43	6.85	10.8	17.0	32.9	95.4	25
30	2.43	3.24	4.32	5.74	7.61	10.0	17.4	30.0	66.2	237	30
40	3.26	4.80	7.04	10.3	15.0	21.7	45.3	93.1	267.0	1470	40
50	4.38	7.11	11.5	18.4	29.5	46.9	117	289	1080	9100	50

This table shows to what amounts $1.00 invested now will grow at the end of various years, at different rates of growth compounded annually. For example, $1.00 invested now will grow in thirty years to $5.74 at 6 percent. In other words, $5.74 due thirty years hence is worth now exactly $100 at a 6 percent rate of interest per year. If you invest $100 now at 10 percent, you will have $1740 in thirty years. The entries in this table are the reciprocals of the entries in Table 7–1; that is, they are the entries of Table 7–1 divided into 1. You really don't "need" this extra table, but having it saves some calculations. Formula for entries in table is $1(1 + r)^t$.

Therefore, the present value of the three-year series is $2.67, given in Table 7–3. The present value, or present price, of a series of amounts due is often called the *capital value* of the future series.

Technical jargon is useful for convenient subsequent analyses. The *sequence* of *future* amounts due is called an *annuity,* a word that suggests annual amounts. A two-year sequence is a two-year annuity. A person who has purchased the right to a stream of future annuities or amounts due—for example, his pension benefits—is sometimes called an *annuitant.*

What is the capital value of a 6 percent, four-year annuity of $1 each year? Inspection of Table 7–3, column for 6 percent and row for year 4, gives $3.47. A five-year annuity would have a present value of $4.21, because the dollar received at the end of the fifth year is now worth 74.7 cents. For 10 years, you will find (in Table 7–3) that at 6 percent interest the capital value of a 10-year annuity of $1 each year is $7.36.

Table 7–1 gives the present value of each separate future payment in the annuity. But for convenience, Table 7–3 gives the cumulated sums, which are the present capital values of annuities of various lengths, where the payment at the end of each year is $1.00. For example, the entry for two years at 6 percent is $1.83, the sum of .943 and .890 (derived from the data of Table 7–1).

If we extended the series to 20 years (still with $1 of receipts at the end of each year) at 6 percent per year, the present capital value would increase to $11.47. It is significant that the present capital value of the *last half* of that series (the 10 amounts due beginning in the eleventh through the twentieth years) raised the total present value by only $4.11 (= 11.47 − 7.36). This means that at 6 percent interest per year, $4.11 *today* will buy you $1 a year for ten years, *beginning after* the tenth year.

Installments to Repay Debt

Table 7–4 lists the annual amounts of annuities of various lengths with a *present* value of $1. For example, $1 *now* will buy $1.49 annually for the next *ten* years, at 8 percent interest. (The entries are reciprocals of the entries in Table 7–3). Also, you can use this table to answer the following kind of question. "How much must I repay every year, beginning in one year, to repay a debt incurred now of $1000, at an interest rate of 8 percent per annum?" Look for the entry in the 5 percent column and the 10 year row, .130. That means that 13 cents a year for 10 years is equivalent to $1.00 now. Hence 13 cents a year for 10 years will repay $1 borrowed now. A debt now of $1000 would require ten equal annual payments of 13 cents × 1000 = $130. At the end of the first year the payment of $130 would cover the interest due that year, $50, and $80 would be applied toward reducing the debt to $920. Each year a diminishing part of the $130 would be applied toward a progressively diminishing interest; in the second year, $46 = .05 × $920, and the increasing remainder ($84 at the end of the second year) of each annual payment would be applied toward reductions in the principal until at the end of the tenth year the debt was extinguished. You can also use this table to find out how much you must set aside every year, beginning one year from now, in order to accumulate $1 (or any multiple thereof) in *n* years. For example, how much must be set aside annually at 5 percent interest

Table 7–3. Present Capital Value (Price) of Annuity of $1, Received at End of Each Year

Year	3%	4%	5%	6%	7%	8%	10%	12%	15%	20%	Year
1	0.971	0.960	0.952	0.943	0.935	0.926	0.909	0.890	0.870	0.833	1
2	1.91	1.89	1.86	1.83	1.81	1.78	1.73	1.69	1.63	1.53	2
3	2.83	2.78	2.72	2.67	2.62	2.58	2.48	2.40	2.28	2.11	3
4	3.72	3.63	3.55	3.47	3.39	3.31	3.16	3.04	2.86	2.59	4
5	4.58	4.45	4.33	4.21	4.10	3.99	3.79	3.60	3.35	2.99	5
6	5.42	5.24	5.08	4.92	4.77	4.62	4.35	4.11	3.78	3.33	6
7	6.23	6.00	5.79	5.58	5.39	5.21	4.86	4.56	4.16	3.60	7
8	7.02	6.73	6.46	6.21	5.97	5.75	5.33	4.97	4.49	3.84	8
9	7.79	7.44	7.11	6.80	6.52	6.25	5.75	5.33	4.78	4.03	9
10	8.53	8.11	7.72	7.36	7.02	6.71	6.14	5.65	5.02	4.19	10
11	9.25	8.76	8.31	7.89	7.50	7.14	6.49	5.94	5.23	4.33	11
12	9.95	9.39	8.86	8.38	7.94	7.54	6.81	6.19	5.41	4.44	12
13	10.6	9.99	9.39	8.85	8.36	7.90	7.10	6.42	5.65	4.53	13
14	11.3	10.6	9.90	9.29	8.75	8.24	7.36	6.63	5.76	4.61	14
15	11.9	11.1	10.4	9.72	9.11	8.56	7.61	6.81	5.87	4.68	15
16	12.6	11.6	10.8	10.1	9.45	8.85	7.82	6.97	5.96	4.73	16
17	13.2	12.2	11.3	10.5	9.76	9.12	8.02	7.12	6.03	4.77	17
18	13.8	12.7	11.7	10.8	10.1	9.37	8.20	7.25	6.10	4.81	18
19	14.3	13.1	12.1	11.2	10.3	9.60	8.36	7.37	6.17	4.84	19
20	14.9	13.6	12.5	11.5	10.6	9.82	8.51	7.47	6.23	4.87	20
25	17.4	15.6	14.1	12.8	11.7	10.7	9.08	7.84	6.46	4.95	25
30	19.6	17.3	15.4	13.8	12.4	11.3	9.43	8.06	6.57	4.98	30
40	23.1	19.8	17.2	15.0	13.3	11.9	9.78	8.24	6.64	5.00	40
50	25.7	21.5	18.3	15.8	13.8	12.2	9.91	8.25	6.66	5.00	50

An annuity is a sequence of constant amounts received at annual intervals. This table shows with each entry how much it takes today to buy an annuity of $1 a year at the rates of interest indicated. For example, an annuity of $1 a year for 20 years at 6 percent interest could be purchased today with $11.50. This amount would, if invested at 6 percent, be sufficient to yield some interest which, along with some depletion of the principal in each year, would enable a payout of exactly $1 a year for 20 years, at which time the fund would be completely depleted. And $1000 a year for 20 years would, at 6 percent compounded annually, cost today $11,400, which is obviously 1000 times as much as for an annuity of just $1. Formula for entry is $[1 - (1 + r)^{-t}]/r$.

Table 7–4. Uniform Annual Payments to Be Paid (Received) at End of Each Year
per $1 Borrowed (Paid) Now

Year	3%	4%	5%	6%	7%	8%	10%	12%	15%	20%	Year
1	1.03	1.04	1.05	1.06	1.07	1.08	1.10	1.12	1.15	1.20	1
2	.524	.529	.538	.546	.552	.562	.578	.592	.613	.654	2
3	.353	.360	.368	.375	.381	.388	.403	.417	.439	.474	3
4	.269	.275	.282	.289	.295	.302	.316	.329	.350	.386	4
5	.218	.225	.231	.238	.244	.251	.267	.278	.299	.334	5
6	.185	.191	.197	.204	.210	.216	.230	.243	.265	.300	6
7	.161	.167	.173	.179	.186	.192	.206	.219	.240	.278	7
8	.142	.149	.155	.161	.168	.174	.188	.201	.223	.260	8
9	.128	.134	.141	.147	.153	.160	.174	.188	.209	.248	9
10	.117	.123	.130	.136	.142	.149	.163	.177	.199	.239	10
11	.108	.114	.120	.127	.133	.140	.154	.168	.191	.231	11
12	.101	.106	.113	.119	.126	.133	.147	.162	.185	.225	12
13	.0943	.100	.107	.113	.120	.127	.141	.156	.177	.221	13
14	.0885	.0943	.101	.108	.114	.121	.136	.151	.174	.217	14
15	.0840	.0901	.0982	.103	.110	.117	.132	.147	.170	.214	15
16	.0794	.0862	.0926	.0990	.106	.113	.128	.143	.168	.211	16
17	.0758	.0819	.0885	.0961	.102	.110	.125	.140	.166	.210	17
18	.0725	.0787	.0855	.0925	.0990	.107	.122	.138	.164	.208	18
19	.0699	.0763	.0826	.0901	.0971	.104	.120	.136	.162	.207	19
20	.0671	.0735	.0800	.0877	.0943	.102	.118	.134	.161	.205	20
25	.0575	.0641	.0709	.0781	.0855	.0935	.110	.128	.155	.202	25
30	.0510	.0578	.0649	.0724	.0806	.0885	.106	.124	.152	.201	30
40	.0433	.0505	.0581	.0666	.0752	.0840	.102	.121	.151	.200	40
50	.0389	.0465	.0546	.0632	.0725	.0820	.101	.120	.150	.200	50

An annuity is a sequence of annual amounts received at annual intervals for a specified number of years. The entries in the table give the possible annuities of various lengths, for various interest rates, which have a present value of $1. For example, for $1 present value or cost, at 6 percent interest, one can receive an annuity for *one* year of $1.06, or of 54.6 cents for each of two years, or 37.5 cents for each of three years, or 28.9 cents for each of four years.

Another way to use the data is to treat annuities as payments. For example, a debt of $1 can be paid off, at 6 percent interest, with $1.06 in one year, or 54.6 cents annually for two years, or 28.9 cents annually for four years, or 10.2 cents annually for twenty years.

to accumulate $1 in 10 years? The answer is obtained by multiplying (a) the entry in this table in the column for 5 percent and the row for 10 years (which is $.130) by (b) the corresponding entry in Table 7–1 (the corresponding entry is .614). The product ($.130 × .614) is $.080. This means that 8 cents at the end of each of 10 years beginning one year from now will accumulate to $1 in 10 years. (If you start the payments right now, without waiting a year, the fund will amount to $1 upon making the tenth payment at the end of the ninth year, one year earlier.)

Even an annuity that lasted forever—called a *perpetuity*—would have a *finite* capital value—namely, only $16.67 (at 6 percent interest). It is easy to remove the mystery from the fact that an infinitely long series of $1 amounts due yearly has a finite (limited) price today. To get a perpetual series of payments of $1 every year, all one has to do is keep $16.67 on deposit in a bank, if he can get 6 percent per year. Every year the interest amounts to $1 which can be taken out, leaving the $16.67 principal. In effect you pay $16.67 today to purchase a never-ending sequence. From Table 7–3, you can see that the first 50 years of receipts (a 50-year annuity) has a present value of $15.80. The *subsequent* entire part of an infinitely long series of $1 receipts, beginning 50 years from now, is worth *today* only about 87 cents. Small present amounts can grow to amazing amounts in the distant future.

Illustrative Applications of Capitalization Principles

1. Are U.S. Savings Bonds Your Best Investment?

For miraculously being "best in class," you are awarded a $100 U.S. Savings bond payable in 10 years. It pays no *explicit* interest in the interim. If the market rate of interest for equally secure bonds is 6 percent per year—which is about what it has been for several years—at what price now could you sell it to someone else? What would someone else offer if he could invest elsewhere in equally secure bonds yielding 6 percent per year? Answer: Exactly as much as it will now take to grow to $100 at 6 percent interest compounded each year for 10 years. In banking terms, how much would have to be put in a bank account today, if the bank pays 6 percent annually, and if the interest were allowed to accumulate, with interest being earned on the accumulated amount, so as to total $100 in 10 years? The answer is in Table 7–1, which gives the *present* values of a future $1.00 available at specified years in the future, at different interest rates. Since the number of years is 10 and the interest rate is 6 percent, look in the column for 6 percent and the row for the year 10, and you will find $.558. That is the present amount that will, in 10 years at 6 percent interest compounded annually; grow to $1.00. Thus .558 × 100 = $55.80 is the amount for which you could sell your prize.

But if you were in fact to buy a $100 savings bond from the U.S. government, you would have to pay about $70. What interest is implicitly being paid on that $70 for the duration? Look again in Table 7–1 along the row for 10 years and find the number closest to .70. You will find it in the first column, headed by 4 percent. At about 4 percent, 70 cents would grow to a dollar in 10 years. You would be earning about 4 percent per year if you bought a $100, 10-year U.S. Savings Bond at the government price of $70. Not an attractive buy— compared to a savings account at over 5 percent, or a regular government bond at about 6 to 7 percent, or a General Motors bond yielding about 8 percent.

2. Why Buy Stocks?

It is a fact that a dollar invested in stocks on the average, over all stocks of the New York Stock Exchange, yielded more than 10 percent per year over the interval 1915–75 (or 8.5 percent from 1929 through 1975, and 11 percent from 1946 through 1975). Some years gave more and some years less; some stocks were better and some worse. But the average over the 60 years and over all the stocks exceeded 10 percent per year. Instead of investing $70 in a government savings bond at 4 percent to get $100 at the end of 10 years, or in a savings account at 5 percent to get $114 in 10 years, what would you have gotten in stocks? Look in Table 7–2, the Compound Amount of $1, under the column for 10 percent interest and the row for 10 years; the entry is 2.59, meaning your investment would, on the average, be worth 2.59 times the initial amount, or $70 × 2.59 = $181.56. But the risk is higher: You might end up with much more or less.[2]

[2] Pages 445–449 present further examination of investments in common stock.

3. Built-In Obsolescence?

You manufacture for 50 cents and sell for that price a light bulb that lasts one year. You then invent a light bulb that costs you the same but lasts two years and gives the same light for the same power usage. For how much can you sell this new bulb? Assume that buyers value a light bulb's services at 50 cents during each year of service. But the second year's service is over a year away, so, if the rate of interest is 10 percent, they will offer you *now* about 45 cents for the anticipated second year's services. (Remember, the present value of a receipt deferred one year is the amount that would grow at 10 percent annually to the future deferred amount. This is obtained by dividing the future amount, 50 cents, by $1.10 or by looking in Table 7–1 for the amount in the 10 percent column and in the row for one year: .909, which, when multiplied by 50 cents, gives 45.45 cents.)

So, you can sell a two-year bulb for 95 cents now. A three-year bulb would sell now for the present value of three years of service. The third year's service value (50 cents) is worth *now,* two years in advance, $.413. You can compute that by dividing 50 cents by $(1.10)^2$ or by looking in Table 7–1, in the 10 percent column and in the row for two years: .826, which multiplied by 50 cents, gives 41.30 cents. Therefore, three-year bulbs would sell now for $1.37.

And now comes the important lesson. If you could produce the three-year bulb for the same cost as a one-year bulb, would you do so, even though it meant selling fewer light bulbs? Of course, because to sell three bulbs, each lasting only one year, would cost you almost three times as much as producing *one* three-year bulb, but you would not take in any more receipts (in present-value terms).[3]

Another surprising application of this lesson is to textbooks. If a text can be resold and used by a second student, the *initial* sale price of the book, just like the light bulb, will include the second student's use value, adjusted to present value terms. Suppose there were no costs of arranging a resale of this text to the next student (an assumption we make to bring out the essential features). If the first user values his use of the book at $5 and the second also values his use of the book at $5, the publisher could have sold the new book for $9.50.[4] The first student would be willing to pay $9.50 for the book knowing that he can later sell it for $5 to the second student—for a net user cost of only $5. (Remember, $5 a year from now is equivalent to $4.50 now.)

As for the author, suppose he gets 15 percent of the sales value. He gets his 15 percent on $9.50 initially rather than 15 percent of two successive $5 books. So, the two-life book (costing less than two one-year books) would sell new for $5 plus $4.54 (the present value of the second year's $5 value discounted at 10 percent interest rates) or $9.54, which is worth two $5 receipts, one coming now and the other in a year. Clearly it is an efficient used-book market that permits this.

You are willing to pay more for a Volkswagen because of its high resale value, and, similarly,

more for texts that can be resold. Killing the resale value of a book (or an automobile or refrigerator or TV set), either by abolishing used-book markets or by quickly issuing "new editions," is not profitable for authors and publishers because costs of books are lowered by fewer, more durable books—a fact that many authors of texts seem not to know.

4. Pay Now or Pay Later

During the recent energy confusion several legislators proposed to prohibit the sale of air conditioners that used more electricity than higher-priced models (though having the same cooling capacity and use life). Lower-priced air conditioners are made with less-costly cooling systems that require more electrical energy when in operation. Actually, prohibition of those high-energy users could be wasteful. Why? Table 7–5 shows

Table 7–5. Energy Cost Example

Machine	Purchase Cost	Annual Energy Cost (Over 10 Years)	Present Value at 6% of All Costs
Energy User A	$60	$24	$60 + $176.64 = $237
Energy User B	$100	$20	$100 + $147 = $247

hypothetical data for air conditioner A, a machine with a low purchase price but high in annual electrical usage. The same information is shown for a higher-priced, energy-conserving air conditioner, B. Only the initial purchase price and the

---

[3] "Almost," because you would be able to produce two of the bulbs later, and therefore the present values of those later costs is less than 50 cents each. Their present cost is $.50/1 + r$ and $.50/(1 + r)^2$. If $r = 10$ percent, the present value of costs is $.50 + $.45 + $.41 = $1.36.

[4] Assuming an interest rate of 10 percent, $9.50 = $5.00 + $4.50.

subsequent annual electrical energy costs differ, with other factors (for example, length of service life, expected repair costs) being the same for both machines.

For each machine the present value of the total outlays for the next decade is shown, based on a 6 percent rate of interest. The *present value* of all the present and future outlays for air conditioner A—the one with the lower initial price but the higher in energy use—is *lower* than for the one with the higher price but lower in energy use. The difference in present values, $10 = ($247 − $237), is what would be saved in total resources over that interval, counting all costs—materials, labor, and energy. Why? The difference in purchase prices is $40 (= $100 − $60); at a 6 percent interest rate, this would earn the equivalent of an annuity of $5.43 each year for 10 years—which is more than enough to cover the extra $4 cost of energy for the high energy user.[5] In this example, the lower-priced machine uses less in total value of *all* resources (of various kinds and at various times). It is wasteful to save energy worth less than the other resources that could otherwise be saved.

This example illustrates two principles. The first principle is that it is incomplete and hence inefficient to look at only *one component* of costs —for example, energy. There is no economic sense in minimizing energy costs if that raises costs of other required components even more.

[5] Either Table 7–3 or Table 7–4 can be used to calculate the 10-year, 6-percent annuity purchased with the $40. (A) In Table 7–3, the present value of an annuity of $1 per year is $7.36; since we here spend $40 on the annuity, divide $40 by $7.36 and obtain the yearly return of $5.43. (B) In Table 7–4, the annuity purchased with $1 is $.136; with $40, we purchase $.136 × $40 = $5.44.

The value of the energy saved here is only $4 per year, but that costs other resources worth $5.43 annually.

As we shall show later (in Chapter 15) when exploring production, it is never economical to minimize the cost of some one input, for that entails excessive increases in the costs of some other inputs by even more than the savings in the one input. Nor does it pay to *maximize output* per unit of some one of the many inputs of production, for that entails increasing the costs of other inputs by more than the gains. Such technological output–input ratios (or efficiencies, as they are often called) are descriptive of an end result rather than useful for making decisions.

The second principle illustrated by the example is that expenditures at *different times* must be converted to uniform values, as if of one common time, before adding them. Capital values are thus costs incurred at various times all corrected to uniform measures. The lowest capital-value cost method is the lowest cost method. If that method is used, more of other things will be available than if any other, higher-cost method had been used. Costs are sacrifices of other goods; lowest cost means the *least* sacrifice of other goods. That is also all that is meant by "efficient"—that is, no waste.

5. Honor Thy Parents

Your parents, having reached age 70 with savings of $50,000, plan to retire on that fund. They want to use it up at a rate that permits them to draw out the largest possible uniform amount each year for 15 years. After that, if they are still alive, you will shoulder your moral responsibility. How much can they spend each year for 15 years? The question can be rephrased in the terms we've been using: "What 15-year annuity is equivalent to a present value of $50,000?" If you invest at 10 percent, the present capital value of a 15-year $1 annuity, as seen in Table 7–3, is $7.60. Since there is now $50,000 in the fund, $50,000/7.60 = $6570, the amount of each annual payment. (This is an approximation, since $6570 is really the amount that could be spent at the *end* of each of fifteen years, not *during* each year, but the difference is slight.) If they want to use up the fund in 10 years, they can get $8140 (= $50,000/6.14) at the end of each year. If they earn only 4 percent, they can get a fifteen-year annuity of just $4500 (=$50,000/11.1).

6. Eat Your Cake and Have It, Too

In some colleges you can borrow (say $1000) for tuition and expenses without paying any interest for eight years. Should you borrow? Of course! Put the money in a savings account paying 5 percent per year. Each year you can draw out the $50 interest and throw a party. At the end of eight years, you can draw out the $1000 plus the last year's interest, repay the $1000, and have $50 for a last party.

In fact, you are being offered a $50 eight-year annuity. Even at so low a rate as 5 percent, its present value is $50 × 6.46 = $323.16. (See Table 7–3.) This means the possibility of borrowing $1000 at *zero* interest for eight years is equivalent to a gift of $323.16 upon entrance to college.

7. The Whole Is Less Than One of Its Parts

After 10 years of working for one employer, you change jobs. During these 10 years your em-ployer contributed (that is, he diverted from your wages) $1000 each year to an account for your retirement (a fringe benefit), and you contributed a matching amount each year. The fund earned 4 percent during that time, and its value now stands at $24,000. Two options are open. (1) You may leave everything in that fund to grow at 4 percent annually until retirement in 30 years. (2) Your other possibility is to take out the cumulated value of "your" contributions, which is $12,000 (one half of the total of $24,000). You can do as you wish with the money you take out, but the other half will revert to the benefit of remaining employees. In other words, you can give up $12,000 today for the sake of getting the other $12,000 with which you may do as you like. Which shall you choose?

One thing the answer depends on is the growth rate you can get on your own fund. Suppose you believe you can get 10 percent per year. Should you take the opportunity to get 10 percent on $12,000 (rather than 4 percent on the whole $24,000) for 30 more years? At 10 percent, that $12,000 will grow to $209,392 in 30 years. If you leave your money in the first employer's fund, the *total* $24,000 fund will grow to only $77,842 in 30 years. (See Table 7–2, 4 percent, 30 years.) Shocked?

Only if you failed to earn over 6.4 percent would your own $12,000 fund have been smaller at the end of 30 years than the whole $24,000 fund at 4 percent. Today almost all company or union funds credit the accounts with barely 5 percent a year, while the average annual rate of return available on the stock market just by random investing, including interest and profits, has exceeded 10 percent a year.

8. Arab Oil Policy: Friend or Foe?

In 1974, political hysteria accompanied the rise in oil prices to about $12 a barrel. The oil-producing countries seemed to have stopped expanding output to get higher prices and revenues on the assumption (well-founded) that the world demand for oil had less than unitary elasticity. Arabs contended they did so as a tactic associated with the Israel-Arab war. But suppose the Arabs had instead said that they began to suspect that the future supply of petroleum was not large enough to satisfy future demands at prevailing prices in the world markets. Since they estimated the price would be substantially higher, say $18 a barrel in 1985 (even without inflation), that would mean that a barrel of oil 10 years prior, in 1975, would be worth about $12.16, assuming a 4 percent rate of interest. That projection of the future energy situation and the future value of petroleum would mean that no producer should extract oil now in 1975 unless it sold for at least $12.16. It is socially responsible to conserve petroleum for the future rather than overconsume it now in uses that are less valuable than its uses will be in 1985.

No consumption is now being curtailed in uses whose current values exceed this present value of projected future values—allowing for the interest rate, which measures the value of differences in times of uses.

Under this hypothetical interpretation, the Arabs could argue that they have done us a service: By preventing excessive exploitation of oil they are preserving the appropriate amounts of it for the future, as conservationists contend should be done for beaches, forests, and other natural resources.

The point of the example is to illustrate how the present price of a durable, storable good depends on expected future values of that good. The price *now* will rise (and curtail consumption) if the expected future price is higher than the present price—until the difference just covers the expected costs of storage and interest. Whether the forecasts of future oil supplies and demands are correct—or more realistically, how small their error is and in what direction—is unknown. But no person or agency that can do better than open-market competition has yet been discovered. Present prices respond to beliefs about the future and influence current consumption. Some people propose to levy special taxes to reduce present consumption, as if the present market price underestimated future values and uses.[6]

Wealth, Income, Consumption, Saving, and Profit

We are now prepared to introduce some more economic concepts that are crucial to economic analysis.

[6] In fact, for the past half century at least, people have overestimated future prices of natural resources. A study of prices of 15 natural resources 50 years ago (aluminum, bauxite, coal, copper, petroleum, gold, iron ore, lead, lime, magnesium, natural gas, nickel, silver, tin, and zinc) shows that *every one* was overvalued relative to their values at the present, so that people were *under*consuming and *over*conserving those resources, relative to their values at the present time. Will the future be different? (Data provided by C. Maurice and P. Gramms.)

Wealth

Physical *wealth* is the current stock of economic goods. The *market value* of that physical wealth is the sum of the market values of the individual goods. *Wealth* is sometimes used to refer to the market value of the goods and at other times refers to the collection of the goods. (Remember also the still greater total personal use value.)

Standard Income

If the physical stock of wealth is put to what the market predicts is its highest-valued use, in exactly one year hence it will, we shall suppose, be capable of increasing by 10 percent. During the year society could have consumed that increase in wealth and still have kept the initial amount of wealth at year's end. This market-forecasted sustainable rate of increase in wealth is the *standard income* available from the wealth of the economy. If wealth is $100 and the rate of interest in the economy is 10 percent, the foreseeable, permanently sustainable annual income is $10 per year. By definition, standard income, wealth, and the rate of interest are related as follows: $I = W \times r$, where I denotes standard income, W is the value measure of wealth, and r is the annual rate of interest. Any two of these define the third.

Saving

Saving is the nonconsumption of some of that standard income. By saving (that is, by not consuming) some of that income, wealth will accumulate. If initial wealth is $100, then with a 10 per-cent interest rate, the standard income is $10 per year. If you consume less than that (that is, save), you will end the year with more wealth than you started; if you consume more than your standard income (that is, dissave), you will end the year with less wealth.

Profits and Losses

The market value of wealth may increase by more than the accumulated savings. Any gain in wealth that is not accountable for by savings out of interest income is *profit*. If we assume no inflation and wealth grows in one year from $100 to $106 while the interest rate was 6 percent, the standard income is $6 per year on that wealth. The source of all the new wealth may have been saving. But if the market value increased by more than what savings accounted for (that is, to more than $106 if all the income had been saved, or to over $100 if all the $6 standard income had been consumed), the net gain is called *profit*: the change in wealth not accounted for by savings out of standard income. For example, if some stock of wealth quickly rose in value from $100 to $106 in two days, that could not have been explained by the accumulation of two days' income at 6 percent per year (which would in fact have amounted to 3.29 *cents* in two days to $100.0329). The profit over that two-day interval is $106 − $100.0329 = $5.9671 (almost $6). Had the wealth risen in two days to exactly $100.0329, profit would have been zero.

We commonly express this succinctly, but ambiguously, by saying that any rise in wealth that is "unexpected" by the market is a profit—and any fall is a loss. We call it "unexpected," for the market value would not initially have been so low (and then the wealth increase by so much) if that future value had been expected by market participants. Of course, it is possible that some person had confidence in his own foresight and bought the wealth for $100 and then got a profit when it rose more than the rate of interest could account for. The fact that he was able to get it for so low a price demonstrates that whatever made that wealth value grow was not fully or accurately expected by the market. We explain it by imperfect foresight.

Suppose an asset has a market value of $150 at the beginning of a year and $200 at the end. At an interest rate of 6 percent, the predicted value would have risen to $150(1.06) = $159 *if all* of the earned interest were saved, and the unpredicted rest of the increase in value, $200 − $159 = $41, would be profit. Alternatively, if *none* of the standard income had been saved, the value would have been expected to remain at $150, then all of the $50 increase in actual value would have been profit. In general, then, profit equals achieved value at end of a period minus initial value and minus saving.

If your wealth today is $100, and unexpected good news develops about future yields or demands for the services of the goods you own, market value of the goods will jump to, say, $120, all at that moment. Your unpredicted (by the market) $20 increase in wealth value is a capital gain, or *profit*. Thus, at a 10 percent interest rate, you now foresee that you can get $2 more standard income per year every year thereafter—$12 per year instead of $10. That profit can be *expressed* either as a wealth gain of $20 or an increase in the standard income flow of $2 per year. Both are different ways of expressing and measuring a *gain*.[7]

Capital Values, Property Rights, and Care of Wealth

Anticipations of future events affect present prices of goods (assets). In the stock exchange these revisions are made especially apparent, because the price of a share of common stock—a share of ownership in a business corporation—is the capitalized present worth of the anticipated future net earnings. If it is newly anticipated that higher taxes will be placed on cars, the capital value of General Motors stock will drop now, imposing a loss of wealth on the *current* owners of resources specialized to General Motors.

Both private-property rights and capital-goods markets (in which ownership of assets can be bought and sold) are essential foundations of the free-enterprise system; if either the rights or the markets are suppressed, the resulting system will lead to actions that appear to be "wasteful or shortsighted," especially in maintenance and investment. The houseowner will maintain and repair his house now even though the repairs may not give him better housing now. He will do so because the market price anticipates the lower subsequent maintenance expenditures that result

[7] More detailed exposition of the sources of profits and alternative means of expressing it are given below on pages 229–231.

from the present repairs. The value of the house is thereby maintained.

This suggests that a tenant would not maintain the premises as would an owner. However, the owner is not blind to this, and, therefore, he takes precautionary contractual countermeasures. The rental contract will provide incentives for careful use by the tenant.

Another illustration of how different types of property rights have different effects is provided by the modern business enterprise. The owner is influenced by all anticipated effects—present and future—that change the wealth of his enterprise. Foreseeable future developments or consequences of present acts will be capitalized into the owner's wealth, which is more specialized to this firm in its usefulness than are its current employees, who are therefore less motivated by long-run consequences to the enterprise. To make employees' actions more responsive to the total span of effects, two claims systems are sometimes added to the wage system. One is a *stock-option;* those employees who have the most influence on the long-run effects and wealth of the firm have rights to buy shares of stock at preassigned values. Because the later, long-run effects of their actions will be anticipated and capitalized in the present value of the shares of stock, those employees will pay more heed to their long-run effects than they would without stock-options. The second system, *profit sharing,* in which employees share the annual "earnings" of the firm, does less than the stock-option to emphasize the future effects of present behavior, because current "earnings" do not include capital-value changes of the firm. That is, because current accounting "earnings" do not include the *wealth* effects of the longer-run implications of present events, "earnings" fail to direct full attention to all the wealth-changing consequences of current employee behavior.

Human Capital

Capital includes people as well as nonhuman goods. However, we see and measure values of wealth of a *non*human type more easily and clearly, because rights to inanimate goods are bought and sold. A person normally sells only his current services as they are performed. Yet each person is wealth—a source of a future flow of services. Although there is not commonly a market sale of people by which that value can be observed, measured, or exchanged for other forms of wealth, there are some *indicators* of values of human wealth.

One measure is life insurance. The amount of insurance a person buys is correlated with his estimate of the value of the services he can sell over his remaining life.

If a person could literally sell claims to his future services now, he could immediately exchange his claims to his future earnings for other, present forms of wealth. As it is, he must keep a major portion of his wealth tied up in the form of his own potential labor services. This is a disadvantage that "free" people must live with. They usually must bear more of the risks of unforeseen developments that may change the value of their human wealth, whether they want to bear that risk or not—usually but not *always.* Occasionally, some people manage to sell rights to some of their future labor services. Classic examples are professional athletes who receive "bonuses" for signing with some ball team to play exclusively for that team.

W. Walton received $2 million for the exclusive right to his future basketball services. He sold the risk on his future services to the person who now "owns" them. Kareem Jabbar sold his future basketball services for over a million dollars. That he will also receive annual salaries does not affect the fact that he sold (capitalized) part of his future services and was able to diversify a portion of his (potential labor services) wealth into some other marketable kinds of wealth.

Star entertainers make exclusive service contracts for many years at specified minimum salaries. Although they cannot be forced to render specific performances, they cannot legally work for anyone else and can be sued for damages if they do. These contracts help the employee to exchange some of the present value of his future services for other wealth. Also, the employee can borrow *larger* amounts of money now with which to buy a house and other present goods. In that way, his human wealth is more exchangeable for current services or other goods.

Borrowing has advantages that its critics often fail to see. These advantages may best be explained in terms of one particular group of people who find it difficult, even today, to borrow against their human wealth—college students. If students could offer lenders ironclad rights to collect from their future earnings, many lenders would be more willing to make loans to students. After all, a young person now entering college represents lifetime wealth on the average of about $150,000–$200,000, which is probably greater than for those who do not go to college. If that seems large, compute the present value (at, say, 10 percent)

of an annual stream of wages (corrected for inflation) of about $20,000 for the next 40 years—which is almost surely an *under*estimation of the average for those who have this book as a text.

If at any time your earnings potential proves to be much higher than anyone expected, your wealth will jump—except that you won't see it recorded in some formal "human labor" market. Would you call that unexpected increase *profit*? You should. If you had formed a business firm to sell your services, the firm would have become more valuable. Its larger (your) future earnings would be expressed as a higher value of your firm. But almost no one goes through that formality; so we typically do not speak of profits to labor—only to owners of inanimate goods. And if you should unexpectedly learn that your current job will end in six months, your wealth at this very moment will have fallen, even though there is no market to register the fact. You will not wait until your wages fall before you readjust your consumption. You will adjust it immediately. Your behavior will reflect that loss of wealth, which is a reduction in your standard (permanent) income flow.

Since human capital has no market-revealed capital value, as it would if people were bought and sold, human wealth and income to labor are difficult to measure. Consequently, a proxy measure of income to labor is typically considered (for example, for income-tax purposes) to be the current rate of money earnings. The various connotations and interpretations of the word *income* are troublesome. Occasionally, *measured current income* is used in economics to refer to this *current-earnings* rate, while *permanent* or *equalized* income refers to some long-run or lifetime average of earnings, or standard income. Sometimes *current measured income* is called *transitory income*, because it may fluctuate temporarily around some long-run average trend—the so-called *permanent averaged income*. A change in *permanent* income would result from some unforeseen change that induced a revision of beliefs about that long-term average. Not every fluctuation in current earnings is unexpected, hence not every change in *current* income is to be interpreted as a change in *permanent* income or as affecting consumption.

Some Confusions about Interest Rates Clarified

If we are to be financial geniuses, we must avoid a common confusion about the relationship between inflation and the rate of interest. Though we will analyze inflation later, an initial understanding of its effects on interest rates can be indicated here. You lend $100 for a year, at an interest rate of 5 percent per year. The $5 interest to be paid you will vary in purchasing power as the general price level falls or rises. If the price level should increase during that year by 3 percent, this means that of the 5 percent interest ($5), about 3 percentage points (or $3 in real terms) is eroded away by the higher prices you must pay for goods and services. In real terms, you have realized only about 2 percent interest on your $100 loan.

If, however, you and most other people had *anticipated* that the price level would rise 3 percent in that year, you would not have been willing to lend at so low a nominal rate, and the borrower

would have been willing to pay a higher rate. As a result, the agreed-to nominal interest rate on the loan would have been higher, say, 8 percent per annum, allowing 3 percent for adjustment of the principal amount to be repaid and on which interest is to be paid, given the anticipated price level rise, and 5 percent for interest in real purchasing power terms.[8]

Roughly speaking, the *nominal* interest rate—indicating the number of dollars to be paid annually per dollar of principal value of the loan—reflects two considerations: (a) the interest rate that would exist if zero inflation were anticipated; and (b) the adjustment for the anticipated percentage rate of rise in the price level. As this is written, in 1976, the *monetary* nominal rate of interest being negotiated on first class (AAA) long-term industrial bonds is around 9 percent. (In the financial community, the best bonds are given the rating AAA—triple A—with less-secure bonds being rated AA, A, and B in descending order security.) It is widely believed (if we judge from financial newspapers and other evidence) that the public anticipates that inflation will continue at about 4 to 7 percent per annum; it has been occurring at those rates for the past several years. If currently negotiated *nominal* interest rates incorporate that anticipation, the promised real rate of interest is about 2–5 percent—not an un-

---

[8] For *one*-year loans, the relationship between the promised "real" interest rate r, and the promised nominal money interest rate, R, if the price level is *anticipated* to increase at the rate of p percent a year, is $(1 + R) = (1 + r)(1 + p) = 1 + r + p + rp$. If we consider rp to be negligibly small, then $R = r + p$. In Argentina, where inflation has exceeded 100 percent per year, interest rates of over 100 percent per year are common. In Chile, with inflation rates of over 500 percent a year (about 15 percent per month), interest rates have been about 15 percent per month or over 500 percent per year.

usual real rate, judging from the past century of experience. What the *realized* real rate will be depends on what the actual inflation rate happens to be. The confusion between the nominal rate (which *includes* anticipations of inflation) and the real rate is a source of political mischief and confused nonsense from newspaper and television commentators. Avoid it, if you can. Later we shall explain the factors affecting the stock of money and the anticipated rate of inflation—and thus the nominal interest rate.

14, 15
16, 17
18, 19
20, 21
22, 23
24

Summary

1. Capital goods render services now and in the future. The current prices of capital goods reflect the value of current services and the value of the future expected services.

2. Earlier availability is typically more valuable than later availability of services because of anticipated larger future output in general and because of ability to generate a net increase in future services by appropriate investment and use of current services.

3. The interest rate is: (a) a measure of the relationship between present amounts of a good and the amounts of future goods for which the present amount can be traded; (b) a measure of the maximal growth rate of wealth; (c) a measure of the price of earlier availability of a good relative to later availability; (d) the time premium paid for borrowed wealth; and (e) the percentage rate of standard income available from a stock of wealth.

4. The higher the rate of interest, the lower is the present price of any future service.

5. $P(1 + r)^t = A$ is one way to summarize the relationship among Present value, Rate of interest, Time, and future Amount.

6. Standard income is the predicted maximum constant rate of consumption feasible without reducing wealth. It equals the product from multiplying the stock of wealth by the rate of interest.

7. Savings are nonconsumption of standard income and an accumulation of wealth at the rate of savings.

8. Profits are defined as the change in wealth in excess of the savings accumulated out of standard income. Since wealth can be expressed in terms of an income flow, profits can also be measured as the *increase* in flow of standard income above that caused by savings.

9. Under private-property rights, there is present capitalization on foreseeable changes in the future value of services from some existing good; that capitalization will take the form of a revised current price of the good and will impose those wealth changes on the owner of the good at the time the future consequences of any act are foreseen, rather than later when they occur. By far, the major portion of marketable services comes from human capital—people who can render present and future services. Approximately 80–90 percent of our wealth is human capital; the remainder is nonhuman capital.

10. The nominal rate of interest would normally be positive and between 3–7 percent per year on secure, almost-sure capital; but with expectations of inflation the nominal interest rate usually includes a premium to allow for the expected rate of inflation or depreciation

of the money in which debts will later be repaid.

Questions

1. You invest $350 today. At the end of one year you will get back $385. What is the implied, or effective, rate of interest?

2. To how much will $250 grow in three years at 7 percent compounded annually? How long will it take to double? (Use the rule of 72).

3. At the end of a year you will get $220. At 10 percent interest rate, what present amount will grow to that amount? In other words, what is the present value of $220 deferred one year, at 10 percent?

*4. In what sense is interest the price of money? In what sense is it not the price of money?

5. What is the present value of $2500 due in five years at 4 percent?

6. What is the present value of $2500 due in 10 years at 4 percent per year?

7. What present amount is equivalent to $1000 paid at the end of each of the next three years, at 6 percent interest? In more useful terms, "What is the present value of a $1000 three year annuity, at 6 percent interest?"

8. You borrow $1000 today and agree to pay the loan in five annual equal installments at 6 percent interest rate. Using Table 7–3, determine the amount of each payment, the first payment to be due in one year.

9. If you can borrow $1000 from college at a zero interest rate for six years, what is the present value of the "gift" to you, at the market rate of interest of 5 percent? (Hint: Each year you can earn $50 interest by investing now at 5 percent. What is the present value of that six-year annuity of $50?) Which would you rather have—an outright gift of $250 or that loan?

10. You buy a house by borrowing the full price of the house, $20,000. Your annual installments in repaying the loan are $1754 for twenty years at 6 percent. (Do you agree?) Check with Table 7–3.

a. At the end of the first year, how much of the house's value is yours—what is your equity? (Hint: On $20,000, the interest for the first year at 6 percent is $1200 but you paid $1754 at the end of the first year.)

b. At the end of the second year, what is your equity?

c. At the end of twenty years, assuming the house is still worth $20,000, what is your equity?

11. Two refrigerators are available for purchase. One costs more to buy but less to operate.

Purchase Price		Annual Operating Cost in Each of 10 Years
A	$400	$100
B	$340	$120

Which is the cheaper source of refrigeration over a 10-year period?

*12. If the value of your buildings or common stock should fall, how can you tell whether there has been a rise in the rate of interest or a fall in anticipated future net receipts? (Hint: Look at the bond market. How will this help give an answer?)

*13. Which do you think will have a bigger influence in revising your annual *consumption* rate—an unexpected gift of $1000 or an unexpected salary increase of $50 per month? (Hint: What is the present value of each at, say, 6 percent per year?) Why did the question say *"unexpected"* gift and salary increase?

14. You own a building worth $10,000. You receive word that the value of your building has fallen to $5000. One possibility is that the interest rate has risen to twice its former level. A second possibility is that the building has been damaged by a fire. In either event your wealth is now $5000. Do you care which factor caused a decrease in your wealth? Why?

15. Mr. A has an income of $10,000 per year. At Christmas his uncle unexpectedly gives him $5000 in cash.

a. What is his income during that year?

b. Is the $5000 gift a part of his income?

c. How much is his annual rate of income increased as a result of the gift of $5000 (at interest rates of 10 percent)?

16. Estimate the present value of your future earnings. Project your earnings until age 65. Then obtain the present value of that projection, using a 10 percent rate of interest. Can you promise your fiancée that you are now worth over $200,000?

17. Your wealth today is $1000. At 10 percent interest rate, what is your standard income?

18. If your income from nonbusiness wealth is $500 a year, what is your nonbusiness wealth, at a 10 percent interest rate?

19. If you consume all of your income for two years, what will be your wealth at the end of two years, if it is $1000 now with 5 percent interest?

20. If you announce today that you intend to save all your income for the next year, what will happen to the value of your wealth now? In one year?

21. You contemplate purchase of a house in a new suburban development. You may buy the house for $40,000, but title to the land will remain with the developer and you must pay $1000 per year for land rent, and at the end of 50 years the developer will get the house. You estimate the land is worth $15,000, and that in 50 years the house will be worth $40,000. Or you may purchase the *land* and the house now for $65,000. At 6 percent interest, which is cheaper?

22. "The employees of the South Bend Lathe Co. were able to buy the entire common stock (and hence ownership) of the company for $10 million in cash. The employees used a federal government plan known as Employee Stock Ownership Plan, or ESOP, whereby the ESOP employee group was able to borrow the full purchase price of $10 million, of which $5 million was lent by the U.S. government to the ESOP for 25 years at 3 percent annual interest, and the other $5 million was obtained from Indiana banks at 4 percentage points above the prime rate (then at about 9 percent)." In effect the $5 million loan from the federal taxpayers at 3 percent for 35 years was a gift of how much in present value terms? (Use 10 percent as the relevant cost of interest, even though the employees must pay 4 percent above the prime rate which ranges around 7–8 percent in 1976.)

*23. Do you know of any products that have become more expensive over the past several decades or centuries because of the exhaustion of cheaper ores or resources from which that product is obtained? (One answer is "oysters.") Is it true for copper, iron, oil, tin, diamonds, coal?

24. A retired person has $100,000 to invest in stocks and expects to get an income of about $10,000 a year (since interest rates are 10 percent). If you advise him to buy stocks that pay out no earnings as dividends, he complains he will have no income. How would you explain to him that he does have an income of 10 percent?

8

Production, Specialization, and Prices

Though at any instant the amount of goods is virtually fixed, in time it changes by production, consumption, or decay. The term *market period* denotes any interval in which the current amount available is fixed and not responsive to a price change. An interval long enough for a price change to significantly alter the amount supplied (with existing productive equipment) is usually called a *short-run period*. A *long-run period* usually refers to the interval distant enough in the future for changes in the stock of productive equipment. We now leave the market period and investigate production.

People can change their stock of goods in purposeful ways. In a word, they are productive and resourceful. We can produce more desirable goods by changing their form or even their location. We can produce more of this at the cost of less of that. Also, man invents better ways of producing goods and invents new goods. Though we lack well-established propositions about the determinants of inventive resourcefulness, for production of more of this good rather than some other good, some regularities are known as *laws of production*.

What determines the amounts of goods to be produced, how they are produced, and who produces them? To mention only a few possibilities: A dictator could direct his subjects; or people could work cooperatively in communal property systems, directed by custom or inherited position; or they could act within a capitalist system. In a capitalist economy, owners of resources have entitlements to decide how their goods and services shall be used; these entitlements can be exchanged with those of other people. If access to markets is reserved to favored groups or re-stricted to existing members of an industry who regulate themselves or who can decide on admission of new suppliers, the system is a *cartel-mercantilist* system. A few examples are the medical, legal, milk, transportation, and public-utilities industries. Socialism is a system in which decisions about uses of resources are determined by government or political processes. A few examples, in our society, are the postal system, television, water and power in many communities, education, and roads. Every society is a varying mixture of free enterprise, cartel-mercantilism, and socialism. The mix of systems is determined, in part, by attitudes toward the question of who should bear risks; by the degree of tolerance for idiosyncratic individual behavior; and by the ability of competing groups to acquire or influence government power.

Certain concepts are essential to the analysis of any and all systems or mixtures of them: for example, the concepts of *demand, costs, marginal costs, efficiency,* and *specialization*. With these fundamental concepts, we can understand how production is controlled and coordinated in a private-property, free-enterprise economy. That system will be explained because it is the dominant system in the United States. Also, economic analysis of that and the cartel-mercantilist systems has been more fully formulated and verified, while economic analysis of socialism, unfortunately, is still tentative and untested.

The variety of institutions through which economic activity is conducted—such as corporations, labor unions, credit buying, suburban shopping centers, trading stamps, discount houses, franchises, factories, and advertising—may obscure the basic principles that underlie the organization of production, but they do not in fact upset them. So, in this and the next chapters, do not think that the simplicity of our presentation means the principles are not applicable to the real world. They are. As with all theory and analysis, the ability to simplify things to their essentials aids understanding how economic activity is planned, ordered, and coordinated without conscious organization and direction by a central planner.

Production and Exchange

In the broadest sense, production is the act of improving one's situation. In that sense, even the *exchange* of existing goods is productive, as we have seen. Production also can occur when the attributes of resources—including their time of availability, place, or form—are changed. Transporting water from a well into a house is productive; carrying coal from the mine to the furnace is productive; tilling the soil, planting seeds, or caring for the crop is productive; so is harvesting, cleaning, grading, transporting, preserving, and distributing the crop to retail stores; so is advertising, displaying, wrapping, and making delivery to the consumer's home, and so are a housewife's many activities.

Our first task is to explain the increase in productivity when people appropriately specialize in their productive activity. Adam Smith, in his famous *An Inquiry Into the Nature and Causes of the Wealth of Nations* (published in 1776), called this *division of labor*.

Costs: Value of Best Forsaken Alternative Opportunity

Inherent in any choice, including choice of productive activities, is the concept of *costs*. In contemplating act *X,* we weigh it against the highest-valued of the possibilities that could *otherwise* have been pursued. To rephrase our oft-repeated definition of cost for this context: The highest-valued, forsaken alternative opportunity *is* the cost of act *X.* An *efficient* system of controlling production means that *X* will be performed if, and only if, its value exceeds the best alternative value—by definition, the cost of *X.* For example, a farmer could produce wheat *or* beans *or* alfalfa, or go hunting, *etc.* A business enterprise may produce radios; otherwise, resources could be released from making radios (including those resources that were released from making equipment that is used to make radios) and diverted to production of other goods. *Every* chosen act entails a cost—the best, or most highly valued, of the alternatives (outputs or activities) thereby forsaken. As long as there is an option there is, by definition, a cost!

We caution that "labor, toil, trouble, and pain" are not what is meant by costs. "Bads" associated with an action are not its costs; they are part of the act or its consequences. For example, a swimming pool yields the pleasure of swimming and the undesirable consequences of neighborhood children splashing the yard. These undesirable splashes are the "bads," but not part of the *costs.* The desirable and undesirable both are taken into account in the *valuation* of a pool. The *value* of any act reflects not only such things in

the act as material goods, but also cultural, social, political, and personal amenities—that is,
all the desirable *and undesirable* features. Any
choice among acts means, by definition, that *cost*
will necessarily be incurred. An opportunity will
necessarily be forsaken—the highest-valued *forsaken option,* which is comprised of "goods and
bads."

Many people carelessly talk as if costs are only
sacrifices of material things normally bought and
sold in the market. However, the concept of cost
includes the entire set of elements in the best
of the forsaken options. In more rigorous terms,
the cost of any act includes all the aspects of
the best forsaken option *or state of the world*
that could otherwise have been realized. To say
the cost of act *X* is $10 means that to perform act
X (with whatever benefits it brings) requires forsaking some other desirable aspects of the "state
of the world," whether in terms of material goods
or services, *or* in leisure, environmental circumstances (views, fresh air, cleanliness), cultural
qualities (crime rates, divorce, immorality) or
features of the state of the world to which anyone
attaches value—that are worth the equivalent
of what one could get for $10. The cost is not
the $10 of *money;* it includes *all* the forsaken
qualities, features, or material goods. It is a mistake to think of costs as only the material goods
that are typically bought in the market.

If *not all* costs are imposed on the person au-
thorizing or initiating an activity, such as the production of *X,* the costs that *he bears* or is induced to heed are incomplete. But the concept
of costs as used in economic analysis is not incomplete. It is the social failure to impose all the
components of cost on the decision-maker that
produces the consequences deemed distressing
and objectionable. That failure is what contributes to "excessive" pollution and "shortsighted"
activity. For the moment, however, we assume
that full cost is borne by the actor. Later we shall
inquire into the conditions permitting, and those
preventing, the full cost to be perceived, borne,
and heeded by the actor.

Once the meaning of costs (including what they
are not) is understood, it logically follows that
minimizing the *cost* of any given activity *maximizes* the value of the other output one can have
along with this activity.

Marginal Costs

The principles of coordinating production processes, under any economic system, can be most
easily made familiar by a simple, but valid, toy
economy example. We first meet Mr. A, whose
distinguishing attribute feature for us is not sex,
color, age, religion, height, weight, marital status,
eye color, blood type, political affiliation, or personality, but his *production* ability. Table 8–1
shows his productive ability. His set of resources
could produce, at most, 10 *X* daily, or if all of it
were devoted to production of something else he
could produce daily other services and goods
worth $14.50. Or he can also produce some of
both. For example, if he produces 1 *X* daily, he
would sacrifice the production of $1 worth of
other goods, which means, in other words, his
cost of producing 1 *X* daily is $1. That $1 worth of
other "goods" is not necessarily only physical
goods; it could be the value of leisure or some
other activity. If he produces 2 *X* daily, the value
of the sacrificed alternative output would be
$2.10, which is to say the cost of 2 *X* daily is

Table 8–1. Daily Potential Outputs and Costs of Producer A

Output of X	Total Cost	Marginal Cost	Average Cost	Value of Other Concurrent Output
0	0	0	0	$14.50
1	$1.00	$1.00	$1.00	13.50
2	2.10	1.10	1.05	12.40
3	3.30	1.20	1.10	11.20
4	4.60	1.30	1.15	9.90
5	6.00	1.40	1.20	8.50
6	7.50	1.50	1.25	7.00
7	9.10	1.60	1.30	5.40
8	10.80	1.70	1.35	3.70
9	12.60	1.80	1.40	1.90
10	14.50	1.90	1.45	0

$2.10. So the $1 total cost of 1 X increases by $1.10 to $2.10 for 2 X daily. If 2 X are produced daily rather than only 1 X, the $1.10 increase in total cost is called the *marginal cost* at 2 X. Marginal cost is the increase in *total* cost for increasing production by one unit. The size of that increase depends upon what the rate of output was before the one unit increase. For an increase from 5 X to 6 X the total costs increase from $6 to $7.50, so the marginal cost at 6 (or of the sixth, as it is sometimes called) is $1.50. This concept of marginal cost is extremely important. Learn it well.

Figures 8–1 and 8–2 show Mr. A's productive possibilities and his marginal costs. Note that marginal costs at 1 X and 2 X add up to the total costs at 2 X. And the first three marginal costs at 1, 2, and 3 add up to the total cost at 3 X (which should be obvious, if you understand the meaning of marginal costs).

Figure 8–2 portrays producer A's marginal costs by the bars over the quantities 1, 2, 3, etc. The increasing heights depict higher marginal costs at larger outputs. At 10 units of X the total cost would be $1.90 *more* than at 9 X daily: that is, the marginal cost at 10 is $1.90. The total area of all those marginal-cost bars between zero and any output of X represents *total* costs for that rate of output. For example, the *total* cost of producing 6 X is measured by the sum of all the marginal cost bars up to and including 6 X, representing a total cost of $7.50 (the value of other potential goods and services forsaken). The *marginal* cost at 6 X is $1.50, which is how much more it costs to produce 6 X daily rather than 5 X.

The *average* cost at six units of X is $7.50/6 X = $1.25 per X; average costs are indicated by the dotted line in Figure 8–2. (The mathematical relationship among average, total, and marginal costs is suggested by an analogy to successive

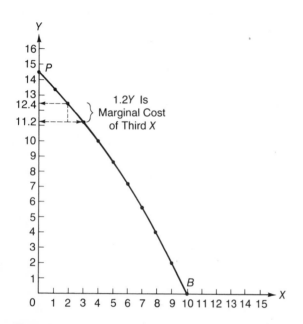

Figure 8–1. Total Production Possibility of Producer A for Production of X and Y

For any specified output of X, the height of the line measures the maximum output of Y feasible. The larger the output of X, the smaller the total output of Y. And the steepening slope at larger X shows that greater and greater sacrifices of Y are required for each extra unit of X produced. That is, the marginal cost of X increases at larger outputs of X.

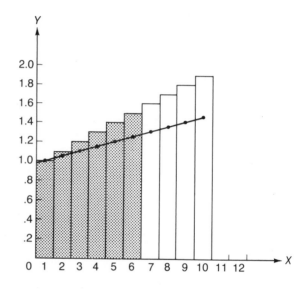

Figure 8–2. A's Marginal and Average Costs of Producing X

Bars show marginal costs and the connected dots show the average cost at each output, based on data in Table 8–1. Accumulated areas of bars to any output of X represent the output of other goods forsaken to produce that amount of X. A major purpose of this figure is to emphasize the difference between the concepts of marginal and average costs.

test scores during a semester. Your total score accumulated to any test is the sum of the successive individual test scores. If the successive scores for each test increased, as our marginal costs do, your average score per test would also be increasing. The current average of all of the tests taken would be less than the score on your most recent test, because of your good fortune in having successively higher test scores (or your bad fortune in having started so low).

A second producer, Mr. B, in our society (two producers are enough for present purposes) has productive capabilities that are summarized in Table 8–2 and Figures 8–3 and 8–4. As with A, his total costs increase with output, as do his marginal costs. The productive capability of B differs from A in two significant respects: (1) B's productive resources will yield at most only 8 X; or, if no X are produced, $9.60 worth of some other output can be produced. Producer B is not totally (or "absolutely") as productive as A in producing X or anything else. (2) B's marginal-cost schedule differs from A's. In particular, his marginal costs

Table 8–2. Daily Potential Outputs and Costs of Producer B

Output of X	Total Cost	Marginal Cost	Average Cost	Value of Other Concurrent Output
0	0	0	0	$9.60
1	$ .50	$ .50	$ .50	9.10
2	1.20	.70	.60	8.40
3	2.10	.90	.70	7.50
4	3.20	1.10	.80	6.40
5	4.50	1.30	.90	5.10
6	6.00	1.50	1.00	3.60
7	7.70	1.70	1.10	1.90
8	9.60	1.90	1.20	0

are lower at low outputs but grow more rapidly than do A's. This difference in the *marginal* cost schedules is important, even if it is often ignored in laymen's analysis of economic events. Of the two differences—the total output possibility of each good, and the difference in the patterns of marginal costs—the former tells who can be richer, but the latter indicates who will produce how much of what. Marginal, not average, costs are a key to coordinating production among producers to achieve efficient production. To that we now turn.

1, 2 3, 4 5

Production Efficiency by Marginal-Cost Equality

Coordination by Authority

Assume for the moment that a dictator controls these two producers and miraculously knows all the data in our tables. If this dictatorial central planner wanted 4 X produced daily, how much would he order to be made by A and how much by B? If the dictator knew the cost data for each producer and could induce A and B to do as he says, he would assign to A a production quota of 1 X daily and to B a quota of 3 X; the cost would be $3.10 ($1 by A plus $2.10 by B). He would not assign equal quotas (of 2 X each) because that would be more costly—$3.30 ($2.10 by A plus $1.20 by B)—and would incur a sacrifice of almost 7 percent of otherwise available goods and services. (We ignore the feelings of A and B by assuming they don't care what they are asked to produce.)

How about 6 X? B should produce 4 X and A should produce 2 X. At these respective rates each would be producing at the same marginal cost. If B produced all 6 X, the marginal cost of his fifth and sixth would have exceeded the costs saved when A does not produce his first and second. The total cost would be $6 worth of Y. So the dictator who wants 6 X will assign B to produce 4 X and A to produce 2 X, for a total cost

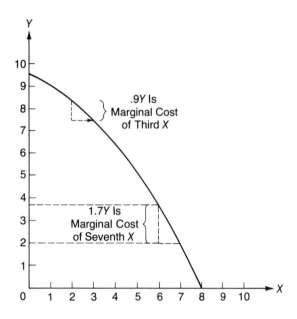

Figure 8–3. Total Production Possibility of B

Taken from data in Table 8–2. For any specified amount of X (on horizontal axis) the curve shows the maximum of Y achievable (on vertical axis). The more of X that is produced, the less of Y that can be produced.

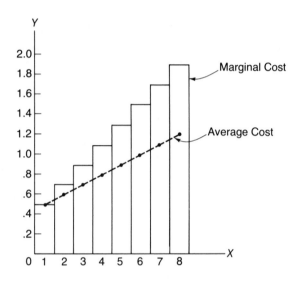

Figure 8–4. B's Marginal and Average Costs of Producing X

Bars show marginal costs and dots in each bar show average cost at that output, for data from Table 8–2. Note that the accumulated areas of the bars to any output represent total cost—the total alternative output sacrificed. A major principle is the increasing marginal cost at larger output of X.

of only $5.30 ($3.20 for B and $2.10 for A). If 7 X were desired, B should produce four and A three, for that would be cheaper (less of Y would be sacrificed) than any other possible assignment. (Try to get seven units in a cheaper way; you can't.) Table 8–3 gives the totals.

The general rule is simple: To minimize the costs of any specified amount of X, produce it with the lowest marginal costs. That is, have each produce an amount of X at which his marginal cost does not exceed that of any other producer of X with which the desired total is achieved. In brief, producers should produce amounts that

equate their marginal costs (or comes as near as possible to equating them). That will result in no waste—that is, in minimum cost.

Diagrammatic Analysis

The principle of minimizing costs by equating marginal costs is illustrated by a diagram with two producers' *smoothed*, generalized marginal-cost curves. (Smooth lines permit graphic clarity.) The curves in Figure 8–5 labeled marginal costs for A and for B portray smoothed marginal costs. As shown in the diagram, when each produces equal amounts, B has a lower marginal cost at

Table 8–3. Total Efficient Outputs of Y and X by Producers A and B

X	Y	Y's Produced by A and B	Marginal Cost of X
0	24.10	= 14.50 + 9.60	0
1	23.60	= 14.50 + 9.10	.50
2	22.90	= 14.50 + 8.40	.70
3	22.00	= 14.50 + 7.50	.90
4	21.00	= 13.50 + 7.50	1.00
5	19.90	= 12.40 + 7.50	1.10
6	18.80	= 12.40 + 6.40	1.10
7	17.60	= 11.20 + 6.40	1.20
8	16.30	= 11.20 + 5.10	1.30
9	15.00	= 9.90 + 5.10	1.30
10	13.60	= 8.50 + 5.10	1.40
11	11.10	= 8.50 + 3.60	1.50
12	10.60	= 7.00 + 3.60	1.50
13	9.00	= 5.40 + 3.60	1.60
14	7.30	= 3.70 + 3.60	1.70
15	5.60	= 3.70 + 1.90	1.70
16	3.80	= 1.90 + 1.90	1.80
17	1.90	= 1.90 + 0	1.90
18	0.00	= 0 + 0	0

his output than does A. Therefore, if B expanded and A contracted, B's incurred marginal cost would be less than the marginal cost avoided by A, as A reduces his output by a matching amount. The *total* social output of X would be the same, but the cost is lower (that is, more of other goods are available). Society is better off. The shaded area under the marginal cost curve for B represents his increase in cost for his expansion of output while the *larger* shaded area for A shows the larger saving in cost when A reduces his output by a matching amount. If any producers of X are at such outputs that their marginal costs are not equal, an expansion by one and a reduction by the other will reduce the total cost for that same total output. When each producer's outputs are such as to equate the marginal costs among producers (though the output rates of A and B are not the same) and the total output is the desired amount, total cost is minimized.

With this kind of diagram, any central planner or dictator who knows every possible producer's marginal-cost curves could assign production quotas to each producer to get the desired total amount at lowest cost (that is, efficient assignment) by assigning output quotas at which marginal costs are equated. He would first add the marginal cost curves horizontally, as illustrated in Figure 8–6. The result, the new extreme right-hand curve, is called the *industry supply* curve. It is the *sums* of the horizontal distances of all the individual marginal cost curves at *common* (equated) marginal costs. The dictator then notes the height of the supply schedule at the total desired amount of X on the horizontal scale. That is the common marginal cost, indicating the output that each should produce to give that total. For example, in Figure 8–6, for a total of X_T units, the amounts that A and B should each produce are indicated where the horizontal line at that marginal-cost height on the supply schedule above X_T intersects the two individual marginal-cost curves. That indicates X_a by A and X_b by B. Any other quotas totalling X_T would be more costly because one producer would have a higher marginal cost than the other. The difference between the higher and the lower marginal costs is a source of saving if the producers would revise their individual output rates to equate marginal costs.

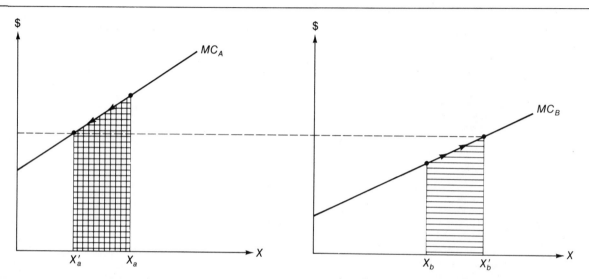

Figure 8–5. Gains by Producing at Equal Marginal Costs

A and B produce the same amount of X ($X_a = X_b$). Marginal cost for X_a is greater than marginal cost for X_b. If A reduces output to X_a' as much as B expands to X_b', the total costs over both producers will be reduced, as can be seen from the fact that extra cost to B (area occupied by horizontal lines) is less than savings of costs by A (area occupied by cross-hatching) over quantity $X_a - X_a'$. Total amount of X is the same as before. Total costs of that output are minimized because marginal costs to A are the same as for B.

The principle of achieving minimum costs of production by having each producer produce at that output at which his marginal costs are equal to that of every other producer is simply a mathematical proposition that holds for all situations in which the total output and total cost is simply the sum of the output and cost of each producing source. The significant economic problem is finding a cheap and effective means of directing the several producers to produce at the appropriate rates. In the ensuing text some alternative means are explored.

Production Inefficiency by Authority?

In 1974 the U.S. national energy board ordered each oil refinery to reduce production of gasoline and to produce more heating fuel. (Crude oil, remember, can be refined into heating oil and gasoline in varying proportions.) You can interpret heating oil as *X*, and gasoline as *Y*, and A and B as two different refiners. The data in Tables 8–1 and 8–2 illustrate the consequences. To simplify the arithmetic, assume that a 50 percent reduction is required. If A and B cut back by 50 percent from a total of 6 *X* to 1 *X* by A, and 2 *X* by B, they produce a total of 3 *X* at a cost of $2.20 (= $1.00 by A plus $1.20 by B). A little calculation and extrapolation will indicate that if B produced 3 *X* and A no *X*, the cost would be only $1.20, a social saving of $1 over the equal-proportion cutback rule.

Why did the energy board use an inefficient principle? One possible reason is ignorance on

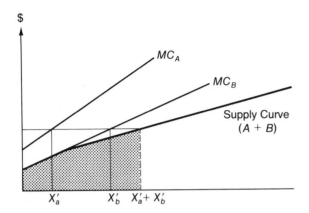

Figure 8–6. Outputs at Equal Marginal Costs Aggregate to Supply Schedule

Summing outputs of each producer at equal marginal costs over all producers gives the efficient aggregate supply schedule. If each producer is at an output with different marginal cost, the total is not being produced at lowest aggregate cost.

the part of the energy board. But ignorance of what? Not of the above principles, but of each refiner's cost conditions. Not all refineries have equal marginal-cost structures for fuel oil and gasoline. The energy directors' answer might have been, "We did not know the cost or production-possibility data for *each* refinery. Therefore, the government should require oil companies to report pertinent data so that production of fuel oil and gasoline could be efficiently determined." "Not so," the refinery owners could reply. "One alternative to data-collection or central planning is quicker and, in addition, determines the *total* amount of heating oil and gasoline that consumers want in the light of relative values and costs of gasoline and fuel oil." That method, which is

not centrally coordinated, is the market-exchange, price-directed system. Adam Smith first identified and aptly dubbed it the "invisible hand." It would better have been called the "invisible planners."

**Production Efficiency by
Decentralized Coordination**

Let producers A and B revolt successfully and depose the dictator. After the revolt, at first, everyone lives independently, self-sufficiently, and with private-property rights in his productive resources. What then guides individual productive activity? The self-interest of each producer. Everyone produces as much of each good, say good X, as is worth producing for *his own* consumption. Everyone is self-sufficient. The situation is graphed in Figure 8–7, showing the costs of producing X by person A and his demand for that good. He produces up to where his marginal personal value for an X falls to his (rising) marginal cost of producing X. To produce more X would cost him more than the extra units are worth to him. He self-sufficiently produces what he consumes. Similarly, person B produces an output where his demand and marginal-cost lines intersect. In this self-sufficient world there is no coordination problem.

The producers would each stay at that output if they could not communicate and exchange with each other in a market. But if they can, they will discover B has an amount of X such that he has a higher *marginal* personal value on X than does A. This would be revealed to A by the fact that B is willing to offer A greater payment to buy some X than an X is worth to A. The best way to show this graphically is to combine the two persons'

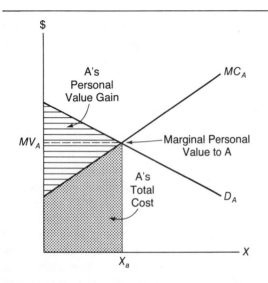

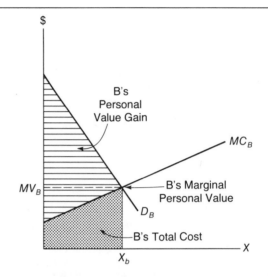

Figure 8–7. Independent, Self-Sufficient Equilibriums

Person A self-sufficiently produces X_A. His total personal value of X_A is the area under his demand curve and exceeds his costs (the area under the marginal-cost curve). The net total personal value to him of X_A is the horizontally shaded area. His personal marginal value at X_A is MV_A. Person B, also self-sufficiently produces quantity X_B and gets the net total personal value shown by the horizontally shaded area. His personal marginal value at X_B is MV_B.

demands into an aggregate-demand curve and also combine their marginal cost curves into an aggregate- (or market-) supply curve, as in Figure 8–8. The aggregate-, or market-demand and -supply curves are horizontal summations of the individual demand curves and the individual marginal-cost curves (which are in effect their supply curves). The total amount demanded and supplied would be equated by a price at the intersection of those two aggregate curves. At that price B would be induced to produce more X than he consumes—selling some to A—and A would produce less X than he consumes—buying the difference from B. (A pays with the other goods he produces.)

Their output decisions are coordinated to achieve the intersection output by the self-motivated incentive, guided by the market price. B will get profits by producing some more X, which he can sell to A at a price greater than their marginal cost to B. Similarly, A has the incentive

to reduce production of X and shift to other goods with which to purchase the X from B at a price lower than his marginal costs of making those X. Figure 8–8 shows the situation explicitly for good X. Figure 8–9 enlarges and isolates the situations for party A and for party B. This market system can coordinate production so as to avoid waste. When the output of each person equates his marginal cost with everyone else's, no other production assignments for that total amount of X will be as efficient, that is, get as much of other goods. Total costs of producing any amount of X

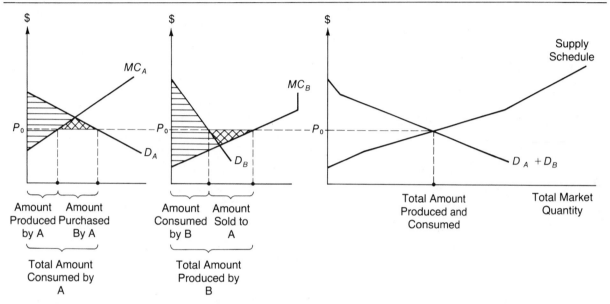

Figure 8–8. Gains from Specialization and Exchange with Interdependence

Trading between A and B as in a market results in larger output of X and other goods and gains to A and B over their self-sufficient, independent status. The extreme right-hand panel is Aggregated Demand and Aggregated Supply (marginal costs). Price is P_o, at which A buys all his consumption of X and B produces more X than when self-sufficient and sells some to A.

The gain to A is the ability to buy more at a lower price and to save production costs by purchasing at a lower price some that was formerly produced by himself at a higher marginal cost. Similarly, the gain to B is comprised of the ability to sell more at a price greater than his costs of production as well as selling some at a price greater than those units of the good are worth to him in personal consumption.

A produces less of X and more of other things, while B produces more of X and less of other things for a larger total social output with larger total personal values. For person B, the gain in the cross-hatched area is comprised of two types: The left part is gain from selling some to A at a price greater than its value to B, and the right part is gain from transferring resources to producing more units of X, which are sold to A at a price greater than cost to B, which cost is simply the (lower) value of other output forsaken.

The gains to all parties from using the market rather than being self-sufficient are the cross-hatched areas. Note that X is now produced at equal marginal costs by both A and B, which is also equal to the market price. Result is efficiency in production. No other "assignment" of production quotas to A and B would be efficient for this particular total output of X.

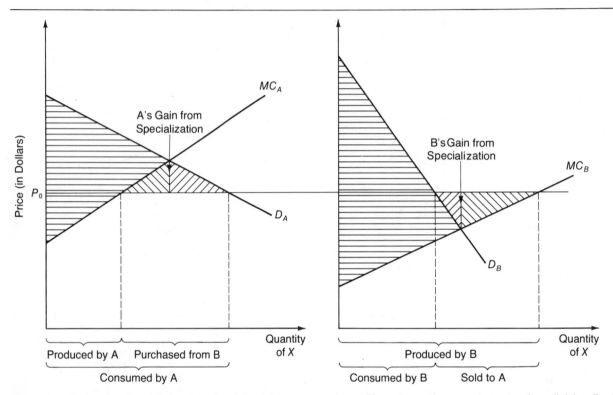

Figure 8–9. Further Details of Gains from Specialized Production and Exchange

This enlargement of the left-hand and center graphs in Figure 8–8 shows two sources of gains to A and B. A gains by being able to buy more at a price that is below the value of the extra amounts purchased and consumed; he also gains by being able to reduce his output of X and produce other goods while purchasing the displaced X at a price lower than his own marginal costs of producing that amount had

been. These two gains are shown as the adjoining lined triangles.

B gains from two sources. The increased output of X is sold at a price that exceeds his marginal costs of production, and some of X that B formerly consumed is sold at a price that exceeds its personal value to B when consumed by him. These two areas, for A and B respectively, are shown as adjoining lined triangles.

are minimized if all producers do so at equal marginal costs. (This situation was first achieved in our earlier example, under the dictator.) Equating the marginal cost of producing X among various producers is achieved in the market system if each producer looks at a common market price and adjusts his output of X to bring his marginal cost to equality with that common, perceived price—in his own pursuit of private profits.

The departure from self-sufficiency lowers the cost of living to both parties in our example and permits *greater social value of output* than with self-sufficient, independent producers. Thus do market prices serve as both coordinating guides and incentives to producers in affecting what and how much they produce—as well as the amount they demand. At the equilibrium free-market price the amounts produced equal the amounts demanded—without a central all-knowing authority. Individual self-interest, the incentive to achieve greater gains or profits and lower costs of what one buys, is what achieves this situation.[1] The necessary institutional features for such a system of control and coordination are an accessible *marketplace* in which *prices* of *exchangeable* goods can be *revealed,* with *private-property* entitlements in productive resources.

You can be excused if all this seems a tediously involved way to say that whoever can pro-

duce one good at lower cost should do so and sell some to other parties in exchange for whatever they can produce at lower cost. The reason we did not put it that way is that the meaning of *lower cost* is usually misunderstood. Some people think it means lower *average* cost—and that leads to error. To see why, reexamine the data in Table 8–1 and 8–2; you will find that although B's average cost at 5 X (90 cents) is less than A's ($1.00) average cost at 1 X (the efficient assignments for 6 X), it would not be efficient (that is, it would increase *total* costs) if B increased his output of X and A reduced his. Always precede the word *cost* with either *total, average,* or *marginal* if you want to increase your chances of correct economic analysis.

6, 7

8

Some Erroneous Meanings and Measures of Costs

If the preceding exposition were perfect and hence thoroughly understood, the following comments would be unnecessary. See if they are.

1. *Technological Ratios or Inputs per Output.* The person who specialized in producing X was not the person who could produce the most X. B, who specialized in X, could produce only 8 X whereas A could produce 10 X daily. It might be thought that since A could produce an X in less time than could B, A must be the lower-cost producer of X. Not so. Cost is *not* time used up. No one *saves* time; he merely uses it for something else. The alternative *use* of that time—not the time itself—is the cost. This error—measuring costs by time used—occurs because people for-

---

[1] Had Adam Smith lived today, he might have called this the "Don't-do-it-yourself" principle. Smith's book, published in 1776, did not contain a logically correct exposition; instead it contained a masterfully persuasive statement of the results of specialization. Robert Torrens, some 40 years after the idea had been "sold," demonstrated its logical validity. Possibly, had Smith tried to give a logically airtight demonstration, instead of a suggestive plausible interpretation, he would never have made his "point" popular.

get the meaning of *cost*. The error is so widespread that it pays to expose it further. The *value* of the labor time used (and that does differ among people according to the value of what they would otherwise have produced in the time involved) is pertinent—not the amount of time. One person whose time is worth $10 an hour, and who can produce 10 units of *X* in an hour, has a marginal cost of $1 for each extra unit of *X* produced. Another "cheap, low-wage" worker whose hourly services are worth only $2 an hour elsewhere and who can produce only 1 *X* in an hour, incurs a marginal (and average) cost of $2 for an *X*. In this case the person producing the most in an hour happens to also be the lower-marginal-cost producer. But suppose the person who produced 10 *X* in an hour could produce $50 worth of other goods in that hour; now his cost of an *X* is higher, $5, though the time used is the same! The relative costs of our two producers now are reversed. So beware of measuring costs simply by hours of time: The *forsaken* output value is critical, and that is measured by multiplying the value of the alternative use per minute by the number of minutes of time used. Thus, for example, when people say that cheap Asiatic labor produces at less cost than American labor because the Asiatics earn very low wages per hour, you should remember to ask, "What is the cost (value) of the labor time used to produce goods?" This cost is given by (hours of labor to produce a unit) $\times$ (value of an hour of labor). The latter component alone is insufficient.

The same applies to any productive inputs like kilowatt hours per unit of heat, or pounds of steel per car, or hours of labor per house, or pounds of cotton produced per acre. Those so-called technological-efficiency ratios *completely* ignore the value of possible alternative outputs of that input. Yet that error of comparing technological ratios—physical inputs per unit of output—is very common. For example, during the past few years many people have been computing technological energy ratios, such as number of kilowatts per hour of light, decibels per watt in audio amplifiers, or gasoline per mile (usually reversed as miles per gallon). These are often called *technological* efficiencies. People who look at these ratios urge us to lower them, that is, to improve the technological efficiencies. But to do so requires higher costs of other jointly used inputs. It is not the cost of one input but *all costs* that should be of concern in measuring the true cost of any output.

Even if the cost of some *particular* input used in producing an *X* is correctly calculated, other inputs are also used to produce *X*. For example, some people compute the cost of energy for heating a house and conclude that whatever method minimizes *that* cost is better. But *energy* cost is not the total cost of heating. Other inputs are also used in the process: Insulation, copper, motors, metal—all are jointly used inputs. If electricity costs were reduced by increasing the other jointly used inputs at a greater cost (forsaken output value), the result is wasteful. Yet many people assert that we ought to conserve energy with devices that have lower costs *of energy* for whatever the device produces.[2] That advice is worse than

---

[2] Why necessarily *conserve?* If it's available we should *use* it, in the most valuable ways, not in less-valuable ways, and that most valuable use *may* be—but need not, absolutely, be —to store it for the future.

nonsense (which says nothing)—it is dead wrong. It makes people worse off, for it involves higher costs of other inputs to permit the reduced energy costs. It is wasteful to save $1 of energy costs by incurring $1.50 costs for something to substitute for that energy. Please, don't respond by saying energy is scarce and limited. Of course it is; but *all* economic goods are scarce and limited. There is nothing special about the scarcity of any economic good, whether it be energy, land, paper, or potatoes. All are scarce. It is wasteful to save *any* of them by using a greater-valued amount of some other goods.

Some people who complain that we Americans are too materialistic (wanting bigger, more comfortable cars) are themselves being materialists in contending that some particular material— gasoline, energy, or environment—is the *only* resource worth caring about.

2. *Everyone Has a Lower Marginal Cost in Some Activity.* Producers at lower marginal costs of *X* will have higher marginal costs of producing other goods. Why? If my marginal cost of producing one more *X* is $10 (the worth of other goods that could have been produced) and yours is $5, this means I could produce $1 of other goods at a cost of only .1 *X* while you would have to sacrifice .2 *X* to produce $1 of other goods. You are the cheaper marginal-cost producer of "other" goods. To say that my marginal cost of producing *X* is *higher* than yours is to say my marginal cost of producing the other good, *Y*, is *lower* than yours. By the definition of costs, it is impossible for one producer to be able to produce every good at lower marginal costs than every other producer. Each producer will have some product or rate of output for that product at which his marginal costs are lower than someone else's. We challenge you to prove otherwise.

3. *Wealth and Costs.* Low or high *marginal* costs are not reliable indicators of a producer's potential wealth. That depends upon his *total* production capability. In our earlier example, A could produce 10 *X* or, at the other extreme, $14.50 of *Y*. B could produce only 6 *X* or $4.20 at either extreme of specialization. A can do everything that B could and more, so far as *total* output is concerned. A will certainly be richer than B. Yet, as we saw, greater wealth does not mean that A is more competitive than B (that is, can produce at a lower marginal, average, or total cost) in *all* products. You hope you were born with great production power, and you hope to develop comparative advantages (that is, lower marginal costs) for those particular products that you hope will be highly demanded when you work for a living.

4. *What Quality of Product?* It is not necessarily sensible to try to reduce the true costs per unit of some *particular performance* aspect of a product. For example, it is a mistake to minimize the costs of transportation from automobiles. Those costs can certainly be reduced, but only by reducing the quality of service. Quieter, smoother, faster, more comfortable, safer, prettier, more flexible kinds of travel are more expensive. Yet these are valued aspects of an automobile, and to reduce their quality is not reducing *costs* but, rather, *output*. Every good has a set of qualities and attributes that can be altered if cost is to be cut by producing a different, lower-quality product. Lowering cost per mile makes sense *only if every* aspect of the product and its quality of performance is left unchanged. It is not

sensible to reduce cost if that means lowering the qualities of the good more than the cost saving is worth. (How do you reconcile this with Congressional legislation requiring more miles per gallon in automobiles or *more* insulation in homes to save energy?) Throughout our analysis *lowered cost* always means a situation in which *all* aspects of the final product are left unchanged

9, 10 | for the worse. Thus we rule out false economies.

What Is Meant by Quantity of Output: Rate or Volume?

The relationship between output and cost shows some general features that we can put as propositions for use in later analysis. *Cost Proposition 1:* Larger output costs more. *Cost Proposition 2:* Marginal costs are higher at larger output rates. *Rate* here means speed or flow of production (later we shall investigate the cost effects of total quantity or volume that is produced). Whatever the total amount to be produced, the higher the speed or rate of production, the higher the total cost of that total amount. That is perfectly consistent with a lower per-unit cost (at the same rate or speed) if the total amount is larger, as with mass production methods rather than by custom production. The same fact holds in either case: Whether the method is mass production (with larger total output at lower per-unit costs) or custom production (with smaller total output at higher per-unit costs), the faster the rate at which a particular quantity is produced, the higher is the total cost of that quantity (volume). Doing something more rapidly costs more than doing it less rapidly. So do not confuse

speed (rate) of production with the total amount (volume) to be produced. Of course, the two will move together if we assume production is to continue for some definite fixed interval of time, because then a higher rate for that given length of time will mean a greater total volume. Most of the examples in this book assume just this situation, so higher rates will here *also* mean higher total volume or quantity.

Why is cost higher at larger rates? Two different forces operate, either of which is sufficient to raise the cost. First, to increase the output *rate* of X, more resources must be diverted from other activities at the same time. For example, to produce more grapes per year, more land and labor must be diverted from other productive activity, say, producing chickens. But not all land or labor is identical; so it will be economic first to shift to vineyard work the particular land and labor that is *relatively* better for vines than for chickens, such as rocky but well-drained land. Less-well-drained, heavy clay soil is relatively better for chickens, and thus should be the last converted to vineyards. Similarly, the labor of caring for vineyards may require more physical strength than does chicken-farming, so some people will be better for vines than for chickens. As the more appropriate resources for vines are shifted first, any further desired increase in the annual output of grapes will require shifting more resources that are less appropriate to vines. So, higher rates of grape production will be accomplished by addition of less-appropriate (higher-cost) resources than those already assigned to vineyards. The higher the rate of production, the less appropriate are remaining resources available for transfer from other activities. Economic or efficient production of any good, by definition, requires that successively higher rates be accomplished by shifting the next most appropriate resources to the higher-rate activity. But, by definition of *cost,* that means the marginal cost will be higher at greater rates of production.

The second reason for rising marginal cost is that even if all laborers or all acres of land were identical in productive ability, congestion of the fixed input (for example, land) will yield smaller increases of output, and that simply is higher cost for each unit of increase.

Whatever the extent to which this second force is operating, the first force is operative and sufficient to result in rising marginal cost.

Differential Earnings

We have seen that the total supply from an industry is the sum of the quantities from all the individual suppliers' marginal cost schedules—where each supplier looks at the same price. (This was diagrammed in Figure 8–8, using only two suppliers because many essential features can thus be shown more readily.) If there were several producers instead of just the two shown in the diagram, the market, or industry, amount supplied would be the sum of the quantities from each supplier's marginal-cost schedule at a common price.

Now we can ask the question: If marginal costs are so crucial in efficiently coordinating producers, why do we pay any attention to *average* costs? While all may be producing outputs at which marginal costs are equal, the *average* costs incurred per unit of output will *differ.* For example, Table 8–1 and 8–2 show that if A is producing two units while B is producing four units,

each has the same marginal cost, $1.10 (the same increment to total cost for the marginal unit being produced). But their average costs at those outputs are different: $1.05 for A and 80 cents for B. If price were $1.10, net earnings of A would be 10 cents (= 5 cents x 2) and net earnings to B would be $1.20 (= 30 cents x 4). A superior producer (that is, the one with larger net earnings) will soon receive offers from other producers for his services regardless of why he is superior—mental ability, diligence, effort, or whatever—because they expect he could do for them what he is doing for himself. But they would have to bid at least as much as those earnings. Thus A would be offered 10 cents while B would be offered $1.20; the competition of other people to buy or hire the services of that superior talent will reveal a price or salary for that talent, and that price must then be treated as a measure of the cost (forsaken alternative) of keeping this special talent here. The net potential earnings of *superior* talent thus gets figured into the *costs* of production and a higher income (differential earnings) to that superior talent.

There is a common, erroneous tendency to call that differential earning power a *monopoly return,* to suggest that there are so few of them. However, *monopoly* is not properly applied to superior resources that remain so scarce as to command a persisting premium relative to inferior goods. Instead, *monopoly* is a term applied to: (1) any situation in which price is above marginal revenue and remains above marginal cost (for reasons we shall examine later), or (2) a seller who gains protection from competitors by imposing on them extra, possibly prohibitive, costs as a condition of their entry. For example, another potential seller might be prohibited from entering the market, or allowed to enter only after paying a special imposed cost that existing sellers won't and didn't have to incur. This second meaning of the term monopoly refers to the *means* of keeping out competitors, while the first refers only to a particular price, marginal revenue, marginal cost relationship. Neither meaning of *monopoly* implies the other!

A piece of especially fertile land is superior, but we do not call it a monopoly. If we did, we would be tending to call every different resource a monopoly, and that is not useful. As it is, things are bad enough with these two different meanings in the term monopoly. (Later we will clearly separate these meanings by using the terms *market power* or *price searcher* to refer to a seller whose price is above his marginal cost, while reserving the term *monopoly* for an existing producer protected by artificially imposed extra costs on any potential new entrants.) If someone is a superior producer, we do not call his higher differential earnings monopoly profit, for it is not caused by any artificial, contrived restraint on competitors (nor associated with a special pricing situation, which we shall discuss later).[3]

More Producers:
Net Gains or Transfers?

Just as two people gain by specialization and exchange between themselves, the entry of more people will increase total community output, to the benefit of *all* parties. Who receives most of

[3] In honor of one of the great early English economists, David Ricardo, who first made this distinction, the differential earnings of superior talent are often called *Ricardian rents*.

that enhanced production and benefit depends on circumstances that can now be revealed with our analysis. A new immigrant, C, enters the society, with productive capabilities described in Table 8–4. In every potential output he is smaller than A or B and will be poorer. But his marginal cost pattern of producing X differs from theirs; it starts lower but does not go as far before reaching his maximum potential of 5 X.

The results of his entry can be analyzed by Figure 8–10, according to which C will discover a market price higher than his marginal costs at his initial output of X, as panel C shows. Therefore, it is profitable to produce some X to sell to A and B. The intersection of the new aggregate supply and demand (including C in the aggregate), shown in the extreme right-hand panel, D, is at a larger output of X. The new equilibrium price is lower.

Party A gains by being able to buy more X at a lower price, and also by diverting some resources from producing some X to other, higher-valued uses. Party B loses. As a large producer of X, he experiences a lower selling price of X. This loss to B is a *transfer* to A because A's purchase price of X is lower. Some of the loss to B is offset by his own newfound ability to get some X at a lower price and to produce other goods with those of his resources that were displaced by C's successful competition. (That resource transfer permits some true social gain, which others share in by lower prices of other goods now more abundantly produced.) The increased social output resulting from C's entry (above the social total of A and B *and* C, when C was not part of that economy) accrues mostly to C.

Thus overall are several consequences of C's entry into the market. (1) There is a gain to C, the newcomer, consisting mostly of the total gain in output. (2) There is a gain to the consumers of what the newcomer produces, because they can buy at a lower price; the transfer is mostly a retention of income formerly going to the higher-price suppliers. (3) The prior producers of the good produced by the newcomer suffer a loss of income, which is transferred to, or retained by, their former customers (this effect is a counterpart to 2). (4) Some social gain is provided by the release of some resources by former producers of X to other output.

However, there is in principle a redistribution of income away from the initial beneficiaries, A and C, to B which, *if it occurred,* would make B better off while still leaving A and C better off than before C entered the community. For example, a fee imposed on C and distributed to B could leave everyone better off than if C had not entered the community at all. But rarely are such taxes or fees in fact imposed on new entrants to a community or nation. Nevertheless, the generalization is that every new entrant to a community will enhance the productive power enough to make everyone better off, though in fact the actual distribution of the increased output will almost always be concentrated on the newcomers while the heavy consumers of what the newcomers produce at lower costs will gain transfers of income from old producers by lower prices. The newcomer can expand along a marginal-cost curve for X that is lower than for those already in the community, while these established producers shift some resources to producing some other products at a marginal cost lower than that at which the newcomer could produce those other goods. This fact is the fundamental source of the social gain from entry of C. *Always* the ad-

Table 8–4. Daily Potential Outputs and Costs of Producer C

Output of X	Total Cost	Marginal Cost	Average Cost	Value of Other Concurrent Output
0	0	0	0	$4.50
1	$ .30	$ .30	$ .30	4.20
2	.90	.60	.45	3.60
3	1.80	.90	.60	2.70
4	3.00	1.20	.75	1.50
5	4.50	1.50	.90	1.00

mission of a newcomer increases the social total above what it would be if he were excluded from the market, and he usually captures most (although not all) of the gain.

The larger productivity from specialization in larger markets (that is, composed of more producers) is the fundamental *economic* argument underlying advocacy of the free market with free access to anyone who wants to produce and sell goods. (There are also cultural, ethical, and moral arguments in favor of such a market.) The basic argument against restrictions on entry, tariffs and import controls, restrictive licensing, or minimum wage laws is illustrated by the preceding mini-economy example, because those enactments restrict market access and reduce the production potential.

The newcomers would be exaggerating their contribution if they included in it all the gains to the consumers of X, because, as we have seen, part of the gain to those consumers is an *income transfer* by lower prices from the old producers. Do not overlook this distinction between the *real output gain* (most of which is captured by the newcomers) and the *transfer of income* from old producers to consumers.

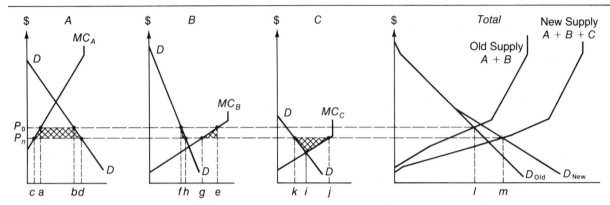

a = amount produced by A before C entered the market.
b = amount consumed by A before C entered the market.
c = amount produced by A after C enters the market.
d = amount consumed by A after C enters the market.
e = amount produced by B before C entered the market.
f = amount consumed by B before C entered the market.
g = amount produced by B after C enters the market.

h = amount consumed by B after C enters the market.
i = amount produced and consumed by C before C enters.
j = amount produced by C after C enters the market.
k = amount consumed by C after C enters the market.
l = total amount produced and consumed before C entered.
m = total amount produced and consumed after C enters.

Figure 8–10. A New Producer Enters the Market

When C enters the market, the price is greater than his marginal cost at his existing output, i. So he increases his output of X to j to make some profits. The new market supply curve is shown in the right panel. The intersection of the new supply and demand curves will be at a larger output and a lower price, since C initially had lower marginal personal value for the amount he produced before joining the market. The benefits to A are indicated by the crosshatched area, representing his lower cost of purchase of the former amount of X he consumed, plus his ability to buy more at that lower price (the right hand tip of his crosshatched area) and the gain from release of resources from some production of X for his own use to other more valuable production (the left hand tip of his cross-hatched area).

B, the larger producer of X, suffers a loss of income as a large seller of X because his selling price falls as C enters and expands the supply. B's loss is only partly reduced by his ability to transfer some resources to other output (the right hand cross-hatched triangle under his marginal cost curve over his reduced output of X) and by his ability to

consume more at the lower price (the left hand cross-hatched triangle).

C, the new entrant, gains as shown by the crosshatched area in his panel of the diagram. C gains by ability to produce and sell more of the X at a price greater than his cost and to sell some of the X he formerly consumed at a price higher than that X was worth to him.

It is important to note that the gains to A are in large part simply a transfer (or retention) of income formerly spent in buying X from B. Hence the major part of the gain to A is a transfer from B and not a true social gain. Conversely, most of the loss imposed on B is not a true social loss but is that transfer to A. Most of the actual gain resulting from C's entry is obtained by C, though some is obtained by A and B as explained above. Moral and caution: Do not add transfer gains to some consumers to the social gain consequent to entry of new producers, for that would over-count the social gain; nor subtract the loss to former producers not partially displaced by the new entrants, for that is not a social loss, but merely a transfer.

Monopoly Restraints

You can now see why existing producers seek laws prohibiting or restricting entrants into "their" businesses. Immigrants would be kept out, *if* the immigrants are likely to compete against existing producers—just as doctors restrict the practice of medicine in the United States by immigrants trained abroad, or Mexican seasonal labor is kept out of U.S. lettuce and grape fields to protect local lettuce and grape pickers. Or existing producers might simply prohibit the sale of the product by any new suppliers—just as taxi companies in most cities manage to have the city government exclude new entrants; or cattle raisers succeed in prohibiting importation of foreign meat; or sugarcane or oil producers place quotas on imported sugar or oil from lower-cost foreign producers; or American textile workers prohibit (or place a tax, called a tariff) on the importation of textiles from Korea or Japan to protect the incomes of those domestic textile workers. All these restrictions are usually imposed under the guise of protecting the American standard of living from competition that drives down wages. But you should no longer be fooled by that self-serving argument. *Some* American *producers* are protected—those who already are producing the goods in this country—but consumers are prevented from having more goods at lower prices. The consumer's standard of living is reduced while the *protected* American producers have theirs kept up—at a net social loss.

Artificial, contrived restrictions against the entry of potential producers or resources into any market, protecting the wealth of existing specialized producers from competition of newcomers, are called *monopoly* restraints. Frustrated would-be entrants must turn elsewhere and produce something of less value. This loss of potential value of output is called *monopoly distortion* or *monopoly inefficiency.*

If every producer has this protection, wouldn't we be richer, since every consumer is a producer, too? No. The total social loss from each such restriction on producers is greater than the gains to the producers. (It's the reverse of the gains from new producers, discussed above.) Ultimately, everyone would be worse off. But we aren't going to prove that here. Instead, we hope that you not only see it to be plausible but also true. But remember that in each particular restriction, the gains are concentrated in a small group and usually are a substantial portion of their wealth. The losses, on the other hand, are so dispersed as to be too small per person, relative to his costs of preventing them, to make it worth trying to prevent them. This disproportionate, unbiased incentive in political competition for legislation which would protect producers' interests from competition in the market is not present in economic market competition, where everyone can express his value preferences, easily and effectively. No procedure exists whereby our individual personal values about legislation can be constantly reflected by effective offers and bids in the political, as in the economic, market. This may be as it should be. But it means that the interests of everyone are not as fully recorded and effective in preventing special interest political favors by political action, as individual interests are in directing market activity. Until (if ever) some method is discovered to avoid that bias, producer (income earning) groups will in general dominate the political processes.

Although our toy mini-economy example included only producers A, B, and C, our analysis is very general in its applicability to the real world. It applies to America, Britain, and China and explains the coordination and gains from international trade; or Albany, Buffalo, and Chicago for interregional trade; or Aluminum Company of America, Bulova, and Continental Container Company, for interfirm exchange, or just plain persons A, B, and C with simple interpersonal specialization and trade.

13, 14
15, 16
17

Absence of Transferable Property Rights

A major obstacle to the operation of the market is the absence of market prices. Suppose that a producer of X believed that the cost of X was not fully revealed by the market measure of costs. People would produce more X than otherwise because *their* perceived costs do not include all the costs. Suppose the costs not being included were the water, air, or noise pollution. By producing the X, people are using or polluting some water or air or disturbing the neighborhood. They are imposing costs on others. If those valuable forsaken goods are not fully priced and salable in a market, their value is not impressed on those who would diminish them. Even if revealed fully, the responsible party would ignore them unless he had to compensate those who own or would otherwise have that forsaken output (or quality). But no one owns the rights to those forsaken things. If someone did, he could make the user pay a price equal to that cost, thereby forcing the user to give *full* weight to the value of the goods he is sacrificing when he makes more X. Less X would then be produced, if the forsaken things are worth more—that is, if the costs are greater. If no one owns rights to that resource, there is no way that the market can protect those goods and make users heed the highest use value of that resource—as we do for things we own, like labor, eggs, wine, cotton, etc. The problem is not that markets or market prices are inherently misleading, but rather that property rights, and our legal system of enforcing them, are incomplete: Transferable property rights over some goods are not sufficiently defined or enforced so as to prevent excessive use in less-valuable ways.

Information Obstacles

Imperfect information about productive capabilities is often mistakenly presumed to cause inefficiency. But information is not free. Like any other resource, it is scarce, valuable, and expensive to obtain. To define efficiency as requiring full and perfect information is as foolish as to assume there are no costs of producing steel and hence to assert too little of it is produced. If resources (for example, people) differ in their productive abilities, as they certainly do, how do we *discover* who has how much of each ability? Slowly, erratically, and expensively. How can anyone know whether an apparently superior person or resource truly has superior ability or is only transiently lucky? Initially, for some interval of time, a person's true ability will be underestimated by the rest of the world (the market). As evidence accumulates that he is more than lucky, others will begin to offer more for his services, bidding up his wages if he is an employee, or bidding up the value of his business if he is the operator-owner. Little is known about how fast the rest of the world detects true superior ability and rewards it with more appropriate market prices, but incredible riches await anyone lucky enough to buy truly undervalued resources or smart enough to detect them before the rest of the world. (We suggest you rely more on hard work.)

Brand Name, Advertising for Product Information

We shall temporarily assume that information, prior to purchase, about the qualities and attributes of goods and services has zero cost. After we have studied production and business firms, that assumption will be modified. For some perspective, let us suggest why information costs are important.

When reliable information cannot be obtained merely by looking at a good, or if the purchase price is not definitely known prior to commitment to purchase, or if performance of the good or service that is below expectations may lead to serious consequences, information about the good's qualities prior to purchase becomes more valuable.

How is prior information provided *economically*? How is the purchaser protected from loss? One can sample or rely on past performance, but that experience can be too costly to risk. Insofar as quality cannot be determined by simply looking at the good or service before or when it is purchased, we will attach to the *maker* a reputation for a particular quality of performance if his product tends to be of some consistent quality. Brand names and trademarks become associated with expectations of a particular quality. Reputations based on consistent past performance economize on the costs of information about the anticipated performance of a good. Thus consumers will sensibly use the brand name or reputation of the maker as a basis for choice. The greater are the possible losses from poor performance of a good, the greater is the value of that brand name as a predictor of quality of performance.

Without brand names or other means of identifying makers, consumers would face larger risks and incur greater costs of information. Obtaining expert information can be more costly than the use of brand names. All this is analogous to using a lawyer of a "recognized" firm rather than trying, ahead of time, to learn all there is to know about some legal problem or about the capabilities of unknown lawyers. As we shall see, it pays to specialize in knowledge rather than to become an expert in everything.

Just as *production* of goods is costly, so is getting information. And it is not because the producers are trying to keep their performance or quality attributes a secret. On the contrary, they spend substantial resources (advertising!) trying to inform potential consumers. An often cheaper alternative is to identify themselves with brands. Don't make the error of assuming that only the information obtainable in school should have a cost and that all other useful information is, or ought to be, available free. All this is simple enough and easily understood. Less obvious are the information-economizing and assurance-providing marketing and pricing activities that this induces, which we will examine later.

Are Specialization and Efficient Production "Good"?

The wealth of specialists depends upon other people's tastes, activities, and willingness to trade. To specialize more effectively requires investments in specific goods and kinds of training. Specialization seems to increase risks, because if other people's demands or willingness to work in certain tasks should change, some specialists will lose much of the value of their investment in specialized goods and training. They will end up poorer than if they had specialized in something else, or possibly poorer than if they had been more self-sufficient like the farmers of olden days. But do not make too much of this point, for the losses of overinvestment in certain goods and skills are not the consequence of specialization. They are the consequence of imperfect foresight. And even a self-sufficient person must invest in productive skills and hence runs risks in estimating his own future demands.

Is Response to Market Demand Desirable?

Efficiency in production is desirable in the sense that more goods are preferred to less. But are you sure the demanded good is "good"? For example, children are permitted only restricted access to the market, because, if unrestricted, children buy goods adults believe they should not. If some paternalist believes other people do not know reliably what is good for themselves—as evidenced by differences of opinion about the use of tobacco, alcohol, narcotics, gambling, low-brow television programs, comic books, pornography—he may seek to prohibit producers from responding to market demands. Many highly educated, socially conscious people do try that. To them, the standard of efficiency (the absence of waste) is useful only insofar as "right" goods are wanted by others. (Still, doing the "wrong" thing efficiently is *not* necessarily undesirable, because whatever the amount of the "bad" good produced, it permits more "good" goods to be produced.) But, in any event, economics does not say what is "good" or "bad" (though some economists do).

Specialization, Tedium, Alienation, and Socialism

Monotony and tedium are said to be more likely —though rewarded by greater wealth—for those who specialize. It would be nice if there were some way to get all that increased output without any of those effects of specialization and exchange. Like everything else, there are trade-offs —we weigh "more of this against less of that."

Karl Marx asserted that specialization of production with market exchange "alienated" producers from understanding their social role and interrelationships with other people. Each worker-producer was said to feel he was producing solely in response to impersonal market prices rather than for human wants and values (as if prices did not reflect such human desires!). Marx contended that, since it is primarily through exchange of their products that producers come into social contact with one another, "persons exist for one another merely as representatives of, and therefore as owners of, commodities. The process of production has the mastery over man instead of being controlled by him." [4]

To eliminate alienation and the alleged "mastery of production processes over man," Marx advocated control of production and distribution by centralized directives in accord with a central plan, as if society were a single huge factory. Hence, Marx called for socialism (that is, government ownership of all the productive resources) believing this would eliminate "alienation."

As we bear sweat, pain, discomfort, or risk of injury, we also bear alienation, because what we gain exceeds the value of what we would lose if we did not. The useful question is "What is the right amount of alienation (or sweat or toil or injuries) in view of what we get from bearing those ills?" To complain about alienation is like complaining about too much work. If you can find a way to reduce alienation or work *without* reducing productive output through specialization, fine and dandy. But when viewed as inevitable, there is nothing special about alienation. Everything is a matter of degree—with trade-offs.

A second claimed motivation for socialism is that socialized (government-owned) production and political regulatory controls better enable politicians and government employees to retain office, acquire wealth, and control society. A third, more recent but unsubstantiated, contention is that centralized government control of productive resources is more efficient and gives a more rapid growth of output.

[4] *Capital*, Vol. I (New York: Modern Library, Random House, 1959), pp. 93, 97.

18, 19
20, 21
22, 23
24, 25
26, 27
28, 29

Summary

1. Specialization is the production of more of some goods and less of other goods than a person consumes himself. Production is efficiently organized if for specified rates of production of all goods except one, that one is maximized; or if it is impossible to increase the output rate of any good without reducing that of some other.

2. Specialization in an open market leads toward efficiently organized production. A central planning and directive agency is not necessary to achieve efficient organization of production and consumption.

3. The gains from specialization are distributed as lower buying prices to consumers and profits to producers. The latter are competed away by lower prices to consumers and larger payments to the productive resources.

4. Marginal costs are the change in costs consequent to producing one more unit—a marginal change in output.

5. Costs are the forsaken alternative output.

6. Producers do not all have identical marginal-cost schedules. Efficient—nonwasteful—production of a good by several producers requires that each producer be producing at any output whose marginal cost is the same as that for all other producers.

7. At each possible price the amount supplied is that for which the marginal cost by each producer equals the price. The sum of the outputs of a good over all producers at any given price forms one point on the industry- or market-supply schedule. The sum of outputs so obtained at each possible price is the

supply schedule to the market by the industry.

8. A market in which price can be determined and revealed to all potential producers is a necessary condition for efficient supply under a capitalist system.

9. Newcomer producers to a market (1) lower the market prices of goods they produce, enabling the consumer to buy more at lower prices, (2) which results in a transfer of income from prior producers of that good to consumers, and (3) the newcomer gains over his situation if he had not been allowed to enter the market. Part of (1) is the transfer from prior producers, as listed in (2) and should be subtracted to get the total gains from all the public. The net gains are more than large enough to permit full compensation to prior producers, but that feasible (in principle) compensation rarely occurs in fact.

10. Monopoly restraints, preventing some potential producers from being able to produce for the market, can preserve or increase the wealth of existing producers at the sacrifice of net social gains, as listed in the preceding point.

11. The analysis of the chapter presumed low or near-zero transactions costs and information costs, and secure private-property rights.

12. Specialization via market exchange and price will enhance total output, but some people may prefer to have the output be smaller—especially if they think some of the goods are kinds other people should not have so plentifully available.

13. The quantity of some input per unit of output is not a valid measure of cost, or of less-wasteful production. The value of *all* inputs for an output must be used—a complete rather than partial measure, because some inputs can be reduced per unit of output by increasing other inputs at an even greater cost.

14. Because not all producers have identical marginal-cost schedules, each producer will always have a lower marginal cost at some activity.

15. A single measure of output is usually not possible since production varies in many ways—for example, rate of production, and volume, to name only two. Higher rates or speeds of production of a given total volume of output are more costly because more resources must be used simultaneously, with the higher-cost ones being brought in only to obtain higher rates.

16. More-productive or higher-quality productive inputs obtain higher incomes because they produce more. They earn a differential income, not one due to monopoly restriction of entry by competitors.

17. Specialization can cause more "alienation" and inability to see what a consumer gets from one's productive effort. But as with all goods and bads, the question is not whether such ill effects should be eliminated but what is the appropriate amount of each, given the gains of productivity from specialization.

Questions

1. Smith's production possibilities are indicated by the following table:

Alternative Daily Production Possibilities by Smith's Resources		
Oats		Soybeans
10	and	0
9	"	1.0
8	"	1.9
7	"	2.7
6	"	3.4
5	"	4.0
4	"	4.5
3	"	4.9
2	"	5.2
1	"	5.4
0	"	5.5

a. What are Smith's marginal costs of producing oats, if soybeans are worth $50 a bushel?

b. If the price of oats is $20 a bushel, how many oats should he produce to maximize the value of his outputs?

2. "Cost is an opportunity concept and exists wherever a choice exists." Explain.

3. "A businessman's costs for material, labor and equipment are simply measures of the highest-valued alternative output producible by those resources he buys or hires." Evaluate.

4. Why are costs not measured in terms of labor hours?

5. What is meant by efficient production?

6. a. For producers A and B in the text, how many units of output of X should each produce if a total of 6 units is desired?

b. Did your solution conform to the equality of marginal cost principle?

c. What would the price of X have to be to induce a total output of 6 units?

7. The following questions involve the production data of the two people given in Tables 8–1 and 8–2.

a. If the price of an X were $1.10 and the price of a Y were $1, what should each person produce in order to maximize his wealth?

b. Would the resulting assignment of tasks be an efficient one?

c. If the price of an X is $1.60 and the price of a Y rises to $2, how much X would each produce in order to maximize his wealth? (Hint: recompute costs of X.)

8. The production-possibility schedules are:

Mr. A			Mr. B		
X	and	Y	X	and	Y
5		0	3		0
4		1.5	2		1
3		2.9	1		2
2		3.8	0		3
1		4.5			
0		5			

*a. Convert these two production possibilities into marginal and average costs of X.

b. Who would be the first to produce profitably some X at a lower price of X? Who would be last?

c. Who would be first to produce profitably some Y at a low price of Y?

d. At what ratio of the price of X to the price of Y would Mr. B switch from production of all X to production of some Y?

9. "It is better to buy from a firm that is losing money than from one that is making a profit, because the former firm is charging too low a price while the latter is charging more than costs." Evaluate.

10. Legislatures of several states started to set energy standards for electrical appliances requiring that they yield at least a specified amount of output per kilowatt hour used. The federal energy agency has stated that automobiles must yield at least 18 miles per gallon (for the average of all cars sold). Why will that almost certainly be wasteful of our national productive resources so that people will be worse off?

11. An obviously most relevant measure of output is not always characteristic of production of various goods. Although in the text we usually refer to both rate of output and the volume of output, in any actual problem often several dimensions of output are relevant. Each particular problem should be investigated more thoroughly and completely in order to determine which one (or several) of possible dimensions of the output is most important. If you are analyzing costs of operating an airline, for example, what measure or measures of output could you use?

12. Which of the following are differential earnings to superior productivity and which are from monopoly sources?
    a. The Beatles' wealth
    b. Bob Hope's labor income
    c. Kareem Jabbar's wealth
    d. Jack Nicklaus's golf earnings
    e. F. Lee Bailey's legal service's income
    f. Dorothy Hamill's income

g. J. Paul Getty's wealth
h. Senator Hubert Humphrey's income
i. McDonald's income
j. Holiday Inn's income

13. In the discussion on pages 188–192, let Mr. C be a resident of Japan, while the others are residents of the United States. Mr. A is a tuna-boat owner and fisherman; B are American workers in other American industries. Let Y be "tuna" and X be "other products." Mr. A persuades his congressman to induce other congressmen to pass a law prohibiting the importing of Japanese tuna—product Y produced by Mr. C. Who gains and who loses by a tariff or embargo on Japanese tuna? (This example captures the essence of the purposes and effects of tariffs and embargoes.)

14. The three-person problem can also be interpreted as a case in which admission to the market for sale of one's production of Y requires a license from the state, and this license is given only if the current output from those now in the production of Y is deemed "inadequate to meet current demands." Who gains and who loses? Can you give some real examples of this situation?

15. Would the three-person new entrant problem also serve as an example of the effect of apprenticeship laws that prohibit a person from acting as a "qualified" carpenter, meat cutter, etc., until he has served a specified number of years as an apprentice? Explain.

16. In California it was proposed that the state should finance education of more doctors because the value of more doctors in terms of lower costs to patients would exceed the education costs. Explain why that is an in-

correct comparison for determination of whether the costs of the education would result in a social gain.

17. "The increased output of specialization is distributed as profits and as a lower price to consumers." What determines the portion of each?

18. What is meant by a subsistence, self-sufficient economy as contrasted to a specialized, interdependent economy?

19. Does efficient production assume that perfect knowledge exists? Explain.

20. When a group of Russian officials touring American farms persistently asked who told the farmers how much to produce in order to supply the appropriate amounts of goods, the farmers said that no one told them. But the Russians were convinced the farmers were concealing something. What would you have told the Russians?

21. "It's wrong to profit from someone else's misfortune."
a. Explain why, if that were taken literally, we would *all* be poorer.
b. Does the doctor profit from your illness? The farmer from your hunger? The shoemaker from your tender feet? The teacher from your ignorance? The preacher from your sinfulness?
c. How are their earnings different from those of the liquor producer, the race-track owner, the burlesque strip-teaser, and the dope peddler?

22. A capitalist system presumes enforcement of certain institutions or rules. What are they?

23. The following remark is commonly made about some rich people: "He is an indepen-

dently wealthy man." From what is he independent? Does his wealth not depend upon other people's demands?

24. a. Do you think specialization will be carried to greater extent in a large city or a small one?
b. Why?
c. Give examples of what you mean by greater specialization.

25. A premier or prime minister of a new "emerging" country bragged that he was going to make his country self-sufficient and independent of foreigners. Do the principles of this chapter suggest anything about how you as a native of that country might be affected? Explain.

26. Evidence of the very great extent of specialization of knowledge is provided by Albert Einstein's assertion just prior to his death (*Socialist International Information*): "The economic anarchy of capitalist society as it exists today is in my view the main cause of our evils. Production is carried on for profit, not for use." Give evidence of your superiority over Einstein by exposing his error in economic analysis.

27. A steals from B successfully.
a. Is that "production"? Why?
b. If you say "No, because someone is hurt," what would you say about the case in which a new invention displaces some other producers?
*c. Are there some kinds of production which you think should not be allowed?

28. Recently India proposed to build a steel mill, and asked the United States government to finance the project. In defense of her request,

an economist serving as American Ambassador to India wrote: "Although it would be a large mill, there is no doubt that the steel is needed. While the plant would be costly, it would soon pay for itself in the imports that it would save. To import a million tons of steel products would cost the Indians about $200 million. The proposed mill with an annual capacity of 1 million tons would cost $513 million to build. Three years of operations would thus recover the dollar cost of the mill and more. Since India combines her pressing need for steel with an equally acute shortage of dollars, the economic attraction is obvious. She could not, in fact, afford to import the steel that the mill could supply." Explain why every sentence of that quotation —except the third and fourth—is wrong, nonsensical, or irrelevant.

29. "Every profit represents the gain from moving resources to higher-valued uses." Do you agree? If so, why? If not, why not?

*30. Dr. John H. Knowles, President of the Rockefeller Foundation said after a trip to China in 1976, "China is now able to meet all of its energy needs and is even in a position to export." Is that a meaningful statement? If so, does it mean China is better off than if it imported sources of energy? Why?

9

Organization and Coordination of Joint Production

Joint, Team Production

We examined specialization in the preceding chapter; now we examine another source of enhanced output, teamwork. People work with other people or with other people's resources to jointly produce something. Two of us, navigator and pilot, operate an airplane. Two of us operate a steel mill, I as crane operator, you as rolling mill controller. Three of us operate a fishing boat, as helmsman, as engineer, and handler of the nets. Four people perform surgery on a patient: a surgeon, anaesthetist, surgical aide, and attending nurse. Five lawyers work together on a law case jointly creating their strategy. The magic of increased output from joint physical or mental effort is taken as a fact that need not be explained here. (We need not explain, for example, why two people pushing a car can push it farther than one person could push it for twice as long.) Instead we examine how people are guided to teamwork, on a team that is known as a *business firm.* We also inquire into what influences how those firms are organized and internally controlled, and how each member's reward (pay) is determined. We first examine a few control techniques; we assume temporarily that all possible participants are identical in ability.

In exploring these basic issues, we can ignore features such as whether the enterprises are small or large, unionized or nonunionized, conglomerate or single-product, local or multinational, new or old, retailing or manufacturing, corporation or proprietorship. We pass over administrative problems like how to select personnel; to plan production schedules; to arrange for

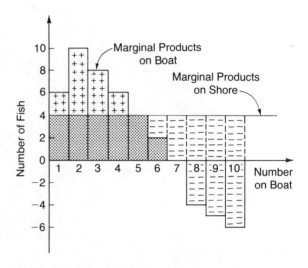

Figure 9–1. Marginal Products on Boat

The vertical bars represent the marginal product (in fish) on board the boat. The horizontal line at 4 fish is the marginal product (in units of fish) on the shore. The areas occupied by plus signs denote the gain by having fishermen on the boat, while the areas marked with minus signs are the losses of having too many people fish on the boat.

purchases, storage, keeping tax and accounting records; to persuade politicians on proposed legislation or regulation; and an incredible array of varied tasks that occupies a businessman's time.

To isolate essentials, assume that 1000 similar people in a community do nothing but fish from the shore, each always catching four fish daily no matter how many people fish. A boat is found; some can now fish out on the ocean. Everyone is interested only in how many fish are caught; fishing from shore or a boat is equally pleasant or arduous. Table 9–1 summarizes the details. The discoverer and sole user of the boat catches

Table 9–1. Catch of Fish on Board *

Number of Men on Board	Total Catch (on board)	Marginal Product (on board)	Average Product (on board)	Net Social Marginal Product	Social Total (Shore plus boat)
0	0	0	0	0	4000 + 0 = 4000
1	6	+6	6	2	3396 + 6 = 4002
2	16	+10	8	6	3392 + 16 = 4008
3	24	+8	8	4	3388 + 24 = 4012
4	30	+6	7.5	2	3384 + 30 = 4014
5	34	+4	6.8	0	3380 + 34 = 4014
6	36	+2	6	−2	3376 + 36 = 4012
7	36	0	5.14	−4	3372 + 36 = 4008
8	32	−4	4	−8	3368 + 32 = 4000
9	27	−5	3	−9	3364 + 27 = 3991
10	21	−6	2.1	−10	3360 + 21 = 3981

* Anyone fishing from shore catches four fish, and there are 1000 people.

six fish, two more than had he fished from shore like any of the others. The *social total* is two fish larger. But if another person joins him on the boat, the pair can catch a total of 16—10 more, so, with two crew members, the marginal product *on board* is 10 fish. Marginal products are graphed in Figure 9–1. Since the second person forsakes the four fish he would have caught fishing from shore, the social total increases by six fish with a second person. That is, with two on board the *social marginal* product is six fish; the social *total* is eight more than without the boat. Who gets the eight fish?

If the two people apportion the fish equally between themselves, each has four *more* fish than each shore fisherman. No one else is affected. Or the gain of eight fish could be divided among all 1000 people so everyone could have

4.008 fish. But whatever is done, at least a third person could profitably switch to the boat, as is indicated by Figure 9–1. That would increase the boat total by eight fish to 24 fish (the marginal product with three crewmen is eight fish) while forsaking only four more fish from the shore. The social total increases by four—the difference between the marginal product on the boat and the forsaken four-fish shore-marginal-product. A fourth crewman could transfer to the boat, since the marginal product *on the boat,* six, with four members is greater than the forsaken marginal product on shore, four—a net *social* marginal product of two. With four boatmen the total product on the boat is 30 (= 6 + 10 + 8 + 6), which, subtracting 16 forsaken fish from the shore (four from each person who shifted to the boat) yields a *social* gain of 14 fish. How the net social gain of 14 fish is divided will be important, as we shall see.

On a *social* maximum output (no-waste) criterion the optimal number of fishermen on the boat is four or five. (There could be five, since the marginal product, four fish, with a fifth crew-member on the boat would exactly offset the lost marginal product, four fish, from the shore. For arithmetic convenience we shall arbitrarily take the larger crew size whenever there is this equivalent double possibility.) The *no-waste social-maximum output* rule is to enlarge the boat crew until the marginal product on board decreases to that on shore. (When people aren't fishing, they sleep, eat, rest, and bask in the sun. Only fish are produced and consumed.) In Figure 9–1 the marginal social gains are the areas of plus signs in the first four marginal-product bars.

Control, Property Rights, and Incentives

Now we come to the point of interest: How many people *will* be allowed on the boat and who gets the increased output?

Share and Share Alike with Controlled Entry

In our first scene of this fishing saga, assume the boat discoverer is entitled to decide how many persons can be on board, and all those on board will share alike in the total catch. Our discoverer will allow only one or two other people, for then the *average* catch on board, which he and each other person gets, is at the maximum:

eight fish, four more than each could catch on shore. He will not tolerate four men (counting himself) on board because the average (which each gets) on board would fall from 8 to 7.5 and he would have less fish—even though the social total would increase. The fourth would enable six more fish for a net social gain of two over the total if that fourth person had stayed on shore. The self-interest of the boat controller here prevents a larger social catch. Indeed, if we changed the rules and allowed *all* those who are on board to decide whether any more will be allowed to come on board, the outcome is the same. The first three would not admit any more, because another person reduces the average to be shared by all from 8 to 7.5.

This is a characteristic problem of socialist firms; "workers" control the enterprise *and share* the net income equally, and newcomers are admitted only by permission of the existing group. This is also a common danger in many labor unions and professions; longshoremen, electricians, musicians, doctors, lawyers, and a vast host of other professions admit new members only by permission (through certifying boards) of present members.

Instead of a boat yielding fish, imagine a college yielding earning power from knowledge and that the ocean shore is the rest of the economy where you could earn income. If extra students reduce each present student's learning (that is, reduce the average quality), how many should be admitted? Before drawing conclusions, continue with our scenario.

Private Property

As Scene Two of the saga of our fishing society opens, the boat-discoverer has been given entitlement to collect a fee from those fishing on board. In effect, the fishing crew must rent space on his boat. Suppose *each still gets an equal share* of whatever is caught on board. How many will the boat owner allow on board and what price will he charge? (For simplicity, assume the owner stays on shore and catches four fish from shore while the boat users are at sea.) He will allow four (or five) people on board and he will charge each a fee of almost 3.5 fish which each person will pay from his equal average of 7.5 fish obtained from the day's catch. That will leave each person with just a smidgeon over four fish. The total payment to the boatowner of almost 3.5 fish times 4 people equals almost 14 fish—almost the entire social gain.

A fifth person (still assuming the owner stays on shore) could be admitted, but that would not be more profitable for the boat owner. If their total catch is divided equally among all five fishermen, each would get 6.8 fish, which is only 2.8 more than the four each could catch on the shore. So they would each offer at most 2.8 fish for the right to be on board. With five people that again gives the owner exactly 14 fish. If you examine the table, you will see the fifth person has a marginal product of four fish, exactly what he could catch on shore. So there is no social increase by adding him, nor any loss. The rental value of the boat is still 14 fish per day. That is exactly the maximum gain in fish that can be caught through use of the boat. Essentially, all of it is paid to the boat owner. But, of course, he is part of society.

Review again Figure 9–1, which shows the *gains* in output *on board* as more crew members are added. The constant marginal-product line of four fish indicates what each one could have earned on shore. As long as another crew member would yield a marginal product on the boat in excess of the four he could catch on shore, he would offer to pay the boat owner some part of that excess of the marginal product over his shore catch for the right to fish on board. Competition for the right to fish on board would bid up the offers to transfer essentially all that excess to owners of the boat. When five people are on board, the marginal product on the boat equals the marginal product on shore. The gain, obtained by the owner, is the shaded area out to where the two marginal products are equal. The total payment to the owner is at a maximum when the number of fishermen on board gives a marginal catch on board just equal to the marginal catch on shore.

If six had been on board, the marginal on-board catch would be two, but four fish from shore are sacrificed with a net social loss of two fish. The fee from each would be at most 2 ($= 6 - 4$, the per capita average on board minus what could be caught on shore). That difference—the fee he could charge—from six people is 12 ($= 6 \times 2$), and is less than the 14 with four (or five) people on board. So the boat owner would refuse six on board. Under the present private-property arrangements, five at most are allowed on board; the community catch of fish is maximized, with all the gain going to the boat owner by people's competitive bidding to get on board. The social total is 4014 fish. (Remember there are 1000 people fishing, either from shore [995] or on board [5].)

What is pertinent in this example is that five fishermen on board is the number that maximizes the social total. That is achievable only if: (a) someone has the right to determine how the boat is used, that is, how many are allowed on board, *and* (b) he is allowed to charge a price for access to the boat, and (c) keep the receipts. A private-property scenario permits those conditions. Private ownership of firms is dominant in most non-socialist countries and will be examined in more detail later.

Employees or Renters?

The same situation could be described differently. Instead of saying *fishermen rent* the boat, we could say the boat *owner hires* the fishermen. In the latter case, he must pay them four plus a smidgeon of fish each to fish on his boat while he keeps the total catch, minus those wages. Of a total catch of 34 fish with five people, each is paid four fish, a total wages bill of 20 fish, leaving him 14 fish. There is *no* difference in this example between fishermen renting the boat or the boat owner hiring fishermen as employees!

Is there, then, no difference between Macy's hiring clerks as *employees* or the clerks *renting* Macy's building and facilities and paying rent (and inventory-use costs) to the owners out of the total daily sales—leaving the clerks with the same income in either case? No difference, *if there is certainty about the output performance.* But someone must bear the consequences of mistaken estimates of the catch, and that does make a difference. For the moment, the important point is the identity between the two payment methods, renting and hiring—assuming certainty about performance.

Uncertainty about the prospective catch introduces a major difference. If fishermen rent the boat, renters bear the consequences of not catch-ing enough (or the boon of catching more than enough) fish to pay for the day's rent and have at least four fish. If the boat owner hires the fishermen, he (the employer) bears the risk for the *day* on which he has guaranteed the fishermen at least four fish. Why do we emphasize "day"? To see, look again at the rental case: The rent set the *following* day for use of the boat will be adjusted to match the *expected* net catch. If the rent is set per day, the fishermen lose only one day's error in estimated catch. But the boat owner will suffer or enjoy the entire *future projected changes* in catch, as profits or losses in the value of his boat. The boat owner cannot escape projected future change—not even by selling off his ownership, because the new buyer will adjust his offer price to take all that into account. By making *short-term* rental arrangements, the renters who use the boat avoid being stuck with an unexpectedly bad future. As employees, on the other hand, they are always guaranteed four fish, which they could always catch from shore, regardless of the fortunes on the ocean deep. You can probably conjecture that if the boat were for sale it would be bought only by a person who was more optimistic about the potential catch, or who thought he knew better than anyone else how to use the boat so as to get the largest catch—or maybe the best kind of fish.

Public, Communal Property

Scene Three of our saga opens with the public enviously confiscating the boat owner's rights. The boat is declared public property for public welfare rather than some owner's personal profit.

Now anyone can board the boat, just as he can use streets, parks, and the beach. People will crowd onto the boat as long as the *average* catch (which each gets) exceeds that on shore. In our example, eight people would be on board with four fish each to take home. But now *no one* is better off than before the boat was found. What happened to the extra 14 fish? They aren't caught, because there is too much congestion on board (instead of the catch-maximizing amount of congestion).

It is easy to see what happened if you examine the data in Table 9–1. With each person on board sharing equally in the total catch (the average of the total catch for whatever number are on board) people crowd on until the *average* catch no longer exceeds their individual catch on shore (where the marginal and average are the same: four fish). So a sixth, seventh and eighth person will go on board; the sixth, because with six people the average catch is six fish; the seventh because the average is 5.14, and with eight people, the average is four. Every person's catch (the average) is reduced as more crowd on board, but each newcomer ignores the harmful effect on other people so long as he gets more than four fish, until with eight persons on board no one else would gain by joining the crew. Allowing a sixth person on board causes a social sacrifice of two fish (his marginal product on board, two, *minus* his sacrificed marginal product on shore, four). A seventh causes a loss of five fish (his negative marginal product on board, −1, and his sacrificed marginal product, four fish, on shore); and the eighth person on board causes a social loss of eight fish. The total social loss is 14 fish ($= 2 + 4 + 8$) as compared to the social *gain* of

14 fish when the crew size is four (or five) people. Thus the potential gain (formerly obtained and received as profits by the owners) is entirely dissipated by overcrowding the boat.

Overcongestion can be shown graphically in Figure 9–1. The social gain is indicated by the plus-marked area, representing the "marginal products on board" in excess of the "marginal products sacrificed on shore," maximized (at 14 fish) with five people on board. With more people, the marginal product on board will not match that on shore. That potential loss is represented by the shaded area below the marginal product on shore and above the "marginal product on board." Unrestricted communal access is common for highways, beaches, sidewalks, parks, air, rivers, lakes, oceans. The reason for the overcongestion should be obvious—inappropriate property rights. With communal or public property, no one has adequate incentive to heed those overcongestion effects. They are left "external" to each person's interests, and are called "externalities." As long as everyone is entitled to, or gets, the average catch—on a share alike basis—everyone will respond to the *average,* not the total (or the marginal).

If, somehow, on board fishing could be limited to five people, all could share in the potential gain of 14 fish, formerly collected by the boat owners. So, in the absence of private-property rights, a government agent is appointed to control the number of fishermen.

Government Control for Profit?

Scene Four opens with the new government agent being told to maximize profit from renting the boat (which is the same as total rent since we assume the boat is costless to operate). He charges a fee of 2.8 fish per person for the right to be on board. With an average catch of 6.8 out of which each pays 2.8 and keeps four, only five persons will want to be on board. Now the 14-fish rent (social gain) goes to the government and is distributed however the government sees fit. It would appear that the only difference between this and the private-property control system is in who gets the 14-fish gain. The private owners, seeking personal profits, also achieved the maximum social output.

However, if our government agent takes life easier and doesn't charge the right fee, what will he lose? The loss is imposed on the public as a whole. But who in the public or government has an incentive as strong as a private owner to detect opportunism or shirking of prescribed duty? In contrast to the private owner, a political authority suffers less loss of potential personal wealth in being less attentive to nonownable gains. And if there is uncertainty about the potential catch on board, he would permit extra people on board if that made him more popular and enhanced his hold on political office. Or to make his personal life easier, the authority might allow too few on board because that permits shorter working hours for him (like closing on holidays and earlier in the afternoons) and not operating the boat as fully as would maximize profits. Soon we shall see how *incentives* and *uncertainty* about future potential production are critical influences on methods for coordinating and controlling joint production activity.

But when has a government agency been supposed to maximize *profits*? It is usually, or always, told to "maximize public welfare and benefit." (The agency might be a nonprofit corporation for hospitals, colleges, or the post office.) How is "maximize public welfare" interpreted? In our example, maximize the number on board? Or maximize the catch on the boat? Or the social total? Maximizing the catch *on board* would, as we have seen, result in marginal products on board that are less than on shore, thereby reducing the social total—a *social* waste.

The ambiguous goal "maximum public benefit and welfare" is sturdy and widespread, because its ambiguity permits the authorities wide latitude of interpretation and hence of measuring performance. It is commonly mandated for government authorities who control access to the television and radio electromagnetic spectrum, air space for airplanes, postal service, highways, national and state parks and beaches, airports, harbors, schools; it is even applied to federal forests, off-shore oil, and federal land. Zoning commissions that control the use of land (such as how congested it can be) are similarly instructed to maximize public usefulness. But hardly any government authority is instructed to maximize profits: not the post office, or the water, electricity, gas, or bus company. All are instructed to "serve the public," or "break even"—with consequences that are now more explainable.

Imperfect Predictability of Performance: Risk Bearing

For two reasons the actual productivity of any group cannot be predicted perfectly. First, natural causes alter the catch: good weather, few schools of fish in the area that day, etc., are causes no man can control. Secondly, members working as a team can shirk and affect the outcome, often letting others bear some of the consequences. Since performance is not perfectly predictable or controllable, it is difficult to know whether it is a team member's negligence or everyone's bad luck that altered the outcome from what was expected. To allow for, or to control, those forces, institutional and organizational arrangements have been developed. In the remainder of this chapter we shall consider responses to the unpredictability caused by sheer luck or nature. We examine the way shirking or opportunism by team members or agents is countered and brought under control in a later chapter on the business firm, one of whose main functions as an institution is to permit team production while controlling shirking and opportunism.

(1) In Scene One of our boat scenario, the three mutual sharing and controlling fishermen bore the risks of fluctuations in the amount caught.

(2) In Scene Two, with private-ownership rights and control, if the *crew* rented the boat for a total of 14 fish (2.5 for each of the five people on board) they bore the day's consequences of catching less (or the benefits of more) than expected. Alternatively, the *boat owner* could pay (assign to each of) the five people a wage of four fish. The boat owner is then an employer paying employees, and he bears the risk of the size of the total catch. With uncertainty of future performance, the allocation of risks depends on whether the boat owner rents his boat to fisher-

men or rents fishermen by paying them prespecified wages.

(3) Under the communal system (Scene Three of our scenario), with anyone entitled to come on board, the risks are borne equally by everyone on board. And the total social catch will, as shown earlier, be smaller because of overcongestion.

(4) Under the government authority (Scene Four of our scenario), payments could, in principle, be arranged exactly as with private-property rights. Crewmen could rent the boat and bear the risks of the size of catch. Or the government authority could hire the crew for an assured wage with risk borne by everyone via their government, according to the political system, taxes, and government expenditures. In general, without a good theory of what government agents really do, who will bear which risks cannot be predicted.

One thing that can be said is that under government control no member of the public can avoid bearing whatever that risk is in the government control system. If you do not like that contemplated risk, you cannot sell your share or interest to some other party. You can't sell your interest in Yosemite National Park, the Postal System, or the Tennessee Valley Authority. If it is profitable (or subsidized) you gain (or lose) depending upon the tax laws and distribution of government services. The risks of changes in the values of various government-controlled resources are not open to convenient realignment in accord with "individual" attitudes toward risks of various resources, because shares in public or government property cannot be traded, except by geographic mobility (that is, by moving to another county, state, or country, depending on the geographic distribution of a given risk-bearing).

1, 2
3, 4
5

Insurance: Pooling Risks

Because of risks of losses of wealth from physical damage (such as from fire or flood or theft), people often insure. They *share* losses by spreading them over the group that bears the losses in the form of sure, regular, small fees, called the insurance premium. These accumulated premiums are supposed to be large enough to pay sufferers of any insured, actual losses. In general, insurance trades each person's small chance of a large loss for the certainty of a small loss—the insurance premium.

Insurance also may induce people to change the probability of the contingent event. Each insured person is often required to take special precautions as a condition of getting insurance. Otherwise, precautionary incentives might be reduced with insurance; for without insurance, we may devote more resources and care and anxiety to protection than with it. So insurance may either decrease or increase total social accidental losses. Yet even if total losses are greater with insurance than without (as they may well be), the avoidance of precautionary resource-use and the reduction of anxiety may exceed the increase in accident losses.

Some accidental losses are not insurable because they are not accidental enough. Insurance against bad business or loss of customers would entice a retailer to be less productive while relying on the insurance to indemnify him for his increased shirking. He could too easily and covertly "influence the chances of the loss." This "moral" hazard diminishes the feasibility of insurance. Claims for indemnity against losses would exceed the insurance premiums an insurance company could get from voluntary insurees.

Risk Allocation by Ownership Allocation

Though many hazards are not formally insurable, other methods are used to escape the risks. You can't buy insurance against your oilwell going dry, or *not* finding gold on your land, or having other people's tastes and demands shift away from your services, or divorce, or dull children, or marital infidelity. You can't *buy insurance* against these risks, yet you can *insure* for some of these events. For example, the risk of an oilwell's unexpectedly drying up can be transferred to someone else. Just sell the well to him. You will get the present value of that oil that other people *expect* is there. If the oil well does dry up, the buyer bears the loss, not you; if it lasts longer he gets the profit.

By choosing not to own certain goods, you avoid the hazards of changing values (profits and losses) of those goods. With a private-property system, risks can be transferred to the most willing, optimistic people—the new owners. People can exchange ownership entitlements to goods and the risks to bear on them on a selective, discretionary, personally preferred basis. By renting a house monthly instead of owning one, you avoid having so much of your wealth depend on the future service potential of that house. By renting goods, a person can select his ownership of goods and risk-bearing more independently of his consumption patterns.

In some countries (Mexico, for example) some farmers (called *ejidos* in Mexico) cannot sell the land they farm and occupy. They can use it and sell the crop, but they cannot sell or borrow against the land. (If they could borrow against the land, they could borrow and then default, letting the lender take the land—circumventing the ban on sale of the land.) They have only *usufruct* rights. These restricted rights to resources do not permit as much discretionary risk-sharing and re-allocation. Furthermore, the incentive to improve or invest in the farmland is weakened, since the prospects of value increases cannot be transferred to those most optimistic or willing to bear them. These *ejidos* invest in more children as a source of future income—not a surprising substitute!

Attitudes toward property rights and their exchangeability by contracts are, in part, based on how the rights and contracts permit *distribution* of risky consequences—profits and losses. Since profits and losses occur regardless of the form of property rights, the issue is whether one is for or against a given system of: (a) distributing the risks of profits and losses (and the profits and losses themselves) over various people, and of (b) stimulating the uses of resources that increase their value. The bearing of profits and losses could be assigned by the political system, in which case the assignments will depend on one's political power. Because socialism is a political allocation of profit-and-loss risk-bearing, part of the issue between the private-property and socialist property systems is over the desirability of their respective risk-distribution institutions. In a private-property system, those who de-termine the uses of resources are more likely to bear the (upward or downward) capitalized value effects of future events.

Risk Allocation by Contracts within a Firm: Wage and Employment Security

The so-called owners of the firm borrow or hire resources as well as use their own. They buy equipment; they lease it; they hire (rent) labor. In each contract the risk-bearing depends on differences in attitudes toward risks, beliefs about the prospects of success, and the ability to usefully direct and to monitor performance of the resources.

For example, some employees make longer-term contracts (formal or tacit) at agreed wages. Most resources (and people are resources) face fluctuating demands for their services. Transient, imperfectly predictable fluctuations in demand will create either (1) instant changes in wage rates if employment is not changed, or (2) instant changes in employment if the wage rate is not changed. Neither alternative is necessarily as acceptable as (3) a steadier job at a lower, but more assured, wage. In the first two arrangements, employed inputs bear more of the risks of varying incomes over the future; like stockholders, they bear the risks of the market value changes of their own resources. The third arrangement, however, indicates that some employees act more like moneylenders who are promised a fixed interest rate (though lower than the average on riskier common stocks) regardless of the firm's fortunes. They agree to more as-sured employment at an assured (but slightly lower than otherwise) return. The employer then bears more of the risks of the future transient fluc-tuations in the net value of the products, net of the relatively constant, assured costs of those in-puts. The employer maintains the wages and em-ployment by using fluctuation-smoothing buffer inventories of goods and borrowed funds. When demand for products of the firm fall temporarily (the owner hopes), he retains those employees—at various, probably less-useful tasks. And during transiently high demand, the employees with these arrangements have tacitly agreed on their part not to leave the firm for transiently higher wages that might be available elsewhere.

There is an understanding that despite the *usual* transient shocks, misfortunes, and events, each would stay with the other, with the employer bearing the risks of those fluctuations and assur-ing a relatively steady income to these "tenured," higher-security employees over the longer in-terval. During short recessions, the firm would not so quickly lay off those employees and would maintain their wages. Other unemployed people would, of course, like to get those maintained jobs during that transient recession. But the em-ployer would not hire them, even at lower wages, to displace his "tenured" employees. We there-fore observe many employers retaining workers at wages higher than those asked by other people seeking those jobs during transient decreases in demand for the firm's product. He honors his tacit agreement with his "tenured," senior em-ployees. Otherwise, he would increase his long-run costs of getting employees during future normal conditions, because employees would not so willingly work for contract violators.

A relatively stable business will have less risk in providing such assurance. A firm that makes a larger variety of products with higher probability of offsetting fluctuations in the demand for its various products can give more employment se-curity by transferring employees from one prod-uct line to another.

Governments and some nonprofit enterprises which respectively derive incomes from taxes or investments rather than from customer sales give greater security of employment for lower wages. Initially government jobs with greater security paid less, as in the post office. But recent legisla-tion requiring pay equal to that of private firms will create an excessive demand for those jobs if that equality of pay is not offset by disadvantages in other features of the more secure job.

Other resources employed by the firm, even the initial capital, are hired on a similar variety of terms, though usually with more explicit con-tracts. Firms hire (that is, borrow) capital funds for investments in plant and equipment. The stated interest rate on longer-term loans is con-stant over a long period and the firm continues to employ the funds even during recessions when the rate on new loans is lower. The firm also uses short-term loans, usually bank loans, of a few months' duration at interest rates that are more sensitive to short-term business conditions than are the long-term borrowing rates. These short-term loans are paid off ("laid-off" or "unem-ployed") when the firm reduces output in tran-sient recessions.

Every resource used in the firm is available under a variety of risk-bearing, insuring arrange-ments. Labor seems to make risk sharing ar-rangements with the employer, probably because of the higher costs (less security) for an employee to borrow single handed against the value of one's labor, as contrasted to borrowing against the security of one's house or other salable assets. The employer in effect becomes a financer of short-term "loans" to his employees when he retains them at the prestated (but otherwise too high) wages during recessions, while the employees repay by continuing to work during boom periods at lower wages than they could have obtained transiently elsewhere.

Employees who are more steadily valuable to employers over intervals of business fluctuations —for example, administrative, nonproduction, security, and maintenance staffs—are more likely to have job stability. Employees who have acquired special knowledge about this particular firm and whose replacement would involve new costs of familiarization are also more likely to be maintained. People who have worked with the firm longer will have more job security (seniority) since they have shown a greater probability of staying with the firm without insisting on transiently higher wages during transiently higher demands. Younger people just entering the market, still searching out career features, are less likely to remain employees of a given firm. An employer's ability to judge their future productivity is less than for "proven" employers, and hence the likelihood of such contracts will be lower.

Those who are self-insuring providers of services to the firm suffer greater fluctuations of income than do those whose income is insured by the employer. During recessions, losses of the firm will increase as the firm continues to pay employed inputs more than they are worth at that moment—but at other times earnings are larger because insured incomes do not rise as readily.

6, 7
8, 9
10, 11

The consequent larger fluctuation in returns to the firm's owners is not some necessary, natural consequence of the world. It reflects voluntary, contractual risk-sharing by the contracting parties—given that future demands and economic conditions are not perfectly and costlessly predictable. For example, a lender of money to a business firm can make a very short-term loan for a fixed interest rate. Normally he will be repaid on time and bears little risk of any interim events that might affect the security of that loan. Others may lend for a 20-year period and expose themselves more to longer-term risks and greater changes in the sale value of that bond in the interim. Others may choose to invest in some firm as an owner rather than as a lender, and experience a wider range of potential values of his investment depending upon how well the firm does. Similarly, employees—sellers of their services to a firm—can make contracts on a shorter- or longer-term basis for a fixed wage or an adjustable wage that depends on business conditions.

Summary

1. Teamwork, another source of increased output over independent production, requires team organization, supervision, and monitoring.
2. Team organization, monitoring, and supervision can prevent wasteful team sizes.
3. Different property arrangements of jointly used resources affect the efficiency of team sizes. Private-property rights to resources permit efficient team organization. Communal rights can lead to excessive congestion and overuse of facilities.

4. The results of team productivity under government control cannot be deduced because a valid theory of the reward and incentive structure for government agents is not available.
5. Among equally efficient property structures and types of contracts among team members, some will be preferred in accord with willingness to bear risks or degree of optimism about the team's productivity.

Questions

1. What is the measurement problem in joint teamwork that is not present in specialization of the type examined in the preceding chapter?
2. a. Why is zero congestion wasteful?
   b. What social institutions prevent too much congestion and achieve optimal congestion?
   c. What is the meaning of "optimal" congestion?
*3. Cite examples of privately owned overcongested resources, and some that are undercongested. Can you explain why each occurred? Cite examples of governmentally controlled overcongested resources, and some that are undercongested. Can you explain why each type occurs?
4. Which of the following are examples of the type of excessive congestion when more than five people are on the boat?
   a. traffic jams
   b. crowds at public parks in summer
   c. air traffic at J. F. Kennedy airport at about 5 P.M.
   d. pollution of Hudson River near New York
   e. deer hunting on opening day
   f. public tennis courts on Sunday afternoon
   g. full house in a movie
   h. citizen band two-way radios
   i. sidewalks at Christmas time
   j. New York subway at rush hour
   k. air in New York and central Los Angeles
   l. buzzards eating a dead wolf
   m. residential crowding in a large city
   n. customers in a store during a sale
5. Suppose in the fishing boat example in the text, people discovered how to make boats that were good for one day and that cost the equivalent of two fish. Assume all property was privately owned, and there are 1000 people.
   a. How many boats would the community use each day?
   b. What would be each person's income?
   c. What would a boat's selling price be and how many boats would a boat maker have to be able to make in one day in order for it to be worthwhile to do so?
*6. For what events is the distribution of risk the same in socialist and capitalist systems? (Hint: How about divorce, cancer, baldness, homeliness, having children all of the same sex, being left-handed?)
7. Contrast socialism and private property as means of distributing risks of profits and losses.
8. What is the relationship between the right to buy and sell and the distribution of profits and losses?
*9. Our laws and customs reflect the assignments of risk bearing. A person who owns land as private property must bear the con-

sequences of changes in the value of that land if people move away or no longer value that location so highly. Similarly, if he catches cold or breaks his leg or becomes hard of hearing and can no longer earn so large an income, he must bear the consequences.

a. Would you advocate that people bear the wealth losses to their private property regardless of cause (aside from legal recourse to violators of property rights)?

b. Would you want a homeowner to bear the consequences of a meteorite's falling on his house? Fire from using gasoline in the house? Flood damage to houses near rivers? Income loss from cancer? Blindness?

c. Who do you think should bear the loss if the individual does not?

d. Why would you draw the line differently in different cases? What is the criterion you used?

e. In each case, do you think people's behavior would be affected according to the risk bearing involved?

f. Would you allow people to agree to take on certain risks in exchange for not bearing other risks, if two people could make a mutually agreeable partition and exchange of such risks? How would that differ from a system of private-property rights?

*10. a. In your first job after college would you rather have (1) a lower wage with more assurance of not being laid off during a transient recession in the first year—with an implied understanding on your part that you will not leave until after a year even if you found a better job, or (2) a higher wage with no such assurances?

b. Which preference would imply greater unemployment for you?

c. Who is likely to prefer (1) and who (2)?

11. "Private property permits selective, discretionary risk bearing." Comment.

10

The Business Firm: Control and Coordination of Production

Predicting Best Production Opportunities

Searching for the most valuable activities a person can perform; coordinating joint efforts among team workers; controlling opportunistic shrinking; assigning risks; distributing rewards according to productivity; negotiating and enforcing legal contracts—all of these activities are costly. The business firm has developed to perform them more economically. Suppose you, a carpenter, wanted to know which of your services would yield the highest value, and where. Should you search the entire market by yourself, or use a specialist in collecting and interpreting information about the values of carpenters' potential services? Keeping up with shifting future demands requires continuing, daily activity. Why not rely on the same specialist on a continuing basis for information and guidance? He may be more optimistic or more accurate—that is, an efficient "entrepreneur." And if carpenter services are best performed by a *team* of carpenters, you may use a specialist who is superior at discovering, directing, and monitoring other appropriate carpenters as team members. You could do all these tasks yourself, but performing the tasks of your specialization is often more productive. Providing information about better opportunities for work, selecting good team members, directing joint production, monitoring performance, and arranging for risk-sharing are some functions of the business firm.

Detecting the Realized Value of Production

Often it is more economical to police (detect and measure) the service value of other members in a jointly performed act by observing and directing their production techniques rather than by examining the final product. If production is carried on by a team of several jointly cooperating workers, detecting and controlling shirking is a problem. Whatever their talents, people can be trusted to shirk. The more difficult it is to detect each person's marginal product performance, the more will the members tend to shirk (even though each wished no one else would). Indeed, each would prefer to work with a group in which no one, not even himself, would shirk—if only there were some way to detect any such opportunism.

Monitoring Performance

A simple technique for adapting to shirking (rather than completely eliminating it) is for the employer to anticipate its average extent and then pay each member a smaller wage to offset his opportunistic shirking. Just as money wages will be smaller if room and board are provided, so will money wages be smaller if various fringe customs of behavior are allowed for—such as personal use of company phones, longer coffee breaks, tardiness, etc. These are acceptable by the employer as long as no employee exceeds the average extent of such fringe "benefits." The explicit wage will be compensatingly lower for each person. But if deviations from the average are excessively difficult to detect, some employees will benefit from *undetected* shirking.

Another technique that reduces shirking is competition from potential replacements who, if they can detect opportunistic shirking, will offer to work better or for lower wages. Competition reduces cheating. Competitors must detect and evaluate performances, inform potential customers of superior alternatives, and persuade employers to believe the alternatives are superior. But that valuable information is not acquired without cost. Markets do aid in collecting and transmitting information, but they are not the only means. (The costs of these activities are carelessly said to prevent markets from being "perfect" or "ideal." So what? It is just as silly as saying costliness of producing steel and gasoline keeps the world from being "perfect" or "ideal".)

If the employer is to monitor performance, who monitors him? Monitors shirk, too. Competition by other potential monitors to replace detectably shirking monitors is one method of keeping monitors effective. Another, self-restraining force will be imposed on the monitor if he is entitled to residuals of the team's product after prespecified, assured payments to other members. The better he supervises and monitors, the bigger will be that residual. To be effective, a monitor must not merely watch and direct other team members, he must also replace inappropriate members or renegotiate the wages, fees, or rents. This means he must be a central, common party to the contracts of each member. He decides which members stay and which do not. He is given the leadership in selecting what the group should produce, who the team members are to be, which

are worth their pay, and which should be replaced. He is typically called the "owner of the firm"—the boss, the employer.

The Firm

A capitalistic firm is a group of resource owners, bound by contracts, with the following characteristics: (1) the inputs of the several owners are put to joint, team use in directed production effort; (2) there is one central party common to all contracts with owners of the joint inputs, with rights to renegotiate any contract independently of the other contracts; (3) the central party holds the residual claim beyond prespecified obligations; and, (4) the central party can transfer or sell its position in those contracts. Modifying any of these characteristics changes the firm from a capitalist one to, possibly, a nonprofit firm, or a socialist firm, or still another kind (to which we will pay little attention).

Will the central party be the most knowledgeable or the most optimistic person who places the highest probability on a positive residual? It is tempting to say "Yes," and assert that new firms spring up and *survive* whenever some resource owners *correctly* estimate the value of their potential services as being higher than estimates by existing firm owners. But that is a characteristic of a superior monitor; to be a superior monitor is to measure more accurately the marginal value of each input as well as to know how to *direct* activities. If he is an excellent monitor only in detecting what has been happening, and is not so good in knowing what to produce, his survival (profitability) as a firm owner is unlikely;

he would instead be a good supervisor. To survive as an effective, superior owner, he must have a superior ability to predict consumer demands as well as a superior ability to detect performance—at least of good supervisors. Economics calls him an *entrepreneur.*

In socialist firms, too (whether they be Russian, Yugoslavian, or an American post office or public school), values of alternative products must be predicted, inputs must be directed, and opportunistic shirking must be controlled. Socialist firms also use centralized-agent contracts, but with less of the *residual claims* assigned to the central agent and more to the employees. Without a residual claim his incentive to efficient self-monitoring is weakened. The residual, whether a plus or a minus, is shared more by all team members. As a result, nonproprietary or socialist firms (such as your college?) seek other means of restraining shirking.

This interpretation of the private-property, employer–employee type of entrepreneurial firm differs from the commonly voiced interpretation whereby employers exploit employees. If you are persuaded of this latter interpretation, why not test it by reversing the argument? Claim that employees exploit employers by making them do the guaranteeing and risk-bearing, because supervising monitors won't be disciplined monitors unless they are "forced" to bear those unpredictable gains and losses. Pejorative interpretations substitute emotion for cognition.

Another fact is important: If consumers do not value a firm's product above the costs (values of best alternative uses) of the resources and labor used, the firm will not survive. The owner of the firm is a middleman *forecaster* and planner between consumers and productive inputs. He will

sustain payments to the inputs as long as consumers value the product more highly than the costs (highest-valued alternative uses of those resources). When a firm owner objects to an increase in the cost of inputs, he is reflecting his anticipation of consumers' objections; for he could cover the costs if consumers did not object. When businessmen object to higher costs, or restrictions on what they can produce, or requirements that quality be higher or products be safer, they object only in so far as they believe consumers will object. For example, General Motors would be delighted—and profited—to add expensive bumpers and safety equipment if consumers valued them above their costs. But because consumers have not valued those items above their costs, the auto producers have strongly objected to them. Producers objected because they that believed consumers would not buy the products in such quantities, and that reduced sales would reduce the values of resources specialized to the production of automobiles. The businessman is essentially a middleman conveying to productive resources his predicted value of their products.

The Corporation

Private business firms commonly assume one of three contractual forms: individual proprietorship, partnership, or corporation. A proprietorship is owned by one person responsible for all debts of the firm, usually to the full extent of whatever wealth he owns—that is, with unlimited liability. A partnership is a joint proprietorship of two or more people, each of whom usually has unlimited liability for the entire firm and can individually make business-related contracts binding the other partners. A corporation has transferable, divisible ownership rights with liability of the corporation limited to only the wealth of the corporation.

With approximately 65 to 75 percent of the total sales of U.S. production, corporations are by far the dominant form of business enterprise, whereas proprietorships account for only about 15 to 20 percent. But in numbers of firms, the proportions are reversed. Almost half of the five million business firms are (wholesaling and retailing) proprietorships. And another five million unincorporated proprietorships are in agricultural and professional activity.

The largest 10 corporations have from 100,000 to 600,000 employees each. The 100 largest industrial corporations employ over six million people, or about 10 percent of all employees. Each of the top 50 corporations exceeds $1 billion in sales annually, with assets of about the same value.[1] Because today's business firms are much larger than those of 30 years ago, we might conclude that it is now harder to organize a new business. However, people are wealthier; organizing a $100,000 capital fund for a new business venture is probably no harder than gathering $10,000 was 50 years ago. Each year for the past 50 years, new firms have been organized at a ratio of about one new to ten existing firms. Half the new firms are terminated in five to ten years because of losses.

A few hundred large corporations "produce" nearly half the value of final industrial output. But this fact must be interpreted carefully. For example, General Motors buys components from thousands of smaller firms. When these parts are assembled into a Chevrolet, should it be said that General Motors produced—or assembled—the Chevrolet? Thousands of firms were involved in designing and providing parts and equipment to that giant assembly line known as General Motors. If we see only the final assembler, we might say that General Motors sells ("produces"?) 50 percent of the cars. If we see all its suppliers, then over one thousand firms "produce" those cars. What, then, does General Motors contribute in that productive sequence? Whatever it is, does it control the automobile industry in determining prices, styles, quality, and employment policies for other producers? Is there less response to consumer demands than if there were scores of assembly firms in place of one General Motors? Would improvements occur more often? Do General Motors' decisions about its production make wages, prices, or total output any different than if there were a hundred firms all responding to the same market forces? Answers to these questions will be suggested in the later analysis.

If the corporation elects to sell its common stock (which is the form in which shares of ownership are expressed) to the general public, it usually must first receive approval from a state or federal regulatory agency (for example, the Securities and Exchange Commission). The promoters must reveal information useful to any prudent investor. Also, if the regulatory commission thinks the corporation is not "strong enough," in some states it can prohibit the sale of stock to the general public.

[1] General Motors has about $25 billion in sales, followed by American Telephone & Telegraph, Exxon, Ford Motor Company, General Electric, Socony Mobil, Chrysler, United States Steel, Safeway Stores, and International Business Machines.

Limited Liability

In England, the name of the corporation is usually followed by "Ltd." (as in Rank-Xerox Ltd.), which is an abbreviation of "limited" to indicate limited liability. A corporation may be owned entirely by one person, as Ford Motor Co. was when Henry Ford was alive; that person therefore owns all the shares of common stock and his liability for debts of the corporation is limited to only the assets of his corporation. If owners (of common stock) of a corporation see opportunity for more profitable investment in the business, they may put in more of their own wealth or may borrow from others, by issuing bonds of the corporation to the lenders; or they may sell more shares of common stock in the corporation.

We can immediately see that the more the corporation borrows (by issuing bonds), and therefore the less of the invested wealth is (proportionally) their own, the more the owners (the persons who own the common stock) would be tempted to make investments that promise bigger payoffs but at greater risk. They would do so because all the profits will be theirs, while losses, if any, are limited to the corporate wealth. In the event of losses, bondholders cannot claim the stockholders' private, noncorporate wealth. Bondholders (lenders) are aware of all this. They therefore ask and get a higher interest rate, but equally, or more important, they put restrictions on investments the owner can undertake. Their effects are therefore thrust back on the corporation owner-manager in the form of greater interest rates, increased restrictions, and reduced value of their stock ownership.

The corporation can tap another source of investible funds by issuing and selling more shares of the corporation's common stock. Existing owners will share the corporation ownership with the new shareholders. A new problem arises: The more people who share the ownership, the lower is the fraction of costs the initial operator–owner bears for any shirking, relaxing, or failure to get as large profits as possible. Every dollar of profits forsaken costs less than a dollar—say 80 cents of the $1 if he shares ownership with other shareholders who have 20 percent of the common stock. Because common-stock holders are the residual claimants with rights to earnings or profits, the more sharers of these residuals there are, the less of the realized profits will the initial entrepreneur obtain. His costs of shirking or taking nonpecuniary (nonprofit) sources of utility will be lower. He will have less incentive (less reward) to make as big profits as otherwise.

These effects on behavior are present in all society and all people, and are not consequences of the corporate structure. They are evident wherever self-interest is diluted—as it is in marriage, the family, and all social life where consequences of one's actions are not entirely borne by him. In legal terms these are effects of what are called "agency" and "trustee" enforcement costs.

Transferability and Continuity

Unlike a partnership or proprietorship, a corporation is not terminated by the sale of ownership or stock to a person or persons other than the initial entrepreneur. Moreover, transfer of shares by sale, gift, or legacy all can be done without permission of other current owners, whereas in a partnership, permission of the other partners must be obtained. Sales of already outstanding stock of many large corporations are usually negotiated in a stock market (such as the New York, American, and several local exchanges). The shares of most corporations are sold so infrequently that they are not traded in formal stock exchanges. These lesser-known corporation shares are sold by private negotiations, often through a geographically dispersed but close-knit set of independent stockbrokers known as the "over-the-counter" market.

"Separation of Ownership from Control" or "Efficient Partitioning of Ownership Rights"?

Ownership usually refers to entitlements to: (a) authoritatively decide the use of a specified set of goods (that is, as against the decisions of other people); (b) transfer those rights to some other person(s) in exchange for other rights to other goods; (c) bear the changes in the usefulness or market value of those entitlements to the goods, whether the value changes because of physical change or exchange values.

A corporation—even General Motors—is not only equipment but also a set of contracts among owners of inputs. Is there an *owner* of that set of contracts, or just some common party to all of them? It is tempting to say the "common stockholders," who have the residual claim, are the owners; they are party to all the contracts through their director–manager. However, stockholders often sell some components of that set of ownership rights to other people. For example,

they often sell part interest in the residual earnings to *preferred* stockholders, persons who become part owners but without the rights to appoint directors or rights over specific goods or rights to operate the enterprise (as the common stockholder can do himself, especially if there is, say, just one stockholder). In fact, common stockholders make a variety of contracts with some inputs of labor, such as high-level administrative assistants, whereby those employees share in residuals (profits or losses) but lack other rights of ownership. Directors—who are elected by stockholders on a one-vote-per-share basis, not on a one-vote-per-person basis—are authorized to make contracts (that is, to select and authorize operations) in the name of the corporation.

The common practice of partitioning the set of ownership entitlements and features will be efficient if people differ in their talents. Though the partitioning among different talents creates conflicts of interest among the holders of the partitioned rights, the benefits of specialization in exercising the various rights can exceed the costs of satisfactorily controlling and resolving those conflicts. Therefore, such partitioning of private-property rights does not necessarily lead to inefficient separation of "ownership from control" or inefficient corporate economic activity, as has often been alleged.

Nor does ownership of a corporation by thousands of stockholders, no one of whom owns a majority of the stock, imply inefficiency.[2] Directors

[2] In 1975 General Motors had 1,350,000 stockholders (800,000) (employees in parentheses), General Electric had 530,000 (400,000), General Tire had 52,000 (40,000), General Foods had 97,000 (48,000), General Mills had 29,000 (50,000), General Telephone had 500,000 (200,000).

rather than stockholders are said to control the corporation (while stockholders bear the risk of changes in the value of the assets of the corporation). But that does not imply the director–managers run the corporation with inappropriate attention to stockholders' (and others') interests. On the contrary, a different interpretation is possible—as we have already seen in respect to employer–employee risk-bearing. Many people want to share, by investment, in the prospects for profits of ventures managed by especially skilled persons, relieving them from some risks. Wary investors or "outside" shareholders are not left "holding the bag" or "submitting to the control of others." They are "investing in other people" or "sharing profits" or "sharing ownership" in the corporation.

Conflicts of interest occur within the corporation as they do in every group. The more diffused the stock holdings and the larger the corporation, the higher is a stockholder's cost of policing the corporation's internal management as thoroughly and effectively as in a small proprietorship. This problem resembles that of the taxpayer whose cost of policing government employees relative to his gain is ludicrously high. There is a difference, however. In contrast to a taxpayer or a citizen in a socialist state, the capitalist corporation shareholder has a salable right in a capitalized value of the future consequence of his actions. That salable capital value of the common stock will reflect more of the entire projected future consequences of corporation members' present actions. The capitalist shareholder therefore has more cause to monitor corporate action. More widely dispersed stock holding does not necessarily impose losses on stockholders, for

they have discounted its effects into a lower initial offer price for the stock.

Still another potent force makes managers responsive to stockholders' interests—competition among managers. Management is not a monolithic bloc of persons scratching each others' backs and tolerating shirking and inefficiencies. Each is interested in his own fortune. If he went along with any such presumed inter-employee "collusion," he would sacrifice opportunities to attract job offers from other corporations. And *that* is the source of his rapid advancement. Even a college faculty member would be careful in his work despite the fact that his employer may be relaxed and inefficient in surveillance of the teacher's performance. Why? To attract offers from other schools. We work *for the world* at large; our current employer is only one of the intermediaries in the vast constellation of specialized activity. We advance by appealing not only to his interests but to the interests of other potential intermediary employers as well. Teachers have interests in excelling and in letting others know of their excellence. This holds for managers, too.

Competition from other people applies to stockholders also. If present stockholders are lax in exercising control, the value of the stock will fall, and this will attract other people to buy a sufficiently strong block of the stock to vote out the existing management. You will hear of "take-overs" (stock offers by one corporation to exchange its shares for that of the acquired—merged—corporation, in order to remove and improve the management in the acquired company), proxy battles for voting rights of the common stock, and tenders (offers to buy a block of stock at a stated price somewhat above the current market price). All these activities, and the threat of them, help to discipline or displace poorer management. The improved management, if so it is, will result in a rise in the stock prices, thereby rewarding all the stockholders. Of course, existing management will not approve of raiders and will be happy to see their efforts frustrated by regulations and laws prohibiting such offers or takeovers. (The Securities and Exchange Commission has promulgated rules that make takeovers more difficult, to whose benefit we leave to your imagination.)

The politically regulated or not-for-profit enterprises permit more departures from market-value disciplines, because consumer demands become less influential the less managers are judged by their effects on the profits of the firm.

Yet popular discussions (to be distinguished from economic analyses) abound in suggestions that the large, private-property corporation with thousands or millions of stockholders is run inefficiently and to the harm of stockholders, and is not responsive to consumers' valuations of the corporation's services.

Finally we face the ultimate question about ownership of a firm: What do the owners *own*? One is tempted to say the residual—the possible profit or losses. But that is only part of the answer; it doesn't explain why owners of a firm can persistently receive a net over all the costs of renting equipment and services and interest on borrowed funds, and a normal return on any physical assets owned in the firm. Why have competitors not bid away all those responsible resources (even as a package), or at least bid up the resource prices and rentals and eliminated any net return to the current owners? What asset is yielding the owners some return?

An answer lies in the sources of knowledge available to consumers about the products and service of that firm. Potential buyers want some knowledge of the quality and future performance of goods and services offered by each seller. Some predictability of future performance is valuable. One source of predictability is the past performance of the producer. Past performance builds a present reputation which is an assurance to the customer of a predictable quality of product. That respectability is identified and conveyed, not created, by its name—for example, Cadillac, Kodak, Sony, GE, Squibb, Texaco, IBM, McDonald's, Holiday Inn, Coke, J.C. Penney, Safeway, Tiffany. Imagine that General Motors secretly produced the same cars in the same way but with new names on the cars, so the public did not know it really was the same General Motors product. How many cars would be sold? At what price? With what confidence for consumers? Consistent, proven performance at some level of quality—not necessarily at the highest level but at a predictable level—is what counts. For example, the names Travelodge and Intercontinental are equally reliable predictors, one for a medium quality and price and the other for a higher quality and price. Both names are valuable to consumers as identifiers of sources of reliable products or services at lower costs than such identification and information could otherwise be obtained.

That name is owned by the firm's owners. Its information value has been built by incurring costs for more reliable services and products. The investment in creating the reliability of the product sold under that name is what they are getting a return on, a normal return on investment in an "intangible," but an intangible that is just as real as a building.

Once a trade name, by representing a known reliability, becomes valuable, its owners can even rent it to others by what is called a franchise. The Hilton Hotel firm is willing to rent the name Hilton, for say three years, to a hotel owner (franchisee) on the condition that the franchisee operate the motel according to the standards of service for which the Hilton name stands. Without the owner's control over the service rendered under that name, the franchisee would tend to provide inferior service, making temporary profits while ruining the name that he doesn't own, much as one would mistreat a rented house if the landlord didn't provide for penalties and standards of upkeep. If the franchisee operated the hotel at the same standards as Hilton's but under a different unknown name, he would not be able to attract so many customers because they have no way as cheap as use of the name Hilton to tell them what kind of service and accommodations they would get.

When Standard Oil, New Jersey, changed its public trade name from Esso (to avoid legal conflict with other Standard Oil companies) it took great pains to make clear that the new name, Exxon, was merely replacing its former name Esso, and was not the name of some new company. To have introduced the new name without indicating which company it represented would have failed to transfer to it the consumer's valuation of the Esso name as a predictor of a quality of service.

The value of the name of the firm is often called goodwill, but that value is hardly ever fully recorded in the accounting records. Instead it is contained in the market value of the common stock of the corporation. If one could subtract the sale value of all the other assets of the corporation, the remainder would be goodwill. But that calculation is prohibitively difficult.

Fundamental Sources of Profits

Because foresight is imperfect, changes in market values are inevitable; profits and losses will be realized. Profits and losses occur in all economic systems. Not even a change from a capitalistic to a Communist or socialist or feudal society will hide their profits and losses; it will only change the determination of who bears them. Only if uncertainty is eliminated will the situation be different; and certainly no earthly revolution will remove uncertainty.

For exposition we group the sources of uncertainty into two opposite classes: (1) extraneous, uncontrollable events, and (2) deliberate innovative activity by resource owners.

Foresight is imperfect: Innovative activity and extraneous events alike yield results not entirely foreseen by the public at large. These unforeseen events, whether innovative or extraneous, change the values of the pertinent assets, since those new values had not been fully discounted into the prior existing price. Innovative activity deliberately seeks to raise resources that are at one value to more highly valued uses or conditions—the difference being profit. If other people had foreseen the event, the resources would already have been at that higher value (discounted by the rate of interest).

Prospects of profits motivate innovative activity. Yet one person's innovation and resultant profits, or a shift in demand, may cause a loss to another person. For example, the invention of the automobile reduced the value of buggy whips, and the innovation of television reduced the value of theater buildings. The loss in value of the theater building is more than offset by the social gain from television. But the theater owner who bears that loss, if he is not somehow compensated, is no better off than if a fire damaged the theater. When losses are the result of improvement elsewhere, is the bearer of this loss always compensated, even if in principle it is possible to do so? As we shall see, in every social and economic system the answer is "No." Still another question is whether or not one should try to compensate him; but that is a question of normative policy, and we shall postpone discussing it.[3]

Profits of Labor

A distinction between profits and the wages of management, or between profits and wages in general, does not mean that labor is not a source of wealth to its owner. *Wages* are payments or receipts for personal services, while *rent* is payment for services from inanimate goods. Both a flow of wages and of rentals have present values (wealth), reflecting anticipated future receipts. The present value of my future wages may be $200,000. If I have an accident and fracture my skull, I will suffer reduced prospective future receipts; and the present value of my wages will fall, say, to $150,000, a loss of $50,000.

[3] Discussed in Chapter 16.

We see and measure profit of nonhuman wealth more clearly because inanimate goods can be bought and sold, whereas a person does not sell himself; he typically sells only his current services. If he could literally sell his future services now, he could convert (or "cash in") his profit to other forms of wealth. But since he cannot, he must risk the value of his wealth in the form of his labor. Even though a person can't sell his future services now, he *can* borrow now against his future wages.

In a sense, all profits—or values—are values of people rather than of inanimate goods. Goods are valuable only because of how people use them. People with superior talents know better how to use resources to make them more valuable. If, for example, General Motors hires a superior designer to design a car of greater value, the increased value of the cars at first shows up as a profit to General Motors. But if we keep our analysis correct, we must recognize that the designer was obtained for a salary less than his worth proved to be to GM. No one knew in advance just how valuable his services would be. GM had to accept the initially uncertain value of his services. GM's ability to hire him for less than his ultimately revealed worth reflected differences in opinion about that worth among General Motors, other potential employers, and the employee himself. But now GM cannot continue to purchase his services at less than they are revealed to be worth unless *all* other potential employers remain ignorant of his real ability—and he will not let his ability stay hidden. The proven high value of his services will accrue to him as other employers bid for his work, driving up his wages and raising costs to all who thereafter use him.

None of this means that GM or any other employer makes profits by paying less for resources than they are worth. What resources are paid is what the rest of the market thinks they will be worth *at the time* they are bought or hired. Always, too little is bet on the winner and too much on the losers. If anyone makes a profit, it follows by definition that the earlier value placed on the resource was too low. And losses result from earlier overvaluation.

Profits: Luck or Superior Ability of Operators of the Firm?

Some firms have larger net earnings because of lower costs or better products: (1) They were able to get resources at prices less than their real productivity, or (2) the owners of the firm put resources to new higher-valued uses than anyone had formerly perceived, or (3) both (1) and (2) were true. The entrepreneurs either had better ability or were lucky, or both. Whatever the case, when the rest of the world catches on, it will bid for the responsible undervalued resources, thereby bidding up the input prices (and hence costs) to more fully reflect their true values. This bidding up absorbs the profits into higher wages, rents, or purchase prices of those inputs, and brings down prices of the final products when more is supplied.

Persisting differential earnings among inputs or firms are attributable to unequal ability, so the differences in earnings are labeled *differential earnings,* or *Ricardian rents,* of superior talent. The concept emphasizes the distinction from *monopoly rents,* which are enhanced earnings to some sellers by prevention of other people from bidding for the responsible inputs and thereby raising input prices—and lowering product prices —to what they would have been with open entry by competitors. An example of differential Ricardian earnings or rents is the difference between Frank Sinatra's earnings and those of "second rate" singers. In contrast, examples of monopoly rents were those of owners of football or baseball teams who were able to hire star athletes at lower salaries (high as they may nevertheless be) because other team owners were restrained from bidding up the salaries of the star players—under rules of the professional athletic leagues (rules known as the Rozelle rule, reserve clauses, or player drafts). "Monopoly" rent will be explored more in the next chapter.

How fast is the superior ability of a person, asset, or enterprise converted to a higher price for its services? As fast as the rest of the most optimistic other people come to believe that the superior ability is really there and not just a one-time lucky experience. One of the authors made a hole-in-one the first time he played golf. No one immediately offered him a professional contract; 20 years later he is still looking for his second. An author who writes one successful book has high probability of not writing another one as good. The "regression fallacy" is not committed by the market.[4] People recognize that great suc-

---

[4] The regression phenomenon is the tendency for good luck to be followed by normal luck. For example, of 100 identical salesmen some would have higher sales in one week by good luck. In the next week they would more likely have their usual luck and would get fewer sales, nearer their long-run average. Similarly those with very bad luck the first week would not have such bad luck the next week, and so their sales would improve the second week. The very lucky in the first week tend to *regress* toward their longer-run average— because they cannot continue to have unusually good luck. Those below their long-run performance level because of

cess is unusual, so initial success is not immediately extrapolated into confidence of ensuing success with a salary of value justifiable only by the (extrapolated) continued high success. On the contrary, it is expected that later performance will regress back towards true ability, as the person is decreasingly lucky. Only a continuation of superior performances yields sufficient evidence of real, inherent superiority. In the interim, a really superior resource, be it a person or a nonhuman asset, will be undervalued—but ultimately will rise in value. Anyone who knows which ones are undervalued could make a fortune hiring or buying at initially undervalued market prices.

Accounting
Records of Earnings

What rates of earnings (profits) do businesses create? Ask anyone at random and be prepared for answers like 30 to 50 percent of sales, or 20 percent on the investment. Public samplings reveal that these are typical opinions. The facts,

---

unusually bad luck in the first week will show better results in the second week. This tendency to *regress* toward the long-run average, after either unusually good or bad luck, is called the regression phenomenon. It assumes that the differences in performance in the first week were at least partly affected by transient luck.

One of the classic ways of taking advantage of this is to invite people to take some performance test—say a reading test—and to tell those who score below average to take lessons in "reading improvement." After the lessons their test performance will on average improve because some of their performance on the first test was due to unusually bad (nonrepetitive) luck. But their performance would on average have improved whether or not they took reading improvement lessons.

however, are that, on average, earnings are about 1 to 5 percent on sales and about 5 to 10 percent on investment, for *successful* firms. As much as 20 percent of all firms report losses in any one year.

Earnings as a *percent of sales* are highly misleading. First, if a person invests $1 to produce some product in one day and sells it for $1.01 (a rate of 1 percent on sales) and repeats the action every day for a year, he will have had sales of $368.65 in the year with net earnings of one cent each day, or $3.65 throughout the year. That is 1 percent of sales per year, but it is a very large return of 365 percent per year on the $1 investment. The relevant measure is the return on investment, the amount of wealth devoted to earning the $3.65 over the year. Second, a very small margin of earnings on sales does not mean it will be wiped out by a slight rise in costs, for the price may also be affected in the same direction, depending upon general supply and demand conditions (such as we have already analyzed). Many businessmen with very small margins of net earnings on sales use that as an indication they are not earning "excessive profits." Whatever the facts, "excessive profits" is merely an emotive term suggesting profits are larger than someone thinks they should be.

Financial accounting provides a record of the company's business activities, such as the amounts of money spent or committed to future payment, and the goods and services obtained in exchange. But *not all* of the foreseen and predictable receipts and expenditures are recorded. All past expenditures and receipts are included in the accounts, but only *some* of the future commitments for expenditure and foreseeable future receipts are included. Noncontractual future prospects of receipts or expenditures are excluded, for very good reason, as illustrated by the following scenario.

With $31,000 I buy land and oil drilling equipment ($10,000) and pay wages ($21,000) to the drill workers. In a year we strike oil. What should our accountant do? Should he record an estimate of the present value of the unknown amount of uncaptured and unsold oil? If I could now get $100,000 on the market for the land and oil rights, then *whether or not* I sell, my wealth has increased to $100,000 plus any resale value of the drilling equipment (which we shall assume is now $6000—down $4000 from its assumed initial price of $10,000). My wealth is $106,000 and since I have no liabilities, my wealth gain (my profit) is $75,000 (= $100,000 − $21,000 − $4000).[5]

However, the accounting records will show a *loss* of $25,000 during the year! (We used up $4000 of oilwell equipment and $21,000 for wages and related services but have sold no oil.) The accountant is unwilling to record a value of the prospective *future* oil sales, because the oil has not yet been sold at a definite price. If the oil is to be valued, *accounting custom* dictates it should be valued at cost ($25,000) and called *book value,* $25,000. If we didn't understand the custom, we might think the $25,000 represented the *market* value of the oil field, but the usual accounting convention is *not* to record any value over costs at all (or at best only up to a formal $1) until there is a clearcut sale and receipt from that asset. Also, a zero (or $1) valuation is

adopted if the asset is not a physical, tangible thing but an idea, design, patent, new product, trademark, or reputation or "quality assurance" or personality. For example, the value of the name "Kodak" was established by a consistently reliable product; the name identifies a product of reliability, thereby attracting sales. How should that expensively created, fragile, valuable asset, the name "Kodak" be valued? At the advertising cost? At the cost of having created reliable products? At zero? Or at some estimate of its assurance value to future customers? Convention prefers the zero value—false though that value certainly is.

Regardless of accounting convention, we know that the prospect of future sales *is* part of the value of a firm. Ford has no contract with future customers for sales of Ford cars next year. Nor does any retailer or manufacturer have any contract that says the public will continue to buy his product. Nevertheless, we can be "sure" that sales will occur. To be "sure" means only that we are prepared to "bet" on it. I am prepared to bet that Ford will have many sales next year, and I am prepared to back my bet by buying some share of common stock in that corporation. I pay for (bet on) the *prospect* of successful *future* operations. In fact, the market price of almost every good is a present bet about prospects.

11, 12
13, 14

Wages, Interest, and "Profits"

There is much confusion about the meaning of income, earnings, and profits. Do not treat receipts, after paying for all services or materials

---

[5] For simplicity of numbers we ignore interest cost over the year. If $10,000 were paid initially and $21,000 at year end, with a 10 percent interest rate, interest costs would be $1000 (.10 × $10,000). Profit would be $1000 smaller—$74,000.

provided *by other people,* as "profits," or net income. If the owner owns some resources which he has invested in the firm, he must count as costs what he could have earned had he invested that amount to the best alternative use in the market. Their forsaken earnings are costs of using them in this firm. That is given by the rate of interest. Thus if he had invested in equipment worth $1000, he must count his forsaken interest, which, at a competitive rate of interest of 5 percent per year, is $50 per year ($= .05 \times \$1000$).

What about his own labor services? If these are counted, and they should be, we can assume for example, they amount to $25,000 per year. These costs total $25,050. If, after all that, he still has a surplus of product value, he has a profit. That excess occurred because he was able to produce more than the *market* (that is, everyone else) expected he could produce with all those resources. It is a pure profit, something the market did not expect to occur, or else the rest of the public would not have let him buy those services so cheaply if any other person could have done so.

When reading that some enterprise has "net earnings" or "income" or "profits," you must investigate in each case to determine whether they have also counted the costs of interest on their investment and their implicit wages. Usually, the reported net earnings is the net *before* that interest on the investment is deducted—and sometimes before the implicit wages of management of the owner.

Expected Current Losses

If you examine the annual reports of business firms, you will find assertions like: "We have started production on a very promising new product and are currently operating at a loss, but we expect that in a year we shall be covering costs and making profits." If that statement were taken literally, one would wonder why they hadn't waited until next year to start operations. Translated into our terms it means: "At the present time the rate of receipts is less than current expenditures, but the present outlays will bring larger future receipts that exceed future outlays. We believe the new product will promise a net flow of actual receipts in the future that will increase our wealth. In fact, the investing public is now of the same opinion, and that is why the market value of our shares of common stock has increased during the current year, so we have really had a profit. Hooray!"

The Quick Pay-Off Period

"It takes three years for us to recover our investment before we can start making a profit." Such a statement implies some *payout* or *cost-recovery* period: Money outlays exceed the money receipts during the first three years, and only in the fourth year do total receipts begin to overtake the total expenditures. But who cares? The important thing is that the *present wealth value* of the receipts should exceed that of the outlays. There is no need to be concerned about the length of that cost-recovery period: A short payout or cost-recovery period has the virtue only of reducing the time one has to wait to find out whether the new venture really will do as well as hoped.

Other Definitions
of Profits

Difference between
Wholesale and Retail Price

To the ordinary businessman *profits* do not always exactly correspond to how they are defined here, since no one has a copyright on the term *profit.* The term is used for a wide variety of relationships between expenditures and receipts. Sometimes a retailer calls the difference between the price that he pays for goods and the price at which he sells them "profit." More normally, that difference is called *markup,* as an indication of how much above the purchase price the selling price must be if all the other attendant costs are to be met. To ignore those other costs is to forget about space, shelter, management, sales clerks, inventory for display and immediate delivery, record-keeping, security, insurance, advertising, taxes, light, heat, fixtures, breakage, pilferage, packaging, returns, employee training, and many other costly activities. *Overhead costs* commonly refers to some of those costs. Yet some people ignorantly say that the sale of a good at a markup of 100 percent (of the wholesale purchase price, or 50 percent of the retail price) represents a profit of 100 percent. Even U.S. Congressional reports have said so.

Profits before Taxes

Another error is to count all costs except taxes, thus calculating "profits before taxes." Remarkably, this concept was used by a government agency, apparently unaware of its implications. Does it not suggest that taxes are not really a part of costs—that they are payments for no service? It is difficult to believe that the government agency would want to suggest that taxes are merely tribute collected from those obtaining profits. One would hardly be more surprised if a labor union published a graph of "profits before wages" as if to assert, falsely, that wages are not a part of costs.

Profits, Monopoly
Rents, and Changes in
Monopoly Rights

Not every gain reflects a transfer of resources from lower-valued to higher-valued uses. Suppose I manage to have a law passed preventing other people from producing goods that compete with mine. The reduced supply from a reduced number of competitors will raise the price of my goods, giving me a gain. This can be done by levying special taxes on my competitors—in the form of, for example, interstate tariffs on goods produced in other states that compete with mine in domestic sales.

The "profit" that results from my competitors' constricted access to the market is called a *monopoly rent—monopoly* because of the legal restriction on market access; *rent* because it (monopoly rent) is not allowed to induce an increase in supply. The legal monopoly restriction on entry will raise the market valuation of assets already in the protected industry. The restriction prevents more resources from being transferred to artificially higher-valued uses. The result, from the consumers' point of view, is the same as would occur if costs were higher than they really are. The "privileged" or "licensed" resources earn their owners a higher value, while the excluded resources receive a lower value.

How much of the current value of a resource is *monopoly rent?* This is an interesting, important, but unanswered question. Some estimates, based on evidence, range up to $3000 of monopoly rent for an acre of land on which tobacco can be grown and sold in the market, because of restrictions on permissible tobacco production. This is nearly 50 percent of the total value of that acre of land. In New York City, where entry into the taxi business is legally restricted, the monopoly rent of one taxi is over $30,000. In California and Florida the monopoly rent of a liquor license ranges from $10,000 to $100,000, because the number of licenses is restricted by law. In most states the present value of banks, insurance companies, airlines, and all public utilities reflects a monopoly rent of various amounts, depending upon the extent to which entry is restricted. Value also depends on the extent to which the monopoly rent is taxed away by the government, or prices are kept down by law so that the legal monopolists cannot realize the maximum market value of their monopoly situation.

We must be careful not to confuse monopolists of this kind with others who are also called monopolists in the economic literature—*market-power price-searchers.* Almost all retailers and manufacturers, large and small, have market power because they face a negatively sloped demand curve for their products.[6]

15, 16
17, 18
19

---

[6] To be explained more fully in Chapters 13 and 14.

Summary

1. Employer–owners of business firms provide information to potential employees about best productive opportunities.
2. Business owners predict values of productive services; they bear risks of losses from paying producing services more than the worth of products, and they bear gains from producing services worth more than the costs.
3. Business firms are cooperating groups of productive services under special contractual agreements about monitoring, assembling, supervising, paying the group, selecting output, and dividing the value of that output.
4. In the capitalistic firm the cooperating members are bound by contracts such that (1) inputs of the several owners are put to joint, team use in a directed production effort; (2) one central party is common to all contracts with owners of the joint inputs, with rights to renegotiate any contract independently of the members; (3) the central party holds the residual claim; and (4) the central party can transfer or sell its position in those contracts.
5. In value of output, the corporation is the dominant organization of a firm. The owners, called common-stock shareholders, can transfer their rights independently of other members, and have no liability beyond assets of the firm. In short, it has limited liability and continuity, usually with several joint owners.
6. The separation of ownership from operating management creates agency costs of monitoring actions of managers. Owners do not suffer from this since they pay a lower price

to reflect monitoring costs of assuring con-
formance of managers' actions with interests
of owners. Advantages of specialized managers to operate firms more than offset incurred agency costs. This is true for any form
of organization, corporation, proprietorship,
government agency, or nonprofit institution.

7. In a capitalistic firm with private stockholders,
the capital value of perceived present and future consequences of managers' actions are
more identifiably assigned as present marketable wealth of owners, who therefore have
more incentive and reward for more effective
monitoring and supervision arrangements
with managerial agents.

8. The ownership value of a firm is the value of
the quality assurance of that enterprise's past
record to consumers and the anticipated continuing organizational superiority in the assembled team of cooperating inputs. To the
extent it is not possible to hire away that
organizational superiority except by hiring
away the whole team, no single member can
obtain that value by adequately large competing offers from other employers.

9. Imperfect foresight of the future value of any
productive resource will result in losses or
profits to that input as the future is revealed.
This is true for labor, nonhuman capital
goods, and owners of a business organization. Usually the gains or losses to individuals
from their labor services are called simply
changes in wages, even though those
changes are profits and losses.

10. Innovative activity may result in greater profits or losses. Therefore, some profits or losses
occur because of superior or lucky (or inferior or unlucky) innovative activity. Distin-

guishing superior ability from luck is not
always possible. As superior skills are discerned, superior inputs obtain higher prespecified incomes and less in the form of
profits.

11. Monopoly rents obtained by restricting competitors to enhance one's own income—the
increase in which is a monopoly rent—are
often called profits.

12. Competition among firms for resources responsible for value of output in excess of
what is being paid to those resources will bid
up their prices to match the value of the
product of those resources. In short, profits
are converted into incomes of responsible inputs as firms compete for them and bid up
their incomes to the value of their marginal
productivity.

13. A primary task of businessmen is not reading known tables of costs and known demands for goods and services. Instead, it is
the striving to detect, predict, and gain from
more accurate determination of what goods
and services are most demanded or most
highly valued by consumers. Successful prediction and striving means using resources
worth less elsewhere for output worth more
here—with a profit to the businessman, or a
loss if he fails to find a greater valued use.

Appendix: Interpreting Financial Statements

Most business firms periodically (commonly every
three or six months and annually) issue financial
reports of their activities and current status. Re-
produced below is a slightly modified (for teach-

ing purposes) balance sheet reported for the United Nuclear Corporation for March 31, 1976. A *balance* sheet presents a listing and valuation, according to the company's books, of its assets, liabilities, and ownership structure. *Assets,* as we know, are the resources owned and used by this corporation. There are always claims held by other people against a business; these claims are called *liabilities.* The net (of liabilities) value to the owners of these assets is called *proprietorship, capital, equity,* or *net worth.*

The basic definition is:

$$\text{Assets} - \text{Liabilities} = \text{Equity},$$

which can be rewritten:

$$\text{Assets} = \text{Liabilities} + \text{Equity}.$$

The firm's situation is then presented in the form of a balance sheet, with items classified as assets on the left side and liabilities and equity on the right side. What do the items mean?

Assets

Cash. The amount of money held, including checking accounts.

Accounts receivable. These are the past sales yet to be paid for by customers for the company's products; charge accounts or credit extended to customers allowing them, usually, 30 days to pay.

Reserve for bad debts. Very likely some customers will fail to pay their debts when due. To express this fact and to estimate the expected amount of receivables that will become "bad," the accountants subtract an amount called a "reserve for bad debts" or "doubtful accounts." This is called a "reserve" because it expresses a "reservation" or "qualification" about the value of the

receivables. Reserves in accounting statements do *not* represent collections of money or particular assets that have been reserved (in the sense of set aside) for some particular purpose. This balance sheet later shows "reserves for depreciation," which is a way of expressing a reservation about the value of the assets. It represents the total depreciation so far accumulated; it is *not* a fund set aside for new equipment to replace the depreciation. As used in bookkeeping, the word *reserve* almost never denotes a setting aside of cash or actual reserving of assets. It is almost always used to express explicitly a reservation or adjustment in the stated value of some asset or liability.

Unbilled costs. The corporation is making some nuclear reactors to custom order; and as a reactor is gradually completed the corporation records the incurred costs as claims accruing against the customer, for which a bill will be submitted upon completion and delivery to the customer.

Inventories. The corporation refines uranium ores. This is the value of ore removed from its mines and not yet sold, plus any other unsold products. In general, this records values of products on hand.

Prepaid expenses. The corporation has paid in advance for some goods and services yet to be obtained. These are rights against other people who have contracted to deliver goods and services for which the corporation has already paid. This is an asset. For example, when you prepay a magazine subscription, you would record that asset as a prepaid expense in your personal balance sheet.

Marketable securities. These are typically U.S. government bonds or notes payable in the near

United Nuclear Corporation
Balance Sheet, March 31, 1976
(in Thousands of Dollars)

Assets		Liabilities	
Current		**Current**	
Cash	$1,929	Accounts Payable	$11,923
Accounts Receivable	4,669	Notes payable	2,358
Reserve for bad debts	—600	Accrued liabilities,	
Unbilled costs	13,335	future production	10,200
Inventories	7,515	Current liabilities	24,481
Prepaid expenses	756		
Marketable securities	5,577	**Long-Term**	
Current assets	33,181	Long-term debt	48,623
		Minority interest	3,974
Long-Term		Long-term Liabilities	52,597
Investments	9,334		
Government contracts	18,244	**Equity**	
Plant and equipment	69,877	Preferred, convertible stock,	
Less reserve for depreciation	—7,000	10,000 shares (5%, $100)	1,000
Other	538	Common stock ($.20 par)	
Goodwill	100	5,175,000 issued	1,035
Long-term assets	91,093	Capital surplus	28,658
		Retained earnings	18,538
Total assets	124,274		47,196
		Liability + Equity	124,274

future, common stocks of other companies, or bonds of other companies. In all cases, these securities are saleable on bond or stock exchanges.

Investments. United Nuclear Corporation owns some stock of another company. Usually, the particular investment is identified in footnotes that accompany the balance sheet.

Plant and equipment. This is original amount paid for the physical property—mines, mills, etc.—of the corporation. Sometimes this is the *cost of replacing it,* especially if there have been dras-

tic changes in costs of this equipment since purchase.

Reserve for depreciation. The property, plant, and equipment have been used and partly worn out. An estimate of the portion of the plant so consumed is called "depreciation." Subtracting depreciation from the initial price gives the "book" value of equipment. (See above: *Reserve for bad debts*.)

Other assets. These can be almost any kind of asset—mines, land, buildings, claims against others, patents, or even U.S. government bonds. Usually footnotes to the balance sheet will give clues. While usually this item is not large, sometimes it is enormous, especially if there are some unusual temporary holding assets. In the present case it is larger than usual when compared to past balance sheets for this company.

Goodwill. Patents and trademarks are often given some small or token estimate of value and called goodwill. Sometimes the continued success of a company is reflected in certain intangibles, for example, its reputation or brand name. This may be recorded as a goodwill item. Usually the *recorded* value is not significantly large.

Liabilities

Liabilities are conventionally categorized into *current* and *long-term* liabilities, with the former usually representing claims that must be paid within a year.

Accounts payable. The corporation has purchased goods and equipment for which it must yet pay. The amount still due is recorded.

Notes payable. The corporation has borrowed, and the amount due is shown. This item may also include any long-term debt that will fall due within a year.

Accrued liabilities. At the present moment (the end of the month), the corporation has accrued obligations to pay taxes or wages at some near future date. For example, if wages are paid on the fifteenth of the month, then at the end of the month it will owe about half a month's wages, to be paid in two weeks.

Long-term debt. The corporation has issued bonds to borrow money. In the present instance, these will run until about 1985.

Minority interest. The corporation is the primary owner of a subsidiary company, the entire value of which has been recorded among the assets. However, since United Nuclear Corporation is not the sole owner, it has recorded here the ownership rights of the other owners of this subsidiary mining company. Usually every balance sheet has an appended list of footnotes or additional information giving further details. In this case the report happens to tell us in a footnote that the subsidiary company, which has a recorded value of about $14,700,000, is all included in United Nuclear's reported property, plant, and equipment ($69,877,000) on the asset side. $3,974,000 of that belongs to other people—the subsidiary company's other owners, the *minority interest*. This recorded minority interest offsets part of the value shown on the asset side.

Equity

Many firms include more than just equity under the heading of *Equity*. Some, like this one, include also a special form of debt, "preferred convertible stock." We shall first explain what that is and then explain the way the pure *equity* is presented.

The first item shown is *preferred, convertible stock.* "Preferred stock" is a fancy name for what is simply a debt of the company. It is called preferred stock because the holders of that stock, in the event of bankruptcy, have a preferred claim against the company, prior to that of the common stock holders. This might have been called bonds of $100 denominations paying 5 percent per year —except that preferred stock often differs from a bond in that if the $5 "interest" or "dividend" on the preferred is not paid, the preferred stock holder cannot institute legal foreclosure proceedings against the company. He simply has preference to the earnings, if any, for payment of interest before any dividends can be paid to the common stock holders. Sometimes the preferred stock is "cumulative," which means that any arrears of unpaid dividends (or interest, if you will) accumulate, and until they are paid, the common stock holders cannot take any dividends. And, as in the present instance, the preferred stock may be "convertible," which means that the preferred stock holder has the option to exchange (convert) it into common stock at a preset exchange rate. In the present instance, the exchange rate is ten common for one preferred stock (information usually given in a footnote to the balance sheet). Thus the present preferred convertible stock has a par of $100 with 5 percent, it pays $5 preferred dividends each year (if earned) and may be converted to 10 shares of common stock.

A person who buys a share of preferred convertible stock for $100 has some hope that the common stock will rise above $10 a share; by converting to 10 shares he will then have more than $100. As the price of a common share approaches $10 in the stock market, the selling price of preferred convertible stock will rise above $100, reflecting both the current value of the preferred "dividends" due and the present values of further future possible rises in the common stock price. A purchaser of *convertible* preferred common stock is in fact a partial common stock holder or owner. A purchaser of nonconvertible preferred stock is simply a creditor of the company.

Finally, some preferred stocks (and bonds) are "callable"; that is, the company has the option to pay it off prior to its due date. A $100 callable preferred stock will usually be callable at some price slightly above $100, but the premium diminishes as the due date approaches. The owner of a "callable, convertible, cumulative, preferred stock" (of $100 par value, at 5 percent, convertible at $10, and callable at $105 within five years) will collect $5 a year dividends, if earned; he may be offered $105 for the stock (which he must take unless he decides to convert); he can convert it to 10 shares of common stock (since 10 shares of common at $10 per share will equal the $100 par value of the convertible preferred share). As you can see, all sorts of terms are possible in a "preferred stock."

The remaining three items show the equity proper, which usually is expressed in three parts: *common stock, additional paid-in capital,* and *retained earnings* (sometimes the last two are combined and called simply *capital surplus*). We already know that equity, by definition, equals the difference between assets and liabilities (including preferred stock as a liability). In the present instance, if we subtract the liabilities (current plus long term) from the assets ($124,274,000 − $77,078,000), we get $47,196,000, which is the *book value* of the common stock holders' equity. How was it attained? Initially, when the stock was issued, $29,693,000 (= $28,658,000 + $1,035,000) was paid into the company. The figure recorded for legal and tax purposes is $1,035,000 as the *initial par value* and $28,658,000 as the *additional amount paid* originally for that stock. This division is of no economic significance and reflects some technically legal quirks. We mention it here to avoid any impression that the par value reflects some true economic value.

What happened to that $29,693,000? It was spent (along with proceeds of loans) for property, wages, equipment, etc., and at the moment the results of that activity are shown as assets on one side and as incurred obligations on the other.

Retained earnings. The corporation has *invested* $18,538,000 of its own net earnings to purchase new equipment and facilities. It may also have paid out some dividends to common stock holders, but we can't tell from the balance-sheet data. (Retained earnings are often called *earned surplus*.) If it had losses, they will reduce this figure.

Such is what the historical balance sheet record of the United Nuclear Corporation indicates. If we divide the recorded *book value* of the ownership, $47,196,000 (= $1,035,000 + $28,658,000 + 18,538,000) by the 5,175,000 shares outstanding, it comes to about $9.12 a share.

It is tempting to conclude that a share of common stock is worth about $10; but don't yield to that temptation, or else you are rejecting everything you have learned in this book, and especially in Chapter 7. Why? Because the figures in the balance sheet's asset column are the historical outlays for the equipment (adjusted for depreciation). They do not tell us what the company will be able to do in the future. How do we know that the uranium mine—which *cost,* say, $1,000,000 to find and mine—is not going to yield $100,000,000 in receipts, or maybe nothing?

None of this is revealed by the balance-sheet asset records—unless the corporation directors decide to make a prognosis of that future receipt stream, discount it into a present value, and record it under "goodwill" or "profits." But they don't do this, simply because they know how unreliable that is. Instead, they issue a report of operations and events along with their balance sheets. For example, United Nuclear Corporation once reported: "The outlook for widespread civilian and military use of nuclear energy for both power and propulsion improved greatly during the past year. The capability of the industry in the free world countries, based on presently known or reserve information, is estimated to be about 20,000 tons annually. This in the face of a projected annual amount demanded of 40,000 tons, excluding military purchases." But the directors did not foresee that a proposal to build another nuclear-powered airplane carrier would be rejected, or the current fear of nuclear hazards. All the directors could do was report what was then known and make some clearly labeled forecasts, which other people can accept, reject, or revise at their own risk.

The book value is a measure only of the past costs of accumulating the assets—adjusted by a formal depreciation method. It is *not* a measure of what the assets would sell for now if disposed of piecemeal if the company were to be liquidated. Nor is it a measure of the value of the company's future net receipts from its business operations. The present value of its future operating earnings may be far above the costs of the assets it uses. An excess of stock price over book value is an indication of profitable prospects; it is not an indication of deception of the stockholders. Nor is a stock price below the book value any evidence that it is a safe investment in the sense that if worse came to worst the company could sell off its assets and collect enough to pay each stockholder the book value. The book value is a measure neither of the piecemeal disposal value nor the value of the going enterprise as a whole. It is instead merely a formalized means of indicating the past costs of the owned assets, adjusted for depreciated use value by some formal

---

United Nuclear Corporation
Income Statement, Year Ended March 31, 1976

Sales		$83,261,000
Costs and Expenses		
Costs of goods sold (labor, materials, power)	$67,929,000	
Depreciation of equipment and depletion of ore	4,599,000	
Selling and administrative	6,079,000	
Interest on debt	4,105,000	
		82,712,000
Operating net income		534,000
Share belonging to minority interest		111,000
Federal Income Tax		25
Net earnings		422,075
Earnings per share		$.08

---

method that often bears little if any relation to the future earnings prospects or the decrease in current market demand for those assets. In 1976 the price had risen to $40. Moral: Forget book value for all practical purposes and look deeper into the company's situation.

At the time the balance sheet situation is disclosed the company also issues its *Income Statement,* a statement of its receipts and expenditures during the year ending at the date of the balance sheet. United Nuclear reported net earnings of $.08 per share of common stock for the year ending March 31, 1976. That is less than 1 percent per year on the value of a share of stock, hardly a competitive return compared to yields available on secure bonds (about 7 percent) or on common stocks (around 12 percent). Why the difference? The current earnings may in the future grow to large earnings. It is the present value of all those future earnings that is reflected in the stock price.

A company with expectations of rapidly rising future earnings will have a high present value on its stock, but low *current* earnings. Stocks with different patterns of future earnings should not be compared by looking at only their current earnings. A company with negative earnings this year but with superb prospects of large positive earnings in the future could be worth more than one with positive earnings this year but no prospects for future earnings growth. The ratio of stock price to current earnings is a highly misleading basis for comparing two stocks—although many people naively use that ratio.

Questions

1. A friend of yours, a brilliant engineer and administrator, is operating a business. You propose to bet on his success and offer him some money to expand his operations. A cor-

poration is formed allotting you 40 and him 60 percent of the common stock. You invest $30,000. This is often described as separation of ownership from control, since he now has the majority controlling vote. Would you ever be willing to invest wealth in such a fashion— that is, give up control while retaining ownership to 40 percent of the value of this business? Why?

2. Is it a disadvantage of the corporation that not every stockholder can make the controlling decisions? That the control is dispersed? That some people who own less than half of the corporation can make controlling decisions?

3. A criticism of the modern corporation is that the management or directors, by virtue of their central position, are able to collect proxies (rights to cast votes of stockholders) from the other stockholders; and as a result the management is in a powerful position and cannot be easily dislodged. It has been said that "the typical small stockholder can do nothing about changing management and that under ordinary circumstances management can count on remaining in office; and often the proxy battle is fought to determine which minority group shall control." Take the assertions as being correct.
   a. Does it follow that stability of management in "ordinary circumstances" reveals some losses to stockholders?
   b. Does it follow that a typical small stockholder "should" be able to turn out management?
   c. If a minority group succeeds in getting a majority of stock votes, does this mean that a

minority controls or that a majority controls through the medium of a minority group? Is this to be interpreted in the same way that political parties consisting of a group of organized politicians have elections to see which minority group shall control the government? Why or why not?

4. "Very few corporations lose wealth, and still fewer go broke." Do you agree? What evidence can you cite?

5. a. In analyzing the behavior of corporation management and directors, why is it pertinent to distinguish among nonprofit or publicly regulated, profit-limited corporations on the one hand, and private-property, for-profit business corporations on the other?
   b. Which do you think would be more marked by self-perpetuating management and stockholder lethargy? Why?
   *c. Which do you think would show more discrimination in employment practices according to race and religion? Why?

6. Joseph Thagworthy has a stable of race horses and a breeding farm. The two, although operated as a business, lose him over $50,000 annually. Yet he continues year after year because he enjoys the activity more than if he spent a similar sum for travel or conventional types of consumption activities.
   a. Would it be correct to say that he is maximizing his wealth in that business?
   b. Would it be correct to say he is maximizing his utility?
   c. Do you think an increase in the losses would induce an increase in that kind of activity? What does economic theory postulate about that?

7. An actress, after years in the movies, suddenly hits it big and obtains an enormously larger salary.

a. Has she a profit?

b. Three months later she begins to get fat, and in a year her contracts are canceled. Has she experienced a loss in any sense different from that suffered by Ford when it introduced the Edsel?

8. A young college teacher hits upon a sparkling teaching style and is rewarded with a higher salary. Has he had a profit? Explain.

9. "Under a socialist system, profits and losses are eliminated." Comment.

10. "Paper profits and losses are not real profits or losses." Do you agree? If so, why? If not, why not?

11. The process whereby secret information is revealed by the stock market is exemplified by the following episode: On March 7, 1954, the *New York Times* reported a test in which a new bomb of enormous force had been exploded on March 1, 1954. On March 31, 1954, Atomic Energy Commissioner Strauss reported publicly for the first time the nature of the new bomb and its dependence on lithium. Weeks prior to his announcement, the price of the stock of Lithium Corporation of America, one of the producers of lithium, increased substantially. How is this rise in price consistent with the fact that everyone connected with the corporation and the test really kept the secret?

12. General Electric and Xerox each recently sold their loss-ridden computer subsidiaries to Minneapolis Honeywell because the subsidiaries were unable to avoid losses. Why would anyone *pay* for a business that is *losing* money? It should have a negative value. One would think that General Electric or Xerox would have to pay someone to take on a business that is losing money. Explain the behavior of these firms. Can you find some explanation that doesn't make the buyers foolish companies? If your explanation makes the buyers look sensible, is it consistent with General Electric and Xerox selling their computer divisions rather than continuing with them?

13. You buy some stock for $100. A month later it has risen to a high of $150. Another month later it is down to $125. Have you had a profit or a loss?

14. Kawecki-Beryllium Corporation common stock sells at a price 80 times as great as the accountants' reported current annual earnings. The stock of Allegheny Ludlum Corporation, a steel producer, sells at less than 10 times its reported "earnings." Assume that the same accounting principles are used in each firm. What do you think will happen to the price of each firm's stock if in the next reporting period each firm reports earnings that are *unchanged* from the preceding period? Explain. (What would the price-earnings ratio be in some year of losses?)

15. A liquor-retailing license in Florida was recently sold for over $110,000. The seller was the person who initially got the license from the state at a cost of $1750. Did the subsequent buyer get a profit in the form of a monopoly rent? Did the initial licensee get a profit in the form of a monopoly rent?

16. a. Which of the following represent some wealth based on monopoly rents? A TV station in Texas, United Air Lines, General Motors,

teamsters in Teamsters' Union, General Electric Company, American Telephone and Telegraph Company, Frank Sinatra, beet-sugar farm land owners, local electric company, Aluminum Company of America, savings and loan banks, professional baseball teams.

*b. In each case in which you think wealth based on monopoly rent is present, how would you test for its presence? And how would you measure the amount of monopoly rent?

*c. In each case where you think it is present, who gets it?

17. "Capitalism encourages deceitful advertising, dishonesty, and faithlessness." Do you agree? If so, why? If not, why not?

18. Suppose it were true that rich people got rich exclusively from profits. Suppose further that those who received the profits were no smarter, no more foresighted, no nicer, no harder working, no more productive than other people. Does this mean that their profits are "undeserved" and that the rich people performed no service?

19. Taxes are often levied on corporations. What in fact is being taxed?

11

Costs and Production

This chapter may be skipped if you are not interested in detailed production decisions and if you are willing to accept the following nine propositions:

1. The higher the selling price of any good, the greater the amount that will be induced from producers.

2. Marginal costs determine the output rate. The total cost per unit determines only if the firm could produce profitably.

3. Marginal costs are higher: (a) at higher rates (speeds) of production, and (b) for quicker changes in output.

4. Average cost per unit and marginal costs decrease for larger planned volumes of output— no matter what the output rate for that entire quantity. Thus 10 airplanes of a given model will cost more per unit than if 100 airplanes were made (similarly for refrigerators, automobiles, suits of clothes, shoes, etc.). The reduction of average and marginal cost through larger planned *volume* is called *economies of mass production*. The increase in marginal and average cost through higher speeds of production (of whatever planned volume) is called increasing costs of higher *rates* of output. Do not confuse the two.

5. If both speed and volume are larger in a production plan of some product—so that the volume is larger in the course of a year's planned production because the rate of production is also faster during that year—the mass-production effects of larger volume tend to dominate until very high rates are involved. No well-established generalization or law is available, except that there is some high rate of use of current resources at which their costs increase and begin to dominate the mass-production effects. Thus although it is possible to get more at lower unit costs, getting it faster will cost more.

6. A short-lived output from existing production facilities can be produced at lower cost if the value of those facilities for other tasks is less than in its present uses. When the facilities wear out, their replacement costs must be covered for production of longer duration.

7. Money prices are *measures* of costs because the buyer must pay at least the value of what the owners of resources think could otherwise have been produced with them. Economists emphasize this by speaking of *opportunity costs*. The word "opportunity" can be omitted, for all costs are opportunities forsaken. Yet to remind ourselves of this, now and then "opportunity" is used as an adjective to "cost."

8. The term *implicit cost* is used if no money payment is made at the time the good is used—it having been obtained long before. If, for example, I already own a garage and use it to store my automobile, the storage costs are not zero even though I pay no money rent to someone else. I could have rented my garage to someone else or used it for some other purpose. The highest-valued forsaken alternative use of the garage— whether by someone else or by me for some other purpose—is the cost of using my garage to store my car. The term "implicit" is used to remind us that the cost is present though not necessarily explicitly evidenced by a current money payment.

9. Finally, and inconsistently with what we shall do in this text, the concept of costs should always be expressed and measured in terms of present value or wealth. The unavoidable present and future forsaken opportunities consequent to having committed to some present action are mea-

surable in terms of the value of reduced claims to future services and goods. This is done by discounting the values of forsaken opportunities into a present capital-value change in wealth, as explained earlier in Chapter 7.

One's present wealth—which is nothing but a *measure* of the present and future services available from his existing resources—will be lower because of that reduced future potential—the cost he incurs by his present action. So the correct and most useful measure of costs is in terms of present value of one's wealth—one's claim to available services and uses now and in the future. Those sacrificed options are measured in the reduced present value of his wealth.

Actions and Costs

Businessmen contemplate future possibilities and, in the light of their estimates, conjectures, hunches, guesses, hopes, and past experience, they invest for some anticipated output program. How large should one plan his initial venture to be? For what rate of sales? At what selling prices? With what marketing tactics? If we could answer those questions, we'd be billionaires advising satisfied clients: Ford would not have produced the loss-creating Edsel, nor General Motors the Corvair; neither General Electric nor Xerox would have entered the computer business at a great loss; Kodak would have geared up for three times the number of Instamatics it first estimated; Wards would have expanded immediately after World War II, when Sears did. And thousands of other people would never have entered business and subsequent bankruptcy. We will now examine a few of the output decisions

and their costs. In later chapters we consider how these costs affect pricing tactics, output, competitive behavior, and wealth.

Cost of Acquisition: Transactions Costs

Normally, we call the purchase price a cost. We also think of cost as the using up (that is, reduction) of some of our personal wealth. If you pay $1000 for a bond, you do not reduce your personal wealth. You exchange wealth in the form of money for wealth in the form of a bond. *Cost* is the forsaken opportunity, so the cost of the act of *acquiring* the bond is zero (ignoring commission costs) only *if* you could turn right around again and sell the bond for $1000. You forsake no opportunities, since everything you might have done you still can do.

Suppose you contemplate buying a Ford at a purchase price of $4000. The top half of Table 11–1 lists all the pertinent expenditure data, which we shall explain. The immediate resale value is $3700. If you kept the car for two years (without using it) the resale value at the end of two years would be $2500. If you use the car at the rate of, say, 10,000 miles of travel per year, the resale value will be only $2200 in two years. What is the cost of acquiring the car? It is $300, the difference between the price and the *immediate* resale value. (See bottom half of Table 11–1.) Once the car is acquired, this cost is "sunk" or "fixed."

Continuing Possession

Once the car is acquired, what is the cost just of continuing its possession for two years? It is

Table 11–1. Expenditures and Costs for Acquisition, Possession, and Operation of Car for Two Years

		Expenditures		
	Now	End of First Year	End of Second Year	Present Value
Purchase Price	$4000	—	—	$4000
Resale Value				
Not driven	(3700)	—	2500	2066
Driven 20,000 miles	—	—	2200	1818
Tax and insurance	200	200	—	382
Gas, tires, repairs	—	500	700	1033

	Costs	
1. Acquisition	$4000	
	—3700	
		$300

2. Possession for two years; zero mileage (that is, without operation)

Current resale	3700	
Final resale (present value)	—2066	
Depreciation	1633	
Tax and insurance	382	2015
Acquisition and continued possession without operation:		2315

3. Operation (20,000 miles in two years)

(Extra depreciation because of mileage)	$2066	
	—1818	
	248	
Gasoline, oil, tires, etc.	1033	
Operation		$1281
Total costs of acquisition, possession, and operation		$3596

the difference in the value of the car now and the *present value* of its resale value in two years. Do not subtract $2500 from $3700! They are values as of *different* dates. If you learned your lesson well in Chapter 7, you will know that the two figures must be compared in contemporaneous values. Therefore, convert the $2500 of two years hence to a present value. At 10 percent annual rate of interest, the present value of $2500 deferred *two* years is .826 x $2500 = $2066 (use Table 7–1).

Subtracting this from $3700 gives $1633 as two years' depreciation.

To add more realism, assume taxes and insurance must be paid if the car is possessed. At the *beginning* of each year $200 is due for the year's tax and insurance, whether or not the car is operated. Converting these two payments to present values gives $100 + (.909)$100 = $381.80, the present value of taxes and insurance if the car is possessed for two years. The cost of two years' continuing possession, *given that the car is already acquired,* is $1633 + $381.80 = $2014.80. The cost of *acquiring* and *keeping* (but not using) the car for two years is ($300 + $2014.80) = $2314.80.

Operating Cost

But you are not managing a museum of cars; you want to use the Ford. Other outlays, listed in Table 11–1, will be made for repairs, gasoline, etc., and will be paid at the *end* of each year, as if they accumulated on a credit card. (Note that we call them expenditures and outlays—not costs.) Since we cannot properly add outlays now to outlays a year later without adjusting for interest, we convert all outlays to present values. They sum to $1033[1] (see Table 7–3). The resale value of the car will depreciate more if the car is used. We assume it will decrease to $2200 at the end of two years rather than to the "nonuse" $2500. The extra depreciation over the two-year interval is $300, which has a present value of $248 (at 10 percent rate of interest). Adding this $248 to $1033 gives $1281 as the present value measure of costs of *operations.*

[1] ($500 × .909) + ($700 × .826) = $1033.

$1281 is the cost that could be avoided if operations were stopped (but the car was kept). The figure would vary according to the actual use of the car (we assumed 10,000 miles per year). You can see why this figure is sometimes called the *variable* cost; the cost will depend on the actually performed service. The other cost, $2315, is independent of the mileage performed, and is therefore also commonly called "fixed" (which gives us a second concept of a "fixed" cost). The sum of $1281 and $2315 is $3596, the total cost in capital-value measure, for acquisition, continued possession, and provision of 20,000 miles of service in two years. These distinctions are important for answering such questions as (1) whether to enter the business and (2), once one has entered the business, whether to get out of business if receipts fall short of expectations or to shut down temporarily until conditions improve.

We now have the following classification of costs for the two-year, 20,000 mile output program:

Cost of acquisition = $300 or 1½ cents/mile.

Cost of possession = $2015 or 10.07 cents/mile.

Cost of operation = $1281 or 6.41 cents/mile.

Each of these costs has several different names and keeping them all straight is a tedious task. We list their most common names:

Acquisition cost ($300):
sunk; fixed.

Possession cost ($2015):
overhead; constant

Operation cost ($1281):
 direct; operating; out of pocket; variable.

Especially ambiguous are the terms "fixed" and "variable," which are used in several conceptual senses. The above list of names is not exhaustive. You will simply have to deduce from the context what specific cost is meant if you hear one of these terms, or some other one, used. Or else ask the user.

1, 2
3, 4
5, 6

Costs and Output Size

We next give an example of how costs depend on the particular output and we explain (with a little more detail than in Chapter 8) the concepts of marginal and average variable costs, which are important for understanding how production responds to demand and price. The purpose of these examples is not to present realistic cost data. In every actual case the marginal and average cost will be something the producer will have to ascertain as well as he can.

What do we mean by a larger output? It could mean a faster rate of production per day (or any unit of time), or it could mean a larger total volume or amount produced over a longer period of time without necessarily speeding up the rate at which that larger volume is produced. If the rate of production is increased from, say, 10 units per year to 15 units per year, for a whole year, both meanings are implied: (1) More will be produced (a larger volume), and (2) production is at a faster rate (15 units in a given time instead of 10 in the same period).

Cars, or hamburgers, or anything can be produced in a volume of, say, 1000 units at many different rates. The faster the rate, the less the time required to produce the 1000 units. But producers often think in terms of a given length of time. Production of cars, for example, may be planned for a year's production. If the length of the period of production is fixed, then an increase of the volume means the *rate* of production must be increased during that period.

The appropriate production technique will depend on both the planned rate and volume. General Motors decides to produce 150,000 units of a new economy car during the coming two years. Having planned a *volume* of production for the two years it has also necessarily picked an implied rate of production, that is, 75,000 per year if it produces them throughout the two-year interval. Many production techniques can yield 150,000 units in the desired time. The producer wants the least-cost production technique—no easy task, if it can be identified at all. Information about prices of various inputs and the technical substitution possibilities among the inputs must be obtained. Even after a production technique is selected, time will be used to assemble or adjust existing equipment, raw materials, and labor to the desired technique. The more rapidly that is done, the more expensive it is.

Thus at least these three dimensions of output are of concern to the producer—the *volume* of output, the *rate* of output, and the *date* by which the production must begin. We now summarize their effects on costs.

**First Production Generalization.
The greater the planned volume
of production, at an unchanged
rate of production, the lower will
be the average unit cost of output.**

This generalization is commonly known as the *economies of mass production.* It says that if Sony produces TV sets at the constant *rate* of (say) 500 per day, the larger the total number of sets of that model to be produced at that rate, the lower can be their average cost. Of course, production of a larger volume at the constant rate of 500 per day means that more time is required. Two main factors are responsible for economies of mass production: (1) Large-scale (that is, large-*volume*) production techniques are not mere duplications of small-scale production methods. If only two cars were to be produced, it would be cheaper to use a custom workshop technique, but for thousands of cars, one would not duplicate the custom workshop methods; an assemblyline would be used. If one car is to be painted, the least costly technique is to use a spray gun. If 1000 cars are to be painted, it is cheaper to set up a paint bath into which the cars are submerged. But one could not construct a 1/1000 portion of a paint bath unit to paint one car. (2) The more an activity is repeated, better ways of doing it are learned. Improvement and learning by experience are evident in managerial functions, production scheduling, job layouts, material-flow control, and manual-dexterity skills. The rate of learning is usually greatest at first and then diminishes as it approaches a plateau.

**Second Production Generalization.
The faster the rate of production,
for a given volume of production,
the higher will be the average
unit cost.**

You might think that for a given volume of output the same amount of materials must be used in production whether it be produced quickly or slowly. However, a higher (faster) rate of production uses more productive material *in a given time,* creating coordination problems that increase costs. Also, as more resources are brought in, only more costly (less-efficient) resources for this kind of work are likely to be available. And less time is available for the identification of best inputs. Furthermore, resource owners insist on higher pay for overtime as more leisure is sacrificed. Thus we have the "law" of increasing costs with higher (i.e., faster) speed or rate of production.

Proportional Increases in Both Rate and Volume

Some producers plan production in terms of definite lengths of time, so a larger volume of production during the period will mean a higher rate of production. We shall use this kind of output variation—one in which the larger volumes of potential outputs are made with proportionally higher rates of production over a fixed length of time. For example, a doubled volume is achieved by a doubled rate of production. A typical be-

Table 11–2. Measures of Costs of Production

Output	Total Constant	Total Variable Cost	Total Cost	Marginal Cost	Average Variable Cost	Average Constant Cost	Average of Total Cost
1	10	1.00	11.00	1.00	1.00	10.00	11.00
2	10	1.95	11.95	.95	.975	5.00	5.975
3	10	2.85	12.85	.90	.95	3.33	4.28
4	10	3.80	13.80	.95	.95	2.50	3.45
5	10	4.80	14.80	1.00	.96	2.00	2.96
6	10	5.85	15.85	1.05	.97	1.67	2.64
7	10	6.95	16.95	1.10	.99	1.43	2.42
8	10	8.10	18.10	1.15	1.01	1.25	2.26
9	10	9.30	19.30	1.20	1.03	1.11	2.14
10	10	10.55	20.55	1.25	1.05	1.00	2.05
11	10	11.85	21.85	1.30	1.08	.91	1.98
12	10	13.25	23.25	1.40	1.10	.83	1.93
13	10	14.75	24.75	1.50	1.13	.77	1.09
14	10	16.35	26.35	1.60	1.19	.71	1.88
15	10	18.05	28.05	1.70	1.20	.67	1.87
16	10	19.85	29.85	1.80	1.24	.63	1.87
17	10	21.75	31.75	1.90	1.28	.59	1.87
18	10	23.75	33.75	2.00	1.32	.56	1.88
19	10	25.95	35.95	2.20	1.36	.53	1.89
20	10	28.45	38.45	2.50	1.42	.50	1.92
21	10	31.45	41.45	3.00	1.49	.48	1.97

Average (per mile) variable costs, average constant costs, and average total costs are in the last three columns. For example, at 10 output units, the average variable operating cost is the total variable cost $10.55 divided by 10, or $1.055. The average constant cost is $10/10 = $1.00. The average of total cost is $20.55/10 = $2.055. The average of total cost also equals the average variable operating cost plus the average constant cost.

havior of costs for such cases is illustrated in Table 11–2, which we will use in combination with possible selling prices to ascertain how the output will depend on the selling price or market demand for the product of this producer.

The meaning of the various costs—average and marginal—are the same as those given in Chapter 8, but with the difference that we now separate the components into constant and variable costs. The constant cost (cost not affected by the output rate) is $10 per period. We assume zero acquisition costs so that we can concentrate on other costs. The total variable operating cost is $1 at one unit of output and increases with higher output. Marginal costs (the change in total costs) start at $1, fall to about 90 cents at an output of

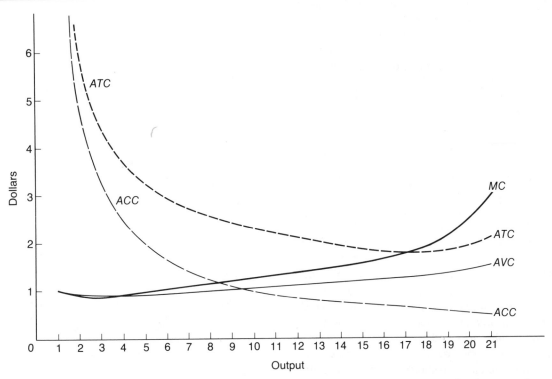

Figure 11–1. Stylized Representation of Relationship among Cost Curves: Average (per-Unit) Total Cost, Average Variable Cost, Average Constant Cost, and Marginal Cost

In any actual situation the cost curves will have different shapes than those shown here. Nevertheless it is always true that when a rising marginal cost line intersects the average total cost, average total cost will begin to rise also; the average variable cost plus the steadily decreasing average of the constant total cost is the average of total costs.

three, and thereafter increase. This difference from the example in Chapter 8 (where marginal and average variable costs rose steadily from the initial unit) tends to arise from the joint effect of a larger volume and a larger rate of output. (But we shall not delve extensively into this feature.) The data are graphed in Figure 11–1.

7, 8
9, 10
11, 12
13, 14
15, 16

Costs of Quicker or Slower Adjustments in the Output Program

The producer cannot be sure that a planned production program will continue to be most profitable. Demands change, and he will have to adjust. His speed and extent of adjustment to a new program affects his costs. More rapid adjustments are more costly—even if possibly more profitable than a slower adjustment. Furthermore, the persistence of a change in demand is uncertain. The expected persistence of the demand will affect the kind of productive equipment he purchases and uses. That, too, will affect his costs of production.

Short Runs and Long Runs

In economic jargon, a *short run* refers to two different concepts: (1) quick *adjustment* of production, rather than a slower, ultimate (long-run) adjustment to a new output program; (2) a short-*lived* run production, rather than a long-lived, long run of production, no matter at what rate of speed the shorter-lived new output is initiated. And, of course, *long-run* can mean either the longer, slower adjustment period, or a long-*lived*, long-run of production. Keep those important distinctions in mind to avoid misunderstanding.

The costs of some new production program initiated after a *quick* adjustment (using initial equipment more appropriate to a different program) are greater than with a longer adjustment and preparation interval (though of course the quicker may prove to be more timely and profitable). This higher cost after a quicker adjustment is indicated in Figure 11–2, showing some marginal- and average-cost curves. The long-run average-cost curve, *LRAC,* shows the average cost of production of each possible output *if* the producers were to have *initially correctly* anticipated and used precisely the most appropriate (that is, lowest-cost) production technique for the selected, persisting output. The lowest-cost technique of producing output q^*, for example, would

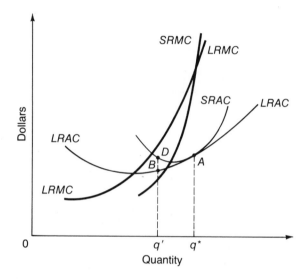

Figure 11–2. Short- and Long-Run Average and Marginal Costs

A change from the output q*, for which existing facilities are optimal, to, say, q', will raise average costs above what costs would have been if existing equipment had been optimal for new output.

have resulted in average costs equal to the height q^*A.

If a producer's plant and equipment happen to be optimal for, say, output q^*, the lowest average cost possible for *that* output is shown by point *A* on the *LRAC* curve. If the producer later faces a changed demand or price and decides to produce an output other than q^*, he would not have the best equipment for sustaining the new output. His average costs for sustaining that new output will be higher than if he had initially planned and set up for that new, revised output. But originally he obtained plant and equipment for the initial output q^*. If he decides to change his amount of output to q', by continuing to use the equipment appropriate to q*, he will experience average costs of production (the height q'D) higher than q'B. The SRAC curve shows short-run average costs of revised outputs, given that he started at q*. If the new revised output continues or is expected to persist for a long time, plant and equipment will be altered (a long-run adjustment) until *ultimately,* for indefinite continuation of that program, his future costs become the lowest costs, called the long-run average cost (LRAC) of producing that output.

As can be seen from the curves labeled SRAC and SRMC (the short-run marginal-cost curve), a larger output would have a higher average and marginal cost if produced with a shorter-run adjustment (using old, existing facilities best suited for the initial program). Looking at the marginal cost for outputs *larger* than the initial planned output, q*, we see that the short-run marginal cost (quick adjustment) exceeds the long-run marginal cost (for output expansions achieved less quickly). For outputs below that for which existing equipment is best suited, the short-run marginal cost is *less* than the long-run marginal cost, because *reducing* output in that way would result in a smaller saving or smaller reduction of production costs than if achieved by the most appropriate equipment. The marginal cost is the difference in total costs between those two outputs. Therefore we expect any reduction in output to reduce costs, and we expect a longer-run adjustment to reduce production costs more (that is, to *save more*) than a swifter, short-run adjustment. This means that the output-response to a price change is greater after the longer-run than the shorter-run adjustment period. In economic terms, *the elasticity of supply in response to a price change is greater in the long-run than in the short-run (adjustment period).*

The graph of costs in Figure 11–2 is a highly stylized picture useful primarily in exposing the relationships among the marginal, average variable, and average total costs. In fact, the particular shape of the curves (all are mathematically interrelated) will depend upon the particular production techniques and equipment. The marginal cost curve (and the average curves) may have long ranges of nearly constant marginal costs. Each case must be investigated on its own. But in any event the general interrelationships will hold among the various cost measures.

Joint Products with Common Costs

Production processes do not all yield only one product. Many give several *joint* products. Beef and hides are joint products of cattle. Cotton and cottonseed oil; kerosene, fuel oil, and gasoline; butter and milk—these are joint products. They are interdependent in supply; generally, more of one involves more (or less) of the other. More beef also yields more hides. More cotton yields more cottonseed oil; but for joint products that increase proportionally, a higher price for one of the outputs will lead to an increased output of the joint good: A higher price for cotton will induce a larger output of cotton, and thus more cottonseed. Thus, the supply of a good is dependent not only on its own price, but also on that of other goods—especially of its joint product.

Yet we mustn't overdo this jointness; even for these joint products, more of one can mean less of the other. Meat, hides, and fat are joint products, but they are substitutes in that different breeds of cattle yield different ratios of meat, fat, and hides. One could change the ratio and get more hide and less meat by selecting different breeds and slaughtering ages. These propositions hold for gasoline, kerosene, and fuel oil—all of which are obtained by refining crude oil. Different refining methods permit different ratios of output. Cotton and cottonseed are also variable, though joint, products. Depending solely upon which of the joint products one is primarily interested in, the other is often called the by-product.

Impossibility of Apportioning the Cost of a Common Input to Each Product

If two products are produced jointly with a common input, the costs of the common resource cannot be allocated to each of the joint products. If, for example, hides and meat are produced from one steer, and if the feed and care of the steer is a common input, or a common cost, to both products, what portion is the cost of the hide and what portion is the cost of the meat? If an airplane carries passengers and cargo, what portion of the common costs of kerosene, of labor, and of facilities is assigned to each? Calling one product the by-product and assigning all the common costs to the other, the "basic" product, is simply a play on words masking an arbitrary allocation. If common input costs can't be allocated, then how can one tell what the costs are of each product? He can't. Then how can he tell how much to produce? Things seem to fall apart at the "joints." In fact, however, the presence of common costs that cannot be allocated uniquely to the joint products does not upset anything (except possibly some mediocre accoun-

tants). He can still tell how much of each joint product to produce or the ratio in which they should be produced.

Pricing and Output Decisions Are Independent of an Assignment of Common Costs

One function of market prices is to ration the existing supply of joint product among the competing claimants. Rationing is accomplished by the separate market prices. Prices, as we have seen, do not depend on costs; they depend on demand and existing supply. Thus it is absolutely no problem that common costs cannot be allocated.

A second function of prices is to influence what goods get produced. Again, no allocation of the common costs among joint products is necessary for this problem. All that is necessary is a comparison of the *changes in total* costs of the whole *set* of joint products with the *changes of total* revenue from their sale. If the total revenue does not cover the total costs, the loss of wealth will induce some producers to stop production, leaving a smaller output and resultant higher prices of the various joint products, until revenue exceeds total costs of the set of joint products.

How Much to Produce of Each?

If the ratios can be varied, what are to be the most profitable output rates of each of the joint products? To make this decision, the producer still does not have to allocate common costs among each joint product; he requires only a measure of *marginal* costs for each of the joint products. If he expands output of any of the joint products, either singly or jointly, how much do total costs increase? The answer to that does not require any allocation of common costs. It requires knowing only how much the total costs change if the output of any one of the joint products is changed. If that marginal cost (including any *change* in the total unallocated common costs) is less than the marginal revenue from that extra output, that output will be expanded profitably. Otherwise, the output will be contracted. In other words, the wealth-maximizing output determination requires knowledge only of the effects on total costs and total revenue. No output or pricing decisions require separability or bookkeeping allocation of the cost of any input shared by the joint products. This bears repeating: Pricing and output decisions do not require that portions of common costs of a common production input be assigned to the products that are jointly produced. Nothing is lost, except an answer to an impossible question: "What is the cost of producing one of the joint products?" To say that the question is unnecessary doesn't mean it isn't frequently asked.

Depreciation, Obsolescence, and Resource Uses

Depreciation is the reduction in the value of an asset as it suffers physical deterioration from use or aging. Depreciation is a cost—even though it is neither an expenditure nor an obligation to spend. Because it is a reduction in value of an asset, it is a cost. If the value of an asset falls when it is used, by that use the owner is forsaking the opportunity to have sold the asset and used some of the value for something else. And even if he doesn't sell it, he has forsaken some future uses. We emphasize that depreciation is a cost because many people mistakenly think that costs occur only when money is spent. In contrast to depreciation are the unexpected reductions in value caused by *unanticipated* developments, whether physical damage or a new, superior competing product. This obsolescence is a *loss. Obsolescence* also often denotes something else—the effect of *anticipated* future improvements in new products. But since those future developments and their effect on future earnings are anticipated, their effect is taken into account as a reduction in the initial purchase price (the initial value) of the existing asset. The purchasers therefore do not later suffer a decline in value as the new, anticipated developments occur—all of which is in accord with the principles of capital values explained earlier in Chapter 7.

Unexpected improvements in competing assets do not necessarily idle existing assets. Instead, the value of the old machine falls enough to permit its continued economical use in the face of competition by the newcomer. This is why today propeller airliners can still fly economically, despite the existence of superior jet aircraft. As another example, suppose some machine is now available that can be used to produce 1000 units of X before it "falls apart"; its value will decline in proportion to its use. Suppose also there are associated costs for materials and labor of 20 cents per unit. Finally, suppose the product sells for 30 cents per unit, so the nonmachine costs are covered by a margin of 10 cents per unit. The machine is then worth $100 (ignoring interest discounting for simplicity).

Soon after purchase of the machine for $100, as luck would have it a new machine is unexpectedly introduced for the same price. The new machine will produce 1000 units before it falls apart, but the associated labor and material costs are only 16 cents per unit, 4 cents less than the 20 cents with the old machine; so total costs with the new machine are 26 cents per unit. The old machine will continue to be used until the price of the product falls below 20 cents per unit, under the impact of an increased supply as more of the new machines come into use. The value of the old machine will drop, because its value is the difference between the new (lower) price of the item produced and its own 20 cents of associated labor and material costs of production. If the old machine could still be used for 1000 items, the machine's value would be only $60 (equal to 1000 units times the difference between the product price of 26 cents and its 20 cents of nonmachine costs). When the price of the product falls to 20 cents, that difference is wiped out; there is nothing left to impute to the old machine. The old machine is then worthless. It will be retired from use if the price of its products falls below 20 cents—the nonmachine costs associated with use of that machine. These decreases in the value of the machine because of the unforeseen reduced price of the product are losses, not depreciation.

17, 18
19, 20
21, 22

Summary

1. Acquisition, possession, and operation are different acts, each with its own costs.

2. Production costs can be comprised of costs, some of which are constant and some of which vary with the amount of production.

3. Changes in the amount of output can be measured in terms of several different magnitudes of output, such as rate or volume, to mention but two.

4. Economies of mass production refer to the falling average cost for larger planned volumes of output.

5. The greater the rate, or speed, of an output, the greater the marginal cost.

6. The quicker the adjustment to a new output, the greater the cost of the adjustment.

7. The terms *short run* and *long run* can each be used in two different contexts. A short run can mean either a quicker adjustment or a short-lived run of production. Similarly for *long run.*

8. Some costs cannot be assigned to particular portions of an output and are called *joint* and *common* costs. The marginal effect on those costs can be determined, however, and that is sufficient for purposes of determining appropriate output.

9. Long-run marginal costs change less in response to long-run adjustments in output than do marginal costs of short-run, rapid output changes.

10. Any cost not associated with a current expenditure is called an implicit cost.

11. Depreciation is the reduction in the value of an asset consequent to use or aging.

12. Reductions in asset value due to the unforeseen development of new competitive techniques are often called obsolescence.

13. The stylized U-shaped average-cost function with output is a conventional means of pre-

senting the relationship between marginal, average variable, and average total costs. The curves may be flat over a wide portion of the output, but ultimately, at very large outputs, the marginal and average curves will rise.

Questions

1. To incur a cost is equivalent to saying that one has sacrificed an opportunity. Do you agree? If so, why? If not, why not?
2. Why are capital values used as a measure of costs?
3. Why cannot money expenditures be identified with costs?
4. A house can be purchased for $20,000. At the end of a year it could be resold for $21,000 if you had also spent $1000 for a concrete fence, $300 for landscaping, $800 for air conditioning, and $1200 for carpeting; otherwise, the house could have been resold for $19,000. Taxes of $300 must be paid in any event. Assume that all these expenditures—except for the taxes, which are to be paid at the end of a year—are paid at the moment you buy the house. The interest rate is 10 percent.
   a. What is the cost of owning a house for one year—if you do not install fence, landscaping, air conditioning, and carpeting?
   b. What is the cost of owning the house if you do install those improvements?
   *c. What is the year's depreciation on the house without the proposed improvements?
   d. Express this cost of ownership of the improved house for one year as a constant two-year annuity.
   *e. Express the cost as a perpetuity.
   f. Express the cost as a five-year annuity.
   g. Which of these is the correct way to express cost?
5. You operate a cleaning establishment. A new cleaning machine has a price of $5000. You estimate its resale value at the end of the first year to be $3000 and $1500 at the end of the second year. The rate of interest is 10 percent.
   a. What will it cost to purchase and own the machine for one year?
   *b. For two years?
   c. What is the present value measure of the depreciation on the machine in the first year?
   *d. In the second year?
   e. If you use the machine, you will incur expenses during the first year of $6000 for labor, power, and repairs; and the machine will still have a resale value of $3000 at the end of the first year. The same expenses will be involved in the second year, and the resale value will be $1500 at the end of the second year. Assume that all expenditures are payable at the end of the year in which they are experienced. What is the cost of having and using the machine for one year?
   f. For two years?
   g. What is the cost of the second year of possession and operation?
   h. If, immediately after buying the machine, you should reconsider and decide to sell it, the resale value would be $4000. What cost would the purchase of the machine "fix"

upon you? This is called "fixed," "sunk," or "irrecoverable" cost.

*i. After purchasing the machine, you can either keep it idle or use it with the attendant expenditures indicated earlier, in (e) above. As between these two alternative actions, what is the fixed cost?

*j. What are the variable costs; that is, the costs incurred over and above the "fixed" costs?

6. "Don't buy your business cars. Lease them from the A and A Leasing Company. You can lease a Chevy for $60 a month. Avoid the loss of depreciation and necessity of tying up capital funds in the purchase of capital items." This is an accurate paraphrase of leasing advertising. What errors of analysis does it contain? Would the reasons given provide any advantage to a businessman? Explain why not.

7. A firm plans to produce 2 million cameras in the next six months. What is the volume and what is the rate of output?

8. If that rate in question 7 is continued for one year, what will be the volume?

*9. Give some examples of how the selected technique of production will depend upon the *volume* to be produced. For example, what about methods of producing letterheads, cookies, holes for fence posts, dresses, airplanes?

10. What happens to marginal and average cost per unit for larger rates of output with constant volume?

11. What happens to marginal and average cost for larger planned volumes with unchanged rates of output?

12. If it were illegal to sell automobiles outside the state in which they were made, would cars be cheaper or more expensive in the United States? Give two reasons for your answer.

13. Why do manufacturers produce a few standardized models rather than a much larger variety of custom-made, custom-designed models?

*14. Give some examples, if you can, of average costs being lower with large-volume production. Can you cite from personal memory the price history of television sets, transistor radios, surfboards, aluminum, penicillin, Polaroid cameras, ball-point pens?

15. If a business firm finds its selling price and output so related that larger output is associated with lower selling price, is this an indication that it has lower costs with larger volume or that the demand is such that more can be sold only if the price is lower?

16. "New business firms can underprice older firms, because the newer firms can buy the latest equipment and are not burdened with the older, less economical equipment which older firms must retire before they can economically adopt the new. This is why continued technological progress contributes to maintaining a competitive economic system." Explain the errors in both sentences.

17. Your car will depreciate by $500, we shall assume, regardless of whether you use it for recreation or business, and regardless of whether you drive it 5000 or 10,000 miles. Each mile you drive it, you will also pay 8 cents for gasoline, oil, tires, repair, etc. (not counting the depreciation). If you drive the

car 10,000 miles, the depreciation cost amounts to $500/10,000 = 5 cents per mile. If you drive it 5000 miles, the depreciation cost is 10 cents a mile. Suppose you drive it 5000 miles for recreation and 5000 miles for business.

a. What is the cost for the recreation mileage, and what is the cost for the business mileage?

b. Should you allocate half of the depreciation to the recreation?

18. Heat and light are joint products of an electric light bulb that uses electric power at the rate of 1000 watts. In one hour the cost of the power is 5 cents.

a. How much does the light cost? How much does the heat cost? How much do the light and the heat together cost?

b. If you were selling the heat to someone, how much would you charge him? And if, at the same time, you were selling the light to someone else, how much would you charge him?

c. Suppose that you are getting 4 cents for the light and 2 cents for the heat. You discover a new light bulb that gives more light and less heat, but this costs 6 cents per hour to operate. You can sell the extra light for 3 cents more, but you get a total of only 1 cent for the available heat. Should you use the new device? (Forget the cost of the new bulb—to simplify the arithmetic.)

*d. But now the *light* buyer complains that you are charging him a total of 7 cents, which is more than enough to cover all the costs, while formerly you charged him only 4 cents, which did not cover the whole costs.

He contends that the price should be lower and that the buyer of heat should pay part of the costs. What is your reply?

*e. Having told him to take it or leave it, you find he leaves it! Why? (Answer: Because someone else can duplicate your service and charge him a lower price to get his business. The price will, with open markets, be cut to the point that total receipt from the joint products are just sufficient to cover the cost of production. And the total amount produced will be of such size that another joint increment would not bring in quite enough new receipts to cover the marginal cost of producing that joint increment of output.)

19. Meat, wool, and hides are joint products of sheep.

a. What assurance do you have that the prices paid for meat, for wool, and for sheepskin are just adequate to cover their cost of production?

b. What assurance do you have that meat users are not paying a disproportionate share of the common costs?

20. You operate a cleaning establishment and expect to obtain $8000 revenue from use of a new cleaning machine during the first year. (Assume you receive all of it at the end of the first year.) Also you expect to receive $15,000 at the end of the second year. For convenience, all the cost and revenue data are summarized in the following schedule:

	Beginning of 1st Year	End of 1st Year	End of 2nd Year
Purchase	$5000	0	0
Expenses	0	$6000	$6000
Resale of Equipment	0	0	1500
Receipts	0	8000	15,000
Net Receipts	—5000	2000	10,500
Present Values	—5000 +	1818 +	8678 = $5496 (profit)

a. What is the present value of cost implied by your expectations? What is the present value of revenue?

*b. Suppose that within a month after you have installed the machine, other people form expectations consistent with yours; however, despite their efforts to open similar cleaning establishments, your revenue forecast will still be accurate (since it was in part based on anticipations that other people would soon copy your techniques). At that time the capital value of your business will be revised upward with a profit of $5496. When do you realize that profit?

21. "The price of a new organic chemical depends on how badly it is wanted—precisely as conceived by classical economic theory, except for reversal of direction. The bigger the demand, the lower the price. A 1000-lb-per-day process operates more efficiently than a 1000-lb-per-month process—which is obvious to you but wasn't to Adam Smith. Old Adam set down the rules for our game in ignorance of elementary chemical engineering and advanced advertising." Quote from an advertisement for Eastman Kodak Co., *Scientific American,* May 1964, p. 57. Explain wherein the ad writers for Eastman Kodak are doubly confused—on both the demand and the supply side.

22. The following is a quotation from the *Scientific American,* 1963: "Recently a number of steelmaking organizations in Western Europe and the U.S.S.R. have eliminated several costly steps in the manufacture of steel by advancing the technique known as continuous casting. U.S. steel firms, which account for about a third of the world output, were for the most part content to observe these developments. They were inhibited by a paradox of industrial supremacy: the huge sums already invested in established methods made experimentation with the new technique seem impractical. The smaller producers, whose competitive position might have been enhanced by continuous casting, could least afford to build the pilot plants."

Assume that the facts stated in the first sentence are correct. The second sentence describes the alleged behavior of U.S. steel firms in response to these facts; and the remaining sentences strive to explain that behavior. Do you agree that the last two sentences present an economically acceptable explanation of the events in the second sentence? Explain why they do not.

12

Free-Market Control of Production and Prices: Price-Takers (A First Approximation)

Business firms have two, often consistent, roles: (1) a conscious, *purposive* role of increasing the wealth of the members of the firm, and (2) an un-intended social, *functional* role of planning and producing the goods most highly valued by the community. Yet, it is surprising how often many people contend these roles are inconsistent. Indeed it was Adam Smith's great contribution to show wherein they are consistent. We will now see how production can be related to consumers' demands.

Information Is Not Free

No one knows everything about all goods: the demand for them, their existence, location, ultimate performance, or the asking prices by different sellers. Since perfect information is not available costlessly (else why go to school?), how is information more cheaply and reliably disseminated to potential customers? Shoppers squeeze bread, smell cheese, heft oranges, bounce golf balls, shake walnuts, pick grapes, slam car doors, bounce on sofas, try on clothes, feel cloth, but still they are not sure. They also read advertisements, ask for warranties, rely on the seller's reputation and brand name, use return privileges, and sample and select from inventories.

The absence of costless, perfect information about a good means that not every difference in price between two ostensibly similar goods will induce a buyer to buy the lower-priced good. There is value to doubts about how identical goods are: such doubts prevent gullibility. It is rational for buyers not to switch immediately to any seller who asks a lower price for the "same" good. Some of us sensibly never incur the costs

to discover if a particular lower-priced good really is equal to the higher-priced good. Imagine what it would cost to learn everything about every good so that anytime we saw a price difference we would know whether or not it was worth it—or to know the prices of every possible seller (for example, the gasoline prices at *every* station in town). Weighing the costs and benefits of reducing ignorance, we can see that there is an optimal amount of ignorance. The lower the cost of information, the more of it we have; the more it costs, the less we acquire. That is our old first law of demand. Why else do we not all acquire the information that would turn each of us into first-class physicists, physicians, or mechanics?

Costliness of informing potential buyers of a lower price or true qualities of a seller's goods reduces the effectiveness of a lower price in attracting more buyers. The fewer the extra units sold by a price cut, the smaller is marginal revenue relative to the price. (Review the relation between marginal revenue and price explained on pages 56–58, if this is not obvious.) These sellers are called "price-searchers" or sellers with "market power" because in their quest for the best price they have the power to try various prices. However, as we shall see, they have little power to control that best price. Furthermore, they tend to be pushed to a price at which the profits are competed away by competition from other sellers of similar goods. Ford, General Motors, Eastman Kodak, your local power company, even your local grocer experience that.

To help potential buyers learn the qualities of goods and sellers, sellers will use advertising, salesmen, inventories, free trials, return privileges, warranties, brand names, franchises, retail price fixing, and a variety of other devices too numerous to name here. Unfortunately, many of those are widely regarded, *erroneously,* as means of taking advantage of—rather than reducing—the ignorance of customers, an error that rests on the false presumption that information about all characteristics of goods can be had at zero cost.

Another source of a price-searcher market is that one or a few sellers of easily identifiable goods comprise so large a part of the supply that their effect on price makes marginal revenue significantly less than the price of extra units they could sell.

However, there are cases in which producers can sell their entire stock without significantly affecting a known market price—essentially the same price as any other seller. Buyers are so well-informed and identification of product quality is so cheap that they, the buyers, can detect whether price is the only significant difference among sellers. Furthermore, any one seller sells so little relative to the market that only a trivial price effect (cut) will be required to sell all he wants to sell. For example, buyers of wheat, cotton, soybeans, and natural gas are so well-informed and can test batches of goods so cheaply that only a slight difference in price will suffice for a seller to win sufficient buyers. These cases are called *pure-price* competition or *price-taker* markets: *Pure* because pure price is all that distinguishes possible sellers; *price-takers* because the seller can take the going price as the price at which he can sell—or more precisely, the price can be taken as virtually equal to his marginal revenue on any extra amount he might try to sell.

Price-Takers: Cheap Information, Small Relative Size, and Price Equal to Marginal Revenue

We begin our analysis of production control and response to consumer's demand with the *price-takers* model for two reasons: First, we will examine some actual goods for which the individual sellers are closest to being price-takers; for example, in agricultural products like wheat, oats, corn, soybeans, cotton, etc., two factors are important: Individual producers are a small part of the market for goods; and the goods are easily identified for what they are. Several types of labor, particularly the less highly specialized or skilled, are more like price-takers in their services. The second reason for starting with the price-takers model is that it is simpler for adequate analysis of several important economic phenomena. In fact, we have already used this model in explaining specialization in production, the rationing problem, effects of prices in controlling consumption, and control of resources under various types of property rights. It is also useful for analyzing: (a) how market prices and capital values control and coordinate output; (b) how anticipated future demands affect current plans for future production of food, energy, shoes, etc.; (c) how taxes affect output prices and the distribution of wealth; and (d) how making it illegal to use markets for a good or service forces resort to more-costly, less-reliable substitutes. The increase in cost and sacrifice of reliability then tend to be erroneously attributed to the prohibited activity rather than to the legal prohibition itself, almost regardless of what the activity is. To these issues we now turn.

Horizontal Demand

A simple, useful way to analytically characterize the price-taker is to represent him as faced with a virtually *horizontal* demand curve for his product at a readily known market price. Whatever amount he supplies, the price would be virtually unchanged and equal to the $10 price shown by the height of a horizontal, straight demand line in Figure 12–1.

If he asked a higher price, he would sell virtually none since other sellers would quickly expand to displace him. That is what a virtually horizontal demand line to *one* seller reflects. And that is a good approximation to some markets.

Infinite Elasticity of Demand

You will remember from Chapter 3 that the elasticity of demand is a measure of the percentage responsiveness of amount demanded consequent to a small percentage change in price. If a slight (one percent) reduction in asking price increased the amount demanded far beyond that which the seller could supply at that price, then, as far as he is concerned, the percentage increase in quantity is indefinitely large, relative to the price; and the percentage increase in quantity is indefinitely large, relative to the price change. So a price-taker can be characterized as any seller who is faced with a demand for his product with virtually infinite elasticity.

Marginal Revenue Equals Price

Another way to describe the price-taker's situation is in terms of his marginal revenue. If the price is essentially unaffected by additional sales,

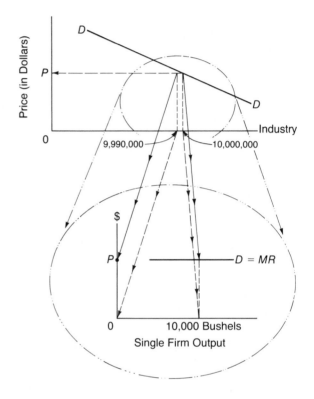

Figure 12–1. Demand and Marginal Revenue Situation Defining a Price-Taker

DD *is the demand facing the whole industry. With the industry supply the price is determined. Each firm takes that market price as the only price at which it can sell, for two reasons: First, a firm is so small a part of the industry that any reduction in its output would change the market price by only a trivial amount, and the firm, being so small, would have a marginal revenue essentially equal to price. Second, if a firm did cut output to raise price, other firms would expand and restrict the price rise. Competition from other sellers and the small size of each firm relative to the market makes the existing market price the only price worth contemplating and makes marginal revenue practically equal to price. All this is often summarized by saying that the individual firm sees the demand for its product as essentially a horizontal line at the market price, with marginal revenue equal to price.*

Table 12–1. Measures of Production Cost*

(1) Number of Units	(2) Constant Total Cost	(3) Variable Cost Total Cost	(4) Total Cost	(5) Marginal	(6) Average Constant Cost	(7) Average Variable Cost	(8) Total/Unit Average Cost
0	$1	0	—	—	—	—	—
1	1	$ 9	$10	$ 9	$1.00	$9.0	$10
2	1	17	18	8	.50	8.5	9
3	1	23	24	6	.33	7.67	8
4	1	27	28	4	.25	6.75	7
5	1	34	35	7	.20	6.80	7
6	1	47	48	13	.16	7.83	8
7	1	69	70	22	.14	9.86	10

* Simplified cost data to illustrate relationships among classifications of costs, and how price will affect more profitable output. Total cost (column 4) is sum of constant cost (column 2) and variable cost (column 3). Marginal cost is change in total cost—due entirely to change in total variable cost. Last three columns are costs per unit of output.

each extra unit would sell at that essentially unchanged price. Therefore, his increased revenue from one *more* unit would be equal to what he gets for that extra unit—its price—because he did not have to lower price significantly on his prior existing sales. His marginal revenue of that one additional unit sold equals its price. This can be contrasted with the case of the price-searcher, for whom an increased offering would have significantly reduced the price of all units sold. The lost revenue from that cut in price on his entire prior quantity would have to be subtracted from the price he gets for that one extra unit. The *net increase* in revenue—the marginal revenue—from selling one more would be less than its price. But a price-taker can take the market price as an excellent measure of his marginal revenue on an extra unit of output. He *takes* price in two senses: He takes it as given by the market, and he takes it as a good measure of his marginal revenue on greater output.

[1,2 3,4]

Response to Market Price

How is a price-taker controlled by the market price? We shall initially assume that the producer knows his costs of possible output programs and that he is already in business with acquired equipment with the simplified relationship between costs and production shown in Table 12–1. The greatly oversimplified data are useful for present purposes because although they could be replaced with far more complicated, realistic data, none of the essential points shown by the simplified example would be altered.

Column 4 lists the total production costs, which are composed of constant cost of $1, listed in column 2, and the variable cost, listed in column 3. (No acquisition is assumed.) Marginal costs— the increases in total costs at each unit of larger output—are in column 5. Finally, average costs are in the last three columns: per-unit average constant costs (column 6), average variable costs (column 7), and average total costs (column 8). Average total costs and marginal costs are graphed in Figure 12–2.

What planned output will maximize the producer's wealth—that is, maximize his profits? Since we assume he is a price-taker, there is a market price that will not be affected by his output. He will produce at a rate beyond which one more unit would increase his daily costs by more than his receipts—the price received for that unit. For example, if the price were $13, he would produce six units daily. To produce one more daily (seven per day) would increase total costs by $22 but would bring in extra receipts of only $13, the unchanged price of an extra unit. If he produced less, at a marginal cost less than price, he would forsake an opportunity to make profits, for the receipts would have exceeded the costs. In sum, he produces an output at which one more would have marginal costs in excess of the extra receipts obtained by selling one more. In our price-taker model, we know that the price is the marginal revenue—the increase in receipts when he sells one more unit. That marginal revenue is the price, because there is no reduction in price on any of his units in order to sell that last unit. To put it most accurately: He produces to that output at which his marginal cost is brought to equality with marginal revenue (which, in the price-taker's case is the same as the unchanged price of that last unit produced and sold). Notice the characteristic shape of the curves. They *may* fall at first, *may* have a near-flat portion (possibly over a large range of outputs), and ultimately for larger outputs certainly *will* rise until an upper limit to the productive capacity is approached (cost increase becomes practically infinite). Noth-

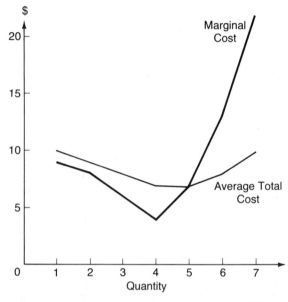

Figure 12–2. Marginal and Average Total Costs at Different Outputs

Where marginal costs are less than average total costs, average total costs will be declining, but where marginal costs have increased to above the average total costs, average total costs will increase—which happens at the largest outputs of producer's capabilities.

ing more should be inferred from the particular shape of the curves used here.

Wealth-Maximizing Output

At a market price of $13 the wealth-maximizing output is six units, as shown in Figure 12–3. The marginal cost exceeds the $10 price beyond six units. Total costs are $48. Total revenue is $78. Profit is $30, or $5 per unit. At other outputs the profit is smaller, as you can check for yourself.

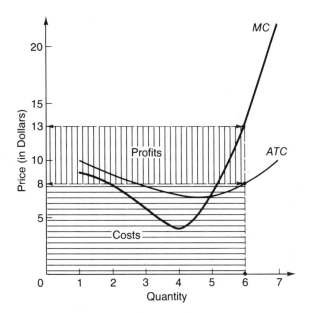

Figure 12–3. Output, Price, Cost, Revenue, and Profits

This diagram shows graphically the measure of profits and costs at the profit-maximizing output when price is $13. The costs are the rectangle over the base of 6 units of output and an average cost of $8, for a total cost of $48. Total revenue minus cost is the profit (the rectangle above the cost rectangle). (Can you see that any other output at that price would give a smaller profit? Producing 7 daily would raise costs by the marginal cost of $22 but bring in only $13 more. Reducing output to 5 would reduce costs by $7 but would reduce total revenue by $13.)

If price were $22, seven would be produced and profit would be $84. If price were $7, no profit would be possible. The *output response* of a *price-taker* producer to a market price is given by his *marginal-cost curve.* That curve says that at a higher price a larger amount would be produced.

A sufficiently low price will stop the production of each firm, as suggested in the preceding chap-

ter. That limit is the lowest average *variable* (that is, yet to be incurred) cost of all possible contemplated continued outputs.

The portion of the marginal-cost curve *above* the minimum point on the average-variable-cost curve (and the relationship between the two dictates that they must intersect at the minimum average-variable-cost) indicates the supply schedule of this producer. It shows the outputs at each possible price above that lower limit. When price is below the per-unit *total* cost (but above per-unit variable cost), the producer will say he is losing money—meaning that his past (regretted) decision to enter the business loses him wealth. He will nevertheless continue temporarily to produce even at that low price below the per-unit total cost, since he will lose less than if he shut down immediately. As long as price exceeds the *minimum* per-unit *variable* operating cost, any excess obtained from a price over the variable cost is better than shutting down, because at least he is covering more than his current operating costs. (In Table 12–1, the minimum is $6.75 at 4 units.) Ultimately, as his equipment wears out, he will face costs of new acquisition or substantial repair. Because at the low price the projected receipts would not cover new acquisition or repair costs, he would quit production.

Warning: The very large profits in this illustrative case are for computational and expository simplicity only. In fact, most business firms do not make such a large net income over cost—which is more typically a net of 2 or 3 cents on the dollar, in contrast to our absurd example of $3 out of the price of $10. Most retailers net about 2 to 5 cents on the dollar. Their so-called large "markups" of 30 percent represent other costs they incur in addition to the wholesale price of the goods sold. (Review the material on p. 232.) The same relative net earnings apply to most manufacturing. Some firms do much better, others do much worse. Some new products that are "hot items" when introduced may command very high prices and high net earnings per unit, but with entry of new firms these fall rapidly—as with transistors, calculators, ballpoint pens, panty hose—and probably everything that once was a new product. And some producers, of course, never find a market demand capable of supporting a price that exceeds costs. They lose wealth and fade away unnoticed.

Quasi-Rents

Any excess of price or receipts over the short-lived variable operating costs is an example of what we earlier denoted as *quasi-rents.* The excess is rent in the sense that it is not necessary to induce some short-lived production with the existing equipment; it is called *quasi* to indicate that it is unnecessary only for a short-lived run of output. But no excess exists over the costs that must ultimately be covered in a longer run of output.

Industry Supply to the Market: Aggregated Supplies of All Firms in the Industry

The market supply is provided by the many firms that comprise the *industry.* Since a higher price induces a larger output from each firm, higher prices induce greater industry output, because the output of all firms is the industry output. The schedule of prices and associated total outputs of all firms in the industry is the industry or market supply schedule. To illustrate this, stylized, smoothed *marginal-cost* data are portrayed in Figure 12–4 as a smooth line labeled MC_A for Firm A. Also in that figure is the marginal-cost schedule (MC_B) for Firm B, which produces less at any given marginal cost. The total output of this industry (for diagrammatic convenience we pretend that there are only two firms in the industry) is obtained by *adding the output (horizontal distance on a graph) of each firm's marginal-cost curve at any specified price above the lowest average (variable) cost output of that firm* (above the lower average of variable costs for short-lived adjustments in output). The summed curve, SS, is the price-takers' industry supply curve. If the price were \$2, the maximum-wealth outputs of Firms A and B would be X_A and X_B. At prices below \$1.30, Firm B would immediately shut down, while A would not shut down immediately unless prices were as low as 85 cents. These lower limits are at their respective lowest average variable costs—the only costs they need cover in order to operate for a short time despite not covering overhead temporarily.

Figure 12–5 shows, in addition, an *industry* market-demand curve, *DD*, which intersects the *industry* supply curve at the price of \$2. The outputs by Firms A and B are indicated by the distances OX_a and OX_b. In earlier chapters, we saw how price rationed the existing stock among competing claimants. Here we see that price also affects the production by each firm. Market price both rations existing output and assigns production.

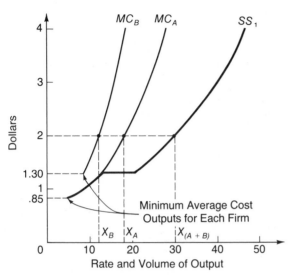

Figure 12–4. Industry Supply from Two Firms

If price faced by these producers were $2, output of each would be 11 by producer B and 19 by producer A, for a total of 30. The horizontal sum of the individual marginal-cost curves is the total industry supply (where no producer would produce at a price below his lowest average variable cost.) Can you also see that if the two producers were producing outputs at which marginal costs were not equal, the producer at the output with the higher marginal cost should reduce his output and the one at an output with lower marginal costs should correspondingly expand?

Only two of the firms are shown. In fact, there are probably scores of producers, each with some marginal cost curve. All would be summed to get the industry supply curve, and each firm would take the price in the market as the price that it regards as unaffected by its own output rate. We imagine only two firms to keep the diagram from becoming too cluttered. The basic principle illustrated is that the amount supplied is determined by market price and marginal costs within each firm, with output being adjusted to that at which marginal cost equals price.

If the demand schedule, *DD*, shifts to the right in Figure 12–5 to D_1D_1 and stays there, price will be bid up—in the absence of laws effectively preventing price changes. The higher demand raises price, which induces and sustains an increased output from existing firms at higher prices (and marginal costs). Also a new producer, C, is attracted. Conversely, reduced demands yield lower prices, reduced output, and fewer firms.

When demand and, hence, price changes, not all firms change output in the same proportion, because some have more sharply increasing marginal costs. If price should fall in response to a persisting decrease in demand, some firms will shut down, the earliest ones being those with higher minimum average variable costs—*not* those that are poorer or smaller or that have less money on hand. Whether rich or poor, each firm shuts down not when wealth is exhausted but when continued operation at low prices would *reduce* wealth more than shutting down would.

Price and Supply Predictability

In Chapter 5 we noted that fluctuating prices increased customers' search and planning costs. Though demand fluctuates transiently around some longer-term average, market price will not follow these transient fluctuations around some fixed average. A local retailer would lose customers if he let price vary instantly in response to transient demand fluctuations, rather than maintaining an accommodating inventory. Economic theory does not say price is changed instantly to equate the amount currently demanded to current production. Instead, sellers maintain buffer inventories of finished products or standby capacity to

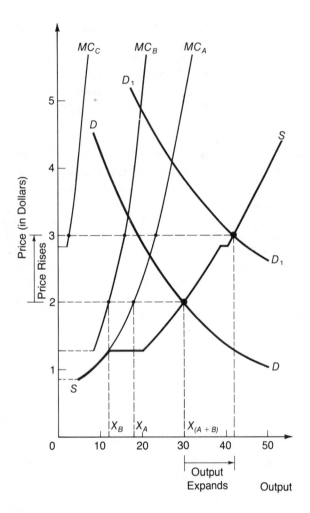

Figure 12–5. Demand and Supply and Output Determination in Price-Takers' Markets

As market demand increases, new firms are attracted by higher prices and wealth prospects. At a price of approximately $3, Firm C will be able to produce profitably. Supply of output by industry shows increased output with higher price because of (1) increased output by each firm, which increases output to point where marginal costs equal price, and (2) increased number of firms as price rises above anticipated minimum average costs of new potential firms. SS, the supply line, is the horizontal sum of the three firms' marginal-cost lines, above their minimum average costs.

feeding into an inventory that buffers transient reversible fluctuations of purchase.

Consumers, and many manufacturing and retailing firms, buy at varying, imperfectly predictable intervals. A seller does not interpret every fluctuation in his daily sales as a changed *consumption* demand by customers, be they consumers or other business firms. Consequently, the seller will strive to make price more predictable over transient fluctuations in daily purchase rates. The lower the storage and inventory costs, and the smaller the size of the transient reversible fluctuations relative to economic size of inventories, and the more likely a fluctuation is believed to be reversed shortly, the more will it pay businessmen to keep prices stably predictable. Only if enough sellers believe there has been a persisting change in the underlying consumption demand is price more likely to change.

On the other hand, farmers who produce and sell a crop once a year, have little incentive or rewards for stabilizing price to buyers who come around once a year—an interval so long that it is unreasonable to expect demand not to have changed in the interval.

fill transient differences between the rate of current purchases and the steadier production rates, thereby providing more stable, predictable prices. Production can, in the meantime, be carried on more economically at a relatively constant rate

If the changed sales rate has persisted for some time before impressing sellers as something that is going to continue into the future, production will respond to adjust inventories. The more quickly sellers perceive or believe a change in sales is going to persist, the more quickly production will be adjusted. Then, insofar as production rates change and involve different costs, the new flow of goods will come at new costs—higher for greater output rates or lower for smaller rates. Prices will have to be adjusted to a new level matching the marginal costs of that new output rate, or else that new production will not be sustained.

The pattern of actual price behavior depends on several features, only some of which have been identified here. In any event, do not conclude that because prices show some stability despite fluctuating demand, economic theory is negated. Unless you knew better, you might interpret the theory as saying that the price is always changing so as to be at the intersection of a transient, fluctuating market demand schedule and production supply. Then any stability of prices, despite fluctuations in sales, would be erroneously regarded as a defect of markets.

Long-Run Supply
Response: Entry of New
Firms and Equipment

The longer a higher demand and higher price are expected to persist, the more new producers are attracted and existing facilities expanded. Since every firm finds it profitable to expand its output

to that at which its marginal costs have increased to the higher price, they would all be operating at the same marginal cost (equal to the new market price seen by each seller) despite having different output rates. Firms with higher minimum average costs will be regarded as "marginal," "fringe" firms, for if demand falls, the lower price will induce them to shut down earlier. (If demand *stays* high or if they learn how to reduce their costs, these firms become recognized as "established" firms, and in turn look on higher-cost firms as constituting the new fringe of "marginal," "unreliable" firms.)

Many simple examples are observable. At big football games, the fees for parking near the stadium are higher, and there are more high-cost parking lots as more local residents rent space in their driveways and yards. These "fly-by-night," fringe operators are disliked by the "established" operators. They appear when demand and price are high; prices are lower than if they did not appear. Charter airlines appear in the summer. Seasonal variations in demand are met by temporary entrants in construction, harvesting, summer resorts, auto rentals—indeed in every industry. When demand for buildings or farm products increases, the number of building contractors and farmers increases, as does the output of each group.

Established parking lots are sometimes legally prevented from raising their prices with transient demand increases; instead, the temporary sellers often sell at higher prices than established firms. How can higher-priced fringe operators contribute to lower prices—if they are the ones who charge the higher price? First, they increase the amount supplied and reduce the pressure for higher prices. Second, to the consumer, price includes more than monetary payments. People who cannot park in the standard lots overflow to surrounding areas and incur the cost of walking farther. The cost to the patrons of parking still farther away and walking is greater than the higher parking fee of the fringe operators. How do we know? Because some people do pay the fringe operators and walk a shorter distance. Without the services of the fringe operators, the sum of pecuniary and nonpecuniary costs imposed on patrons who have to park even farther away would be even higher—especially on those whose time is too valuable to come early enough to park in the established parking lots that are near the stadium.

In Washington, D.C., hundreds of people with full-time jobs elsewhere become taxi operators during "rush" hours. Steel mills operate their more costly blast furnaces only during peak demands. Barber shops have chairs that are "idle" most, but *not* all, of the time. The chairs represent high-cost, but *not* excessive, capacity. Some firms use second and third shifts when demand warrants it, even though they are higher-cost ways of production. Later, if demand falls, the lower price makes it impossible to maintain so high a rate of production and still cover costs. Therefore, all firms reduce output and some begin to withdraw from that business. The displaced resources regretfully and complainingly revert to their next-best sources of income (which served as a measure of their costs).

"Sick" Industries

Another useful application of this economic analysis is to industries that are commonly called "sick"—industries that allegedly have an "excessive" number of firms; "excessive" because most of the firms do such a small volume of business that most of them lose wealth. As rapidly as old ones lose and leave, new ones enter—with the same mortality risk. There seems to be no long-run adjustment that restores the industry to a profitable, or at least a nonloss, balance. The more commonly cited examples of "sick" industries are small retail groceries, bars, restaurants, night clubs, coal mines, gasoline stations, textile manufacturers, and farms.

People who make this argument point to long-term declining demand, foolish overestimation of one's ability, excess capacity, plain ignorance, or the low cost of entering the business. These explanations do not hold up under closer study. First, all firms in an industry could be losing wealth when demand is falling unexpectedly; there is nothing "sick" about a decreasing demand. Second, all firms could be losing wealth if the business provides a sufficiently large amount of nonpecuniary satisfaction, as is said to be the case for horse racing or novel writing or acting or owning baseball clubs. One man grows orchids and makes money and considers it a business; another grows orchids and loses money but regards it as a hobby or consumption activity. Everyone could lose money (relative to what he could earn elsewhere) if this business operation were more pleasant. These considerations help to explain why some industries or occupations can run at a "loss."

Third, there is a more powerful consideration: In some industries the profits may be large for only a few winners, with the rest losing money. In acting, writing, painting, and sports only a few persons seem to make a big success, while the vast majority never make enough to cover the cost. Nothing in economic analysis says that an industry in which only a few make vast fortunes should not have a vast number of "failures." These failures (or is it more accurate to call them nonsuccesses?) entered hoping they could join the favored few, and they often remain despite years of frustration and disappointment. In general, half of all new ventures fail to survive to their fifth year!

How Consumer Demands Affect Values and Uses of Productive Resources

Competition among sellers pushes the price toward the minimum unit cost. If all firms had the same cost conditions as were shown in Table 12–1, the price would be $7 at the long-run equilibrium. In fact, of course, not all firms have identical cost curves. Nevertheless, competition among all firms for productive resources will affect the price of every input so as to make every surviving firm's minimum average cost of production equal to the market price of the output. How will this occur?

When market demands increase (say for sports cars, compacts, miniskirts, wigs, polyunsaturated fats), prices of materials used to produce those goods respond. The values formerly placed on the productive inputs prove too low, as evidenced by profit to those who could get those inputs at the old prices. The greater demand for them will bid up their market prices until no sure profit prospects remain. Through competition the profit has been absorbed into higher input costs. It is

not a contradiction that profits (a gain in wealth) lead to increased input prices and costs. Profits are unpredictable (but sought-for) gains in wealth, but the new, higher value of output from those resources will bid up their prices. To say that current profits imply higher future costs is to say both that the output is of greater value and that the cost of keeping the responsible resources will be bid up by competing demanders.

If I discover oil on my land, the value of my land rises. I am richer by those higher land values. The cost of using that land in any other way will increase at the same time that its higher value made me richer. Anything that becomes more valuable also becomes, by definition, more costly to use, since the user must forsake the greater value he could have had if he sold it to someone else at that new, higher value.

Profits and losses are unforeseen changes in value of particular resources. Desires for greater wealth direct resources to those higher-valued uses (as judged ultimately in the consumers' market of its services)[1] by making it more costly to keep the resources in the lower valued uses. The more quickly, completely, and broadly known is the market's revaluation of assets (hence its recalculation of costs), the more fully and quickly

---

[1] In Chapter 8, where we defined the cost of a given use of resources by one person as the highest *alternative* sacrificed value of output of those resources, we seemed to exclude the value of their *present* use. But we now see that a more general conception of costs consists of imputing to a given resource a market value that reflects its highest possible value in *any* line of activity, including the present one. Costs of resources in a particular occupation stem not only from *alternative uses,* but also from alternative *users.* Even if my land is good only for oil production (that is, it has no alternative uses), it still has a value, which must be taken into account, because other users will bid for it.

will resources be directed toward highest-valued uses.

The control of resource uses by consumer market values extends through a web of substitutions. For example, if an increased demand induces more wheat to be produced, resources must be taken from production of other goods. Resources are transferred to wheat production as their owners seek greater wealth. Land transferred to wheat is taken from oats, corn, and building sites, and as the supply of land for these uses falls, their prices increase. Other land will then be used for corn and oats—land formerly used for, say, cotton, barley, cattle grazing, parks, and potential housing or industrial sites. Also, labor and other resources are diverted to wheat. Laborers who would otherwise work as cattlemen, carpenters, or gas station attendants switch to wheat production. And their places are partly filled from still other occupations. The substitution and shifting is broad and extensive. The many economy-wide effects are so diffused as to be hardly noticeable among the many other everyday events that influence the output of any other particular good. For this reason we are sometimes misled into thinking that more of a good can be produced without producing less of some other, be it leisure or lingerie.

Consequence of Basing Output on Wealth-Maximizing

According to the data in Table 12–1, although the wealth-maximizing output at a market price of $10 is five units, this producer could produce as many as seven and still cover his total costs. But in the interests of his own wealth, he does not. There is an erroneous temptation to call this restriction socially wasteful. However, although the price does exceed average costs, it is less than *marginal* costs for more than five units of output. To expand his output beyond five units would use resources worth more than $10 (the measure of marginal costs). He would be selling to people who value the extra output at only $7—which is less than the costs of the extra output. A larger output of this good (worth $7) is valued less by consumers than the value ($10) of other goods (marginal costs) that would be forsaken. Therefore, the price-taking producer, by holding his output rate to 18 units per year in order to maximize his wealth, is not "underproducing," in any socially wasteful sense, even though he could "afford" to produce more without wiping out all his profit. To produce more would be wasteful, for the costs to society would exceed the value of this extra output here.

Ironically, this implication of wealth-maximizing by price-takers with free access to a market was developed in response to challenges by socialists. Socialists asked what "should" be the output, and when they used the criterion that resources should provide the greatest value as judged by individual consumers and producers, they derived the implication that a private-property system of wealth-maximizers with free access to a price-takers' open market gave precisely that result. Everyone was embarrassed— the socialists because this provided an "argument" for private property and markets and the capitalists because, much as they would have liked this "justification" of their activity, not all of them could validly claim to be selling in open markets—or even defending open markets. Although some of the discussion and argument about each system hinges on this kind of criterion of productive and allocative efficiency, there are other important considerations: definitions of freedom, culture, and characteristic patterns of social behavior, none of which shall we discuss here.

Adjustments without Full and Free Information

With market-revealed values of goods, it is not necessary for anyone to have full information about society's demands or about costs of all possible output programs (that is, industry capacity) in order for higher demands and prices to induce greater output. In the first place, many producers, by compiling data with which to estimate costs, increase their probability of being near the wealth-maximizing output. They know that when demand rises and permits a higher price, an expanded output becomes more profitable, even if they may not know exactly how much larger the output should be.

Second, the wealth-maximizing output is larger, whether or not each producer knows exactly how much larger. All the forces are now more favorable to enlarging output or to sustaining one that was formerly too large. Even for those who may not compute costs to try to find the wealth-maximizing output, the increase in demand means that the set of profitable output programs is larger than before. Even if (as does not in fact happen) every firm picked outputs at random, those that picked larger outputs would be more profitable and grow relative to those that picked smaller outputs. Witness the growth of Sears

relative to Wards after World War II. Sears chose expansion as potentially profitable, Wards chose not to expand. Neither knew in advance what was going to be appropriate.

Third, imitation of more profitable producers will expand output. Such imitation would not be motivated by exhortations to promote national or social interest. Greater personal wealth can be realized either by changing production in the indicated direction toward greater wealth, or by selling one's resources to others who will—if the resources are salable as private property.

Summary of Output Responses

How an increase in demand affects production and market-price can easily be summarized. Output can be more quickly increased only at higher costs; with time it can be increased less expensively. This relationship of costs to time can be suggested graphically by two supply curves: one for the early reaction, and one for the later limiting response. Figure 12–6 shows "before-and-after" situations. Demand, at D_1 with price at p_1, has increased to D_2. As it did, price rose to the long-run equilibrium at p_n. We cannot indicate the exact timing or path of price. Depending upon the size and speed of the demand increase, price will move in some fashion toward the long-run equilibrium at p_n as the output adjustment takes place. By definition, long-run equilibrium requires that price and minimum average costs be equal. Some firms will be expanding and others contracting (when, for example, an owner is aging, or the firm has lost its special abilities, or population is shifting).

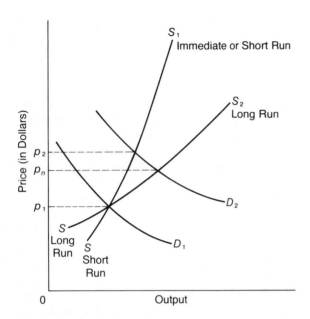

Figure 12–6. Supply Curves for Various Adjustment Dates for Various Outputs

Starting at the initial equilibrium situation, with price p_1, as demand increases, its intersection with supply will slide along S_1, the intermediate, or short-run, supply, which shows increased production from existing firms. In time, new firms will be attracted or new productive equipment will be installed by incumbent firms, and outputs will be indicated by the long-run supply curve, S_2. The short-run supply curve is the summation of the incumbent firms' marginal-cost curves. The long-run supply curve is the sum of the amounts firms (including new firms with new equipment) could produce at each price without losses.

Illustrative Analysis: Effects of a Tax

Uses of resources and outputs of consumer goods are affected by many factors other than changes in demand. Technology of production, or supply of productive resources may change. One factor that especially lends itself to instructive analysis is the imposition of a tax. As we shall see, the legal location or item on which a tax is levied is not necessarily the item that bears the tax.

Tax on All Producers in an Industry: Price and Output Effect

Suppose the producers of playing cards are taxed 50 cents on each deck. This tax increases each firm's marginal costs by 50 cents, and it adds 50 cents to the average cost of each deck. Summing the new, higher marginal-cost curves over all the firms in the industry yields a higher-cost (or lower-output) supply curve, as illustrated in Figure 12–7. Before the tax, the price was 75 cents. Each firm, now operating on a higher marginal-cost curve, would reduce its output *at the old price* from X_1 to X_2. The reduced *industry* output (that is, reduced market supply) would push up price, which would induce each firm to restrain its output reduction to X_3. Our first conclusion is that the higher tax raised costs, but price rose *only because the supply to the market decreased*. The effect on price is through the effect on industry supply to the market. Only because the higher tax decreased the industry supply could a higher price be sustained. The same analysis could be used for anything that raised the marginal costs of production, such as higher wages for labor, or higher prices of material, power, or transport.

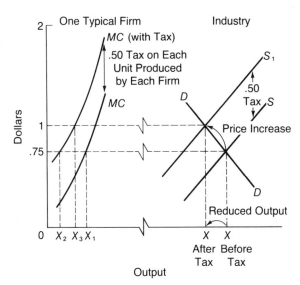

Figure 12–7. Price and Output Effect of Tax on Each Unit Produced or Sold

Tax is levied on output of playing cards of all firms in industry. Supply curve shifts upward to incorporate taxes of 50 cents per unit. This reduces output at the old price and the price moves up to $1. Higher price results from the smaller supply function. Unless tax affects supply curve, price cannot be affected. Price rises by less than tax because, at smaller output, marginal and average costs are lower. Part of tax is revealed as a higher price to consumer and a smaller rate of consumption; another part is reflected in reduced wealth value of resources specialized in production of this taxed good. Tax is borne by consumers and by owners of capital goods and labor services specialized to this industry.

Wealth Effect

In the playing card example, the price is increased by less than the tax on each deck— namely by 25 cents (to $1 from 75 cents). The output is reduced, by sliding back down the higher marginal-cost curve. But this means some

resources used in producing playing cards are no longer so useful to the firm. This decrease in their useful value reflects their lower net value to the playing card producer.

We can see that the total tax receipts (tax per deck times number now produced) are accounted for in part by a higher price to consumers and in part by a lower value of, and payments to, resources used especially to manufacture the taxed good. Clearly taxes are not all ultimately borne by the consumer of the taxed good. Instead, only part of the tax in this case is borne by consumers as higher prices and fewer decks of cards; the other part is borne by the owners of the resources specialized to card production. Those resources could be machines, people, or even land. Their incomes fall to the extent that their excess value in card production over the value of alternative uses is reduced; that excess is what is meant by their being "specialized to card production."

But this is not the end of the adjustment. In the longer run the equipment devoted to producing cards will be further reduced, and the output will be smaller than the immediate or short-run response, as can be seen in Figure 12–8. The longer-run adjustment in price and output includes the adjustment in all the resources in all the firms making cards. When this final adjustment is achieved, the price of cards will be sufficiently higher to cover the tax and the cost of replacing or maintaining new equipment. Some resources that would have produced cards are now directed to less-valuable goods.

Do not confuse the effect on the wealth of those who own resources specialized to card production at the time the tax is announced with

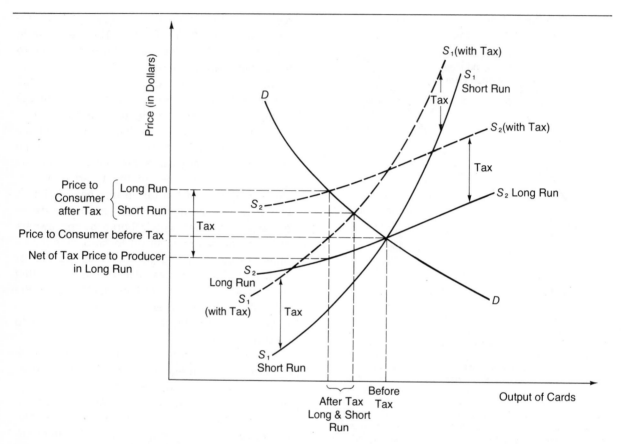

Figure 12–8. Price and Output Effects, Long-Run and Short-Run, of a per-Unit Tax on Playing Cards

The more time allowed after a tax is imposed or cost is increased, the greater will be the effect on the amount supplied (reflecting withdrawal of resources from the industry).

In any event, the higher input price or tax results in higher price to consumers, smaller rate of card consumption, and reduced income and wealth to owners of productive re-sources specialized to card production. The diagram shows price and output effects but not the wealth effects.

the effect on the wealth of those who purchase those resources afterward: New buyers will make offers that reflect the lower capital value of the future receipts *net* of the taxes that must be paid as long as the tax exists, which we assume is "many" years. The wealth-loss to the owners of these special resources occurs at the announcement of the tax.

Tax on One Firm Only

Suppose the tax had been levied on *just one* producer. Without a similar tax on the other producers, the *market supply* from the *industry* does not shift by a perceptible amount. The taxed producer has no way to recoup part of his wealth by a higher price. If he tried to raise his price, buyers would shift to other sellers. In this case, his output and his wealth fall more than if the tax had been levied on all card producers. Price is not significantly affected unless supply is.

Passing on Higher Costs?

The above analysis shows what is erroneous in the common belief that all cost increases are passed on to consumers. This misconception rests on a misunderstanding of the connection between costs, supply, and demand. What is necessary to raise price is that increased costs must reduce the total supply schedule significantly. The greater the number of suppliers whose costs are increased, the more a rise in costs will reduce market supply. To raise the costs of just one supplier, who is but a small part of the total supply, will affect the total supply by a negligible amount with no appreciable effect on the price. And even if every supplier is af-

fected, price will not rise as much as the cost because (1) the demand schedule is negatively sloped—less will be sold when price is raised; and (2) the supply schedule is positively sloped. (See Figures 12–7 and 12–8). So price is raised by less than the rise in costs, and less is produced and sold.

The fallacious idea that a producer can simply pass on increased costs probably arises from confusing his cost increase with *inflation* (which increases *everyone's* dollar measure of costs and also increases market demand by a matching amount). It is not safe to assume that any increase in *your* cost is accompanied elsewhere in the economy by equal rises in costs and demands. That way lies bankruptcy or poverty for you, unless—aha! There is an "unless"! The "unless" is to close the market to your competing suppliers. If you could exclude competitors (whose supply in the market makes your selling price lower) you could raise your price. (But there is no point in waiting until your costs rise to do that.)

14, 15
16, 17
18

Summary

1. Increased demands and higher prices induce larger outputs. The supply relationship between price and output of each firm is given by a firm's marginal-cost curve above the minimum average variable (for the short-run) costs for existing firms. For entering firms it is the portion above the minimum total per-unit costs.

2. At a firm's wealth-maximizing output, marginal cost is equal to marginal revenue—

which is the average revenue or price to a price-taker.

3. Firms will temporarily produce even if price does not cover the total costs (including the fixed acquisition cost of already-possessed equipment, which is a sunk, no longer relevant cost). The decision to enter or acquire the equipment for production was a wealth-losing decision, but if production is nevertheless continued temporarily, the loss will be minimized. When the *minimum* variable per-unit cost is pushed above price as higher maintenance or replacement cost occurs, the firm will shut down.

4. An industry is the collection of firms producing a particular good. The industry short-run supply curve (which excludes new firms) in a price-takers' open market is the sum of the amounts given by each firm's marginal-cost curve at the market price—that is, those portions of each firm's marginal-cost curve above its minimum variable per-unit cost.

5. The long-run supply curve reflecting entry and acquisition of new productive equipment is more elastic.

6. Entry of new firms occurs not only when new enterprises seek to replace or compete with other firms by producing at a lower per-unit cost, but also when price rises in response to demand increases.

7. Industries that have a high turnover of firms are sometimes mislabeled "sick" industries.

8. Profits are imputed, by revised market prices, back to the responsible productive resources. In this way costs of subsequent use of the resources are revised to reflect higher value of the resources. Thereafter, returns to producers just cover the new, adjusted, revalued costs.

9. Unless resources are directed toward their market-revealed highest-value uses, the owner will not maximize his wealth. Wealth-maximizing use of resources to determine outputs is economically more "efficient," the more fully market values reflect the values of all the consequences of each possible use.

10. A per-unit tax on a good reduces its output (releasing resources for use elsewhere). The tax results in: (a) wealth reductions to the owners of resources specialized to the taxed product, and (b) wealth reductions to consumers of the product, who now pay a higher price for the smaller supply of the taxed good.

11. All responses and actions analyzed in this chapter were of price-takers in open markets.

12. An increase in costs to a particular seller cannot be passed on as equivalently higher prices because one producer has trivial effect on industry supply and hence a trivial effect on price. The more general the cost increase among all producers of a product, the more the supply schedule is affected and the more the price will be affected. But price will rise by less than the cost increase unless the supply curve were horizontal and shifted upward by the full amount of the tax or higher cost.

Questions

1. This question is designed to explain the demand situation facing an individual seller in

atomistic, price-takers' markets. The community demand for wheat is shown below, in the vicinity of the market price, $2 per bushel. (Conventionally, wheat prices are expressed to the nearest eighth of a cent per bushel.)

Demand Function

Price	Quantity
$2.01	9,986,000
$2.00\frac{7}{8}$	9,987,000
$2.00\frac{6}{8}$	9,988,000
$2.00\frac{5}{8}$	9,990,000
$2.00\frac{4}{8}$	9,992,000
$2.00\frac{3}{8}$	9,994,000
$2.00\frac{2}{8}$	9,996,000
$2.00\frac{1}{8}$	9,998,000
2.00	10,000,000
$1.99\frac{7}{8}$	10,002,000
$1.99\frac{6}{8}$	10,004,000
$1.99\frac{5}{8}$	10,006,000

a. You have 1000 bushels. If the rest of the suppliers provide 9,999,000 bushels, could you detectably affect the market price by withholding all or any of your supply from the market?

b. If you tried to sell at $\$2.00\frac{1}{8}$ while the market price was $2, would anyone buy wheat from you?

c. What does the demand curve for *your* wheat look like?

2. Suppose you had 6000 of the 10,000,000 bushels provided by all the farmers.

a. Could you sell *any* wheat at a higher price than $2? How much would you sell if you asked $\$2.00\frac{1}{8}$? If you asked $\$2.00\frac{2}{8}$? $\$2.00\frac{3}{8}$?

b. Would it pay you to ask for a price of $\$2.00\frac{1}{8}$ in view of the effect on the sales revenue? What is your marginal revenue?

c. What does the demand curve facing you look like? Would you agree that it is, for all practical purposes, essentially regarded as a horizontal line at the market price?

d. Suppose you owned 1,000,000 bushels of the 10,000,000 bushels of wheat. Could you now affect the market price to a significant extent?

3. You own 1000 shares of General Electric common stock. If you try to sell some, you find you can get a price of $\$61\frac{1}{2}$ per share for all 1,000 shares. If you offer only 500 shares, you can get a price of $\$61\frac{5}{8}$—$12\frac{1}{2}$ cents more per share. By reducing your amount sold by a half, you can get a price that is higher by about $\frac{1}{500}$. And if you sought a price of $\$61\frac{3}{4}$, you would sell nothing. This is an insignificant rise in price for you, but effective in reducing amount demanded as a result of withholding one's supply. Is this a price-takers' market? Compute your marginal revenues as best you can with the given data. Is the elasticity of demand for your shares high or low?

4. In a price-takers' market, does the marginal revenue of each seller approximate the average revenue (price)? Why?

5. Most elementary arithmetic books contain the following type of question: "Mr. Black, the grocer, can buy bread for 15 cents. What price should he charge to make a profit of 50 percent?" Without worrying why Mr. Black should be content with 50 instead of 500 percent profit, wherein does this question ignore

a basic economic fact of life? Suggest a formulation of the problem that will enable students to learn how to manipulate percentage calculations without being taught erroneous economics.

6. Explain why the marginal-cost schedule above the lowest average variable cost is the supply schedule of the firm in a price-taker's market.

   *a. What is the supply schedule of the firm in Table 12–1?

   *b. If price were $22, what would be the rate of profits?

   c. How low a permanent price would make this firm stop production permanently?

   d. How low could price be temporarily without this firm suspending production?

7. "Marginal costs serve as a guide to how much of a good to produce, while average costs help indicate whether to produce the good at all." Explain.

8. Is there a short-run cost and long-run cost for a given output program, or are there two different contemplated output programs, each with its own cost?

*9. If, in some industry, there were 100 firms exactly like the one whose cost data are given in Table 12–1, what would be the industry supply schedule—assuming a price-takers' market?

10. The following describes the market demand in the price-takers' market for 100 firms each with costs given in Table 11–2 of Chapter 11, on page 252.

Demand Schedule					
Price	Quantity	Price	Quantity	Price	Quantity
$5.00	450	$2.80	810	$1.40	1400
4.50	500	2.60	850	1.20	1700
4.00	560	2.40	900	1.00	2100
3.75	610	2.20	950	.90	2400
3.50	660	2.00	1000	.80	2800
3.25	710	1.80	1100	.70	3300
3.00	770	1.60	1200	.60	3900
		1.50	1300		

a. What will be the equilibrium price?

b. What will be the rate of output at that price?

c. If price is somehow kept below that equilibrium, what will be observed in the marketplace?

d. At the equilibrium price of the current problem, will new firms be attracted into producing this good?

e. If new firms can enter this business, each one having the same cost conditions as firms already in the business, to what value will the market price move? (Hint: In the long-run supply curve, price will equal average cost of each firm, including entry of new firms. Assume all firms are identical.)

f. As new firms enter, what will happen to the output of the existing firms?

g. What will happen to the costs of the firms whose minimum average cost curves were lower? (Hint: What happens to the profits of those lower-cost firms?)

11. Suppose the average cost of the resources used in producing an X is $5, where cost is interpreted as the highest sacrificed use

value. On the other hand, if these resources were to be used elsewhere, their sacrificed value of output here is $6. What will make these two different "costs" of the same resources converge to the same value?

12. "The free-enterprise, capitalist system is a system of consumer sovereignty. Consumer preferences determine what shall be produced and how much shall be produced." Evaluate.

13. You are a public employee operating a publicly owned golf course, or swimming pool, or taxi service, or gun factory; and you have the costs indicated by the data in Table 11–2. Furthermore, you are selling the product in a price-takers' market.

a. At a price of $1.50 you would choose to produce not 13 units but about 21 units. Why do we predict that you would produce about 21 units? (Hint: How do the rewards and punishments meted out to you as an operator of a nonprivate-property firm depend on, or vary with, the selected output program? Compare this with a privately owned business.)

b. Suppose you are *told* to maximize profits. Would you? Why?

14. A tax of 1 cent is levied on each pound of peanuts grown by farmers.

a. What effect will this have on the output of peanuts?

b. How will it induce that effect?

c. What will happen to the price of peanuts?

d. Will the land on which peanuts are grown fall in value—in view of the facts (i) that peanuts are grown from plants that must be seeded every year, and (ii) that the land can be used for other crops?

*e. What will happen to the value of *existing* machines used for harvesting, shelling, roasting, packaging, and crushing peanuts? Why?

*f. Explain why these changes in value will not be permanent even though the tax is permanent.

*g. Does the temporary drop in value mean that the wealth-reduction effect of the tax is only temporary? Why or why not?

h. The proceeds of the peanuts tax is used to finance purchases of this book for free distribution to college students. Who is paying for the books so distributed? (The answer is *not* that those who lost wealth from the revised valuation of existing resources are paying for books. That loss of wealth is not offset as a gain to anyone else.)

*i. Who gains what as a result of the tax and expenditure of the proceeds?

15. Suppose that the tax in the preceding problem is levied against only *one* producer of peanuts.

a. What will happen to the price of peanuts?

b. To the output?

c. To the wealth of the various peanut producers?

d. Whose wealth will be affected by this tax?

16. Pittsburgh put a 20 percent tax on gross receipts of private commercial parking-lot operators while exempting competing publicly operated lots. The 1975 U.S. Supreme Court held the tax constitutional even though its enforcement may destroy particular businesses. The Court also concluded that, in any event, a shortage of parking spaces in Pittsburgh would enable private lot operators to pass the 20 percent gross receipts tax on to

Firm A		Firm B		Firm C	
Output	Marginal Cost	Output	Marginal Cost	Output	Marginal Cost
1	$1.00	1	$ .20	1	$ .10
2	1.10	2	.40	2	.15
3	1.20	3	.60	3	.20
4	1.30	4	.80	4	.25
5	1.40	5	1.00	5 is impossible	
6	1.50	6	1.20		
7	1.60	7 is impossible			
8	1.70				
9	1.80				
10	1.90				
11 is impossible					

their customers. The burden of the tax thus will fall upon customers. Is the Court's economic analysis correct? Explain.

17. Above are shown marginal cost data for three firms, A, B, C, constituting the entire industry producing X. Each firm acts as a price-taker.

*a. Compute the supply schedule of this industry. (Hint: At each possible price indicate the amount that would be most profitably produced by each firm. The sum of those amounts gives amount supplied by the industry at each price.)

b. What is the general rule used to derive the supply schedule for an industry comprised of price-takers? How does wealth-maximizing behavior by each firm yield that?

c. The amount supplied at each price by the *industry* in the above example is produced efficiently. What does that mean?

18. Using the same numbers as in question 17 for firms A, B, and C, reinterpret them as fol-

lows: The "output" is now clean water. Each firm produces steel; it uses water and changes the chemical content. To "produce" clean water requires some special cleaning action or the reduction of some production of steel. Mill A could clean *one* of the 10 gallons of water it uses, abuses, dirties, or pollutes at a cost of $1.00. It can do so either by cleaning the water after it is used or by reducing the output of steel in order to not dirty that one gallon of water. In either case the cost of getting that clean gallon is $1 of what could otherwise have been had—in line with the general definition and meaning of costs. Similarly, a second gallon per day could be cleaned or not be dirtied at a cost of $1.10 more. The marginal cost of a second gallon of clean water is $1.10. Similarly, the marginal costs of more gallons of clean water are given by the remaining data for this mill and for the other mills in the appropriate columns for each mill. It is important to understand that, by *not* using water (or by not abusing it), the mill is in effect producing clean water at a sacrifice of other goods (steel) that could be had if the water were in fact used. If the steel is produced and the water used and dirtied, then the costs are the costs of removing that dirt. If the water is not dirtied (and the steel not produced), then the value of the steel forsaken (net of the other costs that are also involved in making steel) is the cost of having clean water.

a. The problem is as follows: If clean water is worth 75 cents a gallon, how many gallons of clean water should be "produced" or permitted by these steel mills? Which mills?

b. If each mill were required to pay 75 cents for each gallon of water that it polluted, how many gallons would each mill use and clean before discharging water? Or how many gallons of clean water would each mill not use that it otherwise would have?

c. If, instead of a pollution fee of 75 cents, polluting water were simply made illegal, would that be better or worse? In what sense? Assume clean water is worth 75 cents a gallon no matter how much is involved here.

d. Would it be better (than a pollution fee of 75 cents) to tell each mill that it must clean up 20 percent of its discharged water? Or that each must discharge at least two gallons of clean water?

e. What is the principle for the efficient amount of clean water?

f. If someone owned the rights to the water and could sell it to users, would that affect the amount of polluted water?

g. Is pollution to be interpreted as any use of a resource without compensation to the resource owner, or is it "excessive" use—beyond what would be used if compensation were required?

13

Market Power: Price-Searchers in Open Markets

The simple price-taker analytic model is adequate to explain several important features and operations of an economic system: for example, output response to present and anticipated consumer demands; effects of taxes on prices, output, and wealth; the function and means of risk-bearing; the role of property rights, specialization, middlemen; capital valuation of assets; "excess" capacity or inventories; effects of price controls; meaning of costs; price as a controlling and rationing device, philanthropy—and it could be used to explain such things as inflation, international trade, the money system, business fluctuations, etc.

Some other phenomena require a more detailed, more complex analysis. A *market-power, price-searcher* model is our next step up the analytical chain (which is like a physics student's moving from a frictionless model to one with friction). We are moving to a model in which costs of information about product qualities, availabilities, and alternative offer prices, and transactions costs and economies of scale are significant. A few other new elements are also added. We emphasize that the phenomena already examined, and their implications, are not significantly affected by this next step. Rather, some previously ignored phenomena can now be explained.

**Market-Power
Price-Searcher**

A seller whose selling price will be significantly affected by the amount he offers is often said to be a *price-searcher* with *market power,* which is

Table 13–1. Demand Facing Price-Searcher

		Revenue	
Price	Quantity	Total	Marginal
$20	1	$20	$20
19	2	38	18
18	3	54	16
17	4	68	14
16	5	80	12
15	6	90	10
14	7	98	8
13	8	104	6
12	9	108	4
11	10	110	2
10	11	110	0
9	12	108	−2
8	13	104	−4
7	14	98	−6
6	15	90	−8
5	16	80	−10
4	17	68	−12
3	18	54	−14
2	19	38	−16
1	20	20	−18

defined as that effect on price. He has power to affect his market price. But what use is that power? If his costs are sufficiently high or demand is sufficiently low, he will not make profits no matter what his market power. Thus he must do some searching to ascertain what price and quantity (and what quality of good?) are most profitable. He has a larger range of possible prices than the price-taker. Finding the marginal revenue and the best price (maximum profit) is not easy. If he lowers the price to sell more, his increase in total sales proceeds on the extra unit sold will be *less*

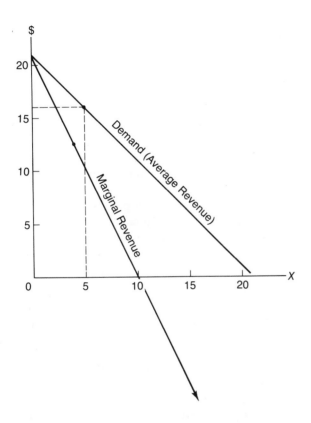

Figure 13–1. Demand Schedule Facing a Price-Searcher

The line marked "marginal revenue" indicates how much the seller's total receipts change when he sells one more (or one less) by appropriately changing his selling price on all the units he offers for sale. At any number of units sold, the marginal revenue is less than the price (unless only one unit is sold). It is the lower line, the marginal revenue that the price-searcher concentrates on. But we call him a price-searcher because he must search for the optimal (the profit-maximizing) price for his wares. And he can come closer to finding that price if he has a good estimate of his marginal revenue at any possible price.

gallon with total revenue of $20. The seller could instead have sold only 10 gallons at a price of $11 per gallon and receive $110 daily, some $90 more. The problem facing this seller is that if he sells an extra gallon he must accept a lower price on every gallon of water formerly sold at the higher price. Thus, to sell 11 gallons daily he must cut the price to $10 on all 10 units that he was selling at $11 per gallon. The *increase* in revenue, the marginal revenue, is zero, even though the eleventh unit sells for $10. That $10 price received on the eleventh unit is wiped out by the required cut of $1 on the 10 gallons that could otherwise have been sold for $11.

Our well owner would offer only 10 (or 11) gallons daily. To offer more, at a still lower price, would reduce his total revenue—his marginal revenue would be negative. To offer less, say nine gallons, would bring him a price of $12 per gallon, but that would be a total of only $108. The tenth unit sold by cutting price to $11 brings a marginal revenue of $2, although its price is $10. A seller keeps his eye on *marginal revenue,* not simply on *price,* in deciding how much to sell.

The seller refuses to sell more water even though its marginal cost (zero) is less than the value to the customer of the unsold water—value

than the price received on that extra unit, because the price cut will also apply to the quantity formerly sold at the old higher price.

To illustrate, suppose a total daily supply of 20 gallons of fine drinking water comes from one well. (Once more to keep the essentials in clear view, assume there are no costs of operating the well or bottling or selling the water.) Assume the community's market demand for that water is the schedule in Table 13–1, shown as a graph in Figure 13–1. If the well owner were to sell all 20 gallons he would have to accept a price of $1 a to the customer is measured by price, not by marginal revenue, which is the value relevant to the seller. The excess of price over the marginal cost is a measure of waste in the sense that the extra gallon has a value to consumer greater than the cost. The discrepancy between value to consumer and cost of production arises because the seller heeds marginal revenue and not price. So long as the marginal revenue to the seller is less than price, the seller will be underproducing in the sense that the marginal costs of extra production are less than the value of that potential product—measured by the price, not by the lower marginal revenue to the seller. And marginal revenue will always be less than price if the seller faces a demand situation in which to sell more he must accept a cut in price on all the units he sells.

All the water could be used if price could be reduced on only the additional units sold while maintaining the price on the first 10 gallons. Later we shall investigate some ways of doing that. In fact, a reason for explaining the price-searcher's marginal revenue is to understand those pricing and sales tactics, some of which, despite this effect, have at times been declared illegal by the courts and government agencies probably through misunderstanding marginal revenue.

Monopoly: Open and Closed Market, Price-Searchers

Warning: The terms price-searcher and seller with market-power are synonymous. There are still others. In one of its senses, the word monopolist is another synonym. However, as explained earlier, monopoly has another, very different meaning to a seller of a product who is protected by legal sanctions from any other person trying to sell that kind of product in the market. Patents, copyrights, and exclusive franchises are legal arrangements designed to keep out sellers of the same product. Political-legal closures or restrictions of the markets to outsiders are widespread. In some states the state government is the sole seller of alcoholic beverages. In most cities, electricity, water, gas, telephone, buses, taxis, and television stations are monopolized by sellers; laws keep out newcomers. The monopolist may be a municipal agency or a private firm. In every such instance the demand curve facing the seller for his product is negatively sloped significantly. Such a seller illustrates both conceptions of monopoly: (1) legal protection from competitors, and (2) a negatively sloped demand for his products such that his marginal revenue is significantly below his selling price.

To avoid confusion of these two notions of monopoly we use the term market-power price-searcher to describe a seller facing a negatively sloped demand with marginal revenue significantly below price and without legal restrictions on competitors. We would like to use the term monopoly to describe only the case of legal restrictions on competitors, so we would refer to price-searchers with legal protection (monopoly) against competitors as monopolists. But, in fact, the term monopolist is popularly used to refer to every seller whose marginal revenue is less than price, that is, with a negatively sloped demand for his products, whether he be in an open or a closed market. Of course, only a few markets are literally closed to competitors: Either bribes and payoffs to legal authorities (which are not so rare) permit additional sellers, or the restrictions on entry were not intended to close the market completely. Nevertheless, to reduce the possibility of confusion we shall use the extreme terms, *open* and *closed markets* (or *unrestricted* and *restricted markets*).

Why Market-Power Price-Searchers?

Even without legally restricting the entry of competitors to the market, why are so many sellers and producers market-power price-searchers? Why does the corner grocer, filling station, druggist, clothier, restaurant, or General Motors have marginal revenue less than price? Why is each seller so large a part of his market? One factor is economies of scale; another is transportation costs; still another is costs of information about attributes of goods and their availabilities. Without economies of scale, there could be so many small sellers or producers everywhere in large markets that each small seller could attract sufficiently more consumers from other sellers with a minuscule price cut, or lose all his customers if he tried to raise his price, at essentially zero cost to those consumers. (But that, of course, assumes buyers have full information costlessly.)

Economies of Scale in Production, Administration, or Retailing

For technological reasons, some products are more economically produced, made known to the public, sold, and serviced with firms of larger size. Although retail stores may be relatively small and may face more elastic demands for their merchandise, the production of automobiles involves such technological effects as volume, design, engineering, and geographic location that make large-scale enterprises more feasible.

Differences in Tastes, Products, and Information

Differences in Products and Tastes

The feel, look, and weight of an aluminum beer can makes it more acceptable than the steel can. Don't call that irrational, silly, or uninformed. Are Fords the same as Chevies, Cokes the same as Pepsis, and is Palmolive the same as Lux? All men are created equal; yet buyers are disconcertingly choosy. The difference between mink and rabbit fur is "slight"—except perhaps to minks and rabbits—yet the public's preference between them is enormous, even if it is all a matter of looks and feel. Are spouses chosen on more substantial grounds? Differences that do not matter to each of us will matter to others—and they may think that what matters to us is of no matter. You may think it really is of no matter whether you eat pork or beef or vegetables, or worship this deity rather than that, or rest or work on Sunday; but people have warred over such "trivial" issues, and still do so. You could declare them prejudiced, ignorant, or discriminatory, but all you mean is that their tastes or preferences differ. And this should give us pause before confidently avowing that discriminators among brands of cigarettes, aspirin, paper tissues, soap, corn flakes, service stations, retail stores, or sales people are uninformed.

Much product differentiation is "natural." Raquel Welch, Barbra Streisand, George Blanda, and Arnold Palmer have unique attributes. Each is a price-searcher. Streisand can raise her fees and still perform, though less frequently. No laws prohibit anyone's trying to copy her, but enough consumers can tell the difference without trademarks or copyrights.

Product Information
Differs among People

Consumers differ in their information about a product or a seller's services. Some are more reliably informed about this product and some about others. The Sears portable electric typewriter is actually a Smith-Corona, but with a different exterior shell. The prices for the two are different, if you don't shop around for sales or special discounts. To say all that reflects ignorance is to say nothing useful, since practically everything we do reflects a lack of perfect knowledge. Why else are you in school? It is more useful to say that the cost of acquiring some more information exceeds the value of the extra information. Why do I buy gasoline from the local station when it is selling at a lower price three blocks down the street? Well, how am I supposed to know that if I drive those three extra blocks I'll find a cheaper price? Extra costs of information often exceed the expected value of the additional information.

When it costs something to get information about product qualities, consumers will differ in information. Some buyers who don't know as much about availability and substitutes as do other buyers will pay higher prices before they switch. This behavior is not irrational, stupid, or an imperfection in the economic system. It simply doesn't pay to try to acquire *full* information, just as it doesn't pay to satiate oneself in any other costly, "non-free" good. We also specialize in our information. It pays your authors to be ignorant about care and repair of automobile engines in order to be more informed about economics and teaching techniques. We may pay higher prices for auto repairs than if we knew enough to astutely evaluate quality of service, but not as much more as it would cost us to become more informed about every repair place and service. If that sounds silly, why not write your own economics text, or teach yourself, or repair your own television set? Could you save more than the tuition and TV repair costs if you tried to serve yourself? It depends in part on the value of your time in other productive uses. To think that information is costless and freely available is equivalent to thinking that steel is costless and freely available. In fact, both are costly, but for some inexplicable reason, people often talk as if information were—or should be—costless. Even if economies of scale were inoperative and consequently there were a very large number of producers, all would be regarded as different if full information were costly.

**Brand Names: Reducing
Costs of Information about Products**

A powerful reducer of the costs of information about the qualities of products is the brand name. Reputations are built and maintained on past reliable performance. Though a newcomer or unknown producer says his product is just as good, how can you be sure? Information or evidence is costly to establish and distribute. Brand names—Kodak, American Express, Howard Johnson, Holiday Inn—identify goods and services of verified, predictable standards of quality—not necessarily of the best or highest quality, but of *predictable* quality. People who heed brands are using economically efficient sources of information about *differences* in product performance. For example, one well-known brand of canned food (S&W) includes riper (tastier) and more expensive goods than another brand (Libby's) that denotes a slightly lower quality and sells for 20 percent less. Make the test. Both are reliable predictors of different qualities. You may think the difference not worth the cost—but then you aren't the only person whose preferences count. In any event, the lower-quality, lower-price products are reliably indicated by their brand-name reputation.

Imagine shopping without knowledge of the brand-name reputations. Many agricultural products like lettuce, potatoes, tomatoes, squash, onions, etc., are unbranded—or were, because their quality is relatively easy to detect at time of purchase. More recently, as labeling has become cheaper and shoppers' time has become more valuable, branding has increased as a cheaper means of indicating quality. More obviously, the name of the *retailer*—as for diamonds or meat—is used to identify the expected quality of product. The more difficult it is to predict the performance of a good at the time of purchase, and the more serious the consequences of deviations from expectations, the more one will rely on the reputation of the seller—which is intelligent economic behavior.

The brand-name value will be eroded by defective performance. By past and present performance the producer must establish and maintain credibility of future performance. He has an incentive to produce goods of reliable, predictable quality insofar as *his* performance will be associated with *his name,* be distinguished from others, and bring him repeat or new customers.

Yet despite his efforts not everyone will be equally informed about his quality of service. He must incur higher costs to give more customers more information about his product quality. In addition, people demand some assurance against unpredictable defects in his product. Will he repair or make good? Though written insurance and warranties can be explicit, it is difficult to identify in advance all the risks that are really worth covering. An alternative to explicit insurance contracts is reliance on the producer to make good in a reasonable way out of his own self-interest for future business based on the reputation and knowledge of his probable reasonable performance. As long as he can establish a reputation for good service he will have incentive to provide such service, if he can be uniquely identified thereafter. A brand name or trademark associated only with him and his products is an efficient way to identify him. (If you doubt this, try buying goods in Communist countries where products are not branded but sold simply as stockings, pickles, bread, canned soups. One experience like that and you'll develop a profound understanding of the value of brand names to both consumer and producers!)

Price and Output for Price-Searchers in Open Markets

In our first example of pricing by a price-searcher or monopolist (p. 290) we explicitly assumed zero production costs without explicitly considering information costs as one reason for the existence of price-searcher markets. But now assum-

1, 2
3, 4
5, 6
7, 8
9, 10
11

Table 13–2. Average and Marginal Costs
at Different Outputs

Output	Average Cost	Marginal Cost
3	$18.00	$9
4	16.00	10
5	15.00	11
6	14.50	12
7	14.28	13
8	14.25	14
9	14.33	15
10	14.50	16
11	14.73	17
12	15.00	18
13	15.30	19
14	15.64	20
15	16.00	21
16	16.38	22
17	16.76	23

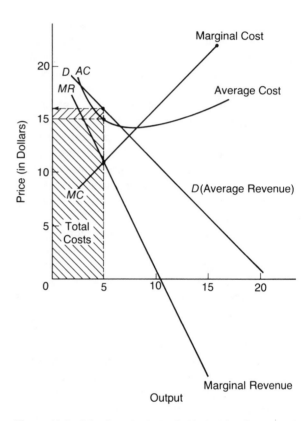

Figure 13–2. Price-Searcher's Profit-Maximizing Output and Price

A price-searcher, whose marginal revenue is less than price, has a profit-maximizing output where marginal revenue equals marginal cost, at eight units of output in this numerical example. The per-unit price at which eight units sell is $16, which yields a dollar net above the costs of $15 per unit. (Marginal revenue and cost are both equal at $11.)

ing that there are costs of production does not change the general results, as we shall now illustrate. (Assume that contemplated output programs are for one year and that any increase in the output *rate* will involve a proportionate increase in volume.)

The *costs* of alternative one-year output programs are in Table 13–2 and represented by the cost curves drawn in Figure 13–2. The average-cost and the marginal-cost curves are labeled *AC* and *MC*. The demand conditions are those from Table 13–1 and are fully known to the seller (an assumption we will later abandon). The producer's demand curve and its marginal-revenue curve are *DD* and *MR*. The output that maximizes the firm's profit is five units, each sold at a price of $16.00, with average cost of $15.00. The total

profit is $5. If a larger output (say six units) were produced and sold, the price on all units would be lower, and the average cost not sufficiently lower. Total profit would be reduced because the marginal revenue at the sixth unit does not cover that marginal cost. The output program of five units is the profit-maximizing output, because at larger outputs marginal costs exceed marginal revenue.

The seller could charge any price if he were prepared to bear the consequences. For example, at a price of $18 he would sell three units and net zero profits, and at a price of $14.50 he can sell six and a half units with the same zero profits. At higher or lower prices he would incur losses. Market demand and cost conditions, along with his desire for wealth, control him and induce him toward the price of $16, a price he searches for, because it is his profit-maximizing price.

"Monopoly" Distortion: Inefficient Output Ratio

At his profit-maximizing situation the price-searcher's output has a marginal cost that equals the marginal revenue, but his marginal revenue is less than price. We know the value of an additional unit to consumers is the price, not the lower marginal revenue to the seller. But the seller heeds the smaller marginal revenue, because that is what he would get if he sold an additional (sixth) unit (*and all his output*) at that new price. An additional unit is worth $15 to consumers; the resources that would be required to produce it are elsewhere producing other products whose value to consumers is only about $12 of the marginal cost at six units. That is what marginal costs measure. Resources are therefore being used elsewhere to produce what is worth only $12 whereas they could have produced here a product worth $15 to consumers—

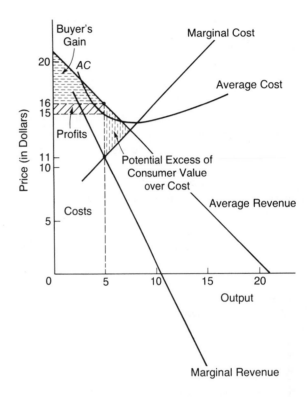

Figure 13–3. Output Distortion if Marginal Revenue is below Price

The excess of price over marginal cost is a wasted potential value unachievable if seller's attention is on marginal revenue rather than price. But there are sales tactics that can increase sales by reducing the price on some extra units without cutting the price on all units already being sold. This permits marginal revenue on extra units sold to be closer to price and above marginal costs, inducing a larger output.

a sacrifice of a potential social gain of $4. (See Figure 13–3.)

This lost value is often misleadingly called the result of monopoly distortion, although it is not a result of "closed" or restricted markets. The distortion arises because the seller heeds the marginal revenue rather than price of the last unit produced and sold. Since the extra receipts to the producer would not equal the price, but instead would equal the lower marginal revenue (because he must cut the price on all the units sold in order to sell more), he refuses to produce more. If he could somehow sell more of what they are worth to consumers—the prices at those outputs—without at the same time having to cut prices on all the former rates of output, the extra revenue would then be equal to the *price* of those extra units rather than to the lower marginal revenue when prices are cut on all the units sold.

A Method to Reduce "Monopoly" Distortion

Businessmen are not fools. They try to lower the price without cutting prices on all sales, as long as the marginal costs of the extra output are less than the price received. One way is to offer some "free" special service to new buyers. If the marginal costs of that special service are less than the excess of existing price over marginal costs, the seller and the customer will gain.

We can illustrate with our present seller, where the price is $16 with a marginal revenue of $12 and a marginal cost of $11 at five units of output. Suppose now that the seller is a hotel operator. Let him attract a sixth customer at the old price of $16 by offering him a free ride from the airport. If the ride costs $1.50, the customer gets something worth $16.50 to him ($15 value of hotel room plus $1.50 taxi; remember, this extra buyer values a room at only $15). All customers pay $16.

The seller's marginal revenue is $16, which after deducting the cost of the taxi yields the hotel owner $14.50, which in turn gives him a net gain of $2.50 over the $12.00 marginal cost of the room to a new customer. The new patron got a package worth to him $16.50 for $16.00. The gains to the patron, 50 cents, and to the seller, $2.50, total $3.00, exactly the formerly wasted difference between the $15 value of the extra unit and its marginal cost of $12.

Buyers who do not take these "free" services do not pay for those that other people get; the extra buyers pay for those services and receive a lower price on the basic item. Free parking, credit cards, delivery, warranty, return privileges, the extra time of clerks and larger inventories for "picky," "choosy" customers, advertising, loss leaders, giveaways, or trading stamps do not necessarily raise costs to consumers. Whether they do depends upon how many of the customers use the free services; if every customer took every free service with every unit purchased, that would be equivalent to a price cut on every unit sold, and this scheme would not work.

Warning: Remarks about waste or underproduction of some goods relative to others—called monopoly distortion—are normative. They assume that consumer valuation is the proper value criterion. You might be surprised to know that we have many laws to *prevent* full exchange "efficiency" in accord with consumers' valuations—for example, compulsory licensing of doctors, prohibition of pornographic literature in many locations, alcohol in some states, and marijuana in most states, availability of many drugs only by prescription, nonenforcement of contracts with minors, and ordinance control of business hours. Perhaps, after all, exchange efficiency is not "good," if it means that people will be more able to trade and consume the goods which *you* think, for their own good, they should not.

12, 13
14, 15

Demand Changes and Effects on Output and Price

Short-Run Response

Suppose demand increased so that more was demanded at each price, while costs were unchanged. In Figure 13–4 the marginal-revenue curve associated with the new, higher demand curve lies to the right and above the old marginal-revenue curve. It intersects the unchanged marginal-cost curve at a larger output, and the price for that larger output is higher. This increased demand induced larger outputs, larger profits, and higher prices.[1]

Though the formal diagrammatic analysis indicates a rise in output and price in response to an increased demand, is it price or output that increases first, and what is the process? In earlier sections we have explained how demand impinges on sellers: Given their buffer inventories to keep price more stable and predictable with quick availability of goods as a convenience to buyers, a persisting higher demand will reduce

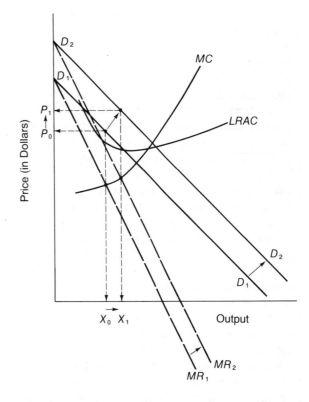

Figure 13–4. Price-Searcher's Output, Price, and Profit at Long-Run Equilibrium

In long-run equilibrium, the demand curve becomes tangent to the average-cost curve at some output, X_0. At that output the best possible price, P_0, equals, rather than exceeds, average cost. Imitative behavior by competitors induces this result. Innovative activity by this seller can push demand or cost away from that situation.

---

[1] Warning: Not every upward change in demand will imply higher prices. A twist in the demand curve toward a less elastic, more vertical line can result in a smaller output and a higher price; or a twist toward a sufficiently flatter, more elastic but bigger demand can result in a lower price and a larger output. But any upward shift must result in at least one of the two—price or output (and probably both)—being greater.

retailers' inventories more surely than will transient variations around a basically unchanged community consumption demand. Correspondingly, wholesalers' and manufacturers' inventories will decrease as retailers purchase more to replenish their unusually low inventories. When manufacturers' inventory depletions are greater than expected, production will be expanded. This output response to sustained increase in demand requires the employment of more resources at a higher cost, whether because they are less appropriate or because they must be attracted from other firms or into the labor market. That will provoke offers of higher wages, with higher costs and higher prices—all because of higher demand (unless the increased demand for this good is a shift in demand away from some other goods). Economics still has not adequately identified factors that explain precisely the speed of response of output relative to price. For the present it suffices to note that output often rises *before* prices because of the information problem—the problem of getting clear signals that quickly distinguish persisting demand increases from transient fluctuations.

The cheaper it is to provide stable, predictable prices and shopping convenience by buffer inventories and production capacity, the more likely is a demand increase to affect output before price; the more expensive are inventory costs or output alterations, the more likely is a demand increase to affect price before output. This will be especially important later when we analyze the effects of aggregate, national changes. As we shall later see, a *general, economywide demand increase (or decrease) for all goods* will increase (or decrease) output and employment before prices.

Long-Run Response: Capacity and Cost Response to Demand Changes

So far the analysis has concentrated on the response of existing firms to changed demand:

Existing firms expand with higher demand. But the increased wealth of existing firms cannot be long concealed. Firm salesmen know who is doing well. In various ways, the word gets around. Other firms imitate this firm. Employees organize their own company, taking part of the company's know-how. Hundreds of firms have been created by former employees of older electronic-computer companies. If the production of electronic organs, of pianos, of Cokes, or of Arrow shirts becomes more profitable, others will produce close substitutes and dissipate the profit of the first producer as some customers switch to the substitutes.

Profit streams of innovators and lucky firms are reduced and finally terminated as competing producers enter this market and bid up prices of responsible resources: assemblers, supervisors, designers, production engineers, salesmen, managers, and research staff. As all of these employees respond to competitors' offers, their wages rise, and hence their current employers' costs of keeping them rise. Formerly undervalued inputs are paid more, absorbing the profits into costs and terminating the undervaluation of resources. Their owners are richer. This is as true for land, buildings, and labor—whether the labor be plumbers, managers, or teachers—as it is for resources owned by a business. Even the cost of an owner's own services in his business must be valued at a higher figure; the more he can earn in his own business, the more others are willing to offer for his superior services. Those sacrificed options in other jobs with higher pay are costs of continuing in his own business. Figure 13–5 is a sample of a zero-profit long-run equilibrium, with price equal to average total costs.

If demand falls, the events are reversed. Values

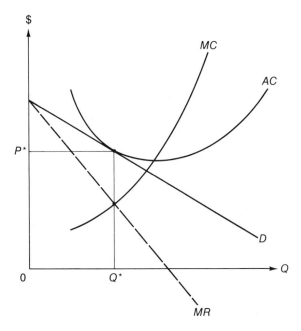

Figure 13–5. Price-Searcher's Output, Price, and Profit at Long-Run Equilibrium

No other price than P* and its output, Q*, would avoid losses. Imitative competition, making similar products available, pushes demand toward this situation. Innovative activity can push the situation away from this result, setting in forces tending to restore it.

imputed to currently used resources fall. Those resources will be shifted to other activities where the values of their services are not so low. Business owners and all other resources whose values are affected will be poorer because consumers' demands for their prior services are lower. To keep them at their old jobs at the former income would require compelling consumers to continue to buy things they no longer value so highly. And that can't be done in a free-enterprise open-market system. But it can be done if suffi-

cient government authority can be exerted to control what consumers can or must buy or support by special taxes to subsidize those producers—a topic we shall explore later.

The zero-profit solution shown by this diagram assumes that no special services are given to some customers (as explained earlier, p. 298) to achieve the output at which marginal cost equals price.

The Search for the Wealth-Maximizing Price and Output with Incomplete Information by Seller about Demand Conditions

If businessmen had better knowledge of present and future demand and costs, the shift toward wealth-maximizing outputs would be telescoped. Businessmen would have better anticipated future developments and initially taken more appropriate action with prices that more correctly anticipated all those foreseen events. There would be smaller profits or losses, because all resources would have been initially more correctly valued with better knowledge of future events. The economic analysis of the revaluation process and search for higher-valued products is appropriate to the real world of *uncertainty, partial ignorance,* and *costly information,* which is *not* to be confused with stupidity or irrationality. Producer-sellers must feel like gamblers at the racetrack: A horse will win, but *which one?* What price and what production of what good will increase one's wealth?

Consider a company that has designed an airplane it believes will be a good replacement for the 707—the first Boeing jet passenger plane.

What price and what scale of production should it plan? This is precisely the kind of question faced by Lockheed with its L-1011 and by Douglas with its DC-10. Boeing had earlier calculated sufficiently well to get a profit on the 707. How close it was to *the* profit-maximizing price no one will ever know. The demand for the Boeing 707 did lie above the cost curve for a region that Boeing managed to find, whereas if the demand curve for Convair's commercial jets ever did lie above their cost curve, they weren't able to find where. If they had known, they would have saved the stockholders scores of millions of dollars. Apparently Douglas was luckier with its DC-10.

Ford misjudged the Edsel demand and lost millions, but guessed right (that is, profitably) with the Mustang. General Electric invested in computer design and production and produced poorer stockholders. Chrysler designed automobiles in the 1950s for which the demand curve was under the average-cost curve, and lost at least $100 million. Not even the alleged consumer manipulations of advertisers could adequately sway buyers, despite easy allegations to the contrary.

Kodak sacrificed large profits in grossly underestimating the enormous demand for its Instamatic cameras. Hewlett-Packard flubbed in underestimating the demand for its electronic handsize computers. But they made some profits. Not only the giants display uncertainty, ignorance, and error. The corner grocer, druggist, and clothier must decide what product to stock. Farmers must guess next season's price in deciding what crops to plant now. Students must select careers. Only in the search for the *present* marginal revenue does the price-taker have an advantage.

Demands are reliably revealed by consumers only after the actual offer of new goods. Producers propose; consumers dispose. Transistor radios were invented and produced before consumers had gone to potential producers with advance orders. The same is true for many, many products: stereo and quadraphonic sound systems, electronic musical instruments, power steering, miniskirts, automatic transmissions, color television, Frisbees, instant coffee, frozen foods, credit cards, electric wrist watches, cordless electric knives, no-iron fabrics, synthetic fibers, stretch clothes, coin-operated dry-cleaning machines, water-based paints, zippers, etc. In each case, the hope of increasing his wealth provoked someone to invest in producing some new item that he thought people would demand. Venturesome, greedy, optimistic individuals are willing to risk their wealth to produce new goods for which they hope revealed demand will be sufficiently great to cover costs.

Product Interdependence

Are demands for some goods not revealed or heeded because they must be used jointly with some other good that would first have to be produced by someone else? Congress enacted a law requiring every producer of television sets to sell *only* sets that receive all 83 television channels, from 2 to 84. Presumably that law was passed because there was not enough incentive to make all-channel sets, and until sets were made to receive all 83 channels, there would be insufficient incentive to telecast on the higher-frequency channels. A vicious circle?

Neither historical facts nor economic analysis

support it. Automobiles, radios, and TV did not wait for "stations"—that is, guaranteed outlets, or workers. Nor did FM receivers for FM transmitters; in fact, they developed despite laws restricting FM broadcasting. Did stereo records await stereo players? Did FM stereo stations and receivers futilely await each other? Did automobile repair shops and automobiles? Did frozen foods and freezers for home use? Did color television require a law compelling all manufacturers of sets to include color capabilities? [2]

How is the alleged vicious circle of new-product interdependence overcome? It isn't there in the first place. Specialization of production is the rule in an economy in which exchange and access to the market are permitted. Specialization implies reliance on other people to produce jointly used products as they mutually and independently seek opportunities to increase their wealth. Interdependencies are not ignored in the economic system. Specialization does not imply lack of coordination, nor that opportunities for profit from joint products will be ignored. In fact, jointly used goods will be more effectively produced if specialization *is* permitted rather than if one person or firm must do the whole task. The vicious-circle bottleneck among jointly used products is a de-

[2] No law required—until 1974!—radio manufacturers to make only FM–AM combination radios. As the design technology improved in the 1950s, FM sets became easier to tune, cheaper, and more reliable. Transmitters "magically" expanded. For a long time the Federal Communications Commission *prohibited* color broadcasts until it could decide on the "best" kind of color system. And when it decided, it chose wrong! Fortunately, the Korean War forestalled production until the superiority of the electronic scan system became more obvious. Color television did not require a law compelling color transmission or receivers with color capability. (Can you guess who lobbied for FM–AM radio receiver requirements in 1974?)

lusion arising from the erroneous beliefs that output must be carried out on a large scale from the beginning, and that people are unwilling to invest now in anticipation of future receipts, *implying that present capital values are irrelevant.* These ignorant suppositions are disproved by events in the real world. A factory is built and others quickly build homes and stores in the area. Only if one forgets the incentives and exchange opportunities in a marketplace will he fail to see the coordinated anticipatory activity of other people.

Developers and Speculators: Risk-Bearing Predictors and Representatives of Future Consumers

An especially instructive, yet misunderstood, example of anticipating and representing future market demand for goods that are as yet unproduced and undemanded is the "speculative" land and housing developer. Future renters and buyers usually do not order construction of their future rental space. Instead, speculative (that is, anticipatory) developers build in the expectation that these new goods will have a demand in the future. Suburban developers are charged with being interested in a quick dollar—a true charge. But a quick dollar is a result of an accurate prediction and timely response to anticipated future demands for, say, houses and apartments. The anticipated future demanders living far away in other areas will move to the area—even as unborn generations. If you could ask those people if they will demand those new buildings, they could honestly say they don't know what their future demands will be. But *some* of them *will* later have a demand for them. Ladies' dress manufacturers make dresses months in advance of shoppers' actual demands, and hence are speculative clothing developers. Similarly, land developers are agents for expected but unidentified future buyers. Competition among anticipators of the future demands of those *unidentified, anonymous* people establishes current land values as the capitalized value of that latent future demand as judged by developers—the foresighted representatives of the future. It is not they who drive up land values; it is the future demand that they are discounting to a present value that establishes current land values. (What a difference an understanding of capital values can make in your interpretation of some economic activities!)

Selection of Maximum Product Values or Survival of Best Activity?

Do not overlook the profound implications of the preceding discussion. It is *not* a primary task of a businessman to read known cost tables and demand schedules to select the wealth-maximizing output. Instead it is risking his wealth in estimating what production techniques, products, and outputs really will have sufficiently low costs and high demands to yield a profit. If you ask a businessman about marginal costs and marginal revenues, he is likely to wonder what you are talking about. To hit exactly on the best production technique or the most profitable product, let alone the most profitable price and output amount is a gamble that is very rarely achieved. What we,

as economists, have done is show how underlying factors—to which the businessman is exposed—will affect what he can continue to do with greater or with fewer profits or losses. We can discern in what direction input prices and demand will affect his most profitable output rate. Competition in the market between alternative suppliers with different production techniques eliminates the poorer and retains the better of the *tested* methods. Untested techniques or products may be still better, but we won't know. (If you think other techniques should be tested, who should bear the risks of failure or success?)

Businessmen, whether they manage giant corporations or small lunch counters, whether they be employers or employees, do not *know* the best opportunities from some infallible "Book of Opportunities." They conjecture (and hope) after study, experience, diligent work, or sheer guessing that they are undertaking a profitable activity. They will find out at a risk. If they make profits, should they be content or should they try to do still better? If they incur losses, should they try a new technique or should they shut down as if there were no likely method they could use at sufficiently low cost. We offer no answers to those questions. That is why we are authors and not rich businessmen—or bankrupt ex-businessmen. Economic analysis does not assume that the producers of the world zero-in exactly on the best production opportunities and achieve the maximum of feasible profits.

Economic analysis uses the maximum profit and wealth *presumption* because the closer a businessman is to that output and price, the more profitable he will be, the more rapidly he can grow, and the more dominant he will be. What we were able to do by analysis is see how external changes would affect costs and revenues and thus predict how the competitive selection process selects *surviving* businesses.

The actual behavior of producers can be described as a frustrating search by hardworking, diligent people who are not perfectly informed, perfectly foresighted. They sensibly tend to stay with whatever action was profitable rather than immediately shift in response to every possible change to another in the confident belief that they can do still better. Will those whose fortunes shift against them be induced to try something new, changing their techniques or products, because the old, if continued, imposes losses? What is disheartening for the producers and businessmen nevertheless validates economic analysis: Even if people try this or that technique at random, with only the accidentally discovered more-appropriate techniques and outputs being successful, the surviving firms will have more of the characteristics implied by economic analysis. Each individual firm may have shifted around willy-nilly in every direction at random, but only those that moved toward what proved to be the right direction will prosper and flourish. A still stronger validation of theory is that even if individuals do not shift, the changing environment (shifts in demand and supply) will make the ensuing fortunes of some wax and others wane into oblivion, by forcing them to abandon loss-incurring activities.

Insofar as producers *and consumers* are denied open access to the market to express their demands and their offers for various services, the test of superior performance (in cost *and* in quality of product) will be weakened and the production process and product set will be less effective than it could otherwise be (however much there be failure for some and great gains for others). Through the markets for goods and services, people *select* and thereby determine which suppliers will flourish and survive or be left with losses because of inappropriate output or methods, however much the competing suppliers may be energetic, lethargic, foresighted, or ignorant. Of course, the more energetic, the more venturesome, and the better-informed are the producers and consumers, the greater will be the national output and the less will be wasted on inappropriate methods and products.

Some Common Misinterpretations of Modern Markets

Obviously, not all the misinterpretations of economic events can be discussed. However, a few are sufficiently common and popular to deserve some evaluation. So we examine them.

1. Arbitrary Administration of Prices

A modern myth has grown up about modern price-searchers' markets, because their prices fluctuate less than do price-takers'. When prices of each seller do change, they change at about the same time, and the largest firm usually is a price leader. These facts have been used to support the myth that dominant firms administer or set prices, and unless they do so with responsible self-restraint, government must intervene to protect the public interest. It has been said that U.S. Steel, General Motors, and large drug companies set the prices of their products by arbitrary administrative decision. Such sellers do, indeed, announce their prices. The Aluminum Company of America announces its price of aluminum; R.C.A. decides the prices of its radios and television sets. But what determines those prices?

The poorest common laborer or retail clerk or employee *could* charge too high a price and be poorer; but because he, too, is greedy and wants more wealth for himself, he charges whatever price will give him the maximum of income. Thus, DuPont does *not* set the highest price at which it could sell *any* of its output; it seeks the wealth-maximizing price permitted (but not readily disclosed) by market demand and competition. It cannot discover this price as easily as the price-taker can; it resorts to trial and error, never being sure. Because of feasibility of charging prices above or below the most profitable price, some think that Du Pont, U.S. Steel, or other sellers have the *market power* to set whatever price they please.

What kind of market power is that? The price-searcher cannot raise price at will—if he also "wills" to have more wealth, for too high a price will mean smaller wealth. Although the term *market power* correctly states that the seller has power *in principle* to raise or lower price, the seller is in fact constrained as to what price he does set by his powerful drive for more wealth. That kind of market power is as relevant as the "power" each of us has to give away most of his wealth.

2. Economic Power

Being a large or a dominant seller of some good with the power to affect price significantly by altering the amount supplied should be carefully distinguished from the economic incentive or probability of doing so. General Motors could raise the prices of cars by producing fewer. But what incentive does it have to do so? Other producers would gleefully fill the void and GM stockholders and employees would lose. Ability should not be confused with incentive. The ability to raise price is like the ability to throw my money away. (Willingness to do so is another matter.) Though a price-searcher has *power* to raise price by altering his output, it does not follow that he has the incentive to do so. Instead he is driven toward the wealth-maximizing price.

Whether sellers are described as using their "market power" to "set" prices or are merely searching for the best (wealth-maximizing) price in the light of market demand is a matter of semantics. Call them "monopolist-administered prices" if you want to regard the seller as a selfish, noncompeting, economic royalist. Otherwise, call them "market-revealed, demand-and-supply-determined prices." Neither self-restraint nor concern for interests of other people determines his prices. It is the effect on his wealth that restrains him if higher prices will lower his net receipts. *All* prices in *all* markets are administered in the sense that each person decides at what price he shall sell (in the light of market demand). But that crucial phrase must not be forgotten: "in the light of market demand." Sellers (and buyers) watch each other closely and, like dogs chasing a rabbit, move together, even in those cases where there is no leader, simply because they seek the same quarry: more wealth.

Another misunderstanding associated with beliefs about effects of large firms is the notion that big firms make bigger profits because they are big, rather than that firms making big profits will become big firms. Being big does not in itself enhance the probability of making profits. That, at least, is what economic theory indicates, and the evidence is consistent. It is easy to think that one can refute this evidence by pointing out a big firm like General Motors, which has earned profits in the capital-value sense during many years (and in that same sense has had losses during many years). But some very large firms have lost wealth in many years (Chrysler, Ward's), and some very small firms have had spectacular growth (Hewlett-Packard, Texas Instruments, Xerox, Control Data). The total of evidence is that, in the *next* interval of time, large firms and small firms have the same probability of showing a profit (unforeseen capital-value gain in its wealth). This predicted pattern is true as well for price-takers and price-searchers—and is even true whether the firm's access to the market is restricted or free. All the foreseeable events have been capitalized into the present valuations; only the unforeseen ones remain to be revealed.

The idea that it is possible to know which firm or class of firms is more likely to earn profits is self-defeating. If they were detectable in advance, it would pay to buy the firms immediately, pushing up their values *now*. Consequently, any statement about which class of firms will in the future experience unusual wealth increases, as profits, is a statement with which the general public (and especially the wealth-holding portion of it) is in disagreement. It is in disagreement because the statement implies that there is today a class of firms whose assets or resources (stock prices) are systematically undervalued. If you know of that class, you have a good road to profits for yourself; but beware, for you are betting against the judgment of the rest of the community.

3. Absence of Price Competition

Another contention is that an industry of a very few sellers, called an *oligopoly,* is characterized by weak price competition. Although it is never made clear what is meant by weak price competition, the context suggests that any one seller is aware that if he cuts price, others will quickly match him, and everyone's profits will take a beating. So instead, a seller holds his price at some "reasonable" level.

Thus, one must not confuse what makes several competitors charge nearly the same price with what determines the *level* of the common price of the few sellers. A common price can mean simply that it is not profitable to charge a lower price (or a higher one!) than others are charging—just as for price-takers. A nearly identical price—or indeed an identical price—among sellers is consistent with both independent competition and a collusive pact among sellers. In such cases other features are the distinguishing characteristics between competition and collusion, and we shall investigate some of them in the next chapter.

4. Price Rigidity

Evidence does not confirm charges that price-searchers administer prices regardless of demand and supply—or that more concentration of the output of an industry in a few large firms raises prices or makes them less flexible. Indeed, the number or size of firms in a price-searcher industry shows no connection with the flexibility of price change. Yet many people—lawyers and members of Congressional committees chief among them—argue that administered prices are rigidly set in concentrated industries.

Why is it argued thus? What was the evidence? The price of automobiles was reported to be stable and invariant because the list (or recommended) price announced by the automobile companies stayed unchanged throughout the model year. But one of the first things a person learns in shopping for a car is that the list price is, at most, the selling price only at the beginning of the new-car season. Salesmen's pencils are sharpened for "special" deals, which are offered to everyone who says he is going to shop around.

The printed, catalogue prices of the thousands of varieties of steel sometimes do not change for many months. Yet the actual transaction prices for steel vary frequently and substantially. Discounts for cash payment vary; speed of delivery and special services vary from week to week; quantity discounts are common. A steel purchase is a complex transaction. Extensive studies of actual contract prices of steel show that the actual prices are highly variable from day to day, despite constant catalogue prices.[3]

The current assessment of the price-rigidity allegation has been summarized by a president of the American Economic Association:

Economists have long struggled to find a rational explanation for prolonged price rigidity, which is in general as inadvisable for profit-maximizing monopolists as it is impossible for "price-taker" industries. Putting aside minor or special circumstances (the cost of a price change; the procedural delays in cartel or public regulation), they have failed to discover any such explanation. It appears that the real world has been equally remiss in supplying the phenomena they were seeking to explain.[4]

5. Concentration and Profits

Another myth or misconception is that greater concentration of an industry in a few firms increases profits; for example, if 90 percent of an industry's sales are by the four (rather than say, 20) largest firms, industry profits will be increased. As evidence, some more-concentrated industries with few firms were observed to be more profitable than some less-concentrated industries with many firms. A conclusion is suggested: to wit, the more concentrated the industry and the more effectively prices were kept up, possibly by advertising, collusion, and barriers to entry, the greater are profits—a not very sound conclusion.[5] There are several reasons, which we now discuss in turn.

[3] One factor that tends to relate high concentration in a few firms to price rigidity is in fact a statistical fallacy. For example, the fewer the firms, the higher is the concentration of output in those fewer firms. And the smaller the number of firms, each with equally flexible or frequent price changes, the fewer the *total number* of price changes; this *frequency* of recorded price changes merely reflects the number of *different* seller's prices to count. So one would see more changes if there were more sellers, even though the flexibility of any one seller's price is the same and is equally responsive to demand changes, regardless of degree of concentration. Thus, the more sellers, the more it *seems* the *market* prices change.

[4] George J. Stigler, "Administered Prices and Oligopolistic Inflation," *The Journal of Business* of the *University of Chicago,* Vol. 35; No. 1 (January 1962), p. 8.

[5] In the photocopy business, Xerox made enormous profits. It and a couple of other "copiers" have a very large share of the market. (But have they a large share and large profits because they developed superior products? Unusually superior products can explain several cases of high concentration and large profits.)

First, having a large fraction of sales of some industry does not mean that those sellers own the same large fraction of resources capable of entering and producing those products. One income tax firm, for example, does about 40 percent of the commercial income tax preparations, yet it has an insignificantly small fraction of the resources quickly capable of producing income tax services. That firm could not raise prices monopolistically and make profits, because the mass of other capable and potential suppliers would quickly take over. High earnings in this case are attributable to superior or lower-cost service, not to power over supply. Do not confuse a large fraction of sales of a product or service with a large fraction of the resources capable of producing it. Such an identification would be appropriate in the nickel industry (in which there is essentially only one owner of nickel ore) but not in very many others.

A second, more fundamental reason for a positive correlation between profit rate and concentration is that the superior performance of a firm will make the firm larger. Profits flow only to the firms that perform well. Because more-efficient firms become larger, their productive superiority tends to produce a major share of the industry's output. But if the sources of higher profits in concentrated industries were collusion and restriction of entry of new firms, higher profit rates should be enjoyed by every firm in the industry—small as well as the largest, for they all benefit from the collusion and entry restriction. What are the facts? The best available evidence (which supplements earlier studies that were less detailed, comprehensive, or rigorous) is that the largest firms are more profitable than the smaller firms in any industry, no matter what the degree of concentration in that industry.[6] That is what one would expect if the more-efficient, more-profitable firms grew in size and became the major suppliers in that industry. Indeed, the industry would become more concentrated by the larger growth rate of those firms relative to the other firms. Thus, the true case would be the reverse of what was alleged: instead of the concentration of the industry in a few firms being the source of higher rates of earnings, it is the relative growth of the superior firms that has caused the concentration in the first place. Furthermore, the more concentrated the industry, the higher will be the rates of earnings for the industry as a whole. If some firms are very efficient and grow to large size with their high earnings, their unusually high earnings will raise the *industry* earnings, and their growth will make the industry more concentrated. Furthermore, if concentration is the result of tacit collusion among the big firms which restrict their own output and raise prices, the smaller firms should *gain.* The evidence does not support the theory of concentration by collusion but rather the theory that concentration is the result of superior performance with larger profits, which leads to larger firms.

Third, not all concentrated industries show higher profit rates than other, less-concentrated industries. Some industries are concentrated because to be efficient the firm must be large. Some products—like automobiles, electric turbine gen-

---

[6] Harold Demsetz, *The Market Concentration Doctrine,* American Enterprise Institute for Public Policy Research, Washington, D.C., and the Hoover Institution on War, Revolution and Peace, Stanford University, 1973; and ''Industry Structure, Market Rivalry, and Public Policy,'' *Journal of Law and Economics,* XVI (April 1973), 1–9.

erators, computers, airplanes—are so expensive and so complicated to design, engineer for production, sell, service, etc., that the firm's large size is more economical, especially if the product can be used on a nationwide basis. More-concentrated industries tend to be similar in every variety of economy. This suggests that concentration is a result of larger firms being more appropriate to certain types of activity, as just explained, rather than a result of some superior firms' idiosyncratic behavior.

Fourth, it is commonly argued that the fewer the firms in an industry, the less effective are competitive forces in keeping prices and costs down and in maintaining quality because two or three firms don't engage in so much competition of price or quality. It can indeed be conjectured that two firms that dominate an industry would be more likely to tacitly or explicitly collude to prevent profit-destroying competition than if there were many firms in the industry. But there are equally sensible models that imply the opposite. So anything may be conjured as a mental exercise. No correlation has been established between number of firms and degree of market competition that affects prices, costs, or performance. Indeed, no theory has been validated that describes the conditions that favor effective collusion among firms. Nor are the conditions understood that enable industry members to get the government to prevent entry or price competition (a topic we take up in the next chapter). One reason why people think the number of firms is inversely related to degree of competitiveness in market prices and products is that in some industries the one major firm has a patent or is a government-regulated public utility protected

from the entry of other firms (water, power, taxes, railroads, airlines). In these cases the *fewness* of firms is incorrectly interpreted as a reason for the lack of market competitiveness; the correct interpretation is that the government protects the existing firm by patent or by preventing new entrants. But this topic—*closed entry* monopoly—is for the next chapter.

The preceding analysis and evidence suggest that productive efficiency is in considerable danger—with no gain in competitiveness—if political policy should rely on the popular but obsolete and discredited doctrine that alleges concentration leads to "less competition" and higher profits by collusion, advertising, or barriers to entry.

Advertising: Education and Information

In a world of specialization, communication is necessary and takes several forms: education, news, and advertising. Information of interest only to a narrow group is disseminated in specialized ways rather than as general news. A new drug or TV set would be reported as news for merchandisers in a trade journal (for example, *Variety, Electronic Products, Textile World*) but would be advertised by the manufacturer in a general newspaper.

To convey news of interest to only a few, unknown persons is often more expensive, per person, than general advertising, even though in both cases much is "wasted" on uninterested recipients. For example, you are taught much in school and in college that not all of you will use in a direct, practical way. That is not wasteful unless there is a cheaper way to identify in advance what will be useful to whom.

There are many ways in which others are signaled or informed about someone's probable future performance. By its expensive decor a new jewelry store signals its intention of being in business a long time. The initial expenses resemble a hostage. Through them the owner says, "If I don't perform as suggested, I'll lose thousands of dollars. That is my bet that I am going to satisfy you and get repeat business." He is more likely to fulfill his implicit promises than is a sidewalk merchant. Initial advertising of sizable amounts is an investment in information, one not worth making by a seller who plans to operate temporarily. The college degree you are purchasing at great personal cost will be a signal to others that you have above-average abilities—otherwise why would the college have accepted you and permitted you to stay?

Does advertising create product differentiation, increase costs, reduce elasticity of demand for advertised goods, thereby reducing competition and increasing the seller's market power? While it is true that all of us can be misled by advertising (and by our teachers and parents), it is another matter to show that the result is to mislead people or conceal information from them more than if there were no advertising.

Advertising is a means of communicating the existence of alternative sellers and the characteristics of goods. Their attributes, availability and prices are thereby more widely and cheaply known. The greater our awareness of alternatives, their availabilities, prices, and characteristics, the less are we bound to any one seller. Sellers of inferior products will be less able to retain customers, and will not survive long, for their brand name will be worthless and their advertising will cease. We therefore expect a positive correlation between continued advertising and quality of product and profitability: Good products allow profitability, which favors advertising and the significance of brand names. The opposite, that advertising alone can increase profitability, is not a sound argument. It is hard to believe that more advertising creates larger profits and to observe firms that increase their profits without increasing their advertising. Advertising can call attention to the availability of some product and by making claims about its quality induce you to try it, but profitability rests on subsequent, continued consumer acceptance—at least for products that continue to be available for any length of time under the same name. Recent studies confirm rather than dispute the notion that the profitability of good products *allows continued* advertising; it would be a mistake to condemn advertising as leading to monopoly and concentration and higher profits.

Do not misunderstand. Advertisers are not assumed to be any more honest than anyone else. Like us, they are less honest the less they are penalized by competitors for their dishonesty. The issue is, "What reduces the costs of discovering more complete and accurate information?" We rely to some extent on government actions to prevent dishonesty, fraud, and theft. But just as we are self-reliant in protecting our property when we use locks, safes, walls, cash registers, fences, grills, and private watchmen, we also rely on private actions and interests to uncover falsities and misleading statements. We rely on the self-interest of one seller to unmask discreditable competitors, as one newspaper's self-interest and profits induces it to reveal the lies or errors of competitors. Giving a newspaper, TV station, or any advertiser a monopoly right to transmit "honest, unbiased" information (as is common in some other countries) is to restrain a powerful, truth-testing force—open competition by others whose self-interest is furthered by exposing truth. (Do you remember Watergate—or any political campaign, for that matter?) If not restricted to a favored few, advertising is a means of providing and testing information. Open competition and access to the market of ideas does not presume honesty and goodwill toward one's fellows. It presumes the opposite. But open competition in the market for ideas and information by self-serving competitors renders dishonesty more discoverable and self-defeating, thereby helping the public discover the truth more cheaply and surely. In essence, whether honorable or not, honesty pays—that is, is profitable—*if* there is competition to reveal dishonesty.

Advertising occurs in our speech. What tends to induce honesty, besides the moral force? Door-to-door salesmen do not expect repeat sales in the future. They have little economic motive to heed the long-run loss of repeat business. A fixed seller will gain more from good, honest performance because dishonesty will lose him his future business prospects. The greater one's future value from present honesty, and the greater the incentive of the other party to check for honesty, the greater is the extent of honesty. The greater one's capital value of future earnings, the greater the loss from dishonesty. General Motors would lose more from dishonesty than a short-lived gain it would make if there were a short-lived increase of business. The present value of General Motors averages over 10 times the earnings of any one year. It is unlikely some person who lied or cheated would be able to help General Motors to 10 times its income in one year. On the contrary, the loss would be enormous and not tolerable.

Is mass advertising wasteful? Mass teaching, mass communication, like mass production, is cheaper than custom teaching, communication, and production. The advantages in lower costs offset the monotony and repetition of what we see and hear in advertising and in the classroom. It is a cheaper method (that is, saves us more of other goods and services we would have had to sacrifice) for communicating information to obtain the gains from specialization in production in a larger society.

Advertising with Communal Rather Than Private-Property Rights

TV and radio advertising, which annoys many people, is the result of the way in which radio and television are paid for. Theaters rarely show commercials, because the patron pays and guides the producers' acceptable actions. Pay television (which is still illegal in most areas) would give viewers more program control. (Imagine what you would experience in movie theaters if theater owners could not charge admissions.) Programs on pay TV would appeal to smaller, specialized groups because a minority could concentrate its "dollar votes" on preferred programs. Because of the diversity of those groups, diversity of programming would increase. If newspapers could not be sold, they would have even more advertising, as is evidenced by the ratio of advertising to news in neighborhood throwaway newspapers.

Much of the criticism that politicians level against advertising on radio and television (and of the resultant programming) is really criticism of how television and radio programs are paid for—and is also a criticism of the politically imposed limit on the number of stations and restrictions on cable systems for pay-TV—imposed by those same politicians.

Billboards and roadside advertising seem to run a close second to TV commercials as objects of criticism. (What about bumper stickers and advertising on cars, buses, and taxis?) But it is not the advertising itself that is objected to, but, rather, its being thrust upon people in places, circumstances, and ways that seem unwarranted by the general benefit. Roadside signs are a prime example. But there is a basic reason for the prevalence of such signs. Roads do not have private owners, so there is less reward to anyone to meet the demand for roads without signs. The technical problems have prevented discovery of how to make such a "good" a resource that is controllable by normal market operation of the property system. And that, of course, is a reason for using nonmarket, political controls.

Advertising Controls or Censorship

Fear that advertising will mislead people suggests that political authorities decide what is permissible advertising. We already engage in censorship. We expose our children to censored ideas when we control by authority what public schools teach them. The continuity of a culture requires that it pass on to the younger generations its customs, taboos, and habits. However, this censorship applies to children, and all parents have a large say in it. We censor our children's channels of communication because they are children—and this brings the crux of advertising content control to the fore. Are we to extend the concept to adults? Each of us may differ in our judgment. We may not like the way others behave when exposed to ideas and persuasive thoughts. But authoritarian control of advertising content is censorship of ideas; of that there is no dispute. The dispute is how much of it is good or bad. Economics has no answer.

17, 18 19

Summary

1. Inventories, price stability, price-searching activity, and advertising are implied for price-searchers' markets.
2. Price-searchers are monopolists in the technical sense of facing negatively sloping demand functions with respect to price.
3. Transient, fluctuating-demand functions imply inventories by price-searchers for price predictability.
4. A seller who perceives a marginal revenue significantly below his price will underproduce only to where marginal cost equals marginal revenue rather than price—its value to the public. This is called monopoly (marginal revenue less than price) distortion.
5. Transient purchase changes over time and among producers make it difficult to detect shifts in consumer demand that would sustain new prices. To permit quick availability at predictable prices as a convenience to customers, producers hold buffer stocks and vary production to maintain those stocks. When demands shift in a persisting manner, output will usually have responded before the price

is adjusted. For products for which buffer inventories are held to aid customers, output changes typically precede price changes.

6. Price predictability and stability over time for some goods does not necessarily mean excessive price rigidity or price control by a few large firms. Rather, the price stability desired by consumers in the face of transient shifts in purchase rates means that price changes occur only when demands shift in a persisting way to induce different outputs at different costs. The absence of instant variation of price should not be confused with failure of price to respond to persisting shifts of demand and cost of supply.

7. Some producers are price-searchers because of economies of scale in production, administration, or marketing, or differences in tastes and costs of ascertaining perfectly every characteristic of every possible good that might be purchased.

8. Brand names and producer identification are means of providing quality assurance to buyers prior to purchase.

9. Several fallacious interpretations of market behavior are common:
a. "Price-searchers administer and set prices." In fact, they do administer and set prices, but the prices that they can sustain are determined by demand and supply conditions, not by sellers' arbitrary decisions.
b. Economic wealth gives economic power but the use of wealth in costly, inefficient, loss-incurring ways for big firms is just as costly and restrained as for small firms.
c. Competition for customers at relatively unchanging prices does not mean no price competition. It can be extreme price competition

where none can survive at lower prices, and it can mean price competition *plus* quality or service competition.

10. More highly concentrated industries do not make higher profits by virtue of greater control over supply. Instead, more efficient, profitable firms grow and tend to become major suppliers to a larger part of the market, leading to greater concentration. In some industries the technological aspects of organizing production, distribution, and product service imply economies of scale, leading to larger firms and more concentrated industries, without implying larger profits as a result of getting market power with concentration.

11. Advertising is a means for less-well-known and well-known firms alike to make availability of their wares and their characteristics more widely known. Accumulated evidence indicates advertising lowers consumers' costs by reducing the costs of acquiring information about available goods and services and prices.

12. Communal property is sometimes used by advertisers—and by auto drivers who congest highways, by bathers who congest beaches, and industries that pollute air. The source of the trouble is not advertising, driving, bathing, or production, but the absence of a means of pricing the use of the communal property.

Questions

*1. a. Can you suggest some good for which the differences among various brands are insignificant? (Hint: sugar, flour, aspirin, tires, dog foods, bread, milk, soap, corn flakes, cigarettes, canned peaches, banks at which you can have a checking account, beer.)

b. Obviously you will not agree that *all* these are examples of goods whose brands are of insignificant differences. Are any? If so, does this mean that when you buy this kind of good, you purchase at random without regard to brand?

c. If not, what do you mean by an insignificant difference?

d. What makes you prefer one brand over another at the same price?

e. Can you name any good and two of its brands for which you believe no one in his right mind could have a "good" reason for preferring one over the other?

2. You are buying trees to landscape your new home. The following demand schedule characterizes your behavior as a buyer:

Price of Trees	Quantity Demanded
$10	1
9	2
8	3
7	4
6	5
5	6
4	7
3	8
2	9
1	10

The price is quoted at $6. Accordingly, you buy five trees. Then *after* you buy the five trees, the seller offers to sell you one more for only $5.

a. Do you take it?

b. Suppose, strange as it may seem, he then offers you an opportunity to buy more trees (*after* you have already agreed to purchase five at $6 each and one more for $5) at the price of $3. How many more do you buy?

c. If the price had been $3 initially, would you have bought more than eight trees?

d. Suppose you had to pay a membership fee of $5 to buy at this nursery, after which you could buy all the trees you wanted for your own garden at $3 each. How many would you buy? (Assume price at other nurseries is $4, with no membership fee.)

e. If you could buy trees at $3 each from some other store without a membership fee, would you still buy only eight trees—saving the $5 for use on *all* your consumption activities?

f. Now explain why, according to the demand schedule, your purchase of eight trees at $3 each, at a total cost of $24, is a consistent alternative to your purchase of eight trees under the former sequential offers, in which you pay a total of $41 (five at $6, one at $5, and two at $3). (In this example we assume we can slide down an *unmodified* demand curve, because the required modification by the change in wealth is slight.)

3. Answer the following questions concerning the demand schedule on p. 316.

a. Complete the total-revenue, marginal-revenue, and average-revenue data.

b. What happens to the difference between selling price and marginal revenue?

c. How many units would you want to produce and sell if you could produce as many

Price	Quantity	Revenue		
		Total	Marginal	Average
$20	2	$40		$20
19	3	57	$+17	19
18	4	72	+15	18
17	5	—	—	—
16	6	—	—	—
15	7	—	—	—
14	8	—	—	—
13	9	—	—	—
12	10	—	—	—
11	11	—	—	—
10	12	—	—	—
9	13	—	—	—

as you wanted at an average cost of $8 per unit and if you wanted to maximize your net receipts (revenue minus costs)?

d. What price would you charge?

e. Could you charge $18 if you wanted to? What would be the consequences?

f. What are the consequences of charging $14?

4. a. How can a price-searcher be searching for a price, when in fact there is available a wide range of prices—any of which he can charge?

b. What happens if he is not good at finding what he is searching for?

5. On a television interview a prominent theatrical producer expressed delight that tickets for his play had been sold out for the next four months. Explain why he might have cause to be very sad, rather than happy.

*6. Change the data in Table 13–1 as follows:

From every indicated "quantity purchased" at each price, subtract 6. If the new number is negative, simply call it zero.

a. Recompute the total and marginal revenue.

b. What is the new wealth-maximizing output for this producer if he has zero costs?

c. What is the new wealth-maximizing output for this producer if his marginal cost is $8 at every output.

7. The difference (for pricing and output behavior) between price-takers' and price-searchers' markets can be characterized by a difference in the demand curve facing each seller. Describe the difference in the demand curve.

8. Is it true that for some products you prefer one brand over the other if both have the same price, but if there is any price difference between them you will take the lower-priced one?

*a. If this is true for some goods, does it suggest something about the basis for or "strength" of your preference?

b. Would you say that you "discriminate" among brands?

c. Is that "justifiable" discrimination?

*9. In France, Italy, Spain, Hong Kong, and New York individual bargaining over the price of a good is commonplace.

a. Would you prefer that custom to the more common one in the United States of not bargaining?

b. But on second thought, can you name three goods that are commonly purchased in the United States by bargaining?

c. How would you explain the simultaneous

presence of two different customs?

*10. Compare and evaluate the following two assertions:

a. "Advertising and brand names create impressions of differences among competing brands where no significant difference really exists. As a result, because of consumer ignorance, sellers face a less elastic demand and can raise price without losing all sales to competitors. Creation of impressions of significant product differentiation by advertising is a social waste."

b. "Advertising and brand names identify rather than create differences among products. They permit customers to know more surely, cheaply, and fully the differences among various products. Otherwise, customers would select blindly, letting the price difference be their only reason for choosing one over the other, much as people would choose purely on the basis of price among superficially identical goods. By identifying products and their makers more fully prior to purchase, brand names and advertising permit customers to be more, not less, discriminating about qualities with less costly other investigation into product details. Hence advertising and brand names that make demands less elastic because they identify more fully differences in product and quality assurance are a social benefit."

11. "General Electric announces a new 11-inch, 12-pound portable television for $99.50." "Parker '45' Pens are sold at an announced price of $5." "Sunbeam appliances are sold at retail prices set by the manufacturer." Explain why the above statements do not imply price setting by the seller. That is, explain why the prices were not instead, say, three times as high.

12. Using the data of Tables 13–1 and 13–2, suppose that your costs of production are changed by a reduction in the cost of materials or labor so that at every output your marginal costs are $5 less.

a. What will this do to the marginal-cost schedule?

b. What will be your wealth-maximizing price and output?

c. What are your profits?

13. Suppose a $5 tax is levied on your business —an annual license tax of a flat $5 regardless of how much you produce.

a. What will be your price and output?

b. What is the amount of your profits?

14. As a superior student you provide a tutoring service. The higher the price you decide to charge, the fewer the hours of work you get.

a. Are you a price-taker or a price-searcher?

*b. Assume that your time, when you are not tutoring, is worth an equivalent of $2 an hour. The daily demand for your tutor services is not perfectly predictable; it varies at "random" around a mean rate of daily demand which depends on the price you can charge. If, at the price you charge, you find that all your available time is always used, and there are occasional applicants whom you must reject because you are fully booked up, do you think you are charging the wealth-maximizing price? Explain.

*c. If you are charging a price at which you

occasionally have idle time, are you charging too low a price?

*d. Given a fluctuating demand, how can you be sure that you have charged the "right" price?

15. In what sense can the marginal-cost curve of a price-searcher be considered a supply curve?

16. A year after the steel-price hassle of 1962, the federal government, in response to complaints from domestic steel producers about low-priced imported foreign steel, initiated hearings to determine whether foreign imports were being provided at less than the foreign costs—with nothing explicit as to what is meant by costs. The hearing determined that imported steel was being sold at prices below cost (below whose cost?), so taxes were imposed on the imported steel. Within a month, the domestic steel companies began raising the price of steel, in a discreet manner, with only lip-service complaint from politicians.

a. Do you think it likely that the higher prices proved to be more profitable?

b. Why did the government at one time object to higher prices of steel and then within a year take action to reduce the imports of steel, thereby enabling a higher domestic price?

17. Let the demand schedule of question two represent the characteristics of the demand for your service as a gardener, and suppose you sell in a price-searchers' market.

a. What price should you charge per garden to maximize your daily net receipts if the "cost" of caring for a garden is zero?

b. If your time is worth the equivalent of $3 per garden maintained, what price would you charge?

c. Is this the "highest" price the traffic will bear, the highest price possible, the lowest price possible, or a "reasonable" price?

18. You are constructing an apartment building. You can build one with many units and have vacancies sometimes, or you can build a smaller unit and have a no-vacancy sign all the time.

a. If the latter behavior is profitable, can the procedure of having vacancies sometimes be even more profitable?

b. Would you interpret an average vacancy rate on apartments of 5 or 10 percent as evidence that they are oversupplied, overpriced, or neither?

*19. "Much advertising is deceitful, dishonest, misleading, fraudulent, and disingenuous. Therefore, it should be subjected to government regulation." If you accept that conclusion, would you accept the same conclusion for daily conversation, political talks, lovers' pleadings—which are subject to the same charges? Explain why or why not.

14

Monopoly Power: Restricted Markets

Employees, employers, and politicians do not passively submit to open competition. They attempt to reduce competition by (1) collusive action with existing rivals, and (2) legal restrictions against potential competitors. In this chapter we investigate the methods of some of these attempts.

Methods for Changing Market Competition

Collusion among Producers

Eliminating *market* competition does not eliminate competition. It shifts the form and location of the competition. In the case of collusion, for example, competition is shifted from the marketplace to the conference table, where it takes the form of dividing the gain and preventing cheating —by no means easy to achieve. The potential gain from *effective* collusion, or restriction of market competition, is illustrated with our earlier water-demand example of Chapter 13, page 291. There, the competitive price is $1, but if all sellers could enforce a price of $6 per gallon, the group's income would be larger. But achieving that control over the whole market supply is extremely difficult. Furthermore, unless the market or industry demand for the product has low elasticity, there is not much to be gained by colluding to restrict output. Restriction of output by large amounts would achieve minor increases in price.

Whether open or secret, collusion—sometimes called a *cartel*—is faced with formidable hazards, even in the absence of legal prohibitions against cartels:

1. Who are the relevant competitors? If you were trying to organize doctors, what would you do about interns, chiropractors, registered nurses, druggists, dentists, and drug companies? All are substitutes for some medical service. If doctors raise fees, people will ask more aid of their druggists and use self-prescribed drugs. Or suppose you are a steel producer. What would you do about aluminum, brass, plastics, wood, and concrete substitutes? And what about firms that make their own steel for their own use? They will expand and sell steel to other steel users. Nonmember firms will profit and grow under the umbrella of higher price and restricted output by the cartel members. Too many of these outsiders can nullify the collusion.

2. Suppose, however, that you decide to include only the 10 major steel companies. Of the more than 1000 companies producing scores of thousands of kinds of steel in the United States, 10 produce 90 percent of the total output. The rest will not grow rapidly enough to upset your plan too quickly, you hope. Nevertheless, not all of the 10 will agree about the best price, nor what their share of sales should be. That depends on each firms' cost-output relationship, elasticity of demand, and growth prospects. Lower prices are more advantageous to lower-cost firms with prospects of growth than to higher-cost, smaller-output firms. Many explorations of, or attempts at, collusion never pass this obstacle.

3. Each member is alert to the gains from competition in ways not controllable by the cartel —for example, quality changes, delivery charges, warranty and repair services, credit, and trial and refund privileges. Controlling *all* forms of competition is prohibitively expensive.

Even with a federal regulatory agency to enforce a U.S. domestic airline cartel, there has yet to be control of competition in quality of airline attendants, special fares, services, types of planes, and other fringe benefits to passengers. All this kind of competition must be controlled by some enforcement technique, or else the potential cartel gains will be dissipated in competition services to customers.

4. The potential profitability of secret price-cutting is very high and the probability of success is related to product and market characteristics. In any event, some technique for enforcing the agreement—and punishing violators—must be available. If all colluding members *pooled* their output, sold it through a central sales agency, and split the proceeds, secret or implicit price-cutting could be controlled. *Secret* price-cutting enables the price-cutter to get profitable business while his competitors, not knowing why they are losing customers, continue to maintain their high prices. And, of course, any sellers who are not in the collusion can sell more because others have raised their prices.[1]

[1] The notorious electrical-equipment case of 1962 involved sales to government agencies that make purchases on the basis of *sealed bids.* Accusations of collusion against sellers of meat, flour, water, pipe, steel, office furniture, cement, milk, banking services have all involved sealed bids to government. A favorable occasion for collusion (in *open* markets) is that of sales to government by sealed bids. The government solicits bids from several sellers and opens them all at one time. No rebidding is allowed (in sharp contrast to the purchase of a car by a private party who solicits bids from various sellers *and* gives each a chance to undercut the others). Furthermore, if any colluding sellers do not bid as agreed, the others will find out immediately since all bids are revealed. It does not seem accidental that most cases of established effective collusion have been on sales to government agencies or government-regulated public utilities.

5. Internally, competition would exist over the share of sales allotted each member. Younger, growing firms want an *increasing* share. An alternative to pooling all output for sales via a central agency is to assign each buyer to one seller. This would reduce the incentive for price-cutting (though not entirely, for by cutting prices, you would enable your customer to undersell his competitors and in this way you indirectly take business from your fellow conspirators).

6. Costs of creating new facilities may dissuade new competitors from quickly entering the business. This lag would appear to make effective collusion more profitable; but there is a counterforce. If expensive facilities are involved, the colluders will lose their own *large* investment value if new entrants do appear—an effect that will continue after the collusion has ended, for, in these circumstances, once a competitor has entered, the greater his effects on the collusion. Such are some of the inherent contradictions, obstacles, and hazards to *attempts* at effective collusion. We emphasize *attempts* because many exploratory attempts to collude simply never come to fruition. Proposals are discussed and agreements reached, only to be rendered ineffective by those hard realities.

Thus simultaneous price action by several firms or price leadership by one firm is not evidence for or against the existence of *effective* collusive agreements. Price behavior, whether it be simultaneous convergence or a chase behind some apparent "price leader," is irrelevant in itself. What is good evidence? The use of a costly enforcement technique: Costs incurred to enforce prevention of prohibited actions are strong evidence that an effective collusion exists—one effective enough to make it worth the costs of enforcement. Restrictions on new investments and penalties for noncompliance with the terms of the collusion are enforcement devices. Self-regulation or self-policing by members of an industry with state-enforced laws or standards provides a weapon of enforcement. Members who do not comply are denied right to do business; licenses or special privileges can be revoked for "unethical" behavior.

A strong implication of the foregoing is that an effective collusion could be organized and enforced by an organization in which membership is essential for staying in business. The organization may provide special advantages (government subsidies, tax favors, pooling of patent rights, rights to do business with the government, exemption from strikes by unions, control over entry of newcomers, or simply legal licenses for doing business). For example, the American Medical Association gives its members sufficiently great special privileges (access to certified surgical hospitals) to enforce observance of its strictures against certain types of competition. Similarly, business firms in Germany from the turn of the century up to World War II were compelled by the state to belong to Chambers of Commerce as a condition of the right to engage in business. Strictures against types of market competition could be enforced by expelling from the Chamber (and thus from the market) any firms that violated the strictures. It is no wonder that Germany was typified by many collusive cartels. In the United States, most airlines find it nearly essential for various reasons to belong to the Air Transport Association, which then serves as a policing

agent to punish cheaters in the cartel of airlines.

An alternative is to get a law passed to regulate the industry in the "public interest"—such as to eliminate quackery, shoddy merchandising, dangerous products, or disorderly pricing. The regulatory agency can then use the law to enforce what is essentially cartel, collusive behavior. A few examples are the Securities and Exchange Commission, Federal Power Commission, Interstate Commerce Commission, Federal Communications Commission, Civil Aeronautics Board, Food and Drug Administration, Federal Trade Commission, National Labor Relations Board, U.S. Department of Agriculture, state liquor control boards, state and local public utility commissions. Later in this chapter, some of these will be detailed.

Collusion by Employees

A commonly successful collusion is that among some sellers of labor. If the employees of a firm or an industry agree not to offer their services at less than a certain wage, they face the usual obstacles to successful collusions. They may strike in order to enforce the goals of their collusion again. A strike is a refusal to work *combined* with an attempt to prevent *other sellers of labor* from offering their services at rates lower than (or working conditions inferior to) those sought by the striking employees. Access to the labor market by any other sellers of labor is restrained by the "peaceful" *threat* of violence to the person or property of would-be strikebreakers, including any striker who might be tempted to cheat on the agreement. The market is closed to other laborers. The right to strike is currently an accepted part of our economic and legal institutions. While laws do not authorize strikers to physically restrain workers, crossing a picket line incites retaliation. Therefore, to avoid violence at the strikers' picket line, anyone who tries to cross a picket line and thereby provokes violence may be jailed along with the strikers for contributing to a disturbance of the peace. The police will not always hold aside the picketing strikers and permit strikebreakers free access to the market for work (at lower terms than those sought by the strikers), for that usually leads to violence.

If the preceding sentences seem antilabor, the reader is injecting his own judgment. They are no more critical or disapproving than the statement that hydrogen is lighter than lead. They do not say that employees ought not to engage in strikes. They do differ from common folklore in their explicit recognition of the role of violence (even if it is only a "threat") in closing out competitors.

Unions acquired legal "closed-monopoly" power when allowed to strike and picket effectively. This was decreed in 1914 when unions were specifically exempted from the 1890 Sherman Antitrust law. The Norris-LaGuardia Act of 1932 legalized group picketing and boycotts. The Wagner Act of 1935 required employers to deal with unions and made it legal for employees to form or join the union of their (majority) choice. And the National Labor Relations Board was created to enforce the conditions of those acts. Is there any reason why the people who seek to collude or to eliminate competitors should be only, for example, tobacco growers, milk producers, liquor sellers, taxi owners, lawyers, morticians, doctors, teachers, radio and television station owners, rather than teamsters, carpenters, auto assemblers, retail clerks, or dock workers? If one

group can ethically rely on political, state (police) power, others will feel justified in resorting to private violence to deny access to the market.

Mergers

A merger superficially appears to be an ideal vehicle for collusive action. Simply merge with your rivals into one big firm and thereby control output so as to get a bigger profit, which can be divided among the merged firms. Again there is the difficult problem of who pays how much to whom in the merger terms. But supposing this can be resolved, is it effective? Most firms make more than one kind of product. Is it worth merging with rivals for *one* of these products at the cost of reduced productive efficiency in others? Your superiority in other product lines is dissipated in the merger. Other firms will enter this business if existing firms merge and hoist prices above competitive levels. The merged firms may make a dollar more per year for, say, four years, but with new firms attracted, later earnings will be smaller than otherwise. A dollar gain for even as long as four years, with a subsequent income that is 60 cents smaller than if there had been no merger, constitutes a *loss of present wealth*. The present value of one dollar a year for four years is $3.46 (at 6 percent), but the present value of 60 cents a year for 10 years thereafter (the loss) is $3.50, a net loss in present wealth.[2]

However, it is important to keep the proper perspective: Many mergers are profitable because

[2] The 60-cent decrease per-year perpetuity has a present value of .792 × $4.42, because the stream is deferred four years (which accounts for the .792 factor). Check our calculations and reasoning by refreshing yourself on the capital-values principles (Chapter 7). These principles are essential for solving practical problems.

they enable more efficient combination and use of resources or because they bring new, superior management to firms that had been operated less successfully. Mergers and takeovers—by stock purchases, exchange of stock, or direct purchases of assets—often represent competition among managers and entrepreneurs in seeking out inefficiently operated firms that can be improved with profits and social benefits.

If there is something bad about collusion, is there not also something bad whenever people voluntarily pool their private wealth to form a corporation that is big enough to affect the market price by its offerings of some good? Every corporation and partnership uses jointly owned resources in wealth-maximizing ways. Why is effective collusive agreement among several businesses different from creation of a business? It isn't. Then why have we devoted the past several pages to a discussion of collusion, as if it were different from the formation of a corporation or partnership? To show the obstacles to any group's controlling market behavior, either by collusion or by buying up firms until only one firm is left—*in the absence of legal compulsions requiring producers to join a collusion as a condition of access to the market.*

[1,2]
[3,4]
[5,6]
[7,8]

The Law and
Market Competition

The Sherman Antitrust Act of 1890 prohibited "monopolizing" and "combinations or conspiracies to restrain" trade. Since it did not define "monopoly" or "restraint of trade," interpretation depended on *ad hoc* arguments in any given case. At the turn of the century, the Standard Oil

Trust, the U.S. Sugar Trust, and the American Tobacco Trust were successfully prosecuted by the U.S. government's antitrust division and were split into smaller companies. It is still uncertain whether these "trusts" did charge higher prices or bought for lower prices. By 1914 confusion had reached the stage where the U.S. Supreme Court could seriously declare that only "unreasonable" restraints of trade were illegal. In 1961 the DuPont Company was compelled to divest itself of ownership of a substantial portion of General Motors. Bethlehem and Youngstown steel companies were dissuaded from merging when told by the antitrust division of the Justice Department that the proposed merger would be prosecuted in court as a violation of the Sherman Act. More recently, the Brown Shoe Company was forced by court order to divest itself of ownership of a former competitor. All were results of judicial opinion or argumentation that these mergers "tended to reduce" competition without any clear conception of what that means. Now, the law even says it is sufficient to show that competition "might probably" be reduced. No great understanding of economics is required to perceive that such a law is ambiguous, vague, and conjectural—the marks of bad law.

In a futile effort to reduce ambiguity, the Clayton Act (1914) prohibited both "price discrimination" and mergers "reducing competition" (but exempted labor unions from antimonopoly laws). As we have already seen, price discrimination can increase the efficiency of resource use. Mergers can enhance the competitive efficiency of firms in the market—and have done so—with benefit to consumers and producers.

Complaints by some businessmen against competitors resulted in the 1914 Federal Trade Commission Act, which declared some marketing tactics illegal and created a commission to investigate businesses to dissuade "illegal" or "unfair practices" by issuing "cease and desist" orders that prohibit future continuance but do not penalize for past practices. Not surprisingly, what is and is not an "unfair" practice often cannot be determined in advance by the businessman or by anyone else.

In 1938 the Wheeler-Lea Act authorized the Federal Trade Commission to prohibit still other "unfair practices"—those "unfair" to the consumer, such as "false" advertising. For example, it is illegal to artificially color margarine without saying so on the label (but it is permissible to artificially color butter without labeling). Exceptions are often responsive to political clout!

During the Depression of the 1930s many (still existing) laws were passed to *prohibit* market competition! But in fact, they encouraged sellers to get together and raise prices, with penalties on those who did not comply. That legislation has done much to thwart open-market competitive forces. It is widely used for many agricultural goods: wheat, tobacco, cotton, peanuts, raisins, milk, peaches, eggs, sugar, etc.

Protection of or from Competition?

One of the principal effects of political regulation of business has been to confuse protection *of* competition with protection *from* open-market competition. For example, the Federal Trade Commission relies heavily on complaints of one business against another. Complainants will try to protect their wealth from market competition rather than preserve open-market competition. They complain of "unfair," "destabilizing," "disorderly," and "cutthroat" competition—which means one's competitors are more successfully catering to buyers' preferences in open markets. Therefore, you contend that he is driving you out of business and "tending to reduce" competition (by *you*).

Advertising Restrictions

Although you may have a legal right to sell in the market, any obstacle to informing potential customers about your offers will protect better-known sellers already in the market. Advertising is primarily a means of informing potential buyers of the presence of a seller and of the attributes of his goods. It leads to lower costs of informed purchases.

If General Motors wanted to restrain the growth of American Motors or Volkswagen, it should seek to prohibit advertising to make it more expensive for newcomers to inform consumers. Holiday Inn, a nationally known motel firm, is favored by bans on local highway advertising. It is significant that the American Medical Association, American Bar Association, and American Dental Association prohibit advertising, yet the Bar Association is elsewhere so solicitous of "free speech." Examine the yellow pages of the telephone directory and compare the advertising in various professions. Would you regard restrictions on advertising as helpful to newcomers (either sellers or customers)? Advertising of prices for gasoline, reading glasses or contact lenses, for example, is illegal or severely restricted in many states and cities. Prices there are higher. The ban also increases information costs to consumers.

Patents and Copyrights

Patents and copyrights are grants of exclusive rights (that is, a closed monopoly) to sell certain goods or ideas.[3] A patent is what a *statutory monopoly* used to be called. The principle of Polaroid film is patented; the patentee has exclusive rights, but can license others to produce and sell that film. The patent, given for a period of years, usually 17, is occasionally renewable for 17 more. The income potential from patents and copyrights is intended to induce discovery and use of knowledge: If a person invented a way to kill flies, show three-dimensional television, or cure the common cold, and others could use the idea without paying him, he would have less incentive to spend his talent and time on his invention. Even though many people try to invent or do research without that incentive, the prospect of gain will attract more people and resources into such activity. The patent holder is authorized to use his idea as a *monopolist*. What is the right amount of reward? The absence of a clear-cut criterion for "proper" reward leaves room for considerable dispute about how long a patent should be protected and what kind of pricing and use of the patent should be allowed. No proposed solution has yet been very helpful.

Suppression of New Ideas?

Sometimes an inventor discovers a new idea that will make obsolete what he currently owns. If I owned a cable pay-television system and then discovered a cheap means to eliminate the cables, would I use the wireless system or suppress it? What I would do depends upon the relative costs. Since the wires are already installed, their remaining cost of continued use is low (until they must be replaced). If it costs less to produce and install the new than to continue to use the already-installed old system, I would immediately abandon the old system. Otherwise, I would not use the new system until the old wires had to be replaced or repaired. This delay in introducing a new idea is sometimes regarded as "unjustified." But, in fact, it reflects the truly lower cost of using up existing equipment first.

It is a commonplace of modern folklore that gasoline producers have discovered a high-mileage fuel or carburetor that would enormously reduce the demand for gasoline, and to protect their wealth they have withheld the device. Is this likely? If the invention were not patented, then a person who knew about it could manufacture the device and make an enormous fortune—more than the existing companies would find it worth their while to pay him to not produce. And if the device or idea were patented, it would be public knowledge; but there is no patent record or any other evidence of such a device. And if it did exist, one could make and sell it at a price reflecting the value of the gasoline saved, a net profit to the owner, be he oil or auto producer.

Nonpatentable Research
and Development

Most research and development is conducted without the incentive of patents or copyrights. Most businessmen have to rely on being first and profiting before competitors come in. The super-

---

[3] Patents do not prevent other people from using some idea or device if they use it for themselves and not to produce something for *sale* to other people; only commercial use is forbidden.

market, the double-pump arrangement in gas stations, drive-up windows in banks, colored soaps, open-all-night stores, discount houses, stretch knits, and a host of cost reductions or quality improvements are not subject to copyright or patent. No generally accepted, objective rule exists as to what range of exploratory activity should be given patent and copyright monopolies.

Political-Legal Restraints on Market Access

We examine now some controls placed *on consumers* as a result of political power. We call these consumer controls rather than the almost universally used term *producer controls* because, if producers are restrained from selling something to the public, the producers are no more restrained from selling than the consumers are restrained from buying. The term *producer control* gives the impression that the laws and regulations are devised to control producers in the consumer's interest. It is convincingly arguable that the opposite is the intent and effect—restrictions to benefit certain producers from consumers who could otherwise purchase from potential competitors.

Sanitation Standards

Laws prohibit the sale of foods and drugs that the Federal Food and Drug employees deem unfit for human use. Government agencies promulgate and enforce standards of cleanliness; thus the private, individual costs of collecting information are reduced. But on reflection, there are other consequences of this law. Some consumers prefer cheaper goods (for example, imported dates), even though they are produced in less-sanitary conditions (cleanliness is not costless). Consider the fact that the Food and Drug Administration refused to allow the sale of a cheap, high-protein, biologically sterile food made in powdered form, because the Food and Drug employees said it was a filthy food—being made from *whole* fish. Yet people eat whole oysters; pigs and chickens are converters of garbage, insects, and worms. No one can object to more cleanliness, if its cost is not "excessive." But a high-priced barbershop that uses a new protective apron for *every* customer will find itself underpriced by one that reuses the apron with a new piece of paper around each customer's neck. The higher-priced shop would do well to insist on higher standards of cleanliness to keep out lower-cost competitors. A requirement of high standards is a restriction on buyers who prefer lower-quality, cheaper service—usually the poorer people. Insisting on higher quality means more of the higher-cost quality goods and less of the cheaper, lower-quality goods, like insisting that only Rolls-Royces be sold and banning VWs. Which is better for the poor and for the rich?

Quality Control

Until about 1950 margarine could not be sold in some states; it was a "low-quality" substitute for butter. And in many areas it could be sold only as a *white* spread—even though butter is artificially colored and flavored. Major milk-producing states had the strongest bans on margarine. (Do you suspect milk producers are big political campaign contributors?) Even mayonnaise was at one time similarly protected from competition of the "inferior" (and cheaper) substitute, salad dressing.

Codes in every city control materials used in buildings. New York City's building code was overhauled only after 30 years, long delaying use of new, better, cheaper construction methods. Rapid development of mobile trailer homes can be explained partly by the fact that they are not covered by building codes. Now, under pressures from the housing industry unions, codes are being expanded to include mobile homes.

Some early television manufacturers who used expensive, high-quality materials proposed to prohibit lower-quality television sets. Speakers would be larger, picture quality better, tuning easier, repairs less frequent. But the set would cost more.

"Bad goods drive out the good."[4] That common belief is incorrect. When *both quality and price* are permitted to be determined in open-market competition, neither drives out either— instead the price reflects the difference.

The medical profession restricts entry to the market for medical aid by state licensing laws administered by the licensed doctors to assure higher quality. If a law permitted the sale of only Rolls-Royces, Cadillacs, and Lincolns, we could certainly have the best-*quality* automobile service in the world—and the most pedestrians. The medical profession emphasizes that it has brought the United States the highest-quality

medical care to those who get it. There would be fewer deaths if more mediocre medical aid and hospitals were also available, because at the present time even worse substitutes are all that can be used—nurses, druggists, books, self-medication, faith-healers, friends, hearsay, phone calls, instead of the choice of either personal inspection or *no* medical attention at all.

It is hard to separate sincerity from duplicity in the professed desire to protect other people. (For example, do you regard the remainder of this paragraph as sincere?) Like health, wealth can be ruined by carelessness. If a person breaks his leg, it can be reset. If he breaks his budget, it can't be reset. Wealth, like health, must be protected from personal ignorance. If a person invests $1000 in some business, and loses, his family suffers. Therefore, before making *any* investment every person ought to be required to consult a licensed, certified economist, who will prescribe how wealth should be invested. He can then take the prescription to the stockbroker. Without this safeguard millions of people every day make foolish investments and irrevocably lose their wealth and harm their families. Many people follow the advice of economic quacks— stockbrokers, politicians, friends, and tip sheets. They overinvest without consulting economists, who could prevent their going too far into debt or buying in the wrong area or taking the wrong job or the wrong kind of insurance.[5]

---

[4] This old saying known as Gresham's law—the bad drive out the good—was developed for situations in which the *prices* of the good and the bad were *not* allowed to reflect differences in quality. In that case, "too-low" prices of higher quality goods reduce incentives to produce those goods and increase incentives of sellers to produce low-cost, inferior goods.

[5] There are signs of "progress." In 1964, the Securities and Exchange Commission issued a report evaluating the securities and stock-market dealers' practices. In the covering letter written by Mr. Cary, the chairman of the committee, is the following prescient passage: "Under existing Federal law there is a right of free access and unlimited entry into the securities business for anyone, regardless of qualifications, except those excluded on the basis of prior securities vio-

Even the most sacrosanct of regulatory agencies, the Food and Drug Administration, has imposed costs that often exceed the benefits. The value of being protected from ineffective drugs or from damaging drugs has not been shown to be worth the loss from delay of new drugs. Studies show that the reduced rate at which new drugs are now introduced, since the requirements of prior proof of their efficacy, has prevented the saving of lives that would have totalled thousands of years. Those lost lives and lost years are not as dramatically visible as the losses from damaging drugs like Thalidomide. Yet the most reliable studies show that the costs and losses of lives and health because of delayed introduction and reduced innovation exceed the losses from premature or harmful drugs. Nothing is free in this world. Greater safety is costly, and the Food and Drug Administration *may* even have made it *too* costly. (Use of the word ''may'' is a common, irresponsible pretension of saying something, when in fact one doesn't know whether it is highly—or only slightly—probable.)

Similarly, according to the only study made, compulsory automobile safety devices for passenger cars have resulted in less-careful driving with more accidents and damage to pedestrians. This is not surprising. But what is disconcerting is that the consequences of our political regulatory agencies over the kinds of services that can or cannot be sold in the market have only recently begun to be studied carefully. The results,

lations. The steady growth in the very numbers of investors and participants, according to the report, has made this concept obsolete. . . . Greater emphasis should be given by the Securities and Exchange Commission and the exchanges and associations of security dealers to the concept of suitability of particular securities for particular customers.'' (Can you imagine what this would do for economists' incomes?)

let alone the appalling rarity of such studies, are dismaying. But do not be misled. Even if the number of fatalities or damage increased, that would not be the crucial test of the desirability of such laws on safety. For example, when airplanes were riskier and fewer people flew, fewer were killed. Now that airplanes are safer, many more people fly and are killed in airplane accidents. Unless you conclude that the increased safety of flying was not beneficial, despite the greater number of fatalities, you cannot conclude that increased accidents and damage accompanying increased required safety is bad—or good. What should be the test?

Control of Employees, Morals, and Service Standards

Laws prohibiting sales during evenings and Sundays ostensibly are to protect the health of employees, the morals of the community, and the quality of service. Sunday selling diverts people from rest and violates the Sabbath. The United States Supreme Court says so. But, in fact, although stores may be open 24 hours every day, no employees work 24 hours. Sunday and evening buying is a convenience to many shoppers. Of course, consumers *could* do all their shopping only between 3 and 7 on Monday, Wednesday, and Friday. Any store able to reduce costs and its price enough by such hours could survive with consumers who prefer the lower prices at those days and hours—except that there aren't enough people with such preferences. ''Blue'' laws are often supported by conventional retail stores that provide more labor service relative to capital than the evening and Sunday discount houses. The extra hours add relatively more to total labor costs of conventional retail department stores than to the costs of "capital-goods-intensive" discount houses.

Orderly Markets

The "orderly market" argument asserts that unless an industry is controlled so as to ensure adequate prices and profits, some firms will go out of business, and when demand later increases there will not be enough firms. Prices and output will swing like a pendulum. Thus, for highly seasonal products like milk (the peak supply of which comes in June and the low point in November), if price fluctuated from troughs in June to peaks in November, the farmers would be driven out in June and wouldn't be available in November to provide adequate milk. Also, when prices are high, fly-by-night producers will enter and "skim the cream," only to leave when prices and demand fall. The "responsible" year-around producers will not survive. Therefore, controls should be placed on entry so that irresponsible short-term producers cannot undermine the long-term stability of the industry.

Can you spot the holes in those self-serving arguments? Any amount supplied is "inadequate" at an adequately low price. For goods with seasonal swings in production, a *stable* price over the year implies an excess amount supplied ("surplus") at peak periods and an excess amount demanded ("shortage") in low-output months—unless storage costs are low enough to store supplies from peak to low-production months and thereby allow relative price uniformity without "shortages." For example, seasonal variations are no surprise. Retail stores predictably do about half their business in the Christmas season. They are not bankrupted by the summer low-sales months—just as they are not by low Sunday sales. Yet the milk industry alleges it must control entry to assure "adequate" supplies at all seasons—as if what is "adequate" does not depend on price. It achieves that with a *uniform year-round high price.* During high-production seasons, the "excess" milk (which would not be "excess" if price were allowed to fall seasonally) is diverted to cheeses. In California the number of commercial milk cows is so restricted by law (because at the high milk prices, dairymen would find it profitable to have more cows) that the *right* to another cow is worth $1500, a measure of the monopoly rent by restricting production. The situation is similar in every major metropolitan area, since federal and state laws permit dairymen to enforce controls. Dairy associations pay part of their monopoly rents to politicians for laws to enforce restrictions on supply (which helps explain why such laws exist). Surprised?

The argument for orderly markets contains two misconceptions. First, it assumes that cyclical and unanticipated changes in demand are viewed by *every* producer as permanent and not transient shifts. Second, it maintains that increasing supplies drive down prices, consequently reducing supplies by which prices are then driven higher. The second misconception thus confuses a shift (an increase) in the supply curve with a move *along* a supply curve as price falls. The error is analogous to confusing a shift in the demand function with a change in amount demanded along a demand curve—a fallacy we belabored in earlier chapters. See Figure 14–1. Nevertheless, error though it is, almost everyone

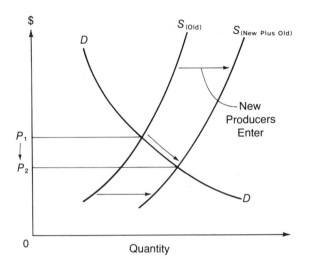

Figure 14–1. Lower Prices Stay Low When Supply Increases

New producers enter a market because of new superior methods of production, shifting supply curve to right from S₁ to S₂. The horizontal distance between S₂ and S₁ is the new output from new firms. As a result, price falls along demand curve, driving down price from P₁ and driving some old producers out of production. But that reduction in amount supplied along the old supply curve does not lead to a subsequent rise in price above P₂, because the total supply is given by S₂, not by S₁.

falls into the trap, especially when it is self-serving. For example, many American industries, like steel, argue that foreign imports increase the supply, drive down prices, and displace American producers, thereby reducing supply and permitting foreigners to raise price even higher than it had originally been. Think it over, carefully.

The "orderly-market" rationale, which denies competitors access to the markets to keep earnings and prices more "orderly" for incumbent producers, has many manifestations in practice.

The Interstate Commerce Commission uses it to regulate truckers. Farm price-support laws—in wheat, cotton, peanuts, and tobacco, for example—control entry of new producers to the market. Farm marketing boards for raisins, peaches, sugar, rice, eggs, oranges, and lemons, to name a few commodities, control the *salable* output of those crops in the *interest* of *greater wealth* for the producers, but in the *name* of *orderly prices*. Domestic sugar (and rice) producers have a law permitting political control of imports, so the domestic price will be high enough to increase the market value of resources specialized to the domestic sugar industry. We shall investigate a few examples in considerable detail—wheat, lemons, cotton, and tobacco.

Agricultural "Surpluses"

When the demand for wheat fell after World War II, rather than take losses and reduce output, distressed wheat farmers resorted to political procedures they would not normally condone in others. But "times are not normal," "this is a special case," and besides, "everyone else does it." Their political action was so successful that it created farm-"surplus" problems. Prices at which wheat could be legally sold were kept above the market-clearing level; as a result, the public demanded less than was supplied *at that price*. There is no sense to the popular claim that farm production exceeds demand. Demand is not a fixed amount; the amount demanded varies with price—a fact we have risked tedium to make obvious to the reader. The American public (not to count the enormous foreign population) would happily have consumed all the current farm output if high prices of those "surplus" farm goods had not been kept up by government purchases of the "surplus" at those high, guaranteed prices. The "surplus" problem arose because the farmers successfully obtained sufficient political power to prevent consumers from influencing output through the market price. It took an inflation and a worldwide crop "failure" in 1973–1974 to eliminate the "surplus," by pushing the free-market price above the old "floor" price guaranteed to wheat growers.

If these seem like words of condemnation, re-read them; there is no suggestion of impropriety by the farmers. Attempts to avoid market forces are not unique to farmers. We examine the agricultural case because it is an instructive example of political efforts to protect wealth.

Holding Crop off the Market [6]

Another example is provided by lemon growers, who sought high prices by withholding some of their output from the market. Their hopes were thwarted by growers who stayed out of the agreement and sold *all their* crop at the raised prices. Furthermore, some superior producers could make more wealth if there were no such restriction at all. How can they and other producers be induced to join? In 1941, a law was enacted permitting a majority of the lemon growers to compel *all* lemon growers to withhold part of their crop from the market. Thus, state police power was used for "self-regulation."

[6] The following analysis is applicable, with minor variations, to many products, for example, milk in almost every metropolitan area, eggs in several states, wheat, cotton, tobacco, rice, raisins, corn.

How much of each producer's output is to be sold? How can the group know that each producer sells no more? One way to police the "quota" is to have a central sales agency pool all the output and itself decide what portion of each producer's output to sell at high prices as fresh fruit in domestic markets and what part to destroy or to sell at lower prices as concentrates or flavorings in domestic and foreign markets. To keep fresh-fruit prices high despite the increasingly larger output, the proportion of the larger supply of lemons authorized for sale would have to be steadily reduced over the years—from 90 percent of the crop in 1942, when the sales-control scheme went into effect, until now, when less than half the crop is sold on the fresh-fruit market.

The success of *sales* controls in raising prices and incomes to lemon growers induced a larger output by each grower and attracted increased production of lemon trees in the absence of *output* controls. The net result has been to raise costs and create larger groves in the competition to get a profitable share of the sales quota. Farmers end up no better off since the potential monopoly rent is dissipated in the increased costs of larger groves. Without this scheme, there would have been fewer, lower-cost producers and a lower price of fresh lemons. The waste is the loss of the forsaken alternative crops like avocados, grapefruit, macadamia nuts, or the forsaken alternative land use like residential housing.

Tax-Subsidized Sales

More political weapons for maximizing income are available to producers. For example, currently the government will buy (out of taxes) whatever part of the crop consumers refuse to buy voluntarily at some pre-specified *parity* price. This method, which denies taxpayers the right of withdrawal from markets, supports the market price (when it would otherwise fall below the *parity* price), of wheat, cotton, tobacco, peanuts, rice, and corn, and it is proposed for more crops.

We exaggerate slightly. Neither the government nor the taxpayer would *buy* the unsold crop. It only lends money to the farmer, using the crop as security. However, if the farmers don't repay, the government can keep the unsold crop—which is, after all, no different from selling the crop to the government. The farmer is assured a minimum price, called the *parity* price, but the maximum is open. Since, in fact, the government was usually left holding the deteriorating "surplus" product, there were *visible* signs that this storage scheme was wasteful. In 1965, the total accumulated crops in government-held stocks had cost the taxpayers over $5,500,000,000, including an annual cost of about $1,000,000,000 for storage. Only in 1973 did the surplus disappear to foreign markets when other countries suffered severe weather and the free-market price rose above the guaranteed price. The "surplus" will return if the market price later falls below the support (parity) price, which is set by political authority.

Production Controls

An alternative is to limit the volume of production to only as much as can be sold at the desired price. (The common euphemism for the desired price is *parity* price.) Output control, if effective, is a very tidy solution because there will be nei-

ther a "surplus" around to embarrass anyone nor a low price to the producers. One way to obtain effective output controls or "self-policing management" is to assign to each producer an acreage he can use for production, say 80 percent of his available land (obviously he will pick the best 80 percent of his land and pour more fertilizer on it). That would reduce the supply schedule and raise the market price. He will even be paid something for the released land if he keeps it idle—a payment called a "conservation" payment. Those who do not restrict their acreage will not be allowed to sell at the resulting high market price. In fact, in the case of tobacco a prohibitive tax of 75 percent of the value of the crop is levied on such excess acreage. This system is called "self-policing" because a voting majority of the growers must agree in order to authorize and enforce the acreage-reduction scheme. In cotton production, the most efficient lands are in the western United States, and the farms are larger. Therefore, the more efficient producers are outnumbered. To cut back the use of older, less-efficient lands more than the newer is obviously not acceptable to that eastern majority. A proposal to cut everyone back by the same percentage of acreage is used instead, and it is ingeniously effective in reducing the newer, more-efficient acreage by a bigger percentage than the old. Why? Suppose you decide to cut all acreage by a percentage of some former amount. Which former amount? The farther into the past one goes for his base, the smaller the base if he is in a recently expanding area. And conversely for older areas that are *declining.* Consequently, the votes of cotton landowners for acreage-restriction schemes fall off dramatically as one moves into the newer, larger, more-efficient western farms.[7]

Acreage control promotes larger use of fertilizer and other jointly productive resources. Production becomes more intensive; the output per acre skyrockets. Acreage must be cut back more than had been expected, because farming becomes "surprisingly productive," and farmers attribute the surplus to induced productivity.

Acreage controls have been most effectively and rigorously used in tobacco production. Land licensed for tobacco growing is marked and policed by helicopters! Since unlicensed producers would have to pay a prohibitive 75 percent tax on the value of the output, there is no tobacco surplus, because the price goes to whatever level will clear the market of the *licensed* (untaxed) output. This output control for tobacco has been extolled by recent U.S. presidents as deserving application to other crops for political, not economic, reasons.

Public Utilities

If larger output can be produced by a firm with ever-decreasing costs *per unit,* the firm is a de-

creasing-cost firm. Two firms producing identical goods would be more costly since one could produce more at lower costs. But if there is only one, that firm could set prices above free-entry costs for a long time, or produce wastefully. That, in brief, is the reasoning behind government regulation of a single authorized firm in an industry—often called a public utility.

Examples of public utilities are electric, gas, water, sewage, and telephone companies, and railroads and airlines. Other industries are sometimes monopolized by law and called public utilities even though they do not have decreasing unit costs at larger outputs. Examples are: taxi, radio, television, and garbage-collection services. Hence the term "public utility" covers whatever you want.

If only one firm is allowed to produce for the market, a legal, closed monopoly is created. (However, any business can produce for itself—as some firms produce their own power.) The closed-monopoly firm is subjected to political regulation of profits, prices, output, service, costs it can incur, and many other details. If the utility fails to make money, the stockholders bear the losses. They may then sell at a loss to new buyers who expect to do better; or the service will come to an end (for example, railroad passenger service, street cars) or may be subsidized by taxes (such as city bus lines, rapid transit, local airlines).

Prohibiting new entrants reduces the likelihood of new products or lower-cost methods of production. It is not that the incumbent monopoly firm refuses to use known lower-cost techniques; instead, the incumbent firm does not know everything. But others, with different ideas about how to produce, are blocked out. Also, the incumbent

---

[7] We interject an ironic note. Although we have been calling the western lands more efficient, some of these lands are more "efficient" only because the costs of irrigation are not borne by the farm landowners who use that water. Some of the water is provided them by federal irrigation projects at prices substantially below the costs—the difference being made up by taxes on the rest of the country. Thus, we see farmers in the southeastern United States paying taxes to enable water to be sold to cotton growers in the western desert areas at less than cost in order to compete with the cotton from the Southeast. And to protect themselves from the consequent lower prices, they appeal for more taxes on the city consumers to finance "loans on unsold cotton"; finally, they appeal for federal regulations restricting production of cotton on those very same western lands for which they have paid taxes to help irrigate at less than cost.

will be dilatory in introducing known lower-cost innovations—not because it is a monopolist. Cost-reducing devices would be introduced *if* the firm could garner the profits; however, if the profits would be denied by the regulatory commission, incentives to reduce costs or revise service for larger profits are blunted. Nor can members of the regulatory commission directly capture the gains of lower costs, so they, too, will be less motivated. It's not that regulators are indolent or lazy; it is just that the incentives in the form of rewards to them for implementing cost-reduction techniques are weaker than if they owned the public utility.

Whose "Utility" in Public Utilities?

An especially instructive example of the incentives and consequences of regulatory agencies is that of the railroads beginning with the creation, in 1887, of the Interstate Commerce Commission to regulate the railroads in the interests of the consumer. What was the basic problem? By 1880, there had been overbuilding of railroads—for example, seven tracks ran between Omaha and Chicago. The high initial investment costs of creating a railroad and the low subsequent operating costs enabled railroads to cut prices far below the long-run total average costs. Rather than shut down if price did not cover "full" long-run costs, some dropped prices to costs of operation with existing equipment. Railroads sought to prevent price-cutting that was self-destructive or involved secret price discounts. Shippers who paid more were at a cost disadvantage. They demanded the government prohibit secret price cuts. Even the railroads wanted—*as a group*—to avoid price competition.

Prices of rail service would have remained low until some rails and equipment wore out and only the more economic, best-routed railroads survived. However, the law of 1887, requiring railroads to charge "just and reasonable" rates and to publicly post those rates, enabled railroads to do what they had unsuccessfully sought to do by private collusion—to prevent individually advantageous but mutually disadvantageous secret price-cutting.

The Interstate Commerce Commission has become the vehicle for maintaining an effective cartel in transportation. Although only three years after the ICC was created the Sherman Antitrust Act declared collusive (cartel) activity illegal, the railroads became a cartel with the aid of the ICC. ICC regulations have provided a legal backup to price collusion (much as if General Motors, Ford, Chrysler, and American Motors had a federal agency that helped them mutually set prices at which all their cars could be sold). In 1920 the ICC acquired power not only to control prices for rail service but to control entry of new competitors and routes as well, thus further protecting the existing railroads. Unfortunately for the rails, other forms of transportation were developing—autos, airplanes, and barges. Because of the high and discriminatory rail freight rates, trucks and barges took much of the business from the rails. So the ICC regulated them, too. The ICC is now authorized to approve interstate rates charged by highway transport, waterways, pipelines, telephone and communication companies, and railroads (and state and local agencies control intrastate and local fares). Any change in service or rates must have approval of the ICC. The administrative regulations and restrictions on competition among these alternative, otherwise-competing forms of services has been estimated to result in the loss of otherwise cheaper services that would have saved over $5 billion *annually*. All this is accomplished with an expenditure by the ICC of less than $50 million annually—not bad as a waste-producing activity.

Additional public utility regulatory agencies exist for airlines (Civil Aeronautics Board), for radio and TV (Federal Communications Commission), for energy (Federal Energy Agency). All these agencies were set up in the belief that open-market competition in these industries was inappropriate or not feasible, and so monopolistic results had to be prevented by regulation. As many people, including even Ralph Nader, have suggested, it is hard to conclude they have not encouraged monopolistic behavior.

10, 11
12, 13
14, 15
16, 17
18

Monopoly Rents: Creation and Disposition

The effect, and often the purpose, of legal barriers to entry is to increase the wealth of those who were already in the market. This increase is *monopoly rent* (here monopoly refers to *closed* monopoly). Closed-monopoly rent is achieved by restricting entry of resources, so that a difference between value of product and costs is created because restricting output raises price. Closed-monopoly rent is not a profit achieved by transferring resources from lower- to higher-valued uses. (See Figure 14–2.)

What happens to monopoly rent? In the agricultural crop-control scheme, it is obtained by the landowners who owned the land at the time the scheme was started. The value of the land

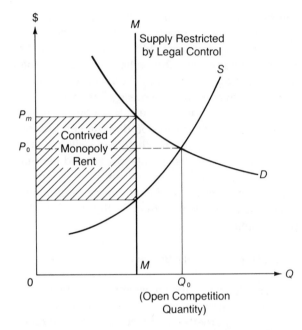

Figure 14–2. Monopoly Rent from Contrived Restriction on Production

Limitations on entry, or controls on supply, restrict output to MM, so price is P_m instead of P_o. Output is restricted to MM, though consumers would prefer to have more out to Q_o at price P_o. The excess of price, P_m, over the average cost at that output is the monopoly rent per unit of output—a rent which would be eroded by lower prices and higher costs at larger output under open market access.

on which the license to grow tobacco is granted is the value of the crop after all other costs of production (labor, equipment, fertilizer, insecticides, management, taxes, etc.) are subtracted. Suppose that *net* revenue from a licensed acre is $400 for each crop year. Recall from the earlier capital-value analysis that an annuity of $400 per year would have a value of about $4000 if the interest rate were about 10 percent. Taking that as a simple assumption, suppose land of the same kind, without a "license," yields a net revenue of $100 annually and has a value of $1000. The difference, $3000, is the capital-value of the monopoly rent.[8] As the licensing scheme is revealed, the favored acre rises in value, and anyone who at that time owns it captures the higher wealth. He can keep the land and the annual higher-income stream; or he can rent the land out for the higher rent; or he can then sell the land (with the "license" for its use) and use his wealth for other kinds of consumption (like living in Florida).

A *new* purchaser of the land gets no monopoly-rent *gain* since he pays a higher price, $4000, to get the land and license. The high monopoly-rent income from tobacco production is equal to a normal competitive return on *his* $4000 purchase price. If the license to grow an acre of untaxed tobacco could be sold "nude" (for $3000) and transferred to a different acre of land, it would be profitable and socially efficient for landowners of less-appropriate land to transfer their licenses, acre for acre, to more appropriate land. Regardless of who captures that monopoly-rent gain, the total costs of the produced tobacco would be lower if transfers to better land were legal. This is not permitted under the law. Why? Some political observers have suggested that sale of bare licenses would expose the monopoly rents provided to the tobacco landowners—just as they *are* exposed in the sale of bare liquor-store licenses, taxi fran-

chises, and radio- and television-station licenses.

The effects of the tobacco program—widely regarded as politically "good" because there is no "surplus"—are: (1) consumption reduced from what it would have been at a price determined by open-market demand and supply; (2) monopoly-rent gains to tobacco landowners (as distinct from tobacco growers); (3) waste; (4) reduced range of choice of occupation for producers.

Competition for Monopoly Status

Monopolists must compete for monopoly status. The monopolist must pay politically for the monopoly rent. Competition in outright bribes, political contributions, higher taxes paid out of monopoly rents, and costs of public-relations men and lawyers to obtain "rights, licenses, franchises, or authorization" may absorb all the monopoly rent. These pervasive payments to both political parties were publicized by the Watergate investigation committee in 1973. They occurred earlier and will continue.

If entry into some business is restricted, would-be entrants will spend money to obtain admission rights. The candidates acquire whatever qualities they believe the authorities use in their criterion of admission. For example, to enter the medical profession you might find that by the time you pay the "costs" of getting "qualified" to enter medical school and finally to practice, the high but short-lived income eventually earned has a capital value, as seen from the date of application to medical school, equal to the average of all college graduates. However, the long queue of applicants to medical schools

---

[8] These are realistic values. Recall that the monopoly rent is about $1500 per cow in the dairy industry in California.

suggests there is still monopoly rent available to those admitted.

In some states, liquor licenses—to sell bottled liquors at retail—sell for an average of over $40,000 though issued for a minor sum ($1750 in Florida). Taxi licenses are worth over $30,000 in New York. Entry into the savings-and-loan bank business in many states is subject to approval of state officials. The value of permission to open a bank once exceeded $50,000 in California, as evidenced and measured by the immediate rise in price on the stock of groups obtaining permission. Radio and television stations are "requested" to provide free coverage of political campaigns, especially at the national level, for the major parties. They are also required to broadcast the kinds of programs that federal government authorities think they should broadcast. (Notice the contrast with newspapers, which do not have to apply for a license. Not surprisingly, they act in ways that radio and television cannot.) Part of the monopoly rent of radio and television is taken not necessarily in the form of money but in the form of power to dictate programming. The owners of a closed monopoly cannot count on getting all the monopoly rent. The political processes that create monopoly rent can take it away in one form or another: through the competition for the right to be a protected monopolist; by taxes or contributions for political campaigning; by personal labor services, production of other goods, employment of special groups, etc.

Recent studies estimate that monopoly rent to favored parties (by restrictions imposed on their competitors—such as licenses to import goods into a country, to build a factory, or open a busi- [19, 20 21, 22 23, 24]

ness) equal about 7 to 12 percent of national income for Turkey and for India, the only two countries for which careful estimates have been made. However, the protected sellers do not necessarily get any gain for themselves. The cost of competition for monopoly rent eats up most of that rent. Indeed, competition for licenses is carried to the point where the marginal cost of the competition absorbs the prospective monopoly rent. If import licenses for raw materials are given in proportion to the size of one's factory, a would-be entrant will overbuild his factory; if licenses are given in accord with the number of applicants, applicants will seek a better chance at an import license by creating firms that are in fact too small. Monopoly-rent seekers resort to bribing officials, or hiring them after they leave government service, or hiring their relatives, or locating their firms in the capital city, hiring lawyers, etc. The winners of monopoly import licenses or other favors are not necessarily any richer after paying those extra costs.

The Sources of Monopoly

Running through this chapter have been two propositions: (1) achievement of monopoly power to raise price by restricting output and preventing entry of new resources is a natural economic result for sellers; and (2) closed-market monopoly power is created and sustained by government power to keep out newcomers and punish producers who expand their output and erode monopoly rents. Which is it?

25, 26
27, 28
29, 30
31

Or are both true? Is government intervention required to prevent monopoly or does it create more monopoly? The answer is unavailable.

Some Market-Power Pricing Tactics

We now investigate in more detail some pricing and selling tactics open to price-searchers. Not all of them require contrived or imposed market-restrictions or closure of markets against competitors.

Intercustomer Price Discrimination

A form of pricing commonly called *intercustomer price discrimination* can sometimes increase the seller's profit. Let a seller have two classes of customers, A and B, described by their two demand schedules in Table 14–1. Both the demands and the marginal revenues for A and B are different. If the seller makes six units at a constant marginal cost of $6 a unit, total costs are $36; if he charges a price of $8 to both customers, A buys five and B buys one, with total sales revenue of $48, and profits of $12.

The seller can do better if: (1) customers cannot exchange with each other the goods bought from our seller, and (2) the seller charges a different price to each seller (but no *multipart* pricing). The seller should set a price of $9 to class A customers, who buy four, and $7 to class B customers, who buy two. The total revenue is $50. Costs are $36, and profits $14, $2 more than before. At those prices the marginal

Table 14–1. Price Discrimination between Two Separable Customers

Price	Customer A		Customer B	
	Quantity	Marginal Revenue	Quantity	Marginal Revenue
$12	1	$12	0	0
11	2	10	0	0
10	3	8	0	0
9	4	6	0	0
8	5	4	1	$8
7	6	2	2	6
6	7	0	3	4
5	8	−2	4	2
4	9	−4	5	0
3	10	−6	6	−2
2	11	−8	7	−4
1	12	−10	8	−6

revenues are equal between buyers, each $6 and equal to the $6 marginal cost. See Figure 14–3.

If you think our seller could transfer some units from the $7 to the $9 customers and get larger revenue, you are forgetting our assumption that to sell more to the $9 customer the seller must cut the price to $8 on *all* the units sold to A in the higher-price market. That means the increase in sales receipts from selling one more (and the former units *also*) at a price of $8 is only $4, the marginal revenue. That unit transferred from B to A had a $6 marginal revenue in the B market, which is greater than the $4 marginal revenue from A, a reduction in total revenue of $2, which accounts for the difference between the revenues of $48 under the common

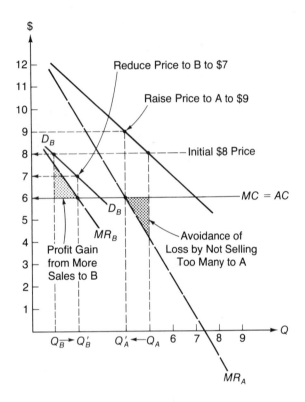

Figure 14–3. Price Differentiation with Marginal-Revenue Equalization

Any seller whose prices to different buyers result in unequal marginal revenues among buyers could increase his profits by changing prices so as to equate marginal revenues. This is shown in the diagram with the gains to seller or avoidance of marginal losses being shaded. This price differentiation is called price discrimination. If it is to be successful, lower-price buyers must not be able to resell to higher-priced buyers.

price and the $50 with discriminatory prices. Clearly, it is not equality in prices but equality in marginal revenues that the seller seeks in his quest for greater earnings.

But the clearest of all are sales by legal monopolies—whose sellers are protected by law from other sellers who might cut price: airlines, railroads, milk producers, the postal service, and telephone company, to mention a few. (Some utilities also use multipart pricing, as explained later.) In each of these cases the price charged

depends upon who the customer is or what the particular item is that he wants to ship by rail or postal service—even though costs are identical. In none of these cases is it legal for a customer to resell to other customers.

Other examples are the higher prices charged to tourists than to local residents at many hotels in Hawaii. Because residents have more knowledge of alternatives, their demands are more elastic, more sensitive to any one seller's price; thus the price from them is closer to the marginal revenue, so that equal marginal revenue from all customers requires lower prices for the more elastic demands of local residents. The same is probably true for price differences to residents and tourists in any country for many goods. Rich persons usually pay more for surgical services. (The services are not resalable.) Is the service they get that much better? Lawyers sometimes charge different fees for the same service to different customers. (But again, are the services the same?) The matter of quality of service is difficult to settle.

Legal monopolies are not necessary for this kind of price discrimination. Some motels charge lower prices to commercial than to noncommercial clients for exactly the same rooms and services. Hertz and Avis have discounts to special customers. Colleges give larger scholarships (tuition price-cuts) to the better students, who are widely sought by other colleges—that is, students whose demand for a particular college is elastic. Does your college bookstore give a discount to faculty but not to students? In each case, ask why the demand by one group is more elastic. What prevents resale by lower-priced to higher-priced customers? What prevents new sellers from upsetting the arrangement—which is to ask: How does the seller happen to be a price searcher in the first place?

Multipart Pricing to One Customer

Other pricing tactics sometimes can be more profitable. To understand the circumstances, examine Table 14–2. It presents the demand of *one* customer facing our seller. Column three is the total revenue at each possible price. Column four is the change in those proceeds—the marginal revenue. Column five gives the *consumer's total personal value* at each quantity. (Review p. 51.) This fifth column will be utilized here. For simplicity, the marginal costs of production are constant and equal to 30 cents.

Suppose the seller set a price at 70 cents, the single price that maximizes his profits ($1.50). The amount demanded (and produced) is that at which marginal revenue equals marginal cost (30 cents). But let our seller try the following tactic: Cut price, but *only* on extra units sold—not on all. That is, after setting a 70-cent price at which the buyer takes four units, allow him to buy *more* at a bargain price of 40 cents each, if he buys

Table 14–2. Demand of One Consumer

Price	Quantity	Revenue	Marginal Revenue	Consumer's Total Personal Value
$1.00	1	$1.00	$1.00	$1.00
.90	2	1.80	.80	1.90
.80	3	2.40	.60	2.70
.70	4	2.80	.40	3.40
.60	5	3.00	.20	4.00
.50	6	3.00	.00	4.50
.40	7	2.80	−.20	4.90
.30	8	2.40	−.40	5.20
.20	9	1.80	−.60	5.40
.10	10	1.00	−.80	5.50

the first four at 70 cents each. This is a reduction in price for the extra units *without* reducing price on all the units. The customer would buy three more at 40 cents each, giving the seller a net of 10 cents (50 cents − 30 cents) on each of the extra three units sold, raising his total profits to $1.90. The buyer benefits because he gets three units more, which he values successively at 60 cents + 50 cents + 40 cents while paying only 40 cents for each of those three—a gain to him worth 30 cents. (The customer and seller are indifferent as to whether the third is purchased, but we assume it is purchased.)

How does this "two-part" system improve the seller's situation? He sells more *without* lowering the price of all the units, so he does not cut his revenue on the former rate of sales, which would have offset part of the revenue from the new units

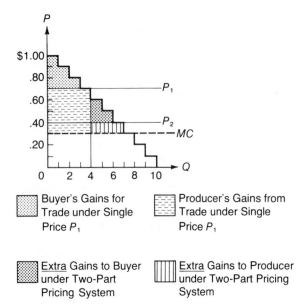

Buyer's Gains for Trade under Single Price P_1

Producer's Gains from Trade under Single Price P_1

Extra Gains to Buyer under Two-Part Pricing System

Extra Gains to Producer under Two-Part Pricing System

Figure 14–4. Effect of Multipart Price on Distribution of Gains of Trade between Buyer and Seller

If seller could charge a single price to the buyer, who could then buy whatever amount he demanded at that price, the price would be 70 cents, and the gain to the buyer would be the shaded area above that price and under his demand line. (This price could be charged because marginal revenue crosses and falls below marginal cost of 30 cents beyond four units. Compute the marginal cost and verify.) If seller could then charge a lower price for units taken in excess of four units on the condition that the first four are sold at 70 cents, the seller could charge another lower price, say 40 cents, and sell three more units for a total of seven, getting additional profits of 10 cents on each of the three extra units, while the buyer gets the extra personal value under his demand line and above the price for the fifth, sixth, and seventh units. (Can you construct another set of prices that would get the same output but with almost all the gains going to the seller? Hint: Try setting the first price at 99 cents, and then construct a series of prices for subsequent amounts.)

sold. Certainly, a two-part price schedule is better for both buyer and seller than a single price at 70 cents, even if not as good for the buyer as a single low price of 40 cents on all units (a price to which the seller would not agree). Figure 14–4 is a graphic exposition of this.[9]

[9] Why not a multi-part schedule? Start at the first unit and go right down the demand schedule as follows: the price is 95 cents for the first one; 85 cents for the second; 75 cents for the third; 65 cents for the fourth; 55 cents for the fifth, and so on until the price is down to 35 cents, just barely over the marginal cost of that lowest-price unit sold, the seventh unit. The buyer, *given no other way of buying this good,* would reluctantly agree, because that is better than refusal to buy at all. The seller has captured almost all the value of the product. He gains all the area under the demand schedule and above the marginal cost. He gets 65 cents (95 cents — 30 cents) profit on the first one, and 55 cents on the second, down to a nickel on the seventh. His total daily

How Should the Gains of Greater Exchange Be Shared?

One effect of this multipart pricing is to increase the extent of beneficial trade. Mutually beneficial opportunities for trade are more fully achieved, but more of the gains are obtained by the seller.

profit is $2.45 (= 65 cents + 55 cents + . . . + 5 cents). Formerly, at a *single* profit-maximizing price the buyer got a larger portion of the gain from trade. The buyer used to buy four for 70 cents each and three for 40 cents each, a total of $4. The total *personal value* to him of those seven was equivalent to $4.90, a gain of 90 cents. The seller, knowing the buyer's personal-valuation schedule, has managed to get from the buyer almost all that each unit is worth. This fortunate seller gets more of the gains from exchange so his profits are larger (now $2.45 instead of the $1.90 he got with the two-part schedule) while the buyer's gain is a nickel on each of the seven (35 cents) which is 55 cents less than before—a neat system if the seller can use it.

But the question about personal wealth distribution, "Should the producer, who after all did produce the goods, get more of the gains, or should the consumer?" cannot be answered by economic analysis. There is no standard of "rightness" of who should get what share of the value of a good being sold. Yet some people argue that the proper division is that which occurs if every seller and buyer is acting as a price-taker. For example, if there had been a single price equal to *marginal cost,* more of the value would have gone to the consumer and less to the producer. Of course, no price-searcher would have set a single price at his marginal cost. If he had to set a single price, he would set one at which the amount demanded has a marginal revenue (rather than price) equal to marginal cost. But there would still be an excess of price on the last unit over its marginal cost, and while the seller would like to be able to sell more at that price because its price and consumer value exceed marginal costs, he knows he would have to cut the price on all units sold and that would reduce his sales proceeds too much. With the best single price (70 cents in our example) his profits were only $1.50, but with two-step pricing he was able to get a profit of $1.90 and he was able to produce more units so that the value of the last unit sold (its price) was closer to marginal costs. He accomplished this by being able to sell the extra units without having to cut prices on the units sold.

Why the division of gains associated with a single price that equals marginal cost should be right and proper has never been demonstrated. It, too, would result in the efficient amount of production and exchange of this good, but so will multipart pricing (if the last bloc is priced at marginal cost). They differ only in the division of the gains from trade among buyer and seller.

Multipart Pricing Does Not Imply Subsidies

Multipart pricing schedules to various customers is not an example of high-price customers paying for the services to the low-price customers, so long as the lowest price to each customer covers the marginal costs of production of what he buys. However, in some cases, public regulatory commissions require that service be provided to some customers at prices below the marginal cost of providing the service. In that case the costs must be subsidized from some other source—by taxes or monopoly rents earned on sales to other customers. For example, third-class mail service to many publications is at prices below marginal costs, and the difference is covered by funds from other sources. No private producer would sell to a class of customers at a price below marginal cost. Giveaways and free trials are not contradictions to this. They are investments made by the seller in communicating information about his product to potential customers, an investment recovered by future business from the customers who like the product they were enabled to sample—something that could be done even if there were no other classes of customers.

Feasibility of Multipart Pricing

Multipart (or two-part) pricing is feasible only if several conditions are satisfied: (1) The seller must be a price-searcher with market power; that is, the demand for his products must have a sufficiently negative slope so that marginal revenue is significantly below price. (2) Customers must find it impossible, illegal, or too expensive to engage in *arbitrage* (whereby some would buy more at the low prices and sell to other consumers who thereby avoid the higher prices). (3) Other sellers of similar products must not be able to undercut the higher-priced sales of a seller using multipart pricing and take away some of his customers. Clearly, multipart pricing is not easy. Having a patent on a sufficiently valuable product is especially effective, say like Xerox copiers or Polaroid film.

The term "cream skimming" is often used to describe the tactics of a competitor who undercuts the high-price units of some other seller who is using a multipart pricing schedule or is charging some buyers more than others. Without such price discrimination, there would be no cream (higher price customer). Almost every public utility offers successively lower prices for larger purchases. Electricity, gas, and water users who are given lower prices on successively larger blocs of power are facing a multipart pricing schedule. The utility company is getting more revenue from the customers. Ever try to resell power and water? Xerox machines offer lower prices for larger volumes of use, charging a high price for the first few, with cut-prices for the next larger groups. Lower prices for large blocs sometimes reflect higher setup costs for small runs, but that is not the case for any of the examples cited.

Is there anything "inefficient" about that multipart pricing system? There can be, if some customers pay higher *last* prices on their multipart schedules than do other customers. The electricity, gas, or water would then be used by the lower-last-price buyers in less-valuable ways on the margin than the potential uses open to the higher-last-price buyers. For example, if I, as a householder, pay 10 cents for a kilowatt hour, while you (industry) pay only 6 cents for your last kilowatts of power, that power is worth more if used by me than by you. My extra uses are more valuable than yours. That would be a social waste of about 4 cents per kilowatt hour, a waste created not by every multipart pricing schedule but by one such that we are not both getting marginal units at the same prices.

A smart power company using multipart pricing would try to tailor a separate multipart price schedule for each customer so that every customer would use as much power as would bring every customer's marginal personal value down to the seller's marginal cost of producing power, say 6 cents per kilowatt hour. The schedules could differ among buyers, but should be such that every buyer ends up in a 6-cents bloc. There would then be no waste of power—no monopolistic restriction of output. Although customers would be paying more to the power company than if all buyers had been able to buy *all* their electric power for a fixed 6 cents per kilowatt hour, there would be no waste or economic misallocation of energy among consumers.

Why do public utilities—producers and sellers of power, gas and water—price that way? They do it to make more money, obviously. But utility companies that are government-owned comprise a large proportion of the utilities and they, too, price that way. Why? It is a form of taxation. The municipally owned utility company is part of the government and so uses this multipart schedule as a hidden tax to appropriate some of the gains from trade as elaborated in Chapter 4. And privately owned utilities are encouraged to do that, too, because their larger net earnings can be absorbed by higher taxes on utilities. Government-political power can help extract those gains from trade by preventing competition among sellers, which would foil these pricing methods whereby the seller gets more of the gains from trade with the buyer getting less of the gains.

Tie-Ins

A subtle device is often used to accomplish indirectly what an explicit multipart pricing schedule would do. So subtle is it that our federal judiciary and many lawyers have not understood it and have misinterpreted its effects. Consider an example. IBM has patents on a valuable computer. IBM is a price-searcher; that is, it has market power. To capture more of the value of that patented product (the area under the demand curve for that producer) than it could get with a simple single-price system, IBM faces two problems: First, it does not know each user's demand curve and hence the total personal value placed on its computer, so it does not know the different appropriate multipart schedules to each user. The second problem is: How can it prevent resale of machines among customers, which would upset the multipart pricing system? How can it know the area under each customer's demand schedule reflecting the value of the patented machine to each customer, collect more of that value, and avoid resale "arbitrage" among users which would upset the attempt? There is a way. Suppose a customer, A, has a very high demand (large value to him) for a computer, while customer B has a low demand (low value to him). If a customer's demand for some *other* good is highly correlated with his demand (value) for an IBM computer, a solution may be available. Suppose, for example, customer A, the higher valuer of a computer, is a large firm, while B is a small firm, and that A uses a lot more machine punchcards in his business than does B. If IBM required each to buy all the cards from IBM *at a higher price than otherwise available,* as a prior condition to being able to rent IBM machines (cards are tied-in to the rental of IBM machines), the customers would agree rather than not have an IBM machine at all. How much would the buyer be willing to pay in a higher card price in order to get IBM machines? Obviously, up to an amount equal to excess of his *value of the computer* (the area under its demand curve for the computer over the price of the *computer*). If the size of that area (value of the computer to him) is correlated with the amount of cards used, IBM would require (tie-in) the customer to buy all his computer cards from IBM at a higher price than the customer would otherwise pay for the cards, and IBM could capture that value with the cards. This *was* IBM's way of *measuring* and *capturing, indirectly via the sale of correlated amounts of higher-priced cards,* some of the value of the computer to the customer. IBM is capturing more of the high value of IBM machines it created for the customer, more than if it had to charge the same price to all customers who value the machine more and are assumed to be users and buyers of more cards. A customer is willing to buy the cards from IBM at the higher price in order to get the machine, and will pay more for the cards—up to *his* value of the *computer* (over the price). This tie-in arrangement will be advantageous to sellers if the assumed correlation of big buyers of cards with the higher valuers of IBM machines is correct and strong enough. What it does is direct the distribution of the gains of specialization and trade toward the producer.

What is important to note is that tying the IBM machine to the purchase of cards does *not* get IBM any monopoly returns from *cards.* It is getting from the buyer, *via* the higher card price, more of what the *machine* is worth. Furthermore, note that IBM is not monopolizing or driving any producers or sellers of cards out of the business. IBM simply could have used existing suppliers of cards to sell cards to its customers at higher prices, reflecting the value of having the *computer,* while the card suppliers pay IBM the difference due to the higher price.

These tie-ins have been declared illegal because the courts judged, erroneously, that the seller was "extending his monopoly power" over machines into the card industry—or was "leveraging" his monopoly power. It should be clear that IBM is *not* getting any monopoly power gains in *cards.* It is collecting the higher value of *computers* by *measuring* the value with card sales—in order to get more of the full value of the computers (not of cards). (IBM no longer uses this system for the additional reason that it now sells its machines and therefore can't enforce the tie-in.)

What is an ethically fair division between the producer and consumer of the excess of a product's value over its costs? There is no principle or criterion. Should multipart pricing and tie-ins be used? This issue must be resolved in terms of division of gains from trade rather than in such misleading terms as "extension of monopoly" or "restraint of trade."

Expenditures made solely to capture a bigger part of the higher value of product might be regarded as "wasteful" since they affect only the distribution of wealth rather than production. If so, it should be carefully noted that the courts do not declare it illegal to get a larger share of the value of product from the buyer by superior bargaining, more information about alternatives, etc. In any event, whatever your opinion with respect to who should get more of that value, the judicial analysis has been misled by poor economic arguments from lawyers.

Tie-ins whereby the buyer must purchase accessories to get the desired good are not uncommon. Gasoline stations often must buy tires, batteries, and accessories from gasoline producers if they are to get gasoline; Xerox and A. B. Dick mimeograph required purchase of their ink, stencils, and paper because they are "more appropriate" for their machines. And they might be right; inferior ink and equipment can foul up the machine. But it might also be a means of capturing more of the value of the copy machine. Tie-ins clearly can serve different purposes.

Another related use of tie-ins is to overcome price controls. During price controls on gasoline, sellers often required that you buy a lube job in order to get the gasoline. That is simply a way to get around the limit on the price of gasoline, and to capture the value of the gasoline—not to "monopolize" the lube business. Still another tie-in can be identified: Many retailers rent buildings and land on the basis of a percentage of the retailer's sales. A retailer with big sales, and who therefore presumably is a higher valuer of the premises, pays more than a retailer with smaller sales and presumably a lower value of the land. This percentage-of-sales method may also be a way of sharing risk about the value of the premises, rather than merely trying to get more of the value of the land to that renter. In either case, the owner of the premises could have achieved the same effect by requiring the retailer to also buy from him all the wrapping paper, or delivery service, or credit-servicing, or any other goods or services that are correlated with the amount of sales. Yet that would probably be declared illegal, while the rental based on percentage of sales is legal and extremely widespread. Lawyers and judges could benefit from a course in economics.

Effects of
Different Pricing
Systems

Though the value of another unit of output to customers is equated to price by the amount the customer decides to buy, the lower marginal revenue is what the price-searching seller heeds and compares with marginal costs. He does not produce enough to bring its value to consumers (price) down to the marginal cost. This "underproduction," called *monopoly distortion,* would be a waste only if there were an economically worthwhile way to avoid it.[10] If it were the result of a legal monopoly, a change of the law would do it. (But what is the cost of getting the law changed, and what were the reasons for the legal monopoly?) In many other cases, where there is

[10] Explained earlier on pp. 297–298.

no legal monopoly, information costs and transactions costs and economies of scale are involved. Because no worthwhile ways are known to overcome these, "underproduction" is not a waste or an inefficiency, because like rain and wintry cold it is economically unavoidable.

If price discrimination is practiced whereby one customer faces a price different from that to another customer, and is prevented (by other than economic costs) from buying in the lower-priced market, an interpersonal *allocative* distortion exists. Why? Both the lower- and the higher-paying customers would be better off if the amounts allocated were revised by having the lower-priced customers reselling to higher-priced customers. But if they in fact resell, that destroys the ability of the initial seller to sell at different prices.

One possible (though probably extremely rare) way to overcome both these distortions is a multipart price, wherein the marginal revenue to the seller on the last unit sold to each buyer is equal to: (a) the price at which it is sold, and (b) the seller's marginal cost. Multipart pricing and a uniform price to all sellers and buyers, who are price-takers, differ only in the distribution of the gains from specialization and trade. Since no generally accepted criterion exists as to the proper distribution of those gains, we cannot objectively evaluate the propriety of one or the other.

Price Discrimination?

We should recognize by now that the words "discrimination," "monopoly," and "competition" are loaded. Yet, the Robinson-Patman Law of 1938 prohibits "price discrimination" where it tends "to create a monopoly, lessen competition, or injure competitors." We should not be surprised that the confusion created by this law has provided lawyers with higher incomes and business firms (and their customers) with extra costs.

Another classic example of misinterpretation of "discrimination" is that in which a railroad charged more to ship goods from New York to Denver than for the longer trip from New York to San Francisco. Naturally, this seems "unjustly discriminatory" against people in Denver. Why did those rates exist? The railroads from New York to San Francisco had to compete with transport by water via the Panama Canal. There was no low-cost competition to Denver.

What a producer can get for his product depends not upon what it costs, but upon what price the supply will sell for when confronted with market demand. The supply of cheaper transportation to San Francisco from New York was much larger than to Denver at any given price. Nature "discriminated" in providing a superb harbor at San Francisco, with none at Denver. To "correct" this "injustice," the law compelled railroads to charge no more to Denver than to San Francisco. So, unable to raise the San Francisco rail rate (because of the cheaper water transport), railroads had to lower the rate to Denver if they were to keep the *legal* right to serve San Francisco. Had Denver been the major terminal of most of the freight, the rate would not have been cut. The San Francisco rate would have been raised, since the railroads would then prefer to lose some S.F. business income rather than all the larger Denver revenue. In that event, fares would still have been "equal," with San Francisco suffering in the cause of "equality."

32, 33
34, 35
36, 37
38

Sometimes, joint products (those having common inputs and hence not entirely separable costs) sell for very different prices. Daytime long-distance telephone demand is higher than at night. There is no right way to allocate the common-facility costs to night and to day service, and, anyway, there is no point in doing so. Phone rates are lower at night because demand is smaller. If night demand were stronger, night rates would be higher than day rates. The relative level of rates depends upon the relative size of the demands to be rationed.

Is it "fair" that night workers should be able to make long-distance calls more cheaply? That theaters should charge less for matinees than for evening performances? That paintings involving the same production costs should sell for different prices? That beautiful people get richer than homely ones, even if both incur identical costs in trying to be more beautiful? These "disparities" arise because of differences in the demand for the good or service, reflecting differences in availability, convenience, or, in the eyes of the demander, quality.

Why doesn't the person paying a higher price instead buy in the lower-priced market? Because using the lower-priced market is not worth the sacrifices (like moving to San Francisco from Denver, or working nights rather than days in order to save on long-distance calls, or learning to ignore superficial beauty). Economic analysis doesn't say what is fair. The words "fair," "just," or "reasonable" have no objective content—Aristotle, Aquinas, the Council of Christian Churches, the President of the United States, or anyone else to the contrary notwithstanding—except, possibly, "The fair price is what I think it should be."

Summary

1. Reduction of market competition by elimination of rivals or by collusion is potentially profitable.
2. Efficient collusion is difficult because rivals find it hard to reach or police an agreement, and keep out new entrants who would be attracted by the higher profit potential.
3. Some labor unions represent effective collusions by sellers (of labor) to raise wages above the competitive level. Wage-cutting and entry is in those cases reduced (though not entirely eliminated).
4. Mergers do not appear to be an important means of achieving collusive action to change market conditions. Rather, many allow efficient managers to take over less-efficient firms or provide certain economies of joint production, none of which involves raising prices as a consequence of the merger.
5. Sealed-bid purchases by government agencies encourage collusion, because they make enforcement of secret agreements easy.
6. The argument against collusion is essentially the argument against monopoly inefficiency (explained in Chapter 13).
7. Under the Sherman Act, the antitrust division of the Department of Justice and the Federal Trade Commission are supposed to prevent "monopolizing" and "unfair" trade practices. Whether these laws have protected the competitive markets or instead the existing marketeers is not clear, and the evidence for either position is extremely weak.
8. Restrictions on access to the market occur for several, sometimes conflicting, reasons: (a) encouragement of invention; (b) protection to consumers, by saving them from incurring costs of discerning undesirable features of goods; (c) prevention of uneconomic duplication of resources, as with *some* public utilities; (d) protection of existing producers from products of other potential producers. While the first three are generally, though not universally, applauded, each serves as a facade for the fourth effect. Therein lies the source of objection to many government and political controls over people who would buy and sell in the open market. Political authorities can create and obtain monopoly-rent wealth through closed, legal monopolies. This enhances the role of competition for political power.
9. Some market controls are ostensibly intended to protect consumers from their gullibility and sanguineness; others are intended to lower individual information-collection costs. This latter objective implies government licensing for "approved" sellers, but not exclusion from the market for nonlicensed sellers.
10. Some market-entry restrictions are designed primarily to protect existing sellers from competition among themselves and from new sellers. Almost every agricultural crop market or production control does this. Although advertising restrictions are intended to protect the buyer from gullibility, they also protect existing producers from new competitors by raising the costs of entry to the market.
11. Closing the markets to new entrants, or to any sellers who would sell below an "approved" price, initially provides a closed-mo-

nopoly rent to the producer. Hence, many of the crop price-support laws intended to help the poor farmers give a greater gain to the larger, richer landowner.

12. Competition to get political power to close markets and get monopoly rents incurs extra costs of acquiring those monopoly rents up to their value, with the result that resources that could be used to produce other goods are diverted to trying to obtain political power to close markets and create monopoly rent.

13. Public utilities are closed monopolies, regulated by the political process, presumably because the product is produced at decreasing cost and more than one seller would be wasteful. The superiority of the regulated monopoly in its overall results (introduction of new processes and goods, reduction of price, reliability of service) to unregulated open monopoly is yet to be established.

14. Pricing tactics most readily used by closed monopolists include price discrimination among buyers and multipart pricing to any single buyer. These tactics often lead to larger output than if a single price had to be charged to all customers. In these cases the tactic is designed to direct a larger share of the gains from trade to the producer-seller than to the consumer-buyer. There is no economic or ethical standard for determining what is the appropriate division of the gains from trade.

Questions

1. Suppose there are ten identical producers of the good being sold in the market charac-

terized by the total market demand given here. Each producer has *zero* costs of production for twenty units; he can produce no more.

Demand Schedule

		Dollar Value of Daily Revenue		
Price	Quantity Demanded Daily	Total	Increment	Marginal (for Unit Increase in Quantity)
$1.00	56.52	$56.52	0	0
.95	62.25	59.14	$2.62	.46
.90	68.39	61.55	2.41	.41
.85	74.65	63.45	1.90	.30
.80	81.36	65.09	1.64	.24
.75	88.17	66.13	1.04	.15
.70	95.45	66.82	.69	.09
.67	100.00	67.00	.18	.03
.65	103.00	66.95	−.05	−.02
.60	110.67	66.40	−.43	−.05
.55	118.60	65.23	−1.17	−.15
.50	127.01	63.51	−1.72	−.18
.45	135.72	61.07	−2.44	−.28
.40	144.48	57.79	−3.28	−.37
.35	153.76	53.81	−3.98	−.43
.30	163.07	48.92	−4.98	−.53
.25	172.92	43.23	−5.69	−.58
.20	182.79	37.16	−6.07	−.61
.15	193.21	28.98	−8.18	−.78
.10	203.92	20.39	−8.59	−.81
.05	214.62	10.70	−9.69	−.91

a. If all are selling in a price-takers' market, what is the price and output?

b. If all sellers could reach an effective agreement to restrict output and raise price, what price should they select?

c. What will be each seller's output and revenue?

d. How much would each seller gain by the effective agreement?

*e. How much (money) would it be worth to each seller to seek means of reaching and enforcing that effective agreement?

*f. How much would you gain if you as *one* seller succeeded in staying outside the agreement or in secretly breaking it while all others raised the price and reduced their output?

*2. Ten concrete-block companies in a certain community were accused by the city attorney of colluding to restrain output and fix the prices of concrete blocks. The accusation stated that the ten producers accounted for 85 percent of the output of concrete blocks in the community. What do you think was meant by "colluding": Meeting and talking in an effort to reach an agreement? Or reaching an agreement? Or those ten firms restricting output and raising prices? Or all firms raising prices?

*3. Assume that all existing firms producing a commodity were successfully and effectively to collude to restrict output and raise prices.

a. What open-market forces would operate to obstruct the effectiveness of the collusion?

b. How can those forces be restrained from operating? Illustrate in the context of the behavior of lemon growers, wheat producers, tobacco growers, longshoremen, carpenters, doctors, retail liquor stores, and steel producers.

c. What devices are used in each instance to keep the supply below the open-market supply?

d. Are these regarded as "proper"?

4. The first case prosecuted under the federal laws against collusion to raise prices involved steel pipe sold to the U.S. government. More recently, an electrical-equipment industry's collusion, which sent some business leaders to jail, was also against the government. What explanations are there for the fact that a majority of prosecuted proven cases involve collusion against the government?

5. What is the difference between collusion, cooperation, and competition? How would you define collusion between two people so as to exclude partnerships and corporate joint ownership from the concept of collusion? Why is collusion considered undesirable?

6. The National and the American Baseball Leagues are two separate leagues of twelve teams each. Teams are owned by different people. To prevent competition among team owners for *new* players, a draft (similar to that used in the football and basketball leagues) has been adopted, wherein each newcomer from a high school is assigned to a particular team. Under this agreement, or assignment, no other team owner will be allowed to sign that newcomer. Once a player signs a contract, he cannot change "employers" at his own volition; but the employer can trade or sell him to another team owner.

a. Who benefits from this arrangement? Who suffers?

b. Why does this system exist in sports and nowhere else?

7. Almost every team in the two baseball leagues is subsidized by the city governments, which provide stadium facilities. If new leagues cannot be assured of access to those facilities, will this have any effect on the income of the existing teams?

8. European coal producers pool their sales through a central agency.

a. Why is that essential for an effective policing of the collusion agreement among the producers?

b. Why haven't some coal producers stayed out of the agreement and taken advantage of the opportunity to sell more coal at the price maintained by the "cartel," as it is called?

*9. Suppose you could live in a society in which trademarks were not protected by law and anyone could imitate the trademark.

a. As a consumer, would you prefer to live in that world or in one where trademarks were exclusively reserved for a particular manufacturer as part of his property? Why?

b. As a producer, which would you prefer?

*10. Milk delivery is sometimes called inefficient because when several firms deliver milk to homes, there is duplication of delivery trucks and labor.

a. For standard items such as milk, would you prefer to live in a community with one centralized delivery service controlled by a regulatory commission to ensure low price and adequate quality, or in one where anyone who wants to deliver milk can enter the market? Why?

b. Apply your analysis of the preceding problem to the case of garbage collecting. Would you feel differently about that?

c. How about mail service? Newspapers? Electric power?

d. If your answers differ, what factor makes you change your preference?

11. a. Do you know of any instances where inferior goods have driven out superior goods?

b. Would any of the following be such cases: compact versus larger cars; margarine versus butter; salad dressing versus mayonnaise; blended versus straight whiskey; plastic cartons versus milk bottles; frozen versus fresh orange juice; ready-made versus custom clothes; office versus home visits of the doctor. Would you consider any of these to be unfortunate developments? Why?

12. It is probably safe to say that a majority of the faculty at any college contends that students are not competent to judge the quality of the instruction in various courses and hence should not be relied upon as evaluators of instructor competence.

a. What do you think?

*b. At the same time, it is probably safe to say that a majority of the faculty thinks its students have come to that college because the students can tell good colleges from bad. Do you see any inconsistency in this pair of beliefs? Explain.

13. The stock exchanges, with the sanction of the U.S. Securities and Exchange Commission, occasionally prohibit (suspend) all trading in a certain common stock, especially when some spectacular news about that company suddenly is heard. For example, if the president of a corporation is sued for fraud by some government agency, with a consequent rush of sell orders by common stockholders, the exchange suspends trad-

ing to permit time for the full news to be digested and to prevent wild swings in the price of stock. The defense of the suspension is that it protects some stockholders from selling in panic at the developing, but as yet unsubstantiated and unweighed news. These sellers would later find the price had recovered—that they had sold at exceptionally low transient prices.

Does that reasoning—as a defense of suspension of trading of the stock—convince you that it would be better for you to be in a situation in which the exchange could stop trading in common stocks you happened to own? In making your decision, consider the risk that the news will turn out to be accurate and the swing will not be temporary. Consider also the effect on the new potential buyers who are restrained from buying. (Incidentally, trading can always go on elsewhere than in the formal exchange markets—whether or not the exchange suspends its trading.)

*14. European countries import inspected frozen fresh meat from Argentina. But the United States limits imports of fresh meat, because some other countries have hoof and mouth disease (a rapidly spreading disease that kills cattle, although it does not endanger human life). Whom does the import limitation benefit and whom does it hurt? How?

15. Texas, which has the legal right to subdivide itself into seven states, surprises us by doing so. One of the new states, Texaseven, with no college in its boundaries, decides to give to every high-school student a four-year annual grant of $1500 to be applied to education costs at the college of his choice anywhere in the world.

a. Would you consider that new state to have the finest or the worst educational system in the world?

*b. Why is that method not used more widely, despite its temporary wide use immediately after World War II as an aid to veterans?

*c. Why is it opposed by the officials of most state universities?

16. Read the first quotation in footnote 5, p. 328.

*a. Why has the growth in numbers of investors made open markets for security dealers and for investors an obsolete concept?

b. If you were a black, a Jew, or an immigrant, would you find this development to your advantage? Why?

*17. Refer to the last passage in footnote 5, p. 329.

a. Restate the proposition of that passage in terms analogous to the control of medication by prescriptions from doctors.

b. Do you think economists should campaign for laws to prohibit any person from buying a security, land, or a house without a prescription from an economist certifying the suitability of that particular purchase by the particular person involved? Why or why not?

18. Gasoline price "wars" have induced many gasoline-station owners to propose a regulatory agency to establish orderly marketing conditions in gasoline markets. Also, they propose that no service station be allowed to charge a price less than costs, and further that no new stations be opened unless the convenience and necessity of the area warrants more stations.

a. Who would benefit and who would be hurt by these proposals, if carried out?

b. If the proposals were carried out, how should the commission decide who got to open a new service station?

*c. What would be your preference about this kind of regulation if you were a black, immigrant, or young gasoline-station operator?

19. Tentatively classify the following, on the basis of your present information, as (a) price-takers, (b) closed monopolists, or (c) open monopolists. (Remember, market closure does not necessarily convert a price-takers' to a price-searchers' market.)

Electric company
City bus line
Airline
General Motors Corporation
Corner drug store
Prescription pharmacist

U.S. Steel Corporation
Lettuce grower
Electrician
Elizabeth Taylor

20. "Retail grocery stores are monopolies." In what sense is that correct and in what sense is it false? "The medical profession is a monopoly." In what sense is that true and in what sense false? Which kind of monopoly implies a higher price?

*21. The market for economics professors in most colleges is completely open. No legal requirements about training or prior experience exist as a condition of teaching. A majority of the profession has opposed certification—under which a certification board, consisting of professors, would administer standards of competence. Consider the following:

a. If all present college professors were automatically certified (under a kind of exception called a "grandfather clause"), but all new entrants had to obtain certification by passing certain tests, would the market be open or restricted?

b. If the number of professors admitted were controlled by the board of college professors, which is what would happen, do you think they would restrict entry to the "needed" numbers and would keep out inadequately trained people in order to protect students? Would this have any effect on wages of college professors? What would be the effect on the number of professors?

c. Similar systems of certification (or admission or licensing or self-policing) are used by doctors, lawyers, pharmacists, architects, dentists, morticians, butchers, longshoremen, psychiatrists, barbers, and realtors, to name a few. What do you think it implies about the wages in these professions relative to wages in an open market? What does it imply about the quality of those who actually practice the professions? About the quality and quantity of services provided the community? Is there a difference between quality of competence of those certified and the quantity of service obtained by the public as a whole?

22. Diagnose and explain the various features reported in the following news story: "An attractive brunette seated in a rear row gave an excited whoop when her name was called Wednesday during a drawing at the County Building. She had good reason to be elated. For $2000 she had picked up an on-sale liquor license with a market value of about

$40,000. She was one of 54 persons who had applied for the 25 new on-sale licenses to be issued in the county this year by the Alcoholic Beverage Control Board. A drawing was used to determine who would get the new on-sale licenses, which permit sale of drinks on the premises. An applicant must have had a premise available and must operate the business for two years before he can sell the license."

*23. Gulf Oil, Baxter Laboratories, Richardson-Merrell, Levi Strauss, Tenneco are a sample of many American firms that made payments to foreign government officials to conduct business abroad.

a. Who extorted payment from whom, or who bribed whom?

b. How is that activity different from paying franchise fees or taxes to do business abroad?

c. Why don't the foreign governments use explicit license fees and taxes rather than insist on covert payments to government officials and their relatives?

d. Almost all the payments made by the companies were to government officials and their relatives. Would it be safer to simply put the official's relatives on the payroll and let him neglect his work?

e. The press called this corporate bribery. What would you call it?

24. As determined by Congressional action, radio and television networks are not required to give "equal-time" rights to any political parties other than the Republican and Democratic parties.

a. Would you consider this a collusion by the two major political parties against the many smaller political parties?

b. Why are newspapers not required to give equal-space rights to the two major political parties? (Hint: The answer is *not* that radio space is limited or a natural resource that "belongs to the people.")

25. Why, despite so much political campaigning against "monopolies," do politicians create closed markets or closed monopolies?

*26. The judicial council of the American Medical Association recommended that it be considered unethical for a doctor to own a drug store in the area in which he practices medicine. It also recommended similarly for ophthalmologists who dispense eyeglasses for a profit. "Any arrangement by which the physician profits from the remedy he prescribes is unethical," in the opinion of the council.

a. Who do you think would benefit if this recommendation were adopted by the American Medical Association and made effective?

b. If it is unethical for a surgeon to profit from the remedy he prescribes, should any surgeon diagnosing a patient be allowed to perform the recommended operation?

c. Should a building contractor be allowed to have any interest in a lumber company? Should any teacher be allowed to use his own textbook? Should a doctor be allowed to own a hospital? Or own an undertaking business?

d. As a patient, would you prefer to deal with doctors who are prohibited from ownership of drug stores? How would this help you or hurt you?

27. The U.S. postal system is a monopoly. No

one else may institute a competitive system of transporting personal messages for pay.
a. Why do you think it has remained a monopoly?

*b. The prices charged are uniform despite vast differences in costs of service to different patrons. Why is this kind of discriminatory pricing practiced for mail but not for food, clothes, or dancing lessons?

*28. Why do union officials object to admitting that their power rests on a closed monopoly, while at the same time opposing any legislation that would destroy that monopoly power? Answer the same question when applied to the American Medical Association.

*29. Moving companies are regulated by the Interstate Commerce Commission; their rates per pound are legally set. Explain why that would entail prohibition of making binding bids, prior to moving, as to the cost of the move? In what manner will they compete for business?

30. Is it possible for an economy to be such that everyone is a closed monopolist yet everyone is poorer than if there were no restrictions on the open market? Explain.

*31. When seeking a replacement for a retiring member of a regulatory board, President Johnson said that he wanted a strong man of action to help strengthen the board, because he had noted that even the regulated industry didn't like weak regulatory boards. Why do you suppose the regulated industry likes a strong regulatory board? (Hint: Who is regulated for whose benefit?)

32. Price discrimination between two markets consists of selling in one market at a price below that of another. That is also called "dumping" into the low-priced market—a very misleading term. The actual purpose is simply to equate marginal revenues, as explained in the text. Yet some observers allege the reason is that the seller is trying to drive some other competitor in the class B market out of existence so he can later raise prices. No such objective is involved. Finally, it is argued that the seller must be selling below cost in the class B market, else how could he sell at a lower price and still cover transport costs?
a. Show how he can.
b. Show that even if it cost 25 cents to ship a unit of the good from the factory—located where all the class A customers are—to class B customers, profits for the producer would increase despite the fact that the selling price is $2 less for class B customers than for class A.
c. Would he ever sell at a price below costs—marginal costs?
Note: Just a few examples of "dumping" favorable to American consumers are Belgian glass; Japanese, German, and Italian cars; Polish golf carts; Korean textiles; Japanese steel; and tuition grants by colleges.

33. Some colleges charge high tuitions, but at the same time they give a large number of tuition fellowships ranging from full tuition payment down to practically nothing. If you apply the principles of discriminatory-pricing techniques of an earlier chapter, can you show that tuition grants are a form of discriminatory pricing of education? Does that make them undesirable?

34. An attempt to impose losses on competitors in order to achieve a monopoly position

with subsequent "above-competitive" prices would be a predatory action. A case frequently alleged to be a predatory action involved Rockefeller's Standard Oil Company in the nineteenth century, when Standard's low prices in selected local markets were interpreted as devices to bankrupt smaller refiners. Would this be an intelligent tactic—that is, wealth-maximizing—even if no law prohibited it?

35. You are the producer of a computer, but to distribute them to the public you first sell them to a distributor who in turn retails them to the public, whose demand for the computer is given by the data in Table 13–1. The retail distributor may choose the reselling price to the public that is best for him. As the producer, you have a uniform marginal cost of production of $4 each, regardless of how many you produce.

    a. Show that the price you should charge the distributor is about $12.50. How many will he buy at that price, and what price will he in turn charge the public?

    b. Show that you and the distributor and the public could be better off if you required the distributor to not charge the public over $13. According to the law a retail price limit is illegal as being presumably anticompetitive because it does not allow the distributor to charge whatever price he wishes for what he has bought from you. Who loses because of that interpretation of the law? (The situation described in the example is faced by some newspaper publishers.)

    *c. Can you think of any of several other products for which this example helps to explain why some firms tend to be vertically integrated (that is, where a firm does manufacturing, distributing, and retailing)? (This is not the only reason for vertical integration.) The problem illustrated in this question is known as the problem of "successive monopoly."

36. Suppose you, the seller, have six units of a good available. At any price you ask of A you must let him buy all he wants, and you must permit B to have all he wants at the price you ask of B; but the price asked of A and B can be different.

    a. What price should you charge A, and what should you charge B, if you want to maximize your revenue?

	Units Demanded		Marginal Revenue	
Price	A	B	A	B
$10	1	0	$10	0
9	2	0	8	0
8	3	0	6	0
7	4	0	4	0
6	5	1	2	6
5	6	2	0	4
4	7	3	−2	2
3	8	4	−4	0
2	9	5	−6	−2
1	10	6	−8	−4

    b. If you charge the same price to both buyers, what is your best price and revenue?

    c. Suppose you can produce this good at a cost of $2 for each unit you make. How many should you make, and what price should you charge to A and what to B in order to maximize your net earnings? How many will A buy, and how many will B buy? What will be your net earnings?

*d. Construct an example of *multipart pricing* with *different sets* of prices to each buyer, so as to get still more revenue than with the preceding policy. Why do you think this kind of multipart plus discriminatory pricing is relatively uncommon? Can you give some examples of it? (Hint: Check the water, telephone, gas, and electric rates charged in your community; what prevents new sellers or customers from reselling to each other in all these cases?)

*37. Consider another ingenious pricing policy. Suppose that you are a movie producer and have made two movies: A, a social-problem-oriented drama, and B, a horror movie. You rent your pictures to various exhibitors, two of whom are "Roxy" and "Drivein." You know the amounts that Roxy and Drivein would pay for each movie rather than not get them.

Maximum Values to Exhibitors		
	Movie	
	A	B
Roxy	$100	$70
Drivein	60	80

We now investigate three alternative price tactics.

a. Set a price on A, with Roxy and Drivein each being allowed to rent at that same price; and set another price on B, with each being allowed to rent B at that price. Under this arrangement the revenue-maximizing prices are $60 for A and $70 for B. Your revenue is $260.

b. Set a price on A for Roxy and a different price on A for Drivein. Also set different prices on B for Roxy and for Drivein. You may have four prices. What is the revenue-maximizing set of prices, and what is that revenue? ($310 is the total revenue.)

c. We come to the third alternative and the purpose of this problem. Suppose that you are *not* legally allowed to charge different prices to Roxy and Drivein. However, you do discover that you can engage in "block booking," whereby an exhibitor must take both pictures if he is to take any from you. What price (*same to both exhibitors*) would you set for the *pair* of pictures as one "block book," if you wish to maximize your revenue? What is the maximum revenue you can get this way? (Answer: $280.)

Explain how you determined the best block-booking prices. (Answer: For each exhibitor compute the sum of the highest amounts that would be offered by each exhibitor for each picture. Charge the lowest of these two sums as the price of the "block." As a seller, it pays to engage in block booking only if your customers assign different relative values to the various products in the block. To show this, try to get a gain—over uniform prices for separate pictures—by block booking when both exhibitors value the various pictures in the same relative way. Remember, in block booking you charge the *same package price* to all exhibitors. You will see that block booking gives no advantage to the seller, and no disadvantage, either, relative to the pricing tactic explained in b.)

d. The exhibitors Roxy and Drivein, who would prefer to prohibit block booking and discriminatory pricing, force you to sell the pictures at the same price to Roxy and Drivein, although permitting a different price for picture A from that for B. (In this case, as we have seen in part a, the most you could get is $260.) In an effort to keep down their costs, Roxy and Drivein complain to the government that under block booking you, the producer, really are "tying" B, the poor picture, to A, the better picture, in order to get rid of your inferior picture. They complain they do not have freedom to buy what they want and that you are an unfair monopolist. Explain why the complaint is in error. Is the procedure forcing the exhibitors to buy goods they do not want? Explain why or why not.

e. What open-market forces reduce your power to engage in block booking? (Block-booking is used by TV networks.)

*38. You invent a photocopy machine. You know that the average cost of making the machine is $1000 and that its operating costs are 1 cent each time the machine is used. You could sell the machine for, say, $2000, letting users pay the 1-cent operating costs. On the other hand, if you can discriminate among customers, and charge some a higher price than others, you can make still more money. In order to make discriminatory pricing ef-

fective, you must not sell machines to the users, for they could then resell them from the "low-priced" to the "higher-priced" customers, and undermine your attempt to get more revenue. Suppose, however, you rent the machine to each user at a uniform fee but charge 3 cents each time the machine makes a photocopy.

a. Would that achieve your purpose? Explain.

b. Selling at different prices is illegal; 3 cents per copy is legal. Why?

c. Is this kind of "discrimination" good?

15

Derived Demand and Substitution in Production

So far we have studied the pricing and production of consumer goods with little regard to the determinants of income earned by productive resources. We now turn to that latter issue and again we use the familiar demand–supply apparatus. But first, to show the relationship between these two areas of study, the circular-flow diagram of Figure 15–1 is useful. The top half represents consumer goods markets, with money flowing clockwise from people as consumers in households through the market to people as producers in business firms or governments in exchange for goods and services going in the counter-clockwise direction. The bottom half represents flows through markets in which people earn income by providing and selling productive resources to business firms. But the analysis, unlike the flows of incomes and goods, is not circular. A mutual interdependent determination of output of various consumer goods and incomes of producers prevails. To show this mutual interdependence and to understand it, we first identify some classes of productive resources, how the demand for those resources is derived from consumers' valuations of their services, and how that derived demand, along with the determinants of the supply of those resources, affects their incomes.

Forms of Income

About 70 to 80 percent of the cost of output is wages and salaries—decidedly toward 80 percent if we include the earnings from labor services of a person running his own business. The rest is paid for services of physical, nonhuman capital goods and is called *rents,* or *interest,* or *dividends,* depending on the kind of good or who its

owner is. If you rent a house from me, you would pay me rent. If I lent (that is, rented) you money, you would pay me what would be called interest, although it is a *rental* payment for the money. A rental payment, whether for money or other goods, is included in the term *dividends,* which are payments by a corporation to its common stockholders. The term *dividend* is applied to all payments by a corporation to its stockholders, including any residual profits that the corporation may have earned and decided to pay out. But in these dividends are also the payments for services of assets owned by the stockholders. Had the corporation rented those same goods from people who were not owners of the corporation, the payments to outsiders would be called rents; but when owned by the stockholders, the rental payment is in the dividend.

Almost all machinery and equipment (*capital goods*) are the results of past labor and ideas. They can be thought of as embodying past labor and intellectual (hereafter included in the notion of *labor*) services in that current consumption services are greater because of past labor used to produce that equipment. Though some capital goods, such as land and raw materials, are not

Figure 15–1. Income Flow
This chart portrays aggregate flows of goods and incomes with some of the institutions. Chapters 1–7 discussed allocation of existing goods (the upper left quarter of the circle). And Chapters 8–14 covered the amounts of goods produced (upper right portion). Methods of determining how goods shall be produced and by whom and for whom (the bottom half of the circle) are discussed in Chapters 15–18. These chapters will also cover determination of individual incomes and wealth. For each case, in the capitalist market system, the communications and controls are channeled via prices and incomes. Fluctuations in the total flow of services and values "around the whole economy" are problems of aggregate employment and national-income and are not covered in this text.

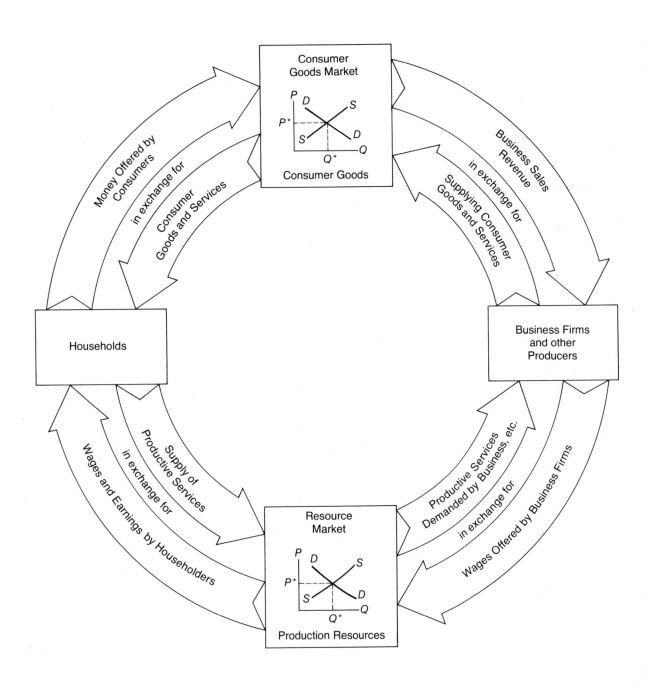

created entirely by man, they are more productive because of past labor devoted to their improvement. Students purchase labor services from teachers to create more productive powers in themselves. Your greater productive power is human capital: You are a human capital good—just as surely as if you somehow could have stuck some machinery inside of you. Converting iron ore to useful machines is identical to converting an illiterate, unskilled person into a literate, skilled person. All of us have greater productive power because of past investment in ourselves.

Capital goods can pretty correctly be considered the product of past labor services *paid for at that time* by someone who hoped to recover at least those costs out of later services of the capital equipment, whether it be in animate or inanimate form (for example, himself, a machine, or an animal). When you produce machine tools this year you are paid now although the value of the services ultimately to be obtained from that machine tool will not be realized until many months later. The person who advances payment to current labor and thereby "invests" in the product (capital good) and risks being recompensed later is called a *capitalist.* The larger the prospective future value, the more of that capital good will be created as people respond to the profit prospects. In the process, wages to the producers are bid up, and as more of the good is created, the value of the end product and capital good is reduced by competition until it equals costs.

Capital and Interest:
Capital Goods and Rents

The role of the capitalist ("advancer" of payment,

or "investor" in machines) is rarely understood. The reason is easy to see. After the machine is completed it is usually used jointly with labor. The joint inputs (*current* labor and machine) yield a product selling for, say, $100. That covers the *current* labor services of, say, $70 in wages. Of the $30 remaining, say, $25 is recompense that may cover the *earlier* invested wages for the earlier labor used to make the machine.[1] This would leave $5 to cover the interest cost of that earlier $25 advance to the earlier labor, which at 10 percent a year would amount to $2.50. That would leave a net of $2.50 (if we ignore his own labor, which we shouldn't). The source of confusion is that this is often described as saying this business man pays $70 for labor and gets $30 for "capital and profit." Actually, the payment to labor services is about $97.50 (in present value terms) for past and present labor, leaving a net of $2.50 (again ignoring his own labor services—which may exceed $2.50, in which case he has a loss).

A capital *good* can be sold, or its services can be rented. For example, the sale price of a house may be $50,000, but the rental price of the *services* of the house may be $1 an hour (which is $8760 per year). In the same way, prices of the *services* of labor are called wages, but since a person is not bought there is no price for a person.

The price of *capital* (*not* capital *goods*) is the rate of interest. But the price of services from a

---

[1] If the machine lasts four years and was created with $100 of labor services a year ago, the depreciation would be roughly equal to about $25 (plus interest on the advance) for each year's full service—in effect, the value of past services now used up.

particular "capital good" is the rental rate of that machine.[2]

So far we have only identified kinds of payment and given them names. What determines their size? We must first note that in a production process of any good, almost invariably more than one input is used jointly. I and a power saw can make lumber. If we do, how much of the lumber did I make? How much did the power saw make? With joint resources it is impossible to assign what is produced by each input. Hence the question of payment according to production assumes the impossible—that is, a clear meaning of what each input produces, just as does the statement that you should be paid according to what you deserve or need. That tells us nothing except that whatever *I* think you should get is what you deserve or need. Whatever the emotional appeal of the statement that people are paid according to their product (or their need), it is a meaningless statement. Instead, what determines the payment for services of an input (that is, its price) is "demand and supply." In this chapter, we first identify a basic demand relationship for productive inputs. Then in later chapters, we introduce supply to analyze the pricing and allocation of these inputs.

[2] Why does economics use the term *capital goods* instead of *physical goods*? Probably to reflect the fact that the physical goods are durable and will be yielding services in the future at prices that must be adjusted for the interest rate if they are to be combined into a total value—just as we did earlier for annuities, present values, and future values in Chapter 7, on capital values. Since the present price or value of a capital good reflects the future services obtainable from it, the term capital value is a synonym for the price of a durable good—a capital good.

Varieties of Production Techniques

To assure that you understand the preceding question we list and illustrate a few basic propositions: (1) An unlimited variety of techniques exists by which any output may be produced. (2) Of these, some are technologically efficient. (3) Of all the techniques, one has the lowest cost, that is, is economically efficient. (4) The lower the relative price of an input, the greater the amount of its services that will be in the new economically efficient technique. (5) The demand for a productive input depends in part upon the amounts of other inputs. (6) The response in amount demanded of a productive input when price is changed is greater in the longer run. (7) Substitution among productive inputs occurs by altering productive techniques and also by altering output mixtures. (8) In a free-enterprise system (whether markets are open or closed) the price received by an input is dependent on its *marginal* productivity. We shall see that the input's marginal productivity depends on *more* than its inherent ability and effort. (9) The value of an input is derived from the market-revealed value of its end product to consumers.

Alternative Techniques Exist for Producing Every Good

Techniques differ in using different proportions of productive inputs. One uses more water and less cooling equipment; another fewer laborers and more power equipment. Houses can be built with varying combinations of power tools, precut lumber, on-site assembly, and common-laborer as-sistants. The variety of available techniques of operating a supermarket is enormous. Fewer butchers can devote their time only to cutting while lower-paid clerks sell the meat to custom-ers. There can be fewer butchers all using power cutting equipment and elaborate facilities, or there can be more butchers and simpler equip-ment. At the checking stand an expert cash-register operator can concentrate on checking purchases, with an automatic machine to deliver change to the customer, plus a moving belt to convey the groceries to the attendant who bags and boxes them. Or there could be more clerks and less equipment, fewer shelves, but still the same amount of grocery sales at the same rate (but at different cost).

This variety of possible techniques often es-capes our notice because we see similar ways in our own everyday experience. But if you travel to other countries or regions and look for these differences, you will see them. Alert businessmen watch competitors and other producers. Trade journals explain ways to improve production. Equipment salesmen and advertisements tell of different ways of doing things and seek to show how their ways are better. Employee representa-tives suggest that things are done differently in other firms. Business consultants and employees hired from other firms help copy different tech-niques.

A fundamental, pervasive property of produc-tion—*the variety of combinations of inputs that can be used to produce a product*—is illustrated by the data in Table 15–1. The table shows the amounts of outputs and different alternative com-binations of two inputs, labor and machines—

each unit of labor (and of machine) considered to be homogeneous (identical to all others of their kind) for simplicity of exposition. Which combina-tion is best?

**Two Types of Input:
An Expositional Simplification**

Just as we were able to use only two people in our earlier initial explanation of the gains from exchange and specialization, we will here speak of two general categories of productive resources —labor and capital resources. The basic prin-ciples are unaffected, but the exposition becomes more complicated if we try to deal with the enor-mous variety of resources.

1. Technological Efficiency

Table 15–1 identifies *some* of the several tech-niques that could produce, say, 277 units of X. It can be done by using 5 M and 2 L, or 4 M and 3 L, or 3 M and 5 L. Other combinations (tech-niques) are available if M and L are divisible (as we are assuming); thus, something like 3.5 M and 4 L will produce 277 X. All these combinations are *technologically* efficient: The outputs cannot be produced with less of both inputs. To produce 277 X with 2 L, the minimum required capital is 5 units. This combination requires .018 ($= 5/277$) units of capital per X produced. It is possible to be even more stringent with capital by using only 4 units of capital with 3 rather than only 2 labor. Then only .0144 ($= 4/277$) units of capital per unit of output are required. A naive person with his eyes set only on capital would use the second method. But there are still other techniques even stingier in their use of capital. For example, it is possible

Table 15–1. Production of X as Function
of Inputs of L and M

		Output of X					
	6	246	304	340	372	395	416
	5	224	277	310	340	360	376
Quantity	4	200	246	277	302	321	333
of	3	171	210	237	259	277	285
Machines	2	141	172	194	214	228	234
	1	100	121	138	152	162	165
		1	2	3	4	5	6
		Inputs of Labor					

For any combination of machines and labor indicated along
the left-hand and bottom sides, the entry in the table gives
the total output of X. For example, for four machines and
three units of labor, output is 277 of X. Note that 277 of X
can also be obtained with three machines combined with
five of labor. (Combinations with fractional amounts are
omitted.)

to require only .0108 ($= 3/277$) units of capital per
unit of X, if one uses the method that employs 5
labor, instead of just 2 or 3 labor. This method is
often called *technically* "efficient" (that is, uses
less) in capital per unit of output because it uses
less capital than the methods that used more
labor. However, it is wrong to think that capital
per unit of output should be minimized by using
more of other resources. If you replace the word
capital by the term "energy" or "BTUs" or "oil"
you will have a perfect example of the fallacy of
calling for "maximum efficient use of energy," as
the National Energy Act of 1975 does.

Rudimentary understanding of production reveals that to use less energy (or capital) we *must*
substitute for it some labor or other materials that
could instead be producing other valuable goods.
Clearly, it would be wasteful to curtail use of

energy by substituting other resources that could
produce more of other things that are more highly
valued than the energy saved.

This fallacy of concentrating on trying to reduce *one* input in production while ignoring the
required increase in costs for other, substituted
inputs is extremely common—so common, in fact,
that no one can read the newspaper or watch TV
without noting that someone recommends *greater*
efficiency in use of energy, gasoline, or you name
it. The least embarrassing interpretation of what
they are saying is that they are advocating the
discovery of some new, as yet unknown, method
of producing more—without more inputs. But saving of *any* input would be desirable. And that
more is better than less hardly requires stating.

2. Economic Efficiency

Among all the alternative techniques that are
technically efficient in energy, or floor space, or
labor, or paper, or you name it, which one is
best? For example, you can produce 277 X with
5 M with 2 L, or only 4 M but 3 L, or with 3 M but
4 L—and a vast number of other combinations. It
would be wasteful to *reduce* the amount of M
required per unit of X if reducing the input of
M requires using more of other inputs, L, which
cost (sacrifice) more than the value of the M that
is saved. It is not sensible to reduce the amount
of energy used in creating X—for example, miles
of travel or number of houses heated—if the other
inputs substituted for the energy will require sacrifice of greater value than the value of the
energy saved. Which of the various ways of producing 277 units of X will get those 277 units produced and at the same time *maximize the*

personal value of output producible with the remaining resources. More precisely, what is the least-cost method of producing 277 *X*? Asking for the least-cost method is simply another way of asking for the *most valuable other output* in addition to the 277 *X*. (Remember: *Cost is the sacrificed alternative value of output.*) To minimize costs is to maximize the personal value of the remaining feasible output. That is why economists often say "value-maximizing" rather than "cost-minimizing." But both are really the same. The personal value of the entire production of this and the other goods produced is maximized.

Rather than being narrow-minded or near-sighted (looking at the input of just one good and ignoring what is happening elsewhere) the economic criterion is of most general scope, encompassing the value of *all* goods—not just energy, or some kind of capital or particular labor. Those values will tend to be ignored only insofar as the goods we want to use are not purchasable in the market—which means: only insofar as property and exchange rights are not attached to those goods.

Many people erroneously think economic values are simply *money* values, that is, the value *of* money. But money is only the *common unit* in which relative values among nonmoney goods are measured. For example, you may recall that saying a barrel of oil is worth $10 and a bushel of soybeans is worth $5 is a convenient way of revealing that a barrel of oil is as valuable as two bushels of soybeans. And that is true for everyone who faces those prices. It does not mean that "money" is the value.

Society penalizes the use of an inappropriate criterion. The appropriate one depends *in part* upon the economic system. In a capitalist, open-market system, owners of productive resources are rewarded with higher wealth if they achieve the higher *market value* of the output obtainable with those resources. The further one is from that market value, the more surely can other people bid away those resources and put them to higher-valued uses. Open-market competition for access to resources makes it expensive to persist in using resources for less than highest personal value uses. You will lose ability to get or retain productive resources as they are bid away by users more successful at discerning wealth-maximizing uses or techniques of production. Your personal desire for more rather than less wealth will "force" you to choose higher-valued, or lower-cost, techniques, or to sell those resources to those who can do so. Whether you judge that to be a desirable solution depends upon your evaluation of the social, cultural, and economic consequences. At any rate, it is the criterion that operates in a capitalist society.

Efficient Production Techniques and Relative Prices of Inputs

If the price of machines were higher, say $45, and the price of labor lower, say $15, the economically efficient (lowest-cost) combination or process would have more of the now cheaper (relative to machines) labor and less of the relatively more expensive machines (5 *L* and 3 *M* instead of 3 *L* and 4 *M*). Conversely, if the price of labor had increased to $50 and the price of machines had fallen to $30, the economic process would have less labor and more machines (2 *L* and 5 *M*).

What is the point of this example? Simply that the lowest-cost (the economically efficient) input combination depends on the input prices; the

1, 2
3, 4
5, 6
7, 8
9, 10
11, 12
13, 14
15, 16
17, 18
19, 20

lower the price of an input relative to others, the more that will be in the new lowest-cost process.[3] The law of demand holds for productive resources—the lower the price of an input, the more that input is demanded in production. (In fact, the law of demand holds even more strongly for productive inputs than for consumers' goods because the various income effects discussed in connection with consumers' goods all operate here to increase the amount demanded as the price is lowered, or reduce it as the price is raised. But a demonstration of that would be too difficult here.)

The Law of Diminishing Marginal Physical Returns

The *marginal* physical product of an input is the *increase* in output consequent to a *unit increase* of that input. The marginal physical products obey the law of *diminishing marginal returns.* This law states: "As any input is increased by unit amounts, the marginal product, although

[3] From one point of view, the question of the appropriate combination of inputs may seem pointless. After all, at any moment there is a given amount of each productive resource in the community and hence a given overall ratio of inputs. With full use of resources the community can't help but use the resources in that given overall ratio. That is true for the community *as a whole,* but consistent with that overall, total ratio of inputs is an unlimited set of different subcombinations of use by the producers of various goods. The task is not, then, to select the average ratio for the economy, but the *specific allocation* for each of the many production enterprises competing for those resources. During the Arab oil embargo of 1974 this problem was made obvious, primarily by the doomed efforts of politicians to solve it rather than letting the market-price system do it. Why did they try it? Your answer is as good as ours.

Table 15–2. Marginal Physical Productivities of Labor

		Amount of Labor					
		1	2	3	4	5	6
Associated Quantity of Machines	6	246	58	36	32	23	21
	5	224	53	33	30	20	16
	4	200	46	31	25	19	12
	3	171	39	27	22	18	8
	2	141	31	22	20	14	6
	1	100	21	17	14	10	3

possibly increasing at first to a maximum (called the point of diminishing marginal returns), will thereafter decrease." Note that it is the increment, not the total, that decreases.

For example, examine the total output data in Table 15–1 *along one horizontal row;* the row with three units of equipment shows total outputs of 171, 210, 237, 259, 277, and 285 as labor increases. The *increments* in total output (marginal physical products of labor) are shown in Table 15–2, which must be read along the *horizontal rows;* each row is for a fixed associated amount of capital. Each unit increase of labor used jointly with the constant amount of equipment yields a higher rate of output. The daily output rate increases by 39 from 171 to 210 as a second unit of labor is applied to three units of equipment. The increment of output of X with the third unit of labor is 27 (237 − 210). The increment of output for the fourth unit of labor is 22.

A graph of diminishing marginal products of labor, for equipment fixed at three units, is in Figure 15–2. Also shown (with dashed lines) is a graph of diminishing marginal products of labor, if equipment were fixed at *four* units. To adjust

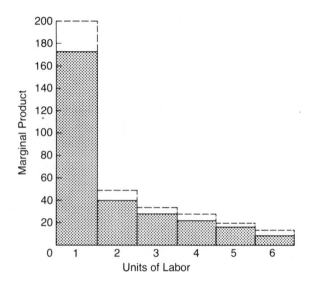

Figure 15–2. Marginal-product Schedules of Labor

Marginal-product schedules of labor with three units of capital (solid line) and with four units of capital (dashed line). Heights of each bar are entries shown in Table 15–2. Diminishing heights, from left to right, portray diminishing marginal productivity.

to this larger rate of input of labor, the equipment can be rearranged to its most effective form for the larger amount of labor.

What Is a Marginal Product? Who Produces It? Whose Is It?

When four units of labor and three of equipment are used, the total output is 259 *X*. How much of that 259 *X* is due to the equipment and how much to the labor? This is not a meaningful question. The concept of *marginal* product does not measure "how much an input produces." What it does measure is something else. For example, according to Table 15–2 the marginal product of four

units of labor (as compared to three units of labor), when used jointly with three units of capital equipment, is 22 units of *X*. Those 22 units of *X* are *not* produced by the fourth unit of labor. Instead, that is the increase in the total when four units of labor are used instead of three units, along with three units of equipment. If a basketball team used six men instead of five, should the sixth man say he produced the extra points? All that can be validly asserted is that six of them produce more than five do, and the increase is what is meant by the marginal product for six people. Instead of the marginal product of the sixth worker, then, we would more accurately speak of the marginal product at six units of la-uct.[6]

Implications of Diminishing Marginal Productivity

All Qualities of Goods Are Used

Suppose that, contrary to the law of diminishing marginal productivity, there were always increasing or constant marginal productivity. With a small plot of the best soil, a farmer could, by adding successive increments of labor to that soil, obtain successively larger or contant increments of output. He would put no labor on any other equally fertile soil since the marginal product would not be as large there—given *increasing* marginal productivity of labor on the best soil. And certainly he would not apply any resources to inferior soil. All labor in the production of wheat would be concentrated on the one small piece of land best for wheat. But in fact inferior

[4] Review the similarity to the analogous concept of marginal revenue.

land is also used for every crop. Farmers do so because the greater amount of labor applied to the superior land has moved the farmer down the diminishing marginal-productivity curve of labor on that land to equality with the marginal product obtained by applying a unit of labor to inferior land. Thus, labor is applied *in varying amounts* to all types of land, not merely to the best. This varied allocation is implied by diminishing marginal productivity, on different qualities of land. And this holds for all types of resources. In sum, we see all grades of resources being used, with superior resources usually used more intensively (that is, with relatively more of other resources).

We must interpret the marginal product in value terms; in our example, the marginal product of a third unit of labor (with four units of capital) is 31 physical units of product. If each unit is worth $2, the marginal-value product at three units of labor is $62.

In general, the relevant marginal product is the marginal *value* product. Anything that increases either the physical output or its price will increase the marginal-*value* product of the input concerned.

More Used at Lower Prices

Diminishing marginal-value productivity is one reason that larger amounts of an input are demanded at lower prices.[5] If the marginal-value product with another unit of labor exceeded the wage rate, it would pay to hire more labor. But if the price of that input were higher, it would pay

to hire less. The appropriate (wealth-maximizing) amount of any input to use in production is the amount at which the marginal-*value* product is brought down (or raised—by hiring less of the input) to equality with the price of the input. Don't spend a dollar more for a nickel's worth of product.[6]

Derived Demand for Productive Resources

Why the demand for an input is called a *derived* demand is now apparent. The marginal-*value* product of an input reflects the value of its final product as judged by consumers. If consumers' valuation of that product should rise, the value of, and hence demand for, the inputs to make that product will rise. To emphasize this dependence of the value and demand for an input on the value of the product to the ultimate consumer, the term *derived demand* is used in speaking of the demand for productive inputs.

Much of the discussion can be summarized by a graph of the *demand for an input* (Figure 15–3). The amounts of the input are assumed to be divisible, and the curve portrays the relationship between the price of the productive input and the amount that would be demanded for production (with allowance for adjustments in output

---

[5] It is not the only reason. Nor is it necessary for every case, but the other factors are too complex to include at this level of analysis.

[6] In symbolic, abbreviated form for labor, L:

$(p) \times (MpL)$ is brought to equality with p_L by altering the amount of L, where p is the price of the product, MpL is the marginal physical product of labor, and p_L is the price of labor.

The same holds true for capital:

$(p) \times (MpC)$ is brought to equality with p_C, and likewise for any kind of input.

21

rate and price and amounts of jointly used inputs). The negative relationship between price
and the amount demanded conforms to the fundamental law of demand for any good. The position and shape of the demand curve depends
upon the amounts of other inputs that can be
most profitably used jointly with this input—in
other words, the curve depends upon the costs
of other inputs.

At any specified price of inputs the amount of
the input demanded will be given by the demand
schedule. Since the height of demand for any input reflects the marginal productivity of that good
at each different amount of the good, the intersection of a horizontal price line with a demand
curve gives the amount of the input employed
and also shows an equality between the price
and the marginal productivity of the input *for the
amount that it is most profitable to employ.*

The italicized phrase is an important condition.
Equality of wage or rent for the input to its marginal product may not occur if the firm is restricted in its choice of inputs at given prices,
or if the firm lacks sufficient information about
the marginal productivity of its inputs.

Determinants of
Marginal-Productivity Schedule

The marginal productivity of any worker is a function not only of his talents and education but also
of the quality and quantity of other jointly used
inputs. This does not mean merely the other
goods he works with, as a seamstress with a
needle, or a driver with a truck. It includes also
the environment provided by the equipment and
the resources of the whole economy. The trans-

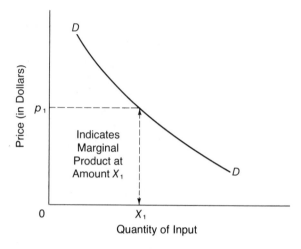

Figure 15–3. Marginal Productivities and Demand Curves for
Inputs

*At amount of good X_1, the marginal product to the buyer is
shown by the height of the curve DD. At price p_1, the amount
X_1 would be bought, at which the marketable marginal product obtained by the employer from using X is equal to the
price of X. At any larger amount than X, the marketable marginal product would be less than price p_1, and wealth of
employer would be decreased.*

portation system, the education and technology
of other workers, the effectiveness of the market
in facilitating specialization and exchange, the
level of honesty, the extent to which contracts are
honored—all of these are examples of *cooperative resources.* Move the carpenters in any small
U.S. city to India, Morocco, Brazil, or Indonesia.
Their marginal productivity would be a lot lower
simply because there is less jointly available
"capital." A richer country with lots of capital
equipment and stable, market-facilitating institutions is a better place for a given amount of labor. While the productivity of the American car-

penters would be less in other countries than in the United States, the productivity would be greater than for natives of those countries—a reflection of the greater education of the Americans.[7]

Speed of Substitution

Substituting and altering amounts of inputs are costly activities. One must learn of new ways, administer decisions, rearrange inputs, and schedule the timing of new inputs. The pace of substitution in response to new prices depends upon adjustment costs; the amount of substitution therefore depends on how much time has elapsed since the price change. The longer the

---

[7] In Table 15–2, the marginal product of labor depends upon which row you read. The more machines (the upper rows), the greater the marginal products of labor. The two resources are said to be *complementary*. The opposite effect could have occurred: larger amounts of machinery might have caused smaller marginal products for labor. Labor and machines then are called *substitutes*. Unfortunately, this is very misleading terminology. Two inputs are substitutes for each other even though they are complements in the sense just indicated. The term *substitutes* has two different meanings: (1) It is possible to produce some specified rate of output with less of one input and more of another. (2) More of one input causes a *lower* marginal product for the existing amount of the *other* resource. It is in the former sense that the term *substitutable* is ordinarily used. A more precise term for the second effect would be *negative cross-marginal productivity*, suggesting that the effect of increasing one resource "crosses over" to another resource and lowers its marginal product. In Table 15–1 there is positive *cross*-marginal productivity and negative *self*-marginal productivity (called the law of *diminishing* marginal returns).

In the interaction between two joint inputs, we cannot tell in advance whether an increase in the amount of one will raise or lower the marginal productivity of the other. But whatever the effect on the marginal productivity, the implied demand schedule for any input retains a negative slope with respect to its own price.

---

time, the more the substitution among inputs. As in consumers' behavior, the demand for productive inputs is more elastic with respect to a price change, the longer the time since the price change. And it can be represented by different demand curves for different times after the price changes.

The demand for an input in the *immediate* period may show little response to prices, because quick changes can be made only at high adjustment costs. But in the ensuing weeks, adjustments can be made at a less costly, more economic pace. Since they are made after a substantial interval, the changes usually fail to be identified as consequences of the input price change. Of course, the employer need not announce that he no longer will buy so much of their services because their price is higher. He simply says that the marginal-value product isn't big enough to warrant their continued employment.

An example is the rise in wages of Chicago elevator operators. Formerly, wages were $1 to $1.25 an hour, until a minimum wage of $2.40 an hour was imposed for operators in downtown (not suburban) Chicago buildings. Owners of some of those buildings then found it profitable to use automatic elevators, which annually cost about $8000. With two shifts of operators, the higher wage of $2.40 per hour raised the cost of manually operated elevators to about $10,000 per year. Clearly, it paid the owner to "automate." This took several months. When the elevator operators were discharged several months later, after having been paid $2.40 an hour for the intervening time, they were not likely to understand that it was a result of the higher wage, since that had been "initiated" a long time ago. They blamed it on "automation." This is not to say that all introduction of automatic equipment is a response to higher wages (as we shall see in the next chapters).

Substitution among Products and among Firms

Substitution among inputs occurs in indirect ways. A lower price of an input leads to lower costs of its products. More of the consumer goods that use more of the now relatively cheaper inputs will be produced and thus become less costly. In this way substitution among inputs occurs through substitution by consumers among the final produced goods. If the price of plastics falls relative to glass, the supply schedule of plastic containers increases relative to that of glass bottles; the price of plastic containers falls; the consumer buys more plastic containers; and plastics are thereby substituted for glass. As another example, higher wages for carpenters will induce more power saws and more standardization with less carpentering service. Wood-paneled walls will be displaced by plaster, and wooden window frames with steel and aluminum window frames. This effect, operating through the consumer's substitution of different consumer goods, is called *interproduct* substitution.

One warning: The productivity of one input may be indirect. It may provide better working conditions for the other inputs so they can be obtained at lower prices, such as provision of sanitary and safety facilities. Its marginal productivity is its contribution to lower costs of getting other inputs —rather than to increased output, as too narrowly suggested by our earlier examples of marginal productivity.

The demand relationship between the price of an input and its rate of employment is a result of more than deliberate adjustments of each producer. Even if no producer were to substitute in response to an input price change, each would experience a change in his wealth. Firms nearer the new, more-efficient combination of input will have a greater increase in wealth than those firms whose input techniques are now less efficient.

Competition in the market tests and *favors the adoption* of the more appropriate existing techniques by rewarding their users with greater profits and growth—whether or not the individual producers themselves *adapt* to the new price situation. Adaptation will occur as productive techniques of the more successful firms are copied. A producer imitating the successful firm may not know marginal productivities of various inputs. All he knows is what techniques succeeded best. Not even the initially successful firm has to know the marginal products. All it has to do is happen to be nearest the "right" combination. Whether it got there through management's calculating marginal productivities via extensive research and testing, with the help of astrologers and consulting economists, or by sheer luck is irrelevant. Being there is sufficient.

Competition among firms with different productive techniques is a selective survival force, just as is deliberate, knowledgeable selection by one producer among alternative available production techniques. Market competition *among* firms adds its force to the adjustment of production techniques in input prices *within* a firm.

22, 23
24, 25
26

Generality of Marginal Product and Derived Demand

Is Total Product Sufficient?

The payment for a unit of productive input is its price. If we multiply the number of employed units by the marginal product, which also equals its price in equilibrium, we get the income to that resource. For example, suppose that in Table 15–1 we were employing three units of labor and one unit of capital equipment, because the price of labor was $17 while the price of the equipment was $138. We now compute the total payments to capital equipment and labor from our firm. Three units of labor at $17 each is $51 while for the one unit of equipment $138 is paid. The total payments to the productive resources are $51 + $138 = $189, an amount that *exceeds* the total value of the output produced, $138. How can a producer continue in this situation? How can inputs be paid more than the total product? The employer of these productive inputs promised them he would make up any loss out of his wealth. That's one of his functions. But it is not something he can do indefinitely.

The "loss-resulting" production will be abandoned. Resources will be discharged from that business and that product. Economywide prices of inputs are bid down or output prices increased as the output becomes smaller. Remaining employers will now be able to break even because the input prices are lower. No inconsistency is inherent in the *resulting* open-market equilibrium.

Abstractions and Validity

We really do not have to assume that there are different, internally homogeneous resources. Every one can be different; equality between the marginal-value product and prices may not be achievable. Instead of equality of marginal-value product and price, an *in*equality condition suffices; inputs will be employed up to the point beyond which the marginal-value product of the input would be smaller than the marginal cost of the input.

Many assumptions commonly used in the exposition of marginal-productivity principles of the demand for productive resources are deliberate simplifications. All theories make overly strong assumptions for ease of logical analysis. They ignore idiosyncrasies in the interest of concentrating on basic common phenomena. For example, a theory relating caloric intake to body weight can assume, as a means of abstracting from incidental details, that all people are alike (for a given age and sex); then certain consequences are implied for an increase in caloric intake. It is doubtful that you would challenge the validity of that implication by saying that people are not exactly alike, or that when caloric intake is increased other events impinge on the individuals—such as their getting sick or other coincident causes. Of course, the complexities could be included; but then the theory would be cumbersome in requiring the use of more complex methods of notation, logic, mathematics, etc. Do not presume that one theory is necessarily better because it is more detailed in its premises and assumptions, and considers more variables.

Pecuniary and Nonpecuniary
Productivity and "Discrimination"

Is the marginal-productivity principle applicable only to capitalist economies? No, it is valid in every economy. In the capitalist economy, the increase in wealth belongs to an identifiable *private* owner or group of owners. If, however, the operator were not able to keep the profits (or did not have to pay the losses) of his business, he would more heavily weigh other potential benefits. He would be more disposed to employ more congenial colleagues (say, only men) if he weren't able to retain the profits of hiring women at lower wages who were equally productive of pecuniary value of marketable goods. For example, a legal limitation on profits or a heavily taxed profit would induce more employment of inputs more loaded with nonmonetary sources of benefit to employers—good looks, racial and religious characteristics, friends, prestige, relaxation, etc. Nonpecuniary discrimination is therefore cheaper and will be more common. Production will be less closely oriented to market demands and exchange values. Marketable wealth is only one of the "products" yielded by inputs. Because government agencies are not privately owned or profit-seeking, they will be more heavily influenced by attributes of inputs less related to the productivity of pecuniary income. If the economic rules only mildly penalize people for not increasing marketable wealth when possible, then agents will be less influenced by market value productivity. The generalized marginal-productivity principle stands, as long as one incorporates all the "products" of inputs.

Nothing in the analysis implies that behavior

27, 28
29, 30
31, 32

that is not responsive to pecuniary value of output is in itself undesirable. That depends upon whether or not one prefers the economic, cultural, and political implications of a noncentrally directed open-market, private-property exchange system. Others may think they could achieve their idea of a better way of life through a different mix of types of competition for resolving conflicts of interests in the presence of scarcity; they can try to reduce the scope of that open-market system. For example, people with certain kinds of personalities may find competition for political power more favorable to them than market competition. They will expect to gain from extension of government authority.

Fluctuations in
Employment and Unemployment

The flow of services from households to firms is not always smooth, although there are powerful forces enabling the desired employment rate for most resources. In general, the market economy has operated remarkably close to that employment situation. In fact, from the preceeding analysis it would be surprising if it did not do so. After all, there are infinitely many jobs available to be performed. (What else does scarcity mean?) The task is to decide which of the infinite range of scarcities one should strive to reduce. But some unemployment and idle resources are with us persistently in varying degree. How can this be explained? Consideration of that is delayed until we complete the analysis of resource-markets operation and the determination of individual incomes and wealth.

Summary

1. Substitutability among amounts of all productive inputs is feasible and pervasive.
2. Wealth-maximizing producers reveal a market demand for inputs inversely (or negatively) related to their price. The inverse relationship with price of the input results from (a) substitutability among inputs, (b) diminishing marginal-value productivity (which reflects both a decreasing marginal physical productivity and a lower price of the output as more is supplied), and (c) consumers' substitution of cheaper for dearer goods.
3. A longer-period demand for inputs is more elastic. The effect of a price change on amounts of inputs used will be less pronounced immediately than with the passing of time.
4. An increased supply of any resource lowers its price, which induces a shift in profitable techniques to more of that lower-priced input. The profitable technique of production is revised toward more use of more-plentiful, cheaper inputs—without central direction or planning—provided producers are not constrained by law to use inputs in proportions other than those that are profitable in the light of market prices.
5. Since income (wealth) of any productive resource is determined by its selling price, incomes of owners of productive resources (human and nonhuman) are determined in a free market by the forces of demand and supply. The demand for resources reflects their marginal productivities in highest-valued uses. For this reason, this analysis is often erroneously called the marginal-productivity theory of pricing of productive resources. More accurately, it is the marginal-productivity theory of demand for productive resources.
6. The marginal productivity of any input depends not only on the amount of the input and on its skills but also on those inputs with which it can work jointly.
7. The marginal-productivity basis for demand applies to all types of economies. Economies based on different systems of control and coordination (different property rights and political authority) differ in the costs borne by decision-makers. This does not destroy the validity of the marginal-productivity theory of demand—whether it be for pecuniary or nonpecuniary services of productive resources. Nor does it have any bearing on how prices are set. They may be set by decree or custom. But the theory is invalid as an explanation of rates of use and assignment to various productive activities if the allocations are controlled by political decree or custom.
8. The demand for productive resources is called derived demand because it is derived from the value of their final products to consumers. The consumer's valuation of the final product, imputed back to the responsible productive resources, determines the value of the productive resources in that activity.

Questions

1. "Chicago, August 10, 1962. A federal judge blocked today the firing of thousands of workers on the nation's railroads pending

final court ruling on the legality of the drastic economy. Judge Perry said, 'I have preserved and protected the right of appeal,' adding that he felt an interim decision affecting both jobs and capital must be resolved in favor of jobs and men." In what sense can it be contended instead that the issue is one between jobs *and jobs,* rather than between jobs and capital?

2. Who is substituted for whom when a firm uses one typist, an electric typewriter, and a copying machine rather than two typists and two manual typewriters? This is called a substitution of capital for labor. Why is that misleading?

3. "The advent of the one-man bus involved more capital equipment: an automatically operated coin box and a door-control device —to name two of the capital goods that replaced the conductor."

a. Is this a case of capital replacing labor? Where?

b. Is it a case of labor replacing labor? Where?

c. Is it a case of no substitution for labor at all, but instead a job revision with a greater total output? Where?

*4. "Invention and the lower cost of power in the home have replaced the domestic servant by capital equipment. Without that machinery more people would be working in homes as 'servants.' But the replacement of domestic employees by capital has not led to the replacement of labor. The released labor is used elsewhere."

a. Can you suggest where?

b. What other goods are more plentiful because of the advent of domestic machinery?

c. Who was aided and who was hurt by the use of the vacuum cleaner, washing machine, water heater, forced-air furnace, garbage disposal, automatic oven, electric mixer, and refrigerator?

5. The electric refrigerator replaced the iceman with capital. By eliminating (making other means cheaper) the job of the iceman, was the total number of jobs reduced? Explain.

6. "Automation does not mean there will be more people than jobs available. It does not mean fewer jobs for unskilled people—in fact a person can be less skilled if all he has to do is punch buttons, pull triggers, and turn steering wheels, compared to driving a team of horses, shooting a bow and arrow, or wielding a chisel." Do you agree?" If so, why? If not, why not?

7. "A molecule of sugar is composed of a fixed ratio of atoms of hydrogen, carbon, and oxygen; it follows that there is no substitutability of inputs in the manufacture of sugar."

a. Do you agree? Why?

*b. Is the reasoning in the preceding question applicable to every other kind of good that can be manufactured—whether or not the good is composed of a fixed ratio of components? For example, is the reasoning applicable to making gasoline, running a railroad, operating a bus, building a house, or selling groceries?

8. Assume that wage rates of gardeners were to double because of reduced supply of gardeners, with an unchanged demand.

a. What substitution for gardeners would occur?

b. Where or from whom could you learn about the available substitution techniques?

9. Why is economic efficiency a more general test than technical efficiency?

10. There are two kinds of economic efficiency—one of cost minimization and one of profit maximization. In what sense is profit maximization a more general criterion of efficiency?

11. In Iowa the yield of wheat is 30 bushels per acre; in Washington it is 50 bushels per acre. Which is better?

12. Jet engines are given an efficiency rating according to the thrust generated per pound of engine weight. Explain why that is an inadequate measure of efficiency.

13. Steers can be bred with such superb qualities that they will sell for about 50 percent more per pound than the standard steers raised for meat. Which type should the farmer raise? Give the answer in terms of technological versus economic efficiency.

14. A high-fidelity stereo sound system is called efficient if it uses a low amount of electric power per decibel of sound generated. Why is that technical efficiency not an adequate efficiency criterion for choosing among sound systems, even if the quality of the sound were the same?

15. A water-storage dam is to be built, and engineers, asked for advice, propose a dam and attest to its efficiency.

   *a. If they attest to its technical efficiency, does that still leave open the question of its economic efficiency? For example, if the value of the water stored is less than the cost of impounding and distributing it, is the dam, though it may be technically efficient, an economically efficient one?

   b. This problem extends the notion of economic efficiency beyond the selection of the cheapest way of doing something. Economic efficiency is extended to include what?

16. The United States Federal Communication Commission says rights to use the radio-frequency spectrum should be assigned to permit maximum usage.

   a. Explain why that statement as it stands is meaningless and useless.

   *b. Would it have been meaningful to say rights should be assigned to achieve efficient use? What would be the criterion of efficiency?

17. After adding 100 to all the output data in Table 15–1, recompute the marginal products of labor and the marginal products of capital. (This is not as hard and long a problem as it may at first seem.)

18. In Table 15–1, the data are *values* of output, where, for simplicity, each physical unit was assumed to be salable for $1. Suppose instead that the output can be sold for $2 each.

   a. Recompute the "marginal value-products" for labor and for capital.

   b. What is the effect of a rise in price of the product on the marginal-value productivity of inputs?

19. Use the data of Table 15–1 to answer the following questions:

   a. Defining efficient production as the lowest-cost methods of production, which method is the efficient method for producing 277 units of X if the price of labor is $60 and if the price of capital is $70?

   b. If the price of capital is $20 per unit and if labor is $10 per unit, which is the efficient way to produce 228 units of X: with 2 capital and 5 labor or with 5.1 capital and 1 labor?

c. Which is cheaper (that is, efficient) if the prices are $2 and $1 respectively?

*d. $60 and $30 respectively?

*e. So long as the prices bear the same ratios to each other, will the same method remain the cheaper method?

20. In Table 15–2, is the law of diminishing marginal returns illustrated by the decreasing values as one reads a row from left to right, or as one reads a column from bottom to top?

21. The law of diminishing returns is a law of diminishing *marginal* returns. What is the difference between diminishing *total* returns and diminishing *marginal* returns?

22. You operate a factory and discover that some resource used obtains *increasing* marginal returns.

a. What would you do?

*b. Does this suggest that we will never find any firm using an amount of resources involving increasing marginal returns?

23. "If the ratio of the price of resource A to the price of resource B exceeds the ratio of the marginal value-products of A to B, it will be efficient to decrease the employment of A relative to B." Explain why.

24. Adjustments in the amount of resources used so as to equate the *absolute* prices of each resource with its marginal value productivity imply more than does the equality of the *ratios* of prices to the ratios of marginal productivities. What is the stronger implication?

25. "If a firm uses resources efficiently, a change in their prices will induce a change in the relative amounts employed." What will induce that change—some directive from a central planning agency, the social consciousness of the employer, or what?

26. "Even if only one combination of productive inputs could be used to produce some good, there would still be substitution among productive resources in response to changes in their prices." Explain what that substitution is and how it would be induced.

27. According to the analyses developed in this chapter, resources will be employed in open markets in amounts at which marginal value-product is not less than price. That also determines their earnings (price times the number of units employed).

a. What ensures that the total earnings will not exceed the value of the total output?

b. Who makes up the difference if payments exceed the value of output?

c. If the payments are less than the total value of output, who gets the difference?

d. In each case, what forces revise payments toward equality with value of output?

28. When former Defense Secretary McNamara recommended against building nuclear rather than oil-fueled airplane carriers because the nuclear system was more expensive, Senator Pastore of Rhode Island is reported to have said that if we had looked at economics we would never have shifted from wooden sailing ships to steel, oil-fueled ships. Whatever the Congressman may have said, is the asserted remark correct? Explain.

29. Suppose you operate a publicly owned factory in which profits cannot be retained.

a. What would be your criterion of resource use in production?

*b. What would induce you to act in accord with that criterion?

c. Would you have any incentive to adjust the use of resources to preserve the equality of the ratios of prices and marginal productivities—that is, to minimize the cost of the output? Explain.

30. "In a socialist state it is difficult for the state to own the producers' goods that are involved in artistic creativity—the human brain and body. Consequently musicians, artists, authors, and poets will be more able to behave in deviant, unorthodox, nonnationalistic ways than those whose earnings are more dependent upon state-owned resources—machines, factories, land, etc. In a capitalistic system this difference would not be present."

a. What premises underlie the propositions?

*b. Would your preference for one system over another be influenced by the validity of those propositions? Why?

31. In Russia and China, two socialist states in which most producers' goods (goods with which you can earn a living) are owned by the government, targets are assigned to factories in terms of the total value of the output (not profits) they are supposed to produce. Plant managers are told to accomplish and overfulfill targets as much as possible. Prices are set by law.

a. Is it desirable to have these targets overfulfilled?

b. Is it more desirable to state a target for each particular good in terms of total value of output than in terms of maximizing profits? What are the differences in performance that will be induced?

*c. Which criterion is more likely to provide a more effective incentive for the manager?

32. Assume that you are a member of a minority group in some country and have reason to doubt that your private-property rights would be enforced and respected in that community.

a. In what forms of capital would you invest?

b. What kinds of skills (as forms of accumulations of wealth) would you encourage for your children?

c. Do you know of any evidence of such actual behavior by minority groups?

16

Wages and Employment

Never Too Few Jobs

Scarcity of goods means that more goods are demanded than available, which means there are too many jobs and tasks still available! The problem is to discover which out of all of them is most valuable to do, rather than wastefully working on second-best jobs. For example: More roads could be improved, more police work would be useful, a lot more national defense activity would be useful, many houses could be repaired and more could be built, more food can be grown by cultivating and irrigating land, more repairmen can be used in service stations, more teachers would enable smaller classes—and so on ad infinitum. Of course, some of those may seem absurd, and they are absurd because obviously they are not the most valuable things to be done with our limited supply of labor and effort. The problem is not finding work—it is too much work, too many employment opportunities, with the result that we devote time and effort to trying to discover which ones are the most valuable activities. An unemployed person could readily find innumerable things to do, but he knows it would be wasteful to do those things when there are other tasks of greater value—if he and others could agree on which ones they were and what their value was.

The preceding paragraph may seem strange and contrary to much of what you had previously heard. But it is correct. Yet it does not mean the unemployed have no excuse for being unemployed or that they are wasteful in being unemployed—nor, on the other hand, that it is entirely someone else's fault. The issues are more complicated, as we shall see in later chapters. But for the moment do not fall prey to the fallacy that unemployment exists because there are too few jobs.

Supply of Labor

In the United States, of 150 million able-bodied adults (over the age of 16) about 90 million (or 60 percent) are in the market labor force—that is, are employed or seeking employment for money wages. The *market labor participation* rate has remained close to 60 percent since the turn of the century. Almost 80 percent of the males are in that labor force. Decreases in participation by teenagers and people over 65 were almost exactly offset by increases in female entry. Over 40 percent of women are now in the labor market, almost twice the rate of 1900, probably reflecting increased education for women, ready-cooked and processed foods, appliances permitting more substitution of capital goods for household labor, and rises in money wages from outside jobs for women relative to their productivity in the home.[1]

Of the 90 million people in the market labor force, most are in *service* (nonmanufacturing) industries—over 45 million, compared to about 30 million in manufacturing industries, with less than

---

[1] Although the preceding data refer to people working in the labor market for pay, perhaps the largest class of workers are housewives managing households as wives and mothers, rather than as hired employees. We estimate that something like 30 to 50 million women are heads of households. It is regrettable that economic analysis and official data have not been directed more fully to the magnitude of their contribution to the national income. Typically, national income is measured in terms of marketed products and services and hence does not include the value of the household head ser-

5 million in agriculture, 2.5 million in the military, and unemployed of about 5 million.

Figure 16–1 shows the labor force allocation by type of goods produced. The distribution by type of skills or tasks is in Figure 16–2. About 24 percent of the labor force had less than a full high school education, while over 25 percent received at least some college education. The former percentage is falling rapidly, and the latter is rising.

Roughly 50 of the 65 million males 16 years or older are employed (most of the remainder are in school), and of the 70 million women 16 years or older about 30 million are employees in the market while the rest are in school, or are not seeking market employment, or are full-time wives and mothers. (About 5 percent of the work force holds two jobs.)

Whatever the population size, the proportion of adults seeking work in the market depends on the market reward for work. The number in the market labor force may respond according to the line SS in Figure 16–3, showing more people entering the labor force or working longer hours at higher wage rates. However, a higher employee income provided by the higher wages may decrease the amount of labor supplied as people seek jobs of shorter hours, or as wives work less because their husbands earn more. Whether we have

vices. We shall only note that estimates of the value of services by household heads in managing and performing the variety of activities of a household (chefs, purchasing agents, nurses, decorators, social service workers, secretaries, gardeners, tailors, chauffeurs, maids, psychiatrists, etc.) indicate a value on average close to about $7000 per family head in 1974. Considering the fact that there are about 30 to 50 million families of various sizes, that is roughly in the neighborhood of, say, $300 billion—about one third the size of the currently measured national marketed income.

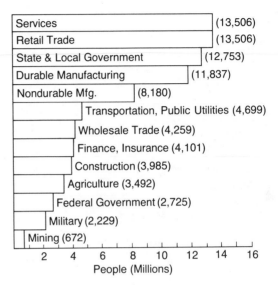

Figure 16–1. Number of People Working, by Industries, 1974

Source: U.S. Department of Labor, Manpower Report of the President, 1975

The overall category of service workers is here classified as subcategories like retail work, finance and insurance, and government employees. The category here called services includes workers in amusement, entertainment, recreation, travel and hotels, education, health, etc.

reached that "reversing" level of wages is difficult to establish. Nevertheless, one component that reduces the amount of labor supplied is the reduced number of hours people prefer to work in a week; it has gradually fallen from 60 to 40 in the last hundred years.

In analyzing how the wage rate affects the amount of labor supplied, we should note two distinctions. The first is between a transient and a permanent rise in wage rates. A temporary increase, say for a weekend or for a couple of months, does not constitute as significant an in-

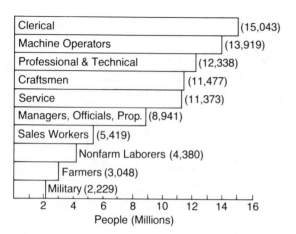

Figure 16–2. Number of People Working, by Skills, 1974

Source: U.S. Dept. of Labor, Manpower Report of the President, *1975*

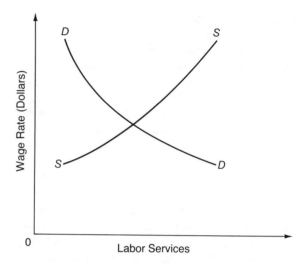

Figure 16–3. Demand and Supply of Labor to Segments of the Economy

For any segment of the economy, be it a firm or an industry, the supply-of-labor curve rises with higher wages, as labor is attracted from other segments or from the nonlabor-force portion of population into the labor force.

crease in wage rates as would a permanent increase. The second distinction is between the supply of labor to an individual employer and that to the economy as a whole. The amount supplied in the total economy may decrease with permanently higher wages, yet the amount supplied may increase to any sector that raises its wages relative to other sectors of the economy.

Labor Service Is a Commodity

"Labor is not a commodity" is a battle cry of some labor groups. Whatever its emotional appeal, the assertion is misleading. Labor *services* are bought and sold daily in the market. What *is* different about labor are the market procedures: the absence of buying and selling of *people,* and the personal involvement among persons during

work.[2] Private-property rights to one's own labor is restricted if he is prohibited from selling his services to other persons at mutually satisfactory terms, or if he cannot migrate to another area to sell his labor services. People are not always allowed to work where or for whom they please on whatever terms are mutually agreeable. Nor is

[2] The ban against selling all one's future services for a single advance payment of the kind for which he could sell other things does not prevent a person from converting some of his future earnings into present wealth. He can borrow now to buy a house and car and repay out of the future income. In this way, he has exchanged part of his future earnings for present goods. Without the right to borrow or to mortgage wealth as security or to buy on the installment plan, people would be at a greater disadvantage in adjusting consumption to the present wealth value of future earnings.

entry into all occupations unrestricted. For example, I could not legally sell psychiatric, medical, or dental services to you. Laws dictate qualifications, permissible wages, hours of work per day, and working conditions.

Economic analysis denies (and very correctly) that, in the absence of legal protection for labor, employers could or would grind wages down to some minimum survival level. An analogy will suggest why. Why are rents on land not ground down by renters to zero? The demands by those who would use the land bid up the rents. Simple competition among users is in operation. And so it is for labor services. The uses and values to which labor services could be put are revealed by all who compete for those services. Potential employers bid wages to whatever level enables them to get an amount of labor that can be put to profitable use. That may be very high if labor is relatively scarce or relatively productive. The price and quantity of labor services employed, like every other good, depends upon demand and supply forces.

Figure 16–3 represents demand and supply forces for some type of labor. The higher the wages offered, the greater the amount of labor supplied. But the higher the wage asked, the less is the amount of labor demanded. Whatever increases demand for labor will increase wage rates; whatever increases supply will reduce wage rates. We know from the last chapter that greater skills and education invested in labor increase demand because the marginal productivity will be increased. Similarly, if the final product is more highly valued by consumers, the marginal value of labor services increases, and hence the demand for labor will increase. Or, if the amount of associated equipment is such that the marginal

productivity of labor is increased, the demand for labor will be increased. So we have three factors that can increase the wages of labor by increasing the demand for labor: (1) increased productive ability by investment in training; (2) increased consumer demand for, and hence higher value and price of, the final output; and (3) increased associated productive capital equipment.

On the supply side an increased number of people will shift the supply curve to the right and lower the going wage. However, if a high market wage were imposed by some outside agency, fewer will be employed in that industry, with the excessive unemployed labor ultimately shifting to other, lower-wage occupations or withdrawing from the labor force.

These simple, powerful propositions are often concealed by the institutional details, customs, and paraphenalia of labor markets. We now give a few applications to see how the underlying open-market demand and supply analysis can be applied and interpreted.

Open-Market Wage Rates

Demand-and-supply determination of wages and employment in open markets is similar in principle, if not in form, to that for any good. People are free agents and can quit or change jobs; they can change jobs when they know of more attractive openings. Employees entertain offers from other employers, also. To retain employees an employer must match offers of other employers. An employer who does so through periodic wage and salary reviews and raises without forcing employees to first seek other offers and then ask for raises (counter offers) will pay no higher wages. Instead, in being known to take the initiative in anticipating market offers, he will find more employees willing to work for him than if he tried to impose all the costs of job comparison on employees.

Many employers periodically review and raise wages without an employee's obtaining a competing offer, or because unions demand higher wages. Thus it may appear that wages are not set by market competition but are instead adjusted simply through "custom" or internal employee pressure. Nevertheless market competition is in fact present; the employer is meeting it by "re-hiring" or keeping his existing employees from going elsewhere, as they would if he did not meet competitive wages and working conditions. It is instructive to consider an example in which the supply of labor changes. Let the labor supply in some occupation *decrease* because some laborers go to other jobs or communities. The smaller remaining supply causes a rise in wage rates. Employers bid up wages to get employees, rather than continue with unfilled jobs (and less wealth). Higher wage rates restrict the amount of labor demanded to the smaller amount available, and they induce substitution of other types of labor or inputs, according to the principles explained in the preceding chapter.

Wage Differences

Some sense of proportion of differences in wages can easily be obtained from available data. For perspective, Table 16–1 shows some 1974 median salaries by occupation and sex.

The range of *average* salaries among occupations listed in Table 16–1 exceeds 10 to 1, from over $30,000 to less than $3,000. Within *each* occupation the range of salaries will also exceed 10 to 1. Is it better to be a very good gardener or a mediocre doctor? Actors and entertainers have a notoriously wide income range from millions down to practically nothing, and the average is probably very low indeed. So of equal importance with the median or average is the available range. Unfortunately there is not much reliable information for ranges *within* various occupations.

Relative Demand and Supply

If first-class musical talent were widely available and the talent (strong back) to be a ditchdigger were relatively rare, some ditchdiggers would get a higher salary than fine musicians. The larger the supply, with given demand, the lower the wages. If the number of doctors were somehow increased enough, their wages would fall below those of window washers, because at that enormous number the marginal-value product of a doctor would fall to very low values. Consequently, given the demand (the succession of lower values of use to which the services of additional workers of a particular skill can be put), wage differentials among occupations or skills reflect differences in available amounts of different kinds of usable talent resulting from heredity and training.

The amount of training (investment in human capital) responds to prospective rewards. Suppose a person could borrow now against clearly perceived higher future earnings he would get

Table 16–1. Estimated Average Actual Earnings Annually in Various Tasks, as of 1974, for Male and Female (In Thousands of Dollars; Not Adjusted to Equivalent Full-Time Earnings)

Occupation	Male	Female	Occupation	Male	Female
Physicians	$34	$15	Telephone Linemen	$10	—
Dentists	29	8.6	Meat Cutters	10	$5
Lawyers	25	12	Auto Assemblers	10	—
Optometrists	23	8.6	Coal Miners	10	—
Airline Pilots	23	—	Surveyors	10	—
Physicists	20	12	Chemical Lab Technicians	9.7	—
Dental Hygienists	19	10	Legal Secretaries	9.5	7.7
Sales Managers	19	17	Truck Drivers	9.5	—
Chemical Engineers	19	14	Registered Nurses	9.5	8.5
Economists	19	11	Airline Stewardesses	—	8.2
Architects	18	9.5	Cabinet Makers	8.9	—
Administrators	18	14	Secretaries	—	6.7
Pharmacists	17	13	(Homemakers, Housewife)	—	(6.6)*
Union Officials	15	—	Dieticians	—	6.0
Accountants	14	8	Upholsterers	8.2	—
Librarians	14	8.4	Typists	8.1	5.4
Tool & Die Machinists	14	—	Bank Tellers	7.8	5.7
Insurance Agents	14	—	Bartenders	7.5	4
Firemen	13	—	Sales Clerks	7.4	5
Electricians	13	—	File Clerks	6.8	4.5
Plumbers	12	—	Nurses Aides	5.9	4.0
Urban Transport Motormen	12	—	Gardeners	5	—
Postal Clerks	12	—	Cashiers	4.2	3.2
Carpenters	10.5	—			

* Value of services—at market cost—estimated and reported by U.S. Social Security Administration and Cornell University.

Source: U.S. Dept. of Labor, *Monthly Labor Review;* U.S. Dept. of Commerce, *Statistical Abstract of the U.S.*

from the training. Then even a poor person could buy education as readily as the rich, by borrowing against his prospective future earnings. Notice, we do not say that the opportunity to buy education will equalize wealth among all people; instead, all could exploit their talents by borrowing against their clearly perceived future poten-

tial increase in earning power. But not everyone who wants to exploit his educational opportunities in this way can do so—for at least two reasons: (1) The future and his performance in it are uncertain. Will more education really enhance earning power and repayment probability? What will happen if the future earnings aren't as big as expected? When creditors want payment will the person repay or plead bankruptcy or undue duress? (2) A large part of one's academic education is obtained before legal maturity. Our legal system and courts will not enforce debts incurred by minors, so lenders are wary of educational loans to young people.

7, 8

Specific versus
General On-the-Job Training

Students are apt to overlook the very large amount of on-the-job training provided in business firms. Apprenticeships are one form of such education. Professional football and baseball players learn during their first couple of years of professional play. In fact, some are paid more in the initial years than their services are worth at that time. Why? Your instructor learned a lot in his first few years. Was he paid more than he was worth in those first years? It depends upon whether the on-the-job education is useful to him only as an employee for that one specific employer or whether it is useful in *general* for other employers, too. *Specific* training is useful only to the current employer and is not a source of higher future income to the employee in any other job. So the employer is willing to pay for it if the employee is not likely to quit soon after he is trained. The military services "give" on-the-job training and some of it is useful for general civilian life. As you can expect, wages paid during training will be lower if the employee receives general training that makes him more productive to other employers.

Employees with predominantly specific training (of value to the current employer only) are less likely to quit or be laid off than untrained or generally trained employees. Their specific knowledge isn't worth as much elsewhere, so they're less likely to quit rather than revise their wages or working conditions. One implication of this is that we would expect to find more of the untrained or generally trained people in the group who most frequently change jobs and go through a period of unemployment while evaluating alternative job options.

Risk-Bearing Differentials

Some people are more willing to give up relatively sure wages in the hope of ultimately earning a higher wage. An architect who gives up a secure job designing conventional buildings and risks coming up with desirable new designs may end up very much richer or poorer. Some choose the risk of ending up poorer for the prospect of being richer. And their choices produce a wide spread of *realized* lifetime earnings.

Wealth-Affecting
Differences in Productivities

Some people have earned over a million dollars in one year for their services. Are the talents and skills of people as varied as their earnings? Does some "force" produce a greater spread among earnings than there is among the "inherent" talents and skills? It has been argued as follows: "The president of General Products receives $500,000 a year. When he retires, someone now getting far less will take his place and will get that high salary. Surely the high salary is a function of the *position* rather than of some differences in abilities." In fact it depends on both. The expected productivity of an input affects what it is offered. As we saw in the preceding chapter, the associated amount of capital or wealth that he directs or uses affects marginal productivity of labor. Consider two managers, one with the ability to make correct decisions 5 percent more of the time than the other. Roughly speaking, that 5 percent superiority is worth about $50,000 in a $1,000,000 business, but only about $5000 in a $100,000 business. The larger business will gain more with the superior man than would the small company. On the other hand, two low-level employees (say typists) who differed by 5 percent in their ability would not be making decisions that differed as much in their effect on wealth as those at the top, and so the *value* of the *difference* in their talents would not be so great. This implies that nonmanagerial skills will be paid more equally in *large and small* companies, whereas the salaries and abilities of top management will be correlated with the size of the company. This is in fact what happens. Notice the explanation provided here is not that the big companies have more wealth and therefore the skilled manager can get more. Instead, larger firms will demand better managers. The bigger the company, the greater is the change in wealth that can be caused by differential talents among managers.

Ricardian Superiority Rents

Differential earnings, whether to personal services or land, if attributable to *natural*, or *inherited,* superior productive ability are called "rents of superiority," or Ricardian rents, after David Ricardo, the eminent early-nineteenth-century economist who first elaborated the concept and phenomenon. We emphasize the concept here to ensure its distinction from *monopoly* rent, which is an enhanced income permitted to some sellers by *preventing* competition from other sellers who would have forced down the selling price of the protected sellers and eliminated the monopoly rent. Later in this chapter we shall explore some cases of monopoly rents to employees.

Geographical Differences

Earnings differ also noticeably among geographical regions and between urban and suburban areas. There is a temptation to think that different areas have different costs of living and hence pay different wages. But that raises the question why more employers haven't migrated to the lower-cost areas to make more profits, and, as more employers spring up to demand more labor, why wages haven't risen to match those elsewhere. It is no answer to say that the weather or environment may be better. That is no answer because rent on the superior located land would be higher.

The higher wages on the North Slope of Alaska are due to the higher productivity of the workers there. They are producing a service of a monetary value great enough to offset the hardships of living there. The costs of providing these people on the North Slope with the quality of life available in, say, California is very high. People have to be paid more to live and work in Alaska. The higher costs can be covered by the higher market-value productivity of their services. Areas with high costs of living must have high productivity of workers if high wages are to be maintainable. However, the wages are high not because the cost of living is high, but because the productivity in those regions is very high *and* not enough people are willing to work there to lower the wages. The high costs of living restrict the supply of labor so that the restricted supply of labor is offered a sufficiently high income to cover the costs of living there in a style that is as good as anyplace else (or that permits enough to be saved so that one can then later live elsewhere). New York City has a high cost of living, and it also has high wages—because of the high productivity there. Its so-called high cost of living is also a cost of high (better) living.

The concentration of large populations in small areas reduces the cost of daily negotiations and transacting of business. The consequent increased productivity of more densely populated areas drives up land rentals, which then absorb part of the higher productivity gains. The high wages in New York are explained in part by the high productivity of people in New York, a result in part of the high concentration. However, they are not better off by all that difference, because land rents are driven up to that point where the costs of land on which to concentrate absorb some (not all) of the higher productivity. To compare just money incomes of people in different areas can be deceiving if those differences alone are used as an index of who is better off.

If wages and income affect the supply of labor, we ought to observe labor moving from lower-wage areas to higher-wage areas relative to living costs. And we do. Nationwide, the movement of people is predominantly to areas with high income; gains in the total population of various counties through migration occurred in the counties with higher median family incomes while county groups with lower incomes had migration losses in both male and female and white and nonwhite populations.[3]

Female–Male Money Income Differences

On average, women earn wage incomes about two-thirds that of men. But that figure is deceptive, since it does not allow for differences in time in the work force, extent of training, and types of work performed. If corrections are made for those differences so that comparisons are made between men and women who have the same amount of time in the work force, the same amount of investment in training, the same record of performance, and the same occupations, the difference is either greatly reduced or eliminated.[4]

But market employment is not the only type of productivity. Women have traditionally excelled in childrearing. Furthermore, if their tasks at home were performed by employees, the staff would contain salaried chefs, chauffeurs, buying agents, interior decorators, nurses, handymen, gardeners, social secretaries, etc., whose costs

[3] Data reported by Gladys K. Bowles and James D. Tarver, "The Composition of New Migration among Counties in the United States, 1950–1960," *Agricultural Economics Research,* U.S. Dept. of Agriculture, January 1966. From 1950 to 1960, counties with lowest median family incomes (under $5000) had a net loss of over 28 percent of their population. Those with $6000–$7500 median family incomes gained 11 percent. The migration was greater for younger people. No doubt labor is attracted by higher-wage areas and repelled from the lower-wage areas.

[4] One study, by J. Mincer and S. Polachek, "Family Investments in Human Capital: Earnings of Women," *Journal of Political Economy,* Vol. 82, No. 2, Part II, March/April 1974, pp. S76–S108, indicates the difference would be reduced to one-sixth. Another study of salaries in college teaching indicates that women with backgrounds and records equal to men get more than the men!

would amount to anywhere from $5000 to $10,000 or more.[5] And those services are tax-free.

How much of the unwillingness of women to forsake their higher productivity in the home will account for less work and investment in the market labor force is unknown. It is tempting to say that larger numbers of women have not entered the pecuniary work force because of prejudice. But that explanation seems to be of little help. For example, if it *were* prejudice, why would all business firms, or so many of them, have been willing to forsake the profits that could be achieved by hiring more women at lower wages? We uncritically accuse businessmen of being greedy for profits, but we then say they are ignoring a profit potential because of prejudice. It is difficult to believe that people would go bankrupt and lose fortunes for that kind of prejudice. Even more telling, the market does hire women in disproportionate amounts in many jobs—as elementary and secondary school teachers and administrators, as office workers, and as clerical and food service workers. How does one explain all that consistently with a *prejudice* against women, a prejudice that presumably reflects no differences whatsoever in performance?

Wage and Nonpecuniary Differences

Employment conditions differ in nonpecuniary features (that is, in differences other than money wage): employer personality, health hazards, climate, type of work, location, congeniality of fellow workers. Higher wages that offset nonpecuniary disadvantages are called *equalizing wage*

[5] As reported by the Social Security Administration studies based on data collected at Cornell University, 1975.

differences. These disadvantageous conditions can persist indefinitely if the cost of equalizing the working conditions exceeds the equalizing difference in wages. For example, people are willing to work in the heat only at premium wages; if the premium is less than the cost of air conditioning, pay differentials will continue.

Employees differ also. Better-looking, more courteous, pleasant, cooperative, and congenial employees provide employers with nonpecuniary benefits. Therefore, an employer discriminates among potential employees with respect to nonpecuniary attributes. If two stenographers have equal pecuniary productivity, but one is brighter, more beautiful, pleasant, well-dressed, with a better-modulated voice, then, at *equal* wages, she would be preferred. Her nonpecuniary qualities will get her a higher wage than the stenographer who is inferior in those nonpecuniary features. Higher pay to the attractive stenographer is the same thing as lower pay for inferior people. And that lower pay enables "inferior" people to get jobs. Equalizing differences in wages, then, provides employment opportunities for inferior employees, just as equalizing differences in wages compensates for inferior, more-hazardous working conditions. Although people recognize differences among employers and working conditions as reasons for employees' discrimination in choice of employers, they resent similar actions by employers on the basis of personal characteristics of employees. Federal laws declare employ*er* discrimination illegal, but employ*ees* may legally discriminate.

Poor paintings sell for less than superb paintings; otherwise, the poor paintings would not be sold. Because Chevrolets sell for less than Cadillacs, Chevrolets can survive in competition against Cadillacs. At the same price for the two cars, fewer buyers would want Chevies. Less-attractive people can compete more effectively by accepting a lower price. You buy some round steak rather than filet mignon because the price of round steak is sufficiently lower to compensate for the inferiority of round steak in tenderness and flavor, even though the nutrient value is the same.

Effect of Technological Progress on Job Allocation and Wages

Although it is viewed with alarm and fought by various labor groups, automation (which has been progressing since man first learned to wield a stick) is a source of increased wealth, easier work, higher real incomes, and a larger supportable population. The plow drawn by oxen (rather than by people) was a great technological advance. What happened to the displaced people who lost their jobs in front of the plow? They turned to what were formerly less-important tasks, like collecting more wood and building more stone fences. And when the tractor replaced the horse and several plowmen, more men were released to produce more of other things. With the advent of new machines, labor's marginal-value productivity was reduced *in the old* jobs below that in tasks formerly left undone elsewhere. Automation or technological progress creates new jobs; but that really is irrelevant, despite overwhelming talk to the contrary. Whether or not the new invention increases demand for workers in that industry, there still will be plenty of jobs—

in fact, more than can *ever* be filled. There are not too few jobs, but *too many* jobs! The problem is comparing and deciding which tasks to perform and which to leave unperformed. Inventions, automation, and progress make us richer, but they do not eliminate the persisting problem of allocating labor to the highest-valued of the remaining tasks.

The real concern is that people whose services are outcompeted by new methods must *shift* to other, next-best paying jobs. We must distinguish three groups of people. Consider the rise of television: (1) Some people get higher wages because they produce or work in TV with the new equipment and programs. They benefit doubly— from higher income and from lower prices of improved products. (2) Some people have incomes that do not depend on TV developments. They benefit from the lower costs of home entertainment, and they suffer no loss of income. (3) Some people are displaced by the advent of TV and transfer to new, next-best jobs. This class can be further divided into three subcategories: (a) Some are better off on net, because they gain from being able to use television as a consumer. (b) Of the remainder who do not reap a gain, even after considering all the effects of this particular innovation, some are nevertheless better off than if they had to forsake *all* new progress since television. They gain through the general dispersal of improvements through lower prices and quality improvements to consumers—despite their income loss. (c) Some employees and owners of outmoded equipment suffer such severe reductions in demand for their services that, even after taking into account the gains from television and from all other technological improvements that will occur during the rest of their lives, they are worse off. This category is more characteristic of older people than of younger.

As yet, we are unable to tell in advance for any invention how many people, let alone which ones, will fall into each class. Even afterward it is often impossible to tell, because other changes impinge and obscure the effects. For example, did the invention of the typewriter increase or decrease the demand for secretaries? The discovery of oil may have attracted labor from coal mines into oilwell drilling, refining, and pipeline work, so that the wages of coal miners *increased* despite the negative effect of oil on the demand for coal. New inventions not only affect the productivity of workers in the affected jobs; they can also attract workers, thus raising wages elsewhere. Spectacular examples are the railroad and the automobile, which lowered costs of transport; as a result, transport increased, as did the demand for workers to provide materials for transportation. Canalmen, livery-stable operators, and buggy-whip makers shifted to better-paying jobs in the new transportation industry. New machines sometimes reduce the cost of products so much that the increased amount demanded raises the demand for labor in that job (for example, typewriters, computers).

Compensation Principle

Out of the net gain from such changes, the whole community could compensate reallocated workers for any loss. This is a logically airtight possibility *in principle,* because the increased value of output exceeds the losses of the displaced factors. However, innovations are too extensive to identify each and every displaced factor and to determine who loses how much. How would we know how much to pay a person who claims to be displaced by the introduction of electronic computers? How could we be sure that he has not taken some easy, low-paying job—in the expectation that he will be given a payment large enough to make up the difference? Only if people's incentives were not changed by the compensation principle, and if there were no prohibitive costs in discovering who gained or lost how much, would that compensation system be feasible. Nevertheless, compensation is not ignored. Today, people pay taxes for a program to retrain and to relocate workers.[6]

If labor is compensated, why not also compensate owners of nonhuman assets? If compensation is paid *out of taxes* for every change in value resulting from innovation, the *owners* of productive resources, human and nonhuman, do not bear the risks of unforeseeable future consequences; instead, the general public becomes the risk-bearer according to the tax load and government services. The compensation principle conflicts with a basic purpose of an open-market society: to enable people to specialize in risk-bearing, to escape communal bearing of all risks of future values of all resources. If I don't want to bear the risks of the future value of some asset

---

[6] This aid is proposed, however, not only for those whose incomes are cut by competition from new, more productive equipment, but for any laborer who lives in an area where there is general decline in demand for services—whatever the reason. A displaced worker in a prosperous *area* is not eligible.

The Trade Expansion Act of 1962 gives the President additional powers to negotiate for tariff reduction and provides for "trade adjustment assistance" for both business firms (through technical assistance, loans, tax relief) and workers (through special unemployment benefits, retraining, loans for moving to jobs in different communities) when injury from increased imports can be demonstrated.

or resource, I simply choose not to own it; in that way I neither capture gains nor suffer the loss. If I wish to bear the risk, I can buy a share of ownership in it. Risk-bearing is then selective and adjustable. I agree to bear all the losses of value of my services, whatever the cause, and in exchange I obtain the right to keep whatever gains might occur in the value of my resources. That kind of agreement is implicitly made by every private-property owner.

Adjustment to Decreased Demand for One's Services

The shift to a new job in a new area, a lower standard of living, and new colleagues and social circles can be a traumatic experience, especially for older people. Those experiencing a reduced market value of output of their current jobs (because of competition of others in the market) often resort to political action to restrain market competition—as we have illustrated in earlier chapters. A very safe prediction is that whenever one's wealth is being lost through market competition from new inventions, changing tastes, or new products, attempts to restrict that market will increase.

Employee–Employer Bargaining Power

Restrictions on market competition are often advocated to protect employees from the employer's presumed superior bargaining power. What forces General Motors to pay the wages it does? The answer is that if General Motors offers less than other employers, it will get fewer employees.

Any employee can get a salary that is at least as high as his services are worth to some other employer. The authors, employees of the State of California, can quit anytime we feel like it and take our best-known alternative jobs elsewhere. Those alternatives, and not the legislators' "reasonableness" is what "forces" the state to pay us as much as it does. The legislators are willing to do so only if our services are worth at least that much to them. "Bargaining power" *is* the highest alternative salary one can get from *other* jobs.

It has been said that the employer who loses an employee loses only one employee, while the employee loses his entire income. In fact, the employee does not lose his entire income; he loses any premium he was getting in his former job over his perceived next-best alternative, plus the costs of moving and job-exploration. Of course, if the employee quits, his own losses can be greater than those suffered by the employer; but such a comparison is irrelevant. Employers hire employees because the employer expects a gain, not because the employee gains less. Do not mistake these remarks. They are not antiemployee, antiemployer, or antiunion; they are anticonfusion.

Labor Unions

"The high wages of the American worker are a result of a strong labor-union movement." Would that it were true. The path to higher income for all workers in poor countries would be open: Unionize and strike for higher wages. However, neither economic reasoning nor actual evidence supports that prescription. The productivity of labor explains high wages. If a community has more

10, 11

natural resources and capital equipment, high educational levels, skilled workers, and a system for organizing productive activity, productivity of labor will be higher. That, and nothing else, is the foundation of high wages. What unions can do in that context is help smooth grievance procedures, provide increased information about job opportunities, help workers improve their skills, provide facilities for joint purchases, and monitor payment of fringe benefits like insurance, retirement, etc.

By no means are these trivial. Anyone working under a foreman knows how an impartial grievance agent helps working conditions. Unions can provide valuable and hard-to-get information about alternative jobs. Insurance or loan services through credit unions are efficient, because that agency, having the member's work record, has a relatively quick means of assessing his credit-worthiness and prospects of job- and income-continuance. These objectives deserve emphasis because some people incorrectly think the only purpose of a union is to enable employees to strike effectively. That, of course, is the union's basic source of strength in improving the wages and working conditions of *some* union members beyond those determined by open-market competition. This power to strike can raise wages of some union members but it does not increase wages in general. It redistributes national income toward some unions but at the same time reduces the total income produced, as we shall explain later.

Unions also influence legislation. Labor unions have existed for a long time, often despite being declared illegal as "criminal conspiracies." However, in 1842 the Massachusetts Supreme Court rendered a precedent-setting decision in *Com-monwealth v. Hunt,* declaring unions to be legal. Presently in the United States 21,000,000 employees (22 percent of the labor force) are in unions. Union membership is charted in Figure 16–4 along with the total civilian labor force. The *fraction* of the civilian labor force belonging to unions has fluctuated, as shown in Figure 16–5. The rise during the late 1930s has been attributed primarily to contemporary legislation (such as the Wagner Act, 1935) compelling employers to negotiate with unions if a majority of the employees voted to be represented by a union. In some jobs, virtually every employee is a union member (musicians, longshoremen, transport workers, construction workers) and in others, nearly none (chemists, typists, economists). A few large unions contain the majority of union membership.

National unions are federations of chartered "locals" to which employees belong. Although the national organization, or federation, has a constitution, the "local" usually has the power to apply membership rules and approve contracts. For example, the national federation constitutions assert membership is open to all, regardless of race or creed, but the actual admission standards are determined by the local members, with much discrimination, especially in craft unions.

Craft unions admit members skilled in the same craft; *industrial* unions admit those who work in one industry regardless of their particular skills or tasks. For example, the carpenters' union is a craft union, whereas the steel workers' union is an industrial union containing members with various skills. Most national craft unions are associated in a national *federation,* the American Federation of Labor (AFL), while the Congress of Industrial Organizations (CIO) comprises mostly industrial unions. A few national unions (team-

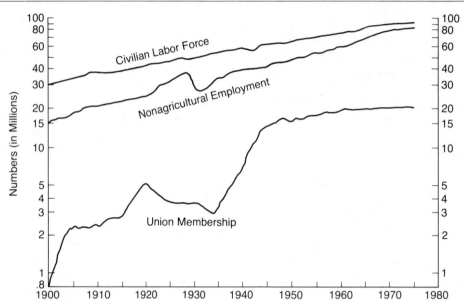

Figure 16–4. Civilian Labor Force, Employees in Nonagricultural Establishments, and Trade Union Membership, 1900–1975. *Source: L. Troy,* Trade Union Membership, 1897–1962 *(New York: National Bureau of Economic Research, 1965). Updated.*

sters and coal miners) belong to neither. The AFL and the CIO have a joint top-level council called the "AFL-CIO." One of its purposes is to define jurisdiction of the national unions to reduce interunion rivalry about, for example, whether an electrical fixture is to be installed by a carpenter or an electrical worker.

Unions are typically comprised of many, separate *locals,* one to each small geographic area. The *local* officers (usually elected by the local membership) maintain membership rolls and expand coverage of the union over more employers, monitor contract terms, and administer routine affairs (pension funds, shop grievances). A "shop steward" is a union member and employee of the firm in which he helps to avoid or settle workers' grievances, much as an agent acts as an intermediary between two contracting parties. Safety rules, working hours, vacation interpretation, "goofing" on the job—these are a few of the perennial sources of misunderstanding and dispute that a shop steward can help to alleviate. The costs of union activity are financed by membership initiation fees and monthly dues. Some initiation fees are hundreds of dollars, with monthly dues usually under $50.

The Wagner Act of 1935 required employers to deal with unions and made it legal for employees

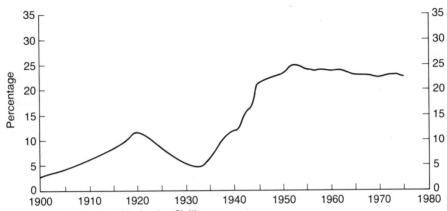

Figure 16–5. Percent of Union Membership in the Civilian Labor Force. *Source: L. Troy,* Trade Union Membership, 1897–1962 *(New York: National Bureau of Economic Research, 1965). Updated.*

to form or join the union of their (majority) choice. Unions are recognized as the *sole* permissible negotiating agent for a specified type of employee in a firm, if a majority of the voting employees so prefer under procedures established by the National Labor Relations Act, as administered by the National Labor Relations Board (NLRB). At present (and probably for many years in the future) one of the major disputes among employers, employees, unions, and the NLRB concerns the Board's scope of authority.

Less ambiguous is the scope of union-membership requirements. Some firms are *closed shops,* meaning that only union members can apply for and retain jobs. Some have *union shops,* in which employees must become union members, or at least pay union fees, if they are to retain a job for more than one month, but they need not be members when applying for a job. *Open shops* do not require union membership in any respect.[7]

In addition to modifying the techniques for negotiating the sale of labor services, unions can impose severe costs on employers to induce them to agree to union demands. A *boycott* is a *concerted* refusal by union members to buy the products of the employer being boycotted. Sometimes, other firms that do business with the boycotted firm will also be boycotted—a *secondary boycott.* The *strike,* which is the ultimate weapon, consists of two parts: (1) employees stop work, and (2) other people are prevented from replacing the strikers. Violence or its threat is re-

[7] Current federal legislation (Section 14-b of the Taft-Hartley Act) permits a state to prohibit union shops. This is called the "right-to-work" law, somewhat misleadingly. This law is under attack from unions, and almost every year attempts are made in Congress to repeal it by prohibiting any state from requiring open shops in all places of employment. About 20 states prohibit union and closed shops.

quired for the second part. Without the ability to prevent others from negotiating for these jobs, strike would merely be a mass resignation.

The Strike as a Market Restriction

It is a tribute to the intelligence and economic acumen of union leaders that they know that the right to strike is crucial to a strong union. It is a tribute to their political skill that they concealed their real purposes behind the facade of "equating bargaining power."

Legislation Concerning
Unions and Strikes

In England and France, beginning with the French Revolution, labor or trade unions were prohibited as "conspiracies." Union members conspired against anyone who undercut the desired higher wages. Although the threat of violence in the strike was basically what anticonspiracy laws aimed to stop, they abolished the right to form a union—which is very different. Joint voluntary action is in most concepts of freedom. Hence, anticonspiracy laws were opposed both by employees who had their sights on the right to strike and by people who had their sights on the ideal of freedom. By 1830, the English anticonspiracy laws had been repealed *and* the right to strike tacitly granted—with the forlorn hope that no violence or coercion would ensue.

The right to strike had its subsequent ups and downs. At times, it was prohibited as an interference with a nonstriker's access to labor markets. Even when legalized, it has sometimes been tolerated only if strikers did not interfere with nonunion people who work at less than the wages demanded by the strikers. Police have at times permitted pickets to block entry. At other times they have protected the nonstrikers. Today some countries (Russia and the Communist bloc nations, for example) prohibit strikes; anyone can quit his job, or the whole group can quit, but others can in no way be prevented from replacing such a worker or workers. In other countries, tolerance ranges from legal restrictions against interference with nonstriking employees to legal support of strikers who prevent nonunion replacements from working.

In the Clayton Act of 1914, Congress intended to restrict judiciary use of antimonopoly laws and "restraint-of-trade" injunctions against some union activities, including the strike. It exempted labor unions from antimonopoly laws. In 1932, the Norris–LaGuardia Act effectively restricted the power of the judiciary to prevent unions from engaging in strikes, picketing, and certain types of boycotts. But subsequently, the Taft-Hartley Act of 1947 permitted the President to prohibit any strike that would create whatever he calls a "national emergency." Section 14-b of the act permitted states to ban union shops. Approximately 20 states have passed "right-to-work" (without joining a union) laws. Such laws do not, in logic, necessarily increase every worker's range of choice. For example, if some employer and all his employees want a union shop, the state "right-to-work" law would prevent it. On the other hand, a group of employees cannot force other employees to join a union against their will.

Voluntary Arbitration

If unable to resolve a dispute, the employer and the union sometimes hire an outsider to suggest mutually acceptable terms, though neither party necessarily agrees to accept the terms. Presently, no law requires employers and unions to submit disputes to an arbitrator for a binding settlement, but about 90 percent of labor contracts provide for some kind of arbitration (though not necessarily compulsory).

Do Unions Raise Union Wages?

Once the power to strike effectively is allowed by law, better wages and working conditions can be sought for *some* members of the striking unions—better than if other people were free to compete in the same market. The association of union bargaining with increases in union wages is not in itself evidence that such bargaining achieves wages higher than would be obtained in an open market. Suppose, for instance, a wage contract were signed two years ago for specified wage rates, and since that time wages in general have risen 15 percent. The employer is ready to offer a pay-raise of 20 percent, to retain, as well as improve, his work force in the face of better wages elsewhere. The employer initially offers 15 percent. Union officials, however, might demand a 25 percent increase. After a ritual of negotiation and bargaining, the terms come out to be 20 percent; and the union claims it has raised wages. However, neither the employer nor the union set the final wage rate: The employer pays that amount because he must in order to get employees; and the union negotiators accept it unless they are prepared to face a loss of job opportunities from this employer, who will be unable to hire so many at a higher wage.

Unions certainly have affected members' working conditions, insofar as a union bargaining agent will help settle employee–employer grievances more efficiently and amicably. As for wages, studies indicate large differences among unions in their effects. Some have raised union hourly wage rates substantially above the open-market; many others have had no detectable effect on union wage rates. The best estimates are that the effect of unionism on the *average union* member's income has been to raise it 10–15 percent above that of equivalent nonunion workers.[8] But this superiority is only *relative* to nonunion wages, which are lower than they otherwise would be. Some unions have had greater effect—for example, the income of *employed* coal miners was estimated to be about 50 percent higher, with nonunion wages being reduced.

How can unions, or anything else, raise *some* wage rates of union workers above those that would have existed under open-market demand and supply? Economic analysis (graphed in Figure 16–6) suggests three primary ways: (1) raise demand; (2) reduce supply; (3) impose higher wage rates.

1. While some unions try to help employers use labor more effectively and raise demand for labor, there is little evidence of significant success.
2. Entry to the labor market is effectively restricted by longshoremen, plumbers, doctors, electricians, projectionists, teamsters, linotypists, and butchers, for example. Apprenticeship limits, compulsory licensing, and limits on union membership are examples of devices for restricting entry.

[8] See H. G. Lewis, *Unions and Relative Wages in the United States* (Chicago: University of Chicago Press, 1963).

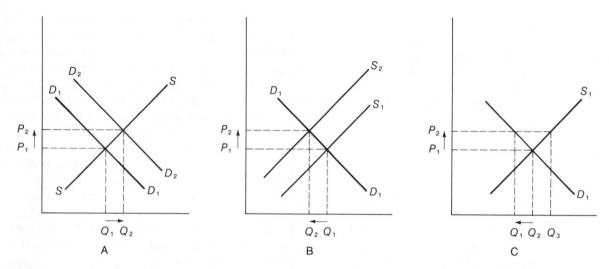

Figure 16–6. Alternative Basic Means of Affecting Wage Rates and Employment

Panel A shows that an increase in demand will increase wage rates from P_1 to P_2 and employment from Q_1 to Q_2.

Panel B shows that a decrease in supply will increase wage rates but not employment. The problem is how to exclude some people from the market in order to reduce supply. Immigration restrictions, licensing, entry qualifications (education, age, sex, residence) are some of the means.

Panel C shows that an arbitrarily higher wage rate negotiated without a change in demand or supply will leave displaced workers whose presence may be sufficiently strong to restrain the possibility of pushing up wage rates. The problem is how to prevent new entrants and displaced workers from undercutting the agreed-upon wage rate. Jobs can be rationed or shared by spreading reduced work over all members, as the musicians' union does.

3. By sufficient potential strike power, the union may force wages higher than an open-market competitive wage would have been in some industry. When unions are effective in raising union wages above free markets for a whole industry, who gains and who loses? Usually it is claimed that the gains come out of the employers' income. But the consequences are spread far more widely. Those employers in the industry who cannot survive at the higher costs sell their assets at correspondingly lower prices to reflect their smaller income. Output diminishes until it is small enough to raise prices to cover the higher wage costs; or a growing industry does not grow quite so much. People who would have been employed in the industry if wages had not been raised shift to other jobs at lower wages or do transient work. Output of products of the higher-wage labor is smaller, and the displaced labor makes more of other less-valuable goods. The national income is smaller. Thus, in a fundamental sense, employees do not compete against employers; they compete against other labor. This is often obscured by slogans of "labor versus management."

Nonwage Rationing of Employment

At a wage higher than the open-market level, the number of qualified job applicants will, by definition of an open market, exceed the number of high-wage jobs available at that wage rate. The high-wage jobs must be rationed more according to nonwage criteria. The common procedure is to assign probationary union members to temporary and seasonal jobs; when demand falls, they will be the first to go. Whatever the other purposes of apprentices and probationary members, they serve as an employment-rationing device that protects senior members. If the reduction in employment is particularly severe, so that some men with "seniority" (greatest amount of accrued time on the job) also are without jobs, work-sharing often emerges, with limitations on the number of hours a week any one person can have. Compulsory attendance at frequent union meetings as a condition of good standing will help to reduce "excessive membership."

Jobs may be rationed through restriction on union membership (through larger initiation fees and more rigid standards: race, age, personality, sex, education, experience, probationary membership periods). "Unethical" job-seeking conduct prejudicial to the senior employed members of the union (whether it be the American Medical Association, the American Bar Association, the Teamsters, or the Longshoremen) can warrant expulsions. Probationary membership also helps to restrict entry into the union. One publicized, self-serving reason for these restrictions is protection of the employer and consumer from shoddy work.

Recent protests by blacks and replies by union officials have elicited undisputable evidence of union discrimination by race. National union officials have promised to try to change the situation. But union locals make the decisions about admission, and as long as union membership is limited, some form of discrimination is necessary in deciding who shall be admitted to the jobs.

If the union is strong enough, it can impose work rules, known as "featherbedding," whereby an employer must employ more laborers than he wants. Teachers decry the use of television in the classroom; hod carriers once refused to carry premixed concrete; typesetters require newspapers to set duplicate type if preset type forms are submitted by advertisers; building codes specify unnecessarily expensive labor-using techniques; standby local musicians must be hired when touring orchestras perform locally. All are expressions of legal monopoly power deriving from the power to strike effectively. Railroad employees have had perhaps the most publicized featherbedding provisions; and this should not be surprising, because the railroads were themselves in a *legal* monopoly position; higher wages were paid out of their monopoly rent.

Strong union contracts that cover all workers have an impact on employment because they reduce the ability of each employee to renegotiate his own wage in the event of decreased demand for his services. If the demand for a firm's product should fall, some employees will be dropped unless wages can be cut sufficiently. But the employee who is laid off cannot renegotiate a new lower wage if he *and* the employer are tied to a union scale. Those who remain employed at the union scale will not want that scale cut just to permit continued employment for those who were dropped. The extra rigidity imposed by a *group* wage scale that can be cut only with approval of a majority of the group will penalize the junior or less-able people who normally are just barely worth the particular scale imposed on the group.

Closed-Market Monopoly Rent: Acquisition and Disposition

Entry into a union may be so restricted that normal attrition (gradual loss) by death and retirement reduces membership. Employers will then bid up wages of the remaining union workers. Limited membership in unions with higher than open-market wages permits "unusual" behavior. For example, suppose the wage rate would have gone up to $5 an hour under the contrived scarcity. However, if the union agent could hold wages down to the contracted $4 an hour, the employer, who would be prepared to pay an additional $1 per hour per worker to get more employees, would perhaps be persuaded to pay the person responsible for assigning union workers to various employers—as is the case for longshoremen. The union agent could demand or accept payments for favoring the short-handed employer. In effect, the cost is just as high to the employer but is not paid entirely in the form of wages to the workers. Reluctant employers can be penalized by not getting many employees.

A different, especially notorious monopoly rent to union officers (for example, Teamsters Union officers) comes from their management of union funds for pensions, health, and recreation. These funds are invested. If the officers make loans with those funds at lower than normal interest rates, borrowers will pay the difference to union officers in the form of special favors, commissions, or business purchases from favored firms with which the agent is associated.

Considerations of equity and morality of the "sharing" by union officials are not simple. Union organizers can claim they accomplished the closed-market monopoly for the union. Why shouldn't they be rewarded with larger salaries, expense accounts, vacation resorts, and homes than the union members, who had little to do with the development of the organization—in fact, no more than the employees of a successful businessman who builds a great enterprise? Economics contains no ethical criteria by which to judge this. It merely explains.

Employers, on the other hand, are quick to exploit opportunities inherent in union labor monopoly. Some will propose to pay the union a special reward if it will withhold workers from competing firms. The favored firm will be able to command higher prices for its services. (James Hoffa, the late former president of the Teamsters Union, used this tactic.) This agreement is known as a "sweetheart" contract. Whether first suggested by the employer or by the union official doesn't matter; nor is it dependent on whether union officials or members get the monopoly rent.

Difficulty of Maintaining Long-Lasting Closed-Labor-Market Monopoly Rent

Closed-market monopoly rent is not easy to maintain. For example, a union carpenter cannot exclude competition merely by prohibiting nonunion carpenters from offering services to *his* employer. Other employers will hire nonunion carpenters and sell their products at lower prices. **Even if** all carpenters joined forces and forced all employers to hire only members of the carpenters' union, product competition would be effective. Plaster, steel, cement, glass, and other building materials can partially displace carpenters' products. Even doctors' attempts to raise fees are partly restrained by the availability of branded or proprietary drugs, advice of friends, Christian Science, do-it-yourself care, faith healers, etc.

Some people believe that participation in market transactions should not be prevented by anyone, let alone one's direct competitors. These critics do not object to unions as voluntary associations of employees for collective negotiation, but they do object to the strike as a restriction on access to the market. It is not clear whether these critics are aware to what extent a union would lose power if strikes were prohibited. Unions could still exist and negotiate with employers, but they would experience reduced power to raise salaries or improve working conditions above the open-market level by preventing access to the market for jobs. When a President of the United States says unions are basic institutions in a free society, the relevant question is still to be faced: "With what kinds of power to restrict the open market for jobs?" And on that issue reasonable, "humane" people differ.

If a labor union prevents nonunion workers from working for less than the wages it seeks, how does the union differ from a medical profession that prevents a free market for medical services? One difference is that the medical profession has *more successfully* defended its actions, in the name of higher quality of (a smaller quantity of) medical service. That it also enables

doctors to get higher wages is obvious and not irrelevant. The second difference is that the medical profession does not have to rely on strikes and private intimidation against competitors who would sell services at "substandard" prices; instead, it has a licensing law. It merely telephones the government for a policeman to restrain the competitor. If laws prohibited the sale of workers' services by anyone except a "licensed" (union) person, or prohibited training except in approved schools, then the union could keep the supply small and wages higher. Were the public police force available, gangsters and hoodlums—the specialists in intimidation—would be of less value. Then union officials would all be as free of the "undesirable elements" and as respectable as are the officers of the medical and legal associations and public utilities, to name only a few closed monopolies.

Union Monopoly versus Employer Monopoly

Union monopoly power is often said to countervail the monopoly power of industry. Unfortunately, this proposition confuses monopoly with open-market, price-searcher's market power. Consider the steel industry; it is a group of independently owned firms—just as a union is a group of independent workers. Yet there is a fundamental difference: Access to the market is open to all steel producers, of which there are more than 1000. Under the law, only *one* union can exist for any class of employees. Other unions may try to take its place, but only one is permitted to exist as the "exclusive" bargaining agent. In this one crucial difference lies the error of thinking that employers constitute a "monopoly," which requires a countervailing union monopoly. Not even for purposes of negotiating with a common "antagonist" is it possible for the steel companies to avoid open-market competition. The industry simply is open to entry. The theory that unions are necessary for bilateral monopoly bargaining is empty unless the employer is a closed monopoly, as in professional baseball.

Public Utilities Are Closed Monopolies

When faced with union strikes, public utilities can, *at first,* more easily yield to union demands, since they can draw on potential monopoly rent. The regulatory commission can allow the public utility to raise its already-restricted rate to offset higher wage costs. True, with higher rates sales will be smaller but the wealth of the utility will not necessarily suffer, if the rates had previously been held below the wealth-maximizing level by a regulatory agency. Any monopoly rent derived from the public utility's protected position can be transferred to the utility employees. Examples are transit systems, whether bus, taxi, rails, or air.

A more serious problem arises when public employees strike against governments. This amounts to achieving government power to tax the public in order to finance their demands. We know of no analysis that determines how much taxation the public will tolerate to benefit those who can withhold services *and prevent anyone else from replacing them.* Of course, the higher the wages the greater will be the number of people seeking some of those jobs, for example,

firemen, police, garbage collectors, teachers. One factor that tends to restrain this higher tax-supported wage is competition among cities or states: Cities with lower wages for unionized public employees will have lower tax bills and will tend to attract people and industry (until they, too, become subjected to that strike power?). Why do legislatures and city councils encourage and even require unions for public employees? Ask your political science instructor, but only after you try examining the economic interests of politicians to see if they get a better hold on political office, income, and power by getting votes in this process from benefited government employees. Again, note that nothing in the preceding pages suggests that unions act improperly.

12, 13
14, 15
16, 17
18, 19
20, 21

Legal Restrictions on Open Markets for Labor

Minimum-Wage Laws

Minimum-wage laws prohibit employment at less than some stated wage per hour. Federal law currently specifies a minimum wage of $2.50 an hour.[9] At the higher minimum legal wage rate the

[9] Some exceptions are permitted. Among the major ones are motion-picture theater workers, highly seasonal amusement area workers, employees in small firms (less than $500,000 in annual sales), restaurant employees receiving a substantial portion of their income in tips, agricultural employees who have a lower minimum, employees of educational institutions, and summer work by college students. It is a challenging problem to explain why these exceptions are granted if the effects of the law are desirable.

quantity of labor demanded will be less than the quantity of labor services supplied.[10]

Some of those whose services are worth less than the minimum wage and who lose their jobs as employees will resort to work as private, independent contractors to their former employer, taking a lower income by means of a low contract price rather than a reduced wage rate. For example, a person seeking a job as a taxi or a truck driver, at the stipulated wage rate of, say,

$100 a week, could instead rent a vehicle from his employer and drive as an independent driver (or subcontractor). He can cut his wages below $100 by renting the taxi from his "employer" for a weekly rental of, say, $20 a week *above* the free-market car rentals (a sort of secret rebate).

People who cannot produce that legal minimum value per hour may obtain temporary jobs when demands transiently rise to make their hire worthwhile at that wage rate. Their vulnerability

[10] Except allegedly in a "monopsonistic" market, a market in which the employer is such a significant part of the total demand that to increase employees he must offer higher wages for new *and* old employees. The graph shows a rising labor-supply curve, *WW*, to the firm. The marginal-wage-cost curve *MWC*, the height of which shows the increase in the *total wage bill* for one more employee, lies above the average-wage curve, *WW*, because the higher wage for the new employee must be paid also to all other employees. The intersection of the demand curve, *DD,* with the marginal-cost-of-labor curve, *MWC*, indicates the wealth-maximizing employment, E_0, at which the wages paid each person is W_0, indicated by the average-wage curve, *WW*. To hire one more employee would increase total costs by the height of the *MWC* curve but would yield a marginal product indicated by the demand curve, *DD*.

If now a minimum uniform wage is imposed at W_1, the employer would be able to hire as many employees as he wished at a *constant* wage rate out to the intersection of the horizontal line W_1 with the curve *WW*. Each extra employee (out to that limit) would increase his total wage bill only by the wages paid that new employee. In effect, line W_1 becomes the average-wage schedule. The marginal cost of more labor is therefore *equal* to the constant average uniform wage already paid each employee. It would pay the employer to hire out to where the horizontal wage line, W_1, intersected the demand for labor curve, *DD*. In the illustrated case, this employment rate at the higher constant wage W_1 is greater than with a rising wage for successive employees (which higher wage must also be paid to existing employees). Both the wage rate and the employment rate are made greater by imposing a *uniform*, constant wage.

So far so good. But there are three, often overlooked, factors to consider. First, the higher wage rate will raise

total costs of operation for the firms; output will be reduced as price must be raised, and, with that, employment will thus be reduced. Second, employers faced with a rising supply curve for labor are often able to confine the higher wage only to the new employee: the old employee has no better option in any event, whether or not the new employee is hired; special fringe benefits or job classifications permit differential pricing without requiring uniform wages for all employees. Third, few employers are large enough relative to the market from which they draw labor to have significant long-term effects on wages by individually varying their rates of employment. Over a longer period, the flow of workers from other employers and areas makes this case of little significance.

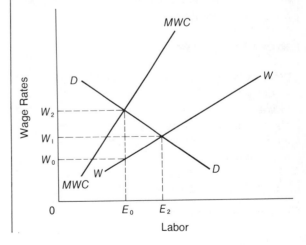

to the vagaries of general business fluctuations is heightened.

A factor tending to soften the effects of minimum-wage laws is the adjustment in conditions of work, which are not controlled by law: health care, vacation, time off for illness, tolerance for tardiness, use of company mail or telephones, coffee breaks, lunches, clean restrooms, parking space, safety, air conditioning, and a vast host of other features. Employees will accept jobs with less of these nonpecuniary features and reduce costs to the employer to offset the higher minimum wages. If this can be done for those who would not be hired at the minimum wage without reducing amenities for those who would have been hired at or above that wage, the minimum-wage law is made less effective.

The groups most severely exposed to all these effects are teenagers, blacks, women, and the aged.[11] It is hard to refute the charge that the minimum wage laws are white, middle-aged, male chauvinist devices. Or as a wit wrote "A $3.50 industrial minimum wage would go a long way toward perpetuating the family farm. . . ."

Equal Pay for Equal Work

Wage differences often reflect differences in working conditions, yet compensating differences in wages are not always welcomed. One of the classic methods of trying to eliminate them is to advocate "equal pay for equal work"—on the presumption that equal work is easy to identify

[11] It follows that since the minimum wage laws are not very effective for household help, a large portion of which is provided by black women, the law hits harder at black men than women.

and that nonpecuniary differences among services by employees or employers should not count.

Many employees seem to express dislike of wage differences based upon nonpecuniary differences. The person who has what are considered "inferior" features dislikes being paid less for the "same" work, even though the wage difference enables him to offset his personal nonpecuniary "disadvantage." "Superior" people complain that compensating wage differences allow "inferior" people to compete for jobs that would otherwise have yielded a still-higher wage to superior people. In many jobs where both men and women might do equally well in pecuniary productivity, men may be hired because of an employer's preference for male employees. Women then have the nonpecuniary disadvantage of being female. But enjoyment of the employer's preference is made more expensive by lower wages for women. Males cleverly advocate "equal pay for equal work"—of course, at the same wages paid to men. Men can profess to be doing this for the benefit of women. Whatever the motivation, the effect is to protect men's jobs and raise their wages by reducing the opportunity for women to underbid men.

This analysis extends to geographical differences in pay. Wages for similar labor are lower in the South than in the North, and lower in Puerto Rico than in the continental United States. How can a northern employee protect his wage from the competition of lower-wage southern labor? And how can a U.S. laborer protect his job (that is, his higher wage rate) from Puerto Rican labor? One device would be to advocate "equal pay for equal work" and for minimum-wage laws. Not surprisingly, such advocacy comes primarily from northerners who profess to want to help southern laborers.

Fair-Employment Laws

Laws for uniform pay or minimum wages transfer discrimination from wage rates to employee types. Pressure mounts for "fair-employment laws," prohibiting employers from choosing employees on the basis of any criterion ruled unethical—usually race, creed, age, and sex. These laws are incredibly difficult to enforce. How can it be determined whether an employer is hiring as many workers whom he and his customers consider "inferior" as he would have if he really didn't think them "inferior"? Furthermore, the employer will be even more reluctant to observe the spirit of the law when he knows it will be more difficult to dismiss those whose services are unsatisfactory.

Fair-employment laws impose burdens on some employ*ees*. If Armenians prefer to work with Armenians, Catholics with Catholics, a black with blacks, or a Mormon with Mormons, these laws make that illegal, for the employer would be susceptible to legal prosecution for *de facto* "discrimination" or segregation.

Immigration Restrictions

Immigration into the United States has been restricted since the late nineteenth century. While it is unwise to admit a desire to create barriers against competition from one's fellow "Americans," it is ancient and honorable to bar "foreigners." Currently, a favorite target is the tempo-rary immigrant Mexican farm worker, who is either excluded or required to work at such high wages that fewer are demanded in the United States. Also many *products* of foreign workers have been excluded; the use of "pauper labor" abroad has been a persistent (but fallacious) argument of American high-tariff proponents (both employers and employees).[12]

Closed Monopsony: Buyers Close a Market to Other Competing Buyers

Monopsony is analogous to monopoly in that it means exclusion of competitors; but in monopsony those excluded are not other sellers but other buyers. So far this chapter has focused on means whereby labor *sellers* (employees) sought to close the market to competitors. In Chapter 14 the collusion involved sellers. But buyers, particularly employers of labor, are anxious to close the market to other employers of labor to keep wages lower. They have had some spectacular successes, many of which have not been recognized. And some of the recognized successes have been regarded as socially desirable.

But most public attention is often drawn to the relatively *ineffective* cases of attempts to lower wages below open-market rates. For example, when asked to name cases in which employers "ganged up" on employees, people usually talk about "yellow-dog" contracts, "sweatshops," and "child labor." In a "yellow-dog" employment contract the employee agrees not to enter a union.

---

[12] This fallacy was exposed on pp. 188–190.

Sweatshops pay low wages. (But lower than what?) Child labor is less productive and therefore earns less. The general objection is that since children have low productivity, it pays to be in school investing in learning to be more productive. The decline in the amount of agricultural labor relative to nonagricultural employment is what accounts for most of the overall decrease in child labor in the past 50 years in the U.S. population as a whole. Child labor on farms has not decreased much.

We turn now to some important, effective collusive actions by *employers* in restricting wages below open-market levels by closing the market to other employers. We call them important because once they affected over half the young men in the entire U.S. labor force.

Hospital Interns

All states require licensing before admittance to medical practice. Membership in a medical association is also required if a doctor is to capture the greater income available from practice in a first-class hospital (other than at a medical school). Suppose the association restrained hospitals from paying interns more than $1000 a month, whereas with open competition among hospitals the rate would be higher—say, $1500. Any hospital that violated the agreement could be punished by withdrawing its "Class-A" certification. The power to *enforce* the price agreement is now established. The gains from secret violations are small relative to the possible punishment, and violators will very likely be detected. All the buyers (Class-A hospitals) of this service (interns) are forced into the agreement. The organization (the American Medical Association) wielding that power was formed for other, more-valuable purposes, not simply to keep interns' wages down, so denial of membership to a doctor or surgeon means a greater loss of wealth than can be gained by violating the intern wage agreement.

One conclusion stands out: It is sufficient to get the power of the *law* on the side of the collusive organization so that "cheaters" of the wage collusion can be *legally* prohibited from buying any of the "service." Without this *legal* constraint, secret violators could go their way, independently taking advantage of the wage agreement by paying slightly more and getting a larger share.

College Athletes and the NCAA

Colleges maintain a very effective but not publicly understood collusion to hold down wages of college athletes. When intercollegiate football became a substantial source of income to colleges, the best football players received money inducements—"wages." Some college administrators opposed all money payments to athletes, because that was "professionalism." They contended amateurism was inherently virtuous. Other administrators, with an eye on the football income, were dismayed that competition among schools was raising athletes' "wages" and reducing net income.

An agreement (athletic "code") among the colleges to restrict wages was reached through the National Collegiate Athletic Association (NCAA). Not surprisingly, colleges switched to athletic "fellowships," "free" room and board, travel to college, sinecures (payments for little or no work), jobs for relatives, clothes, etc. These methods of competition were later restrained by an agreement permitting wages up to $2 an hour. At identical offers, the most distinguished colleges would get the best athletes. The incentive was stronger for the less-distinguished colleges *in metropolitan areas* (large potential gate receipts) to resort to covert offers, and they did so —as evidenced by the frequency with which their violations were detected and punished. To choose one example from hundreds, over a decade ago two California colleges, UCLA and USC were caught "outcompeting" the NCAA code. They were assessed $100,000 fines and prohibited from playing in postseason Bowl games (the most profitable). Even the tennis, basketball, track, and baseball teams—members of which had received no "unethical" payments—were banned from national tournaments. Recently other state universities were under similar bans, for example, the University of California, Berkeley; California State University, Long Beach; Oklahoma; Missouri; North Carolina State; and maybe yours!

How could collusion to restrict wages survive in the face of the great advantages of "cheating"? After all, if television and radio networks tried to suppress performers' wages, other networks could profitably be organized to take advantage of the reduced wages. The National Football League tried to keep wages low but soon found itself faced with other leagues that wouldn't abide by its pay scales. Similarly, the National Baseball League was faced once with a new American League. What rewards of the collusion are greater than those obtainable by not belonging, so that the threat of membership cancellation

can enforce the agreement—on the assumption, of course, that violations can be detected without prohibitive detection costs? (The college athletic conferences—all members of the collusion—hire private detectives and investigators to spy on recruiting activities of students, coaches, and alumni.)

The answer is that any college violating the athletic "code" could find its *academic* accreditation threatened. Any college on probation or expelled would find it more expensive to recruit faculty, and students would be dissuaded from attending. Even Phi Beta Kappa refused to authorize chapters at colleges that gave "disproportionate" amounts of money to athletic scholarships. The survival of the college could be threatened. Why does the present accreditation group have power to prevent formation of a new accreditation system? A very important reason is that colleges do not operate on a self-supporting basis. A college could not expect to survive from football profits if it had to charge competitive tuition to students. No school could get subsidies from the state or major philanthropic foundations without official accreditation by the *present* accreditation group—which is powerful in influencing the *government* and the charitable foundations. We have finally arrived at the source of the value of membership in the NCAA and related organizations: subsidized colleges. The value of the subsidy exceeds the potential football profits, and since control over the subsidy lies partly in the hands of the NCAA, its wrath can mean life or death for the entire college. We emphasize the NCAA was not created to restrict the pay of football players. It was set up for other purposes, but once its greater value for these other purposes could be denied to a nonmember, it became an enforcement agency of a collusive cartel.

Employers' Collusion for Professional Athletes

College athletics is cheap stuff compared to professional sports. The National Football League teams did not bid against each other for players. Players were simply "drafted," and they had to play for whatever team wanted them, or not play in the United States. With the rise of the new American Football League as a competitor, football players began to get their open-market price, which exceeded $100,000 per year for an outstanding athlete, who was paid almost nothing while in college. Subsequently, the two football leagues merged and those open competitive wages (called "suicidal" and "exorbitant" by the team owners, of course) are now "under control."

For many years the two professional baseball leagues tried not to bid against each other for baseball players. Yet, under enormous incentive to get better players, the teams managed to offer side rewards to players, and the system of bonuses developed. More recently the baseball leagues returned to a draft system whereby the teams do not compete with each other in signing new players. As of 1976 there were two professional basketball leagues competing for basketball players, and their salaries reflected it more than do football or baseball salaries.

Military Draft

The most spectacular collusion by buyers was the military draft. From World War II into the 1970s, the United States obtained the bulk of its enlisted men by a draft. A draftee had to work at wages set by Congress—unless he wanted to lose valuable citizenship rights. They required young men to work at less than market wages, when there was no law that required them to do so as policemen, firemen, astronauts, garbage collectors, generals, admirals, or politicians. The draft was a tax young people paid *in kind,* just as the old French kings drafted labor to build palaces and roads. Those who did not bear the tax in kind are those who were not drafted—the old, the smarter, the "physically handsome" who married early and had children, and women.

The costs of military forces are greater with than without a draft, for in its absence explicit money taxes are levied on all who should bear the burden of national defense. Without the draft all who serve are obtained by market money wages for their services—just as airplanes, missiles, munitions, officers, politicians, policemen, firemen, and teachers are obtained. Not only are the true costs of the draft then revealed but they can literally be *reduced* for any specified military capability. Remember what happened in our three-man economy if the wrong people were drafted into producing the various goods. The total possible output became smaller: And so it was with the draft. Without the draft the explicit government-budget monetary tax bill would be larger but the real cost would be smaller. And so it is now with no draft and with a volunteer military.

When the cost is measured more fully in budgeted expenditures, as it more fully is without a forced draft, the military must pay more attention to the true costs of assignments and to means of providing services. Drastic shifts in combinations of inputs occur, according to the principles outlined earlier. At the most obvious level, there is more reliance on civilian employees to provide nonmilitary services. Custodial, food, and sanitation work around military camps is provided by labor cheaper than that of strong young men of greater value as soldiers or in other work. The turnover rate and new enlistee training costs are lower. In short, lower-cost methods are forced into the open. Claims that it is a person's duty to defend his country are beside the point. Everyone has an obligation to defend his country: But it does not follow that the obligation is to pay the tax in kind, which is what those who claim an obligation from only young men are really contending. Specialization in achieving military capability is just as sensible as it is for achieving our food, clothing, and domestic police protection.

Military leaders resist changes that would force them to modify their methods. Any change is difficult, especially if it results only in more efficient methods and provides no gain for those who must revise their way of life. And most politicians find it impossible to ignore that part of costs they are concerned with—the *budgeted* explicit costs, not the total real costs.

Let it be noted that the Union Army in the Civil War, a war in which we used a far greater proportion of our young men with higher fatality rates than in any subsequent war, and in which the men fought with unexcelled valor, was *not* a draft army. It was purchased in the open market: men were "drafted" but every "draftee" had the right to hire someone to take his place, usually by paying that other person a lump sum. The draft

22, 23
24, 25
26, 27
28, 29
30, 31
32, 33
34, 35
36, 37
38, 39

was a means of *assigning the tax* among the young men; once taxed, he could either pay the amount necessary to buy a substitute or he could work it out in the Army. Those who served did so in the cold calculation of the amount of the tax and of the market value of services. Only the heavy tax on young men was imposed by that draft, not the decision as to who would serve in the military.

Summary

1. The source of unemployment is not too few jobs, but too many jobs. Usually what is meant by too few jobs is too few jobs at the salary one would like to or used to have.
2. Labor service is a commodity, subject to the laws of demand and of supply like any other commodity.
3. The demand for labor is a negative function of the wage rate paid for labor. The supply function for labor services is one in which larger amounts of labor can be obtained by offering a higher payment for more services.
4. Differences in wage rates, like differences in prices of various goods, reflect relative demands and supplies of various kinds of labor. *Qualitative* differences in people's productive talents yield differences in relative supplies of those talents and hence in the wages paid. Differences in supplies of various talents reflect inequality in amounts of various *natural* talents, *costs* of training and developing talents, and *willingness* of suppliers of labor to engage in various kinds of work.
5. Differences in *monetary* wages sufficient to

compensate for nonmonetary features of various jobs or of personal traits of employers or employees are called equalizing differences. These differences are sometimes called discriminatory wage differences, in that they discriminate or compensate for differences in the *nonmonetary* attributes of the job and the employer and employees.

6. Much education of people for productive work is on-the-job training. Some wage differences reflect compensation for on-the-job education, since the employee is willing to pay for it by accepting a lower wage. Employees receiving training specific to one employer do not thereby receive lower-than-competitive wages; they receive wages larger than the current value of their current services to the employer and later receive wages less than their value to this employer.

7. Technological progress does not reduce the number of work opportunities. It reduces the value of some jobs and induces people to shift to others formerly left unperformed because of their lower value relative to other performed tasks. Not every producer or employee gains from every technological advance. Some producers gain with higher demand for their services in the new activity. Some, as consumers, gain by lower costs of improved services from the new activity. Some owners of productive goods (labor as well as physical goods) lose wealth by being displaced to new tasks not paying as much as they formerly earned.

8. Compensation to people hurt by technological progress is feasible in principle, but because of exorbitant costs of determining accurately who is hurt and by how much, crude approximations are made by tax-financed compensation schemes or the risks of such effects are distributed via ownership arrangements.

9. Most public discussion of automation and technological advance suggests a "lump-of-labor" fallacy: that there is only so much work to be done, and that every task more efficiently performed with less labor means just so much less worthwhile work is thereby left to be performed. This is identical to saying that currently society could produce all the goods and services it desires, so that any released effort has no other productive uses —an obviously false proposition.

10. Union membership increased from about 5 percent of the work force in the 1930s to about 20 percent at the end of World War II and has remained close to 25 percent since then.

11. Unions affect wage and job negotiation. Wages will be affected insofar as the supply of labor is changed by modified conditions of labor entry to the labor markets. The union shop, the closed shop, strikes, and control of entry to the union affect the labor-supply conditions for employers. Underlying all factors is the power to strike, without which the union would be a relatively ineffective instrument for influencing labor supply to employers.

12. The strike is a concerted action by employees to prevent anyone from working in specified jobs at wages less than demanded by the strikers. The union's power to strike effectively and close markets to competitors is protected by law.

13. Compulsory arbitration would prohibit some

strikes and force an employer and employees to agree to terms set by arbitrators.

14. The effect of unions on overall wages is not definitely known. Estimates are that unions on the average have raised wages of their members about 10 to 15 percent relative to non-union labor but the total overall average was not raised.

15. If wages are set above the open-market clearing level, nonpecuniary productivity more strongly influences job allocation. People strong in desired features are not easily underbid by the people who are poorer in personal traits. Discrimination increases.

16. Wages set above the open-market clearing level yield a monopoly rent. Union leaders find their control over that rent enhanced to the extent that fringe nonmoney benefits are utilized.

17. Union closed-market power appears undesirable because of the way it is enforced—usually by threatened or actual violence. Other professions with closed markets are socially approved because laws authorize closing of markets with police force.

18. Minimum-wage laws transiently raise real wages for some employees, while displaced employees must shift to lower-paying jobs not covered by the laws, or become unemployed. Beneficiaries are those who retain their jobs at the higher wage. Working conditions deteriorate to offset imposed higher wages.

19. Immigration restrictions limit labor supply and keep wages higher.

20. Equal-pay-for-equal-work laws help keep producers who are "inferior" (in some nonpecuniary sense) from higher-paid jobs. Compensating differences in wages are prohibited.

21. Fair-employment laws make it illegal for an employer to choose employees on the basis of age, sex, color, race, religion (but do not prohibit an employee's choice of employer according to these criteria).

22. Collusions among employers have been effective for some special types of labor.

23. The military draft, one of the most effective collusions against sellers, led to inefficiency and a biased measure of the true cost of the military. It was an implicit tax on young, able-bodied, less-educated males.

Questions

1. Almost every year someone proposes that Congress enact legislation "to create more jobs." Of course, it doesn't create jobs, for there are already too many jobs to do and the jobs it presumes to create already exist as useful things to do. What is Congress really being asked to create by that legislation?

2. In almost every city and state during the recent energy flap people were told that unless more energy were conserved or made available, jobs could not be preserved. That statement is of course incorrect. Jobs would in fact be increased by a reduced supply of energy for there would be more work for people to do! What do you suppose people meant, or should have meant, by saying the jobs could not be preserved?

3. "A substantial number of relatively unskilled persons reported that they cannot find work. At the same time, there are many unfilled jobs for relatively skilled people. Apparently,

the problem is that there are more unskilled people than unskilled jobs." What is wrong with the reasoning?

4. In feudal England there was no unemployment—only work and leisure. Employment for wages was rare. But the rise of the commercial system introduced markets for labor services and induced peasants to break away from their feudal ties and to sacrifice their feudal security for the hazards of private contractual employment and unemployment. By the sixteenth century employment for money wages was well established (but maximum permissible wage rates were set by government, and potential employers were exhorted not to offer more and were punished if caught).

    a. What devices do you think developed as a means of paying more than the maximum-wage ceilings?

    b. Why would the government have imposed *maximum* limits to wages?

5. "In the open market, wages are driven down to the subsistence level." That is the iron law of wages. What is meant by "the subsistence level"?

*6. America was founded partly on "slavery" of white men. In early days immigrants "indentured" themselves, pledging to work for the benefit of a master for seven (or some specified number of) years if the master would finance their way to America. Today, this is illegal.

    a. Why?

    b. Who gains and who loses if such contracts are prohibited?

7. "My doctor charges me a high fee because he has to cover the high cost of his educa-

tion and equipment. On the other hand, my golfing teacher also charges me a high fee, even though his education is practically absent." Is either one cheating or fooling me? Explain.

8. "Elizabeth Taylor was paid over $5 million for making a film. Yet Glenda Jackson could have taken her place for, say, $1 million. There must be something wrong with the movie industry." Using marginal-productivity theory, explain how it can be sensible to pay Elizabeth Taylor that much more.

9. A candidate for the office of U.S. Senator proposed that employees be given time off with pay to promote political campaigns of their favored candidates.

    a. Tell under what circumstances you as an emplo*yer* would not care if this were done. (Hint: Remember, there is more than the money pay that attracts employees to a job.)

    b. Who would be paying for the time off?

*10. "Automation is destroying 300,000 jobs a month." Is destroying jobs socially good or bad? Explain why it does not mean that anyone will be left without a job.

11. "In a society where there has not been an adjustment of wages to the savings of time afforded by the use of new techniques, and where such savings may result in an oversupply of labor, an agreement among laborers to prevent such conditions has a lawful labor objective." (Decision by Superior Court Judge Martin Caughlin, San Bernardino, California, in case of *Orange Belt Chapter of Painting and Decorating Contractors v. AFL-CIO Painters District Council 48,* July 1958.) Suppose the introduction of spray and roller painting methods reduced

the amount of man hours in painting a house to 50 percent of its former level.

a. Does the above decision mean that wages should be doubled? Or that the laborers can force the houseowner to hire as many hours of labor with the new technique as with the old?

b. What does it mean?

12. "Technically speaking, any labor union is a monopoly in the limited sense that it eliminates competition between workingmen for the available jobs in a particular plant or industry. After all, all unions are combinations of workingmen to increase, by concerted economic action, their wages, i.e., the price at which the employer will be able to purchase their labor." (Arthur Goldberg, Justice, Supreme Court of the United States, and formerly Secretary of the Department of Labor and counsel for the United Steelworkers; quoted from *AFL-CIO: Labor United,* New York, McGraw-Hill, 1956, p. 157.) Why did he write *"technically speaking"* and "in the *limited* sense"? Is there some other mode of speaking and is there an unlimited sense of monopoly? Does a monopoly (closed or open?) eliminate competition? What does it eliminate and how?

13. "The steelworkers' union and the U.S. Steel Corporation are both monopolies." In terms of the closed and open monopoly distinction, is that correct?

14. You work for a television manufacturer as a welder, and two unions contend for recognition as the sole bargaining unit for welders. One, a "craft" union, would be composed only of welders; the other, an "industrial" union, would admit all employees who work for television manufacturers.

a. In which type of union do you think you will be able more effectively to raise your wages by imposing apprenticeship conditions and other devices to restrict the number of people who can seek jobs in competition with you?

b. Which union do you think will be more able to impose a wage-rate increase upon the employer without first restricting union membership? Explain why.

*15. The National Association for the Advancement of Colored People contends that the building-trade craft unions (among others) discriminate against blacks. The national-headquarter officials of each union reply that the local unions in each city are autonomous and determine membership. The charter provides that there will be no discrimination. The unions reply variously that no qualified blacks have applied, that a new member must be nominated by three members in good standing, that they do have some blacks, that they use a quota system to ensure that all groups are equally represented, and that the present time, when even the white members are unemployed, is not a feasible time to increase entry rates. Given that the craft union has the power to determine who and how many may join the union, some system of choice is necessary—if the number is to be restricted in order to maintain wages above the open-market level.

a. What criteria for selection do you think should be used and declared defensible? Explain why.

b. Would you recommend a quota system? Why?

*16. "Plumbers' and steamfitters' union local 2 of New York has no Negroes, and 80–95 percent of the members are the sons of existing or former members." (News story from *New York Times,* August 2, 1963). What explanation can you offer for this?

17. a. Labor groups were strong advocates of raising barriers to immigration in the nineteenth century. Employers objected. Why?

b. Labor groups were less enthusiastic for tariffs (taxes on imported goods), but some were in favor of them. Why?

18. Walter Reuther, former head of the auto workers' union, contended that automobile producers should lower their prices to benefit the public.

a. Why did he not propose that the current tax (tariff) of 12 percent on importation of foreign cars be abolished as a means of increasing domestic supply?

b. Why do you think Reuther wanted lower prices for products produced by members of his union?

19. Some employers welcome the growth of powerful unions that will be able to raise wages and control number of employees admitted to the union. Why? In answering, show why some employers would be hurt by the elimination of effective unions (even ignoring the conflict in trying to eliminate the union).

*20. "Any craft union that has to resort to the strike to get higher wages is not being operated efficiently. It should instead concentrate on control of apprenticeship rules and admissions in order to assure high-quality, reliable, skilled union members. And it will incidentally thereby achieve its higher wages in a peaceful, democratic way." Explain what the speaker, a highly successful union leader, meant.

21. As a beginning lawyer, would you benefit if fees for the following were set by the bar association: drawing up someone's will, serving as an executor of an estate, arranging for a divorce?

22. A representative of the Congress of Racial Equality advocated raising the minimum legal wage in order to help blacks get higher wages.

a. Would blacks benefit from a higher minimum wage?

b. Would it reduce or increase discriminatory hiring?

23. "The higher the legally constrained minimum-wage rate, the greater the amount of unemployment of unskilled workers." Is this correct? Explain.

24. If in some town the mimimum wage rate for taxi-driver employees were raised to $5 an hour, what would happen to the ratio of cabs driven by the owners to cabs driven by employees of cab owners? Why?

25. You are an immigrant. Would you prefer laws insisting on equal pay for equal work, minimum-wage laws, apprentice laws, or strong unions that have been effective in raising wages above the open-market level? Explain.

*26. The federal government is taxing and paying for job retraining for those who lose a job.

a. Do you think it should provide an apartment renovation service for people whose apartments become vacant?

b. What is the difference between the two forms of aid?

c. Why would you support one and not the other, if you would?

27. As a summer-job-seeking college student, are your chances of getting a job increased or decreased if the wages you can get in a cannery, summer resort, factory, etc., are set by a union comprised of current full-time employees? Why?

28. As a college-age baby-sitter, would you benefit if an association of baby-sitters were organized and a minimum wage of $3.50 an hour enforced? Why?

29. A law is passed requiring each employer to provide hospitalization and premature retirement benefits for his employees who have "heart attacks."
   a. Who will benefit by such a law?
   b. Who will be hurt?
   c. Who will pay the costs? (In answering, first consider the same questions if a law were passed requiring employers to pay for all the housing costs of redhaired employees. Explain why if you were a redhead you would be smart to dye your hair black. Similarly, if you had a heart condition, why would you try to keep it a secret? Does the employer pay for these services—in the sense that his wealth is lower as a consequence of the law? If he doesn't, who does?)

30. Some employment contracts provide the employee with the following: paid time off for jury duty, funerals of relatives, voting, sickness, and vacations; free parking space and work clothes; retirement; two weeks' severance pay; seniority rights over new employees; no discharge for union activities; no discharge if job is displaced by new machinery.

   a. Suppose you were to offer to work for some employer who did not give any of these provisions and who insisted on the right to fire or discharge you at any time for any reason whatsoever. Would you consider working for him at the same take-home pay as for the other employer?
   b. Would the employer be willing to pay you a higher take-home salary for an employment contract without all those provisions listed earlier?
   c. In the light of your answers to the preceding questions, who do you think pays for those fringe benefits listed earlier?

31. The National Teachers Federation, a teachers' union, advocates a single salary scale —wherein every teacher, regardless of specialty, gets the same salary in his first year of teaching, with salary thereafter tied strictly to years of service. Who would benefit and who would suffer if that were made universal: Men or women? Blacks or whites? Superior or inferior teachers? Mathematics or physical-education teachers?

32. "If an enterprise cannot survive except by paying wages of 75 cents or $1 an hour, I am perfectly willing for it to go out of business. I do not believe that such an enterprise is worth saving at that price. It does more harm than good, socially and economically. It is not an asset; it is a liability. So if this kind of business is killed by a minimum wage of $1.25, I for one will not be sorry." (George Meany, Hearings before Subcommittee on Labor Standards, 86th Congress, 2nd Session, 1960, p. 36 of Part 1 of printed hearings.)
   a. How does this statement differ from one

that says, "Any person who cannot produce a product worth at least $1.25 an hour should not be allowed to work as an employee"?
b. Explain why Meany did not suggest that a business that paid wages of $5 an hour was an even greater liability to the community.

33. Laws have been passed designed to prohibit employers from discriminating among potential employees according to race, religion, and, in some instances, age. Why are there no laws prohibiting employees from similarly discriminating among employers for whom they choose to work?

34. Is the analysis of this chapter consistent with the fact of high unemployment rates among blacks in the North? What is the explanation for high unemployment among male blacks, Puerto Ricans, and Mexicans? (Do not answer "low education," "prejudice," or "immobility" since all of those would imply lower wages, not higher unemployment.)

35. "The National and American Football Leagues have finally gotten together and agreed to have a common draft of college players. The draft will eliminate those utterly ridiculous $600,000 bonuses that were paid to untried muscular meatballs from the college campuses. The peace pact will also put a stop to the alarming movement to tamper with the legal property of other clubs (i.e., bid players away from other leagues). The peace pact is welcome. If the cost is high, a continuation of the warfare would have been costlier." (Sportswriter Arthur Daley, *New York Times,* June 9, 1966.)

"Pete Gogolak, the star American Football League placekicker, said today he thought player salaries would not suffer because of the merger of the two leagues. He said, 'The new players who stood to get big bonuses because of the competition between the two leagues may get hurt, but I think the salaries of the other, older players will remain high.' Gogolak had played out his option with the American League Buffalo Bills and then signed with National League Giants at a salary believed to be $32,000." (News item from *New York Times,* June 9, 1966.)

"The common draft, now agreed to by the two leagues, will drastically cut bonus payments and should appease the colleges who have railed against the in-season solicitation and premature signing of college players attributable to the scramble for talent." (Sportswriter J. M. Sheehan, *New York Times,* June 9, 1966.)
a. To which two of the three writers just quoted would you give a flunking grade in economics? Explain why.
b. If General Electric, Westinghouse, and other electrical companies could get together and have a common draft of graduating engineers, would engineers' salaries suffer? Why?
c. If General Electric, Westinghouse, and other electrical companies could get together and have a common draft of college students at a salary of $100 a month and could compel chosen students to work for them or face jail and loss of citizenship, do you think the draft would be regarded as defensible and in the social interest? Reconcile your answer with the existence of the Air Force, Army, and Navy common draft.

36. "An official Defense Department study reported that the elimination of the draft by raising wages to enlistees would cost about $5–$15 billions annually. Therefore the Defense Department in view of that prohibitive cost is recommending continuance of the draft." (News item from *New York Times*, June 1966.)

a. Explain why the first sentence is an incorrect assertion.

b. Would you be willing to assert that raising wages to abolish the draft would *reduce* costs? Why?

*37. Minimum wage laws prevent relatively untrained people, especially teenagers and Negroes, from getting jobs. To overcome this the federal government is going to subsidize employers for hiring these less trained people. The rationale is that the workers hired at the minimum legal wage, though not that productive, will learn on the job and in time become productive enough to warrant that wage. In the meantime, the employer, receiving a subsidy of an amount equal to the difference between the worker's productivity and the wage paid the worker, is providing on-the-job education. Show how this amounts to facilitating a privately operated educational system, with choice by students of the private "school" they will attend.

*38. At many colleges students are seeking membership on committees that appoint or fire faculty members. The faculty usually contends that employment is a matter best judged by qualified people like faculty members. Students contend that the faculty chosen affects their lives and hence they should have a say in the matter. (1) The authors say that neither faculty nor student should have the authority to hire or fire faculty. (2) Moreover, students already have more power than the faculty. Explain in what sense (2) is correct; then defend as best you can the preference expressed by the authors in sentence (1).

*39. The 1977 U.S. National Income estimate of $1.2 trillion annually does not include the value of women's services in the family household. Those services could easily exceed about $.3 trillion. Consider the wages for someone hired to perform all the tasks of a housewife and mother, and do not forget the problem of monitoring an employee's performance to see that it is as efficient and motivated as the housewife's. One reason, possibly minor, for so much self-performance in the home is that the value of that performance is not taxable as an income tax, whereas if performed by a hired employee, taxes would have to be paid. At present income tax rates, women working at home are earning roughly 20–30 percent more (untaxed) than if they worked for taxable money wages. What do you think your mother's services would have commanded in explicit money wages when you were a child?

17

Wealth: Saving, Investing

Wealth is more than inanimate machinery, buildings, fertile land, sheltered harbors, rivers, and good climate. *People* are wealth, too; and so are skills, talents, knowledge, initiative, manners, and customs. To know that the *non*human wealth of the United States has a market value of over three trillion dollars is to know only part of our wealth.

Another form of wealth is the stability of government, reliability of the judicial process, and respect for property rights and certainty of their continuance. Because these forms of wealth are not marketed separately, they have no directly measurable values. Their value is contained, rather, in the value of goods that are sold. For example, people are willing to pay higher rents in cities or neighborhoods with low crime rates.

The sources of greater wealth are savings, knowledge, and efficient coordination of productive abilities. Many areas are rich in natural resources, but these have to be converted to useful form. In this country, the prairie was a forbidding area until man sweated over it with the plow. (With what incentive?) New England's rocky soil, severe winters, and short summers were available to the Indians for centuries, but still the Indians were poor. Resources must be worked with knowledge.

During the Westward advance, people could claim land, appropriated from the Indians, as private property. The land was not held by the government for the "benefit of all the people." Private property was permitted to develop productive wealth. People could sell it or borrow against it; they could "profiteer"; they didn't have to stay on it to obtain the value of their development of the land, as one must today in foreign countries that ban absentee landlords or land sale—for ex-

ample, Mexico, Iran, Egypt, and India. The value of the future consequences of their present actions was capitalized on the owners. The coordinating, incentive effects of a capitalist system were operative. Prices and uses of resources were influenced by open-market competition. In many countries today political suppression of property rights and open-market competition reduces the growth of income and wealth. Could a socialized economy achieve greater wealth than a capitalist economy? Undoubtedly, a higher *proportion* of income can be put into the form of savings by government compulsion. The issues are whether a higher rate is desirable on those terms, whether the saving will be invested as productively, and whether the income itself would be as large. The debate waxes eloquent and emotional; the evidence is not yet conclusive enough to convince everyone.

Note the words of a man who spent 14 years in the "development business," first as a Vice-president of the International Bank of Reconstruction and Development and then as President of the International Finance Corporation:

Let us briefly examine some of the frequently cited causes of underdevelopment. It is often claimed that geography and natural resources are determining. They are of course important. . . . But resources lie inert and have no economic worth except as people bring them into use. It is easy to attribute the progress of the United States to its wide expanse and abundant physical resources. However, other areas—in Latin America, Africa, Asia—have comparable natural wealth, but most of it is still untouched. On the other hand, there are countries in Western Europe with limited fertile land and meager mineral deposits, yet they have achieved high levels of economic life. . . .

Perhaps most often lack of capital is blamed. In the first place, there is in most developing countries more potential capital than is admitted. But large amounts are kept outside, because of political instability. . . . Or it is invested in often underproductive land, low priority buildings, or otherwise hoarded. . . . Over the postwar period immense sums have been made available to the developing areas. Some of these funds have been well applied and have produced sound results, others have not. . . . If [money] is applied to uneconomic purposes, or if good projects are poorly planned and executed, the results will be minus, not plus. The effective spending of large funds requires experience, competence, honesty and organization. Lacking any of these factors, large injections of capital into developing countries can cause more harm than good. The test of how much additional capital is required for development is how much a country can effectively apply within any given period, not how much others are willing to supply.

It is popular in many quarters to charge colonialism with lack of development in territories which have been dependent. This argument seems less persuasive when we observe that a number of countries which have been their own masters for long periods are no further advanced.

I am, therefore, forced to the conclusion that economic development or lack of it is primarily due to differences in people—in their attitudes, customs, traditions and the consequent differences in their political, social and religious institutions.[1]

[1] Robert L. Garner, International Finance Corporation, *Summary Proceedings, 1961 Annual Meeting of the Board of Governors*, September 21, 1961, pp. 4–6.

Sources of Wealth

Having suggested by this quote that the world is a complicated place, we note that those who wish to grow in wealth must do their own saving. Wealth-accumulation involves producing more than is currently consumed. How can wealth be increased? First, a country could build up capital with gifts from abroad or with borrowing, except that outside aid will not contribute to capital accumulation if all of the aid is used for current consumption.[2]

Second, people could be encouraged to save and invest more. But how? Investment might be made by government, financed by taxes, in the belief that private wealth owners refuse to invest enough. But that tends to reduce saving because of a smaller aftertax private disposable income. Furthermore, to escape the tax, people will invest in ways that yield more nontaxable nonpecuniary income. (An example is evident in the

[2] And: "The earmarking of particular foreign loans or grants to specific investment projects may do something to ensure the productive use of funds, but is not by any means a basic remedy. Only if there is no domestic saving at all to start with can such earmarking be fully effective. The Austrian government, so the story goes, asked for the release of counterpart funds to reconstruct the Vienna opera. The E.C.A. [Economic Cooperation Administration, directing the Marshall Plan for postwar European reconstruction] is said to have replied that this would not be a productive investment and that the release could not be granted for this purpose. Then the Austrian government remembered that it was itself financing the construction of an electric power plant in the mountains. It went back to the E.C.A. and asked for a release of counterpart funds to pay for this piece of construction, to which the E.C.A. agreed. So all that happened was a switch: the wily Austrians, having got the E.C.A. to take over the financing of the power plant, now financed the reconstruction of the opera from their own resources." Ragnar Nurkse, *Problems of Capital Formation in Underdeveloped Countries* (Oxford: Basil Blackwell, 1953), pp. 95–96.

United States, where homeowners are not taxed on the "income" from their own homes, whereas pecuniary income from investments in rental apartments or business is taxed.)

Third, political authorities may increase investment in a particular kind of wealth—namely knowledge—through education and research, on the presumption that private investors in the discovery of new knowledge receive insufficient incentive from patent or copyright protection. But this remains a presumption, because patents and copyrights are available, and because the whole conception of the efficient rate of invention or discovery of ideas is still undefined.

A fourth method is to reduce the costs of channeling savings into investments. Just as the costs of distributing food from farmers to consumers are reduced by an extensive network of middlemen, so an extensive specialized network of middlemen collecting funds from millions of savers and channeling them to better investment prospects increases wealth.[3]

A fifth way is to make it more likely that the profits of investment will go to the investor. If rights to profit are threatened or weakened, incentive to invest is reduced. Greater security of entitlements and reduced threat of theft, price controls, or expropriation by taxation enhance security. Many countries have tarnished reputations for security of property. (For example, Brazil, Chile, Indonesia, Kenya, Egypt, Algeria, and Uruguay have reputations that are not yet in the same class as Switzerland, the United States, and Malaysia. Both lists could be longer.)

---

[3] Illustrated later; pp. 440–441.

Property Rights, Growth, and Conservation

To maintain wealth, it is often argued that we should *politically* restrict exploitation of many of our natural resources—forests, seashores, fertile lands, oil, and iron ore, for example. This argument fails both to comprehend the meaning of wealth and to recognize that "using" goods *can* mean converting them into even more valuable forms of wealth. If a tree is more valuable for future use than the current lumber that could be made from the tree now, the *present* (capital) value of the live tree will exceed the value of the lumber in the felled tree. The tree will not be cut now, because goods made from that lumber now would yield less service or income than the growth of the standing tree. Market values restrict wasteful, premature use. People invest in trees, but they can also invest by cutting trees and producing *more* wealth with the lumber. Comparison of present values of the two uses indicates which of the two will give the greater wealth. This explains why it cannot be said that the private-property, open-market system tends to cut trees too fast. It does "conserve" them by capitalizing the highest-valued uses of the tree, whether for lumber, recreation, watershed, or any other use, into the present value of the live tree. By comparison of that value with the value of the lumber if the tree were cut, it is determined whether to cut or not.

But there are circumstances in which people fell trees though the live value exceeds the current lumber value. If no one owns the tree, the only way to capture its value is to cut it and take the wood. No one will have wealth incentives—or legal power—to preserve the tree (rather than cut it prematurely in order to establish rights to the lumber). Or, if no one owns land whose use is affected by trees, the beneficial effect of a tree on the land's value will not be heeded accurately. This is why forests in many parts of England and China were prematurely destroyed. First come, first served. *Lack of well-defined, transferable, marketable property rights,* not personal greed, was responsible for this "wasteful" use of resources.[4]

This same analysis can be applied to fish and game, which, until they are caught, belong to no one. People have an incentive to possess them— killing if necessary to get title—regardless of whether they may be worth more alive. If someone had ownership rights to the live fish, he would have incentive to avoid premature or "over" fishing. Fishing would be restrained, if it is "excessive," as is claimed for tuna, seals, whales, and salmon.[5] As a substitute for property rights in "wild animals," governments have sometimes managed to reach agreements limiting catches to prevent waste. Similarly, as long as no one owns the lakes, rivers, or underground water supplies in the United States, and as long as rights to present and future uses are owned by no one, no one has incentive to use water in its most valuable ways. Instead "first used, first possessed." Everyone dumps garbage in an unowned lake,

since the lost value of polluted water is not thrust upon him or anyone with sufficient rights or self-serving incentive to control pollution. But an owner would suffer that loss of value and would have the right and self-interest to prevent others from excessively fouling the lake. Since most (but *not all*) major lakes are not held as private property, they are excessively polluted with garbage.[6] Water, beaches, and air provide examples. Rights to water are generally, though not universally, assigned only to the person who "uses" it. In California an aqueduct costing billions of dollars was built to move water from Northern to Southern California. The construction of the aqueduct and "use" of the water now was simply an exceedingly costly way of establishing property rights to access to future water. Petroleum was once unowned until taken out of the ground. To remove the incentive to pump oil prematurely simply to get title to it, as with nonowned goods, rights to subsurface oil were prorated to surface area owners.

Let's try to better understand where and in what circumstances we miscalculate or inadequately heed costs because the people responsible for inducing those actions cannot be made to bear the full costs. If a paper mill produces paper worth $10, at a perceived cost of $6, but also pollutes water, reducing the water's value by $5; then the total costs ($6 + $5) exceed the $10

---

[4] Recall pp. 161–162.

[5] Walter Cronkite (or his writers) once said this overfishing was a failure or weakness of capitalism; it is, of course, a result of the failure to *apply* capitalism to fish in the ocean.

[6] One of the authors of this text owned land adjoining Lake Arrowhead and also land at Lake Tahoe. Arrowhead is owned by a private corporation; Tahoe, owned by no one, is divided between California and Nevada. He dumped sewage in one lake, at the other he did not. Why was he "irresponsible" at one lake and not the other?

value of the paper. That is destructive of wealth. But if the fouled water is reduced in value only by $2, then the paper worth $10 is produced at a total cost, or sacrificed value, of $8, a net social gain of $2. When *fully* costed, profitable activity is growth and is always "good" if good means to get what is worth more to people than otherwise would be had. Growth *is* that.

One possibility of assessing, discovering, or achieving growth rather than destruction is to make the calculation of costs clearer and more directly borne by the people inducing the action. Another is to facilitate saving, lending, and investing.

Conservationists, we will presume, are trying to ensure that all costs and all values produced by some activity are fully and accurately assessed, even for resources that lack an owner who would have seen to it that effects on its values are taken into account. Since some resources are not owned, it is often proposed that some government employees should act so as to make users of those resources take into account the values of *all* effects. One way to impress the value of that consequence (cost) on the user is to make him pay a fee (price) equivalent to the presumed loss of value (that is, he purchases a right to pollute). Requiring a payment is a way of ensuring that he really is getting value greater than the loss of value in the resource that is abused. To *prohibit* all use of that air, water, or seashore would be to prevent some uses that yield greater benefit than the damage to the resource. That would be as bad as the old error of not charging any price at all, i.e., placing no restriction on its use. Yet, we have switched to that extreme in our air pollution laws and court decisions which pro-

hibit *any* pollution of air in new areas—regardless of other benefits that would be obtained by some fouling of the air. That reduces welfare just as effectively as overuse of the air. Fortunately, not all our legislators or courts are so ignorant of the lesson of economic analysis. Typically they weigh the change in value in one resource against the benefits obtainable in deciding whether, for example, to permit a lighted parking lot or cooking smells from a restaurant that annoys the neighborhood.[7]

**1, 2
3, 4**

Lending

Anyone can lend some of today's income in exchange for a promise of future income. The lender usually gets a promissory note or a bond as evidence of his claim to future income. The borrower may increase his current consumption, perhaps in the form of a vacation, or buy capital goods. Saving and lending do not necessarily result in production of wealth; some may borrow and consume what another saves and lends.

What is loaned or borrowed is income. You may think that a person can borrow some wealth rather than income; for example, he may borrow your house or your car or money. But all that the borrower gets is the income (service) from that asset.

---

[7] An economist once shocked students (not of economics) by remarking that the best—most valuable—use of Lake Erie may be as a carrier of ore freighter ships, or as a sewer for industrial waste, rather than as a swimming pool for those living next to the lake. It's a matter of which use—and to what extent each use—provides the greatest benefits.

Buying and Selling Capital Goods

A continuing redistribution of capital goods, money, and current services occurs in retail markets (where money is traded for consumption goods), bond markets (where claims to future amounts of money are traded for money now), stock markets (where claims to corporate capital goods are traded for money now), and real estate markets (where land and buildings are traded for money). Because these markets enable asset holdings to be revised, they make a person more willing to accumulate any one kind of wealth. If I could never sell a house once I had built it, I would be less likely to build one. Furthermore, prices in these markets reveal relative values of various kinds of goods.

Interdependence of Lending (Bond) and the Capital-Goods (Stock Market) Prices

Suppose the explicit interest rate in the *lending* market were 5 percent. Suppose also that in the stock market some stock expected to yield $10 a year for the indefinite future were priced at $333, a yield of 3 percent. In that case, you could sell the stock and lend the proceeds, $333, at 5 percent in the loan market and thereby get $16.65 a year instead of $10. For that reason, no one would offer $333 for that stock if they could get $16.65 by lending the $333 at 5 percent. The stock's price would fall, which would raise the realizable rate on that stock from 3 percent toward 5 percent. The ability to practice *arbitrage* between markets by selling in one and lending

(buying bonds) in another brings the yield rates together.

Similar adjustments take place between countries. A higher-interest-rate economy will borrow from a lower-interest-rate economy—as when the United States lends to countries in South America. Also, the South American country will sell future-service-yielding goods to the lower-interest-rate country in exchange for current income.

Prices of common stocks change (even though interest rates may not) because they reflect changed anticipations about the future. It is not always possible to separate factors causing deterioration in future income prospects from those causing a rise in the interest rate. Although different, the two show their effects in the same way —reduced prices of stocks. Therefore, we usually study interest rates by looking at bond markets, where the future payments are less uncertain. If stock prices fall while bond prices stay steady or rise, the cause is likely to have been a deterioration in future income prospects rather than a rise in the interest rate. Regardless of the reason for a drop in stock prices, the effect on capital-goods production is quick.

Investing by Converting Income into Wealth

Wealth is produced in many ways. We can *convert* presently consumable goods to sources of future services. For example, we convert fresh milk to cheese, apples to cider, pork to bacon, grain to whiskey, grapes to wine, olives to olive oil. Or we can produce more durable goods: steel instead of wood buildings, concrete instead of blacktop roads, diamond-tipped instead of metal-tipped record needles, pipelines instead of trucks.

We have talked of saving *and* of investing. When a person saves he is accumulating wealth, that is, he is *investing. Saving is investing,* but the two words describe different aspects of the process. Looking at it as "not consuming," we use the term *saving,* but looking at the particular goods that are accumulated or at the process of making goods to be accumulated, we use the term *investing.* Saving suggests the nonconsumption of income, whereas investing suggests the use of the nonconsumed income.

5, 6

Net Productivity of Investment Activity

A dollar of income used for investment rather than for current consumption often yields *more* than a dollar of future income. That miraculous gain is called the *net productivity of investment.* Plant a seed today and next year have more than one seed, after allowing for all other costs. This net productivity of investment is "economic" productivity. Profitable investment converts—directly or indirectly—energy, or material, to more desired forms. Capital goods usually require the preliminary step of making a tool or a good that is used later to produce consumption services; this is often called a "roundabout" or "indirect" method of production. Though it is customary to see future output increased by use of capital goods, it is also easy to make durable goods or tools that are less productive than their cost. However, obviously wasteful production or investment is undesired, so the capital goods we usually see have net productivity.

A Measure of the Net
Productivity of Investment

If we invest one unit of current income today and thereby get 1.15 units a year hence, the gain is .15 units in one year. In general, for an amount, A, invested today, if we obtain a year later an amount $A(1 + g)$, we define g to be the *net percentage productivity* of investment per year. (In our example, $g = .15$.)

Though we never know in advance what g will be, almost all of us make investments of one type or another—in education, buildings, cars, and business. We "bet" (by sacrificing current consumption or going into debt to others who lend us current income) that the future product will be *sufficiently* greater than the present sacrifice; everyone who invests must gamble. A person's decisions are influenced in part by his estimates of the productivity of investments.

Profitable Investment

Profitable investments are those that yield at least the rate of interest. For example, if the interest rate were 5 percent, and you invest $1 now with a payoff of anything more than $1.05 by the end of one year, your investment would be profitable. An investment is profitable if it gives an increase of wealth at a rate, g, that exceeds the interest rate, i.[8]

Now we can see how crucial information is. You may be sufficiently confident that your investment will result in more than the present

---

[8] Alternatively, the relative increase in future steady *income* flow (not wealth) consequent to a unit increase of current investment—$dY_{(t+1)}/dI_{(t)}$—is called the marginal *efficiency* of investment.

investment cost plus the interest (even though no one else believes it). You may find that within two months other people also become persuaded, so they bid up the value of your asset above your cost (including accumulated interest). That excess is an immediate profit to you. Do not jump to the conclusion that it is desirable for an investor if the rest of the market reacts quickly to his activity. The longer others fail to see what his activity is leading to, the more he may escape imitative competition from other people.

Higher Rates of Investment Tend to Reduce g

The net productivity of investment, g, depends upon many factors: Our legal institutions, property laws, security of peace, knowledge of laws of nature, availability of markets, and mental talents are factors. But one that particularly affects the net productivity is the rate or amount of current income directed into investment.

The higher the rate of investment, the lower is the net *marginal* productivity of investment; that is, each increase in the investment rate will yield a smaller net product than was yielded by the previous increase in the investment rate. Reduced *net marginal productivity* at higher rates of current investment occurs because less-appropriate resources for investment must be diverted from current consumption to investment. Recall from Chapter 11, on production, that the higher (faster) the rate of production of Y, the higher the cost. Similarly, the cost will increase for successive increments in the current rate of investment, which is a way of saying that the net marginal gain will be lower at higher rates of investment.

Demand for Investment: The Most Profitable Rate of Investment

To identify some determinants of the rate of investment-saving that a person or economy is induced to undertake, we resort to the demand-and-supply relationships that relate the value and the cost of an activity to the rate of the activity. The *demand* for investment is a relationship between the net marginal productivity value of investment, g, and the rate of investment. The investment demand schedule shows the feasible profitable rates of investment for any specified g. That relationship has the characteristic that the higher the rate of investment, the lower is the attainable marginal productivity of investment.

In Figure 17–1, the investment demand curve, *DD*, shows for each interest rate the largest rate of investment people think they can make while receiving on the *marginal* dollar of investment a rate of return, g, at least equal to the interest rate. The lower the interest rate the larger is the rate of investment that is most profitable. Why? A lower interest rate should not be thought of as merely a reduction in interest costs when borrowing some particular investment. Many people, noticing that interest costs of borrowed funds may be only a small portion of the total investment, jump to the erroneous conclusion that a lower interest rate has little effect on costs and profitability and hence on the rate of investment. They forget that a lower *market* rate of interest increases *present values of capital goods relative to their current costs of production.* Current income power is used to produce longer-lived capi-

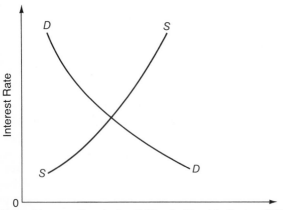

Rate of Income People Are Willing to Divert to Saving *(SS)*,
and Feasible Profitable Rates of Investing *(DD)* at Each
Rate of Interest

**7, 8
9, 10
11, 12**

Figure 17–1. Demands for Investing and Supply of Savings
Are Related to Interest Rate

*The lower the interest rate of the economy, the greater the
most profitable rate of investment that people believe is feasible, shown by the DD curve. The lower the interest rate, the
lower the rate of saving that people are willing to incur,
illustrated by the SS curve. The interest rate is the rate at
which the most profitable feasible amount of investment
equals the amount of savings people would like to perform
by adjustments in production, relative prices, and income
(not graphed).*

tal goods, and *current-service* prices rise less
than *capital-goods* prices when interest rates fall;
therefore that increase in the value of capital
goods relative to their costs of production means
that a higher rate of investment becomes profitable for a *wider* range of capital goods.

We can illustrate this principle. Suppose a concrete building costing about $750 would yield
$100 a year net of all other costs for nine years.
Its *g* is about 4 percent. (See Table 7–3, page 152,
7.44 × $100 = $744, a close approximation to

$750, for 4 percent.) At a 5 percent interest rate
in the market, constructing the building would
not be a profitable investment, for its present
market *value* would be only $711, which is less
than its cost of $750. But if the interest rate were
3 percent, the present value of the building would
be about $780; the investment would be profita-
ble. (Check our calculations by reference to the
data of Table 7–3.) Since most people think of
the interest rate simply as the cost of borrowing
or lending rather than as a reflection of *current
prices of capital goods relative to current service
prices,* we can see why most of them would think
it relatively trivial in affecting general investment
activity.

Savings Supply

The *SS* curve in Figure 17–1 indicates the amount
of current income people are *willing* to save (divert from consumption to accumulation of wealth)
at the different offered rates of return on the vertical axis. The higher the rate of return offered, the
more the savings supplied. People would be *willing* to save at the rate of $3000 a year *if* they
could get, say, 15 percent on the marginal dollar
of saving. But if there were no way to produce so
high a rate of return on the three-thousandth
marginal dollar invested, the *DD* curve would be
lower and would intersect the *SS* curve below the
15-percent rate of interest and to the left of the
$3000 investment–saving rate.

Do not make the mistake of thinking that the
investment-demand schedule and savings-supply
schedule are distinct just because people who
direct the investment are not always those who

save. One curve reflects what is believed to be *feasible* in investment returns; the other curve reflects how much people would be willing to save, if promised that rate of return. Having said this, however, we emphasize that decisions about savings and about investment are in large part made by different people. Therefore, markets or devices are required to coordinate the two activities—saving–lending and investing–producing. If either the savings or investment schedule shifts, not only is the interest rate affected, but serious repercussions for total income and aggregate employment can also follow.

Coordinating Investing and Saving Decisions

Every *person's* behavior is characterized by personal DD and SS curves, summarizing his investment capabilities and savings propensity. In Figure 17–1 the *community DD* and SS curves represent summations over all individuals. Through competition the interest rate is moved toward an equilibrium at which the amount of income that people believe they can invest profitably is equated to the savings (that they are willing to provide).

It would be a mistake to think that this adjustment occurs in just one special market. There is no one market for "savings" or "investment." Instead, those activities are guided in several markets: the lending and borrowing markets, the capital-goods markets, and markets for current production.

1. Increase in Savings Propensity

If preferences for future income increase relative to present consumption, the SS curve shifts to the right, with two results. (1) There will be more offers of loanable funds, with a lower interest rate which allocates the increased savings over the competing borrowers—the same rationing technique investigated in earlier chapters. (2) Prices of assets will rise, because assets are means of getting more future income. For example, prices of steel and concrete buildings (long-lived assets) will rise relative to those of wood. Young, rapidly growing animals will rise in value relative to older, slower-growing ones. Since a yearling steer grows at a faster percentage rate than an old steer, every pound of a yearling represents a greater percentage increase of future beef than does that of older, slower-growing steers. The demand (and price) of yearlings will rise relative to that of older steers; fewer yearlings will be slaughtered, the price of veal will rise relative to that of beef. Less veal and more beef will be supplied.

Consider another example. Suppose the community initially places the value of $710 on each of two goods, one yielding a $100 annuity for nine years and the other yielding $200 annually for four years. This implies a 5 percent interest rate, which you can (and should!) check by using the data in Table 7–3. If the community's preference changes in favor of longer annuities, the nine-year annuity will be increased in value more than will the four-year annuity. If the present value of the nine-year $100-per-year sequence rises to $779 and the four-year stream to $744 (both up from $710), the interest rate will be 3 percent, down from 5 percent. (Check this, too!) Production of the longer-lived goods will be relatively more profitable. The interest rate has fallen in the production activity markets; that is, prices of longer-lived assets have risen relative to current service costs. House prices have risen relative to rental rates for those houses.

2. Increase in Productivity of Investment

Suppose there is an increase in the perceived *feasibility* of producing wealth profitably; new inventions, cheaper refrigeration, more durable and rust-resisting metals are examples of ways to enable more future consumption per dollar of present investments. The *DD* curve (of Figure 17–1) shifts to the right. In the lending and borrowing markets this appears as an increased demand to borrow current income—in the form of money. In terms of the demand and supply of bonds, the supply of bonds increases. The price of bonds falls—that is, the interest rate rises, rationing available savings to the most profitable investment prospects. Otherwise, nonprice rationing would occur wherein allocation would be less heavily influenced by marketable profitability—as we have already studied.

3. Increased Stock of Capital Goods

What would happen if the stock of capital goods increased, possibly by a gift from a foreign country or by the accumulation of capital goods over the years? Don't jump to the conclusion that the interest rate will be lower. The increased stock of capital goods means an increase in current *and* future income. *If* the increase in wealth is heavily weighted by types of capital goods yielding greater future-service relative to the present than for prior existing goods, the interest rate would be higher than otherwise. Why? With a larger ratio of future income relative to present, people are willing to trade more out of future income for present income rights. The proper analogy is of the person who learns he will have more income in the future than he had formerly expected; he immediately borrows against his future. On the other hand, a reduced *proportion* of future relative to present consumption potentialities may be inherent in the increased stock of capital goods. The interest rate would be reduced. (Why?) Thus, we do not know whether a country that is richer in capital goods will have a higher or lower interest rate.

4. Prospects of Reduced Future Yields

Let's take a more difficult case. Suppose beliefs about future yields of existing or producible assets deteriorate; the *DD* schedule shifts to the left. Those who first have this belief will try to sell their common stocks or capital goods to others before the belief is confirmed by ensuing events or more broadly shared. Their efforts to sell will depress stock prices (including prices of capital goods such as buildings and land). Lower prices of common stock and capital goods make investment less profitable, so investment will be reduced. People will switch to assets whose future yields are not expected to deteriorate so much, for example, bonds or money. This will lower interest rates in the bond markets (raise bond prices).

The process is not pleasant, because the future (in our example) is not pleasant. Investment-goods producers (and others) must shift to new jobs with transient unemployment and lower incomes. Savings are reduced. So *both* the *DD* and the *SS* curves shift to the left. Caught in a squeeze of falling asset prices and reduced income and the necessity of paying off debts, firms will seek to borrow money to tide them over the "adjustment." During this "liquidity"-adjustment crisis the interest rate in the loan markets is pushed up *temporarily.* (Why?)

The point of all these examples is that adjustment of the interest rate pervades every market and all exchanges. And a shift in the demand schedule for investment can also shift the savings-supply schedule. Events that change the demand for (that is, the profitability of) investment and capital goods have broad ramifications, which are not confined to one small market. The consequences are more widespread than a change in the demand for tires, wheat, and almost every other good. The interest rate reflects relative demand for *all* types of goods capable of rendering services in the future. And since rights to present and future income can be traded in *many* ways in many markets, the interest rate will affect many markets, with effects on aggregate incomes.

12, 13 affect many markets, with effects on aggregate
14, 15 incomes.

Why the Loanable-
Funds Market Is a
Key Market

Since almost all exchange occurs through the medium of money rather than by barter, people revise the timing of their income or consumption streams not by trading this good now for that good later, but by trading money now for money later. Hence, we can expect almost all revisions in investment prospects and savings willingness to affect borrowing and lending in money markets, where interest rates are most explicitly expressed. That is why factors affecting rates of interest and investment are often analyzed in terms of demand and supply *for money* or loanable funds in the so-called money markets. That is why people tend to refer (very misleadingly) to interest as the price of money. It would be better to refer to interest as the price of borrowing or

16, 17 of *credit.*

The Meanings
of the Interest Rate

The expression *interest rate* is associated with several different concepts. First is the net rate of increase in wealth from a dollar more of investment, which we denoted as g, the net productivity of investment. Second is a personal, subjective valuation of present consumption rights, measured in terms of the amount of future income that is valued as equivalent to one dollar of consumption now. Third is a market rate of return on loans, called a *rate of interest on credit*—on bonds or promissory notes. If this third rate is greater than the second, people will reduce present consumption (save more). If the second is less than the first, investment will increase. Fourth is an interest rate that is implicit in the relationship between present prices of capital goods and their future income streams. All these rates—(1) the net productivity of investment, (2) personal valuation of future income relative to current consumption, (3) return on bonds or loans, and (4) the interest rate implicit in relative prices of capital goods—are brought toward equality by switching activity among the various markets and goods. When all are equal, the common value is the interest rate. If any are not equal, then arbitrage (the simultaneous buying and selling of the same thing by the same person) will induce adjustments of profit prospects in the various markets, pushing them all toward equality. Since the most easily perceived and measured rate is the rate in the market for *secure bonds,* we usually look at the rate in that market to measure the interest rate. This explains why the interest rate is referred to variously as the price of "current consumption," the price of "credit," the price of "savings," the price of "loans," the "rate of time-preference," the "net rate of investment productivity," and the "price of money." Properly interpreted, it is a measure of all these things in equilibrium.

Historical perspective is provided by Figure 17–2, which shows long-term interest rates (on 10–20-year secure bonds) during the past century. Some swings in that rate can be explained by long-term movements in the price level and associated anticipations of inflation; by government monetary policy; and by changes in business conditions. We shall explain later how these affect the rate of interest.

18, 19
20, 21

Explicit Nominal
Interest Rate and Implied
Nominal Interest Yield

We know the interest rate explicitly stipulated in a loan at, say, 6 percent per year may not be the implicit (also called *effective*) rate. For example, if you lend $900 for a promise of $1000 to be re-

paid in one year with a zero interest rate explicitly stipulated in the written terms of the loan, you are in effect being promised a return of 11.1 percent. ($1000 − $900)/$900 = 11.1 percent. If the loan is repaid when due, you will have *realized* an interest rate of ($1000 − $900)/900 = .111 or 11.1 percent per year. The implicit effective *yield* is 11.1 percent per year at the time the loan is made (taking into account not only the stipulated, explicit rate of zero percent but also the initial present amount loaned and the amount due later). You can see that the implicit yield differs from the explicit rate if the present (price) amount actually loaned differs from the principal amount to be repaid (excluding the *explicit* interest). In general, for any *one-year* loan, the *implicit* (or *effective*) yield, i, is given by the following formula:

$$i = [(Ar + A)/P] - 1$$

where r is the interest rate explicitly expressly *stipulated* in the loan agreement; A is both the principal amount on which the interest is to be paid and the amount to be paid as principal when the loan is due; and P is the present amount paid or loaned.

For example, suppose you buy a bond promising a stipulated, explicit 5 percent interest per year on a principal amount of $1000, due and payable in one year. The present price, or amount you pay now, for that bond is, we assume, $900. The *implicit* yield is $[($50 + $1000)/$900] - 1 = .167$, or 16.7 percent per year. If the present price had been $1000, the implicit yield would be 5 percent.

In referring to an interest rate, we shall usually mean the implicit (effective) yield rather than the

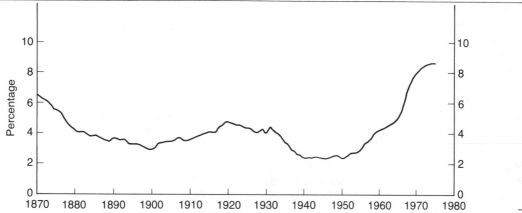

Figure 17–2. Long-Term (10–20 Year) Corporate Bond Nominal Interest Rate (Highest Grade Bonds). *Source: National Bureau of Economic Research.*

The long-term interest rate has varied over a wide range for various, not entirely explicable, reasons. We conjecture that the recent rise to 8 percent is in anticipation of a rising price level in the future, thereby inducing lenders both to insist on a higher money rate and to be willing to pay more in money terms if prices are going to rise in the future. If inflation is curtailed, that recent rise should become a peak rather than a plateau.

stipulated rate. And if the loan is paid on schedule, the implicit effective yield will be the *realized* interest rate yield on that loan.

Default Risk

Some debts have very high assurance the borrower will pay interest and principal promptly. Currently, U.S. government bonds are as high in quality as any available, but not because government officials are more honest or reliable than private individuals. Instead, the government can use the police to collect taxes.[9] (Also, it has the power to "collect taxes" by creating money.) Private bonds usually can be repaid only if the

[9] Evidence of the importance of the ability to collect taxes is that government bonds that are repayable only from receipts of particular projects (such as toll roads) are of lower quality than "general" tax-supported bonds and promise higher yields.

borrower is able to induce people to purchase his products. Bonds issued by private firms like General Motors, American Telephone and Telegraph, and the Santa Fe Railroad are of very high quality because they are almost certain to be paid when due. Bonds of other strong firms promise an implicit yield of about 8 to 10 percent. There is a vast range of riskier bonds that *promise* higher yields.

You will notice that we have referred to "promised yields" and not to the interest rate. Superficially, riskier bonds appear to pay a higher rate of interest. The promised yield includes a risk premium. For example, suppose a potential borrower of $100 offers 5 percent interest per year, and you regard the probability of repayment as being only one-half. To make that an attractive proposition, you could offer to lend him $50 for his promise to repay $105 in one year. Under this arrangement you will get $105 with a probability of .5 and nothing with a probability of .5. *On the average* you would get $52.50, which would be equivalent to 5 percent on your loan of $50, though the *promised* yield on the $50 loan is 110 percent.

For example, in mid-1975 TWA (Transworld Airlines) three-year, $1000, 6.5 percent bonds could be purchased for about $700 on the New York Bond Exchange, which promises the purchaser an explicit yield of about 18 percent annually; New York Central RR, 30-year, 5 percent bonds could be purchased for about $70, giving an implicit yield annually of about 70 percent, if paid; and Chicago Calumet Skyway, 20-year, $3^3/_8$ percent bonds could be purchased for about $450, giving a promised implicit yield of about 30 to 35 percent annually, if paid. All these bonds promise to pay the stipulated interest annually and $1000 principal when due—like the average yield on the *winning* tickets in a lottery!

A test of the validity of this interpretation is provided by events in the bonds markets. If risk accounts for a difference in promised yield, then when a business firm has improved prospects of meeting its debt obligations promptly, the price of its outstanding bonds should rise. And they do.

I may know I will repay a debt when due, but does the lender know it? Some borrowers call the loan market imperfect because *they* cannot borrow on the same terms as their neighbor; and some complain they cannot borrow at all. The lender sees differences among borrowers in the prospects of prompt repayments without extra costs being imposed on the lender. You should not expect a lender to tell you rudely that your promises are too risky. A banker says, "I'm sorry; we just don't have any funds to lend now." The

banker is tactful—and misleading. If he chose to be tactless he could have said, "We think the prospect of your repaying is not high enough. We specialize in loans to people with better credit prospects. To lend to you, we feel that we should ask 25 percent instead of 19 percent to help cover the costs of the collection problems and other activities in defaulted loans. Go to lenders who specialize in higher risks and are better prepared to handle your type of defaults."

Effect of Quantity of Money versus Effect of Increasing Quantity of Money

Often it is said that the larger the quantity of money, the lower the interest rate and the larger the rate of investment. However, twice as much money means twice as high prices of wages, goods, land, and stocks. There will be twice as much debt and twice as much wealth, income, savings, and investment in money terms—but no change in interest rates or in real quantities.

There are transition effects of *changing*—say, increasing—the quantity of money. There are effects, too, from the *way the new money is created and initially spent*. Suppose new money were created by a legal counterfeiter who proceeded to spend it on wine, women, and song—with the result that there was an interim increase in the demand and prices for wine, women, and song, without affecting interest rates. But suppose, instead, our counterfeiter was a dull fellow who used his new money to buy bonds. That would immediately push up the price of bonds, or, if you prefer, lower the interest rate. That creator of the money is a member of the community and he has shifted the community's demand for future income relative to present income by his bond purchases with his new money.

It so happens (as explained in Chapter 19) that the usual process of legally increasing the quantity of money is almost always associated with the purchase of bonds and promissory notes.[10] For this reason, low interest results not from creating and issuing money but from the purpose for which that new money is *initially* spent. The increase of money was initially used to increase the relative demand for bonds. This is why you will frequently read that *increased* money leads to transiently lower interest rates—but only because that new money is first spent for bonds. (If, however, as we shall explain later, increasing money leads to *anticipation* of inflation, interest rates will be higher.)

**Inflation and
Nominal and Real Rates
of Interest**

All the preceding holds valid for periods of zero inflation. If inflation (a general, persisting rise in prices) occurs, the major effect is to raise the nominal (dollar) interest rate above the real (real-goods) interest rate. For example, if you were to lend $100 for one year at 10 percent per year and if in a year all prices were to double, you would suffer a loss in real purchasing power, for you will get back $110, which at the new prices buys

only as much as $55 would have at the old prices. You are being promised a negative *real* interest rate of *minus* 45 percent! The nominal rate was stated as 10 percent per year, but the promised real rate is −45 percent per year. Using more likely numbers, if inflation continues at the rate of 8 percent per year, a loan that promises 10 percent in nominal (dollar) terms is promising the lender only 2 percent more in real terms in one year. The nominal rate is 10 percent, but the real rate is 2 percent. (All this assumes that the principal and promised interest are actually paid as promised.) The *real* rate depends on what happens to price levels. (Don't confuse the *real* with the *realized* rate. The *realized* nominal rate depends on what is in fact repaid, while the realized real rate depends also on what happens to the price level.)

We can now quickly dismiss the commonplace claim that the government can keep the rate of interest low by creating new money with which to buy bonds (lend), thereby driving down interest rates. According to the claim, an increased supply of money to purchase bonds (that is, to lend money) would raise bond prices and lower interest rates. In fact, as you can now see, the increased stock of money will lead to higher price levels, with more money chasing the same amount of goods. The threat of the increased stock of money will create anticipations of inflation and thereby reduce the willingness of people to lend at such low nominal rates, and will increase the willingness of people to borrow at those old, low nominal rates. The nominal interest rates will be adjusted upwards to allow for the reduced future purchasing power of the money interest and principal. Hence, there is a chance of significantly driving down interest rates

---

[10] Most of our money is in the form of commercial bank debts, debts payable on demand by writing a "check" on the bank. Because it is repayable immediately *on demand* at the option of the holder, holders of this kind of debt will get a lower rate of interest *per year* than on a debt payable only after some time.

by increasing the money supply to lend more now against bonds *only* if the public can be fooled into the belief there will be no increase in the inflation rate. What do you think are the chances of fooling the public in that way?

Specialization of Borrowers and Lenders

The people who save are not generally the people who perform the investment activity. Savers (say, families) rely on producers (business firms) to make capital goods. Coordinating these groups—savers of income and producers of investment-goods—is a complex network of financial intermediaries (jargon for "middlemen") who channel savings from savers to investment-goods producers or to consumer–borrowers who utilize the "financing" made available. Financial intermediaries are specialists who collect savings and who can identify or locate demanders of such funds, the investors and borrowers. Because of the diversity of capital goods and producers, there are people especially knowledgeable about borrowers, their credit worthiness, and their likely demands for funds. Similarly, there are intermediaries who specialize only in serving savers, and who use other intermediaries to channel the flow of savings to investors and borrowers. Commercial banks, investment banks, savings and loan institutions, commercial credit and consumer loan companies, pension funds, insurance companies (insurance premiums are composed partly of savings as well as payments for current risks), stock investment funds, bond markets, and stock exchanges with their host of brokerage houses are only a part of the financial intermediary structure. All help reduce the costs of channeling savings to investment activity, thereby making the economy more productive and richer than if each saver had to search out each ultimate investor or borrower and make comparisons among them.

Financial intermediaries also reconcile conflicting desires of savers, investors, borrowers, and lenders about the contract terms. If lenders want to lend on *short*-term—say, for less than one year—while borrowers want to borrow on *long*-term—say, 10-year—contracts or bonds, the intermediaries act as adapters, borrowing on short-term from the savers–lenders and in turn lending the funds to the borrowers–investors on long-term contracts. For example, a saving and loan bank permits its depositors (savers) to draw out funds with very short notice while it lends on long-term contracts. The operators of the bank anticipate, correctly, that the many savers, in their day-to-day offers and withdrawals of funds, will just about balance out with no large, unexpected net drain of funds, thereby permitting the institution to lend the funds on long-term bonds —usually by paying lower interest rates for the collected funds in order to cover their costs of intermediation. Their costs of intermediation are *lower* than the costs lenders and borrowers would incur if they tried to operate without specialized intermediaries.

This role of financial intermediaries can be illustrated by noting a few of the stages in making, selling, and using an automobile. The manufacturer's employees and suppliers want to be paid now so that they can consume now, but they are glad to make a car if someone is willing to pay them now and wait for the future income from the car. If the owner of the business were to finance the work—that is, pay now and collect later—he would have to defer to consumption. But he wants to specialize in production activity, not in saving. He seeks a lender to finance the current production by transferring current income rights (that is, by lending money) to auto producers in exchange for later repayment. Automobile manufacturers borrow by selling bonds to the public and to such institutions as insurance companies that channel public savings. They also borrow from commercial banks to carry them over seasonally active periods. Car retailers also rely on commercial banks. In addition, they borrow from finance companies and commercial credit companies. The ordinary consumer has little occasion to deal directly with some of these financial intermediaries. Yet, because they exist, the car dealer can carry a bigger inventory, allowing the consumer to inspect a larger variety of cars and get quicker delivery with cheaper credit costs.

The typical consumer will borrow to pay for the car. He is likely to deal with a consumer credit company, either directly himself or indirectly through the car dealer who attends to details of the loan. The consumer may borrow from a credit union at his place of work, because the credit union is relatively well acquainted with his personal situation and prospects of repayment. He may borrow directly from a neighborhood bank or from an insurance company with which he has a policy. As goods pass along the line from producer to final consumer, the successive stages are financed by a series of different lenders with special knowledge about successive participants.

An excellent index of a country's wealth and productivity is the sophistication and efficiency of its financial intermediary institutions. These reduce the costs of engaging in secure saving and productive investment—the key to economic development in a private-enterprise society. In authoritarian directed economies, the rate of saving and form of investment is controlled by political processes, whereas in private-enterprise societies decisions about extent of savings and form of investment are made by individuals in the light of feasible rates of return on investments to which property entitlements are relatively more secure. Therein lies a difference between socialist-directed societies and noncentrally directed societies.

Negotiability of Bonds

Lenders who may want to change their minds about deferring consumption until a bond is repaid can sell the bond to someone else, who will thereby defer his consumption. The right to sell an outstanding bond to someone else is known as *negotiability*. Lenders (bond buyers) are willing to accept lower interest for the greater "liquidity." However, a borrower may prefer to have his debts not transferable, since the original lender might be more considerate and lenient in the event of difficulty in repaying a debt. Because of the agreement not to sell the bond to someone else, nonnegotiable notes usually carry a slightly higher rate of interest.

Negotiability of bonds is facilitated by bond brokers and the New York Bond Exchange, a formal, privately owned marketplace where the bonds of well-known, strong American corporations can be bought and sold—not from the corporations but from people who earlier lent money to the corporation, or from those who subsequently bought the bond from the original lender.[11] A large portion of bond resales, however, takes place elsewhere than the Bond Exchange, through bond brokers or dealers. Much like used-car dealers, they maintain small inventories of outstanding bonds of well-known corporations, but they know other people from whom any particular bond can be bought—at a price. These security brokers, relying on telephones and computers, are known as "over-the-counter" security dealers, since they do not operate in a formal, physically compact exchange like the New York Bond Exchange.

Since none of these bond-market transactions transfers money to the original borrower, some people erroneously think these markets serve no useful purpose to *original* borrowers or lenders. But used-bond markets are as important to the production and sale of new bonds (that is, to saving and lending) as the used-car market is to the production and sale of new cars. How many people would buy cars if they could never sell them but had to keep them until they were junked? Because these markets facilitate the transfer of bonds, more people are willing to hold bonds. The initial flow of savings to investors is made cheaper. Negotiability of bonds also permits people to be more discriminating in their risk selections.

---

[11] Prices and amounts of bonds exchanged on the major organized exchanges are reported in the financial pages of major newspapers and in stockbrokers' offices.

Legal Restraints on Access to Loan Market

The existence of a positive interest rate has been variously denied, condemned, or legally prohibited. Aristotle asserted that money is "sterile," so that no interest should be paid for money loans. Yet, interest was paid before and after Aristotle's condemnation—despite religious dogma and other sources of protest, because there were borrowers who offered to pay interest rather than not get loans. And the would-be borrower had to pay it because the demand for savings was greater than the supply at a zero price. Until about the sixteenth century Christian theology "officially" condemned interest as a venial (minor) sin. Christians conveniently borrowed from Jews, whose religion placed no severe ban on taking interest from gentiles. In fact, however, the Papacy itself charged a positive interest— though under the name of "fees," "gratuities," or anything but "interest" or "usury." In the Middle Ages, lords had claims to payments from users of land. Sometimes the lord wanted to sell to the church his rights to future rents. Suppose an annuity of rents was expected to run for at least 50 years. For what price could it be sold? A 50-year annuity of $1 a year would be sold to the church for less than $50—because the rate of interest was positive. In buying lands, the church was charging a positive rate of interest—unless it paid a unit price equal to the expected *undiscounted* sum of the future annuity payments. And it never did that, as far as we know.

Interest-Rate Ceilings and Usury

Economic facts of life have insidious ways of circumventing political laws or decrees. With man's usual speedy perception, it took the church only about 1000 years to lift the ban against interest on loans—but still, state governments decree "unreasonably" high (usurious) rates of interest illegal. In most states, any rate over 10 or 15 percent is called usurious and illegal. (But most were quickly repealed in the past two years when market rates rose over 10 percent!)

Lenders who make riskier loans at a higher interest rate, in the hope of averaging an acceptable return, resort to legal fictions. Pawn shops lend to strangers of dubious credit at a rate of 30 percent per year—not by a "loan," but by a "purchase and repurchase" agreement. You sell your camera to the pawnbroker for $100 (which is less than its market value) and simultaneously obtain the right to buy it back in one year for $130. When, and if, you buy it back, you have paid 30 percent to cover the risk, interest, storage, and transaction costs.

An effective prohibition of high interest rates would prohibit borrowers with dubious credit from borrowing at all. Legal barriers, of course, are not necessarily undesirable. That depends upon one's attitudes toward the consequences of open contracting and open access to markets for lending. Restrictions on the rights of commercial banks to make certain types of loans (long-term business loans, second mortgages, stock-exchange loans in excess of certain amounts) are alleged to prevent bankers from making loans that are "too risky" for their "own best interests" and the safety of their depositors' accounts. Also, banks are legally restricted in the interest rates they can competitively offer to depositors or charge to borrowers. (Do you suppose that is the result of the bankers' political power?) However, a bank that is prevented from making certain

types of loans can still make risky loans within the authorized class of business borrowers. (Laws restricting the class of permitted bank borrowers or the interest banks can charge have not prevented banks from competing with other cost-incurring services.) These restrictions compel many borrowers, especially the poor-risk borrowers, to resort to more expensive sources of funds. Rather than helping borrowers who would normally pay high rates to cover their low-security status, laws that limit the "interest" rates lenders can ask increase the costs of borrowing to poor people by forcing them to less-efficient sources of funds—or prevent them from borrowing at all.

Limits to Borrowing

Some restrictive laws are directed at borrowers. Since some consumers go "too far" into debt, apparently *everyone* should be controlled. Or, perhaps, although it's permissible to borrow for a house, doctor bills, or business equipment, it is impermissible to go into debt "merely to enjoy consumption before one has earned all the costs." Thus, a generation ago considerable publicity and legislation condemned consumer installment loans. But the desirability of earlier over later consumption, and of consuming while earning, replaced the old-fashion virtue of high consumption in one's old age. Today, installment buying is an accepted convenience—which has brought the specialized loan market to the young as well as to the older.

The Board of Governors of the Federal Reserve Banks is authorized to restrict installment debt. It once prohibited installment credit for more than 50 percent of the value of the item purchased, by requiring a 50-percent "down payment." Why? Three reasons have been advanced. First, as we said earlier, it protects the consumer from his own carelessness. Second, the total amount of consumer credit is deemed too large for the "good of the economy"—though it has not been explained why. Third—this reason is advanced by *opponents* of the restriction—the Federal Reserve Board, which is alert to the U.S. government's borrowing problems, wanted to channel more of the available savings to the government: By establishing borrowing limits for private consumers, the government was left with less market competition for loans and could borrow at lower interest.

Higher minimum down-payment regulations reduce installment debt, but they increase other debt. Frustrated consumers increase mortgaged debt on houses or land. The inconvenience and costs of increasing such debts often exceed the costs of installment loans. These loan restrictions have different impacts on different kinds of people: the older, richer, and more-informed are not restricted as much as the younger, poorer, and less-informed about other sources of funds.

Individuals are prevented from "excessive" indebtedness not only as consumers but also as investors. The Federal Reserve Board limits the amount a person may borrow from a security dealer against the stocks and bonds he owns. Why? Not to protect him if the stock should fall, but instead to prevent stock prices from being bid up higher—as they allegedly would be if people could buy shares with lower down payments. This power to control credit assumes the Federal Reserve Board is better able to judge what the prices of common stocks should be than are investors in an open market. It is a most attractive bet that the Federal Reserve Board is not as good a judge of the right prices of stocks as is the open market, but in any event the evidence (and economic analysis) says those margin regulations do not affect stock prices in any systematic way.

It is easy to foil the debt limit. Borrow from a banker (instead of the security broker) using the stock you are about to buy as the pledged security. Your banker can lend more if he wants to, but not for the express purpose of buying stock. The money you get from the banker can be used to pay some other bills, while the money you otherwise would have used to pay these bills is released for stock purchases. Money is fungible.

Not only the United States but most other countries also restrict borrowers. Any person who proposes to sell new bonds or new common stock, but does not give out specified information or attempts to market gleaming promises, can be prevented from selling the securities through the mails or on security exchanges. Without controls on open-market solicitation and sale of investment securities, it is argued there will be more "suckers" in the quest to get rich. Established business firms will find it less expensive to borrow if new, unproved firms cannot compete for funds on those organized markets. *If* some people can select investments better than can other people, *and if* these people can be identified in advance, then giving them power to control the kinds of investments for which funds can be solicited in the market may lead to less error in use of resources; but no evidence exists to support these premises.

The propriety of controls on the stock market cannot be settled by simply weighing their effects on the extent of profitable or unprofitable investments, or on the extent to which dishonest security dealers are detected. It concerns also the question of whether a person ought to be allowed to make whatever investment choice he would like to make, through whatever agency he chooses, as long as he pays for the resources used. Whether he invests foolishly or consumes too much chocolate cake is a decision he might consider his own. Who is right?

22, 23
24

Personal Investment Principles

It is well and good to talk about investment and wealth in general. But both occur in the form of particulars; consider, for example, a widow who finds herself with a small fortune of, say, $100,000. In what form should she keep that wealth to provide herself with an income and perhaps a legacy for her children? What should a young father do to accumulate a fund for retirement?

Dividends or Capital-Gain Stocks?

Should they buy for dividend income or for capital-value appreciation? This question is (except for tax purposes) pointless. Why? Business firms, we hope, have net income which is either reinvested in the firm or used in part to pay dividends to stockholders. Companies that pay dividends do *not themselves* invest all of their earnings, while (capital-growth) companies that do not pay dividends *do themselves* invest all their earnings. But with either kind of stock you could consume the same amount. If the company pays dividends, you can yourself buy more stocks and reinvest. If they invest earnings instead of paying

dividends, you can sell some of your appreciated stock (reflecting the retained earnings) or borrow against it and consume as much as you would have if the dividends had been paid.

For example, suppose you have 10,000 shares in a company that earns $1 per share annually. Assume the stock is now selling for $10 a share. If the company were paying dividends of $1, the stock price would stay at $10. You receive $10,000 annually, which you can spend, and at year-end you have $100,000 in wealth. If, however, the earnings (income) is being retained by the corporation, the stock will rise in value by $1, to $11 at year-end. You can sell 909 shares of the stock at year-end for $11 each and consume the $10,000 proceeds, and you will have 9091 shares left worth $11 or $100,000 in total. In either case, the amount you can consume and the amount you have left is the same as in the case of dividend-paying stock.[12] Whichever yields the greatest "income plus increase in capital value" will provide the greatest income or consumption power—whether it be consumed or saved.

What Variance Risk?

For investment, a necessary choice is whether to invest in assets (we shall speak only of common stocks as an example) that have a wider range of potential future values (say plus or minus 30 percent) in a year, or in assets that promise a

[12] *Nearly,* because of a difference for your income taxes. If you are in a tax bracket paying over 25 percent of the highest dollar earned, you might be well advised to hold nondividend-paying stocks and to realize the income in the form of capital-value proceeds by selling stocks. This is an idiosyncrasy of our tax laws which puts a lower maximum tax on capital gains. There is another difference. The cost of selling some shares is not negligible.

smaller range (say plus or minus 10 percent). The first are called "volatile" and the second are called "blue chips." Suppose you have purchased oilwell stock. If oil is discovered, assume the stock value will go up by a factor of 10; if not, it will fall to zero. That is a volatile (risky) stock. But you could buy American Telephone and Telegraph and almost certainly at the end of a year its price will not be over 15 percent greater or lower. On the *average,* volatile stocks will yield about what the very-small-variance stocks yield, say 10–14 percent a year judging by the record for the twentieth century. However, you cannot count on experiencing exactly the *average* yield, every year on every stock, so if you buy one volatile stock you will probably be farther from the average (above or below) at the end of the year than if you had bought the smaller-variance stock. (For that extra risk of being farther above or below the average, the riskier, larger-variance stocks yield, on the *average*, a slightly higher growth.)

Your choice must be about the extent of variation to which you expose your wealth relative to the average gain. You can achieve near certainty (zero variance) in your future *dollar* wealth position by holding high-grade, *short*-term bonds or savings deposits. (However, while this gives you very high security about the *money* value of your wealth a year hence, it exposes you to a loss in real terms if inflation has not been accurately anticipated in the market, or a gain in real terms if an anticipated inflation does not occur.) What size of *variance* (risk) of future growth (or loss) in wealth will you accept? Against which particular type of unpredictable future events do you want protection? That decision cannot be avoided —although you may refuse to recognize it.

Random Selection, within Variance Class, Because of Information Efficiency

Once you have predicted high- and low-variance stocks from inspection of past behavior, which ones in each set should you buy? A very good rule is: Pick at random! Shocking? It's a very good rule, especially if you confine yourself to stocks sold in the major stock markets. This does not argue that ignorance is bliss, but, rather, that information and evaluation of prospects of various companies are quickly and openly revealed in stock prices, which reflect the opinion of the market at large. Any stocks that *were* "good buys" will have already been bid up to where they are no better than previous "bad buys" whose prices have been allowed to fall until they are equally good buys. Open competition in the open public market *with publicized prices* of actual trades provides stock *evaluation* at low cost to us innocents, for the best opinions of the insiders, professionals, and everyone else are revealed in the actual market prices.[13] The best opinion may be lousy, but unless you think you have access to (1) *better,* (2) *secret* information, and can (3) *evaluate* it better than anyone else can, you had better accept the existing market price as an unbiased reflection of the worth of

---

[13] This means that the price that evolves tomorrow can be correctly considered to be generated by an economic process that is *describable statistically* as a randomly selected price from a whole set of possible prices, whose average value is equal to today's price. Then when tomorrow's price occurs, whatever it may be, the price on the "day after tomorrow" will be "drawn at random" from a new distribution—one which has been changed so as to set its average or "expected value" equal to whatever may have been tomorrow's price. This does not mean prices are merely random values; it means that only the *unpredictable change* is random with zero average value and unrelated to the past change.

various stocks. *Competition makes them all equally good buys in terms of the expectation of future performance.*

The evidence for these propositions is overwhelming and leaves no doubt. Not only is this true for stock market prices but it appears to be true for all assets and securities. It simply means that other people (the market) leave or offer no surefire or above-average prospects of gains above the normal interest growth. Furthermore, there is no tendency for runs of positive or negative changes in stock prices. The price change (plus or minus) in each period (plus or minus) is independent of any other period's price change. This means that drawing charts of stock prices to predict future prices is unprofitable, however popular it may be.[14] Popularity is not profitability. Unless you have inside information that no one else has, pick the stocks at random![15]

[14] Numerous performance tests have been conducted. For a sample, see: E. F. Fama, ''The Behavior of Stock Market Prices,'' *Journal of Business,* Vol. 38, No. 1 (1965), pp. 34–105; E. F. Fama, L. Fisher, M. C. Jensen, and R. Roll, ''The Adjustment of Stock Prices to New Information,'' *International Economic Review,* February 1969, Vol. 10, No. 1, pp. 1–21. See also various recent issues of the *Journal of Finance;* or B. Malkiel, *A Random Walk Down Wall Street.* New York: W. W. Norton, 1973.

[15] We said random selection is a very good rule—and it is. But still better is to pick stocks on the basis of how closely their returns correlate or move with the market in general. Some stock prices tend to move opposite to, or less regularly with, the market as a whole. The variance of the average returns can be reduced by taking that correlation into account. This computationally more expensive method of forming portfolios of stocks promises a smaller variance for a given average rate of expected return than selection without regard to correlations. But left unchanged by all this more sophisticated method are the propositions that current price equals the expected future price; and that no detectable patterns in past stock prices can predict profitable gains in stock prices.

We are not advocating ignorance. We rely on the ability of the *stock exchanges* with their quickly published prices to make almost instantly available to the public at extremely low cost the best information and evaluation of the myriad of stock analysts and investment counsellors. You must pay a commission to use the exchange, which in part reflects expenses of providing evaluations of the stocks in the stock prices as they move from moment to moment. But there is no point in paying for that information twice: once as commissions and again as a fee to an investment counsellor or to mutual funds which will only reproduce that information and in fact do no better than the random sample procedure.[16]

Do not conclude that your stock broker, security analyst or investment counselor is worthless. He reduces costs of access to the securities market. He will also take care of securities you have purchased. Those are significant functions. He searches out company information and keeps the market better-informed. He can provide information to facilitate *diversification* of risks so that with as few as from seven to 12 stocks you can reduce the variance of your portfolio performance to close to that of a very large portfolio—if you wish to reduce the variance. (In the foregoing, we have not written about diversification and its principles, for that would take us beyond the scope of this book; but if we did, none of the principles exposited so far would be vitiated.)

[16] A weighty study showed that of the mutual funds, those that did best spent the least amount for research and commissions in changing stockholdings—thereby having the lowest expense ratio and hence the highest growth! W. F. Sharpe, ''Mutual Fund Performance,'' *Journal of Business,* *39,* Supplement, January 1966, 119–139.

What Is the Mean and Variation of Stock-Price Changes?

Picking stocks at random within variance classes is hard to accept psychologically, but is economically sensible and valid. Consider the question: "If I took from the years 1926–1973 one year at random and then took one stock at random from the New York Stock Exchange, how much would my investment have changed in value during that one year?" We do know what the *average* of all such actions would have been: one dollar would have grown to $1.13, counting the increased value of the stock plus any dividends paid out. You can be almost sure you would not experience exactly that average. What is the dispersion around that mean within which your stock would probably have fallen? In 90 percent of the cases your initial wealth of $1 would have been between 46 cents and $2 at the end of the year. Half the time it would have been between 80 cents and $1.25.

These ranges of potential loss or gain are shown in Figure 17–3. The top section shows the range for .9 of all possible randomly selected *single* stock investments for *one* year. (The thicker bars are for .5 of all cases.) The probability is .9 that the year-end value of *one* stock would be between about .4 and 2 times the initial value. Narrower intervals result if several randomly selected stocks are included in the portfolio. The average of an eight-stock portfolio shows a narrower range of .6 to 1.7. And if every stock on the New York Stock Exchange were somehow held in your portfolio, the interval would be .65 to 1.6.

The intervals reported are for *one*-year investments. If the investment is maintained for five or 10 years, all on the basis of an initial random

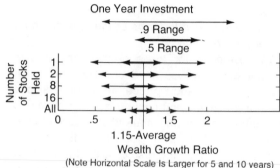

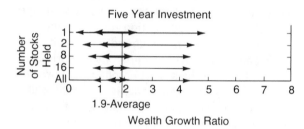

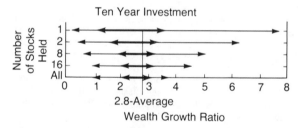

Figure 17–3. Investment Wealth Ranges for .9 and .5 Probabilities for Portfolios of 1, 2, 8, 16, or All Stocks on the New York Stock Exchange (1926–1966). *Source: Lawrence Fisher and James H. Lorie, "Some Studies of Variability on Returns on Investments in Common Stocks,"* Journal of Business *(April 1970), pp. 99–134. More recent data from 1967 to 1973 were included by the authors.*

selection in the first year, what are the average wealth ratios and what are the widths of the .9 (and the .5) probability wealth-ratio intervals?

The *average* end-point wealth ratio for a five-year investment was 1.3 and for 10 years was 2.6.[17] The lower sections of Figure 17–3 show ranges for five- and 10-year investments and for portfolios of one, two, eight and 16 stocks (and *all* stocks as a reference). The intervals are substantially greater for the longer investments, as one would expect. Increasing the number of stocks narrows the probability intervals substantially. That the intervals with only a 16-stock portfolio are nearly as narrow as for the whole market is surprising to most people.

25, 26

Patterns of Personal Income and Wealth Differences

Each of us can incorrectly view his wealth as a division of a predetermined given total. More accurately, the total is a set of individual contributions, some large, some small. What determines who inherits what from past generations? That varies among societies. No doubt, the legal right to endow one's children—rather than the next generation at large or other people of this gen-

eration, through the political forces of government—is an incentive to accumulate wealth for a legacy. Even the form of the wealth is affected. Parents can endow their own children in ways not so easily thwarted: in skills, knowledge, and developed abilities rather than with buildings, lands, or goods, any or all of which could be claimed by the state. Jewish emphasis, for example, on personal skills is said to be a survival trait in the face of hostile people who confiscate nonhuman wealth—an experience which Jews have long experienced.

Whether the pattern of personal wealth and income is fair and equitable cannot be answered, because the meaning of "fair and equitable" is unclear. (Maybe that is why the terms are so popular.) One could ask whether the processes determining how productive a person is and how much he gets for his work (why do we avoid saying "for his product"?) lead to larger incomes, to less social friction, or to a "good" society. If one looked only at the resulting patterns of wealth and income he could assess the end pattern. But like assessing chocolate ice cream relative to bourbon whisky, there is no generally accepted criterion for either the resulting end-pattern or for the process. There are only assertions and personal opinions—of which there seems to be no scarcity.

To illustrate the difficulty in defending an "equal distribution," what would you think if incomes and wealth were equal initially, but some people offered more to Kareem Jabbar to play more basketball or to Liza Minelli to sing and thereby made them richer than other people? The result would not be a redistribution of some fixed total of income, but an increase in the total. Jabbar and Minelli would be producing more; total income

[17] A thorough student will notice that the *average* wealth-growth ratio for a 10-year investment is 2.6 instead of 3.3, which would be obtained by compounding the one-year average growth of 13 percent through 10 years. (See Table 7–2.) What is wrong? Nothing. If you adjust your stock holdings so as to have equal values in each stock at the beginning of each year, selling some of those that went up and buying more of those that went down, the average growth will be different than if the initial investment in each stock were left alone, as it is in five- and 10-year portfolio results reported here.

would be higher. The fans get more of what they want, and Jabbar and Minelli each have more income because they rendered more of their highly valued services. It is an error to treat most differences in income as being a result of some unequal distribution of a fixed total of income, rather than a result of greater production of incomes by some people without thereby making someone else's income smaller. If you argue that no one should inherit more than others, what made Jabbar tall and coordinated and Minelli vocal and vivacious? What about your inherited intelligence, color, sex, and abilities? If you object to the inheritance (but not to the giving?) of physical marketable wealth as unfair and unearned, is it any less unfair if it is redistributed by taxation? No answer.

It is argued that a few very, very wealthy people in a sea of low-income people is unjustifiable. Does that mean their wealth should not have existed? Or should have been given to the poorer? If the latter, would the wealth have been produced in the first place? We have no complete answers to these queries. We pose them to prevent the facile, fatal presumption that answers are obvious or even available.

Socialists say socialism leads to more equitable wealths and incomes and more freedom, with less inequality. The evidence does not support the contention that a socialist state has more equal (let alone "equitable") patterns of wealth and power. Top political authorities have access to the state's wealth and great power over the lives of other people through the police power of the government—something that private wealth lacks.

Table 17–1. 1975 Earnings by Types of Households (32 Million Households)

Family Categories (in Millions)	Median Year-round Earnings
7 husband and wife only	$10,700
6 three persons	12,000
5 four persons	13,100
5 five or more persons	13,200
23 million	
3 female family-head	6900
6 unrelated members	8400
9 million	

Source: U.S. Bureau of Labor Statistics; 1974 data adjusted to 1975 prices.

Income Differences

First, to get some basis for comparisons of people's incomes, Table 17–1 presents median annual incomes classified by size and makeup of family. The median incomes separate the top half from the bottom half of all families in 1975. The range of incomes around the median at any one year is substantial and reflects a variety of factors, some of which we will explore. As Table 17–2 shows, U.S. families in the bottom 20 percent obtained about 7 percent of aftertax national income, while the families in the top 20 percent obtained about 40 percent of the aftertax national income. The middle 60 percent obtained over 52 percent of that income. What may come as a surprise is a comparison of this distribution with those of Sweden and Russia, often regarded as

Table 17–2. Personal Income Shares by Quintile: United States, Sweden, and the Soviet Union (After Taxes and Subsidies)			
Income Units	United States	Sweden	Soviet Union
Lowest 20%	6.9%	7.7%	7.5%
Middle 60%	52.5	56.5	55.0
Highest 20%	40.6	35.9	37.5
	100%	100%	100%
Highest 5%	15.9	12.9	14.0

Source: L. Galloway, "Folklore of Income Distribution," in S. Pejovich, ed., *Governmental Controls and the Free Market.* College Station: Texas A & M University Press, 1976, Chapter 2. Based on data from Bureau of Economic Analysis of U.S. Commerce Dept. and foreign sources.

Table 17–3. Median Family Income by Ethnic Group, United States, 1975

Racial or Ethnic Group	Median Family Income
Japanese	$17,800
Chinese	15,098
White	14,169
Filipino	13,260
Cuban	12,137
Mexican	9907
Puerto Rican	8773
Black	8628

Source: U.S. Bureau of the Census, *Decennial Census of 1970.* 1969 data adjusted to 1975 by price level rise of 42 percent since 1969.

leaders in income equality. This similiarity, shown in Table 17–2, is remarkable. All incomes are aftertax and after income transfers through subsidies. Even these data overstate the degree of income differences within a country because of factors to be considered shortly.

Also interesting is that the distribution of incomes within the white group and the nonwhite are essentially identical; the fraction of total incomes within each quintile is essentially the same for whites as for nonwhites. The difference between the two groups lies in the mean value of incomes; the whites have a higher average. But the relative *dispersions* around their higher average is the same as for non-whites. However, the nonwhite class is composed of many different groups. Separation within the nonwhite group reveals the data reported in Table 17–3. But these data are also misleading, for they combine people from different geographical areas. The blacks are disproportionately more in the South, a lower income area for all ethnic groups. Therefore, separation by geographical areas and ethnic groups gives the data of Table 17–4. Large differences still occur by ethnic groups, but the differences are substantially smaller.

Classification of differences among families according to income received are given in Table 17–5. Less than one-third of families earn incomes over $20,000 annually, while barely more than 10 percent earn over $30,000 annually. For perspective, the average annual incomes of economics professors is over $20,000. Your college's president, if he is at a state university, is most likely in the $30,000-and-over category. Why do incomes differ? Some of the factors can easily be noted.

Table 17–4. Median Family Income by Ethnic Group and Region, United States, 1975

Region	Ethnic Group					
	Japanese	Chinese	White	Filipino	Spanish	Black
Northeast	$15,600	$12,400	$15,223	$15,400	$ 8,500	$10,400
North Central	16,600	15,300	14,600	17,150	13,000	11,000
South	10,600	15,100	12,400	10,800	9,400	6,900
West	18,300	16,209	14,700	13,000	11,800	10,400
California	17,600	15,600	15,600	13,000	12,400	10,600
Hawaii	19,200	20,100	14,900	13,200	11,300	9,512

Source: U.S. Census Bureau, *Decennial Census of 1970,* adjusted by price level for 1975.

Age Differences

If every person has an identical life time pattern of income, rising to a peak at about age 50 or 60, but the population was composed of people of different ages, then at any moment *current* incomes would be unequal. The younger would have smaller earnings than the older. Yet, on a life time basis all would be equally wealthy.

Figure 17–4 depicts the 1975 pattern of incomes, associated with age. Incomes start low, rise to a peak, and then fall off. The figure shows the incomes per week that separate the top quarter, the top half (median) and the bottom quarter of males and of females for 1975. If everyone's income in 1975 were recorded without regard to age, the range between the top and the bottom quartile would be about $150 per week (from $270 down to $120). But if the interquartile range is computed for people of the same age and sex, say at age 50, the range is smaller, by some 33 percent, or about $100 per week. Finally, if everyone miraculously had the same lifetime earnings equal to, say, the median for men, at any moment their age differences would produce a difference in their current incomes, a difference of about $50 per week between the top and bottom quartiles, due entirely to the differences in ages (from $240 down to about $190).

Note the very important implications of age differences for income inequalities. Conventional measures of income ignore the differences in people's ages. The apparent inequalities in income would be significantly reduced if a comparison were made of life time earnings. Almost half of the differences would be eliminated, according to some estimates. The income dispersion in any one year due to the differences in people's ages in that year is not indicative of *life time* earning opportunities. Given that earnings vary with age, as long as there are young people and elderly people, there will always be a poorer (young and elderly) group at any one time, even if everyone had equal life time earnings. An interesting question is how much income in, say, the bottom 20% is simply an age-related low income interval, and how much is the result of really persisting differences in incomes over the life cycle.

Table 17–5. 1975 Estimated Percent of U.S. Families in Annual-Income Classes

Annual Income	Percent of Families
Under 5,000	12
5–10,000	19
10–20,000	40
20–30,000	18
30,000 and over	11
	100

Source: Bureau of Census. Data adjusted from 1972 to 1975 dollars.

It has been estimated that if everyone had equal life time earnings (though they varied according to the age earnings pattern from low earnings at youth to peaks in middle-age and then declining), the bottom 20% of the population in any *one* year (mostly the young or elderly) would earn just 13% (instead of 20%) of the national income of that year. The disproportionately smaller income is a result of many people being in their low income earning ages in any given year. Similarly, for the top 20% of the population, their earnings would account for 25% (instead of 20%) of the total national income in that year. Hence it is only to the extent that the lowest quintile in any one year earns less than 13% of national income and the top quintile earns over 25% of national income that one can have reason to look for differences in earning skills and productivity among people rather than merely differences in ages of equally productive people. Differences still remain, of course, for the bottom 20% accounts in any one year for about 6% of national income instead of 13%, but this is closer to equality than the falsely conceived share of 20%. Similarly, the actually top 20% proportion of 41% of national income should be compared to 25%, and not to 20%.

The major point is that almost all data purporting to show differences in incomes fail to adjust for differences in age, which, because income is related to age, will exaggerate differences in incomes earned over a life time.

Investment and Income Dispersion

Another source of differences in income in a given year is past investment. Some save more at an early age and invest in property, personal knowledge, and skills. At an older age they will have higher incomes than people who consumed more earlier. (Does a person who saves a larger fraction of his income in his youth for high consumption after retirement have a greater "life utility"?) This will increase the dispersion of *old* age income. But it represents personal differences in preferences for temporal patterns of consumption.

Medical doctors, college teachers, and scientists with advanced degrees have larger wealth at age 30 because they consumed less and invested more during college age. If a high-school graduate were to save two-thirds of his income for about seven years, he, too, would accumulate a respectable amount by age 25.[18]

[18] If he earns $8000 a year for seven years (and saves $5000 each year) he will, at 8 percent, accumulate a wealth of about $45,000 in seven years. And this would yield him an annuity thereafter for 30 years of over $5000 a year. Will your college education do as well for you? On the average, it is about a toss-up!

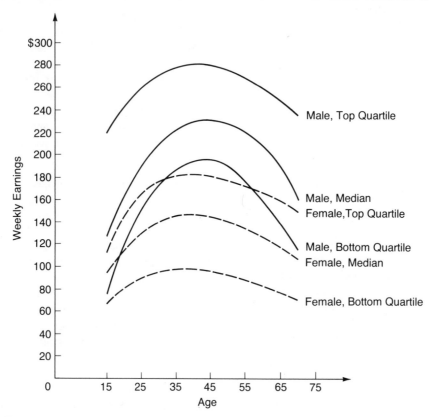

Figure 17–4. Weekly Earnings Differ with Age. *Source: Various issues of* Monthly Labor Review, *Washington, D.C.: Bureau of Labor Statistics, U.S. Dept. of Labor, 1975.*

Chance, Imperfect Foresight, and Choice of Risk

Chance makes for transiently high incomes in some years and lower ones in others, and contributes to the dispersion of earnings in any *one* year. Business earnings (industrial, commercial, and agricultural) are more volatile than the earnings of employees. There is no way to avoid this volatility, given our imperfect foresight. The question is, "Who will bear it?" We can share it by averaging over everyone, so that each of us has a smaller annual variation of income. Or some people can pay others to bear a larger share. That is accomplished with specialization of asset-holdings by property owners. Those who choose occupations with more-risky (volatile) earnings will have a greater dispersion of incomes. For example, some businessmen are wealthy and some are poor; self-employed lawyers have a greater dispersion of income over their lifetimes *and* in any year at any one age than do salaried lawyers. In part, this is the result of a choice of a *chance* for more income relative to a more stable, lower average income.

In addition to age, savings-investment, education, and riskiness, still more forces affect reported annual, as well as life time, earnings.

Market and Nonmarket Income

Reported *money* earnings differ from real incomes because some people receive more of their earnings in nonmonetary form (for example, farmers versus city dwellers). "Income" is taken in different proportions of marketed and nonmarketed services. Also, some people prefer to have more leisure; the teacher with three months of absence from teaching has a smaller money income but less summer work.

The valuable services of housewives are excluded from typical money-income measures. Rearing children, cooking food, shopping economically, managing the home, and planning purchases are services that could be purchased from hired governesses and housekeepers. A husband earning $8000 a year would probably be using services from his wife costing at least $4000, equivalent to half his income. This understates income by a larger proportion for poorer than richer families, so differences in family *real* income are less than in money incomes. Furthermore, the housewife's production of income is not taxed.

Endowment Differences

Though any and all the preceding factors are sufficient to cause dispersion of earnings at any given moment, differences in earnings ability and endowments are also important. Yet, even learning abilities are partly endowed. Your genetic talents are not entirely happenstance. They may be as deliberate a creation as the money wealth you inherited. People seek "good" genetic types as mates in various ways: in choice of college, sorority or fraternity, church, residence, and personal friends—all provide select groups. In your own process of finding a mate you are influencing the genetic types of your children. While difficult to know if the mating processes in our society tend to make succeeding generations more, or less, alike, it is a fact that differences among incomes do, in no small part, reflect differences in inherited talents and, of course, family environment and parental attention. The wealth of the Judy Garland vocal cords, the Marilyn Monroe body, the Namath arm, the Einstein brain, the Kennedy personality were not taxed upon inheritance from their parents; but the Rockefeller or Getty endowment of propertied wealth to their children is heavily taxed.

Property Income and Personal Labor Income

What is the effect of incomes from property, taxes, private pensions, and transfer payments through public assistance and social security? Very little, as compared to pure labor income. To see this, examine the data in Table 17–6. The dominant differential factor is *not* property or transfer income, but is the difference in earned income from wages, salaries, and self-employment. These re-sults lose their surprise when one realizes that total nonhuman property income accounts for only about 10 percent of total national income, and hence does not have a major effect. Notice how similar are the percentages in the last two columns, for income earned from labor and for total income. The evidence points to differences in human earnings as the major factor in income differences.

The Poor

Though the lowest 20 percent of income receivers in the United States are enormously richer than most of the population in India, China, Peru, or Tanzania, there still is reason to ask if the poorest here were being denied opportunities to realize their potential. And even at their potential, some (unfortunately enfeebled or crippled) would have so low an income that some of the rest of us de-sire to help improve their unfortunate lot.

What constitutes "poverty"? In the United States, one criterion (proposed by the Federal Social Security Administration) allowing for family size, ages, and locality has the poverty-family in-come varying from about $1700 for a single per-son on a farm ($2300 urban) to $8000 for a seven-person urban family (about $1100 a person) in 1975 dollars.

The proportion of the population that is in pov-erty has decreased since 1945 from about a third to a tenth, and certainly had long been decreas-ing before that. For the reasons already given, the number in poverty in any one year overstates the fraction that remains in poverty. First, per-sonal incomes fluctuate transiently; in some years the income of a family can fall into the poverty

category, while in other years it will be sufficiently high to bring the average for the whole period above the poverty line. Second, about one-third of the families in the poverty group are families of old people who are consuming their wealth, be-cause of shorter life expectancy. This permits more consumption than their "income" indi-cates.[19] And many college students will be counted in the poverty group, if only current earn-ings are counted. Third, recent immigrants (for example, Puerto Ricans) constitute disproportion-ately high membership in the poverty group—a characteristic of most immigrants in their initial years in the United States. This increases the tran-sient percentage of the population in the poverty group. (While Puerto Ricans are about 8 percent of the New York City population, they represent about one-third of welfare recipients, but no data exist to separate recent from earlier Puerto Rican immigrants.)

Who, then, tend to remain in the poverty group for many years? Undoubtedly people who are in-capable of producing a significantly greater in-come for themselves. And some with normal capacities lack the drive and responsibility to produce and save toward normal contingencies. Some were not given the kind of education in childhood that the rest of us received. Families whose primary source of income is from a woman, an aged person, a farmer, a black, or a person lacking a high school education are more heavily represented in the persistent poor.

[19] Some even give all their wealth to their children to qualify for welfare, relying upon their children also to assure them of support for consumption. A person with a life expectancy of five years and a wealth of $20,000 would report an income of perhaps $1000, although he could consume at the rate of about $6000 a year for five years. Should such a person be considered *long*-term poor?

Table 17–6. Percentage Distribution of Types of Income, by Income
Classes (United States, 1972)

Income Class	Percent of National Total of Sources of Income in Each Income Class				
	Household Units	Property Income	Transfer Income	Labor Earnings Income	All Income
$ 0–4999	16.6	4.3	18.9	2.0	4.1
5000–6999	10.2	4.7	12.4	3.8	4.8
7000–9999	16.8	9.0	14.8	10.7	11.2
10,000–14,999	26.1	15.6	17.7	26.4	25.3
15,000–24,999	23.0	26.6	19.3	35.9	33.9
25,000 and over	7.3	39.8	16.9	21.2	20.7
	100%	100%	100%	100%	100%

Source: U.S. Bureau of the Census, *Current Population Reports,* Series P-60 No. 90, and reported
by Lowell Galloway, "The Folklore of Unemployment and Poverty," 1975.

Responses to these situations differ. Some we help; from others we withhold aid. We do not conclude that for *every* low-income recipient the same corrective or alleviative actions are desirable. To analyze the problems of the poor or of the very poor is to analyze a variety of situations. Family responsibility for relatives is a prime source of aid. Discrimination in voluntary charitable aid reflects judgments about the merits of each case. Social policy via political action cannot display such personal discrimination. When dispensing other people's money, extra care must be taken to ensure that the dispenser observes uniform standards of discrimination. Tax-financed redistributions of wealth are part of our social policy. Graduated income and inheritance taxes take a larger portion from higher incomes. Other taxes, like the sales tax, take larger portions from the lower-income groups. For example, it has been estimated that for families with annual in-

comes of under $2000, federal and local taxes take over 40 percent of income, compared to about 25 percent for middle-income families and 40 percent for high-income families with $25,000 and over. But after allowing for interpersonal transfers of tax proceeds (social security payments, welfare, and unemployment compensation), the under-$2000 families are estimated to get a *net increase* of 80 percent of their pretax income. The group earning between $2000 and $3,000 on *net* has a decrease. And for higher-income groups the net outpayment percentage increases to over 40 percent at very high incomes. The government's *explicit* tax and transfer system redistributes income toward the classes with very low incomes. But some *implicit* taxes and subsidies work in the opposite direction.

Distributions of income after taxes are usually less unequal, at least in that there is less distance between the extremes. Unfortunately, that comparison is defective because it does not include government services. If those services are distributed to the higher income groups in amounts greater than their taxes take from them, they would be aided and the poor hurt. Many government services are in fact received in greater amounts by the richer income groups, for example, publicly subsidized golf courses, better schools, parks, colleges, and roads in richer residential areas. But without more data than are now at hand, no definitive answer can be given about the overall effects of government tax and expenditure activities.

Government welfare activities are intended to relieve the indigent by transferring wealth and fostering rehabilitation or increased productive ability. Some argue that many of the poor have not worked as diligently and been as careful in saving and husbanding their income as have those who are now not poor. Others have argued that the poor are poor for reasons not of their own making: "Poverty is the social by-product of a complex, highly interdependent, dynamic economy; therefore responsibility for alleviating this poverty rests primarily upon society." Both arguments are defective. The first does not imply that nothing should be done for (or to?) those who may be so irresponsible as to be poor. The second is defective in that even more poor existed when society was less complex, interdependent, and dynamic; furthermore, everyone—rich and poor alike—lives in that kind of society, so should everyone be taken care of by everyone else? More germane is what kind of aid to give—in what form, how much, and under what conditions.

Direct money aid to very-low-income groups has been proposed. One form of such aid, known as the reverse, or negative, income tax, would grant to those earning less than a specified standard a subsidy sufficient to meet the standard. This has been proposed as a substitute for the entire welfare system wherein each case is individually examined before giving aid. The negative income-tax plan would be less expensive to administer, but would it contain the purported remedial elements of the current welfare system?

To strike more directly at one cause of low income, more appropriate education has been proposed. Typically, high school education has not provided significant vocational training for those not continuing on to college. More on-the-job training could be subsidized by taxes if such vocational training is not given in the public schools. Or exempting teenagers from the minimum-wage law would permit more on-the-job training apprenticeships as part of their pay, since teenagers' services to employers (while learning) are often worth less than they must be paid under the minimum-wage requirement—though in this case the training cost is financed by the teenager rather than by taxes on the rest of society.

To anyone having read this far, it is unnecessary to emphasize that aid to the lowest-income groups could be obtained also by reducing the extent to which jobs and markets are closed to potential entrants in various unions and businesses. This closure of access to jobs is under heavy pressure—whether or not it is effective pressure is yet to be seen.

Regional and
National Differences
of Income

Collected evidence shows clearly that in the richer countries the rise in wealth and income has not been achieved by a small fraction getting wealthier while the masses did not. The lowest 10 percent have moved up by at least the same multiple as the top 10 percent. But over the past century or two has the *worldwide* distribution seen the bottom quarter move up in the same proportion as the top? The common impression is that it has not. (But if we consider that a poorer person had a very short life expectancy a couple of centuries ago, the increase in life length is a form of greater income and wealth that we must not overlook.)

The poorer areas within a country do not necessarily reflect inefficiency or incompetence. Less-habitable deserts or mountain regions do not permit high productivity. To obtain resources like water or to exploit hilly slopes by terracing is expensive. People shun those areas for others richer in natural resources. If people living in a naturally barren area are not allowed to emigrate to the geographically richer areas, they will use available resources as best they can, but they will not be as wealthy as people in the better areas. Only outside gifts—or invasion of the richer areas—would permit them a higher rate of *consumption.*

On the other hand, all areas would benefit from cheaper interregional trade. The ability of the United States and Japan to trade has benefited many Japanese and Americans. Mobility of resources—even if not of people—enables per-

27, 28
29, 30

capita incomes to be enhanced. Not even the imaginary lines demarking countries and restricting migration alter the consequences of specialization and exchange if trade is allowed. Nor do differences in the color or religion of people engaging in trade.

Summary

1. Growth of wealth is increased if savings are cheaper (more plentiful), property rights in wealth are more explicit and secure, and profitable investments are more readily perceivable and exploitable by investors. Growth of wealth is also aided by institutions for organizing, coordinating, and directing productive activity.

2. Conservation, as preservation of resources in their initial form, is not necessarily a means of preserving or increasing wealth. Conversion of goods to other forms of wealth can be more valuable. Incentive to conserve or convert goods to most-valuable forms is aided by identifiable property rights of goods.

3. Investment and saving are different concepts when used in the demand and supply *schedule* sense: saving represents the rate at which current income will be *willingly* diverted from current consumption to accumulation of wealth at each rate of interest. Investment is the current income that *can be profitably* diverted from consumption at a given rate of interest. In these senses, saving is a positive function of the interest rate, while investment is a negative function. The investment schedule is often called the demand for

savings, while the savings schedule is called the supply of savings.

4. Saving and investing are operative not in a single market for saving and investment but in the loan markets, the capital-goods markets, and the production-activity markets— all loosely called the saving–investment markets.

5. An increase in preference for distant income relative to present implies more willingness to save, an increase in the saving-supply schedule, and hence a lower rate of interest with more investment. An increase in investment demand consequent to an increase in perceived profitable investment opportunities results in a higher rate of investment and a higher interest rate.

6. Since both the supply and the demand schedules depend on the interest rate, it is tempting to think that the interest rate adjusts to equate the rate of investing with the rate of saving. But both saving and investing are dependent upon and affect other variables also (wealth, income, expectations about the future), and these other variables also change when saving or investing schedules shift.

7. An increased stock of wealth has effects on the rate of interest and rate of investment depending upon the kinds of wealth that are increased.

8. The interest rate reflects the net marginal productivity of investment, the personal value of present consumption relative to wealth or future income (often called one's time preference), the rate of return on loans, and the relative prices of capital goods and consumer goods.

9. *Increasing* the quantity of money will transiently affect the interest rate because of how the increase is first spent. But the quantity of money will not in itself affect the interest rate, though the price level is changed.

10. Since our institutional mode of creating money is such that the increased money is spent in acquiring bonds, the typical result is that an increase in the quantity of money leads to transiently lower interest rates.

11. On the other hand, since the nominal interest rate equals the real interest rate plus the expected rate of change in the price level, an expected increase in the stock of money leads to expectations of higher prices (inflation), and this effect dominates the transient bond purchase effect on interest rates.

12. Interest yields are typically combined with a risk allowance, so that riskier loans indicate a higher possible yield.

13. The implicit interest yield on a one-year bond is $i = [(Ar + A)/P] - 1$, where r is the stipulated interest rate and A is the principal amount, both due at the end of the year, and P is the present price of that bond.

14. The capital market for lending and borrowing is a complex network of specialized intermediaries between savers and investors.

15. Negotiability is the legal right of the owner of a bond (creditor) to sell the bond to someone else. Bond exchanges facilitate negotiability; they also facilitate borrowing, because lenders regard negotiability of bonds as a desirable attribute.

16. Like many markets, the lending market is not entirely open and free of restrictions. Interest rates, extent of borrowing, and length of loans are commonly restricted by laws. These restrictions are supposed to protect borrowers

and lenders from their own over-optimism. They do protect one class of borrowers or lenders from open-market competition of other borrowers and lenders.

17. All stocks on the stock market have the same expectation of average gain. If any were thought to have greater expected gain, the current price would have been bid up to reflect that and thereby eliminate any extra from a current purchase of that stock. Extensive collected evidence verifies that implication of a well-functioning market, such as the U.S. security markets.

18. The relative distribution of incomes by families is remarkably similar among different countries and societies, though the average differs substantially.

19. In the United States and in many other countries, the dominating factor in differentiating incomes by families is earned income. One reason is that labor or human capital is close to 90 percent of the productive capital or wealth of a country.

20. The distribution of income is partially a function of the age distribution of the population and the variations of a person's income with his age, life expectancy, investment in personal education and skills, savings, and investment in physical wealth. Even if everyone had an identical earnings potential, at any moment neither incomes nor wealth would be equal.

21. Chance and imperfect foresight of conjectural events lead to choices of risk-bearing that result in differences of wealth of various people. Chance effects that cannot be sold to other people result in differences in wealth that do not reflect a choice of risk-bearing.

22. Market, pecuniary income underestimates "real income" to spending units, because of self-production by, for example, farmers and housewives.

23. Preferences for monetary wealth relative to leisure and less-difficult work contribute to increased differences in monetary income.

24. Different endowments occur in both personal abilities and physical wealth. The accumulation of wealth, not the endowment, is a source of wealth differences.

25. Differences in productive ability are magnified by the correlation between superior abilities and the amount of capital resources submitted to the direction of superior talent.

Questions

*1. You are an unborn spirit offered your choice of country in which to be born. In country *A* all land is owned by its users; absentee landlordism is forbidden. The land cannot be mortgaged by the owner. Everyone is born with rights to use certain parcels of land and these cannot be taken away or contracted to others. In country *B,* absentee landlordism is legal. All land is privately owned and either used by the owner or rented to the highest-paying tenants. Land can be sold or mortgaged. Private-property rights are strictly enforced for everyone. Many people do not own land at all. Into which country will you request that you be born? Why?

*2. In a public park an apple tree yields excellent apples. These may be picked by the public, but not more than one apple per person at a time. When will apples be picked? Why? If the American buffalo had been owned by someone, do you think the buffalo would now be so nearly exterminated? Why?

Do you think seals and whales would be faced with extinction if some person or group were able to buy, as private property, the right to catch whales and seals? Why?

*3. "Extending the three-mile limit now in force for American territorial waters out to 1000 miles would help to conserve sea resources." Explain why. Why not extend the territorial claims out to half way across the ocean up to the territorial claims of other countries, as has been done in the North Sea for oil rights? What would that do to the doctrine of the "freedom of the seas"? What does the doctrine of freedom of the seas do to the efficient use of ocean resources?

4. a. Why will a person who has salable property rights in an enterprise for which he is making decisions be more influenced by the longer-run effects of his decisions than if he did not have salable property rights in the enterprise?

  *b. Does this difference in type of property right induce a systematic difference in the kinds of decisions made by government employees, as contrasted to employees of a privately owned enterprise—even if both are engaged in the same kind of activity (production of power)? Explain why the influence of the salable capital value of property rights will or will not make a difference in decisions.

5. Drying grapes to convert them to raisins is investing. Why is this investing since it merely changes one form of consumption good to another form?

6. Instead of playing bridge, a man works around the house painting and refinishing the walls. Explain why this is a form of investment.

7. By giving up $100 of present income for $105 of consumption rights available in one year, a person gets what g?

8. "Roundabout, more capitalistic methods of production are always more productive than direct methods using less capital equipment. Therefore, any country that wants to develop should start increasing the amount of capital goods it has." Evaluate.

9. A man plants a seed for a tree. The rent for the land on which the seed is planted is 50 cents per year. In addition to that cost, there are other costs—spraying, watering, fire protection, taxes—to be paid over the years. In the table on p. 463, the present value of all those costs is indicated in column 4. The tree, if cut and converted to lumber at the end of the ages indicated, will yield lumber worth the amount indicated in the second column. The third column gives the *present* value of that future potential lumber, at 10 percent rate of interest. Some of the entries are not presented.
a. Compute the missing values.
b. Find the age at which the tree should be cut to provide the maximum *present* value of that tree.
c. What is that maximum present value?
d. How much is a newly planted tree worth?
e. Suppose that the value of the tree rises relative to current lumber prices. What would this imply about the rate of interest?
*f. If no one owned the tree, and it could be

cut by anyone who wanted to use the lumber, when would it be cut?

(1) Age	(2) Lumber Value	(3) Present Capital Value of Lumber	(4) Present Value of Costs	(5) Present Value of Profit If Cut at Age Indicated
0	$ 0	$ 0	$5.00	$—5.00
5	1	0.62	5.70	—5.08
10	4	1.54	6.20	—4.66
15	11	2.63	6.50	—3.87
20	25.0	——	6.60	——
25	60.0	5.54	6.80	—1.26
30	140.0	——	6.82	——
35	260.0	9.25	6.95	+2.30
40	450.0	——	6.96	——
45	650.0	8.91	6.97	+1.94
50	800.0	6.80	6.98	—0.18

10. Some whiskeys improve with age. The following table lists the consumption value of a barrel of whiskey at various ages. For example, if the whiskey is removed from its aging vat and sold now to consumers for current consumption, it will sell for $100. If sold in ten years, it will fetch $250 for *consumption.*

a. How much will the vat of whiskey be worth right now (at 10 percent) if it is to be held until the end of the second year before being bottled and sold?

b. For what length of time should one expect to keep the whiskey in the vat for a maximum present value? (Hint: How much is it worth paying for the whiskey now if it is to be held for five years? For ten years?)

*c. If no one owned the vat of whiskey, how long would it remain unconsumed?

*d. Suppose it were owned but could not be sold: how long would it be kept before consumption?

Consumption Date	Consumption Value	Consumption Date	Consumption Value
Now	$100	6	$205
1 year	120	7	220
2	140	8	230
3	160	9	240
4	175	10	250
5	190		

*11. Goods differ in their rate of yield of consumption services, or in their "durability." Pine lumber naturally deteriorates more rapidly than redwood. If demand for future consumption rights should *rise relative* to present consumption rights, would pine or redwood experience the greater rise in present price? Show why this is expressible as a fall in the rate of interest. (Hint: The interest rate is the exchange rate between present and future consumption rights.)

12. Changes in the rate of interest are detectable in the changes in the structure of relative prices of various types of goods.

a. If the price of raisins (relative to grapes), of prunes (relative to plums), of whiskey (relative to corn), of cider (relative to apples) should rise, would that mean a change in the rate of interest? In what direction?

b. What effect would that have on the profitability of producing raisins, prunes, whiskey, etc.?

c. Ultimately, what effect would the revised production have on the relative values (for example, of raisins and grapes)? What effect would that have on the rate of interest?

13. In a certain country the only productive goods are "rabbits." Either the rabbits are eaten, or the rabbits increase at the rate of 20 percent per year.

a. If there are 1 million rabbits in the community at the first of the year, what is the income of the community (measuring the income in rabbit units)?

*b. What will be the rate of interest in that community?

*c. What is the maximum possible growth rate of the wealth of that country?

*14. "A rise in the profitability of constructing houses and buildings tends to push up the rate of interest." Why?

15. The propositions on costs in Chapter 11 imply that the demand curve for investment is negatively sloped with respect to the rate of interest—that is, that higher *rates* of investment will be less profitable. Why is this implied by the earlier propositions on behavior of costs?

16. "If savings is defined as an increase in wealth and if investment is defined as an increase in wealth, then savings by definition is always equal to investment; for it is merely the same thing looked at from the point of view of two different people." Since this statement is correct, how is it possible to speak of equilibrating the rate of investment and the rate of savings?

*17. "The most important fact about saving and investment is that they are done by different people and for different reasons."

a. Is that why savings must be equilibrated to investment via a demand for investment and a supply for savings function? Why not?

b. Suppose that everyone who invested had to do his own saving and could not lend or borrow or buy capital goods from other people. Would that destroy the principles of demand-and-supply analysis for growth of wealth? Why?

18. If you received a gift of $10,000 in cash, and decided to convert it to some intermediate kind of claim or goods (like bonds and savings-bank deposits) before finally holding more stocks and personal or business goods, give the sequence of effects on the interest rate.

19. The rate of interest helps to equilibrate investing and savings, and the demand for borrowing and the supply of savings; it is the relative premium of price of current consumption rights over future consumption rights; it is the price of money; and it equates the demand and supply of assets. Explain how it is all these things at once.

20. Suppose the world were going to last for just two years and you have wealth of $100.

a. If the interest rate is zero, what is the income available in each of the next two years?

b. If the interest rate is 10 percent, what is the income of each period (again assuming a two-year life to the world)?

c. If the interest rate is 10 percent but the world is going to last for an indefinitely long period, what is the maximum annual maintainable rate of consumption?

21. You are a visitor in some underdeveloped country in which all lending and borrowing

are effectively prohibited.

a. Is there a rate of interest?

b. If so, where could you get data to compute it?

c. How could you tell when it changes?

22. "Large corporations have so much of their own funds that they do not have to borrow in the capital-funds markets in order to make new investments. They are therefore immune to interest rates in the capital markets so that their investments are not screened as are those of investors seeking funds in the capital markets." Explain the error in that analysis.

23. "Most states have restrictions upon the rate of interest that may be contracted for in the absence of special authorization for higher rates. The most common maximum contract rates are 6 percent and 8 percent a year, but a few states permit contract rates as high as 12 percent. Loans to corporations are generally exempt."

a. Who is helped and who is hurt by these laws if they are effective?

*b. Do you think they have any effect on the rate of interest?

*c. What do you think happened when interest rates on excellent bonds exceeded 10 percent in 1974?

24. You propose to buy a house for $20,000. You have $3000 in cash now. So you seek to borrow $17,000 from a lender at 5 percent rate of interest. We say 5 percent because the government of the state in which you live has agreed to guarantee the loan on your house since you are a veteran. The law will guarantee your loan so long as the lender does not get over 5 percent. Unfortunately, no one will lend to you at that rate because 6 percent is available elsewhere. But you are clever enough to find a lender who will lend to you at 5 percent, *after* you make the following proposal: If he will lend you $17,000 at 5 percent (which is, let's say, 1 percent less than the 6 percent rate he could get elsewhere—and thereby costs him $170 a year interest otherwise available; that is, 1 percent of $17,000 is $170 per year), you will buy from him insurance on the house and on your car and life. In doing this, you may or may not realize that you could have bought the same insurance at a lower rate or more conveniently elsewhere.

a. Why do you make this agreement with him?

b. Is he being "unfair" or "unscrupulous" or "unethical"? Are you?

*c. Who is aided or hurt if such tie-in agreements are prohibited?

d. Do you think they can really be totally prohibited by laws? Why?

25. You are trying to decide which of two stocks to buy. One has been falling in price during the past month, but the other one has been rising steadily during the month. Which one should you buy on the basis of that information?

26. A retired person has $100,000 to invest in stocks and expects an income of about $10,000 annually because interest rates are about 10 percent. If you advise him to buy stocks that pay out no earnings as dividends, he complains that he will have no income. How would you explain to him that he does have an income of 10 percent?

*27. If you were a Jew in an Arab country, or an

Asian in Africa, or an Englishman in Indonesia, or an American in Argentina, or a Moslem in India, would you invest for your son in personal human capital or in physical capital? Why?

28. Distinguish between conservation of specific resources and the growth of wealth. Is conservation of specific resources an efficient way to increase the productive wealth of the community?

18

Coordinating
the Economy

So far we have analyzed how markets, prices, and property rights (a) allocate and control consumption, (b) determine the goods produced, and (c) affect the income and wealth of owners and suppliers of productive resources. Though each depends upon the other, we considered them one at a time, assuming the others to be fixed or appropriately adjusted.

If each market were *independently* and simultaneously cleared, regardless of what was happening in other markets, the preceding analysis would be entirely reliable and usable for study of the operation and coordination of the economic system *as a whole.* But the markets and various industries are not independent of incomes and prices in other markets and industries, so coordinated adjustments in each are not achieved costlessly and instantly.

We have also assumed appropriate monetary and government policy. However, the inability to clear all markets instantly and the fluctuations in the demand and supply of money create transient intervals of unemployment for people and resources.

The Magnitude of Employment and Unemployment

In 1975 the United States had over 90,000,000 people with gainful employment of one kind or another. About 65,000,000 worked full time and 25,000,000 worked part time. Approximately 10,000,000 changed jobs during the year. Every month, *on the average,* approximately one in 20 employees quit, was laid off, or dismissed; the same proportion took new jobs or returned to an old job. In this process, over 15,000,000 persons reported themselves as unemployed at some time during the year, although at any one time the number of unemployed averaged about 4,000,000. Some 2,500,000 were unemployed all through the year; 1,500,000 from one to three months; and 3,000,000 from four months to more than six months. Over 5,000,000 had at least two spells of unemployment. These data show a persistent flow of people from job to job, others between jobs, and still others experiencing more-prolonged unemployment with continued reassessment of job options and considerations of possible new occupations.

Unemployment

Unemployment varies substantially as a result of changing business conditions. The incidence depends also upon characteristics of people: age, sex, color, and general skills. Typically, unemployment in the 20–65 year-old male married group is less than 3 percent, while unemployment rates for teenage unskilled nonwhites exceeds 10 percent. The average over the whole labor force rises from what is known as the full-employment percent of unemployment ("natural unemployment") of about 3–5 percent up to about 7–9 percent in a recession. Figure 18–1 charts the percentage of unemployment for the labor force as a whole over the past several years. In the deepest part of the Great Depression, 1932–1933, it was about 15 percent. Figure 18–2 shows the reasons for unemployment.

Table 18–1 presents unemployment rates by

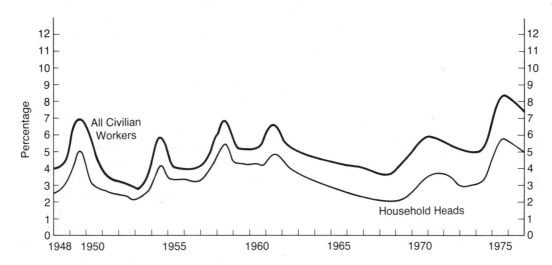

Figure 18–1. Percentages of Unemployment. *Source: U.S. Dept. of Commerce,* Survey of Current Business, *various issues.*

groups of people. Differences among the various groups exceed the variation within a group over time from recessions to booms. Unemployment for some groups is high even in nonrecessionary periods.

What is the normal length of unemployment? Typically, over half are between jobs (unemployed) for less than five weeks, with about a third taking up to three months, and less than 5 percent extending beyond six months.

Why do unemployment rates differ with sex, age, and color? An incorrect answer is that teenagers, women, and nonwhites are not trained for the jobs available. That is wrong because an infinite number of jobs are available—the tasks to be performed in a world of scarcity are un-

limited.[1] Then why are the unemployed not working at the tasks they can do? Because they would rather not work at the wages in the best jobs they know to be available to them; or they have not yet decided what are the best jobs for them; or both explanations may be correct. Some may be

---

[1] Statements about unskilled, untrained people or people with skills that do not correspond to job requirements are misleading. That would have an effect only if wages had to be uniform for all workers and if there were *no* value for *any* of the services that could be provided by low-skilled people. (Warning and disclaimer: Analysis and explanation should not be interpreted as implying that nothing should or can be done to alleviate the situation or that the existing situation is "desirable." The doctor who explains the cause of your back pain to be the high-heeled shoes you wear is not saying that you deserve it or that nothing should or can be done to prevent or alleviate it.)

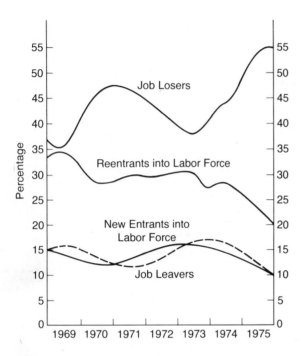

Figure 18–2. Categories of Unemployed as Percentages of Unemployed. *Source: U.S. Dept. of Commerce,* Survey of Current Business, *various issues.*

so low in demonstrated money wage-earning capability at the best-known job that they prefer not to work for wages. Many people simply are not seeking a wage job. Why, then, do sufficiently productive teenagers or nonwhites experience higher unemployment rates? Teenagers shift more than others from job to job as part of their initial search for and evaluation of possible careers. They are often without employment at each job shift. Another factor is the minimum-wage law, which restricts the abilities of employers to employ unproven, low-productivity teenagers as recruits or to bear general job-training costs. For

nonwhites, another factor has been their higher rates of migration. A larger fraction of blacks in a city are new migrants from the South; a larger fraction are engaged in job-opportunity search and evaluation; hence a larger fraction will show up as unemployed.

Clearly, "unemployment" covers many disparate activities or situations: investigation and comparison of various employment opportunities; legal insistence on employment of only those whose productivity exceeds the legal minimum; refusal to continue as an employee at a wage believed to be less than obtainable elsewhere in due time; and still other reasons and sources. Appreciation and recognition of these different phenomena—all called unemployment—is important to understanding economic events.

Frictional Unemployment

When demand for a product falls, if the productive inputs were to immediately shift to other tasks there would be no unemployment and no "idle" resources. But such immediate shifts are not feasible, because of the costs of discovering the various buyers and sellers and exploring their offers, so that each can realize the best opportunities. These costs of information explain a wide class of activity known as frictional (or "natural") unemployment, about 2–3 percent of the total work force during what is called "full" employment. (It is not always the same people who are unemployed.)

Such "unemployment" is consistent with individual efficiency and rationality. Consider the even greater costs if you were *never* allowed to be unemployed during changing conditions of demand and supply. You would not be allowed to

Table 18–1. Unemployment Characteristics

| | Percent of Work Force | | | | |
	1960	1965	1970	1974	1975
All Workers	5.5	4.5	4.9	4.8	8.4
White	4.9	4.1	4.5	4.4	7.7
Male	4.8	3.6	4.0	4.0	6.5
Female	5.3	5.0	5.4	5.0	7.0
Married men	3.3	2.2	2.4	2.4	5.0
Nonwhite	10.2	8.1	8.2	8.3	14.0
Teenagers	14.7	14.8	15.3	12.9	20.0

Period of Unemployment	Percent of Unemployed				
4 weeks or less	45	48	52	45	35
5–10 weeks	21	21	23	19	20
11–14 weeks	9	8	8	10	10
15–26 weeks	13	10	6	9	15
26+ weeks	12	10	6	9	20
Average duration, weeks	13	12	9	11	13

Source: U.S. Bureau of Labor Statistics. *Monthly Labor Review,* various years.

quit and spend a month evaluating other options, because you would then be "unemployed." It is unlikely that you could find the *best* of alternative jobs with *instant* search at *no* cost while working at the old job in order to avoid "unemployment." The activity, called "unemployment," is not *job* seeking; it is job-*information* seeking. We repeat the eternal truth: Many, many jobs are available, but information is sought about still other jobs in the belief that some will be superior. The present job or first alternative investigation may not pay enough to stop you from looking for *better* job opportunities. Therefore, a person engaged in acquiring information for better jobs may be called

frictionally unemployed. Frictional unemployment is applicable to labor, houses, capital goods, or any good whatsoever. It is an efficient wealth-enhancing way to adjust to unpredictable changes in demand and supply.

For example, new college graduates devote much time and many resources investigating potential employers. No student knows everything about every potential employer, nor does every employer know everything about every potential college graduate. Wage offers differ, in part reflecting both pecuniary and nonpecuniary features as perceived by other people—that is, employers. Accepting a first offer reduces the probability of finding the highest-paid job and thus lowers a person's wealth (present value of future earnings) compared to what it would have been if he had taken longer to find more offers. The more firms contacted, the greater is the probability of finding better jobs. Also, the greater the difference is believed to be among potential wage offers and working conditions, the greater the amount of search it would be profitable to perform. Employment agencies help reduce the cost of getting that information by specializing in obtaining and disseminating it.

A person should search for and explore other wage offers until the expected gain (in present value of anticipated future income) equals the cost of continued search. Since the gain from extra search diminishes, there is a limit to the sensible length of search. Although few persons may make detailed calculations, their observed behavior conforms to this explanation. The greater the rate of change in tastes and demands, and the greater the costs of movement, the greater will be the differences among job opportunities, and the greater the gain in wages by more extended search. Hence the greater the rate of "unemployment."

The search process on the employer's side is associated with "unfilled" jobs.[2] If information and transfer costs were zero, they would instantly hire the right people at the appropriate wage. But, information is not free, so an employer who always takes the first available person will have a smaller probability of getting the "best" person.

Some unemployment is an inherent (sensible) part of any society in which demands change and people may select their work and produce at their own volition at open-market prices rather than being tied to jobs as serfs or assigned them by dictators. In the military, everyone always has a job; however, it is not clear that this is more efficient or preferable to an "idle" search for other, *better* jobs. If less attention is paid to seeking most appropriate jobs and workers, it is easier to keep everyone busy. Avoiding unemployment by arbitrary work assignments is called "disguised unemployment."

Some Other Sources of Unemployment

It is misleading to call people "unemploy*able*" when the highest predicted value of their current services is less than a legal minimum wage. Some "unemployed" are excluded from particu-

lar jobs because of apprenticeships or licensing laws. These people call themselves unemployed "electricians," "musicians," "meat cutters," "projectionists," or "bricklayers." Some of these people will remain "unemployed" until they shift to "independent" owner-contractor status or to other, less-productive occupations without minimum wages.

Teenage unemployment is lower in many foreign countries than in the United States, because in those countries wage rates of teenagers are typically lower relative to wages of experienced workers than in the United States. Here, highly unionized occupations have a smaller range of wages than in nonunionized occupations, making it more difficult for teenagers to be employed in those highly unionized occupations.

Another class of "unemployed" people take employment only when demand for their services is high enough to warrant the high wages that would attract them. Some housewives work during seasonally high demands at certain types of labor—in grape-picking, fruit-packing, or clerking in retail shops at the Christmas season. The rest of the year they prefer not to work at the lower available wages. People in short-lived projects, like movies, plays, or construction, are commonly called unemployed between projects—especially if they have qualified for unemployment benefits.

Structural-Demand and Aggregate-Demand Changes

Structural Shifts

Structural shifts are relative shifts in demands for (or supplies of) labor among occupations. Aggre-

1, 2
3, 4

---

[2] The concept of "unfilled jobs"—or "vacancies"—is a dangerously misleading one. The simple fact of scarcity in this world means there are innumerable tasks or productive activities people could perform. So when thinking of unfilled jobs we must ask, "at what wage?" At higher wages the job—or offer to employ at that wage—would not exist. At lower wages the number of jobs offered increases without limit.

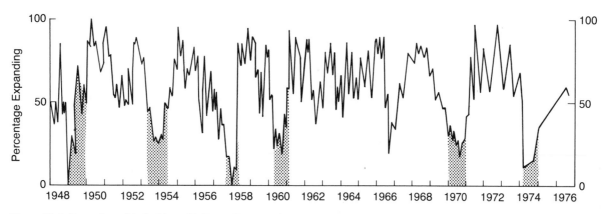

Figure 18–3. Proportion of Industries with Expanding Employment (Shaded Areas Are Recessions). *Source: U.S. Department of Commerce,* Business Conditions Digest, *various issues.*

This graph is based on 30 industries and month-to-month changes.

gate, economywide demand for goods in general may be steady or rising, while the demands for some goods fall, either absolutely or relative to other demands that may be increasing. New production techniques change the relative values of different types of labor in various uses. People and resources whose services fall in value must accept lower wages and rents or shift to other jobs, or possibly both. The change often initiates a job-evaluation search (unemployment).

Figure 18–3 shows graphically an index of the conformity of expansion (or contractions) of productive activity among different industries. The proportion of 30 major industries experiencing an expansion in a given month is indicated. The proportion fluctuates, rarely reaching 100 percent or zero. The curve usually stays within about 20 to 80 percent. (Expansion and contractions among *firms* within an industry show a similar pattern.)

If the line in Figure 18–3 were stable at about 50 percent, it would suggest a relatively steady

aggregate *national* demand, with *relative* shifts balanced among various industries.

Aggregate Demand Decrease

Fluctuations in various industries are correlated rather than entirely independent, diffused, or perfectly offsetting. These correlated fluctuations in employment and production identify what is known as recessions. The graphs in Figure 18–4 show respectively an index of industrial production, the number of employed, and percentage of unemployment since 1948. There were recessions in 1949, 1954, 1958, 1961, 1970, and 1974–1975.

If demand for one good falls, resources can transfer to other activities with a likely fall in real wages earned. But a decrease in demand *in general* (correlated over many products) requires a more difficult adjustment. You are an auto worker; demand for cars has fallen. You can retain your job only if you cut your wages to practically zero—unless all other inputs to autos also

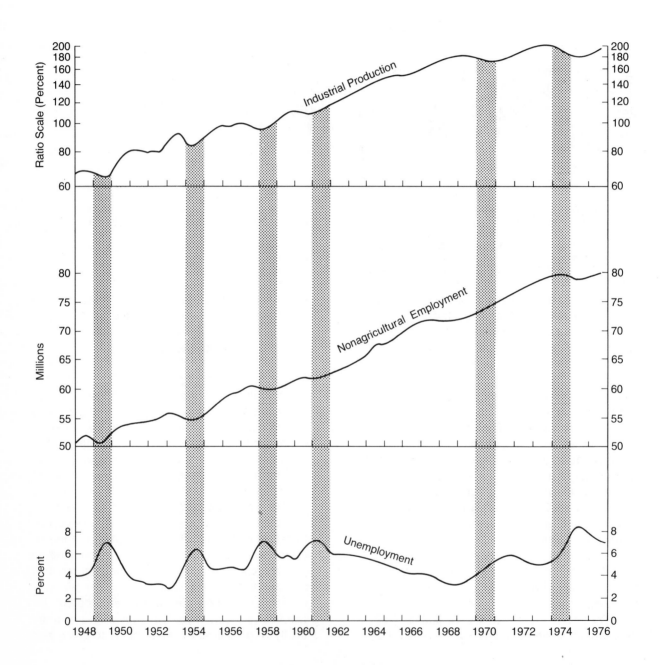

Figure 18–4. Unemployment Percentage, Nonagricultural Employees (Shaded Areas Are Recessions). *Source: U.S. Dept. of Commerce,* Survey of Current Business, *various issues.*

cut their prices at the same time by, say, 10 percent, in which case a 10-percent wage cut would suffice. Do sellers of steel, tires, fabrics, copper, plastics, transport all *immediately* know demand has fallen elsewhere, and adjust prices to permit you to retain your job with only a 10-percent wage cut? No. If your employer asked each of the other input suppliers to cut their prices, they would react as you did. So steel workers' wages and the prices of all inputs in making steel, plus those in tires, copper, plastics, etc., must be cut (by varying amounts); and, in turn, each supplier must have the same occur for all *its* inputs in an ever-widening network. There simply is no way known for all that information about the best alternative price for *each* input to be instantly transmitted to every input. And no one knows how *long* to expect the decreased demand to continue; this fact will affect what each is willing to accept as a price.

Indeed, a new set of prices for all the inputs of the economy (some in new jobs), could, *if it were known and believed by everyone,* immediately restore full employment. No predictive central brain or information network has even been conceived —except in a formal, abstract, symbolic way— that could do so instantly or even in, say, a week. Collecting and testing data involves time before a convergence develops toward a new equilibrating set of prices and assignments of inputs in most-appropriate jobs. That is why a general decrease in demand is accompanied by temporary (though not insignificant!) disorganizing increases

in unemployment. Gradually, over a few months or a year (depending on the reason for the demand changes), unemployment is reduced as new prices and best-available new jobs are discerned and accepted.[3] The coordination problem is awesome, indeed so awesome as to be believed unfeasible by those who do not understand the operation of market prices as controls on amounts demanded and supplied. Still, it does not costlessly reveal the solution *instantly.*

Recessions, Depressions, Fluctuations, and Normal Full Employment

Economic fluctuations (other than seasonal phenomena) are not systematic cycles in the sense that high prosperity creates recession. Prosperity does not breed recession.

If a recession becomes more severe, it becomes a depression, with each person his own authority as to when to call it one or the other.

---

[3] We do not refer to "stickiness" or "inflexibility" of wage rates behind prices of other goods. There is nothing to prevent any worker from immediately adjusting his offer price as low as he wants to: No custom or convention denies him perfect, instant flexibility. But his *notion* of what price he can get lags behind the facts; the cost of getting information makes his *state of knowledge* lag behind the actual equilibrating price that would restore employment. It is an *informational stickiness,* or *inflexibility,* or *lag.* He chooses not to reduce the price of his services because he thinks the equilibrating price is higher than it actually is; or if it actually is as high as he thinks, the cost of search is reduced by a delay between the old and the new job. The lag must be understood to mean the time it takes people to discern the new best price.

Among the main characteristics—and most are highly correlated in behavior—are decreases in aggregate national money income, employment, output of goods in general, asset and common stock prices, profits, and wealth. Typically, any decrease in these variables lasting more than six months is likely to be called a recession, and certainly so if these magnitudes have not recovered in a year. The biggest percentage fluctuations occur in unemployment and business net income. If we speak of employment rather than *un*employment, the fluctuations are small, because a 3 percent decrease in employment from 97 to 94 percent is the same as a 100 percent increase in *un*employment from 3 percent to 6 percent. To some, keeping employment at about 95 to 97 percent of those who desire employment seems phenomenally good; to others, an unemployment rate of 3 to 5 percent seems too high.

We have identified some reasons for variation and suggested why the employment rate tends to move back toward 95–98 percent, like a helium balloon bouncing along a ceiling. Are recessions normally followed by a return to full employment, or does the economy lack forces toward full employment for those desiring employment, so that it wanders along at random levels of employment depending upon chance circumstances? Which is the appropriate characterization? The overpowering evidence is for the first: Downward shocks cause recessions from full employment but they are later overcome as market forces tend to restore full employment. One strong piece of evidence is the high normal rate of employment, around 94–98 percent most of the time, rather than an aimless wandering or tending to sink toward zero.

Another powerful piece of evidence is the size of the upward recovery after a downward shock. If the economy tends to return to full employment, decreases in employment should be followed by upward swings of about the same magnitude, whereas recoveries would not determine the size of the next recession. Declines tend to be followed by the same size upswings. But declines are not correlated with the preceding upswings. An upswing is not followed by a downswing of about the same size. That would be a system in which a "boom" causes a "bust": "What goes up must come down." The economic system does not show that pattern—nor does it simply wander at random with no connection whatever between any declines and rises.

But we add three cautions. First, the ceiling amount of employment is not rigidly fixed, but depends on the number of people seeking employment. More women, elderly, and the very young or the handicapped seek employment during a war. Women's participation in the market labor force depends on education, marital status, number of children, income of husband, and the general cultural attitudes toward female employment. However, a larger number in the labor force does not increase the unemployment percentage.

Second, demand shifts that cause frictional unemployment can be costly to specialized resources in particular industries and communities —textile mill towns, mining towns, Detroit when auto demands fall, Seattle when the Boeing plant experiences a decreased demand for jet planes, Orlando, Florida, when the space program was reduced. These all can be explained by frictional unemployment; but only 1 to 3 percent of the labor force of the nation may be a big proportion of some particular community.

Third, although the evidence is overwhelming for the tendency toward full employment, how fast is the recovery? Can the rate be speeded by conscious government action? Over the past half-century, the actual recovery rate has averaged about 4 percent points per year. That is, unemployment recovered on average from 8 percent to 4 percent or 7 percent to 3 percent in one year, or from 7 percent to 5 percent in six months. Sometimes it was faster and sometimes slower, depending in part on factors that started the downward shock. A dip in employment because of a widespread strike would be followed by a more rapid recovery since almost everyone knew what the best opportunities were when the strike was over. But if the down-swings were caused by some broad changes in supply or demand, as when energy supplies changed, people would have to inform themselves more extensively to find the best alternative options for work, investment, and production. That takes more time.

Some shocks are so minor that the adjustment is hardly noticed. For example, the rise of television and decline of radio occurred without long-lasting unemployment for resources formerly employed in radio. The rise of the automobile, the airplane, and the electronics industry were all integrated without upsetting the economy. Droughts or natural disasters are also typically adapted to with remarkable speed. Because they impose greater physical damage, wars sometimes cause greater adjustment problems. But if one contemplates the speed with which the economy adjusted from war production to peacetime production in 1946 and after other wars, the coordinative efficiency must seem adequate to any shock. However, sometimes a series of successive shocks have caused major upsets in the directive,

coordinative power of the market system—as in the Great Depression of the 1930s. If prospects of a profitable investment act in existing activities decline because of a decrease in aggregate demand, or a fear of unstable governments and insecurity of property and person, the normal savings flow cannot be profitably invested without first acquiring adequate information about the expected future situation. A substantial portion of resources must shift to new tasks. Which new ones? What new products? No one knows. The situation increases the demand for more investigation and evaluation of alternatives and prospective prices prior to new production. For example, the quick adjustment after World War II contrasts sharply with the slow recovery and adjustment after the decline of 1929–1932. One difference was that when the war ended, people knew it had ended. But the severe decline beginning in 1929 did not end with an official announcement in 1932. Who was to know in 1932 that the long period of decreasing money supply would really be stopped that year? Furthermore, a series of new laws and profound changes in economic institutions after 1932 created more uncertainty, which required more information for adaptation to a continuing highly uncertain future. This is to explain not why the recovery was as slow as it was, but rather why it was slower than the adjustment following World War II or most other recessions.

Dispassionate Analysis and Compassionate Policy

Those who lose jobs see a world of reduced wealth. There are fewer jobs of the kind they had been performing at the former pay. To point out that there are other jobs, although not of the kind each person thinks it wise to accept, is not to say that people are foolish for not taking those jobs. Nor does an understanding of the reasons for increased unemployment make it any less unfortunate. Quite the contrary. A clear understanding can help avoid some events that cause recessions or deter recovery.

How large are the losses from a reduced demand for one's services in the economy at large? Recessions imply—indeed, mean—at least an interim reduction in demand for one's services relative to other known options (and to future expected demand). The resulting fall in income, caused by whatever caused the recession, is not trivial. We should separate two elements—(a) changing a job, and (b) the interim, recession-reduced demand.

Cost of Employment Transfer

The cost of changing jobs through interim unemployment may equal quite a modest proportion of the present value of one's lifetime earnings stream. Suppose the present value of your lifetime earning stream is about $200,000 (equal to the present value, for example, of $18,000 per year for the next 30 years, at 8 percent rate of interest, as you can verify from Table 7–3 on page 152). If you refuse a wage cut and seek a new job paying the *old* rate, and if you take two months to find that preferred alternative, you have sacrificed one-sixth of a year's pay, or $3000. Hence, finding the best new job costs about 1.5 percent of the present value of that resource. Compare that with the cost of transferring a car to a new user; its resale costs amount to nearly

20 percent. Or consider the costs of transferring a house from one *renter* to another; the *relative* normal costs of changing tenants (including the rent forsaken during vacancy, and the costs of finding new tenants) is about the same as for labor. The cost of transferring shares of common stock from one person to another via the New York Stock Exchange is about 3 to 10 percent of the value of the stock. We introduce these facts not to suggest that costs of search and transfer are insignificant, but instead to give a sense of proportion about the costs of resource reallocation, both in absolute terms and relative to transfer costs of other resources.

Cost of Recession

Some measure of the recession effect can be obtained by stock-market prices. Prices of common stock reflect the current expectations of future income. If investors expected an annual average stream of earnings of $5 per share for some corporation and were capitalizing that at 10 percent, the market price of the corporation's common stock would be $50. Now a recession sets in, and for the next year the earnings are expected to fall to, say, a negative amount of −$3 per share, with an expectation of a recovery in the following year to +$2 and then back up to $5 in the third year. The price of the stock would immediately fall from $50 to $41.[4] As a matter of fact, when a recession sets in, no one knows how long it will continue, but when recovery can be foreseen, stock prices rise. The later recovery,

[4] The change of earnings to a $3 *loss* is an $8 reduction in the earnings stream for the first year, and earnings in the second year are $3 smaller than formerly expected; these reductions, when discounted to present values at 10 percent, total to a reduction of capital value of about $9.30.

however, does not restore the lost wealth.[5]

Reductions in wages, earnings, rents for physical goods, stockholders' wealth (nonhuman assets) are the money-income measures of reduced production during the recession. Physical indices, such as industrial production, employment, and labor income, move in roughly similar patterns, but stock prices and net earnings of business experience bigger percentage fluctuations.

Determination
of Aggregate Demand

What makes *aggregate* production fluctuate instead of being nearly constant with shifts from one product to another offsetting each other? Why and how do expansions in one industry or sector set up forces for expansion in other sectors? A decreased output of final goods in one industry will decrease the inputs bought from supplier industries. A decreased demand for cars will decrease the demand for steel and a host of other services, with some consequent further effect on the demand for cars. That several sectors contract in close step should not be surprising.

Another particularly serious shock occurs when the supply of money is reduced (for the moment assume the reason is unimportant). Existing prices are then too high to permit profitable output, but that fact must first be discovered. Again,

an extensive search for a new coordinating pattern of prices must be conducted. Even worse, demand for goods is reduced when the money supply is decreased; forces tending to depress output and employment at existing prices and patterns of employment are overwhelming, and possibly reinforcing. The monetary system—the industry that produces money (cash, paper money, and checking accounts)—is a uniquely critical industry. Its controlling agency, the Federal Reserve Bank system, forced large unexpected decreases in the supply of money in 1929–1933. That was the primary reason for the Great Depression. Furthermore, the recovery after 1932 was impeded by unprecedented legislation, however well-intended. That misconceived legislation set up many restrictions on access to the market as a protection to existing firms and employees against newcomers. Incidentally, the rate of recovery has been widely underestimated because measures of unemployment included people who remained employed on new government projects. We cite this fact not to deny the severity of the depression in 1933, nor to fully explain the slow recovery (which has not yet been satisfactorily explained), but to refute the belief that forces to full employment were absent.

If our monetary system creates large increases in the money supply, as it did from about 1965 through 1975, inflations occur, as we shall see in the next chapter. Whether inflation will continue into the future, and at what rate, is impossible to predict, because the money supply is controlled primarily by political forces. Our (the authors') possibly naive theory of political processes leads us to believe it will continue for at least a few years, and therefore the economic analysis in the next chapter may continue to be timely.

---

[5] For example, when the stock price in the preceding footnote rises, a couple of years later, back to $50, the stockholders are not back to where they would have been if no fall had occurred. Had earnings been maintained at $5 per year, stockholders would have had either more consumption or a greater wealth than $50 at the end of the recession—about $62.50.

8, 9
10, 11

Summary

1. Unemployment is not a sign that there are no jobs or work worth doing. It is, rather, a job-relocation process that involves a search over other job opportunities to find the *best* one.

2. Contrary to what would be implied in a world of free information and no cost of quicker adjustment, reductions in demand do not imply that prices will be *immediately* reduced to market-clearing levels with sustained total employment and use of all productive resources. Instead, unemployment and idle productive resources are implied as modes of adjustment to changing demand and supply conditions.

3. Unemployment occurs for several reasons: (a) Restraints on markets (such as minimum-wage laws) that prevent some people from working at wages that reflect their marginal productivity. They shift to "noncovered" jobs or become self-employed "contractors." (b) Restraints on people working at jobs without a license or authorization (such as regulations for union membership or apprenticeship). (c) The fact that some workers are willing to work only during seasonal peak demands when wages are high. (d) Shifting of relative demands or supplies that induce job shifting. This is called structural unemployment. (e) Falling *general* demand that requires reduced wages and prices. This is called *aggregate demand deficiency* unemployment. (f) Resources often appear to be idle, or "unemployed," in order to economize on the costs of physical readjustments to unpredictable fluctuations in demand.

4. Unemployment of resources can be reduced by reducing the extent to which *general* demands fall. General demand decreases are a major source of the severe unemployment that is characteristic of depressions.

5. Major general recessions reflect "malfunctions" in the monetary and political institutions, rather than any real decreases in general wants.

Questions

*1. In deciding who is an unemployed person, would you consider the following:

a. Is he now working for someone else as an employee? If his answer is "Yes," would you classify him as unemployed or as employed?

b. He answers "Yes" to the preceding question, but answers "No" to the question "Is your current job your usual kind of work?" He reports that he is working at a service station, while looking for a job as a lathe operator. Would you change the classification?

c. Next he is asked, "Are you willing to take an available job as a lathe operator at a wage of $5 an hour?" He answers, "No, I used to work for $10 an hour and I'm an experienced operator, not a novice." Is your classification of him still the same? Why?

d. If you do not call him unemployed in the preceding question, then how can you call anyone unemployed? For there are always jobs available at some sufficiently low wage —a wage he would call "ridiculous," "un-American," or "below standard."

2. The usual criterion of an unemployed person is "not employed by someone else and actively looking for a job." It says nothing about the range of jobs or wages he refuses

to consider. What do you think the criterion implicitly assumes to avoid being completely useless?

*3. "A man who loses his job through no fault of his own should not have to bear the losses of unemployment. The government must see to it that he does not." This is a quotation from a campaign speech of a major candidate for governor of California.

a. Is the candidate proposing that there be no unemployment or that anyone not currently employed should be given an income equivalent to what he was formerly getting?

b. How can either of these be accomplished?

4. Is a person who loses his job through no fault of his own also unemployed thereafter through no fault of his own? Explain.

*5. "Unemployment is a wonderful privilege. Without it we would all be slaves to tyrants."

a. Can you interpret this "ridiculous" statement so as to make it not ridiculous. (Hint: There is no unemployment in the military. There is reputed to be none in Russia. Distinguish among the factors that shift demands, those that make job information costly, and the losses of wealth consequent to those demand shifts and costliness of job information.)

b. Would you prefer to live in a community in which unemployment is forbidden? Why? (Later we shall analyze ways of reducing unemployment without forbidding it.)

6. a. What different kinds of unemployment (with respect to why unemployment exists) do you think it is relevant to distinguish?

*b. Why?

7. Suppose the daily sales of each of 50 firms are determined by a process simulated by the turn of a roulette wheel with numbers from 0 through 30. Further, suppose that the firm will on the next day seek to hire as many employees as the sales of the preceding day. Thus, if sales are 20 on the first day, the firm will seek to hire twenty people on the second day—given the wages of $25 per person per day. If there were fifty firms, the number of employed people would be $50 \times 15 = 750$ on the average.

a. Would that employment rate stay constant day after day despite the independent additive random process for determining the number of employees demanded at that wage rate?

b. If those who were laid off by one employer took a day to select a new job, would there always be some unemployed?

c. Would there always be some unfilled vacancies?

d. Would the number of unemployed equal vacancies?

e. What would happen to the number of job seekers and to the number of vacancies if the top five numbers on the roulette wheels were erased?

f. What would happen if all the numbers had been increased by 5?

g. The change from day to day in the totals of the 50 firms, with an unchanged roulette wheel, and the change when the roulette wheel is changed are two different kinds of changes. Which would correspond to a correlated decrease in general aggregate market demand for goods?

*h. How quickly do you think a person would detect a changed wheel, that is, a general demand change?

8. On the average, the cost increment of each extra job investigated increases. Also, on the average, the gain in wages from another job investigated diminishes. If these two propositions are true, then what must be the relation between the increment of gain and the increment of cost in order to conclude that it will pay to always take the first job investigated?

9. Employment agencies charge about 50–60 percent of one month's salary for their services for jobs paying about $600 per month. For jobs paying about $1000, the fee is one month's salary. If this is paid to the employment agency by the employer, does it mean the employer bears the costs? Do you think this fee is too large? Why?

10. Is the analysis of this chapter consistent with the fact that unemployment among blacks is higher than among whites? Does it explain the level of employment at "full employment" or the massive changes in the unemployment rate?

*11. When requesting a Congressional investigation into the methods, charges, and quality of services of private employment agencies, Mr. Abel, president of the United Steelworkers of America said, "A man or woman should not have to pay—often a large sum —for the privilege of obtaining a job." He also asserted that society and government had an obligation to make it possible for "every willing and able individual to work at or near his highest skill." Evaluate those remarks in the light of economic analysis.

19

Inflation

Inflation, like death and taxes, appears inescapable. What is inflation? Why does it occur? What are its effects? How can you protect yourself?

What Is Inflation?

Inflation is a rise in the number of dollars required to purchase a given standard of living—a prolonged reduced purchasing power of dollars. If prices of gas, sugar, and shoes rise, while those of computers, television sets, and fruits fall, the lower prices may offset the higher. People will switch more to the relatively lower-priced goods. Since we don't know just how much substitution of cheaper for more expensive items would leave people as well off as before, we can't actually compute the costs of the new equivalently desired combination. Changes in quality add more difficulties. If people switch from black-and-white to color television at three times the price (while black-and-white prices do not change), is it the cost or the quality of living that has risen?

Can we never know, then, whether inflation has occurred? A useful clue is provided by the money costs of a particular fixed pattern of consumption from month to month, on the assumption that changes in quality or substitution have been *relatively* insignificant. The U.S. Bureau of Labor Statistics publishes a monthly Consumer Price Index (CPI) as an approximation to month-to-month changes in the *dollar* cost of a particular basket of goods for lower-income people. The course of such an index over the past 140 years is in Figure 19–1. Because of sampling coverage, quality changes, and purchase-pattern shifts, to name a few factors, a dollar cost rise of 2 to 4 percent

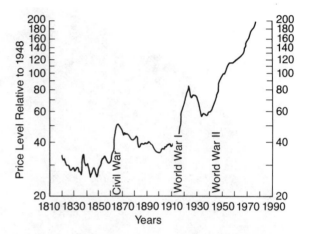

Figure 19–1. Consumer Goods Price Index, 1820–1970 (1948 = 100). *Source: U.S. Department of Labor,* Monthly Bulletin.

over one year for that rigid consumption combination could occur even though the nominal dollar cost of living did not change after allowing for substitution possibilities and quality changes. A change of some 90 percent within a few years, as happened in the United States from 1941 to 1947, and 60 percent, as happened from 1964 to 1975, certainly is not caused by sampling or quality changes. Major swings in that index are taken to be indicators of inflation and deflation.[1] The inflations in several other countries have been more pronounced and spectacular. For example, since World War II several countries show the rises graphed in Figure 19–2.

[1] The major inflations and deflations have been great enough that their dates can be fairly well noted by any of several closely related measures of price levels—we hope. A major defect is that the index does not include prices of capital goods (it covers primarily prices of current services). The severity of bias or degree of error resulting from this omission has not yet been determined. Nevertheless, the conventional, though incomplete, measure is commonly cited.

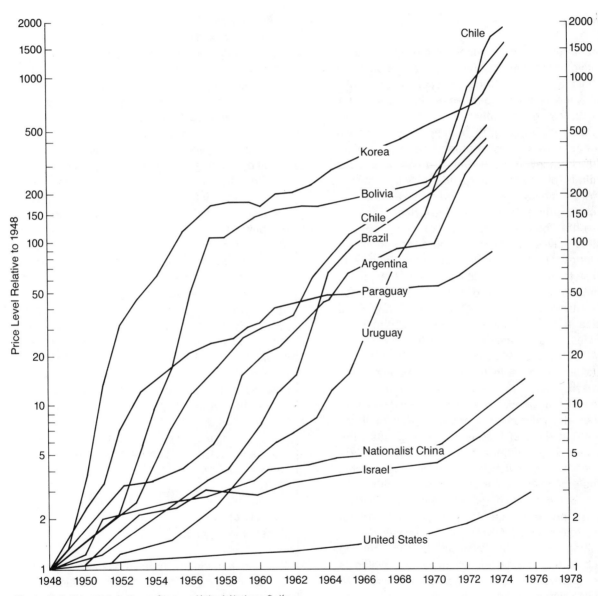

Figure 19–2. Recent Inflations. *Source: United Nations Bulle-of International Financial Statistics. Slopes of lines indicate annual rates of inflation.*

Why Inflation?

Inflation occurs if the supply of money increases relative to the amount of money that people want to hold at existing prices. If each of us awoke with twice as much money as on the previous day and no less of any other goods or services, we would spend some of the money for other goods to reduce the excessive proportion of our wealth held as money. But not everyone can reduce his holdings of money by spending, which merely transfers money from one person to another. As a result, prices (and wages are prices, too) are "driven," "pushed," "pulled," or "bid" up. We find ourselves wealthier with more income in *dollar* terms. On the average, wealth and income in money terms will be about twice as high, because only then will we want to retain the larger money amounts we in fact have. (Typically, in the United States, the public, on average, over all firms and families, holds money equivalent to three or four months' income. What is your figure?)

But an increase in the stock of money is not necessary for an inflation. A *reduction* in the stock of real goods with an unchanged stock of money also raises money prices. A drought, flood, or natural disaster may reduce real goods without changing holdings of money. With no less money, but fewer goods, people will spend some of their money to replenish stocks of other goods. Since someone else receives what one person spends, prices will be bid up as people try to get more real goods (of which there are fewer). The resulting inflation is "caused" by the reduced stock of real goods relative to money, which is also expressible as an increased amount of money *relative* to the supply of real goods.

A historically significant inflation occurred during the black death, or bubonic plague, in England in the fourteenth century. A substantial percentage of the population died, but with no corresponding decrease in the money supply. Wage rates rose spectacularly, but prices of other (nonhuman) goods rose not nearly as much, since their supply had not decreased as much. Survivors got substantial per-capita increases in real income because of the reduced population relative to other goods—not as a result of the accompanying inflation. In this case, inflation (caused by the decrease in population relative to the physical stock of other goods *and* the money stock) was accompanied by a *rise* in living standards for the survivors. At other times England has experienced a *decrease* of real, nonhuman wealth because of agricultural crop failures, with less to eat but no less money in the nation. That, too, changed the ratio of goods to money, so an inflation occurred. Common sense would suggest that the reduced crop (*without* a corresponding decline in money) induced the inflation of prices. Nevertheless this kind of decrease in real, per-capita wealth has been carelessly called an *effect* of inflation. On the contrary, the correct sequence is that inflation was the result, not the cause, of a reduced crop and stock of real resources.

Quantity of Money and Inflation

If the stock of money increases at about the same rate as the real stock of goods, inflation is not likely. If the money stock increases more rapidly than the normal growth rate of real goods and population (about 3 percent per year), inflation occurs. If the real output transiently falls below the normal amount while the money stock continues to grow at the normal, say 3 percent rate, a transient rise in prices will occur. Such a transient decrease in real agricultural output contributed to a transient increase in inflation in 1973–1974. But from the early 1960s the money stock has more steadily and persistently grown at a rate substantially and increasingly higher than real income and population—about 5 to 8 percent per year with a growth of real income of about 3 percent in the 1960s. From 1970 to 1975 the money stock has grown faster at about 10 percent per year, and inflation, not surprisingly, was about 7 percent, rising even to 10 percent when real supplies fell transiently in 1974 through bad crop harvests and oil embargoes.

Though many factors other than an increasing stock of money affect the price level, they are rarely big or long enough to induce a *persistingly* increasing price level. Figure 19–3 shows the strong and persisting correlation between the average annual rates of persisting increase in the quantity of money and prices for each of 65 countries for the period 1948–1974. The picture would be even more overwhelmingly impressive if it also showed extreme inflations of the kind that occurred in Germany in 1923, when prices rose by a factor of about 100 billion in one year, while the amount of money increased by a factor of 10 billion. This is equivalent to a doubling of prices every two weeks. Similar episodes occurred in Greece in 1944, in Poland in 1923, in Russia in 1921–1923, and in Hungary in 1923 and again in 1946, to mention only a few. The Hungarian in-

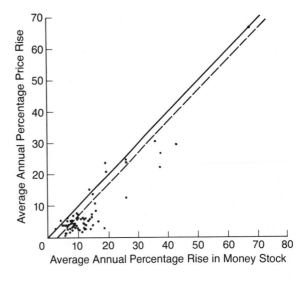

Figure 19–3. Money-Supply Increase and Price-Level Rise (Average Annual Percentage) for 64 Countries, 1948–1974.

Source: International Financial Statistics, Supplement, International Monetary Fund, 1976.

The general correlation between increases in money and the rise in the price level is vividly illustrated by this chart. The straight-dashed slanting line is the line of equal proportional changes in prices and quantity of money after allowance for a 3 percent annual growth of the physical stock of goods.

Inspection shows that, on the average, prices do not rise exactly in proportion to the increase in the amount of money. If they did, the points would cluster around a 45-degree line out of the lower left corner. Instead, most points lie below it. Because of a growth of population and nonmoney goods of about 2 to 4 percent a year, the price level will rise about 2 to 4 percent a year less than the rate of change in the amount of money. This implies that the points should lie around the dashed line drawn on the figure, and they do.

flation of 1946 saw prices doubling on the average every two or three days. Plotting these experiences would require an enormous graph, but, as expected, the plotted points would be in the far upper right of Figure 19–3, if extended.

Increasing the Stock of Money

Never has inflation lasted several years without an increase in the money stock, relative to other goods, and never has such an increase in the money stock happened without an inflation. No other factor is associated with sustained inflations. It is the disproportionate absolute growth in the money supply that has sustained inflations, such as almost all nations are now experiencing.[2] But how does the money stock increase so rapidly?

The answer is that governments print and issue money more rapidly than real output grows. But why? Political forces: It is easier to print money than explicitly levy sufficient taxes to balance government budgets. This has been a fact since time immemorial and doubtless will continue in the future—in varying degrees. The long sweep of history shows an upward growth of money created by governments to finance expenditures, and at a rate exceeding the society's growth of real income. To understand the mechanics (if not the politics), see how we do it in the United States.

Our coins are minted and paper money (called Federal Reserve Notes) is printed by the U.S. Treasury and delivered to Federal Reserve Banks,

its banking agents. The Federal Reserve Board of Governors is authorized by law to spend the new money to buy government bonds, not surprisingly —but not copies of this textbook, unfortunately. The Federal Reserve Banks are legally and purportedly independent of the U.S. government, but are in fact responsive to it. (And unless the Banks buy bonds when the President and Congress "advise," new officials will soon be managing Federal Reserve Banks.) So when U.S. government administrators decide to sell some bonds (borrow money) to finance its deficit—that is, the excess of government expenditures over explicit taxes— they urge the Federal Reserve Banks to buy the new U.S. government bonds with new printed money, which is then spent by the government. Though the institutional details are complex, the practical effects are exactly as indicated. In essence, the Federal Reserve Bank system issues new money when it "lends" to the U.S. government in exchange for some promissory notes (U.S. bonds). Of course, those bonds are really never repaid; they are renewed (exchanged for new bonds) when due. The issued money stays outstanding in the hands of the public (except when worn-out bills are exchanged for crispy new ones). This strange, roundabout method of creating and issuing more paper money developed by historical, but convenient, political processes that we ignore here.

This is known as "monetizing" government debt, a clever way of creating money for the government. New money is created by a "central bank" (the "Fed") for the U.S. government. Thus, a deficit, *only if financed by money creation,* is a source of monetary and price inflation. Most other national governments are less circuitous: They simply print and spend money, period.

---

[2] With the exception of the few massive gold and silver discoveries, history records no major, persisting inflations in the absence of money-creation by governments.

It's really almost that simple—almost, because we ignored bank checking account money. Checking accounts are called *demand deposits,* because they are payable by the commercial bank on demand. Checking accounts increase in very close proportion with paper currency, for reasons we can ignore here. Therefore, a 10 percent increase in the stock of new money issued by the Federal Reserve Banks will lead very quickly to a similar percentage increase in the total of the public's checking accounts. (In 1976 checking accounts were about $230 billion, while paper and coins held by the public were about $70 billion, a total of about $300 billion.)

The important implication of all this is that the size of the U.S. money stock is technically controllable by the Federal Reserve Bank authorities —who, however, cannot easily, if at all, refuse what the President and the Congress "advise." It is easy to see why, when the government wants to spend more (that is, when your representatives respond to political forces exerted by you and the rest of the public), there is an irresistible temptation to create money rather than levy enough explicit taxes to cover all expenditures. It follows that it is technically very easy to stop inflation: Just stop increasing the money stock faster than the normal increase in real output— except that the Federal Reserve Bank officials would soon be induced to resign. Some members of the Board of Governors say the Federal Reserve Banks really can't control the quantity of money in existence. If "can't" means they haven't done so with deliberate design, no one would dispute them. But it is undeniable that they have the technical power and ability to do so and have determined the amount—no matter what they may say to absolve themselves from blame for some of the large increases and decreases in the stock of money.

"Sources" or "Causes" of Inflation

At one time or another you will hear that foreign aid, agricultural support programs, social security, and our space, military, energy, or unemployment and welfare programs are inflationary. Whether they will "cause" inflation depends whether they involve an increase in the quantity of money. Whether (1) the program itself, or (2) the increase in the quantity of money to finance the program is called the "cause" of the inflation depends upon how one defines *cause.* Is the money increase *the* cause? Or is the *cause* of the money increase *the* cause? The moral is: Carefully distinguish between the increase in the money stock and the factors that induced monetary authorities to increase the money stock. Call either one—the money increase or the reason for increasing money—the cause, but don't confuse the two.

For example, especially current in public discussion is the highly plausible belief that a "wage-push" or "administered" prices have caused inflation. The belief is that some wages and prices are increased because some "market power" is in the hands of "key" people, and all other prices must adjust to these key prices. Steel prices or union wage rates are often cited as examples. Analytic rigor—and much factual evidence—reveals no key commodities to whose prices the prices of other goods adjust. For example, an imposed rise in the price of steel will reduce the amount demanded. Employment in steel mills will fall. Some resources used in steel production will in time shift to other goods, whose prices will fall as supply is increased. The price level remains unchanged. There is a rise in the price of steel goods but a fall in others. However, inflation will then occur if the transiently unemployed resources persuade political authorities *to create new money* to spend for the products to return the unemployed to their old jobs. Then the increased quantity of money will raise all prices up to match the prices that had first been arbitrarily raised. In this way, the monetary inflation restores the former structure of relative prices.

Looking at one particular higher price and saying it causes inflation is to confuse consequences with cause. For an inflation to occur there must be an increase in the money supply relative to the demand for money. Thus an increase in the quantity of money must be kept distinct from the *motivation* for increasing the quantity of money. In our example, the motive was to *assure* employment even at the new, higher imposed prices. If government authorities keep an eye on the rate of unemployment in the *steel* industry, it is easy to see that steel could be *called* a key industry. If the government assures full employment for some other group of employees, they too, could be called the key group—regardless of whether they be teachers, custodians, or actors.

In principle, it is easy to stop inflation: Reduce the growth rate of money. But it is not easy to adopt that policy. That would require abandoning the political promises of full employment even for those who ask high prices. Our political, government programs contain that promise, and if it is fulfilled you can be sure inflation will occur as the government prints more money to finance its expenditures designed to maintain adequate demand for those who are unemployed at whatever high prices or wages they are asking. A policy that assures people they will be rescued by increased government spending to preserve their jobs regardless of the wages or prices asked is a major "cause" for inflation.

Inflationary Redistribution of Wealth

Though odd names are given to inflation (creeping, galloping, runaway, and hyper-), a critical distinction is between *unanticipated* and *anticipated* inflation. Anticipated inflations are those for which people on average correctly foresaw its timing and future duration. Unanticipated inflations are those that were incorrectly foreseen. That is, loans were made prior to anticipation of inflation and without increasing either the principal amount to be repaid or the interest to offset the lower purchasing power of dollars. As a result, debtors gain in real purchasing power and the creditor loses in being repaid in money of lower purchasing power. Unanticipated inflation transfers wealth from creditors to debtors. But exactly what is meant by being a creditor or a debtor?

Monetary assets are claims to a *fixed* number of *dollars* in the future. They take two forms: (1) money, and (2) claims to fixed amounts of money, such as bonds, promissory notes of fixed payment, constant-dollar retirement pensions. Monetary liabilities are the other side of that claim: obligations to pay that fixed amount of money.

On the other hand, real assets (or liabilities) are claims to (or obligations to deliver) goods and services whose dollar prices change with inflation. Owners of real assets do not suffer a loss during inflation because real asset prices on average rise with inflation.

For example, consider the effect of a completely *un*anticipated inflation of 10 percent if a person's monetary assets are $100 in money and $1000 in U.S. bonds yielding 5 percent. The price level rises 10 percent. A year later his $100 in cash has depreciated to the equivalent of $100/1.10 = $90.90 in real terms. His bond, which pays $1050 (principal plus interest) in one year, will return $1050/1.10 = $954 of purchasing power—a loss of purchasing power of $9.10 on the cash and $96 on the bond. But if he also owed somebody, say $1200 at 5 percent interest, he could pay that $60 interest and $1200 principal with dollars that are 10 percent less valuable in real purchasing power. So he has $1260/1.10 = $1145 in obligations (in new real value)—a transfer to him of $115 (= $1260 − $1145) in real purchasing power. Since he loses $9.10 on his cash monetary assets and $96 on his credit (the U.S. bond) but gains $115 from his monetary liabilities, he has a net gain of $9.90 (= $115 − $96 − $9.10), because he was *a net* monetary debtor. He was not evenly balanced in a "neutral" monetary status. If you wonder about the *real* assets he owns or owes, they change in dollar terms on average by the amount of the price-level change—so on average he neither gains nor loses from his real assets or liabilities.[3]

[3] Let R and M be net real and net monetary assets, respectively, and E the initial equity. Thus: $E = R + M$. If E' is the new equity when prices rise by proportion P, then: $E' =$

A common way to be a net monetary debtor is to buy a house with a *large* mortgage. If a person has a $20,000 house with a mortgage of 5 percent on $10,000 (a monetary debt) the following two balance sheets show his situation before and after an unanticipated doubling of the price level. He initially holds $100 of monetary assets (money) and $20,000 of real (house and land) assets, a monetary debt of $10,000, and he has an equity (net wealth) of $10,100. With a doubling of prices, his equity increases from $10,100 to $30,100, giving him *real* wealth equity of $30,100/2 = $15,050 in original purchasing power dollars, a gain of $4950 (= $15,050 − $10,100) in terms of original purchasing power dollars.

If inflation were anticipated to occur at 100 percent over the next year, a lender would insist on being paid about 100 percent more dollars to compensate for the depreciation in the purchasing power of dollars when prices rise 100 percent. The borrower would agree, so instead of getting back the normal, say, 5 percent interest in money, the lender would get back an additional *inflation adjustment premium* of about 100 percent more of the *principal* on which the promised interest

$PR + M$. Finally, let Q be the proportionate increase in the money value of the equity: $Q = E'/E$. Now, substituting and rearranging,

$$Q = \frac{PR + M}{E}$$

$$= P\left(\frac{R}{E}\right) + \frac{M}{E}$$

$$= P\left(\frac{E - M}{E}\right) + \frac{M}{E}$$

$$= P - (P - 1)\frac{M}{E}.$$

Balance Sheets Before and After
Unanticipated Inflation for a Net
Monetary Debtor, Showing Real Increase in Equity

Before Inflation

Assets		Liabilities	
Cash	$ 100	Debt	$10,000
House	20,000	Equity (Net Wealth)	10,100
	$20,100		$20,100

After Inflation
(Doubling of Price Level)

Assets		Liabilities	
Cash	$ 100	Debt	$10,000
House	40,000	Equity (Net Wealth)	30,100
	$40,100		$40,100

is to be paid. The inflation adjustment is applied to both the principal and the interest—but is usually all expressed in the "interest" rate (actually an interest *and* inflation premium) on the principal amount due. So in this case the interest on the one-year loan would be expressed as 110 percent. The lender gets back $210 ($100 + $110) on his $100 loan. At twice the initial price level, the $210 is equivalent to $105 in original purchasing power, a 5 percent real return. If the extent of the inflation is underanticipated, lenders lose and borrowers gain, because the explicit nominal interest rate is too low. And the opposite happens if a coming inflation is overanticipated.

If interest rates received on all monetary assets (and therefore, paid on all monetary liabilities) could be adjusted for the correctly anticipated inflation rate, there would be *no* wealth redistri-

4, 5
6, 7
8, 9
10, 11

butions. Neither borrowers gain nor lenders lose. Thus, from 1960 to 1975 long-term interest rates have risen from 4 percent to about 9 percent. Was inflation anticipation increasing to about 5 percent per year?

**Illustrations of Inflation-
Induced Wealth Redistribution**

Substantial evidence collected from inflationary periods of the past 50 years in the United States establishes that the inflations were unanticipated or incompletely anticipated, so that a transfer of wealth occurred from net monetary creditors to net monetary debtors. Strong evidence is provided by the experience of business firms. Annual balance-sheet reports show which firms are net monetary creditors and which are net monetary debtors. The former have a larger total of cash and accounts receivable than they owe in accounts payable and bonds, while the latter have the opposite balance.[4]

[4] An example of a net monetary debtor was Reynolds Metals Corporation. As of December 31, 1970, it possessed monetary assets totaling about $270 million (cash, government securities and loans to others, and accounts receivables); and it owed in monetary liabilities about $1.131 billion (bonds, preferred stocks, and notes and accounts payable). On net, Reynolds was a net monetary debtor to the extent of $861 millions. With 16.6 million shares of common stock outstanding, each one bore a net monetary debt of about $85. You could buy a share of common stock at that time for about $25, becoming a net monetary debtor to the extent of about $60, over twice your equity. In effect, you had claims to about $110 of real nonmonetary goods, offset in part by the monetary debt of $85, leaving you an equity of $25. It is as if you had bought a $110 good by paying $25 down and borrowing the remaining $85. If the price level rises 10 percent, your equity would increase by $11, which

During an inflation, as at any other time, a host of factors affect the fortunes of every business firm—new products, changes in demands, new management, fires, inventions, etc. Nevertheless, one steady differentiating factor contributing to a gain for all the net-monetary-debtor firms is the wealth-redistribution process just outlined. On the average, the price of a share of common stock (share of ownership in the equity of the corporation) in firms that are net monetary debtors should rise *relative* to those of net monetary creditors during unanticipated or incompletely anticipated inflations.

Since almost half the business firms on the major stock exchanges were net monetary creditors while the other half were net monetary debtors, we could test for that wealth-transfer effect. Data of stock prices and assets and liabil-

is a 44 percent increase relative to your $25 equity. Thus a 10 percent rise in the general price level would increase your wealth by 44 percent, giving you a net gain in real wealth of 35 percent (the net gain of 44 percent in monetary terms adjusted for the rise in the price level). Inflation would increase your real wealth if you held Reynolds common stock, *unless* other people had anticipated the inflation gain and had already bid up the price of Reynolds common stock —in which case you would neither gain nor lose if the inflation did occur.

An example of a net monetary creditor was Filtrol Corporation, which on December 31, 1970, was a net monetary creditor to the extent of $22 million ($24 million in monetary assets minus $2 million in monetary debts). With 2.2 million in common shares outstanding, this is $8.50 a share, onethird of the $25 price of the common stock. In effect the owners had paid $25 for $16.50 of real goods and $8.50 of monetary assets (equivalent to cash). In the event of an inflation, only the $16.50 in goods would increase in value, giving one a smaller percentage increase in his $25 equity. An unanticipated inflation would hurt the stockholders of Filtrol. If the inflation were correctly anticipated, then the stock price of Filtrol would be lower initially and someone who bought after the inflation was anticipated would not lose from the inflation.

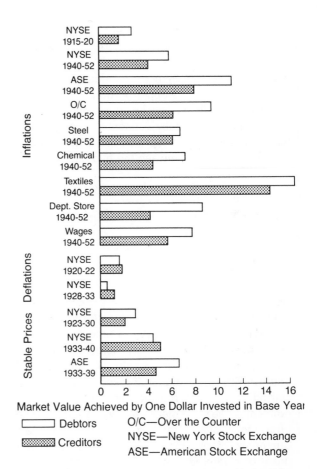

Figure 19–4. Effect of Unanticipated Inflation on Market Value of Equity for Net Monetary Debtor and Creditor Business Firms. *Source: A. Alchian and R. Kessel, "Redistribution of Wealth through Inflation," Science, Vol. 130, No. 3375 (September 4, 1959), p. 538.*

During every inflation, net monetary debtors experienced an increase in the value of their equity more than did net monetary creditors. During deflations, the opposite effect occurred. During periods of stable prices, no dominance by either debtors or creditors was evident. Attempts to perform the same measurements for corporations in the 1960s and 1970s have been thwarted because almost all business corporations have become net monetary debtors.

ities for thousands of firms over the period 1914–1952 bear out the analysis. Figure 19–4 presents the evidence. In every sample, net monetary debtors did better than net monetary creditors, as can be seen in the upper portion of that figure. The opposite effect is observed during deflations. Finally, as is implied by economic theory, during the episodes of stable prices there was no significant difference between the two classes.

Inflation: Taxation without Legislation

Tax on Government Money

Coins and paper money yield no explicit interest. This makes government-produced (noninterest-bearing) money more costly to hold during inflation. Those losses to money holders during inflation are equal to the wealth the government gets with the new money it issued. So, inflation started by the government's spending new government money is a means of levying *a tax* on the prior stock of outstanding government money. But much of our money is private money that does pay interest—in particular, checking-account money. Commercial banks *do in fact* pay more implicit interest on checking accounts when interest rates rise, as in the past five years, by giving more services: Charges for checks are reduced; mailing costs for deposits are covered; free parking and lounge rooms are provided, as are lower-cost travelers checks, notary services, and safety deposit boxes for big checking-account holders. If these appear trivial, remember that 6 percent interest on an average balance of

12, 13

$400 is equivalent to $2 a month of special "free" services and since that isn't *taxable* interest-income, only about $1 to $1.50 of such services per month on a $400 balance is required to make it a competitive interest return.

To summarize: During *underanticipated* inflations, net monetary debtors gain at the expense of net monetary asset holders. During correctly *anticipated* inflations, monetary assets that do not pay interest (explicitly or in kind) decrease in real value. The principal monetary assets that do not pay interest explicitly or implicitly (even during anticipated inflation) are coins and paper money. Inflation, anticipated or not, is a tax on holders of existing noninterest-bearing, government-issued money. The tax on money equals the gain obtained by the government by creating the new money that caused the inflation.

What is meant by saying the "government gains"? The government is not *a* person; everyone is somehow involved. Strictly speaking, the government is part of the wealth structure of every person. People gain from inflation to the extent that their other explicit taxes are not raised, and to the extent they are beneficiaries of however the government uses the increase in its wealth. Even though no one may include his latent tax obligations in a balance sheet of his wealth, an inflation reduces the "real" value of the amount of future taxes that must be collected to pay interest on existing bonds.

Graduated Income Tax and Capital-Gains Tax

Besides the tax on money, as just explained, inflation increases the taxes on people in three other ways:

1. Graduated income taxes tax higher incomes at higher *percentage rates.* As inflation progresses and people move into higher dollar income brackets, they pay a larger fraction of their income as taxes. This automatic tax increase with inflation is taxation without legislation.

2. Taxes are levied on increases in the capital values of any asset (collected when the asset is sold). So if you buy a painting (or some common stock) for $1000 and then three years later sell it for $2000 because all prices of all goods have doubled on average, you are not wealthier in real terms, but you must pay up to 40 percent of that $1000 capital gain in dollar terms to the government as a tax. You end up poorer. But had there been no inflation your later sale of that painting at $1000 would not have imposed any tax on you. This capital-gains tax can be especially severe if you recognize that a tax of 40 percent on capital gains would amount to a tax of 20 percent of all wealth when prices double (40 percent of the nominal value gain is 20 percent of the unchanged real value). Prices in the United States have increased by over 60 percent during the past decade—constituting an increase in capital-gains tax liabilities of up to 15 percent of wealth (40 percent of the 60 percent rise in nominal value corrected to real terms by dividing by the price rise of 1.6) even though there was no value gain in real terms.

3. A similar tax is one on business firms. As inflation progresses, the old nominal value of their assets cannot (under income-tax laws) be properly adjusted upward in terms of new prices to more accurately reflect the higher costs in dollar terms of replacing the depreciating equipment. That overstates the reported dollar earnings in terms above their real purchasing power. The overstating of nominal profits, because costs are understated, forces business firm owners to pay a higher tax—again without specific legislation—which explains why stock prices tend to dip when inflation fears increase.

Business firms do not gain in wealth by selling inventories at higher prices when inflation occurs than they earlier paid for their inventories. The reason they don't is that the firm, while taking in more money, must also pay out more in higher prices to replace the inventory. In real terms it gains absolutely nothing. Higher money receipts merely enable it to avoid a loss of real wealth. The correct statement is that the firm's nominal earnings in *dollar* terms are bigger but by no more than the rise in the price level: It has no increase in real profits or real wealth, like everyone else whose wages, rents, or sales prices rise in inflation. Computing dollar profits as receipts at new prices minus costs at *old* prices overstates dollar profits so that taxes increase more than in proportion to prices. Therefore, business firms with inventories costed at earlier low prices suffer heavier real taxes on unchanged real profits during inflation. Correctly attempting to put inventory costing on replacement cost is known as "last in–first out" (LIFO) inventory costing.

Living with Inflation

The Nonexistent Wage Lag

A common fallacy about the effects of inflation is that wage rates typically, if not always, lag behind prices. Exhaustive examination of available historical evidence fails to support that belief. During some inflations real wages indeed fell (money wages rose less than prices), but there were as many inflations in which real wages rose (money wages rose more than prices).

What creates the persistent belief that wages lag behind prices during inflations? First, anyone whose wages do not rise as much as other people's—whatever the reason—will seek some scapegoat. If there is an inflation at the time, there is the excuse. (During that same time, people whose wages are rising more rapidly will attribute the rise not to inflation but to their own "just desserts.")

Second, even if there were no change in any wage *rates,* upgrading employees from lower- to higher-paying jobs would increase *realized* wages. Concentrating only on particular hourly wage rates rather than on the *earnings* of employees can be misleading.

Third, everyone—whether he is selling labor, pencils, or automobiles—will notice that the price of what he sells lags behind the *average* of other prices most of the time. His prices change sporadically, whereas the *average* of all other prices, being an average of a host of sporadically changing prices, will change more smoothly and steadily. Of course, at the moment his price is adjusted, it "leads" the general rise. The *average* of all wages does *not* systematically lag behind the average of all prices.

Fourth, often governments shift demand—for example, from peacetime goods to armaments, or from consumer goods to space vehicles. The shift in demand increases prices and wages of those goods (armaments and wages of armament workers) relative to other prices and wages. These are responses to shifts in relative demands. Yet, if shifts in demand are accompanied or facilitated by the creation of money, inflation also will occur. As demand is shifted from retail clerks, teachers, etc., to welders, machinists, and aerospace engineers, it is easy to see why there is a relative decline in wages of teachers, and why that could be mistakenly considered a result of inflation, rather than of the revised demand. During the last 60 years the U.S. government has accomplished that revision in demand by creating new money to spend for more desired goods.

Fifth, it is often believed that a rise in the demand for some good will "filter down" and affect wages of employees only after the product price has increased. This error is based on the assumption that the economy is a simple sequence of production steps from raw materials with equal supply elasticities to final products. In fact, some goods are inputs for earlier stages and outputs from later stages of production (for example, gasoline is used to make steel to refine oil to get gasoline, etc.) so that one cannot tell whether a good is at an earlier or later stage in a production process. Furthermore, the sequence of price rises is not necessarily from consumer goods to labor-input wages. Recall the example of the rise in consumers' meat prices in response to demand increases (in Chapter 4): A demand increase does not necessarily invoke a series of price rises starting at the *consumers'* end of the distribution process. "Filtering down" is not what happens.

"Rippling out" to many interconnected industries is a more accurate metaphor.

Sixth, the wage-lag belief has been fostered in part by fallacious economic reasoning. For example: "Inflation increases the resources at the command of government or the agency creating the new money; it follows that there is less left for the remaining segments of the economy. They must consume less, since less is available, so the prices at which they buy must rise relative to their incomes." Where is the flaw in this analysis? Though the government takes private wealth from the public, and the public must consume less, this does not mean that the public's income from *wages* must fall relative to prices of goods it buys. Instead, its *wealth* has decreased. Money holders lose part of their *money-wealth* value and will therefore consume less; their wage *incomes* do not lag; prices do not rise faster than incomes from productive resources. Inflation is *not* a tax on wage earners or on money *incomes*. Money-wage incomes rise with the price level. Holders of monetary assets issued by the government (currency and government bonds) lose wealth equivalent to that obtained by the government by inflation.

If the inflation is a result of a crop failure or disaster, like an oil embargo, that reduces physical output, the value of money falls as prices rise; so a loss of purchasing power is borne in accord with the quantity of money held at the time prices rose. Though practically all other goods also rise in price, they do not rise as much as the price of the good with the decreased output. So all other resource owners, wage earners included, suffer some loss. Since everything rises in price relative to money, money holders suffer the greatest real loss per dollar of initial wealth.

15, 16
17

It is the decrease in *real* output that initiated this inflation. The reduced real wealth is a result of the crop or good decrease, not of the inflation—which only reveals the decreased output through higher prices.

No "Forced Savings" in Inflation

There is the fallacious "forced-savings" doctrine which contends that the "lost income" from the alleged "wage lag" goes to profit receivers in businesses, who invest it in new equipment. People have argued that it brought about the industrial revolution of Western Europe. During World Wars I and II this doctrine provided popular support for special taxes on business profits. Profits were interpreted as unwarranted gains from "forced savings" imposed on employees by a lag of wages behind prices or from inventory gains. Neither economic analysis nor empirical evidence supports such a notion. On the contrary, it is denied by both, as the preceding discussion shows.

Real Incomes Not Reduced

Another fallacy is that inflation erodes our real income in the following sense: The U.S. Department of Commerce reported in 1974 that the median income of Americans had at last exceeded $10,000 annually, up 11 percent from $9000 the year before, but the 8 percent inflation eroded away all but a 3 percent real income growth. The fallacy is in not realizing that the increase in money income was a result of the inflation in the first place. Had there been no increase in prices (no inflation), average money income would have risen only 3 percent, not 11 percent. The inflation raised that 3 percent of real income to an 11 percent increase in money terms. Inflation did not erode away 8 percent of any potential real income that would otherwise have been available had there been no inflation. The U.S. Department of Commerce press release had the cause and effect turned around: Inflation was the cause of the 11 percent, rather than a 3 percent, rise in *nominal* earnings. Inflation did not reduce the real income from 11 percent to 3 percent, nor even determine the 3 percent real growth.

Savings Are Not Eroded

Another confusion permeates errors about inflation: the belief that inflation destroys the value of savings. The confusion is between savings and the form in which it (wealth) is held. If held as nonmonetary assets, there is no loss from inflation. Only wealth held in the form of claims to monetary assets will suffer a loss, if the interest rate or principal amount to be repaid is not indexed or anticipated for any ensuing inflation. But a person can put his savings into nonmonetary assets such as houses, cars, buildings, or stocks with a neutral net monetary status portfolio.[5] It is true, however, that people who had invested their savings in *monetary* assets years ago will lose wealth because of the form in which they earlier chose to hold that wealth—fixed money pension rights during an underanticipated inflation. "Widows, orphans, and old people" suffer from inflation only to the extent they put their wealth into the form of monetary assets—some-

thing that they do no more than any other people. It is not marital or parental status or age that determines whether one loses or gains from inflation; it is the kind of wealth.

Data collected for families in 1962 showed, somewhat surprisingly, that over half the families that had below-average income, or were middle-aged, or married, or homeowners, or male-headed would be net monetary debtors (and gain from inflation). For the members of the opposite classifications (above-average earners, rentors, etc.), over half were net monetary creditors and would lose from the underanticipated inflation.[6]

**How to Avoid the
Inflation Tax and Wealth Transfer**

In what form should wealth be held to reduce or avoid the inflation money tax and the wealth transfer? Less in money and more in nonmonetary assets—stocks, houses, land, art, or any other goods whose market values are not *fixed* in money units regardless of inflation. A lot of people with only a few hundred dollars of savings usually hold savings deposits paying low rates of interest that are constrained by federal law not to respond competitively to interest rates on open loan markets. They tend to suffer when an inflation occurs.

There is no way people who invested in monetary assets can avoid losing wealth if inflation occurs at a faster rate than anticipated—unless they had arranged, when making the loan, to have the principal amount increased or "indexed" by the

[5] To be neutral means the total monetary debts are equal to the monetary assets of the fund.

[6] Data collected by Federal Reserve Board of Governors and analyzed by P. Chen and C. Nisbet in Chen, *Understanding Economics*. Boston: Little, Brown, 1974, p. 34.

amount of any subsequent rise in the price level—a form of indexing of the principal to some measure of the cost of living. Unfortunately, measures of the cost of living are not reliable—especially if produced by any group on which pressure can influence how the index is computed. (This is not a fanciful conjecture. It has happened in the index used to measure the cost of living for farmers in computing the farm price supports that the government provides them.)[7]

A more basic and inescapable defect of an index is that it requires some particular, specified set of prices and weights reflecting the amount of each good considered appropriate for the real purchasing power of the interested parties. What is a relevant, appropriate set of goods will differ among people and, most seriously, will require prediction of those goods that will be of interest in the future; that in turn will depend on their relative prices in the future. Predicting which relative prices will change in which way (and some will fall relative to others, no matter what the rate of inflation) poses an intractable problem in finding an acceptable, reliable means of indexing the amount that should be repaid to allow for inflation. This is one reason why it is so rarely that bonds and loans are indexed in dollar terms to adjust for a future inflation during the life of the bond.

Shortage of Money or Too-Rapid Money Growth?

With money *known in advance* to be depreciating in value (that is, becoming more expensive to hold), people will strive to hold lower "real" amounts of money in order to avoid some of that depreciation, just as they would with any good that has become more expensive to hold. This smaller real value of money balances results from efforts to economize on resources that have become dearer to hold.[8] Prices will be higher than in proportion to the increase in nominal money—often expressed as a reduction in the *real* stock of money—despite larger nominal amounts of money.

The inconvenience of a smaller amount of "real" money is borne in order to avoid higher costs of deteriorating money. In sum, persisting *anticipated* inflation destroys part of the real money capital of the community. An analogy is illuminating. A tax on gasoline would collect wealth for the taxing agency, but people would then use less gasoline; thus, the *cost* of the tax is not merely the pecuniary wealth transferred to the taxing agency but also the reduced level of convenient transportation.

These inconveniences of holding less real money are superficially ascribed to a "shortage" of money. Yet, as we have seen, the reduced amount of "real" money is the result of each person's rational response to anticipated deprecia-

---

[7] Shorter-term loans are less affected by *changes* in price-level anticipations because there is a shorter future life over which *changes* in anticipation are capitalized into the present value. Also, there is some evidence that short-term rates of about 90 days seem to forecast inflation pretty accurately. The evidence is not overwhelming, but it does suggest that short-term loans therefore involve smaller wealth transfers.

[8] People will want to hold an amount of money equal to, say, four weeks' income rather than five. If they try to do so, prices will jump by 25 percent so that at the higher incomes the old stock of money now matches only four weeks' instead of five weeks' income.

tion of dollars. Strangely enough, some people contend that the way to alleviate this "shortage" of money is to print more money—which, of course, would instead increase the rate of anticipated inflation and drive people to hold even smaller *real* money balances. Instead, the increase in nominal amount of money should be reduced—so as to reduce the anticipations of inflation—a solution that is paradoxical only to those who forget the difference between relative and absolute (or real and nominal) amounts of money.

Dying with Inflation

Price and Allocation Controls

A predictable gut response to inflation is the political imposition of wage, price, and allocation controls (called euphemistically "incomes policy"). The controls are often initially hidden under the sham of "voluntary" controls. Their use may stem from the mistaken impression that inflation is caused by greedy, powerful businessmen and labor unions seeking higher prices and wages. If you still think unions or big business ("monopolies" is the usual epithet) raise prices and cause inflation, reconsider. If a union or business raises its wages or prices, what determined the height to which the wages or prices will be raised? There is some optimal (*not maximum*) price. Suppose the wages and prices are set at that seller's optimal height. If next year he raises them again, what raised the new *optimal height* to which the wages and prices are being pushed?

1. If nothing happened, the optimal level would not have changed.
2. If the union or business has a smaller supply to sell than previously, where have the productive resources gone? Wherever they went, prices and wages there will be lower; the price level as a whole will not be higher.
3. If supply conditions in this union or business did not change but the demand increased,
   a. it must have been falling elsewhere when demand shifted to this industry, so lower prices elsewhere will maintain the same general price level without inflation.
   b. or, if demand increased in this business *and* elsewhere, a general increase in market demands has occurred. How could that happen except by an increased money demand for goods? The general increase in demand (requiring a larger money stock) is what causes the general price level to increase.[9]

Far from preserving the value of money, price controls actually *reduce* it. Controlled prices below those that would exist in open markets are *not* prices at which people can get amounts demanded at those prices. Money is less effective in

---

[9] There is one other possibility than an increase in money supply. People may demand more of nonmoney goods in general and less of money, possibly because of an increased confidence in the future value of goods. This will cause an increase in demands for goods in general, and will raise general prices. But this possible case is a one-shot affair, occurring usually during recovery after a prior recession. As conditions return to normal, prices will stop rising because people then find their wealth and incomes have risen enough to make the amount of money they demand match that which is in existence. This will not cause a continuing inflation.

getting goods. The inevitable shortages, outages, and delayed deliveries are reductions in the power of money and exchange of command goods. Other forms of competitive power, or rewards to seller, will compensate for the reduced exchange value of a dollar: Political power, status, personal characteristics, and standing in line are examples, as explained earlier in Chapter 4.

The irony is that price controls, which are presumed to preserve the value of the dollar, in fact reduce its value by making it less relevant for exchange, *and* thereby reduce the roles of personal preferences and exchange as social control institutions. Which is better: a low but less-accurate and less-influential exchange price, or a higher, more-accurate, more-powerful price? Inflation without legal price controls reduces the value of a dollar; but it retains the power of money and market prices in directing exchange and production.

In Germany, three years after World War II, when price controls were removed, the economy responded with spectacular increases in production and efficiency. Japan and Italy had similar experiences. These increases could not be attributed to recovery from war damage, but instead were sufficiently isolated and abrupt to reveal how severely market-price constraints reduce the effectiveness of the market as an informative, allocative, incentive system. In 1974 West Germany did not impose price controls on gasoline during the Arab oil embargo. Prices rose; there were no "shortages." In the United States there were price controls—and shortages. When the United States removed price controls, gasoline became available with all the side services at the higher prices. Was there ever a better example of the effects of price controls?

Perhaps the most noticeable (and undesirable?) effects are those that follow from the adoption of price and wage controls: allocations of use by political authority, because suppression of market prices also suppresses transmission of information, reduces the extent of exchange and specialization, creates shortages (whatever the amount supplied) and outages at controlled prices, and induces people to establish rights to available supplies by means that are costly but less reflective of the consumer's highest-valued uses and more reflective of the opinions of the politically powerful.

It is a fact that in all countries, inflation is almost invariably accompanied by political controls of wages, prices, and uses. To judge by its relative frequency, we have to conclude that most countries "prefer" political control of wages and prices to open inflation. Or is it to be explained by economic ignorance or by the political processes?

Are those who will exercise more political power the same ones who most clamor for price controls? Is it a battle between the politically ambitious and the economically ambitious? Many people who propose price controls find themselves (not unexpectedly) employed as price controllers, or are the politically favored groups. Many politicians who disapprove of economic competitive power of private interests propose price controls to increase their own political power. Again we warn you: This should not be taken as condemnation. Who is to say what is the best form of competitive power for controlling behavior and for allocating resources and goods? That the various forms operate with different effects on total productive potential and the culture does not prove any one of them to be necessarily the desirable one, whatever may be your own preference.

The Case for, and against, Anti-Inflation "Guidelines"

Price and wage guidelines (called incomes policy) have been invoked by every President since 1932 and by almost all European governments. The guidelines say people should ask only for wages or prices that would be consistent with no inflation. If productivity of inputs in real terms is increasing at the rate of 2 or 3 percent per year, then *input* prices could rise 2 or 3 percent per year *on the average* without increasing the price of final output.

We have seen that a necessary and sufficient condition for inflation is an increase in the quantity of money relative to the amount demanded (which is correlated with the supply of other goods). If the supply of money does not increase, higher prices will not be sustainable with the same stock of goods. Hence, it would be unnecessary to exhort people not to raise prices; their own inadequate sales would "control" their prices. Price raisers would find themselves priced out of the market. Why bother to "jawbone" them if the inexorable forces of demand make higher prices nonprofitable? On the other hand, if the stock of money does increase, all the talk in the world will not stop prices from rising if that is profitable. Then why all the desire for "guidelines"? There can be a reason. To see it, we use (1) the distinction between anticipated and unanticipated infla-

tion, (2) the power of a monetary authority to determine the quantity of money, and (3) a government policy of assuring full employment by increasing the stock of money, regardless of any resultant rate of inflation.

Suppose some people agree to long-term contracts—say labor union wage contracts for the next three years. Suppose, further, that these employees and employers now agree to higher *future* wages in expectation of future inflation. Assume also that a severe disappointment in sales would be required to induce an attempt to change the contract, a lengthy process that might take six months to a year. It would take time to convince enough people that the anticipated inflation had not occurred *and* is not going to. Under these conditions the monetary authorities are in a bind. If they are prepared to increase the quantity of money sufficiently to validate those expectations and thereby make the agreed-upon future prices consistent with high employment, the inflation anticipations will be validated. If there is a commitment to always increase the money supply sufficiently to avoid an increase in unemployment whenever any prices are raised, monetary inflation by the monetary authorities (government) is necessary unless the *future* prices contracted for can be restrained. This requires convincing people that there will be no future monetary inflation. They must be convinced that the government authorities will not increase the money supply sufficiently to validate high future-price commitments to assure full employment at those higher prices.

Guidelines are essentially announcements of the degree of inflation that the monetary and government authorities are prepared to tolerate and permit—if you believe them. Politicians and the Federal Reserve Board may announce guidelines indicating the rate (zero or whatever) of inflation they would validate by increasing the money stock. But what assurance is there that they would not really inflate the money stock any faster? Regrettably, not much! The record is reliable for the unreliability of such pronouncements.

In sum, *if* (a) guidelines did persuade people not to make long-term contracts with *future* prices higher than would occur simply from increased productivity, and *if* (b) governments did not inflate the money stock to finance government expenditures greater than tax collections, then most inflations would be avoided. Those "ifs" are not consistent with history, ancient or recent.

Anti-Inflation Monetary Reforms

Once the money stock has increased, only four policies are available: (1) Suppressing prices by controls will mean that people can't spend their money and get what they want at freely negotiable prices. Money and wealth lose some of their competitive rationing power because their market exchangeability is restricted. Other forms of competition will be more influential. (2) If prices and exchange are not suppressed by controls, as in an open inflation, higher prices will reduce the real wealth value of money, again imposing the wealth loss on money holders. But the role of competitive market offers of wealth relative to other forms of competition in affecting production and allocating goods will not be changed. (3) A third alternative, monetary reform, is simply to cancel a portion of the money, which means

money holders lose. (4) The fourth alternative is to impose a special tax on general wealth (not on money alone) and then to destroy the money proceeds. But, if this kind of general tax could have been imposed, the money probably would not have been created in the first place.

Transient Side Effects of Changing the Rate of Inflation

A *change* in the rate of money increase to a lower rate than was *anticipated* will slow down the increases in demand in the market. As a result of the unanticipated change, a *transient* decrease in employment and output will occur as side effects until the public learns that the increase was below the expected rate, reduces its forecasts, and properly reduces the rise in anticipated future prices—that is, reduces the inflation-adjusted interest rate. Then the transient reduction in employment and output will end. The stronger the anticipations of persisting inflation, the greater and longer will the transient reduction in output probably be, unless the inflation-reducing monetary policy is somehow convincingly and demonstrably invoked so as to change beliefs quickly.

The episodes in 1970 and 1975 are instructive. Prior to each, the money increase nearly stopped for over half a year. Recession set in and price rises were abated. Responsive to public complaints about recession, monetary authorities then made large increases of money partly to enable the government to embark on recession-combating expenditures by again increasing the money stock. The upturn in demand, output, and prices lasted until 1974, when again the monetary authorities brought the money growth down from 10 percent annually to nearly zero. Again a transient recession set up new demands for transient recession-combating inflationary measures. Back we went to money increases, and inflation was fired up again.

We want no inflation; if we have inflation, we want no transient recession as a side effect to ending the inflation (and we know of no way to avoid that side effect, any more than we know of a way to avoid a bed-rest recovery after an appendectomy), and we want to continue expanding government expenditures beyond explicit tax collections or borrowing from private savings. There is simply *no way* to achieve *all* those things in a free society. We simply will have to give up *some* or all in some degree.

19, 20

What Can You Do to Reduce Inflation?

Nothing any person or group can do in a private capacity will reduce or prevent inflation, nor should it be tried. A refusal to raise prices as a seller or as a competing buyer will reduce your welfare and help no one else by as much as you are hurt. Such is the lesson that should be carried over from the earlier chapters of this book. That may sound selfish and antisocial. In fact it is social in that it speeds the discovery of market-clearing prices—with the consequences already developed in the early chapters on exchange and production. It is social in that it undercuts the errors and political confusion of those who argue that the private citizen should restrain himself and not spend his money—so the government authorities can spend money at lower prices than the goods are worth to those who are told not to buy so much.

What little you can do is to act in your political capacity to try to deny office to those who would create money to finance government expenditures. That is the *only* way to stop inflation, despite self-serving political oratory and popular media nonsense to the contrary. When the issue is so clearly stated, you may be moved to ask, "Do I want inflation stopped if I must give up some of what the government is doing, or if new explicit taxes must be levied?" The answer may very well be, "No," but in any case it will, or should, depend upon evaluating the effects of inflation and possible price controls against the effects of reduced rates of government activities or new taxes.

Recessions Can Occur during Inflation

Recent recessions in the midst of inflation surprised many people who thought rising aggregate market demands and prices stimulated output and avoided recessions. Inflation combined with recession persuaded some people that the economics like that presented in this book is wrong. However, recessions during inflation are completely consistent with the economic analysis presented in this book.

During noninflationary times, and if people expect no inflation, investments must yield salable products worth about 5 percent more in a year (if the interest rate is 5 percent). Otherwise their full costs will not be covered. If, in this noninflationary case, aggregate demand falls below expectations (*absolutely* in this case), recession will set in until a new expected rate is perceived by enough people to induce agreement and discovery of new appropriate prices for full employment at tasks with highest earnings prospects. And the initial expected inflation rate that was unfulfilled could have been zero or very high.

For example, if enough people expect inflation at the rate of 15 percent a year and a real interest rate of 5 percent (with the nominal interest rate being 20 percent), any investments or initial outlays must return a sales value that is rising at the rate of 20 percent a year, otherwise not all costs will be covered. If aggregate demand does not rise enough to maintain that expected growth, people will not be selling enough to cover their costs at existing prices and wage rates. Only after enough people discover that the demand growth in the economy-wide aggregate has lagged below that expected rate, and only when enough of them revise expectations, will new prices and wages be found that are acceptable and appropriate to full employment in the best discerned employment prospects.

Those who thought an inflation was necessarily stimulative (even one that was lower than a former rate of inflation) were confused by thinking that wages and costs lag behind selling prices, so that profits would presumably be created by any rate of inflation, large or small. There is no inherent lag of wage rates behind other costs or other input or consumer-goods prices; nor is there any *contractual rigidity* that makes wage rates in general less mobile upward or downward than prices of other goods and services. Production changes because of a lag in enough people's *discerning* that existing price and wage rates and production activity are not consistent with the new revealed aggregate de-

mands. That information lag is not a result of stupidity or stubbornness. For reasons explained earlier (pages 468–478), every fluctuation in sales of some product cannot be immediately tested for persisting generality over other segments of the economy, as distinct from transient fluctuations. What are believed to be transient, reversible sales fluctuations are handled by variations in finished or intermediate buffer inventories, thereby permitting a more stable, more economical production. If inventories or sales change beyond expectations, the individual producer will be induced to revise his output. He can't alone change his input prices because resources he buys or rents have other, almost equally valuable uses, or so they believe. Not until enough people experience the general deterioration in aggregate demand elsewhere will they be willing to agree on new prices, wages, and products appropriate to the new nominal relative demand.

All this can occur during inflation or in its absence. It does not depend only on the actual rate of aggregate demand change. What counts is the difference between the anticipated rate and the actual perceived rate, and how fast enough people can correctly readjust their beliefs and discover the advisability of new appropriate prices and jobs. Indeed, many economists have long been warning politicians of the error in believing that higher employment can be sustained simply by inflating.

Even hard experience doesn't necessarily teach a person, unless he has a good analytic basis for understanding. We hope your experience with this book and your instructor has enabled you to improve your understanding and ability to use economic analysis. And this, gentle readers, is the end of this book. What did you expect, a pot of gold?

Summary

1. Inflation is a rise in the general level of prices of consumer goods. Measurement difficulties arise because of quality changes, substitutions among consumer goods in response to relative price shifts, ascertainment of actual prices, and determination of unchanged levels of utility at which to compute costs.
2. Effects of inflation should be distinguished from effects of factors causing inflation.
3. Anticipated inflations are those for which people correctly foresee the extent and timing. Incompletely anticipated or unanticipated inflations are those in which the anticipated rate of inflation is less than that which actually occurs. The effects of inflation are different, depending upon whether or not the inflations are anticipated.
4. Monetary assets are claims to fixed amounts of money; monetary debts are obligations to pay fixed amounts of money.
5. If one has more monetary debts than monetary assets, he will get a wealth gain from an incompletely anticipated inflation at the expense of net monetary creditors (those who hold more monetary assets than monetary liabilities).
6. Holders of money lose wealth during an inflation (of any kind—as long as interest is not paid on money) to those whose credit constitutes the money or to those who issue token or fiat money (governments).
7. Government, being a very large net monetary debtor, gains wealth from incompletely anticipated inflation.
8. A common fallacy is that wage rates typically, if not always, lag behind consumer goods prices. Extensive evidence lends no support to that proposition. The illusion or allegation arises, we conjecture, because:
   a. specific wages are erroneously compared with the average prices of consumer goods,
   b. demand shifts under circumstances that induce an inflationary policy,
   c. job changes are ignored,
   d. it is erroneously believed that prices of consumer goods always rise before the prices of components, and
   e. because of the fallacious belief that if the government gets more of the community's wealth and income by issuing money and raising prices, real wages must have fallen (which is false—the transfer of resources to the government comes from the *wealth* transfer, not from a shift in wages relative to consumer goods).
9. Inflation does *not* reduce the value of saving. It reduces the real value of monetary wealth, and savings need not be held as monetary wealth.
10. Inflation occurs because the supply of money increases *relative* to the amount of money that people demand to hold, given their existing wealth and income. The absolute supply may increase or the demand may decrease possibly because of loss of wealth from plague, drought, or disaster.
11. Causes of inflation usually refer to reasons for an excessive increase in the stock of money.

But the technique of creating an inflation must be kept separate from the motive for using that technique.

12. Inflations are not caused by cost-push or administered prices. Saying so confuses the *motives* for resorting to increases in the quantity of money with the *increase* in the quantity of money. The former alone will not cause an inflation. The latter will, regardless of the motive for the increase in the stock of money. Every significant inflation (over 10 percent in one year) has been caused by an increase in the absolute quantity of money. Reductions in real wealth are usually of relatively minor significance.

13. Anticipated inflation avoids the wealth transfer from net monetary creditors to debtors because the interest rate on debt was fully adjusted to allow for the price-level rise. But it leads to resource distortion in that people try to reduce the "real" amount of money wealth, giving rise to the phenomenon of a "money shortage" and making exchange more difficult (expensive), thereby sacrificing some of the gains from fuller specialization in production and exchange. This effect does not occur in an open and unanticipated inflation, though a wealth transfer does.

14. Wage and price controls do not reduce the transfer of wealth from net monetary creditors to debtors, because the exchange value of money is reduced by restricting the *ability or right* to offer it in the market. Open inflation achieves a similar effect by increases in prices. Repressing price changes leads to reduced use of the exchange market and to reduced market-directed specialization and exchange. Repressed inflation enhances the political controllability of resource use and allocation.

15. Antiinflation monetary reforms are confiscation or taxation of money forms of wealth. Such reforms involve no transfer of wealth to net monetary debtors, which would occur in an open inflation.

16. Stopping or reducing a rate of inflation that has become expected results in transient reductions in employment and output, because future demand does not develop as anticipated so future output and its costs are not covered by the reduced demand. As anticipations are revised downward, production and employment are increased again toward full employment (as long as the new anticipations are more accurate).

Questions

*1. Almost all consumer price indices for the U.S. in 1977 report a rise of about 40 percent over the price level of 1972.

a. To test your belief in that—and given an annual income of, say, $10,000—would you rather do all your purchasing from a 1972 Sears (or Ward's) mail-order catalog or from a 1977 one? (If you are tempted to pick the current one because of changes in styles of clothes, suppose the styles were to be altered at no cost.) Which year's catalog would you choose?

b. Remember, if you choose the current one, you are expressing disbelief in the existence of inflation! How could you reconcile your position—if you choose the current one?

*2. When collecting prices for your cost-of-living survey, you discover that not all customers can buy a good advertised on sale because the limited stock was sold out in the first hour. Continuing with your cost-of-living survey, in New York City the rents are controlled; but at the controlled rents apartments are not available to many who would pay the legal price. Why would you not use that legal price as the cost of housing?

*3. "The progressive deterioration in the value of money throughout history is not an accident, and has behind it two great driving forces—the impecuniosity of governments and the superior political influence of the debtor class....The power of taxation by currency depreciation is one which has been inherent in the State.... The creation of legal tender has been and is a government's ultimate reserve; and no state or government is likely to decree its own downfall, so long as this instrument still lies at hand unused" (J. M. Keynes, *A Tract on Monetary Reform,* London: Macmillan and Co., Ltd., 1923, p. 9). Explain in more detail what Keynes meant.

*4. It was asserted that if producers of molybdenum responded to increased demand by raising their prices, the effect would be inflationary. Can you spot a fallacy in that argument? (Hint: Remember the discussion of the way meat prices might rise in response to a rise in demand? Suppose that cattle raisers had not asked for a higher price in response to an increased demand. Would that have meant that meat prices to consumers would not have increased?)

*5. If you were asked for the cause of the inflation in Brazil, how would you revise the question?

*6. Suppose that all colleges were forced to pay professors a minimum salary of $30,000 per year in order to preserve the dignity of professors. Many professors will soon find themselves without jobs. Being of great influence in government, the professors tell the politicians that their salary demands are reasonable and that the basic trouble is insufficient demand. Congress could embark on a program of general-demand expansion by spending more with money creation. If the government assures college professors that they will have full-employment without wage cuts elsewhere, is inflation the inevitable consequence? Why?

*7. "Higher interest rates are higher prices and therefore are an element of inflation." Expose the error of that assertion.

*8. A monetary asset is one whose price can change although the asset is a claim to a fixed value in money terms. Give an example.

9. Which of the following are monetary? Are they assets or liabilities?
   a. money: checking accounts;
   b. charge account at department store;
   c. prepaid subscription to *New York Times*;
   d. long-term lease for land;
   *e. rental arrangement whereby tenant pays 1 percent of monthly sales as rental to the building owner;
   *f. U.S. bonds;
   *g. a share of General Motors common stock;
   *h. house;

*i. social-security benefit rights;

*j. pension rights in a retirement fund;

*k. teacher's salary.

10. If, during an inflation, you held all your wealth in the form of real goods, would you gain or lose wealth relative to the price level? (Hint: What else must you know?)

11. Young movie stars under the age of 21 are ordered by judges to save a fraction of their weekly earnings and buy U.S. government bonds. They are not allowed to invest that savings in stocks.

a. If you were a young movie star, would you regard that as good advice?

b. If you were a judge, would you regard that advice as good?

c. Can you give any reasons why jurists and the legal system are prone to advise investments in U.S. government bonds?

*12. a. If in drawing up your will you were arranging for advice to your widow about investing your life insurance, would you recommend that the funds be invested in bonds or in stocks?

b. How do the risks from inflation differ in each case?

*13. Show how an inflation that doubles the price level will bring to the government more than twice as much in income taxes. (Hint: Estimate the income taxes for a person earning $10,000 a year before the inflation and $70,000 after the inflation.)

14. To test whether average wages lag behind prices of consumer goods, someone examines the record for 30 years of price-level increases. He finds that half the time the wage rates rose less than the price level, while in the other half they rose more. He concludes that the wage-lag effect was present half the time. What would you have concluded? (Hint: If someone said a roulette wheel gave odd rather than even numbers and then on 100 trials he found that half the numbers were odd, would you say his assertion was correct half the time or that his assertion was simply wrong? Is this comparable to the wage-lag assertion?)

15. "Wages must lag behind prices because demand first affects selling prices and then filters down to the prices of productive inputs." Evaluate.

16. "If by inflation government increases its share of national income, there is less left for the private sector. Real wages must be smaller simply because available real income is smaller." Even if it is true that the real income left for the private economy is smaller, there is an error in that reasoning. Who loses what was obtained by the government?

17. a. If you knew that every price was going to rise at the rate of 2 percent a week, would you try to hold larger or smaller amounts of money relative to your wealth and income?

b. Would you resort completely to barter to avoid loss of some money wealth every week?

*c. In 52 weeks how much higher would the price level be? (Use tables from Chapter 7 to compute the answer.) Are you therefore not surprised to see why people will still use money even when they know the price level will rise by that amount in one year?

*d. Are you convinced that even at an anticipated 100 percent per *week* rise in prices, people would still use money?

e. If people reduce their money balances *relative* to their wealth and income from say one-fourth of their annual income to one-tenth (in order to avoid so large a loss of wealth from the decreasing value of the money), approximately how much would prices jump immediately?

18. Emperor Julian exhorted the merchants of ancient Antioch to practice self-restraint in pricing their wares. Today government leaders exhort businessmen and labor leaders to exercise statesmenlike self-restraint. Tomorrow the story will be the same. Why is such exhortation worse than useless?

19. Explain why neither shopping more carefully nor saving more restrains inflation.

20. "Inflation causes price distortions because not all prices are equally responsive to changes in demand. Therefore, a period of rapid inflation causes inefficiencies in the economic system. Evidence of the distortion is clear if one looks at the fact that, during inflations, relative prices change." Would you consider that as evidence for the proposition that inflation causes a change in relative prices? Is there some other reason why you would expect the beginning of an inflation to be associated with greater relative changes in prices more than during the subsequent inflation or during periods when price levels are constant? (Hint: Why did the inflation occur? That is, what events caused the increase in money stock relative to demand for money?)

Answers to Selected Questions & Index

Answers to Selected
Questions: Chapter 1

1. False. It is because people are reasonable and act in accord with their interest that there are economic problems and wars.

2. a. Highest valued.

   b. Expressed in a common denominator or measure of value.

   c. In general, no. Not if more than one thing could have been produced—including leisure.

4. The first statement is true, but the second is wrong. The value of an hour is the highest valued use one could have made of that hour. Hence the cost of an act taking an hour is the value of the best alternative action forsaken during that hour. (A common, though not always accurate measure of the value of time, is the earnings one could have obtained during the time.)

5. Costs are not the undesirable consequences of an act; they are the highest valued forsaken opportunity.

6. All costs are private. Social costs are simply the total of all private costs. If a person does not bear all the costs of his action, then the social costs exceed the total of the costs he bears (because some of the costs are borne by other people). The statement means all costs of a decision are borne by the decision maker.

7. William the Conqueror, Julius Caesar, Napoleon Bonaparte. You can add scores of others easily.

8. a. Promises to raise or lower taxes (affect other people's wealth) in order to benefit those who vote for you. But the politician can't offer to sell services as a businessman can.

   b. Will letters of recommendation help you get a better grade in this course? Does your past record influence the teacher of this course in making grades? Does wealth of parents?

   c. Employees can offer to work for a lower salary to get a job with a favored employer in a preferred town. Will this work in fraternities? How about a candidate's ability to increase the wealth of the fraternity?

9. a. Yes.

   b. We know of no institution with the dominant power of coercive violence that is not the government in any country. Government is an institution for enforcing certain rules and procedures for resolving interpersonal conflicts of interest. The making and enforcement of laws and the judicial settlement of disputes are behaviors that support the propositions. (Note that the second statement says government is an agency, not the only agency. For example, many social disputes are resolved by social ostracism, and by agreement to use an arbitrator.)

10. a. You should first want to know the behavioral consequences of each kind. More than that we can't yet say.

    b. The only kind of competition made illegal by a price ceiling is that of offering more money (and all that can be bought with it) than the legal limit as means of offsetting weaknesses in other attributes in competing for goods. Fair-employment laws (prohibiting choice of employees by color, creed, or age) prohibit competition in terms of personal attributes. Pure food and drug laws prohibit offers of inferior food at lower prices or of new and possibly better but untested (by government) foods and drugs. Private-property rights prohibit competition by violence and involuntary dispossession of goods deemed to be private property. Socialism prohibits competition in terms of offers of types of services and goods that individuals privately prefer, without having to obtain authorization of government officials for propriety of producing the services. These are merely examples of types of competition that are ruled out—not a complete chronicle, and certainly not an evaluation of the desirability of the various types.

11. Greater use of factors other than willingness to pay is enabled by the fact that colleges are not privately owned, for-profit institutions.

13. a. Until you define what "socially preferred" means, you cannot answer this question. We don't have a definition to offer.
b. We do not know what socially preferred means. For example, does it mean that a majority prefer it, or that the most important people prefer it, or that everyone prefers it, or that the speaker thinks everyone should prefer it, or that he prefers it? Beware of any expression referring to the preference of a group.

15. a. No.
b. Socialism is full of competition through political processes.
c. Competition is the interpersonal striving for more of what is scarce and desired—by production, by purchase, by striving for political power, etc. Cooperation is a joint activity with mutual striving for a common end.

16. They will be explained in the course of study. The query is intended to whet your interest in what is coming.

17. a. They are different—because these all involve social, interpersonal interactions. As such, one person's behavior with respect to these characteristics or attributes will affect other people, and their responses to his behavior will vary accordingly. Their response and their ability to influence his actions will depend upon whether or not there is private property—for reasons we shall see as we progress through the book.
b. Nothing like this question to kill a discussion! (Remember, evidence does not consist of one's idiosyncratic memories or ad hoc examples.)

19. a. A theory is logically valid if all its elements are logically consistent with each other or with some broader theory with which it is associated.
b. It is empirically valid if its implications about observable phenomena agree with the observed phenomena.
c. Neither implies the other.

20. All societies use force and compulsion. The pertinent issue is: What kinds of coercion and force do various economic, political, and social systems use? The capitalist system uses the force of self-interest; it is coldly impersonal in its market effects; it is a severe and unforgiving taskmaster. He who produces at a loss is forced out of business into some other tasks, perhaps with less compassion than under a socialist dictator, who could spread the loss over other people. More sensible than the question of which system uses less force is the question of what effects the various kinds of forces (incentives, rewards, signals, orders, and penalties) have on the economic, cultural, and political behavior. For

example, how are freedom of speech, job mobility, social fluidity, individual dignity, religious worship, search for the truth, etc., affected? The effects on all the various goals of a person must be considered.

Not even reference to the use of the rule of law versus the rule of arbitrary dictators is a basis for ultimate judgment. Here, too, the question is: What law and what rules will be enforced by the ruling law—the rule of private-property rights, the rule of socialism, or some other?

Differences are implied about the kinds of opportunities or "freedoms" provided to individuals living under each system. The implications are that an open-market system gives individuals a greater range of consumption patterns or goods from which to choose. Whether it is "good" that individuals should have such a range of options to explore is a question that economic theory cannot answer. A greater range of choice can be regarded as a greater range of temptation, risk, error, regret, and deviant behavior. Just as a parent restrains his children's choices for their own good, we may prefer to restrain the choices of adults because everyone retains some childlike impulses. Whether you wish to regard one system or the other as giving more freedom depends upon your meaning of "freedom." In one sense, freedom can include protection from the costs of resisting temptation and from making unfortunate choices; in another sense freedom might include the right to bear those costs and to make those choices and explore tempting alternatives. Whatever your interpretation, the implications derived from economic theory

about the factual consequences of different allocative systems will be helpful in forming a judgment.

Answers to Selected Questions: Chapter 2

1. a. Each has a common goal.
   b. We're sure he has more goals.
   c. No, quite the opposite, because it's a matter of *more* of some goals relative to *less* of other goals. It's not a matter of first fulfilling one goal and then turning to the next.
2. Individuals, not abstract things called "colleges," make decisions.
3. Yes; no.
4. No one wants *more* of a good that is so plentiful as to be free, by definition of a free good. But we do want the amount we have. Only if we don't want *more* is it a free good. The question tends to confuse *more* or *less* of a good with all or none. Life is almost entirely a choice of more or less, not all or none.
6. The first statement contains no implication about any thought process. It would also apply to rocks and water obeying the law of gravity. The second statement suggests some mental calculation and choice among alternative possible actions. Neither statement has the slightest dependence on the concept of free will or independence of behavior; both are red herrings in respect to the present problem. Economics does not have to assume the second statement as a basis for its theory, despite common arguments that it does.
7. It is.
8. a. One artichoke is worth 5 steaks, or 1 steak

has a marginal personal value of .2 artichokes given that I have option A or B.

b. Between B and C my personal marginal value of artichokes is 6 steaks, greater than between A and B, because I have fewer artichokes at B or C than at A.

c. Increases the amount of meat that expresses the personal marginal value of artichokes, because I have fewer artichokes (and more meat).

9. a. Yes.

b. We don't know that any of them do.

c. Behavior of bees, ants, and baboons.

d. No.

10. No. It does not imply what is good, bad, better, or worse. It implies what will be observed in the real world.

11. Denies none. Power over other people is a goal or good.

12. a. If it is supposed to mean that one area had more of some good than it wanted (could possibly use at all), the statement is dead wrong. And we can't think of anything else it might mean.

b. We propose that the relative supplies were different so that relative values were different, leading to mutually preferred exchange and reallocation of goods among Mediterranean and Baltic people, just as between Charlie and Linus.

13. It assumes that the middleman performs no service to consumers or producers in facilitating exchange and that therefore he can be eliminated without someone else's having to perform the service in which he specialized. Eliminating the middleman is a form of the do-it-yourself principle and as such is not necessarily more economical.

14. Middlemen facilitate exchange and specialization, while "do-it-yourself" is a reduction of specialization and exchange or a case of doing middlemen's activities by oneself.

15. a. No. Middlemen perform services for householders more cheaply than consumers could, and are paid in price paid by consumers, without reducing purchase price paid to farmer. In fact, purchase price to farmer can be raised if these middlemen services save consumers enough to make them want more of the farmers' goods.

b. Not necessarily, because that might be the result of no middlemen services to consumers, thereby transferring to farmer all of the price paid by the consumer, but less than if middlemen performed those services more efficiently than the consumer could for himself.

16. All are denials of open markets.

17. a. Yes, I would.

b. Transfer of monopoly rent to me.

c. Seller of goods might offer me payment to keep out his potential competitors.

18. a. Yes, unless all consumers could agree to pay me more than the one seller to whom I gave the monopoly right. (In principle they could always pay more than monopolist would gain.)

b. The one who helped me most to get elected or offered me the most.

c. Answered in b.

d. No. Their monopoly rents are partly used to aid (pay?) politicians and are also dependent on political favors and support.

e. Once in office, create favored monopoly privileges by prohibiting entry of competitors. As we shall learn later, consumers lose more

than the monopolies gain. But ability of monopoly party to pay politician exceeds that of
consumers, who have more difficulty in arranging payment because there are so many
consumers, each with a small amount involved.

19. The first statement means that *more* of one
goal is achieved at the cost of having *less* of
another. The second statement means that
goals do not exclude each other.

20. See answer to 18.

22. It is the theory and its structure that conform
to laws of logic and rationality. The predictable regularities of response of people to
changes in their environment do not require
they be "rational" any more than the response of water to a slope requires rationality
by each molecule of water.

23. Free speech means a right to speak or communicate with others who are willing to listen,
free of government intervention or prohibition.
It is not a right to take resources of other
people for purposes of communication with
other people. To use college property without the permission of the college authorities
for speech is not a right of free speech; it
is simply appropriation of property as if the
property were free for the taking. Nor is it a
denial of free speech if a college or anyone
else denies the use of resources under its or
his control which others would like to use for
the purposes of communication; it is instead
a denial to others of resources to use in ways
they would like. This does not mean that colleges ought to refuse to allow use of their resources for communication of popular or unpopular ideas; it is simply a clarification of
the difference between free speech and the

proposition that resources are "free" to anyone for the taking so long as they will be
used for communication.

24. a. Postulates 3 and 2 together.
   b. Yes.
   c. Postulate 3.
   d. Postulate 4.

25. By drawing another curve about this one (or
to the right of it) with similar properties (slope
and curvature).

26. Postulate 4, because in the table the marginal
substitution rate between *X* and *Y* is constant
between all the options. In fact, the marginal
substitution rate, or marginal personal subjective value between successive options
changes according to postulate 4.

27. Use the diagram of the constant-utility indifference curve in the Appendix. The values
given will plot as a straight line. But the
postulates say the line connecting equally
preferred points must be curved. So if a
curved line is drawn from option A to C it will
pass under the point representing option B.
You have to draw this as in Figures 2–5 and
2–6 to see the idea.

28. Given a choice between A and B, people do
not choose B.

**Answers to Selected
Questions: Chapter 3**

1. b. No. He values a sixth at .50¢.

2. a. No. Only a second.
   b. Yes, at 90¢.
   c. He can choose to buy one or two or more
   at the price of 90 cents. He chooses to buy

two, so the second must be worth the extra 90 cents he pays for it. Value is the amount of some other good one is willing to give up to get this good whose value is being defined.

3. He adjusts his rate of *consumption* or *rate* of purchase over time, not the *amount* purchased at a given moment.

4. He increases his rate of use or he replaces items more quickly.

5. True.

6. Rate of 18,250 gallons a year.

7. 70 gallons, because he will consume 140 gallons in the week rather than 70 gallons.

8. No. I take longer vacations.

9. First is rate; second and third are stocks.

10. a. Sell 3 at $10; 2 at $9, 1 at $8. Buy 1 at $6; 2 at $5, etc.
    b. He would buy 4 more to have a total of 8.

11. a. No such thing as basic need. We would use more and we could also get by with less security. It's a matter of what price we are willing to pay, and a matter of more or less, not all or none.
    b. We "need" more of everything that is not free. The amount of any economic good we choose to have is a function of its price. To say our children need more schools ignores what we propose to give up to get more schools.
    c. It depends upon the price, whether it is good enough to have at the price. If this says simply that more is better than less, O.K. Otherwise, it seems to deny relevance of alternatives.
    d. Same as comment to b.

12. See answer to preceding question.

14. Difference is that price is ignored in deter-

mining how many golf courses would be demanded (needed?).

15. a. Marginal revenues are successively: $1.00, $.80, $.60, $.40, $.20, $.00, $−.20, $−.40, $−.60, $−.80
    b. Marginal personal use values are successively $10, $9, $8, $7, $6, $5, $4, $3, $2, $1
    c. To marginal personal use value.

16. Because as price is reduced to sell more, all prior units bring in less revenue, and that offsets part of revenues on the extra unit sold at the new lower price.

17. To right of above.

18. All except last one. (Why?)

19. a. Correct.
    b. Correct.
    c. It is conventional to call this an increase in amount demanded, not an increase in demand—which refers to a shift in the whole demand relationship.

20. It is the *ratio* of *percentage* change in quantity in response to a *small* percentage change in price.

21. Demands a and b have the same elasticity at any common price. But the elasticities of a and b decrease at lower prices. Demand c has a lower elasticity at any price than demands a or b, and its elasticity decreases at lower prices. Hint of reason: The slope of b is greater than for a, but the quantity at any price is proportionally greater also. Demand c has the same slope as b but its quantities are larger at any price. Hence for any small price cut, the absolute change in the amount demanded on line c and b is the same, but for c, the increase is a smaller percent of the amount demanded (at that price).

22. a. True. Economic theory says they would. Compare cars in countries with higher gasoline prices. How about extent to which automatic transmissions would be used?

b. Reduced gas usage.

c. Effects would be more extensive in three years than in one year.

23. Whatever provides the impulse; the lower the price of the item, the greater is the probability the impulse to buy will result in a purchase. The higher the price, the less likely the impulse will be effective. Habitual buying is consistent with knowing the price from prior purchases and having settled on a consumption plan which is generally repeated over time. However, let the price of some of the consumption goods rise and the habit will be revised. Inconsistent behavior would be behavior that did not conform to that just outlined.

24. Yes, to all.

25. a. No.

b. The negative functional relationship between price and amount demanded. The explicit numbers serve merely to illustrate the meaning of the negative relationship.

26. It is a fall in the price of candy in ice-cream units. Candy is cheaper relative to ice cream than formerly.

27. The law of demand does not say that every person will instantly respond to every price change no matter how slight. It says a sufficiently high price will induce a response now, and it also says the response will be greater the longer the time allowed. In the case at hand, some people will respond quickly though some will not. Even for a small price rise the aggregate amount demanded over all

people will respond because some will respond. In time all will respond to a sufficiently large price rise.

28. If this happened with *equal* prices for slums and for high-quality spacious apartments, we would be stumped. In fact, however, we find that the prices of the high-quality dwellings are higher, which reduces the amount of the high-quality apartments demanded. Given the law of demand, we see that with a higher price of higher quality apartments, it is possible to reduce the amount people want or demand so that it does not exceed the amount available. Just why the price of slums should be so low as to induce more slums to be wanted than are available is something we shall take up later. For the moment we are interested in showing the implications of the law of demand.

29. a. Demand increases. Schedule shifts upward.

b. Can't tell. Milk production may be so important a source of your income that you consume more when its price rises (despite the higher price, because you are wealthier). But you consume less than if your wealth had increased for other reasons and without a rise in milk prices.

30. Hiring babysitters at, say, $1 an hour and staying out for four hours, will cost $4. Add the cost of two movie tickets at $1 each, and compare that total cost of $6 with the cost of going to the $4 theater. The $4 theater costs a *total* of $12 ($8 + $4) and movies cost a total of $6 ($2 + $4). Taking all costs into account, the $4 theater ticket costs only twice as much as the $1 movie ticket for parents who must pay babysitters. The theater then costs twice as much, but if a couple has no children and no babysitter fee, the theater will cost $8 and the movie $2—a ratio of 4 to 1: theatergoing is relatively more expensive in real terms, i.e., in terms of other goods given up for childless people. (Testing this would be a fine term project if you have lots of time to collect data.)

31. If T_1/T_2 is less than P_1/P_2,

$$\frac{P_1 + T_1}{P_2 + P_2} \text{ will be less than } \frac{P_1}{P_2}.$$

Therefore the price (including transport) of goods in the more distant market will be lower relative to the price of good 2 in the more distant market. More of good 1 will be demanded than of 2 relative to that in the domestic market because the relative price of good 1 is lower in the distant market.

32. Welfare change is not measured by total market value of entire crop. If demand elasticity is less than one, bigger supply will lower total *market* value (total market revenue) while total personal value is increasing because of larger supply. Do not confuse total personal use value with total market exchange value (market sales revenue). Former is closer to welfare criterion.

33. What does invaluable mean? We are reminded of a news item. "This priceless four-strand necklace is now in the possession of Mrs. Lovely, who bought it for $85,000." Rarely do we find such an incongruous juxtaposition of obvious inconsistencies. However, in fairness to those who often use the term "priceless," we suspect they usually mean that the priceless good is not reproducible. Thus, a Grecian urn or an original Dufy cannot be replaced at any price if destroyed. At the same time, one should be careful not to think it can't be bought at a finite price, or that a nonreproducible item is necessarily valuable.

Answers to Selected Questions: Chapter 4

1. a. 0, 1, 2, 4, 6, 8, 9, 11, 13, 15 for prices from 10 through 1.
   b. 4 to A and 2 to B.
   c. Shortage.
   d. Surplus.
   e. All depends upon where price is.
2. a. $7.
   b. 3 to each.
   c. Shortage.
   d. Remove price control.
3. Yes. Any resource with more than one possible use or user has a demand and a supply (its value in the other uses).
4. a. Yes. It is true for all goods.
   b. We have yet to find one.
5. Law of demand relates purchase rate to price. Law of demand and supply states price is at intersection of supply and demand. The former holds generally; the latter not always.
6. Yes, for it does advance the argument (analysis?) to grasp the meaning of scarcity and to understand that economics says nothing about which goods ought to be allocated via the exchange-market form of competition. We leave it to you to try to figure out why the "degree of scarcity" should affect the form of competition that should determine how a scarce resource is allocated among alternative uses and users. We can't.

7. In brief, price is ignored in its effect on amounts demanded and supplied. Past balance or equality reflects the simple fact that *price* was allowed to adjust up or down so as to equate *amounts* demanded with amount supplied. Any particular forecast path of amount demanded (and that is all that a single line can indicate for each year) must presume some particular price in each year. A higher projected price would reduce the amount demanded and raise the amount supplied, raising the "supply" line and lowering the "demand" line to keep them equal. An appropriate path of price over the future will affect the amounts demanded and the amounts supplied so as to keep the two equated. All the diagram says is that price will be kept too low, whereas in the past it was allowed to equate the amounts demanded and supplied. Every such projected future imbalance of amounts demanded (probably labeled "needs," "requirements," or "demand") with amounts supplied of any good (probably labeled "supply," "availabilities," "stocks") is merely a prediction that price will not be allowed to move to equate amounts demanded with amounts supplied—as it has in the past. Beware of being fooled by such utterly worthless diagrams.

8. They probably use phrase "heavy buying" to mean increased demand, or at least so we hope.

9. Shopping several sellers is better because alternatives are what sellers must beat. See A. Jung, "Price Variations among Automobile Dealers," *The Journal of Business,* October 1959, pp. 315–325.

10. Holding down the wholesale price of cattle to the meat processors increases the spread between purchase price and selling price for the processors. The price to consumers would rise anyway because of the increased demand for meat. The wealth that would have been available to cattle growers is instead given to the cattle processors.

11. Price controls do not increase probability that lower-income groups will get more housing. They may get less (and over time with effect on production of housing, housing quality and quantity will deteriorate). Outcome depends more upon possession of nonpecuniary attributes that now play a greater weight in allocative decision.

12. Scarcity is pervasive, but what people call shortages are simply the result of prices that are kept too low. A reduced supply is not a shortage. A reduced supply is a reduction in the amount available—pictured as a shift to the left of the supply curve. Confusing these three different concepts helps create imaginary problems.

15. The belief that money or market-exchange value is the sole criterion of allocation is so widespread, deeply ingrained, and incorrect that it is worth spending some time in examining it. Money is not the only criterion; that much has already been established with our analysis. (That it ought to be or ought not to be is not the issue.) When I dine in a restaurant, I select my dinner according not only to prices but also according to what the item is. I never tell the waitress to bring me the cheapest items only. The taste, nutrition, and looks of the item are considered. Similarly,

when buying a suit, I take into account the style, feel, looks, and fit, as well as the price. For national security, we don't buy the cheapest weapon regardless of what it will do, nor the most modern, expensive weapon simply because it is the most expensive or modern—but not as effective as three units of a cheaper weapon (for example, one B-1 as compared to three missiles).

Only if the options are equivalent in *all* other respects do money costs become the *sole* criterion, simply because cost is the only one that, in this case, makes any difference. On the other hand, if money costs were equal, then only the other attributes would be relevant.

Suppose that I own some land next door to where I live. Of two people who apply to buy the land—one, an ordinary man who offers $1000; the other, a beautiful woman who offers at most only $995—I will sell to the woman. Her presence as a neighbor is worth more than $5 to me. The man could overcome his handicap if he offered $100 more. Money (exchange value) does count, but it is not the sole nor even the dominant (whatever that means) criterion.

A related criticism of the capitalist system says it relies on *market*—revealed money demands rather than intrinsic or humanitarian needs. By now there is no "need" to discuss the nonsense of "needs." But why do *market* demands count so much? The reason market demands are so effective is simply that exchange is a way to increase utility. Every person is free to reject the market demand and to exchange his wealth with "more deserv-

ing" people who offer less attractive market bids. But the market demand for exchange is heeded because people prefer to gain by exchange—not because they are perverted by capitalism or a desire for money.

If private-property rights did not exist, people would not be able to make such extensive market offers, because they would have nothing legally to buy or sell. In a university, the faculty does not have private-property rights in offices and classrooms; therefore, there is no marketplace where classrooms and offices are so easily exchanged. In a socialist system, market money demands are less effective simply because there is relatively less exchangeable property.

16. According to this criticism, a person is so influenced by his interest in his economic wealth that other criteria are dominated. However, the exchanging of goods does not make it difficult for anyone to be influenced by the artistic, social, humanitarian, or cultural uses to which he can put his goods and services.

Playwrights complain that the financial "backer" invokes his crass monetary standards. Artists complain that businessmen want mere display copy, not true art. The architect complains because builders do not want the artistic designs he proposes. What they really are objecting to are other people's tastes and preferences. But the issue is rarely put in so embarrassing a way.

Saying that only lowbrow products sell well seems to suggest that this is a result of the money-value system. But that system effectively reveals and enforces the "lowbrow" tastes and desires of the public. The actors and writers wish the public valued such quality more than it does. Hence, actors and artists are frustrated because other people don't want as much "quality" as the artists would like to provide at the prices they would like to get. Or putting it "selfishly," the artists must admit that the income they can get from "low-quality" work is so high that they prefer to produce low-quality plays and get a big income rather than produce high-quality plays and live with a lower income. In this case, it is also the artists' and actors' own tastes for more wealth, not merely that of the public, that precludes quality.

17. True.

18. Both. Choice is an act of discrimination.

19. All.

20. Sales price, if goods were available at that price at time of sale. Price means exchange prices, not hoped-for price.

21. Price-controlled goods are more likely to be distributed with more political and government influence and authority.

25. You should disagree. A higher price permits a reallocation of existing goods—a reallocation that would not occur in the absence of higher prices. Immorality is a gratuitous judgment. That the profits to those who own the goods when prices rise are "unwarranted" is also a gratuitous judgment. The point is to note that higher prices do have a consequence—real-location—and that personal preferences should not blind one to that fact.

26. All contain rent, so far as existence is concerned.

27. Yes. Land would exist at lower price, but particular use is determined by full payment received.

Answers to Selected Questions: Chapter 5

2. a. Yes.
b. Yes, and it pays not to cut rent to get an immediate occupant (because the cost of his moving soon is greater than wage cut would be worth).

4. Tolls on bridges; parking meters; tollways.

5. Yes, this could be so. While it is not possible to know what is necessarily better, it is true that the total cost of providing parking space could be cheaper if it were not policed as carefully as a park-for-pay lot. A free lot would impose the costs on those who purchase from the persons who provide the free parking lot, but not on those who use the lot without doing any business with the providers of the parking space.

6. *A* is suing for property rights to uncongested streets. Under current law this kind of right seems not to be recognized. Presume we would rule against him. What do you say?

8. If you define access to sunlight as an aspect of land ownership, then it is a strengthening of private-property rights.

9. Either way. No, it shouldn't. In some cases damages have been awarded, but this is rare.

10. Not true. To remove all risk of all accidents costs more than it's worth.

11. a. No rights were being curtailed. Instead rights are being defined and allocated for first time.
b. No, they were being defined and specified.

12. Nader ignores the social gains provided by activities that produce smog and pollution as a by-product. Just as automobiles and airplanes produce death, just as travel takes up land for roads, just as making sheet-steel involves less of other desirable things like leisure, quiet, and rest, just as oil wells create some smell in the neighborhood—so all productive activity involves some undesirable by-products. All of these "pollutions" of our environment are part of the costs of production and could be avoided if we were willing to have a less convenient, more Spartan life. We should not look only at costs and think that something is wrong with those economic activities that involve the largest costs, for they, in general, may also yield the greatest benefits. Relieving one's self in the river may be less valuable than the value of output from a factory that creates equivalent pollution and may be avoidable at lower cost. Similarly, smoggers are producing other services in the process, whereas muggers produce no social service.

The complaint that Nader should develop is that governments and courts have not introduced a system of making people pay for the right to pollute—a system which would induce people to pollute *less if* the gains obtained from activities that yield pollution are worth less than the pollution damage. Just as we could produce less oil or less paper by having less pollution of air and streams, there is a trade off between more or less clean air or cleaner water and more or less other desirable goods output. Efforts to expose that trade off rate and to induce the pollution costs to be taken into account by a system of prices for the right to pollute (by fines) rather than with zero prices or absolute prohibitions (infinitely high prices) are what Nader might more usefully be recommending.

13. a. Camp sites are not privately owned.
    b. Less space per person.
14. a. Privately owned. More of proceeds go to identifiable owner.
    c. Privately owned course.
15. Tendency to price public parks and services at less than a market-clearing price is explanation. Motels, priced higher than facilities in parks, rely on the law of demand to keep amount demanded in line with facilities available.
16. Seats are allocated first come, first served, rather than sold to worshipers—except in some churches, where a person donates a large sum and is given a special pew as a token of appreciation.
19. Nonsense. Property rights are the rights of people to do things with goods and services. They are human rights. Usually objection is made to the way a person uses his property, which means that the conflict usually is between one set of human rights and another set of human rights—not between human rights and property rights.
20. Ignores *prices* at which government goods are distributed. Price of such goods is so low as to create a shortage and appearance of insufficient amount.
21. Depends upon extent to which you want to give parents authority to determine allocation of funds to family members.
23. Building and nonfaculty purposes gain and faculty also gains to extent faculty salaries are raised more than they otherwise would have been raised. Money that would be spent for faculty salary increases can be spent for other purposes.
26. a. Price of stock fell.

c. National and Eastern gained wealth value of the airline route. Taxpayers lost the value of those rights, which otherwise could have been kept by government when it sold those rights—as it sells timber and gas-prospecting rights on federal lands.

29. As many as people want to use or create. No other objective test of the right number.

30. False; it is the consumption of the good that is referred to in the definition of a public good.

31. (c) is correct.

32. Each spectator displaces someone on the outside who would enter—and the theater cannot house everyone.

34. a. Yes.
    b. Yes.
    c. Probably not.
    d. (ii).

35. If good is already produced, exclusion benefits no one.

36. True.

39. The market-exchange system characteristic of private property (capitalism) has been the dominant institutional context of the preceding chapters. The economic theory used in the analysis is applicable to any system of competition (capitalist, Communist, or what have you) for resolving conflicts of interest among people arising from the fact of scarcity. In fact, the analysis of allocation with prices at less than the free-market price is an application of economics to a socialist society in which free-market prices are not used. Think of the actual money price as being zero, or at some level below the free-market price. Then how will goods be allocated among the competing claimants? (Review

Chapter 4.) The relatively greater nonpecuniary "discrimination" should come as no surprise.

Many Communist systems rely on money prices and private property to ration existing stocks of some consumer goods. In Russia, many goods are sold for money, and individuals get money income from wages and salaries—*but not* from ownership of productive physical capital goods and instruments and land. Given a person's money income, he is allowed to choose among a variety of consumption patterns by voluntary exchanges with other people via controlled (as distinct from open) market prices.

The postulates are not idiosyncratic to capitalist systems. They hold for all known societies. The laws of demand and production hold also, whether or not exchange of resources *via* a private-property exchange system is used. We illustrated the use of these laws under noncapitalist situations where private property and open markets were not the ruling institutions for the particular goods and services investigated.

What we are striving to emphasize is the distinction between economic theory and analysis on the one hand and, on the other hand, the institutional (legal and political) circumstances or conditions to which they are applied.

Answers to Selected Questions: Chapter 6

1. Futures price is price agreed to now for claim to future good in the form of a futures con-

tract. Future price is the price that will be formed in the future.

2. Perishable. High storage cost (high perishability) implies larger present consumption supply and smaller future supplies. Increase in new supplies will be greater relative to carryovers, enabling greater increase in rate of consumption and lower prices.

3. No.

4. If we assume the price of the futures contract falls by the same amount as the spot price, he will be able to buy back his futures contract at 35 cents per 100 pounds less than the price at which he sold it. The profit on his futures contract (ignoring contracting costs of about $30) is $175 (35 cents per 100 pounds for 50,000). This will offset his loss on the processed soybeans—if the two prices move together by exactly the same amount.

5. a. Fall months.
   b. Prices lower in November, suggesting new crop is harvested between May and November.
   c. One to two cents a bushel—estimated by differences between prices during interval when no corn is being added to stocks, for example, December to July.

6. a. I bet on the Reds and you bet on Dodgers.
   b. We have shared some risk and reduced range of our resultant wealths; in that sense we have reduced risk. I buy some (half) rights to your parking lot and you buy (half) rights to mine for the World Series days. Neither of us expects actually to help the other operate the parking lot. Instead, each gets half the receipts regardless of which team wins the playoff game.

7. Ask those who consider it immoral. Some people say "Selling what you haven't already got is immoral." A contractor who bids on a building at a fixed price sells what he doesn't yet have. He has sold a promise or commitment. Short sellers do the same thing.

8. a. No. It means there is less reallocation of risks.
   b. Processors, growers, middlemen, and some consumers.
   c. We really don't know why.

9. You should disagree. Open futures markets reveal information for all at a lower cost. Those with superior knowledge could benefit from abolition of futures markets because they could then more readily keep their information secret.

10. a. No.
    b. Less hedging, poorer price forecasts with greater price fluctuations, more erratic supplies to consumers.
    c. Gains to few middlemen whose private information about crop conditions and supplies is less known to outsiders.

11. a. We couldn't think of any method. Can you?

Answers to Selected Questions: Chapter 7

1. ($385 − $350)/$350 = $.10.
2. $250(1 + .07)^3 = $306.25. Would double in about 10 years (72/7 = 10.3).
3. Refer to Table 7–1, present value of $1. At 10 percent the present value of $1 deferred one year is now $.9091. Therefore, the present value of $220 deferred one year is $220 × .9091 = $200.
5. $2055; $2500 ÷ (1.04)^5. Tables have only three digit accuracy.

6. $1686; $2500 ÷ $(1.04)^{10}$. Remember, tables in text have only three-digit accuracy.

7. $2670.

8. Annuity of five years with present value of $1000 at 6 percent rate of interest is $1000/4.21 = $237.53.

9. 5.075 × $50 = $253.75.

10. a. $554.
    b. $587 + $554 = $1141. (Interest in second year is 6% of $19,446.)
    c. $20,000.

11. It depends on the relevant rate of interest. At 10 percent, the $20 higher operating cost for 10 years has a present value of $61.40, so machine A, which would avoid that extra cost of $61.40 but costs only $60 more to buy, would barely be cheaper. At 12 percent B would be cheaper. Indeed at rates above 11 percent, B would be cheaper. At lower rates, A is cheaper. Clearly the extent to which it pays to economize on operating (energy?) costs depends on the rate of interest and the difference in purchase cost of the equipment.

14. Yes. With higher rate of interest you still buy other resources equivalent to your house, but with fire you can buy only half a house or equivalent type of resource. In both cases you do suffer a loss relative to some other resources, but loss is more general in case of fire.

15. a. $10,000 plus interest on $5000 for last 6 days of the year.
    b. No.
    c. $500.

16. Very probably "yes" for college students.

17. $100 per year.

18. $5000.

19. $1000, and it will stay at that value.

20. Nothing now. Next year it will be larger by the amount of income saved in the interim.

21. Pay $40,000 now and $1000 a year rent. And with the accumulated value of lower initial outlay you will have in 50 years more than enough to buy the house and land at that time.

22. Yes, you are paying $50,000 now and then giving it up to the landowner in 50 years. So you are giving up today a claim to $50,000 due in 50 years. At 8% per year that future amount of $50,000 has a present value of only $1065. In other words, $1065 will grow in 50 years at 8% interest compounded to $50,000. This means you are giving up $1065 now for the use of the land for those 50 years. The land is worth $15,000. The annual rental on such land would be at least $1200 every year (8% of $15,000). But you are getting use of that land for the entire 50 years at a once and for all total cost of only $1065 instead of $1200 *every* year. You have a great bargain. Grab it.

24. Increase in value of his holdings is his income. If he invests in stocks that do not pay out any earnings as dividends, all his stocks will grow in value by 10% because all the earnings are reinvested in the company. If he buys non-dividend-paying stock he can sell some of his more valuable shares at the end of the year, equivalent to the reinvested earnings, and still end up with $100,000 in wealth. If he buys stocks on which all earnings are paid out—and nothing is reinvested—he would collect

dividends and have stocks that did not grow in value. In either case he has $10,000 to spend while ending up with $100,000.

The correct way to view the gains from investment is to sum the dividends paid out and the increase in market value of the stock. The sum of those two, however divided, is the earnings. Taxes aside, it makes no difference in what form that earning accrues to the owner of the stock.

Answers to Selected Questions: Chapter 8

1. a. $5 for 1st oats, $10 for 2nd oats, $15 for 3 oats, etc.
   b. 4 oats.
2. A choice means an opportunity among two or more options. The most valuable of the forsaken options is the cost of the one taken.
3. True.
4. Hours of labor have alternative uses. Hours cannot be used. Hence best *forsaken* use *value* of an hour is cost of any hour of use of labor.
5. Production is efficient if the output of one of the possible products is maximized for stated amounts of the other products. Or production is efficient if an increase in output of one of the products can be achieved only by reducing the output of some other product. Roughly it means no waste of potential output.
6. a. 2 by A, 4 by B.
   b. Yes.
   c. 1–10 units of Y per X is Y price of X.
7. a. 2 X and 12.4 Y by A; and 4 X and 6.40 Y by B.
   b. Yes.
   c. 2 X by B, none by A.
8. b. A is lower marginal cost producer up to 3 units by A.
   c. Producer B.
   d. At any ratio below 1.
9. Not necessarily correct. Losing firm may have higher price than profitable firm.
10. Costs of other resources used to reduce gas consumption will exceed value of uses to which the saved gasoline will be put, because people would voluntarily prefer cars that use less gasoline if it was worth the costs. Government energy policy ignores fact that gasoline is worth what we are willing to pay for it and other resources used to save gasoline are also valuable.
11. In the sense of having a greater range of potential future positions with greater probability of having a different wealth than now, I have the greater risk.
12. We believe all are returns to superior productivity rather than monopoly-protected incomes. We know of no evidence that any have power to exclude competition by methods not related to superior performance.
13. B loses compared to what he would have been able to purchase with his income had C been able to produce Y and sell to A. A keeps wealth compared to what he would have had with open access to markets by C. That C lives on an island across the Pacific rather than on the American continent does not change effects.

14. Losers are consumers of the product that would be produced by the newcomer. Potential frustrated newcomer also is worse off. Examples are taxis, interstate airlines, liquor stores, high tariffs on imports.

15. Yes. The law delays entry.

16. Confuses (1) wealth transfer from existing doctors to patients—consequent to increased supply—with (2) social increase in value of extra medical care.

17. Speed of entry of new resources and their similarity to existing resources.

18. A subsistence economy is one in which people consume what they produce. Specialization means people produce more of a good than they consume, and consume more of other goods than they produce. Specialization also means that producers do not produce complete consumer goods but instead concentrate on components or portions of assembly tasks.

19. No. It merely assumes that existing knowledge can be used and subjected to performance tests. Assumes no restrictions on rights to purchase or exchange knowledge. Knowledge is a valuable (economic) resource. To assume it is free is, for example, to deny that schools exist and that teachers perform a useful desired service. A substantial fraction of our wealth is devoted to gathering information of one kind or another. Do not assume that ignorance is irrational, ridiculous, or the result of inefficiency or wastefulness or deliberate lying.

20. Private property rights plus market price knowledge of various feasible crops.

21. a. All exchange benefits *both* parties.
    b. Yes.

c. They are not monopoly rents from restricted entry.

22. Private property and observance of contracts.

23. Don't know. His wealth does depend on other people's demands for services obtainable from his wealth.

24. a. Large.
    b. Greater variety of relative talents and training so that differences between people's relative abilities are more common. Further, the larger market enables a person to sell more of his special output at profitable prices.
    c. Greater concentration of time on same repeated subtasks. For example, hair-shearing for poodles only; specialists in color-TV only; architects specializing only in certain types of buildings; greater number of specialty shops.

25. Suggests I shall be poorer and engage more in "do-it-yourself." Reduced opportunity to trade limits extent to which gains from trade can be achieved.

26. Capitalist society does not restrain production. Production for profit is production for higher-*valued* uses—not just anything for any *use*. Einstein didn't seem to understand what *value* and *costs* meant or how they affected profitability.

27. a. Usually production is used to refer only to activity that is not illegal. We wish we knew of a better answer. The question helps to reveal the hidden normative content of concepts which at first seem to be objective and free of ethical presuppositions.

28. How much steel is "needed" depends on costs. Imports are not costs. Capacity is a variable, not a fixed number. Present values are ignored in three-year calculation. "Need

for steel" and "shortage" of dollars are rhetoric. She could not "afford" to produce at a higher cost than cost of importing steel.

29. No. Ignores monopoly rent possibility.

Answers to Selected Questions: Chapter 9

1. Detection of performance of each member is more difficult.
2. a. Because marginal product, though decreasing, may exceed marginal cost of that marginal product.
   b. Private-property rights that are enforceable and transferable. Also political controls where private rights are enforceable.
   c. Marginal product value from congestion equals marginal cost.
4. All except full house in movie—and possibly last item, "customers in store during sale."
5. a. The number that maximized the average take. With three in each boat, 33 boats (with two on two boats).
   b. 7 1/3 fish (net of the boat cost of 2/3 fish per person per day).
   c. Price would be two fish. $7.33/2 = 3.67$ boats per day.
7. Socialism does not permit selective, discretionary optional selection of wealth holdings by each individual. Profits and losses are borne in accord with taxes, rights to use government resources, and powers of political office.
8. Former facilitates or permits the latter to be revised in accord with personal preferences.
11. Sentence is correct. By selective purchase of assets of personal wealth holdings, people

can vary their mixtures to suit their risk-bearing preferences.

Answers to Selected Questions: Chapter 10

1. Yes, because I am investing in him and his managerial talents.
2. No to all questions.
3. a. No. In ordinary circumstances we would expect stability.
   b. Should the typical voter or minority groups be able to turn out the governor of their state? It is precisely in order to prevent every single person from making his own will count that voting systems are utilized.
   c. It means a majority controls through the medium of a minority of the stockholders to whom a majority gives its votes, as the Congress represents a minority of the American public, being only some 537 people representing 200,000,000.
4. Depends upon what you mean by "very few." Annually many corporations show decreases in the value of their common stock. Approximately 30 to 40 percent of all corporations report losses for the year, although the firms reporting losses are not always the same. Since 1916 the percentage has always been above 20 percent and has been over 50 percent in several years. For all reporting corporations the aggregate earnings (after taxes) normally run about five times that of the losses. For more details consult *Statistics of Income,* U.S. Treasury, issued annually.
5. a. Wealth constraints are different in the two classes of cases.

b. The former, because of reduced possibility of personally capturing capitalized value of improvements of new management—as can be done in private-property corporations via purchase and sale of common stock.

6. a. Probably not.
   b. Probably yes.
   c. Yes.

7. a. Yes.
   b. No.

8. Yes. His services are now recognized by the market for teachers to be more valuable. That increase is a profit.

9. No. They are borne by different people more in accord with political power.

10. Disagree. Paper profits usually refer to an increase in value of some asset that a person has not yet sold in exchange for money. But they are real profits that one continues to keep in the form of the asset whose price has risen.

11. Suppose only the president of the company knew the secret and also owned some shares. He would be less willing to sell at the old price and would be willing to buy more shares. In other words, his demand to hold shares increases and thus affects market demand. Certainly several people in the company knew the secret and several also owned stock in the company. Price would rise because their own demand to hold the stock had increased in the light of the secret developments.

12. No one would pay anything for a losing business—that is expected to continue losing. (1) Buyers are more optimistic about how they can manage the business. Or, (2) the business is really not a "losing business" but instead had already invested more than was worthwhile, in light of subsequent returns. So new buyers bid a sufficiently low price for the business so that on that lower price they will be able to cover those costs out of the future returns. In this case there is no point in selling the business, because the loss from the prior inopportune investment is not avoided by the sale of the business. The lower sale price of the business will make that loss explicit in the accounting records, without really changing anything.

13. Both—you first had a profit of $50; then, by continuing to hold that wealth, you incurred a loss of $25 during the second month. Whether or not you convert it to cash has nothing whatever to do with the fact of your change in wealth—that is, of profits or losses. Only the income-tax people use the conversion-to-money principle, for computing taxes.

14. Price would fall, since future prospects no longer look so good as formerly expected.

15. Subsequent buyer probably did not. First licensee did.

16. a. All. Some by patent rights, some by licensing which limits entry, some by limiting access to open markets for competitors, and one (Sinatra) by natural superiority.

17. That capitalist money-seeking activity cultivates deceitful advertising, false claims, and dishonesty is so serenely believed by some people that it's a shame to waken them. The fact is that dishonesty and deceit often do pay. Therefore, it is sometimes said that free and open competition in the market gives a seller an incentive to lie in order to get customers from his competitors. Yet politicians also lie and don't tell the whole truth when

campaigning or making speeches. They are not more honest than commercial advertisers. The socialist governments are not distinguished for their devotion to the truth. Surely there are good grounds for doubting that capitalism is more conducive to dishonesty than other systems. Nevertheless, it is worth considering the questions "Does capitalism reward one more for cheating than does any alternative system? Is the cheater likely to be discovered in the capitalist system and punished as effectively as in a different system? Is the public more likely to be deceived?"

That everyone has an incentive to lie and cheat is not denied. But is the ability to get away with it affected by the ease of competitors' making counterclaims? The question has only to be posed to be answered. A newspaper will be more careful with the truth if it knows that other news media can challenge its veracity. Politicians are more cautious if they know opponents can challenge their statements. A witness in court is more careful with the statements of facts if he knows he is going to be cross-examined by the opposition. The easier it is for all to enter the market of ideas, the more counterclaims and different interpretations of events will be offered. In open-market capitalism, the incentives to disprove the claims and to submit counterclaims are increased. That is why it is a good rule to talk to a Ford salesman if you want the truth about Chevrolets, and conversely.

18. No. The only remaining sources for their profits is risk-taking, bearing risks others chose not to bear. That is a service. They perform selective risk-bearing function, whether they know it or not. In prospecting for oil, some will lose and some may win. And some of us do not have to commit our wealth to that risky venture. Still, if we want more oil, the "lucky" investors who bear the risks relieve us of that risk. For that function they are allowed, under private-property rights, to obtain profits. As for taxing them away, that depends upon your desire to have risks borne selectively, voluntarily, upon your willingness not to renege on general agreement to let lucky ones keep wealth, and upon attitudes toward differences in wealth among people.

19. The *corporate form* of organizing our productive work.

Answers to Selected Questions: Chapter 11

1. True, by definition.
2. Because they include future foreseeable sacrifices of present actions.
3. Some expeditures are for assets with future service value and with resalable value.
4. a. $2,998 (three figure accuracy) = $20,000 − .909 × (19,000 − 300).
   b. $4482.
   d. Two-year annuity with present value of $4482 is $2591 per year.
   f. $1183 per year.
   g. All correct.
5. a. $5000 − ($3000 × .909) = $2273.
   c. $2273. See answer to a.
   e. ($6000 × .909) plus $2273 = $7727.
   f. ($6000 × .909) plus ($6000 × .909^2) plus $3761 = $14,171.
   g. $f − e$ = $6444.
   h. $1,000.

6. The renter of the car pays for the depreciation as part of his rental charges. He avoids tying up capital funds only in the sense that the leasing company is lending him the car and charging him for its rental, whereas he could have borrowed money, bought a car, and then paid rental on the borrowed money (as interest). The rise of leasing services is primarily a consequence of business tax laws too detailed to go into here. But the point is that renting or borrowing money or paying out of your already accumulated wealth doesn't change the costs at all—aside from idiosyncrasies of the business tax laws.

7. 2 million is volume. Rate is 4 million per year.

8. 4 million units.

10. They begin to increase.

11. They decrease.

12. Volume and greater specialization.

13. Public prefers lower cost more than greater variety of models.

15. The latter—regardless of the relationship between output and cost.

16. Old firms are not burdened by old equipment. They too can switch to new goods. That they don't simply means they can compete by using old equipment, whose value is recapitalized to whatever level will enable it to continue to be used—unless its value must be zero, in which case it will certainly be retired. First sentence is typical of a very common error—an error that ignores market's valuation process of existing goods.

17. a. Impossible to divide costs between these two uses.
    b. Not answerable. Divide it half and half if you wish. But what difference does it make for any real problem? None.

18. a. Can only tell that both together cost 5 cents an hour.
    b. No way to know with cost data only.
    c. Yes.

19. a. None. That they will not far exceed it for long is a result of open markets.
    b. None.

20. a. Present value of receipts is $19,669. Subtracting present value of costs of two-year ownership and operation, $14,173, the difference, $5496, is the imputed profit.

21. The ad writers have mixed up rate and volume effects on costs. A greater supply—volume—implies a lower unit cost and also a lower price. Bigger volume demand yields lower price because it evokes a greater supply (in volume sense). But in the *rate* (or speed of production) sense, higher demand yields a higher price. When demand increases in both the volume demanded and the speed at which that volume is demanded, price may fall (in response to volume effect) but it will be higher than otherwise in order to increase the rate of production. What advertising can do is to affect the volume demanded, but if it also increases the rate at which the good is demanded, it leads to higher prices.

22. Industrial supremacy has nothing to do with reluctance to buy new equipment now. Existing equipment was more economical to continue using. Smaller producers can spend as much as bigger ones when profit prospects appear, for investors will be ready to provide funds and small will become big. An explanation of the behavior of American producers is provided by the author of that article in a subsequent paragraph when he writes:

"No continuous casting plant has successfully produced the low carbon rimming steel that forms such an important part of U.S. steel production. Rimming steel, so named because of a difference in density and composition between the interior of a solidified ingot and its outer rim, is rolled into thin sheets for automobile bodies, tin plate for cans and galvanized sheeting. The continuous casting process is not likely to duplicate the combinations of physical and chemical properties that characterize the 'deep-drawing' rimming steels. It is unlikely that the complete acceptance of continuous casting in the U.S. will come about before the technique is able to produce this important family of steels.

"That day may not be far off. Two plants being built in the U.S. will be used almost exclusively for manufacturing rimming quality steel plate. If these two U.S. plants succeed in producing deep-drawing steel, the last real obstacle to technical feasibility will have been overcome. Nonetheless, U.S. manufacturers will still have to question the economic applicability of the process."

Answers to Selected Questions: Chapter 12

1. a. At $2 per bushel, I could not affect price by withholding my stocks of wheat. Best price I could get is the market price of $2, whether I sell 1 or 1000 bushels.
   b. No.
   c. Horizontal straight line.
2. a. Yes; 4000 bushels; 2000 bushels; none.

   b. No.
   c. Yes.
3. Yes, although in strict terms we assume that there is no rise in price as a result of withholding one's offers. This analytical classification yields implications that are for all practical purposes equivalent to those of a less extreme, discrete classification. For example, in this instance, it would not pay anyone to reduce sales for a higher price. The trivial effects are, for all intents and purposes, equivalent to no effects at all. Hence, in all the discussion it must be understood that we are using an extreme assumption simply because it makes the analysis so much easier without changing any of the pertinent implications. Marginal revenue is about $61\frac{3}{8}$ per share; total revenue difference is ($61,500 − $30,812.50) = $30,687.50 for 500 shares change in sales. This is $61.37 per share.
4. Yes. Trivial effect on price by offering more by any one seller.
5. Ignores demand by consumer. "What number is 50 percent larger than 15?" If the grocer's selling price to consumers was 50 percent over his own buying price of 15¢, what is the price to consumers?"
6. c. $6.75.
   d. $7.00.
7. Marginal costs along with marginal revenue indicate maximum wealth output, while average costs in relation to price indicate whether the profits are positive or negative.
8. Two different programs, each with different costs.
10. a. $1.50.
    b. 1300 units.
    c. Shortage with waiting or rationing.

d. Yes; profits are being earned.

e. $1.87.

f. Contract.

g. Costs will rise as price of resources responsible for lower costs are bid up by new entrants seeking those resources. Profits will be absorbed into their costs.

11. Resources will be increased in production of X until extra value of output of X falls to $5.

12. Not "consumer sovereignty" but "individual sovereignty" is more accurate. Individuals make choices as consumers (buyers) and as producers (sellers). An individual expresses choices about working conditions as much as about consumption goods. If mining is unpleasant compared to cutting timber, so that individuals are more willing to work at the latter rather than the former, the amount of lumber relative to coal will be larger than if individual preferences as producers were reversed.

Because there are so many other people, each of us is usually powerless to affect output or market demand in a significant way. This does not mean we cannot choose among alternative purchases or products to produce. Nevertheless, because we cannot significantly change the range of offers made to us, each open-market producer thinks the consumer (a personification of the market) is sovereign, while the consumer erroneously thinks that producers (personification of supply) decide what consumers can have.

13. We are using here a possibly inaccurate theory of behavior under government control. No validated theory for that behavior is available.

14. a. Reduce the output.

b. At first, if output is not reduced but taxes are paid, the wealth of peanut growers will fall. Higher marginal costs indicate a lower output as the new wealth-maximizing output. Or some who formerly made profit or broke even will now have a loss and be induced to abandon or reduce peanut production.

c. Reduced supply, shown by shift of supply curve to left, implies higher price.

d. Land will fall in value only to extent it was worth more for peanut growing than for next-best use.

h. Peanut consumers.

15. a. Nothing noticeable.

b. Nothing noticeable, since the one producer yields a trivial part of industry supply.

c. This taxed producer will lose wealth of resources specialized to growing peanuts on his farm. Other peanut producers are unaffected.

d. See answer to c.

16. Nothing is implied about that.

17. b. Output of each firm is at same marginal cost. Each firm sets same price, and marginal cost equal to price (for price-taker) maximizes wealth.

c. At each output the maximum value of all other outputs is achieved.

18. a. Mill B would clean three gallons and Mill C would clean four gallons.

b. B would buy three; C buys four.

c. Worse, since A would have to shut down, although producing an output worth more than the clean water obtained by stopping production.

d. No, in sense that total value of output (of all goods and services including cleaner water) would be lower.

e. Marginal cost equals value of extra output.

f. Yes. Would probably reduce it.

g. "Excessive use" is analytically more useful meaning.

**Answers to Selected
Questions: Chapter 13**

2. a. Yes.

b. Two more, for a total of eight trees.

c. No. Remember, an eighth tree is worth at most $3. What you paid for "earlier" trees is irrelevant except insofar as it affects your remaining income and thus your demand for everything else. But this effect is spread over all your purchases, and we assume here it is a trivial amount compared to your total income.

d. Eight.

e. Yes.

f. Marginal price is same under each circumstance, and we adjust to price of extra units.

3. a.

		Revenue		
Price	Quantity	Total	Marginal	Average
$20	2	$40		$20
19	3	57	$17	19
18	4	72	15	18
17	5	85	13	17
16	6	96	11	16
15	7	105	9	15
14	8	112	7	14
13	9	117	5	13
12	10	120	3	12
11	11	121	1	11
10	12	120	−1	10
9	13	117	−3	9

b. It goes to intramarginal purchasers as a lower price. For example, between a price of $18 and $19 with sales of four and three units, respectively, the marginal revenue, $15, is less than the average revenue, $18, by $3. This amount is distributed to buyers of the three units by a price that is $1 lower than formerly.

c. Seven units.

d. $15.

e. Yes. See f.

f. Having smaller profits than if price were set at $16.

4. a. He is searching for the wealth-maximizing price.

b. He is likely to find himself losing money as others enter business and reduce the price-cost spread.

5. A higher price of tickets would have reduced the amount demanded; *but* if the demand were inelastic the proceeds would have been greater, even with some seats unsold for every performance. In any event, the sell-out indicates the price was probably too low and should be raised; the producer has less revenue than he could have had.

7. Price-takers' demand curve is horizontal at highest price at which seller can sell any of his product, while in price-searchers' market his demand curve is a negatively sloped function.

8. b. Yes.

c. It is, when I do it. How about you?

11. Price that maximizes their wealth depends on demand, not on their own desire for more wealth. Prices three times as high would, in opinion of sellers, yield smaller wealth or profits.

12. a. Lower it by $5.

b. Price is $15 or $14. Output is $6 or $7.

c. $90 − $57 = $33.

13. a. Nothing.

b. Reduced by $5 to $28.

14. a. Price-searcher; an open-market monopolist.

15. In the sense that it indicates the amounts of the good that the productive resources would be willing to provide through the intermediary of the businessman. But it does not present the supply schedule of the amounts actually forthcoming at each potential selling price of the good, because the intermediary businessman is heeding marginal revenue rather than price (average revenue). Instead it is the schedule of amounts at each marginal revenue. If marginal revenue is essentially equal to price or close to price, the marginal-cost schedule will approximate the supply schedule and no significant difference will exist between price and marginal costs.

16. a. Yes.

b. The government is not a monolithic agency of just one person. It often does conflicting things at the same time, in response to different pressures.

17. a. Either $5 or $6.

b. $7.

c. None. It is the wealth-maximizing price.

18. a. Yes.

b. Neither.

Answers to Selected Questions: Chapter 14

1. a. Slightly more than 10 cents. (Call it 10 cents for subsequent computations.)

b. Between 65 and 67 cents. Call it 67 cents for subsequent computations.

c. Each would sell ten units at 67 cents each, for $6.70 daily.

d. Formerly received (10 cents × 20 units) = $2 daily. Each gets $4.70 more.

4. Government agencies enforcing laws against collusions concentrate on collusions against government. Second, government uses system of sealed bid, publicly opened. This is ideal for preventing secret price cutting or evasion of collusion by colluding firms.

5. Collusion connotes elements of deception in seeking to negotiate exchanges in the pretense that the sellers are acting as independent competitors. Buyers are misled into presuming sellers are acting independently. If buyers knew sellers were in agreement, buyers would be alerted to incentive of each seller not to bid as he otherwise would. Without element of secrecy, buyers are aware of lack of inter-seller conflict of interest—as, for example, among the two salesmen of the same firm. The pretense of competing with respect to prices and quality is designed to induce buyer to think he is already obtaining advantages of inter-seller competition.

With open collusion, such as mergers, there is no pretense. Buyers are not deceived and can then obtain offers from other independent sellers. Open agreements not to compete are not deceptive and consequently are much less effective in open markets. Partnerships being open are not deceptive, hence do not connote elements of collusion. Element of deception is undesirable.

Competition connotes interpersonal striving about who will get what of existing resources, while cooperation connotes joint action to increase total stock of wealth to be distributed. Some actions do both at the same time. Thus, exchange with specialization is both competitive and cooperative in increasing wealth as well as in allocating it.

6. a. Team owners are able to sign new players at lower wages, since other owners agree not to compete for these players. The team owner's problem is to pay just enough to induce the newcomer to play; he does not have to compete against other owners. The competition is transferred to that of determining the initial assignments of newcomers to each team—by giving the lowest-standing team first choice of the newcomers (high school graduates) and the next-lowest team the next choice. This is the "draft." Although this assignment system is alleged to help equalize team abilities, it does not; players are subsequently sold to other teams, at prices far in excess of that paid the newcomers. The draft is simply a device to pay players less than they would get in open markets, while the resale of the players to other teams at higher prices is a scheme of wealth redistribution among the teamowners. (If the two basketball leagues reach an effective agreement, as seemed to be happening as this book went to press, basketball players will get smaller salaries because team owners will not have to compete against each other.)

The better athletes suffer. Since it is impossible to know in advance precisely how good an athlete will be, the initial sign-up price will be lower to reflect that uncertainty. There is a stipulation in all contracts that wages cannot be cut "rapidly," so those who turn out to be poorer than expected will be overpaid for a substantial time. Those who turn out better than expected will be underpaid thereafter, because other team owners will not bid for their services by offering the player the higher wage, but will instead pay the team owner to get that player.

b. Perhaps this explains why we call these "sports" rather than "businesses." No business could do this. It is a much tougher, and still unsolved, task to explain why other businesses cannot do what sports can do. The existence of laws restricting business firms does not explain why.

7. Yes. Enhances prospect of monopoly rents.

8. a. To control secret violations of sales of a homogeneous product.

b. The law compelled them to join.

11. a. Yes, under price controls, producers reduce the quality of products.

b. No. All are with open competition.

12. a. We think students can discriminate as ably as any other group you would suggest. To the argument that students are prone to take snap, popular, "theatrical" courses, we ask, "What is bad about popular, theatrical courses if the course is nevertheless good?" To say that students select snap courses (meaning courses that are easy—not because teaching is good but because course content is trivial) is to provoke question as to why students do that. To say they are lazy is to presume that they should not be lazy or that only hard-working students should attend a class—a rather presumptive judgment. More germane is question of why students who are able and motivated to go to college should nevertheless sacrifice "good" courses for

sake of an easy grade. Does it suggest something about the criteria imposed on the students by the college administrators? What?

13. Each can judge what is best for himself, we suppose. As for us, we would prefer formal exchanges not to shut off trading in particular securities, thereby reducing exchange opportunities. Under present system, presumption is built up that stock-exchange officials are good judges of what price changes are justified or what news ought not to be allowed to affect decisions of individual investors—a presumption which not even the stock-exchange officials will defend. Rationale for restrictive practice is that wide price swings resulting from news that turns out to be incomplete or exaggerated are often blamed on the stock market, with suggestion that stock-market officials were responsible or that they ought to have prevented such unjustified (with hindsight) swings. In fact, these wide swings are the result of incomplete information, which no one can improve on at the time. On the other hand, if the stock exchange closes trading at such uncertain times, and if the news is verified and does bring a persisting change in demand and supply conditions, the exchange can say that the new price truly reflects the situation. What this ignores is that stopping trading during those times locks existing owners into continuing ownership even though they would prefer to shed the uncertainty by selling to others who are more willing to bear it. Bad news is made more damaging for existing holders in that they cannot sell out as early at the suggestion of worsening conditions. Consequently, it is not correct to say that closing down the exchanges at the arrival of big news (assassination of President, outbreak of war), or suspension of trading in particular stocks, is a good thing.

15. a. The best—by definition, since the students can select from the entire world, rather than just within one state.

16. b. As any of these groups, we would oppose the development proposed.

18. a. Owners of high-cost stations and stations already in existence would benefit. Low-cost stations and those who might enter business are hurt.
    b. Your guess is as good as ours. How about men with the prettiest wives?

19. Distinguish between open-market price-searchers and closed or restricted market access. Closed markets imply higher price.

20. Distinguish between open-market price-searchers and closed or restricted markets. Closed markets imply higher prices.

22. Simply a case of monopoly rent.

24. a. We don't know the answer to this question. But it shows the difficulty of deducing collusion from overt behavior.
    b. Newspapers are privately owned and use privately owned resources. Their right to publish is not controlled by government agency.

25. Enhances political power. (Or ask your political science professors.)

27. a. Read G. L. Priest, "The History of the Postal Monopoly," *Journal of Law and Economics,* 18, 1 (April 1975), 33–80.

30. Yes, because extent of exchange and specialization is reduced, with consequent smaller wealth.

32. a. He need only cover marginal costs with marginal revenue, but marginal revenues are not same as price.

b. As long as initial difference in marginal revenue (at equal prices) exceeds transport cost, it will pay to ship to lower-priced market.

c. No, but see p. 298.

33. Yes, they are discriminatory. Depends on who you are.

34. No.

35. a. He'll sell four units and retail price will be $17.

b. This is known as problem of successive monopoly distortion. Your instructor will probably explain this in more advanced courses.

36. a. $7 to A; $5 to B. Total receipts are $38.

b. $6 to both. Total receipts are $36.

c. Eight units. Sell five to A at $6; three to B at $4. Net earners are $26 (= $42 − $16).

**Answers to Selected
Questions: Chapter 15**

1. Jobs of workers on railroad engines and jobs the displaced workers will accept elsewhere; also, jobs of workers on railroad engines and jobs of workers making equipment that will be used if railroads can revise their work rules and assignments.

2. Labor used to make typewriters is substituted for the typist. Substitution of capital for labor is misleading because it ignores labor used to make machines.

3. a. Yes. Equipment on the bus for a laborer on the bus.

b. Yes. Labor off the bus for labor on the bus.

c. Yes. Total labor is reallocated in its tasks. No labor is released from work force, since that labor is used to produce more of other goods—except to the extent that some now choose a bit more leisure (as total output is larger).

5. No. Unlimited number of jobs available; only those are filled which are highest-value jobs, given present knowledge and resources. New inventions induce labor to seek and move to best of other unfilled jobs. The labor moves to a less valuable job. But at the same time the total wealth of the community is increased. The displaced person, as explained in the text, has no assurance of realizing a net gain from the particular innovation which displaces his most profitable job opportunities; but he does gain from most other innovations that do not displace his job.

6. No. People are released from some kinds of work so they can do some other productive work—of which there is always some as long as scarcity exists.

7. a. Fixity of ratios of kinds of inputs in the final product says absolutely nothing about the ratios in which those inputs will be used to produce the good.

8. a. Power mowers and equipment, smaller gardens.

b. Sellers of power equipment, cement surfaces, plastic flowers, etc.

9. There are many alternative ways of doing something, all of which can be technically efficient. But, of these, only one minimizes the value of forsaken opportunities; that is the economically efficient one.

10. Compares value of what is produced with the cost, rather than merely minimizing cost of what may not be worth even that cost.·

11. Can't tell. Depends on costs.

12. Inadequate because it doesn't necessarily maximize difference between value of the total thrust and the cost of getting it.

13. Can't tell. This tells us nothing about cost. We presume new method is technologically or technically efficient, in that no more could be obtained as output for given amount of specified inputs. But this doesn't tell us output is worth the input.

14. Same as answer to question 12.

15. b. To include exchange efficiency. Values of outputs are being included as judged by what people will pay in an exchange system. Thus, efficiency is broadened to include deciding what to produce, rather than merely the cheapest way to produce an arbitrary output.

16. a. Suppose you had one piece of paper and were told to maximize your use of that paper. What would you do? Is it clear now that the expression has no meaning or that it means anything you want it to mean? Usage is not something you maximize; for usage is not measurable in a single-dimensional sense. In international radio-communications conferences, the statement sounded good to many radio and electronic engineers working for the FCC and for the State Department—precisely because it lets them interpret radio uses however they wish to. It's like having your parents tell you to maximize your time at college.

17. Only marginal products of first unit of labor and of first unit of machine are changed by 100.

18. a. All now twice as large.
    b. Increases them proportionally to rise in price.

19. a. Three labor and 4 capital, but if we interpolate we can do still better by using a little less than 4 capital and a little more than 3 labor—but not as much as 4 labor and 3 capital, which costs more than using 3 labor and 4 capital.
    b. 2 capital and 5 labor.
    c. Same one is cheaper for some output. Relative prices of inputs did not change.

20. Along the rows horizontally.

21. Decrease in total versus decrease in increments.

22. a. Increase the amount of that resource used relative to other resources.

23. See page 371.

24. Maximizes net value of output, rather than minimizes cost of some arbitrary output.

25. The desire for greater wealth and the competition among actual and potential employers for those resources that give greater rather than less wealth.

26. Ratios of final consumer goods purchased would change, thus redirecting use of inputs toward those outputs whose input ratios are more efficient at the new prices.

27. See page 375.

28. No. Ignores meaning of costs relative to value of output.

29. a. Same as before: maximize utility. But, now less profit or net value of output can be retained or taken out by the owner; hence, less attention to profits as a source of utility.
    c. Possibly some, but not as strongly as if enterprise privately owned. Would let it depart from ratio if thereby obtained more util-

ity from other uses of resources rather than for profits or higher pecuniary exchange value.

30. a. Less control by state permits more discretionary behavior by individual choice.

31. a. No, not if waste is to be avoided.

b. No, won't determine whether $1 of one output is worth $1 more of some other output. Profit criterion answers that question.

32. a. Kinds not easily appropriated by government or mobs.

b. Invest in personal intellectual skills, since these are not as easy to expropriate as physical wealth for benefit of politicians.

c. Yes!

Answers to Selected Questions: Chapter 16

1. Demand to employ people at higher wages than now offered in available jobs. This does not mean the current offers in those jobs ought not to be increased by monetary or fiscal policy. They may and they may not be already appropriate; but in any event it is not more jobs that are being created but higher money-wage offers.

2. Productivity in existing jobs would be reduced if cheap energy were available in smaller supply. Indeed, more-expensive (less-available) energy would increase tasks to be done by people. More labor would have to be used, like pushing a lawnmower rather than using a power mower! Remember, jobs are never saved or created by changes in resource availabilities. They are made less or more productive. Labor becomes more or less productive in jobs the more or less other jointly usable resources are available.

3. As in prior questions, there are too many jobs to be filled. The problem is to get productivity and hence wages in each task acceptable to people. Unskilled persons may refuse to work unless they are paid more than they are worth in jobs. The skilled may not be skilled enough for some jobs that could be performed only by very skilled people. I might offer $5 an hour to someone who could keep my computer program working, but no one is skilled enough to do that. Or if they are, they could earn more at other jobs. We can always specify some task that no one is skilled enough to do or offer a wage too low to attract those skills. Though that would mean "unfilled jobs for the more skilled," obviously the wage is too low to attract adequate skills. And at the required wage the job might not be offered.

4. a. Employees were also paid in nonmonetary ways, such as "free" or "low-cost" clothing, food, or housing.

b. Feudal lords wanted people to remain tied to their estates, so they tried to prevent industrial employers from attracting them to more attractive industrial activity.

5. Wages are driven down or up to whatever equates the amount of labor demanded at that wage to the number willing to work. This may be so high as to result in real incomes adequate to support a rapidly growing population that is also getting richer per capita, as has been true for the past 500 years in most countries. "Subsistence" doesn't specify what *level* of subsistence.

7. In each case supply of that talent gets that price, whether because of higher costs of creating that talent or because of natural scarcity. Neither one is cheating or fooling.

8. Producer estimated E. Taylor would attract at least $4 million more in box office receipts— a greater marginal productivity by E. Taylor.

9. a. New employers who are yet to enter business wouldn't care.

   b. Employees would compete down monetary wage offers or other nonmonetary features to get those jobs that now offer more desirable selected nonmonetary features. Only if every adjustable feature of a job could be controlled would such imposed requirements be totally effective.

11. a. Ask the judge.
    b. Ditto.

12. *Technically* often means "accurately and unambiguously." All monopoly is limited in some sense to some class of goods. Monopoly does not eliminate competition. It eliminates certain forms of competition and increases reliance on other forms. In the present case it reduces the scope of wage-rate competition, but increases relevance of age, seniority, etc.

13. Yes, except for the important fact that the union is not an open-market monopoly and U.S. Steel is. (With respect to the world open market, both are closed-market monopolies as a result of immigration laws and tariff and taxes on imports.)

14. a. Craft union of welders.
    b. We don't know.

17. a. It would have reduced the number of laborers and raised wage rates.

    b. Producers (employers and employees) of

goods that could be obtained more cheaply by importation wanted tariffs.

18. a. Members of his union would have to switch to lower-paying jobs.

    b. The number of cars purchased by public would be increased, and if producers responded by producing more cars, the number of employees making cars—and the number of union members paying dues to the union— would be increased. The suggestion also serves as a publicity ploy in preparation for contract bargaining sessions.

19. If the union can eliminate low-wage sources of labor, then firms can be eliminated that would survive with low-wage, low-productivity labor and thus compete against the firms with higher-cost labor.

21. It would be made harder to get business if the fees were uniform among all lawyers. But if fees are set at a point that maximizes net revenue from this kind of business—as in collusive price-setting—the present value of the future receipts may be higher even though present receipts are reduced to younger lawyers (who will get more of higher receipts after they are older, more experienced, and well known).

22. a. Some would. But we conjecture most would not.

    b. It would increase revealed discrimination by color, because currently blacks can compete by taking lower-wage to get job. (Do you think a law prohibiting choice of employees by color or race would be effective enough to offset increased incentive to discriminate and would be enough to offset reduced employment on wage basis?)

23. Those who cannot provide services worth as

much as the minimum-wage rate will have to work as self-employed or commission-basis employees. Thus, in saying that a higher minimum wage reduces employment, we meant employment for wages—not productive work as self-employed or commission-basis employees.

24. Increase. Self-employment is a way of evading wage regulation.

25. We would prefer none of those laws, since they restrict the opportunity of an immigrant to compete against more popular types of residents in seeking jobs as employees.

27. Decreased. The union will set wages higher to keep only full-time employees at work, with less interest in casual, seasonal laborers.

28. Depends upon whether parents prefer college-age people or old people for baby sitters. Certainly high school students will suffer, since they are poorer quality and manage to compete by offering to work at lower wages.

29. a. It will aid people who already are employed and who are going to have heart attacks and who either do not plan to shift to new jobs or who do not appear to be prone to heart attacks.
b. It will make job shifting more difficult, and will hurt those who reveal a higher probability of heart attacks insofar as they want to change jobs. Will help them as long as they stay with *current* employer (with employer at time of passage of law).
c. All new employees will bear some of costs since heart attack is not perfectly predictable. People with a record of attacks will bear heaviest cost, since they will not be able to get jobs at as high a wage as formerly.

30. a. Would not. I would want higher wage.
b. He would offer higher wage.
c. Employees.

31. They lose who would have advanced more rapidly because of personal superiority in job performance as judged by superiors. We conjecture those who would have advanced rapidly are men, whites, superior teachers, mathematics teachers—of the characteristics listed in the question. (What is your conjecture? Do we differ in principles of analysis or in estimation of attributes that would lead to more rapid advance?)

32. a. Doesn't differ except in degree to which it reveals implications of what is said.
b. At $5, reduction in number of employees would be too great. Self-employed do not join unions. Meany depends upon unions.

33. We don't know. We conjecture that employee discrimination is regarded as acceptable; and would be incapable of being prohibited by any law, in any event.

34. Minimum-wage laws preventing employment of low-productivity labor would strike most heavily against those listed in question.

35. a. Flunk writers of first two items. Bonuses paid were reflective of estimated value of players to the teams. "Bidding away legal property" in Daley's article is not ridiculous, for what else does one do when he buys something? Does Daley imply there is "theft"? Not if bid away. If a player is not legal property, like a slave, bidding away is neither illegal nor "unethical." Daley seems to be advocating that employers be allowed to hire employees while employees are not allowed to be paid open-market competitive wages.

b. No. Could pay new firms to enter business and bid away the employees.

c. Probably not. Cannot reconcile this with draft.

36. a. Correct form of statement would be that it would raise the *payments* the federal government would have to record in its budget. Real costs are being paid already by those who are drafted. The income they are sacrificing is the cost and this would be reduced if the draft were eliminated and military personnel were obtained by paying adequate wages to attract men.

b. You should, since it will. By better assignment of people to jobs in this country—which would be a result of using adequate wages for military personnel—the total productive efficiency and output would be increased, which means that our sacrificed output would be smaller. Draft conceals costs—by making federal expenditures lower through device of compulsory service—just as police-department costs could be made to appear lower if police were drafted.

Answers to Selected Questions: Chapter 17

4. a. Longer-run consequences are, insofar as foreseen, discounted into present capital value of the enterprise and are hence borne by the present owner.

5. It permits more future consumption at cost of less current consumption.

6. Current consumption is forsaken for future income from preserved house.

7. 5 percent.

8. Not all roundabout, capitalistic methods are more productive. But many forms are. So the right forms of capital-goods accumulation will enhance wealth in the future.

9. a. $3.71; $8.02, $9.95, $6.80 for col. (3); −$2.89, + $1.20, + $3.04 for col. (5).

b. 40 years.

c. $3.00.

d. Lower interest rate.

e. As soon as its lumber value is positive.

10. a. $115.60.

b. Three years.

12. a. Yes. A fall in the rate of interest.

b. Increase the profitability.

c. Reduce the ratio of the price of raisins to grapes. Raise the rate of interest.

13. a. About 200,000 rabbits.

15. Higher rate of investment means a higher rate of production of some goods, and this implies a higher cost per unit of those goods.

16. Investment is defined as that rate of conversion (of present income) to wealth which can be profitable. The function relating these rates to the rate of interest is the investment-demand function. Saving is defined as that rate of conversion of present income to wealth that the community wants to engage in. This desired rate—or the rate at which the community is willing to divert income from current income to wealth accumulation—is a function of the rate of interest (among other things); and this relationship between the saving rate and rate of interest is the supply-of-savings function.

18. Ignoring the effects arising from the adjustments of the person from whom you got the money and looking at only your own impact, the net effect of the sequence of actions would be to push down interest rates in the bond market as you purchased bonds—but later to be reversed as we sell the bonds preparatory to purchasing other goods. If we assume that the money received was new money issued by the government, then, in addition to the above transient effect, the general price level would be pushed up as the demand for goods experiences a net increase. (Admittedly, $10,000 is a drop in the bucket for the whole economy, but even drops have their ripples.)

19. See pp. 435–436.
20. a. $50 per year.
    b. $57.80—a 2-year annuity.
    c. $10.00.
21. a. Yes.
    b. Relative prices of capital goods and earnings.
    c. Changed price of capital goods relative to current consumption goods; prices of capital goods relative to earnings.
22. Corporation managers do not have to invest all funds within the corporation. They can invest in other companies; they can lend the money. So long as they consider possible alternative investments, they will use funds within the firm only if to do so looks more profitable, as would be the case if the funds were to be borrowed from the market.
23. a. Among those hurt are people whose credit is so poor that they are unable to borrow at these low rates. Among those helped are the better-credit borrowers, since some funds that would have gone to high-risk borrowers are now diverted to the safer borrowers with a consequent lower interest rate to them; corporations are benefited.

24. a. To evade the five percent interest limit in order to get the guarantee.
    b. Is this economic analysis or name calling?
    d. No. Tie-in sales are literally impossible to prohibit completely. (Once upon a time there was a man who rented his house, under rent control, at the legal maximum rent to the renter who also had offered to buy his ailing cat for $1000.)
25. Either.
26. See p. 445.
28. See pp. 426–430.

Answers to Selected Questions: Chapter 18

2. A person should be able to get a job at a salary close to his last salary without a significant cost of finding such a job.
4. No. He chooses not to accept the best alternative job he has so far discovered and is instead looking at more jobs—which is not to say that he is lazy or deserves to be poorer.
6. a. Unemployment from relative demand shifting; from general money demand shifts; from closed markets.
7. a. No. The sum of a random variable, summed over trials (one for each firm), will still be a random variable. Random deviations do not cancel each other exactly.
    b. Almost certainly. Very rarely would every firm have bigger sales on following day.
    c. Almost certainly. Very rarely would every firm experience a decrease in sales.
    d. No, almost certainly not.
    e. Average would be decreased.
    f. Average would be increased.

g. The former.

8. Increment of cost exceeds increment of wealth for second job possibility investigated.

9. Costs borne by both—no matter who pays the employment agency. If you think it too large, why don't more people go into the business?

10. It is consistent with it, but how far it goes toward implying that higher rate is not clear. As blacks move to the North away from smaller towns with fewer employers, they find it profitable to engage in a larger scope of search; also, employers find it profitable to engage in more extensive search of these applicants than in a small town. A major factor is also believed to be the minimum-wage rate, which cuts more heavily against less-skilled persons—which is not inconsistent with the analysis of this chapter. Massive unemployment in response to big decreases in general demand is certainly an implication of the analysis and is a powerful piece of evidence supporting the analysis.

**Answers to Selected
Questions: Chapter 19**

9. a. Monetary asset to creditor; monetary liability to debtor.
   b. Monetary asset to creditor; monetary liability to debtor.
   c. Real to both parties.
   d. Real asset to leaseholder; real liability to lessor; monetary liability to leaseholder and monetary asset to lessor.

10. Are you a net monetary debtor?

11. a. No.
    b. Yes, because legal ethics and principles are concerned only with the nominal absolute value of the funds and not with their real value (relative to price-level changes).
    c. Our legal system seems to be premised on non-inflation as a fact of life—so that nominal value of investment is all that has to be protected by a prudent trustee of your investments.

14. The wage-lag assertion usually refers to a systematic force and not to random events, so lag should be apparent more than half the time. All evidence refutes the existence of a lag.

15. Increased demand does not necessarily first occur for consumer goods. It can be for labor to make buildings, machines, or roads. To think of demand as always having its impact from final consumer goods is to confuse impact of demand changes with value derivation from consumer goods. Furthermore, recall the discussion in Chapter 4 of the effect of a change in demand for meat.

16. Money holders.

17. a. Smaller.
    b. No.
    e. By about 250 percent.

18. It prevents prices from facilitating exchange; it diverts attention from causes to consequences.

19. Neither affects the quantity of money or of real goods and services, nor the demand to hold money.

20. The desire to revise the pattern of demand is often a reason for resorting to a policy of money creation. The inflation does not therefore cause the revised price pattern; instead, the revised demand brought about by the new money causes the relative price changes. At

least this interpretation is consistent with facts about sources of inflations and observed changes in relative price patterns. The statement that inflation in and of itself causes a dispersion of prices because of price rigidities is not entirely false if regard is given to prices that are fixed by law and can be changed only by appeal to a regulatory agency (as with public-utility prices). But assertion usually is made in a more sweeping context, and for that there is no supporting evidence.

Index